WELFARE AND WORK IN THE OPEN ECONOMY
VOLUME II

Welfare and Work in the Open Economy
Volume II. Diverse Responses to Common Challenges

Edited by

FRITZ W. SCHARPF

AND

VIVIEN A. SCHMIDT

OXFORD
UNIVERSITY PRESS

OXFORD

UNIVERSITY PRESS

Great Clarendon Street, Oxford OX2 6DP

Oxford University Press is a department of the University of Oxford.
It furthers the University's objective of excellence in research, scholarship,
and education by publishing worldwide in

Oxford New York

Athens Auckland Bangkok Bogotá Buenos Aires Calcutta
Cape Town Chennai Dar es Salaam Delhi Florence Hong Kong Istanbul
Karachi Kuala Lumpur Madrid Melbourne Mexico City Mumbai
Nairobi Paris São Paulo Shanghai Singapore Taipei Tokyo Toronto Warsaw

and associated companies in Berlin Ibadan

Oxford is a registered trade mark of Oxford University Press
in the UK and in certain other countries

Published in the United States
by Oxford University Press Inc., New York

British Library Cataloguing in Publication Data

Data available

Library of Congress Cataloging in Publication Data

Data available

ISBN 0–19–924091–4
ISBN 0–19–924092–2 (pbk)

1 3 5 7 9 10 8 6 4 2

Typeset by Hope Services (Abingdon) Ltd.
Printed in Great Britain
on acid-free paper by
Biddles Ltd.
Guildford and King's Lynn

PREFACE

Since the demise of the Cold War with its fear of a nuclear doomsday, 'globalization' has become the current specter of public debates in Western Europe, threatening to wipe out the achievements of advanced welfare states in providing full employment, social security, and greater social equality for their citizens. At the same time, these debates have seen an ever more rapid succession of 'model' countries that seemed to have found some miracle solution, and that were displaced by the next one when, on closer inspection, the miracle turned out to be less than perfect. Thus Japan, celebrated as the world leader in industrial productivity, was succeeded by the 'Rhine model' of social consensus and stability, which in turn was forgotten when admiration shifted first to New Zealand's radical liberalization, and then to the 'Great American Job Machine', which subsequently was overshadowed by the Dutch 'polder model', by growing attention to the Danish achievements in defending high levels of employment and social protection, and now by peak-level discussions about 'multiple Third Ways'.

When we first began to talk about the possibility of a joint project that would clarify these issues in early 1997, the academic literature was split between theoretical contributions, some warning of inexorably tightening economic constraints that were reversing postwar advances in the democratic civilization of capitalism, and others celebrating the ultimate liberation of economic dynamics from the fetters of state control. The available empirical research provided either statistical tests of hypotheses focused narrowly on a few quantifiable indicators or case studies dealing in depth with selected issues in one or a few countries. Thus, what was needed in our view was empirical and comparative research that would utilize much more information about specific problems and policy responses of advanced welfare states than was possible in statistical studies, and that would also be more comprehensive with regard to issues as well as the number of countries than had been possible in the available case studies. In a series of discussions among ourselves and with knowledgeable colleagues, we concluded that such a project would have to include at least Sweden and Denmark among the Scandinavian welfare states; Austria, Germany, the Netherlands, Belgium, France, Switzerland, and Italy in Continental Europe; and the United Kingdom, Australia, and New Zealand among the Anglo-Saxon countries. We also decided to focus on employment as well as social policy systems and to cover the period from the early 1970s to the present.

Even though our substantive research interests as well as the geographical reach of our first-hand knowledge were complementary, rather than overlapping, we never thought we could carry out a comparative study of this scope by ourselves. At the same time, the manpower requirements and costs of a project based on original empirical research covering the policy experience of a dozen countries over three decades would have been prohibitive. Instead, we decided to organize a highly structured conference project that would rely on the cooperation of colleagues who are experts on the countries to be covered, and who could draw on their background knowledge plus a limited amount of additional research for the preparation of comparable country reports that could then provide the foundation for comparative analyses. Even so, the financial needs of the project would by far exceed the resources that could be provided by the Cologne Max Planck Institute for the Study of Societies, where the project was to be located.

We count ourselves extremely lucky in obtaining the early, and in many cases enthusiastic, commitment of so many competent colleagues to what turned out to be an extremely demanding common project. At the same time, our needs for financial support were eased by a pump-priming allocation of the President of the Max Planck Society, and then met by a major grant from the Volkswagen Stiftung, a grant from the Fritz-Thyssen Stiftung for a smaller coordinated project, and by the support of the Robert Schuman Centre of the European University Institute for one of the project workshops. We are deeply grateful to all these sponsors. Their support allowed us to bring Anton Hemerijck, Rotterdam University, and Vivien Schmidt for half a year to Cologne, where the project was supported by a highly competent team including Steffen Ganghof, Martin Schludi, Eric Seils, and Torben Vad. Vad and later Ganghof acted as overall project coordinators.

In order to assure a common focus among all participants, we began the project by formulating a 50-page 'background paper' that reviewed the available literature and explicated a comprehensive set of working hypotheses on the possible first- and second-order impacts of changes in the external economic environment on the employment and social policy systems of advanced welfare states, on the likely effectiveness of possible policy responses, and on the institutional conditions favoring effective policy responses.[1] In order to allow contributors to locate their country

---

[1] Fritz W. Scharpf, Vivien A. Schmidt, and Torben B. P. Vad, *The Adjustment of National Employment and Social Policy to Economic Internationalization*, Background Paper (Cologne: Max Planck Institute for the Study of Societies, 1998).

studies in a quantitative context, the Cologne team also compiled a common database consisting mainly of OECD time series on the economic performance, employment, public finance, capital markets, social policy, wages and distributive outcomes for all countries, starting in the 1970s wherever possible.[2]

Both documents were made available to the participants of an 'opening conference' in Cologne, early in 1998, in which the overall design of the project, the questions to be addressed, and their goodness of fit for the countries to be covered were discussed by the future authors and several expert commentators. At the same time, it was agreed that a number of important issues needed to be addressed in special studies. First drafts, which were expected and delivered in the early Fall of 1998, were subsequently discussed in great detail in a series of smaller workshops in Cologne and Florence. Second drafts as well as first drafts of the comparative chapters were then prepared for discussion among all participants and again a number of knowledgeable commentators in a 'concluding conference', convened in February of 1999 in the snowbound isolation of the Max Planck Society's Ringberg Castle in the Bavarian Alps.

By that time, Oxford University Press had agreed in principle to publish the outcome of the project in two volumes—provided we would be able to meet its page limitations and its timetable. This implied that all authors received not only detailed comments from the editors, on themes to be elaborated and additional information to be supplied on the basis of the Ringberg discussions, but also precise instructions about how much of the text had to be cut in producing the final draft that was due at the beginning of the Summer. By the end of the Summer, a second round of comments from the editors and revisions by the authors led to 'final-final drafts' which then went to Jeremiah Riemer, our most demanding language editor, whom we cannot thank enough for his skill and diligence in translating texts from German-English, Italian-English or Danish-English into lucid and elegant American-English.

We have described the process in some detail to show that unlike many conference projects, where participants produce loosely connected papers based on ongoing work, ours did demand a great deal more of contributors, not only because of the range of issues we asked them to address but also because of the very specific guidelines we suggested they follow in writing their papers, the common hypotheses which we expected them to address, the comparative data by which we expected them to contextualize their analyses, and the numerous rounds of editing and requests for

---

[2] Martin Schludi, Eric Seils, and Steffen Ganghof, *Adjustment Data Base*, Paper (Cologne: Max Planck Institute for the Study of Societies, 1998).

revisions under increasingly tight deadlines with which we badgered them. We are extremely grateful for their willingness and ability to produce first-rate contributions under these very demanding conditions. Similarly, we are grateful to the expert commentators in our series of conferences and workshops who were willing to read many and very long drafts and to offer extremely helpful critiques and suggestions, both theoretical and empirical. Their input proved invaluable to the authors and to the project as a whole. Since they will not appear among the authors, we name them here in alphabetical order: Jens Alber, University of Konstanz; Peter Hall, Harvard University; Franz-Xaver Kaufmann, University of Bielefeld; Stephan Leibfried, University of Bremen; and John L. D. Stephens, University of North Carolina.

Our final thanks go to the staff of the Cologne Max Planck Institute without whose support all our efforts would have come to naught. Under the professional supervision of Christel Schommertz, Sonja Jerak and Thomas Pott worked very hard, and in the final two weeks practically around the clock, in order to have all texts, tables, and figures formatted according to Oxford rules in time to meet the ironclad publication deadline. We also thank Jürgen Lautwein and the administrative staff at the MPI for the efficient and flexible management of our complicated project finances, and Christina Glasmacher for secretarial and organizational support throughout.

Fritz W. Scharpf
Vivien A. Schmidt

Cologne and Boston
December 1999

CONTENTS

LIST OF FIGURES

LIST OF TABLES

ABBREVIATIONS

The following abbreviations are used to indicate various countries in some of the tables and figures:

A	Austria
AUS	Australia
B	Belgium
CAN	Canada
CH	Switzerland
D	Germany
DK	Denmark
F	France
FL	Finland
I	Italy
IRL	Ireland
JAP	Japan
N	Norway
NL	Netherlands
NZ	New Zealand
S	Sweden
UK	United Kingdom
USA	United States of America

Other abbreviations used:

EC	European Community
EMU	European Monetary Union
EU	European Union
ILO	International Labour Office
IMF	International Monetary Fund
ISIC	International Standard Industrial Classification of All Economic Activities
OECD	Organisation for Economic Co-operation and Development

NOTES ON CONTRIBUTORS

MATS BENNER is Assistant Professor of Sociology at Lund University, Sweden. He has written several books and articles on comparative industrial and technology policy.

GIULIANO BONOLI is a Lecturer in the Department of Social Work and Social Policy, University of Fribourg, Switzerland. He has recently published a book entitled *The Politics of Pension Reform: Institutions and Policy Change in Western Europe* (Cambridge University Press, forthcoming). His current research is on comparative social and labor market policy.

MARY DALY is Professor of Sociology at Queen's University, Belfast, Northern Ireland. She formerly worked in Germany, Italy, and the Republic of Ireland. She has written widely on the topic of comparative welfare states, especially in relation to gender. Her latest book, *The Gender Division of Welfare*, is published by Cambridge University Press. Her current research interests include welfare state reform and family and labor market policies in comparative perspective.

BERNHARD EBBINGHAUS is Senior Researcher at the Max Planck Institute for the Study of Societies, Cologne (Germany) and 1999/2000 J. F. Kennedy Fellow at the Center for European Studies at Harvard University, Cambridge, Mass. (USA). He is also co-author (with Jelle Visser) of *Trade Unions in Western Europe since 1945* (London: Macmillan, 2000).

MAURIZIO FERRERA is Professor of Public Policy and Administration at the University of Pavia and directs the Center for Comparative Political Research at the Bocconi University of Milan. He has written several books in Italian on comparative social policy and on Italy's welfare state. In English he has recently edited (with M. Rhodes) a special issue of *West European Politics* on 'Recasting the European Welfare State' (2000).

STEFFEN GANGHOF is a doctoral fellow at the Max Planck Institute for the Study of Societies in Cologne. His research interests include comparative political economy, institutional analysis, and European Integration.

ELISABETTA GUALMINI is Assistant Professor at the University of Bologna, where she teaches Comparative Public Administration. Her most recent book publications include *Le rendite del neo-corporativismo* (Soveria

Mannelli: Rubbettino, 1997), *La politica del lavoro* (Bologna: Il Mulino, 1998), and *Salvati dall'Europa*, with M. Ferrera (Bologna: Il Mulino, 1999).

ANTON HEMERIJCK is Senior Lecturer in the Department of Public Administration, Leiden University, the Netherlands and visiting researcher at the Max Planck Institute of the Study of Societies in Cologne. He studied Economics at Tilburg University, and Political Science at Oxford University (Balliol College), where he wrote his dissertation, and MIT, Cambridge, Mass. He has published widely on issues of comparative social and economic policy and welfare reform. Together with Jelle Visser, he wrote *'A Dutch Miracle': Job Growth, Welfare Reform and Corporatism in the Netherlands*, which is now available in English, German, Italian, and Dutch. A Japanese edition is currently in preparation.

ADRIENNE HÉRITIER is Professor of Political Science and co-director of the Max Planck Project Group on 'Common Goods: Law, Politics and Economics'. Recent publications include: *Policy Making in Europe and Diversity: Escape from Deadlock* (Cambridge: Cambridge University Press, 1999); 'Elements of Democratic Legitimation in Europe: An Alternative View', *Journal of European Public Policy*, 1999, 269–82.

JONAH D. LEVY is Associate Professor of Political Science at the University of California, Berkeley. His research focuses on economic and social policy in Western Europe, notably France. Levy's most recent publications include *Tocqueville's Revenge: State, Society, and Economy in Contemporary France* (Cambridge, Mass.: Harvard University Press, 1999) and 'Vice into Virtue? Progressive Politics and Welfare Reform in Continental Europe', *Politics and Society*, 27/2 (June 1999), 239–73.

ANDRÉ MACH is a teaching assistant at the Institut d'études politiques et internationales, University of Lausanne, Switzerland. He is currently completing his Ph.D. on the reform of competition policy and changes in industrial relations in the 1990s in Switzerland. He has published on organized interests and on social and economic policies.

PHILIP MANOW, political scientist, is a researcher at the Max Planck Institute for the Study of Societies in Cologne. He is the author of numerous articles on the German welfare state and has written two books on German health policy. Currently, he is co-editing a book on *Varieties of Welfare Capitalism*. Recent English articles include 'The Comparative Institutional Advantages of Welfare State Regimes and New Coalitions in Welfare State Reforms', in Paul Pierson (ed.), *The New Politics of the*

Welfare State (Oxford University Press, forthcoming); (with Anton Hemerijck and Kees van Kersbergen), 'Welfare without Work? Divergent Experiences of Reform in Germany and the Netherlands', in Stein Kuhnle (ed.), *The Survival of the European Welfare State* (Routledge, forthcoming).

MARTIN RHODES is Professor of European Public Policy at the European University Institute in Florence. His recent publications on employment and welfare issues include 'Globalization, Welfare States and Employment: Is There a European "Third Way"?', in N. Bermeo (ed.), *Unemployment in the New Europe* (Cambridge: Cambridge University Press, 2000) and 'The Political Economy of Social Pacts', in Paul Pierson (ed.), *The New Politics of the Welfare State* (Oxford University Press, 2000).

FRITZ W. SCHARPF, Professor of Political Science, is director at the Max Planck Institute for the Study of Societies, Cologne, Germany. Recent publications in English include: *Crises and Choice in European Social Democracy* (Ithaca, NY: Cornell University Press, 1991); *Games Real Actors Play: Actor-Centered Institutionalism in Policy Research* (Boulder, Colo.: Westview Press, 1997); *Governing in Europe: Effective and Democratic?* (Oxford: Oxford University Press, 1999).

SUSANNE K. SCHMIDT is a research fellow at the Max Planck Institute for the Study of Societies. Recent publications include (with Raymund Werle), *Coordinating Technology* (Cambridge, Mass.: MIT Press, 1998) and *Liberalisierung in Europa. Die Rolle der Europäischen Kommission* (Frankfurt am Main: Campus, 1998).

VIVIEN A. SCHMIDT, Professor of International Relations at Boston University, has written extensively on European political economy and public policy, including *From State to Market?* (Cambridge: Cambridge University Press, 1996); *Democratizing France* (Cambridge: Cambridge University Press, 1990); and articles in journals such as *Publius*, *Daedalus*, *Comparative Politics*, *Current Politics* and *Economics in Europe*, *Government and Policy*, *Governance*, *Journal of Common Market Studies*, the *Journal of European Public Policy*, and *West European Politics*. Currently, Professor Schmidt is working on a two-volume project on the impact of European integration on national economies, institutions, and discourse in France, Britain, and Germany.

HERMAN SCHWARTZ is Associate Professor of Government and Foreign Affairs at the University of Virginia. His research interests focus on public sector restructuring in Australia, Canada, Denmark, New Zealand, and Sweden. See <http://www.people.virginia.edu/~hms2f>.

ERIC SEILS has studied political science at the Universities of Konstanz and Huddersfield. Currently he is a doctoral fellow at the Max Planck Institute for the Study of Societies in Cologne. His research interests include the welfare state and the political economy of the low-wage sector in Germany and the Netherlands.

BRIGITTE UNGER is University Professor at the Department of Economics, University of Economics and Business Administration, in Vienna, Austria. Her research topics are macroeconomics, economic policy and institutional economics, and innovation. At the moment she is revising her latest book on 'Room for Manoeuvre: Choices Left for National Policy' for publication and works on a TSER-project on National Systems of Innovations and the Idea Innovation Chain.

TORBEN BUNDGAARD VAD is a political scientist and works at Danish Commerce & Services in Copenhagen, Denmark as a political consultant with knowledge services as his main area of expertise.

JELLE VISSER (1946) is Professor of Empirical Sociology and Sociology of Labor and Organization at the University of Amsterdam, where he directs the Centre for Research of European Societies and Industrial Relations (CESAR). His most recent publications include (with Bernhard Ebbinghaus), *Trade Unions in Western Europe since 1945* (London: Macmillan, 2000; (with Anton Hemerijck), *'A Dutch Miracle': Job Growth, Welfare Reform and Corporatism in the Netherlands* (Amsterdam: Amsterdam University Press, 1997); and (with Joris van Ruysseveldt), *Industrial Relations in Europe: Traditions and Transitions* (London: Sage, 1996).

1

Introduction

FRITZ W. SCHARPF AND VIVIEN A. SCHMIDT

This book is the second of two volumes presenting the findings of a twelve-country project on the adjustment of employment and social policy systems in advanced welfare states to the challenges of economic internationalization. The first volume contains comparative analyses and attempts to draw general conclusions from the research presented here. One chapter explores how characteristic differences in the socio-economic structures, policy legacies, and policy institutions of different countries have affected their vulnerability to international economic challenges and their ability to adopt and implement effective policy responses. A second chapter compares the greater or lesser effectiveness of actual policy responses, and it attempts to identify characteristic sequences of such responses and their relationship to successful policy learning. The third chapter takes these policy responses as given and explores to what extent they violated pre-existing normative aspirations and national values and whether legitimating discourses were or were not able to gain public acceptance of policy change.

This second volume represents the core of the project and the empirical foundations for the comparative analyses in the first volume. It provides in-depth studies of the adjustment of employment and social policies to changes in the international economic environment in the period from the early 1970s to the late 1990s in twelve advanced capitalist (OECD) welfare states plus special studies on women in the labor market, early retirement, the public services sector, and tax competition. The country case studies cover three countries representing the 'Anglo-Saxon' model (the United Kingdom, Australia, and New Zealand), seven varieties of the 'Continental' welfare state (Switzerland, Austria, Belgium, the Netherlands, Germany, France, and Italy), and two 'Scandinavian' welfare states (Sweden and Denmark). We left out the United States and Japan, which are generally not considered 'advanced welfare states' in the same sense as the countries included herein, and we excluded Canada, Finland, Norway, and Iceland which, though certainly advanced capitalist welfare states, appeared to represent unique cases for a variety of reasons. Ireland,

Portugal, Spain, Greece, and Turkey were left out because during the period covered in our project they were confronted with external challenges that differed from those confronting more advanced economies. In the special studies, we chose to examine more closely some of the issues which are of general concern in the adjustment of the welfare state, but not likely to get sufficient attention in any one country chapter.

1.1. The Postwar Decades

In focusing on adjustments beginning in the early 1970s, we had assumed that the expansion of state responsibility for achieving full employment, assuring social security, and reducing social inequality in the early postwar decades had culminated at the end of the 'golden age' in the late 1960s, and that subsequently these solutions were challenged and increasingly constrained by changes in the international economic environment. As will be seen in the country chapters, this stylized background assumption does not apply in all cases. In some countries, welfare state solutions were exposed to severe international economic challenges long before the 1970s; and in other countries, the expansion of the welfare state continued in the 1970s and even the 1980s. Nevertheless, the specific configurations of employment and social policies of all the countries considered herein, had developed in the early postwar decades under conditions in which the direct influence of the international economic environment on domestic policy choices was very limited in comparison to conditions that had existed before World War I or in the 1920s.

After the rampant protectionism following the Great Depression and the complete breakdown of world markets in World War II, most currencies were not freely convertible, capital transfers were tightly controlled and internal financial markets strictly regulated in most countries. The restoration of international trade in product markets was a slow process. Export dependence and import penetration were still limited, and the range of economic activities that were sheltered against international competition was quite large. Services were protected along with agriculture in most countries, while manufacturing was generally more export oriented—except for Australia and New Zealand, which relied on agriculture and raw materials exports to sustain highly protected manufacturing industries. If the competitiveness of internationally exposed branches became insufficient, moreover, the Bretton-Woods system of fixed exchange rates allowed negotiated adjustments to correct structural imbalances.

While it would be wrong to speak of closed national economies in the early postwar decades, nation states were able to control their own economic boundaries and the conditions under which transnational economic transactions would take place. Behind these protective barriers, national governments and unions could more or less ignore the exit options of capital owners, taxpayers, and consumers. Government interest rate policy was able to determine, and vary, the minimal rate of return that captive capital owners could expect in the market for longer-term investment opportunities. By the same token, the level and the type of taxes that governments could impose on captive taxpayers was primarily limited by political, rather than economic, constraints. And if governments and unions were able to impose uniform regulations, taxes, and wage increases on all competing firms, the higher production costs could generally be passed on to captive consumers without endangering the profitability of capitalist production.

Under these conditions, advanced industrial democracies were able to achieve the 'Great Transformation' (Polanyi 1957) that allowed them to exploit the economic efficiency of dynamic capitalism without having to accept its recurrent crises and highly unequal distributional consequences. Since they were able to control transnational capital movements, most governments learned to dampen macroeconomic fluctuations through Keynesian demand management, and to achieve and maintain relatively high rates of economic growth and full employment. At the same time, national control over external trade gave governments and unions great freedom to shape the conditions of production and employment through regulation and collective agreements, and to redistribute incomes through cross-subsidization in the private sector as well as through transfers and public services financed through either progressive income taxes, consumption taxes, or payroll taxes. Hence, in some countries 'solidaristic' wage policy could compress wage differentials between low-skill and high-skill groups with little regard for actual differences in labor productivity; in others energy policy could require the use of expensive domestic coal in electricity generation; in Europe agricultural policy could be used to keep inefficient farms in business, whereas in Australia and New Zealand, alternatively, external protection was used to maintain full employment in import-substituting manufacturing production.

All countries in our project were capitalist in the sense that the private ownership of the means of production was accepted in principle, and all had accepted their dependence on profit-oriented private enterprise and market interactions for the creation of wealth and economic growth. At the same time, however, they all relied on the state's newly increased capacity for market-correcting action to pursue at a minimum three socially valued aspirations:

- Full employment with 'good jobs' for all (men) who were expected to work for a living;
- social insurance of workers against the risks of sickness, invalidity, unemployment, and old age;
- social assistance to prevent the poverty of those without other sources of support.

Beyond these minimum aspirations, countries differed greatly with regard to the extension of employment opportunities for women, with regard to the coverage and generosity of publicly provided social insurance, social assistance, and social services, and even more so with regard to their commitment to reduce, or prevent, the social inequalities that are continuously generated and reproduced by capitalist market economies. They also differed greatly in the policy instruments employed and the institutions created for the achievement of their market-correcting goals; and in the economic efficiency of their 'golden age' solutions, whether measured in average rates of economic growth, per capita GDP, or employment rates. These differences are explored in greater detail in the comparative chapters in Volume I. What matters here is the fact that in spite of these differences, all countries in our project were able to achieve their respective welfare-state goals without endangering the viability of their capitalist national economies in the relatively benign international economic environment of the postwar decades.

Differences in institutions and policy legacies began to matter from the early 1970s onward, when major changes in the international environment did increase the economic vulnerability of advanced welfare states. This is not meant to deny the importance of other exogenous and endogenous challenges—among them the technical changes that have revolutionized production and consumption patterns, the effects of expanding education, the aging of the population, the transformation of traditional family structures, and profound value changes—that also differed in their impact on different types of postwar welfare states. To the extent that they interacted with the external economic challenges considered here, they will be discussed in the country chapters of this volume, and also in the special study on the participation of women in the labor market (Daly, this volume). But the basic focus of our project is indeed on the responses to challenges caused by changes in the international economic environment. In the period from the early 1970s to the mid-1980s, these challenges were in the nature of macroeconomic shocks, whereas the later period and the present are characterized by intensified competition in international capital and product markets.

1.2. The Challenges

For most industrialized countries, the end of the postwar 'golden age' coincided with the breakdown of the Bretton-Woods system of fixed but adjustable exchange rates and with the first OPEC oil-price crisis of 1973/75. The first created an environment of floating exchange rates and accelerated the growth of 'offshore' capital markets that were not under the control of any of the major central banks. The second confronted oil-dependent industrial economies with the double challenges of 'stagflation'—i.e. the simultaneous impact of cost-push inflation, caused by the fourfold increase within a few months of the price of crude oil, and of demand-gap unemployment, caused by the diversion of purchasing power to OPEC countries that could not immediately 'recycle' their new wealth into additional demand for industrial products. Under these conditions, governments committed to Keynesian demand management were confronted with a dilemma: if they chose to fight unemployment with monetary and fiscal demand reflation, they would generate escalating rates of inflation; but if they would instead fight inflation with restrictive fiscal and monetary policies, the result would be mass unemployment. The dilemma could only be avoided if, in addition to fiscal and monetary policy, wages could also be employed as a tool of macroeconomic policy. What was needed was a form of 'Keynesian concertation' where the government would prevent job losses through demand reflation while the unions would reduce inflationary cost pressures through wage restraint (Scharpf 1991).

The closest approximation to Keynesian concertation was achieved in Austria. In Germany and Switzerland, by contrast, governments were unable to reflate the economy because monetary policy was determined by an independent central bank that was unconditionally committed to the defense of price stability—in which case the bank's tight money policy would neutralize expansionary fiscal impulses. The same was true in countries like Denmark, the Netherlands, or Belgium, where the government tried to stabilize the exchange rate with the Deutschmark. Under these conditions, major job losses were unavoidable. But they could be softened if real wages were quickly adjusted downwards, which was true in Germany and Switzerland but not in the other hard-currency countries practising an imported (and perhaps less clearly understood) version of the Bundesbank's monetarism. In countries where the central bank was willing to accommodate the rise of oil prices, government deficit spending was generally able to avoid major job losses in the 1970s. But then inflation would escalate unless it was counteracted by effective wage restraint—which, in the absence of unemployment, was more than most unions would or could deliver. In most countries, therefore, inflation continued at very high, often two-digit levels. Moreover, the attempt to stabilize employment through demand reflation had left most governments with very high budget deficits at the end of the 1970s.

Thus, by the end of the decade, governments and central banks in most countries had come to define loose money policies and fiscal irresponsibility as the critical policy failures of the 1970s. This increased their willingness to switch to monetarist beliefs and hard-currency policy responses when the second oil crisis of 1979–81 seemed to replay the challenges of the 1970s—with the result that unemployment rates now also rose steeply in most of the countries that had been able to avoid major job losses in the 1970s. Most important, however, was the fact that now the monetary policy of the United States was no longer ready to accommodate oil-price inflation. As a consequence, real dollar interest rates, which had been close to zero or negative through most of the 1970s, rose steeply to very high positive levels—3.1 percent in 1981, 5.4 percent in 1982, 7.2 percent in 1983, and 8.1 percent in 1984. Since the internationalization of capital markets had progressed rapidly during the 1970s, and most countries had become heavily indebted to them, national central banks—regardless of their institutional independence and theoretical orientations—were forced to raise interest rates accordingly in order to avoid massive capital outflows. This had major distributional consequences. Since minimal profits expected from real investments have to be above the interest income from risk-free government bonds, the dramatic rise of real interest rates meant that the share of capital incomes in the national product had to rise at the expense of government and labor shares if investment and business employment were to be maintained. The only question was whether the change in distribution was realized through reduced wage claims and tax 'reforms' favoring capital incomes, or whether it was realized through disinvestment and job losses in the private sector.

On the whole, therefore, the success or failure of countries during the crises of the 1970s depended primarily on their capabilities for macroeconomic management—i.e. on the coordination between the fiscal and monetary policy choices of the state, and on the capacity and willingness of unions to practise effective wage restraint in the face of oil-induced inflation. In the early 1980s, however, the role of fighting inflation had been assumed almost everywhere by a very restrictive monetary policy. Under these conditions, the extent to which unemployment would increase depended primarily on the willingness and ability of unions to accept wage settlements that favored the rise of business profits. By and large, most countries had learned to cope with these conditions by the mid-1980s; and in the latter half of the decade, when inflation, oil prices, and dollar interest rates had come down again, the international macroeconomic environment of capitalist economies seemed once more relatively benign. At the same time, however, the protective barriers that had shielded their internal structures in the postwar decades were now rapidly disappearing.

By the early 1990s, the internationalization of markets for goods, services, and capital was again reaching levels that equaled, and then exceeded, the degree of international economic integration that had existed in the decades before World War I. Capital exchange controls, which had still protected the domestic financial markets of most countries in the early 1970s, had practically disappeared.[1] Moreover, the European Community had decided to liberalize financial services, and most countries had deregulated their domestic financial markets as well. As a consequence, financial capital is now again internationally mobile, and the minimal rate of return that investors can expect is no longer defined by reference to interest rates set by the national bank but rather by the attractiveness of competing worldwide opportunities for speculative, portfolio, or real investments. At the same time, successive rounds of GATT and WTO negotiations had progressively lowered the tariffs and quantitative restrictions protecting national markets for goods, services, and investments. In Europe, the Single Market program had also eliminated the non-tariff barriers that still impeded the full integration of product markets, and it had introduced international competition in a wide range of services and utilities—among them telecommunications, postal services, rail, air and road transport, or electricity supply—which before had been provided either by the state itself or by state-controlled monopolies and cartels. For some of the countries in our project, the completion of the internal market was followed by the commitment to create a Monetary Union which would not only remove monetary and exchange rate policy from the control of national governments and impose severe constraints on the conduct of national fiscal policy, but which also removed the last important barrier to real capital mobility: firms are now able to choose the lowest-cost location of production within the territory of the Monetary Union without having to consider either non-tariff barriers or exchange rate fluctuations that might affect their access to the home market. By the same token, it has become much easier to move mobile tax bases—in particular business profits and other forms of capital incomes—to locations offering the least burdensome tax regimes.

---

[1] According to an indicator of capital-exchange liberalization constructed by Dennis Quinn on the basis of IMF data (where a score of 14 marks total liberalization), in 1970 eleven of twenty OECD countries had scores below 10, and only one country (Germany) had a score of 14. By 1993, only one country (Greece) still scored below 10, and nine countries now had a score of 14.

As a consequence of these cumulative changes in the international economic and legal environment, national governments and national labor unions are now no longer able to rely on the protective barriers that facilitated the achievement of their policy goals in the postwar decades. The internationalization of capital markets had already reduced the effectiveness, and increased the budgetary costs, of Keynesian full employment policies in the 1980s, and by the 1990s the exit options of investors, taxpayers, and consumers were severely constraining the capacity to regulate processes of production and to tax the profits from production. In that sense, it is indeed plausible to conclude that 'Polanyi's Great Transformation is over' (Cerny 1994: 339).

That is not to say that countries have lost all capacity to pursue the welfare goals they had chosen in the postwar decades, but it does imply that these goals must again be pursued within the constraints of international capitalism—and it suggests that in contrast to the macroeconomic shocks of the 1970s and early 1980s, a capacity for macroeconomic management and union wage restraint is no longer sufficient for coping with the new challenges. Since governments and unions are no longer dealing with captive capital owners and captive consumers, national systems of taxation, regulation, and industrial relations have now become vulnerable to the extent that they reduce the attractiveness of the national economy to mobile capital and the competitiveness of nationally produced goods and services in international product markets. The first major impact of these new constraints is on employment in the internationally exposed sectors of the economy (including major service branches), where more intense competition puts a premium on product innovation, productivity increases, and flexibility which, on balance, have negative consequences for employment levels and the conditions of employment in the advanced industrial countries. When overall employment nevertheless increases, the gains are mainly achieved in the sheltered sectors, where services are locally produced and locally consumed. The second major impact of the new international constraints is on the financial viability of the welfare state—which is affected by international tax competition as well as by efforts to increase competitiveness in product markets through reducing the costs of production.

It is here that structural differences among financing and spending patterns have the greatest influence on the vulnerability, and on the need for policy adjustment, of different types of welfare states. These differences and their impact on the effectiveness of policy responses are examined in comparative chapters in Volume I. But comparison cannot provide new insights unless it is based on a thorough understanding of the complex interactions of challenges and responses in the countries whose experiences are to be compared. This is the task performed by the country case studies and special studies assembled in this volume.

1.3. The Country Case Studies

The overall goal of the country studies is to provide a picture of how the postwar social welfare and employment structures (as they had matured by about the early 1970s) have changed under the impact of changes in the international economic environment. Each chapter sets out the main set of problems for the country in question, examines how it went about trying to resolve its problems, and assesses the solutions. The chapters are organized in parallel fashion, to ensure the greatest ease of comparison. They are all based on the same set of cross-national data[2] (supplemented, of course, by additional country-specific data) to guarantee comparability across countries and sectors. They all address questions about how the three main types of pressures from internationalization, that is, competition for shares in the markets for goods and services, competition for investment capital, and competition for mobile tax resources, have affected different segments of national employment, including the 'exposed sector', the 'sheltered' sector, the private sector, and the public sector, and different aspects of the welfare state, including public sector revenue, welfare financing, and welfare expenditures.[3] Finally, the chapters all seek to assess: (1) the greater or lesser vulnerability of national employment structures and welfare-state institutions to the effects of international competition; (2) the greater or lesser effectiveness of the policy responses actually adopted; and (3) the greater or lesser political and institutional capacity of the national policy system to develop effective policy responses.

The country studies begin with a description of the 'golden age' or postwar model of the welfare state, by providing a snapshot of the country's economic structure and policies, industrial structure and governance system, political profile and institutions, welfare and industrial relations systems, and social policies and labor market programs. They then proceed with a chronology of the successive external economic challenges and internal

[2] The data-set consists mainly of OECD comparative time series data, starting in the 1970s, with information on such indicators as wealth, distribution, employment, unemployment, export performance, exchange rates, investment, taxation, social spending, etc. It was compiled and presented by members of the Max Planck Institute project team Martin Schludi, Steffen Ganghof, Eric Seils, and Torben Vad.

[3] These questions were all raised in a preliminary background paper (Scharpf, Schmidt, and Vad 1998) which presented an inventory of hypotheses linking international economic competition to plausible first-order and second-order effects on specific features of national employment and social-policy systems.

policy responses up until today, beginning with the oil crises of the 1970s, which some countries felt more severely than others; continuing with the 1980s, when many countries but certainly not all began the adjustment process; and following on to the 1990s, when all countries felt the need to respond. They end with a depiction of the new model or model in making, if there is one, and an assessment of what went right, and what went wrong.

The chapters focus either on a single country or on two or three countries sharing important characteristics that invite specific comparisons. Thus, for the Anglo-Saxon welfare states, Britain is considered separately, but Australia and New Zealand are paired in order to bring out the differences in countries which at the beginning of the 1970s had similar economic profiles but ended up following quite different trajectories. Similarly, for Continental welfare states, Switzerland, Germany, France, and Italy are considered separately, but Austria, the Netherlands, and Belgium are compared in a single chapter in order to highlight how countries with such seemingly similar institutional configurations could have had such different adjustment experiences. Finally, the Scandinavian welfare states are considered in a single chapter, again to illuminate the differing recent histories of countries that have traditionally been so similar in welfare-state aspirations and yet so different in economic profile and industrial structure.

1.3.1. The Anglo-Saxon Welfare States

Contrary to what many have assumed, there is no single 'Anglo-Saxon' model of welfare-state retrenchment. This is well illustrated in the chapters by Martin Rhodes on the UK and Herman Schwartz on Australia and New Zealand. Although in the postwar period prior to the 1970s, the United Kingdom, New Zealand, and Australia resembled one another in their approaches to social policy, with the 'liberal' welfare state a modest one serving as a safety net for a system based on full employment, they increasingly diverged over time. The UK, as Martin Rhodes explains, started with a comparatively meager welfare state whose expansion was constrained by economic conditions characterized by the need to defend an international reserve currency and by the inflationary pressures of a highly decentralized and conflictual wage-setting system. Neo-liberal reforms in the 1980s by a Conservative government succeeded in changing the structure of industry and breaking the power of unions, but did not fundamentally change the structure of the British welfare state. Rhodes suggests that it is only today, under a 'new' Labour government, that real reforms appear to be underway, albeit with a mix of neo-liberal individualism and social-democratic redistribution.

While the formal welfare states of New Zealand and Australia resembled the British model in the postwar period, Herman Schwartz shows that they differed from it in terms of economic policies, industrial structure, and industrial relations systems. As highly competitive exporters of agricultural products and raw materials, both had chosen to develop highly protected import-substituting industries in order to assure full employment as a complement to the welfare state. When this configuration ceased to work in the 1970s, both countries chose to liberalize their industrial sectors, attempting to achieve price competitiveness through government-controlled wage-setting procedures. Schwartz argues that since New Zealand was less successful in this, its Westminster-type governments turned to radical neo-liberal reforms in the 1980s that went beyond those enacted in Britain. Australia, by contrast, whose federal and bicameral constitution imposed greater political constraints, was able to achieve international competitiveness through corporatist concertation while maintaining and even expanding and its welfare state.

1.3.2. The Continental Welfare States

The seven Continental welfare states considered herein demonstrate as much if not more diversity in their patterns of adjustment than the Anglo-Saxon welfare states. Although all loosely resembled one another in the postwar period, with the 'Christian democratic' welfare state providing reasonably generous income replacement for the male breadwinner, they too adjusted in different ways at different times, because of differences in economic vulnerabilities and institutional capacities.

Among Continental welfare states, the country which one might assume would have had the fewest adjustment problems is Switzerland. It has had the highest per capita income and the highest employment ratios in our sample of advanced welfare states. Its export-oriented industries and services have remained highly competitive throughout the period included in our studies. And it has low tax levels, low levels of welfare expenditures, and a comparatively flexible labor market. Nevertheless, as Giuliano Bonoli and André Mach make clear, Switzerland has also felt the impact of international economic pressures, and sought to adjust. Political pressures from export-oriented business were successful in reducing the tariff and non-tariff barriers protecting the sheltered sectors of the Swiss economy, whose inefficiency was beginning to hurt the competitiveness of internationally exposed firms. However, when the demand for neo-liberal reforms touched on the benefits provided by the—not particularly generous—Swiss welfare state, Bonoli and Mach note that they were stopped not by the 'social partners' as in other consociational/

corporatist democracies, or by electoral shifts in governments, but by the direct democracy of the referendum system. As a consequence, limited retrenchment had to be combined with some important extensions of welfare coverage.

Germany, like Switzerland, has also been much less affected by international economic pressures than many of the other countries in our sample. The main question for Germany, as Philip Manow and Eric Seils see it, is: How can a country which continues to remain highly competitive internationally still suffer from serious adjustment problems, and in particular from such high unemployment? They argue that the impact of unification is only a part of the explanation, and that, ironically, Germany's very formula for success is also the key to its current problems. The manufacturing sector is still the backbone of the German economy. In spite of the job losses of the 1970s, it has been able to maintain the cooperative labor relations on which its international competitiveness depends by using the welfare state's generous exit options from the labor market for older and less productive workers. Given the prevailing mode of welfare financing, however, this required increases in social security contributions that added to the costs of labor throughout the economy. During the 1980s, employment increased again and welfare costs could be stabilized. But since the government relied on the same solution in coping with the massive employment losses in East Germany after unification, non-wage labor costs have risen to a level that can be sustained only by highly productive types of work. Under these conditions, as Manow and Seils contend, the German welfare state imposes severe constraints on the growth of the less productive domestic service sector, and thereby closes off one of the most promising solutions to the problems of unemployment and welfare-state financing.

The French welfare state, as elucidated by Jonah Levy, is financed by social security contributions to an even greater degree than is true in Germany. But unlike Germany, during the oil-price crises of the 1970s and early 1980s France tried to contain job losses by way of employment retention in its nationalized industries and subsidies to private firms. This changed with the decision to abandon *dirigisme* in industry after 1983. Thereafter, the welfare state—made more generous by the Socialist government after 1981—had to expand in order to absorb the job losses caused by industrial restructuring. As in Germany, increasing non-wage labor costs have in turn added to the difficulties of job creation in the private sector—a problem to which the government responded by shifting part of the burden to a special income tax. The purposeful expansion of the welfare state came to an end in the 1990s when the pressures of European monetary integration imposed severe budgetary constraints.

However, the efforts by successive governments to cut back certain types of welfare benefits were often confronted by large-scale protest, with French citizens taking to the streets to prevent the dismantling of the traditional welfare state. The problem, Levy argues, is one of style as much as of institutional conditions. In the absence of corporatist interlocutors, French governments tend to impose their preferred solutions without negotiation, treating the intensity of protest as a test of acceptability. But it may very well be that the more communicative style of the present Jospin government has in fact hit upon a formula for more consensual and successful adjustment.

While the main problems for most countries have come from the outside, with the need to adjust to the impact of internationalization, for Italy, as Maurizio Ferrera and Elisabetta Gualmini tell us, the main problems have been on the inside, and the external pressures from internationalization have in fact acted as an impetus for internal revitalization. Italian business has consistently been able to rise to the challenge of global economic competition. Until the early 1990s, however, the clientelistic Italian state was not able to put the brakes on the spiral of wage increases that were automatically linked to price increases, and that in turn had automatic links to all sorts of public and welfare-state expenditures which—in the absence of automatic balancing requirements—led to the exponential rise in public deficits. After 1992, though, with the sea-change in Italian politics, Ferrera and Gualmini describe a seemingly miraculous new set of dynamics, as labor and business began to coordinate wage restraint and social welfare reform with the state, largely in response to the impetus of European monetary integration. The question for Italy is: Can external pressure be enough to ensure the continuation of internal reform? And what if such pressure recedes?

Although Austria, the Netherlands, and Belgium are so seemingly alike in their tightly coupled, consociational and corporatist democratic structures and in the Bismarckian origin of their welfare states, they have had radically different experiences since the 1970s. Anton Hemerijk, Jelle Visser, and Brigitte Unger show that while the Netherlands, which appeared in the 1970s and early 1980s to be afflicted with a terminal, purely 'Dutch disease', has seemingly been cured, Belgium, with a similar initial profile, has been malingering, and Austria has managed to avoid the crises from which the others are recovering. What is the possible explanation? It cannot be simply economic since the Netherlands and Belgium were initially very similar in their sectoral profiles. It also cannot be purely institutional, since Dutch institutions did not change much between the 1970s and the 1990s. What the three countries have in common is a policymaking structure with plural veto positions that can lead to perverse policy outcomes if the occupants of these positions use their power to pursue and defend narrowly defined interest positions. Under these conditions, the difference between success and failure of the political economy as a whole does depend on the ability of separate corporate actors to adopt action orientations that emphasize common, rather than separate, interests. As Hemerijk, Visser, and Unger show, the Austrian social partners have succeeded in maintaining this 'encompassing' perspective throughout; the Dutch had to relearn it after dismal failures, and in Belgium the increasing salience of linguistic cleavages added to the difficulty of achieving, and acting on, convergent perceptions and interest definitions.

1.3.3. The Scandinavian Welfare State

Among the welfare states in our sample, the Scandinavian countries have consistently been the most generous, with the 'social democratic' welfare state achieving consistently higher levels of employment and greater equality in wages and higher rates of female employment than either Anglo-Saxon or Continental welfare states. Moreover, of the two Scandinavian welfare states considered herein, Sweden has almost consistently topped Denmark in generosity and levels of employment and equality for most of the period under consideration. But very recently, the two countries seem to have changed places. This is the main puzzle that Mats Benner and Torben Vad seek to explain. Sweden, for so long respected as the most successful social democratic welfare state, capable of withstanding the pressures of internationalization through the 1970s and 1980s, fell very far in the early 1990s. At the same time, Denmark, which had struggled unsuccessfully through the 1970s and 1980s to emulate Sweden, has now emerged as the most successful and progressive of welfare states. The superficial explanations seem to emphasize major errors of judgment on the part of Swedish fiscal and monetary policy, and considerable luck in the timing of Danish macroeconomic policy choices. Beyond that, however, Benner and Vad show how Sweden is struggling to defend the previous pattern of a 'decommodifying' welfare state whereas Denmark has switched to active labor market policies that emphasize and enforce the transition from welfare to work. The question they leave us with is: Will this change in places last? Or is Sweden's fall from grace only temporary, and Denmark's rise the result of short-lived, favorable coincidences?

1.4. The Special Studies

Some very important issues cannot be adequately dealt with in the context of single-country studies because significant patterns may only become visible in comparative overviews. A few of these questions are the subject of more narrowly focused and comparative 'special studies' in the second part of this book. These consider: (1) the changing nature of female employment and its impact on employment in general as well as on the direction of welfare state reform; (2) the changing nature of the workforce in view of rising unemployment and early retirement; (3) the impact of liberalization in formerly protected service and infrastructure sectors (transport, telecommunications, etc.) on employment and other welfare values; and (4) the greater or lesser vulnerability of national public-revenue systems to tax competition.

One of the central causes of change in the welfare state has been the changing economic role and employment behavior of women, especially of married women. Factors related to gender, as Mary Daly argues, are the key to explaining labor market variation among the most developed countries. But that picture is a complex one, requiring fine analytic gradations among women and men in different family situations. In explaining how women's presence has transformed labor markets in the twenty-three most developed countries, Daly draws on a wide range of possible factors, including policy packages, historical trends, and cultural norms about the family and women's roles. The analysis is based on a threefold model which includes supply, demand, and country-specific contextual factors.

Another very important factor in the adjustment of the welfare state is early retirement. The main questions are: Why did early exit from work, especially among industrial blue-collar workers, become a widespread practice in many (but not all) OECD countries since the first oil crisis? What problems did it solve? And what problems has it in turn created? Bernhard Ebbinghaus reviews the strategy of early retirement as an adaptation to economic restructuring, mass unemployment, the social needs of older workers, and the employment needs of young and female jobseekers; and he shows how it was facilitated by special state-sponsored programs, employer–union bargained agreements, and (un)intended loopholes in social security systems. Ebbinghaus then goes on to discuss how, as the costs of an increasingly inactive population rose while the expected employment effects failed to materialize, reformers sought to reverse the course of 'welfare without work'. And he explores how, besides blocking the pathways of early retirement, disability, and long-term unemployment, welfare states are now stressing new forms of part-time pension, extension and equalization of normal pension age, and shifting responsibilities and costs to the individual and firms.

The liberalization and/or privatization of formerly highly protected, monopolistic, public utilities and infrastructural services has added to the challenges of welfare-state adjustment. The move to market competition is affecting these industries' historical role not only as providers of public service goods but also as important national employers. Adrienne Héritier and Susanne K. Schmidt provide an initial stock-taking of the consequences of liberalization and privatization for the quality, cost, and availability of utilities and infrastructural services and for employment. They compare the telecommunications and railways reforms of France, Germany, and Britain, analyzing the different mechanisms that were enacted to ensure that public service goals continued to be met, and assessing the performance of the different regimes. In addition, they compare the employment effects of liberalization in the telecommunications, posts, railways, and energy sectors of a wider range of countries.

Finally, one of the factors often regarded as the cause of fiscal constraints on the welfare state is tax competition. But in fact very little is known about its real impact. How have advanced industrialized states reacted to the growing mobility of parts of their tax base? To what extent has tax competition resulted in a shift of burdens to less mobile tax bases? These are some of the questions Steffen Ganghof seeks to answer as he examines the different shape and force of tax competition in different areas of taxation in different countries, and the differing ways in which countries have responded. He concludes that while the pressures of international tax competition are real, so are countervailing economic and political pressures that work against a general 'race to the bottom' in the taxation of potentially mobile bases. And he shows that revenue-preserving strategies of policy adjustment prevented large-scale revenue losses, but partly led to a more controversial structure of taxation.

1.5. Conclusion

The contributions in this book offer a valuable set of insights into the different paths of adjustment of welfare states to international economic pressures. Most clearly, they show that there is no convergence in the welfare state, and that there is no single solution or formula for successful adaptation. Rather, each country must find its own way. And this depends upon a variety of nationally-specific factors. These include a country's economic profile and its level of vulnerability to external economic pressures; its institutional configuration and its capacity to respond effectively when necessary; the policy legacies that shape the available options; and the social learning processes that affect policy actors' awareness and willingness to respond as necessary. But while economics, institutions, and policies are the main factors considered by these chapters, they also note, where relevant, the political events, ideas, and even values and legitimating discourses which affect public reactions to policy initiatives, in order to understand the political dynamics of adjustment and not just the economic or institutional dynamics.

Thus, even though all authors collaborating in our project started from a common set of working hypotheses and a broadly standardized research design, the completed studies emphasize the diversity of national experiences, and the importance of 'historical' explanations that are responsive to the causal influence of country-specific factor constellations. These need to be taken seriously, and the country studies assembled in this volume deserve to be understood and evaluated in their own light. Nevertheless, the overall project was inspired by the expectation that the whole would be more than the sum of parts, and it is gratifying to see that this expectation was fully realized. In fact, the studies in this volume do not only provide analyses and explanations of national experiences. They also constitute a unique and immensely useful body of information for secondary, comparative analysis that permits the investigation of more complex sets of explanatory hypotheses than was previously possible. These explanatory hypotheses in turn enable us to tease out patterns that offer clues to new 'equilibrium models' of the welfare state, ones which have moved from vulnerability to competitiveness. And although our analyses yield no findings of convergence on a single model of welfare state, they do show that certain patterns of success or new 'equilibria' do emerge within each of the three clusters of welfare states (Anglo-Saxon, Continental, and Scandinavian) as well as certain cluster-specific patterns of failure or 'disequilibria'. These patterns are explored in the comparative chapters in Volume I.

REFERENCES

CERNY, PHILIP G. (1994). 'The Dynamics of Financial Globalization: Technology, Market Structure, and Policy Response'. *Policy Sciences*, 27: 319–42.

POLANYI, KARL (1957). *The Great Transformation*. Boston: Beacon Press.

SCHARPF, FRITZ W. (1991). *Crisis and Choice in European Social Democracy*. Ithaca, NY: Cornell University Press.

SCHARPF, FRITZ W., SCHMIDT, VIVIEN A., and VAD, TORBEN B. (1998). *The Adjustment of National Employment and Social Policy to Economic Internationalization*. Background Paper. Cologne: Max Planck Institute for the Study of Societies.

2

Restructuring the British Welfare State: Between Domestic Constraints and Global Imperatives

MARTIN RHODES

Britain has always been exceptional among European welfare states, and it continues to be so at the dawn of a new century. As a predominantly tax-based rather than contributions-based system, with no social partner involvement in the management of social security, the institutional and policy linkages between social policy and the economy have always been fractured and weak. This has had advantages. Unlike the Bismarckian insurance-based systems, Britain has not had a major structural problem of pension liabilities funded from social charges and payroll taxes. But unlike in its Nordic and Continental neighbors, the notion of the social wage has never been at the heart of a social consensus but instead has been the object of social conflict since mid-1940s, making a successful incomes policy impossible from the outset, not simply problematic as elsewhere in Europe with the first oil-price shock and the end of Bretton-Woods.

Britain has also been exceptional in respect of the nature and extent of its internationalization as a former imperial power and early industrializer. This was an economy which was already highly vulnerable to international economic shocks in the early postwar period, and the victim of relative economic decline and macroeconomic turmoil through its 'not so golden age'. Exposure to a turbulent external environment, exacerbated by periods of acute macroeconomic mismanagement, has conditioned the development of the British welfare state from the outset and, combined with ideological opposition to state intervention from an early stage, explains its 'liberal' nature.

I would like to thank Noel Whiteside, Colin Crouch, Jonathan Zeitlin, Michael Moran, Ian Gough, Des King, Fritz W. Scharpf, and Vivien A. Schmidt for their comments on earlier drafts of this article, and the latter two for their patience and forbearance as editors. Thanks too go to Herman Schwartz for being an inspiring partner when, in an earlier incarnation, this article was part of a joint venture.

Against this background, the industrial relations—and broader economic—crisis of the 1970s should be seen as the accumulation of dysfunctions and contradictions generated by a voluntarist industrial
relations system and an incapacity, primarily for organizational reasons,
for implementing incomes policy. Contrary to the impression often given
of a 'consensus' on economic policy priorities and the desirability of a
strong welfare state, in reality 'stop–go' policies and a volatile economic
cycle combined with the vicissitudes of partisan politics to produce an
acute discontinuity in policymaking. The flaws of the system were fully
exposed when exogenous pressures post-Bretton-Woods became more
constraining, full employment became difficult to sustain, and fiscal problems made an extensive industrial policy impossible at a time of widespread crisis in traditional sectors of industry.

Thus, as presented in the first section of this chapter, until the 1980s,
welfare and the economy by and large existed in separate spheres, and
when and where they interacted the result was often dysfunctional. At a
general level, as in all European countries, welfare could be used as part
of an ensemble of public interventions to sustain demand and full
employment and compensate for risks over the life cycle. But in Britain,
while Keynesian policies were always problematic in practice, especially
in reconciling full employment with wage demands and growth with the
balance of payments and exchange rate stability, the lack of consensus on
the social wage triggered industrial relations conflict that fed into the
cycle of macro-mismanagement and decline. Thus, in its disjointed mix
of formal social programs and labor market income delivery, both the
'accumulation function' (promoting growth) and 'legitimation function'
(securing popular support for economic adjustment) of welfare were
flawed.

Thatcherism, analyzed in Section 2.2 below, provided a new and rather
brutal 'institutional fix' that fundamentally altered the logic of the system
and established a new set of linkages between welfare—in both its formal
and informal dimensions—and the economic system. It was not just policy and new legislation that reformed the system but, perhaps with even
greater effect, the decade of macro-mismanagement between the early
1980s and early 1990s which accentuated the economy's vulnerability to
external shocks, devastated much of an already enfeebled manufacturing
sector, and via two massive labor shakeouts, completely transformed the
composition of British employment. In the end, this complemented nicely
the political and policy campaign against all fragile vestiges of British-
style corporatism and collectivism, ending decades of futile attempts to
forge incomes agreements and turning wage determination over to one of
the most completely deregulated markets in the OECD.

The outcome was a welfare state much more clearly connected, indeed subjugated to, the needs of an economy increasingly polarized in terms of employment opportunities, entitlements, and incomes. The new model was one in which, as discussed in Section 2.3, a new 'functionality' was engineered between a social and employment policy system and the demands of accumulation in a liberal market economy. Low corporation taxes and social charges are vital, not just for sustaining Britain's FDI dependent manufacturing sector, but also for meeting the demands of the large low-wage, low-skill, low-productivity sector of the economy, whose employers also benefit from 'in-work' means-tested social security benefits as an effective subsidy. Demand for goods and personal services is sustained by low personal rates of income tax and a high level of credit indebtedness facilitated by a highly liberalized domestic financial sector. In these circumstances, income polarization is not just a consequence of a deregulated employment system, but a key functional component of the current economic system.

In these circumstances, any new government—not just that of Tony Blair—would find itself in a tight economic straitjacket. The potential for progressive innovation is small. The 'new functionality' between welfare and the economy must be conformed with, for on this will partly depend the growth and employment creation that might allow for more equitable policies in the long run. The major paradox—which New Labour is currently struggling to manage—is that demand for quality public services remains high while higher taxes are not just unpopular but 'dysfunctional' for the economic model it inherited. Therein lie both the force behind and the future pitfalls of the Blairite 'Third Way'.

2.1. The 'trente glorieuses' and the Crisis of the 1970s

2.1.1. The 'Model': The Postwar Settlement and Early Vulnerabilities

In any comparative work on the welfare state it is obligatory to begin with a discussion of British 'exceptionalism'. Britain is different in numerous respects from its European neighbors, both in terms of its welfare state and the general 'liberal' political economy in which it is embedded. Only by understanding these distinctive features can we understand the trajectory of welfare-state development and the nature of the 'adjustment problem' with which it becomes identified by the late 1970s. While many states of Continental Europe were constructed or reconstructed in a way which placed social contracts at the heart of their constitutions, in Britain, the sphere of welfare was placed at arm's length. The disarticulation of welfare from the economy has been true at least for the period until the late

1970s. From the mid-1980s onwards, it would become more central to economic regulation but in ways, once again, quite distinct from other European countries.

2.1.1.1. The Nature of the Welfare State

First, the welfare state itself. Although frequently referred to as 'liberal', the British welfare state was less the product of nineteenth-century English liberalism than of an amalgam of traditions, including in 1945 a compromise between the designs of an elitist civil service and pragmatic Labour Party 'socialism'. 1945 was far from being 'year zero' (Parry 1986). The Liberal government's introduction of old age pensions in 1908 and social insurance against unemployment and sickness in 1911 led to union involvement in running the state's insurance schemes alongside their own limited occupational regimes. The one critical change of the next thirty years was the withdrawal of the unions from social insurance management under the pressure of recession and high unemployment.

Thus, when World War II provided the stimulus for a new era of social reconstruction, bolstered by the election of the Atlee Labour government in July 1945, the unions were absent as formal participants from the feast. One of the peculiarities (at least in the European context) of the British system was the consequent divorce between the labor movement and the social insurance system (Toft 1995; Crouch 1999*a*). Combined with 'voluntarism' and organizational fragmentation in industrial relations, this helped prevent the development of the notion of the 'social wage' in Britain. As argued below, this made an important contribution to the more general problems of economic management during the postwar period.

For this reason, it makes sense to separate analytically the 'formal' social policy welfare state—the core programs, that is, of social provision—from the 'informal' welfare of employment and incomes policy and social dialogue (see Whiteside 1996). The formal programs established in the mid-1940s sought to give citizens universal rights of access to equal standards of health care, family income support, comprehensive social insurance (including pensions), public housing, and education.[1] The key elements were the National Insurance system funded by employers, employees, and the Treasury which covers unemployment, sickness, maternity and industrial injury benefits, and retirement pensions. The

---

[1] The major pieces of legislation were the Education Act (1944), the Family Allowance Act (1946), the National Health Service Act (1946), the Town and Country Planning Act (1947), the National Assistance Act (1948), the Children's Act (1948), and the Housing Act (1949).

National Health Service provided free treatment and has largely been tax-financed. These initiatives provided the basic architecture of the system which, in its essentials, persists today.

Their particular character can be explained by a peculiarly British combination of intellectual influence and domestic and international constraints. Like Keynes, William Beveridge (the 'architect' of British welfare) was a 'reluctant collectivist'. His 1942 report on welfare maintained that 'the State in organizing security should not stifle incentive, opportunity, responsibility'. Social insurance and assistance were to guarantee a subsistence income only (Lowe 1993: 16–19). But largely due to Treasury skepticism of National Insurance and pessimism about the economy, the system created by Labour in 1946 was even less generous than Beveridge envisaged. There was also a major reluctance to antagonize British industrialists: in 1950 they contributed the lowest proportion to welfare costs in Western Europe (15.6% compared to 39.7% in West Germany, 65.1% in France, and 70.7% in Italy) (Tomlinson 1998: 72). Though pensions eligibility was more generous under Labour than originally intended, the result overall was an austere system of social security that differed only from former private arrangements in that insurance was compulsory (Barr and Coulter 1990: 274 ff.).

One of the most important aspects of social policy in the early postwar period was on the 'informal' side—that is the commitment to a full and stable level of employment. Beveridge's benchmark measure for full employment fixed unemployment at 3 percent—a level only exceeded as an annual average in 1947 and 1971–72 (Lowe 1993: 68–69). But there lay one of the biggest flaws in the postwar settlement. For successfully stimulating growth and full employment via demand management depended ultimately on the predictable behavior of employers and trade unions. Inflationary pressures in a seller's market for labor could only be contained if the distributional conflict was controllable (Marquand 1998: 44). Yet this assumed—wrongly as it turned out—that the unions would not endanger full employment by bargaining irresponsibly. In fact, organized labor could not be 'encompassed' within the system and the notion of a 'social wage' was neither developed nor institutionalized. This was to make economic management all the more difficult through Britain's 'not so golden age', with important—adverse—consequences for welfare provision.

2.1.1.2. A Vulnerable Political Economy

The British economy was highly vulnerable to external pressures from early on, and this restricted the scope for welfare expansion. A weak manufacturing sector meant that the international economy constrained the elaboration of social policy from the outset. Chronic current account deficits necessitated 'stop–go' policies to preserve the international payments position. Relatively deep, liquid (and impatient) share markets even before the 1970s meant a rapid transmission of financial pressures in the economy when internationalization accelerated. There has also been a high level of dependence on inflows of foreign capital to fund current account deficits and generate new manufacturing investment. Consequently, British governments have been especially sensitive to falling exchange rates, interest rate shocks (including credit rating downgrades), and the problematic distribution of risk between the public and private sectors.

The early postwar years found Britain at a distinct disadvantage. In 1954 it had a debt-income ratio of 175 percent (Germany had its debt written down in the late 1940s and 1950s) and the servicing costs made balance of payments crises hard to avoid (Eichengreen and Ritschl 1998). While poor economic management exacerbated that problem, the root causes of decline are to be found in the micro-foundations of the economy (Hall 1986). The financial system has been internationally oriented and poorly integrated with the domestic economy. Poor levels of investment in manufacturing have long been a serious problem. The financial system, while facilitating mergers and takeovers, has failed to provide domestic finance for regionally-based small and medium-size firms where detailed knowledge, risk assessment, and long-term investment commitments are required. The market-based credit system has kept banks, firms, and the government in different spheres, preventing the development of a state or bank-led industrial modernization strategy (see e.g. Zysman 1983). Partly in consequence, large, well-integrated, modern capitalist firms have been slow to emerge. Britain soon lost its lead in inventions, innovations, and patenting to the USA, Germany, and France in the early twentieth century. The resistance of family-run firms as well as financiers delayed the shift to the mass production paradigm (Elbaum and Lazonick 1986). Mergers from the 1950s on were frequently defensive and incomplete responses to antitrust legislation, often spurred on by financial motives such as advantageous tax treatment for debt capital.

Delayed modernization has also been attributed to an adversarial industrial relations system in which a strong but decentralized, craft-based union movement and a weakly organized employer class have impeded consensus on incomes, industrial organization, and technological change. The proliferation of British industrial relations into hundreds of bargaining units, multi-unionism, and the voluntarist rather than legal basis of industrial relations practice produced an amorphous system bedeviled by mistrust, over which governments could exercise little leverage. Ostensibly based on four pillars—legal support for union membership; legal immunities for unions in disputes and secondary actions; the acceptance of collective bargaining; and legitimate union influence in tripartite institutions—this characterization gives a greater impression of coherence than ever really existed. The tradition of 'voluntarism' has proven impossible to reform: Labour's 'In Place of Strife' initiative (1969), the Industrial Relations Act (1972), the Trade Union and Labour Relations Act (1974–76), the Employment Protection Act (1975) all fell victim to the essential 'disorganization' of the system (see Beardwell 1996).

As King and Wood (1999) argue, the more general problem was one of 'firms embedded in uncoordinated organizational contexts'. Hostile to collective organization and unable to provide supply-side public goods, they developed product market strategies that minimized reliance on such goods. Training is a major case in point. Combined with low spending on R & D, the collapse of the traditional apprenticeships, and the absence of a national training system have led to severe deficiencies in Britain's 'innovation system'. The result has been a 'low wage–low skills' equilibrium (Finegold and Soskice 1988) in which a vicious circle of low skills, low productivity, low profits, and low wages forces reliance on 'price' rather than 'non-price' competitiveness. The state has been unable to steer the economy in a different direction, despite decades of attempting to do so. The creation of various instruments of industrial planning and intervention from the 1950s onwards were all inspired by a rationalist optimism and drew heavily on Continental experience.[2] But all suffered from adversarial, 'stop–go' policymaking and the frequent antagonism of industrialists and the Treasury. Nationalized companies, meanwhile, were poorly managed, lacked clear investment and performance guidelines, and in most sectors became heavily indebted and plagued by chronic industrial relations problems.

2.1.1.3. 'Disorganized Capitalism' and British Welfare

In the British case then, 'disorganized capitalism' has long been the prevailing state of affairs. And within this general context, far from early postwar economic growth and export performance being damaged by the welfare state, it was rather the reverse. The weaknesses of the British economy and the relegation of welfare in the list of postwar priorities heavily constrained early welfare expansion, and subsequently induced a shift away from the original universal ambitions. In fact, by contrast with most

---

[2] These include the National Economic Development Council in the early 1960s, the Department for Economic Affairs (1964), the Economic Development Councils and the National Plan (1965), the Industrial Reorganization Corporation (late 1960s), and the National Enterprise Board (1975).

of its European neighbors, this was always a rather lean—and mean—welfare state. This was partly due to some of its key characteristics: a flat-rate system of pensions payments which, while linked to wage inflation until the Conservatives broke that link, did not prevent old age poverty; under-investment in the NHS which has always had to ration its services; and a concentration on the setting of minimum standards rather than on redistribution that set an effective floor for incomes protecting the poorest in the population.

Claims that an over-generous welfare state damaged Britain's economic prospects (e.g. Bacon and Eltis 1978; Barnett 1986; Maynard 1988) have been convincingly refuted for the early postwar period by evidence that welfare spending had no detrimental impact on investment in the early years of welfare-state expansion (Tomlinson 1995: 194–219). More generally, any increase in government financed consumption comes at the expense of marketed sector consumption, not marketed sector investment, and this is a true for the 1950s as the 1970s (Crafts 1995: 253; Broadberry 1991). As Hall (1986: 31) argues, although public spending as a share of GDP grew from 32 percent in 1950 to 45 percent in 1980, with an annual PSBR (public sector borrowing requirement) of around 4 percent in the 1950s, peaking at 8 percent in the 1970s, there is no causal link between poor growth and public spending. Contending (as do Bacon and Eltis 1978) that public sector activity is unproductive ignores the contribution health policy, education, and national infrastructure make to the health of the national economy.

The informal elements of welfare—resting on incomes and employment policy—were similarly shackled by more general economic problems, and here it is possible to attribute some of the blame for Britain's economic problems. Given the parlous condition of industry, and the disorganized state of industrial relations, contradictions between full employment policy and balance of payments equilibrium made informal welfare not just a victim (as in the case of formal welfare) but also a cause (among others) of recurrent economic crisis. Full employment increased the bargaining power of trade unions—whose membership was equivalent to 43 percent of the workforce in 1950—over both wages and working conditions. In the absence of a workable incomes policy, or effective policies to bolster industrial productivity, the long-term effects could only compound Britain's economic problems.

Thus, despite bursts of growth, poor economic performance meant an insufficiency of economic resources to meet the pretensions of successive governments. GDP doubled between 1948 and 1973, but average economic growth was half that of the EEC, reducing, correspondingly, the resources to be spent on welfare. Despite its wartime defeat and widespread social and economic dislocation, by the early 1950s, Germany spent a larger proportion of GDP on welfare than Britain. By the end of that decade, Britain spent less on social security than all of its major European industrial rivals and many of the smaller ones. Social transfers in 1960 were 6.2 percent—well below the 9.3 percent European median (Crafts 1995: 247). Poor economic performance constrained British welfare. There is no convincing evidence to suggest that the reverse was the case.

2.1.2. *Three Episodes of 'Crisis': U-turns and Retreats in 'Golden Age' Social Policy*

The vulnerability of the economy, poor institutional adjustment capacity, and adverse consequences of mismanagement for welfare can be illustrated briefly by considering three 'golden age' episodes of policy crisis. These episodes illustrate the institutional dynamic at the center of Britain's economic management problems during the 'golden age' and the adverse consequences for welfare:

(1) the maintenance of full employment in an uncompetitive industrial system and in the absence of an incomes policy capacity strongly contributed to the 'stop–go' cycles of the 1950s and 1960s;
(2) when demand was expanded to sustain employment, imports increased, potential exports were diverted to the home market, and a balance of payments crisis threatened (frequently also provoking a sterling crisis and higher interest rates);
(3) given that devaluation was often resisted to protect the trading and reserve roles of sterling, the response was always the same: reduce demand, increase unemployment, and create the conditions for another 'go' phase in the cycle;
(4) in turn, the tax changes used to regulate these fluctuations frequently hit formal welfare provision (Lowe 1993: 109 ff.; Stewart 1977).

The consequence was a subtle interplay between the political and economic climate. Despite policy reversals under both governments, a general consensus on the desirability of welfare (or at least an inability to control it) seems to be confirmed by the fact that social spending rose faster under Conservative than Labour governments. From 1950 to 1980, the seventeen years of Conservative government saw GPD rise 2.9 percent on average and social spending by 4.1 percent. By contrast, thirteen years of Labour saw a 2.0 percent average increase in growth and 3.5 percent in spending (Parry 1986: 223). But this ignores economic constraints. Labour was able to expand spending in the 1960s when the economy grew faster, as were the

Conservatives in 1970–72. Labour is penalized, though, by poor performance in the late 1970s, while the Conservatives contained spending in the 1950s, when growth rates of both social spending and GDP were below the postwar average. In reality, as the following 'mini-crises' reveal, neither party in power was fully capable of controlling the social policy agenda nor of managing the economy in classical Keynesian fashion.

The first crisis was encountered early on. Having created the welfare state and nationalized a large part of the economy (accounting for 10% of GDP and 19% of fixed investment), the Atlee government could more easily exert moral suasion over the unions than subsequent administrations. The government also gave into joint union and employer lobbying for trade restrictions and price controls and against effective antitrust policies. Nevertheless, although a wage freeze was accepted on a temporary basis after the 1949 currency devaluation, this led to attacks by sections of the labor movement that workers were bearing the costs of making British industry more competitive.

The main problem lay in convincing skilled and semi-skilled trade union members to accept either a squeeze in wage differentials or that the expansion of welfare could be traded for real wage gains. Signs of a fragmentation of bargaining had already appeared with a powerful shop stewards movement in the car industry and unofficial dockers' strikes. As long as cost of living subsidies were in place (by 1950–51 they were more expensive than the new National Health Service), union acquiescence could be bought. But attempts to offset the impact of subsidy reductions and price increases with social spending met with union opposition (Whiteside 1996: 90 ff.). When, in spring 1950, Stafford Cripps, the Chancellor of the Exchequer, offered budgetary concessions in return for wage restraint, the TUC General Secretary advised that 'he did not believe the unions would recognize the notion of the social wage' (Jones 1985: 30 ff.). In the absence of such an understanding, plans put in place in the last year of the Attlee government for permanent mechanisms of wage regulation were doomed to fail—as were successive attempts of this kind under both Labour and Conservative governments (for detailed accounts, see Fishbein 1984 and Jones 1985).

In any case, there was little room for bargaining over the social wage. The 1947 sterling convertibility crisis reduced the availability of dollars for timber imports (hitting the government's housing program), while expenditure cuts after the 1949 devaluation reined in spending on health and education. Per capita health spending was virtually static between 1948 and 1954 (and actually fell as a proportion of GDP), while capital expenditure on hospitals fell to one-third of pre-war levels (Lowe 1993: 180). The first new hospital only opened at the end of the 1950s, by which time the hospital bed/population ratio was lower than in 1939 (Tomlinson 1995: 212). In May 1951, a divided government, beset by economic difficulties, introduced charges for dental and ophthalmic care—breaching the principle of a free health service and provoking the resignation of the Health Minister, Aneurin Bevan.

The second episode came against the background of ten years of Conservative mismanagement and early attempts to retrench in welfare. The Conservatives contributed to the disorganization of industrial relations, and at a time when other European countries were implementing the American 'productivity gospel', neglected the inadequacies of training and the weaknesses of management (Tiratsoo and Tomlinson 1998. For a contrasting perspective which is much less pessimistic about the success of organizational change in this period, see Zeitlin and Herrigel 2000). Britain's relative decline massively accelerated.[3] The welfare state began to suffer from its identification as a burden rather than a productive resource, for the Conservatives had already developed a 'Thatcherite' critique of welfare as reducing individual initiative and family and social responsibility and creating disincentives to work (Glennerster 1990: 16). With full employment achieved, what need was there for universal social provision? Thus, the 1954 Phillips Committee recommended the abandonment of a key principle of Beveridge—the rise of flat-rate benefits to subsistence level—and argued that pensioners would have to rely on means-tested National Assistance. In 1956–58 the Treasury attacked universal family allowances for the second child. In 1957 there was a further retreat from Beveridge when the Treasury's contribution to National Insurance was capped (Lowe 1993: 142–43).

In response, the trade unions united in their defense of free collective bargaining and against the introduction of incomes policy measures.[4] The government became caught between two contradictory policies: rising wages were used to justify the removal of universal social welfare, while the welfare state was used to justify appeals for wage restraint (Whiteside 1996: 98). The dual commitment to full employment (and thus electoral popularity) and the strength of the pound contributed to the 'stop–go' cycle of the 1950s: policy lurched between contracting the economy when a failure to achieve balances, above all in foreign payments, threatened sterling, and expanding it when unemployment threatened to rise. The

[3] Growth (per capita GDP per annum) in France, Germany, and Italy increased, respectively, by 2.0%, 2.8%, and 3.3% over that of Britain in 1951–65. This compares with increases of 0.4%, 2.0%, and 0.8% between 1924 and 1937 (Tiratsoo and Tomlinson 1998: 33–34).

[4] These included the Council on Prices, Productivity and Incomes (1959), a National Incomes Commission (1962), and the National Economic Development Council (1963–64).

excessive use of monetary and fiscal instruments to engineer deflation was highly damaging to investment—both public and private. The 1959 Plowden Committee criticized the manipulation of current and capital social expenditure as a means of regulating the economy because of its damaging effects on social provision (Lowe 1993: 109–11). Between 1952 and 1958, the growth rates of social expenditure and GDP were both below the postwar average.

The third episode—the crisis of the Labour government of Harold Wilson (1964–70)—is the most dramatic. In the last years of the Conservative government a 'tacit' alliance with the unions emerged in which wage moderation was exchanged for welfare expansion—in hospitals (where spending/GDP had fallen below the 1930s' level), higher education, and council housing. But the conditions for an enduring and explicit bargain on the social wage still did not exist—as was fully revealed under Labour. Labour planned innovations on two fronts: a state-led modernization strategy, linking planning with industrial policy; and a revival of incomes policy. But both were completely overwhelmed by economic problems. By 1965–66, the economy was overheating and inflation threatened competitiveness. After many years of current balance surplus, a large deficit was recorded in 1964 and low reserves and a weak payments position exposed sterling to crisis on three occasions between 1965 and 1967. The consequent combination of cuts and tax increases diverted nearly £1 bn (or 3% of GNP) from consumption.

International factors loomed large: greater international competition increased the import propensity of the economy and prevented producers from passing on increasing unit wage costs (Woodward 1993: 74–75); and as revealed by the financial disasters of 1965–68, the confidence of overseas bankers and speculators had become at least as important as the state of the real economy. Together speculation and British capital exports accounted for two-thirds of the total negative foreign balance of £3.6 bn in 1964–68 (Pollard 1992: 360).

In consequence, Labour's welfare ambitions had to be abandoned. A promised 'income guarantee' and upgrade in universal benefits were jettisoned. Means-tested claimants and benefits increased enormously, in conflict with both Labour Party policy and Beveridgean principles (Lowe 1993: 143). Prescription charges—which Labour had withdrawn on its return to office—were reintroduced. While Labour's proposals for reforms of pensions, local government, and the NHS foundered, in employment policy, the aims of the 1964 Industrial Training Act were undermined by the absence of consensus among firms on training delivery and a failure to override trade union control of the apprenticeship system (Vickerstaff 1985: 45–64).

There was no new consensus on the social wage. Labour was unable to use demand-management to draw the unions into a voluntary and long-term incomes policy commitment and a fractured labor movement, in any case, provided an unlikely partner in such a project. The TUC could barely influence the strategies of its more than 100 member unions. But more to the point there were by now 200,000 or more workshops, sections, or groups into which two thousand or so plants had fragmented for pay decisions. In 1965–66, wage rates and hourly earnings rose at twice the norm due to plant-level pay increases and wage drift. After devaluation, attempts to introduce a zero norm, deflationary policies, unemployment at over 2 percent and attempts by employers to recoup profitability all led to the strike and wages explosion of 1969–70 that helped bring the Conservatives back to power.

All in all, and despite improvements in social and economic conditions, this was a far from sparkling 'golden age'. The consequence for social policy was what Glennerster (1998) calls 'welfare with the lid on'—that is, a constrained welfare state in which, despite periods of spending expansion, there was little scope for building on the foundations put in place in 1945. Welfare spending grew when and as GDP grew—although the former tended to outpace the latter as time went on. Between 1952 and 1958, social spending and GDP both grew below the postwar average; between 1961 and 1968 they were both above average; in the crisis years of the 1970s both grew on average at 1 percent or less in relation to the average (Parry 1986).

2.1.3. The End of the 'Golden Age': Welfare and the Failure of Economic Management, 1970–1978

In terms of the underlying dynamic of discontinuous economic policy-making, there is no sharp break between the experiences of recurrent 'mini-crises' in the 1960s and the major crises of the 1970s. The first Wilson Labour government had become entrapped in the same vicious circle as its predecessors. The essence of the problem was the failure to maintain productive efficiency in industry, which led to export losses, an increased import propensity, balance of payments problems, and short-term, knee-jerk government responses which further damaged investment and productivity.

In this context, incomes policies in the 1960s, buttressed by the devaluation of 1967, were really attempts to bring prices into line with the weakened condition of the economy as export markets became more competitive. The competitiveness problem itself remained untackled. Wage rises were actually below those in Britain's major competitor countries

(France, West Germany, Italy and Japan) until the 1970s: the difference was that in those countries these increased costs were absorbed by productivity gains that British manufacturing could not generate (Pollard 1992: 366–67). Meanwhile, and contrary to the usual 'golden age' thesis, maintaining full employment in this context—although largely achieved before the late 1960s–early 1970s—was never unproblematic, regardless of fixed exchange rates and the absence of major external shocks (cf. Sentance 1998: 38–40).

In this respect, the 'external problem' facing the economy had been consistent from the end of the 1950s onwards, as the 'seller's market' that British manufacturers enjoyed was steadily transformed into a 'buyer's market' in which they could not compete (Woodward 1993: 74–75). Whereas in 1951 some 51 percent of British exports went to Commonwealth markets protected by Imperial Preference, this fell to 29 percent by 1970. By then, 40 percent of exports were sold on much more competitive European markets. Meanwhile imports also increased as British goods lost their price and quality advantage at home. Also consistent was the other aspect of the difficult external position: the poor ratio of reserves to short-term liabilities that lay behind perpetual sterling crises. Before 1970, gold and dollar reserves never exceeded $4 bn, compared with much higher levels of sterling balances (held mainly by foreign governments), sustained by the international role of the pound. Between 1972 and 1976, this situation became critical, with reserves only sufficient to pay for two month's imports (Burk and Cairncross 1982: 167–68; Cairncross and Eichengreen 1983).

To the extent that both the competitive and sterling reserve problems were longstanding features of the economy, 'internationalization' was not new. Moreover, short-term capital flows had always had a substantial influence over exchange rate policy and the balance of payments. What was new, however, was the importance assumed in the 1970s by the foreign exchange market in determining the exchange rate. This reflected both long-term factors such as the internationalization of capital markets and short-term factors such as the inflow and outflow of OPEC oil revenues after the mid-1970s' price hikes.

The crisis of 1975–77 was significantly worsened by large-scale capital outflows, at a time when the current account was actually improving (Burk and Cairncross 1982: 279–80). Nevertheless, this begs the question of why there was so little confidence among holders of sterling and why Britain suffered so much more than other countries facing the same perilous international economic conditions. This takes us back to the chronic failures of domestic economic management, which, ultimately, must bear full responsibility for the crisis of the British economy. New dimensions of 'internationalization' were complicating and exacerbating factors, rather than causal.

Like Harold Wilson's Labour government before him, Edward Heath's Conservatives came to power in 1970 determined to break with 'stop–go', innovate in labor market policy, and reform the welfare state—including an early but active 'pre-Thatcherite' search for alternatives to state provision in housing and income maintenance. But with unemployment increasing from 2.5 percent in late 1970 to 3.8 percent in the first quarter of 1972, and inflation at 6–7 percent, Heath made two big mistakes. The first was liberalizing credit controls (in the mistaken view that interest rates manipulation could control any consequent burst in bank lending and growth), the second his 'dash for growth' in the form of a reflationary budget in 1972. An unsuccessful attempt to join the European Community's currency 'snake' led to a decision to allow the pound to float, followed by a substantial depreciation, which, given the worldwide commodity price boom, added imported inflation to the domestic wage explosion (Jones 1985: 97). While the classic demand strategy gave the requisite kick to the economy, producing growth of 5 percent by the middle of 1973 and a fall in unemployment, the industrial relations and incomes policies were a dismal failure.

At the same time, Heath became caught in a familiar bind over the social wage. Heath's employment and welfare policies hardly endeared him to the labor movement. First, the Industrial Relations Act of 1971—which sought to bring greater coherence and responsibility to wage bargaining—was rejected outright by the unions. Most reprehensible for the latter was its attack on the closed shop. Further, like previous Conservative governments, Heath's failed to appreciate the political importance of preserving the welfare status quo. For while health and education were ring-fenced, alternatives to state provision were actively sought in housing and income maintenance. The 1972 Housing Finance Act sought to make housing aid more selective, targeting poorer tenants only; the 1973 Pensions Act sought to wind down National Insurance and introduce greater reliance on private occupational pensions (Glennerster 1990: 18–20).

Through 1972, ultimately unsuccessful negotiations saw the unions consciously raise the issue of the social wage and link their agreement to a wage accord with radical welfare concessions. The statutory pay freeze that followed the collapse of incomes policy talks held average earnings at less than 1 percent from November 1972 to March 1973 and prices stabilized, but the government's expansionary policies and falling unemployment led to competitive bidding between firms. Subsequent attempts to keep wage increases at 7 percent linked to a new system of wage indexing were bust apart by a large miner's wage claim and strike. A voluntary policy had become infeasible anyway. For there were now some 5,700 pay settlements in firms employing between 100 and 999 people alone, excluding those in the smaller firm sector (Jones 1985: 97). Wage drift was uncontrollable. And if the miners had not undermined Heath's incomes policy, rising inflation and the autumn 1973 OPEC price hike certainly would have (Jones 1985: 86–96; Brown 1994: 35–37).

Labour came back into power in 1974 hoping (against hope) that by invoking the social wage it would be able to bind the unions to government policy without surrendering its freedom to govern. In fact, that was precisely the problem: inflexibility in domestic policy at a time of unprecedented external pressures. There were thus critical differences between the response of Britain to the crisis and that of other, more successful, countries. In 1974–75, the Wilson government prioritized full employment while relying on an insubstantial incomes policy. By contrast, a tough combination of fiscal and monetary restraint in Germany and the USA was followed by a return to expansionary policies in 1975. Thus, prices and unemployment rose faster in Britain than elsewhere.

After the biggest boom in 1973, Britain went into the deepest recession in 1974–76: zero GDP growth compared with 3–5 percent in France, Italy, and Germany. Productivity growth was stagnant against 10 percent growth in France and Germany (Burk and Cairncross 1982: 221–24). In the liquidity crisis of 1974–75, industrial profitability fell to half that of France, a third that of West Germany, and to a quarter that of Japan and the USA. Labour costs doubled (Middlemas 1991: 10–12). Stagflation, combined with higher public spending and borrowing, reserves well below the liquid liabilities that had accumulated as sterling balances, and, most importantly for market confidence, four years of current account deficit from 1973 to 1976, made Britain the sickest of the sick men of Europe.

It was not meant to be that way. The social wage was at the center of Labour's 'Social Contract'—a bold attempt to bring the lessons and benefits of Scandinavian and Continental corporatism to industrial strife ridden Britain. A new incomes policy was to be based on 'real wages'—pay after tax, social security, and benefits (Middlemas 1990: 374–75). In return for wage stability, Labour promised a wealth tax, price and rent control, more protection against dismissals, a full repeal of Conservative industrial relations laws, 'economic democracy', more nationalization and full employment. Things began relatively well. The first of three budgets in 1974 was slightly deflationary but more strongly distributional, increasing pensions and food subsidies and raising corporation taxes. Labour repealed the Conservative's industrial relations laws and strengthened dismissals protection and the closed shop. The 1975 Employment Protection Act bolstered union recognition, guaranteed pay during layoffs, and extended mandatory notice periods for redundancies (Flanagan, Soskice, and Ullman 1983: 418–24). The 1975 Social Security Pensions Act sought to end massive dependency on means-tested, supplementary benefits by adding a state earnings pension (SERPS) to the basic flat-rate pension to be fully protected against inflation. The 1975 Social Security Act, replaced the Beveridge flat-rate system and introduced earnings-related contributions. This supposedly made it possible to increase benefits and make cash benefits less like actuarial insurance and more like a redistributive tax transfer system (Barr and Coulter 1990: 277–79).

These were major achievements but they were expensive—especially in a hyper-inflationary environment—and the change in philosophy short-lived. An uncontrollable wage and prices explosion, a leap in unemployment, and full recession in 1974–75 led to tax increases, cuts and cash limits on all spending programs. A growing fiscal crisis forced the government into heavy borrowing to meet increased demands for welfare as unemployment rose, undermining foreign confidence and forcing the value of sterling to historically low levels. The postwar commitment to full employment was jettisoned and in the 1978 Supplementary Benefit Review, a renewed emphasis on means-tested benefits was explicitly made (Lowe 1993: 324). This was the most acute example of institutional incapacity in British government in the postwar period. Caught between powerful domestic constraints and overwhelming global imperatives, the loss of state autonomy was complete.

In retrospect, the Social Contract was doomed from the outset. As industrial wages spiraled out of control in 1975, union leaders failed to deliver restraint: decentralized, plant-level bargaining made local shop stewards pivotal. Basic wage rates escalated to 33.1 percent in spring 1975. Phase 1 of the subsequent incomes policy was relatively successful due to a sharp fall in profitability (reducing union bargaining power) and the TUC's determination to penalize free riding (Boston 1985). Incomes policy seemed to work after all. But by spring 1977, unemployment was rising less rapidly, inflation was falling, and the pressure on the exchange rate eased after the negotiation of the $3.9 bn IMF loan which restored market confidence. The unions felt less constrained and attacked the government for abandoning full employment and for IMF induced cuts and spending limits. Phase 4 of the policy—introduced in mid-1978, with perhaps an unwisely restrictive 5 percent pay target (Hopkin 1998)—saw its collapse. Strike numbers rose from 1 million to 4.5 million (Jones 1985: 110–17; Flanagan, Soskice, and Ulman 1983: 434–436). Militant public sector workers and private sector workers joined forces and launched the 'Winter of Discontent'—the first to fight falling real incomes, the second to defend wage differentials. What they got was Margaret Thatcher.

2.2. New Times, New Politics, New Model? Employment, Welfare and Economic Adjustment under the Conservatives: 1979–1997

2.2.1. The Model in the Late 1970s

The analysis above has presented a much less than 24-carat 'golden age' in which the formal welfare state is the victim not the cause of Britain's economic adjustment problems. The industrial relations system, by contrast, is intrinsically caught up in the special pathology of Britain's ongoing economic crises. At the heart of the matter, it has been argued, lay an institutional incapacity to link advances in welfare provision with a medium- to long-term commitment to wages and price stability. It was the absence of a clear notion of the 'social wage' as the crux of social consensus that tripped up government after government and contributed both to the failures of economic management and to the indirect effects of low growth on the expansion of welfare.

Despite its many achievements, the performance of the welfare state gave cause for critique on all sides. On the formal welfare side, the success of British welfare lay in its undeniable contribution to living standards and its eradication of abject poverty, the development of a comprehensive system of education, the creation of a National Health Service which was much more cost-effective than its insurance-based counterparts in France and Germany or the US market-led system, and the avoidance of excessive public sector deficits. The downside lay in the consequences of the process described above: thirty years of development in which neither political party was fully capable of meeting its objectives, and in which continuity was overridden by short-term policy switches and budgetary fluctuations, undermining the government's powers of raising revenue, distributing income, and meeting new needs.

This, coupled with technical and organizational inefficiencies, affected the quality of provision in all services. In health, despite higher spending, the numbers on waiting lists for treatment grew steadily from the 1960s on. In education, despite major successes in increasing the numbers passing public examinations, in the early 1980s some 10 percent of 23 year olds had literacy problems and the deficiencies of technical education were widely acknowledged. Housing policy had rehoused millions from slum areas but often in conditions even more conducive to physical degradation and the proliferation of social problems and crime. Homelessness among certain groups became a major problem from the 1960s on (Parry 1986: 202–8; Lowe 1993: 280–97).

Most seriously—and lying behind many of these problems—was the persistence of major gaps in the full coverage of social need (affecting the long-term unemployed, the low paid with inadequate income support, the disabled, single-parent households, and pensioners), alongside poverty and unemployment traps and a social security system which, by the 1980s, was struggling to deal with the consequences of an increasingly regressive tax system and the expansion of means-tested benefits. Contrary to the nostrums of the New Right, the problem was not so much one of dependency and 'voluntary unemployment'—one of the so-called 'moral hazard' consequences of welfare—but of the prevalence of low-paid jobs, the burden of taxation and National Insurance at low income levels, and the poor take-up by those in work of means-tested supplements. In the 1960s and 1970s, combined tax and benefit changes actually reduced the 'replacement ratio' of benefits to income from work which had never been especially high in the British case (Parry 1986: 196–97; Pollard 1992: 279).

Taxation became less progressive. While taxes on income and capital, including net insurance contributions rose only from 20.8 percent of GNP in 1950 to 23.8 percent of GNP in 1980, taxes on spending—which are regressive in effect—rose from 14.7 percent to 19.3 percent. Between 1945 and 1975, the standard rate of tax fell from 50 percent to 35 percent, with a similar fall in the effective rate of surtax paid by higher income earners. After 1970, due to the withdrawal of 'reduced' tax rates, those who only just passed the tax threshold were paying the standard rate: in 1949 a married man with two children would have to reach 187 percent of average earnings before paying tax at the standard rate. By 1975, this had fallen to 44.6 percent. Tax allowances (e.g. relief on mortgage interest payments) and exemptions (e.g. of company contributions to occupational pensions) all favored the more prosperous classes. Between 1949 and 1975–76, the proportion of post-tax income received by the bottom 50 percent of income earners rose hardly at all—from 25.6 percent to 27.4 percent (Lowe 1993: 282). In contrast, that of the top 10 percent fell from 27.1 percent to 22.3 percent. Evidence does show, however, that inequality was trending downwards from the early 1960s onwards, to be reversed in the period after 1978/79 (Jenkins 1996).

By the late 1970s, the middle classes had become major beneficiaries of the welfare state. Julian Le Grand calculated in the early 1980s that the top 20 percent of income earners were receiving educational and health services worth, respectively, three times and two-fifths as much as those received by the bottom 20 percent (Lowe 1993: 284–87).

In fact, it is in the operation the tax system that we can find one of the few causal links between the operation of the British welfare state, broadly conceived, and the performance of the economy. In terms of revenue sources, it should be noted that corporation tax had long been low and had fallen through the 1950s–1970s, with two effects. First, it meant a steady shift of taxation onto the average wage earner. But second, it may also have had a detrimental effect on employment and economic performance, contributing via generous tax allowance incentives, to low company profitability and a decline of employment in manufacturing industry in the 1960s and 1970s. Between 1955 and 1964, the proportion of total tax revenue raised from companies halved, and did so again between 1965 and 1974, while income tax, employee's National Insurance contributions (as the Treasury contribution fell), and indirect taxes—particularly regressive—assumed an ever greater part of the tax burden (Lowe 1993: 284). Tax allowance incentives to investment were part of government policy to promote full employment and growth. But because of rising labor costs, this led to a substitution of capital for labor within existing technologies and a longer run shift to more capital-intensive ones—and this process continued even as profit gross of tax fell (Maynard 1988: 18–19).

There is also a connection between the effects of the tax-benefit system, the issue of the social wage, and the problems of sustaining wage moderation—again with consequences, albeit indirect, for economic performance. As a result of industrial relations indiscipline and low investment levels in the 1960s and 1970s, British wages rose considerably faster in relation to prices and productivity than in comparable countries, contributing to a rapid rise in unit labor costs and the loss of markets for British goods. Trade union militancy was due in part to empowering legislation (especially that passed under Labour governments in the 1960s and 1970s), rising membership (from 9.3 million in 1950 to 13.5 million in 1979—58% of the workforce), the growth of the closed shop (covering 44% of manual workers in 1980), and the fragmentation of the bargaining system.

But it was also due to genuine frustration with the decline of freely disposable incomes. This was due to the incidence of standard tax rates at low levels of income (described above) and the rapid rise in additional costs per employee in National Insurance contributions and taxes (which rose from 21% to 47% of net earnings between 1960 and 1980). From the 1960s on, the ratio of the net amount transferred by the tax and benefit system to the total turnover of taxes and benefits (the 'churning' index) continued to fall (in 1967 the average household lost 38% of income to tax and recovered 21%, but by 1983 it lost 47.2% and gained 25.3%). As pay increases took workers from the first quintile to the third, the 'churning indicator' fell rapidly from 62 percent to 11 percent (Pollard 1992: 268–73; Parry 1986: 200–201). This reflected government policy to increase the size and range of benefits, leave taxation to pay for them and ignore the cumulative effects on final incomes.

In sum, the absence of any mechanism for regulating the social wage in Britain not only contributed to 'stop–go' and an incapacity for stable economic management. It also produced heavy distortions in the operation of the social wage, with detrimental consequences for incomes—amongst the working poor as well as higher wage earners—and contributed a further twist to the vicious circle linking poor industrial relations with the perennial problems of British economic management.

2.2.2. *'There is No Alternative': Neo-liberalism in the 1980s and 1990s*

Keynesianism and the full-employment commitment had already been abandoned under the Labour government when forced into a strategy of fiscal and monetary conservatism in 1975. But Labour had its back against the wall; this was a party committed to full employment that had discovered, amidst inflation and currency crisis, that Keynesianism—in the form of soft currency policies and an expansionary macroeconomic stance—was no longer possible. The Conservatives, by contrast, hit the ground running in 1979, committed to a reversal of the status quo at all levels: the use of macroeconomic management to determine output and employment was to be abandoned; given the futility of incomes policy, monetarist restraint was considered the only alternative for controlling wages and inflation; and releasing the productive potential of the economy required a reduction in the role of the state—in taxation, borrowing and the public ownership of industry.

While there was no detailed blueprint for change, the enemies—Keynesian demand management, the trade unions, bureaucracy, and welfare—were clearly identified. 'Public expenditure', stated the government's first White Paper, was 'at the heart of Britain's economic difficulties' (HM Treasury 1979, cited in Hills 1998: 3). The welfare state constrained the free spirits of capitalism, sapped the individual of initiative, and created a culture of dependency. As had frequently occurred since 1945, 'corporatist collusion' could deprive the state of its capacity for purposive action; indeed, an important feature of Thatcherism was its determination to 're-empower' the state.

These ideas were not new and had been around in various forms in the Conservative Party since the 1950s. But in the 1970s they were backed by a growing 'advocacy coalition' of politicians, pundits, and think tanks, and with the crisis of the late 1970s, their time had decidedly come. Thus, legitimized by New Right thinking—and electoral victory—a combination of principled and expedient policies, linked to direct attacks on the power bases of the Labour Party and the labor movement, soon melded into what seemed to be a coherent plan to reform Britain forever.

Privatization, new restrictive industrial relations laws, the diminution of the powers of local government, the massive sell-off of public housing all simultaneously strengthened the institutional capacity of central government, sapped the electoral strength of Labour, and helped build a new pro-market social coalition. The latter, with the help of fortuitous events (e.g. the Falklands War), was to keep Labour in opposition for almost two decades and transform the political—and economic—landscape.

A key part of that transformation lay in abandoning the failed and, in retrospect, futile, attempts of governments since 1946 to forge a negotiated link between the formal and informal welfare states around the notion of the social wage. Incomes policies were abandoned (except for the public sector where statutory limits were imposed), the power of unions to influence government policy was radically reduced—indeed eliminated—and a new and instrumental linkage was forged between the social security system and the labour market, by 'activating' benefits and making welfare a tool of employment policy. Meanwhile, even if welfare spending remained at roughly the same level in 1997 as twenty years earlier, its role, as argued below, had in many respects changed fundamentally. The most important long-term results would be an often quite explicit subservience of social policy to the interests of the economy (and where possible subject to market competition), the division of welfare purchasers from welfare providers (e.g. the NHS reforms), the decentralization of responsibilities for benefit delivery (to local government and in some cases businesses), and the concentration of formal powers of control in the hands of central government—trends largely continued, and indeed reinforced under New Labour in the late 1990s (see C. Pierson 1994).

That said, change was much more radical in some areas than others, and economic performance during the Thatcher decade was far from outstanding, raising important questions regarding state capacity—often considered to be the *sine qua non* of the British case. Indeed, until the early mid-1990s it is fair to say that the failure to escape from the classic British 'stop–go' policy put the Conservatives in a similar position to their predecessors. Fundamental weaknesses in the real economy combined with economic mismanagement to frustrate success in their labor market and welfare reforms as well as in broader economic performance.

In 1990—after eleven years of Conservative government and the year Margaret Thatcher resigned as prime minister—Britain had the highest rate of inflation among the advanced economies, the highest interest rates, high and rising unemployment, large-scale bankruptcies, falling output, declining national income, and the largest current account deficit in history. As for rolling back the state, the share of national income devoted to welfare services was still roughly the same as in the late 1970s. The only consistent achievement—held to through all phases of the economic cycle—was judged at that point to be the Conservative's 'reverse Robin Hood program' which transferred 'income from the poor, especially the poorest, to the rich, and especially the richest' (Pollard 1992: 379). Yet once the deep recession of the early 1990s had passed, the more general impact of the Thatcher 'revolution'—its successes (in its own terms) as well as its failures—would become much clearer.

2.2.2.1. Macro-Mismanagement and the Medium-Term Economic Strategy

Given the importance of the economic cycle for understanding the Thatcher–Major period—in terms of public spending, employment, and economic adjustment—a detour into the macroeconomy is indispensable. As described above, postwar governments of both stripes had frequently come to power convinced of the need (and their ability) to break the 'stop–go' cycle but always failed. The Conservatives after 1979 were no exception; but being Conservatives, they did so in Rolls-Royce style. The boom–bust cycle was especially impressive. The deep recession of the early 1980s was followed by a boom which, fueled by the liberalization of credit and hire-purchase controls, was the longest and most sustained episode of its kind in the post-war period—as was the bust of the late 1980s and early 1990s which followed, with all the predictable consequences in terms of bankruptcies, spending limits, and damage to investment and employment, especially in manufacturing. The opportunity of escaping from the main cause of the 'stop–go' cycle—the balance of payment deficits—provided by the flow of North Sea oil, was therefore squandered.

Once again, it was all meant to be very different. The new Conservative government was determined to reject short-termism and develop a medium-term economic strategy, with a focus not on the demand side but the supply side of the economy. A tight monetary policy—to be achieved by focusing on broad money M3 (cash and credit instruments) plus the public sector borrowing requirement (PSBR)—would dispense with the need for an incomes policy, since trade unions would soon realize the consequences of irresponsible wage bargaining: increasing unemployment for their members. The market would set wages, and welfare provisions would be cut, not just to reduce government spending, but to remove the floor below wage levels and allow them to fall. The rate of inflation was the most important target, while the value of the currency and the balance of payments took second place.

The problem of the Thatcher years lay in a clear contradiction between the micro policy supply-side strategy and the deflationary impact of macro policies to restrain the money supply (Pollard 1992: 376 ff.). Indeed, the latter can be said to have 'overdetermined' the former. The severity of deflationary policies was intensified, in turn, by the poorly timed liberalization of credit and exchange controls in the early 1980s and impressive personal tax reductions in an already inflationary environment both at the beginning and end of the decade. Thus, the 1979 budget was deflationary but accompanied by a big shift from direct to indirect taxation: the standard rate was cut from 33 to 30 percent and top rates from 83 to 60, while value added tax (VAT) increased from 8 and 12.5 percent to 15 percent. The abolition of exchange controls in the same year led to an immediate outflow of capital. The rate of inflation rose by 4–5 percent to more than 20 percent in early 1980, stimulating higher wage claims. Interest rates consequently rose, nationalized industries were forced to raise gas and electricity charges and local authorities to raise rents (Pollard 1992; OECD 1982, 1983).

The removal of the 'corset' on bank lending in 1980 and the abolition of controls on hire-purchase in 1982 helped produce monetary growth well in excess of the target ranges (by 9% in 1980–81 and 3.5% in 1981–82) and well beyond any overshoots in 1976–80 when objectives were more or less met. High interest rates and a high exchange rate (bolstered by the flow of North Sea oil) quickly took their toll on industry and unemployment doubled to 12 percent—nearly 3 million—over 1980–82. In 1983 imports of manufactures exceeded exports for the first time since the war. Recession meant a decline in government receipts, an increase in transfer payments as unemployment rose and large PSBR overshoots in 1980–81. Inflation came down rapidly with the recession to around 5 percent and unemployment peaked at around 12 percent in the summer of 1985—during which time, however, real wages continued to rise. Monetary policy, meanwhile, remained unsuccessful, and money supply targets impossible to meet given their poor definition (and thus lack of credibility with the markets), the increasing international integration of financial markets and the simultaneous liberalization of domestic finance. Against this background, large current account deficits (with goods sucked in primarily by a massive shift from private saving to consumption) made the country increasingly vulnerable to shifts in speculative international capital.

As always, economic mismanagement played a prominent role. When in 1988 the standard rate of tax was reduced to 25 percent and all higher tax bands of 45, 50, 55, and 60 percent consolidated into single top rate tax of 40 percent, inflation was already mounting. Unemployment had fallen from 11.5 percent in 1986 to 8.5 percent, with a large increase in jobs (especially part-time and for women) in the service sector, and credit liberalization and easy mortgage finance was feeding a frenzied consumer boom. Between May and December 1988, the Chancellor raised interest rates (the only tool for controlling money supply the government permitted itself) 12 times, but inflation rose to 11 percent in October 1990. The 1990–92 recession had begun. Investment in 1990 fell by 5.4 percent, GDP growth fell to 0.5 percent (before slumping to −2.2 in 1991), while bankruptcies that year rose by 35 percent and housing repossessions soared as the housing price boom collapsed. The unemployment rate (UK claimant count) at 5.8 percent that year rose to 8.1 percent in 1991 and 10 percent in 1992 (OECD 1995). This was the second massive labor shakeout in less than a decade, with major consequences for government spending and the nature of the labor market—and arguably as important for understanding the transformation of the employment system as government legislation.

Aware that its independent monetary policy lacked credibility with the markets, the UK authorities had already been tracking the Deutschmark for several years before joining the ERM in October 1990. In choosing a central entry rate of DM 2.95 the authorities took a hard currency option to bring inflation down while putting heavy pressure in the short run on already suffering export industries. However, with protracted and deep recession in the UK and tight monetary conditions called for in Germany, tensions between internal and exchange rate objectives emerged and together with turmoil in international financial markets led to sterling's suspension from the ERM in September 1992 (OECD 1993). Poor UK economic conditions combined with the consequences of German unification made the situation unsustainable. After ERM exit the UK abandoned monetary aggregates as a nominal anchor and instead followed the New Zealand solution of explicit inflation targets set over an 18-month–two-year period. Both the target and interest rates were now set by the Chancellor of the Exchequer with the Governor of the Bank of England providing policy recommendations. By the mid-1990s policy credibility—in terms of financial market expectations and exchange rate stability—had once again been achieved.

One of the most important consequences of macro-mismanagement and the accompanying currency overvaluations of the early 1980s and the ERM period was the damage done to British manufacturing, producing bankruptcies, closures, and employment losses well in excess of the requirements of structural change and modernization. As Rowthorn (1999) argues, macroeconomic instability and exchange rate fluctuations destroyed even successful parts of the manufacturing sector with potential for long-term growth, while also discouraging new firm entry and damaging service activities dependent on manufacturing. Parts of the north, already afflicted with adjustment problems, were reduced to industrial wastelands, and a large proportion of their workers consigned to long-term unemployment.

Against this background it is unsurprising that the government failed to halt budget expansion as foreseen. In the first half of the Thatcher decade (and regardless of privatization receipts) public spending rose from 34.7 percent of GDP in 1979 to 39.1 percent, in 1982 and 42.6 percent in 1984 as well as against the average of other OECD countries, and with it went tax levels. A rising defense budget (agreed to with other NATO countries) played a part, but particularly important was the big increase in unemployment and increases in National Insurance and social benefits paid to the unemployed. The biggest real spending increases between 1979 and 1989 were in health (35%) and social security (33%). While total spending remained constant over 1980–93, a fall in government consumption and investment was offset by a rise in transfer spending. The share of social spending in GDP rose by 5 percentage points compared with an OECD average of 4.7. Compared to OECD averages, increases in UK spending were lower for pensions and unemployment benefits (areas where the government could successfully cut outlays by ending earnings indexation), close to the average for health care but much higher for disability, housing, and other social assistance benefits (all areas of spending linked to the incidence of unemployment and increases in household poverty) (OECD 1998). Other areas of spending, which were critical for long-term economic performance—most importantly education and training—suffered instead from much heavier restraint.

Again, it was all supposed to be very different. In terms of capacity for achieving broad economic objectives, it was unsurprising that at the end of the Thatcher decade Keith Middlemas (1991: 275) provided the following assessment: 'A government determined to rule by monetarist rules did so to full effect for only a brief period in 1981. What followed suggests that there existed in late-twentieth-century British conditions very serious practical limits to the thesis that parliamentary sovereignty confers effective power on governments to manage the state and control public behavior.'

2.2.2.2. Labor Market and Welfare Reforms

Assessing the situation a decade after Middlemas, it is much less obvious that over almost twenty years of government the Conservatives failed, ultimately, to 'control public behavior' or create the economy they wanted.

The first signs of success appeared in the aftermath of the recession of the early 1990s. By the spring of 1994 the UK economy attained its 1990 peak level of output two years after the start of the economic recovery. But the same level of output was now produced with 1.8 million fewer jobs and greater reliance on female and part-time workers, while modest nominal and real wage outcomes and more flexible employment practices meant that the drop in unemployment was much faster than in the previous

1980–81 recession. After a period of seven to eight years in the first part of the 1980s in which wage behavior seemed unaffected by labor market deregulation, real wages rose surprisingly little in the second half of the 1980s despite the rapid fall in unemployment. Real wages did increase during the 1990–92 recession, at a time when unemployment was rising sharply, but in 1993 wage moderation led to a fall in 'underlying' inflation despite currency depreciation and this helped to 'crowd in' jobs (OECD 1994).

Even allowing for a decline in labor force participation (especially amongst males in manufacturing) (Morgan 1996), this was a big contrast to the 1980s. The unions had been weakened (strike rates in 1993 were at their lowest since records began in 1891!), product market competition had increased, the labor market deregulated, and managerial attitudes changed (Dunn and Metcalf 1996). Productivity was up, as was investment and returns on capital, and export competitiveness, helped enormously by post-ERM sterling depreciation, had markedly improved. Public spending was back under 40 percent of GDP and the overall tax burden no higher than in 1980. The 1970s were just a bad memory. Bolstered by a credible anti-inflationary macroeconomic stance, the upturn in 1993 initiated a period of non-inflationary growth and declining unemployment rates that was to continue for the rest of the decade.

How, and to what extent, did labor market and welfare reform contribute to this change? Before presenting an answer to this question in the next section, a brief survey of the key innovations is appropriate. As discussed, the enemies—including bureaucracy, the trade unions, and the supposedly debilitating effects of welfare (for both individuals and the economy)—had been clearly identified. But the aims of reform on the informal side—industrial relations and the labor market—were much more explicit and conscientiously pursued than those on the formal side, for both practical and political reasons. Public support for radical change in industrial relations legislation and the fragility of industrial relations and labor market regulation contrasted with the popularity amongst the electorate of major welfare programs—especially health—their institutional embeddedness and the variety of client and professional vested interests defending them.

The reform mix consisted of several elements, the interaction of which has radically transformed the nature of the British welfare state, at least in terms of the delivery and composition of the social wage and the interface between the social security system and employment:

(1) trade unions were placed in a legal straitjacket which overturned the tradition of 'labor immunities';

(2) labor market reregulation re-empowered employers and facilitated non-standard forms of employment;
(3) benefit changes provided 'incentives' to find work and remove employment traps; in the 1990s they were increasingly integrated with work or training requirements;
(4) and education and employment policies were intended to correct Britain's massive deficit in skills.

In industrial relations, following Hayek's prescription that 'there can be no salvation for Britain until the special privileges granted to the trade unions three-quarters of a century ago are revoked' (cited by Dunn and Metcalf 1996), the numerous trade union reform acts between 1980 and 1993 removed legal immunities, both for picketing and secondary industrial action and also from civil actions regarding industrial actions not agreed to in advance by a secret ballot. Unions were made liable to injunctions and damages linked to unlawful industrial action. The reforms strengthened the rights of employees dismissed for refusing to join closed shops and introduced secret ballots to approve new closed shops and approve old ones, as well as for the election (every five years) of trade union executive committees (from 1984) and general secretaries (from 1988). Ballots must also ratify union political donations. Since 1990, unofficial strikers can be dismissed and their social security payments deducted and all secondary strikes, boycotts, and closed shops have been outlawed. Since 1993 (when the remaining Wages Councils were also abolished), trade unions have had to give seven days' notice for legal strikes, members of the public have been able to seek injunctions against unlawful action, and employers have been able to treat union members differently from non-members (e.g. provide incentives to opt out of collective bargaining and sign bespoke contracts) (OECD 1986; Rhodes 1989; Dunn and Metcalf 1996).

The barrage of legislation affecting employment rights lengthened the period of employment before unfair dismissal complaints could be made from six months to two years, and removed the onus of proof on employers (1979–82); rescinded various 'fair wages' resolutions (breaking the terms of ILO Convention No. 94) (1982) and (in 1986) modified minimum wage-fixing machinery, removing employees under 21 from cover and ending control over working conditions (entailing the deratification of ILO Convention No. 26). Most restrictions on the working hours of 16 to 18 year olds were removed (1988). It should be noted that temporary and part-time workers were already relatively unprotected in law (or by collective bargaining), but these rights were further reduced in 1989 when they were removed from Wages Council cover. In 1992 (after a decade of opposition by Margaret Thatcher to European social policy initiatives), the Major government negotiated an opt-out from the Social Protocol of the Treaty on European Union to avoid any new labor regulations stemming from EU legislation.

As for benefit changes, despite the lack of evidence that high replacement ratios in Britain were the norm or that they made any significant contribution to rising unemployment from the 1970s (OECD 1986: 32–33), the government was determined to combine its cost reduction strategy with the eradication of 'welfare dependency' and disincentives to work. This has been done in a number of ways, including both 'stick and carrot' methods.

First, as for the 'stick', earnings-related supplements to National Insurance payments introduced in 1966 were reduced in January 1981 and abolished in 1982—removing the third (earnings-related) tier from a two-tier benefit structure (comprising a flat-rate insurance benefit paid subject to contributions, supported by a second tier of income-tested assistance). From July 1982, unemployment benefits became liable to tax. These were just two of 23 changes introduced during the Thatcher decade (out of a total 38—the remainder had a neutral impact) that 'turned the screw' on the unemployed, reducing the amount of social security payments to those out of work by an estimated £500 m (7% of spending on the unemployed) per annum.

In a review of these reforms (including the 1986 Social Security Act, implemented in 1988), Atkinson and Micklewright (1989) noted the shift that had occurred since the 1970s when—in line with the views of Beveridge—there was still a commitment to a contributory system paying benefit as of right. In the 1980s there was a major movement away from insurance benefits towards reliance on incomes-tested benefit for the unemployed, while their role was reduced by contribution conditions and other restrictions and their value cut by taxation and de-indexation from earnings (Atkinson and Micklewright 1989: 39–40). Including other areas of welfare (e.g., child benefit and housing allowances for low-income households), between 1978 and the mid-1990s, the proportion of means-tested to total benefits doubled, with a major shift in this direction after 1988 (Lowe 1993; OECD 1996).

Second, the carrot came in the form of 'in-work' benefits. The first 'in-work' benefit was Family Income Supplement introduced as long ago as 1973, but Family Credit was more generous, in terms of the income supplement and offsets for childcare expenses, and became more widespread, especially when extended after 1995 to childless couples and single adults as 'Earning's Top-up'. The rationale for in-work benefits is that they can reduce the extent of the unemployment trap by increasing incomes for those in work without reducing out-of-work incomes and at lower budgetary costs than general tax cuts, thereby reducing the effective replacement rate without major cuts in benefit which could exacerbate poverty. Such benefit changes have reduced the replacement rate and—arguably—disincentives to work. But while removing the 'unemployment trap', there is evidence that the strategy of 'making work pay' has also bolstered the poverty trap for certain groups (Dilnot and Stark 1989; OECD 1998). On the employer side, incentives to employ the low-skilled, long-term unemployed were introduced in 1985 and 1986. These included a reduction of employer National Insurance contributions for employees earning below a certain level, and a total exemption for up to a year when hiring someone who had been unemployed for more than two years. Although measuring the impact of such changes is difficult, Hart and Ruffell (1998) estimate their contribution to employment to have been about 0.7 percent, or 154,000 new jobs.

And third, in a set of reforms designed with both carrot and stick incentives in mind, new education and training schemes to improve employability were married with a set of benefit changes to coerce the young unemployed into taking up places. On the benefits side, in 1988 those under 18 lost eligibility for Income Support—creating a widespread phenomenon of young people sleeping rough—while unemployed workers under 21 were presented with a choice of participation in youth training schemes or losing benefits (Atkinson and Micklewright 1989). The removal of Wages Council protection (which in 1990 still covered some 2.5 million workers) allowed employers to push down already low pay levels for young people. In October 1996, the new 'Job Seekers Allowance' extended training scheme compulsion to all unemployed people: to cite King and Wood (1999), 'workfare had arrived'.

The main training initiative—the Youth Training Scheme—was launched in 1983 to give vocational training to unemployed 16 and 17 year olds unable to find work. In 1988 responsibility for training was transferred to employer-led Training and Enterprise Councils, overturning the quasi-corporatist institutional basis of training hitherto under the aegis of the tripartite Manpower Services Commission (MSC) which was abolished the same year. A Council for Vocational Qualifications (NCVQ) was set up in 1986 creating five levels of national vocational qualification (NVQs) covering 86 percent of work force. The aim was to ensure that 60 percent of young and adult workers were qualified at NVQ level 3—equivalent to a craft apprenticeship or 2 A-level passes—by 2000 (a rather modest target).

Most assessments of these initiatives have been highly critical. It is true that the 1990–93 recession held back the success of these schemes and that by 1996 3 percent of all employees had an NVQ or were training for one and 30 percent of employers offered NVQs to some or all employees in 1994. The share of employees receiving some training rose from 8 percent to 14 percent between 1984 and 1994. But many left Youth Training with no qualification, NVQ attainments were overwhelmingly at the low level and most employer-provided training remained short, informal, and uncertified (OECD 1995). Despite Conservative claims that they had created a system superior to that of Germany (!), the number of workers with technical level vocational qualifications remained unchanged from the mid-1970s. By the late 1980s, only 30 percent of manual and 25 percent of non-manual workers had some form of qualification, against a German level in both categories of 60 percent (Prais 1995; Cruz Castro 1999). Insufficient funding, employer resistance to a statutory framework with genuine training contracts, inadequate mechanisms for cost and risk sharing among employers and the narrowness of work experience provided have all limited the impact of these initiatives.

2.2.3. Welfare and the Economy after the Conservatives: An Assessment

How have these developments interacted to transform the delivery and composition of the social wage and the interface between the social security system and employment? And what of the impact on the economy? As revealed by the considerable debate on this issue, it is difficult to disentangle the consequences of macroeconomic mismanagement, a secular process of tertiarization (post-industrialization) and the purposive objectives of legislation in explaining developments in the labor market and the broader economy. The knock-on effect of a relatively high level of foreign direct investment—attracted in part by the low levels of corporation tax and employers' contributions allowed by the lean UK welfare state—has also been important. What can be said is that changes in legislation and labor law have dovetailed neatly with other influences to create a liberal market economy with a strong bias in employment creation towards both the high-paid and low-paid ends of the service sector and growing income inequality.

The labor shakeout and manufacturing crisis induced by the cycle of boom and bust in the 1980s and early 1990s certainly hastened that process and made it much more painful. Rowthorn (1999) argues that Britain is a clear and distinctive case of 'negative de-industrialization' in which manufacturing labor is shed but against the background of a stagnant manufacturing output and a much less than full absorption of the unemployed into services. Average labor productivity growth in manufacturing since 1973 has been similar in Britain to the rest of the industrialized world, but output growth has been much lower at an annual 0.4 percent per annum as against 1.4 percent and 2.3 percent, respectively, in the EU and OECD. Output growth closer to the EU figure would have added a further 700,000 jobs to the 4 million currently employed in manufacturing and exerted a positive multiplier effect on employment in services. As it is, 'negative de-industrialization' is responsible for rates of inactivity of 30 percent among men aged 25–64 in the old industrial regions of Yorkshire, the Northwest and Northeast. Among males aged 55–65, the inactivity rate is as high as 80 percent in the Northeast. Even in the prosperous south some 40 percent of this group are without official employment.

Alongside draconian industrial relations laws, recession and the massive reduction in manufacturing employment have clearly contributed to the decline in trade union power, the reassertion of employer's prerogatives over pay and conditions of work and the parallel decline of collective bargaining. Union membership fell from 13.3 million to 8.9 million workers (from 50% to 30% of the workforce) between 1979 and 1992, and the numbers covered by the closed shop declined from 5.2 million to around 0.4 million. Meanwhile the proportion of firms in employers' associations fell from 25 percent to 13 percent and those engaged in multi-employer pay bargaining fell from 27 percent to 16 percent (Dunn and Metcalf 1996). If the impact of the law on ballots on militancy appears ambiguous, that on secondary picketing was manifest—it had virtually disappeared by the 1990s. Industrial strike action in general has diminished enormously, due partly to the law, partly to worker apathy and partly to the psychological impact of major defeats (such as the prolonged miner's strike) in the 1980s. The end of statutory recognition has had a major impact. Work places with trade union recognition fell from 66 percent in 1984 to 44 percent (and just 34% in the private sector) a decade later. Induced by tax incentives, some 75 percent of large firms now use profit-related pay, producing sharper skills-based wage differentials and greater regional wage variation (OECD 1995). The erosion of differentials set by bargaining has led to a dramatic widening of pay dispersion (Dunn and Metcalf 1996: 89–90).

As for the general economic impact of Conservatism, the much-vaunted productivity and employment miracles of the 1990s must also be attributed to a combination of factors and their real effect qualified. The initial impetus for productivity gains preceded the new industrial relations legislation and came from the 'Thatcher recession' of the early 1980s. Hitting the most heavily unionized plants hardest, the slump produced an enduring shift of power on the shop floor (Oulton 1995; Dunn and Metcalf 1996). From 1985 to 1995, UK relative labor productivity levels subsequently rose by 5 percentage points per person engaged and 10 percentage points per hour worked vis-à-vis the United States. But these gains should be put in comparative and historical perspective.

First, the productivity catch-up has been much less impressive against other EU countries. Second, as Rowthorn points out, output per worker in manufacturing stagnated during the second half of the 1970s, rose strongly over the subsequent decade (at 1% per year faster than in 1974–79) but then fell back and returned to its pre-1973 trend. This suggests for Rowthorn (1999) that the underlying rate of growth remains unchanged (see also Glyn 1992). Finally, UK labor productivity is still the weakest of the G7 along with Canada. This is due to a lower level of per capita investment in physical assets and skill acquisition than elsewhere in the OECD. Spending on education and research, and development as a share of GDP has fallen from above the OECD average to about the median level and the stock of qualifications lags behind countries with significantly higher living standards (cf. Robinson 1995). As the OECD predicts, it will take some time for this productivity gap to narrow (OECD 1998). In this respect, the training initiatives of recent years have contributed little given the scale of the problem. King and Wood (1999) conclude that Conservative policies transformed training partly into a means of providing firms with temporary, low-cost labor rather than creating incentives for firms to invest in employable skills.

Part of the UK's productivity improvement is due to the impact of foreign direct investment (FDI) (Griffith 1999). A higher ratio of inward investment to GDP than any other major economy is assisted in part by the tax regime which levies lower corporation tax, payroll tax, and social security contributions on firms than in the country's major competitors (Eltis and Higham 1995). In 1993, the ratio of business tax to GDP was 5.9 percent in the UK, 14.5 in France, 9.1 in Germany, 17.3 in Italy, 7.2 in the US, and 9.4 in Japan. Docile trade unions (and the shift from multiple craft union to single union deals in the 1980s) have also helped. In 1992, foreign companies accounted for 20 percent of the manufacturing work force, 25 percent of added value, 33 percent of capital investment, and 40 percent of manufactured outputs. They produced two-thirds of data processing and office equipment, one-third of vehicles and parts, and one-third of instruments and provided 75 percent of investment in cars and parts and over 50 percent in electrical and electronic engineering.

Combined with the massive level of foreign investment in the UK financial sector, this makes the UK Europe's most internationalized economy. Alongside the contribution of FDI to trade (producing surpluses in sectors such as color televisions and computers), there is also an outward ripple effect in terms of management and human resource techniques, especially from Asia-Pacific firms which embed themselves in the domestic economy via multiple supplier linkages (Williams 1999). But a long tail of UK-owned companies remains uncompetitive and highly vulnerable to exchange rate and interest rates fluctuations (O'Mahony 1995). And although the adoption of Japanese production and supply techniques has improved the efficiency of certain British firms, this only slowly translates into better financial performance (Oliver and Hunter 1998). Meanwhile, even if compensated by surpluses on the services account, the trade deficit on manufactures was more than £20 bn in 1998, with the IMF warning of a £50 bn deficit (5% of GDP) by 2000 (*Observer*, 2 May 1999).

But what of the impact on employment? The general record since the mid-1990s is undeniably good when compared with the 1980s and recent European experience. According to the OECD (1998), by 1996 the 'natural rate of unemployment' was below many European countries as was the non-accelerating wage rate of unemployment (NAWRU), reflected in five to six years of recovery with very little wage pressure since 1993. The unemployment rate has followed the boom–bust cycle, rising from 2 percent to 5 percent through the 1970s, surging to 11 percent in the mid-1980s, dropping to 5.5 percent in 1990, then back to a peak of more than 10 percent in 1993. But by early 1996 it was down again to 8 percent and is currently (late 1999) back to—and perhaps below—the 1990 level. The bright side of such responsiveness to the cycle is that unlike many other European countries, Britain does not have a problem of jobless growth.

The downside, of course, is that the next slump when it comes may see another massive employment shakeout. Moreover, although the participation rate is high by European standards (even if it has not increased over the last two decades), a 5 percentage point fall in male participation has only been offset by an increase in female participation. And those who have stopped participating in the labor market in the 1990s could account for as much as a quarter of the recent fall in unemployment. There has also been a big increase in the numbers classified as unable to work due to long-term sickness. An increase in student numbers and the changing age structure of the workforce (with a marked decline in the activity of older workers) has also contributed (Morgan 1996; Rowthorn 1999).

At the same time, the nature of employment and the distribution of earnings have changed considerably. Numerical and pay flexibility have both been increased and part-time, temporary, and self-employment all grew under the Conservatives (Jenkins 1996; Johnson 1996). Responsibility can be attributed once again to the accelerating effect of the two massive labor shakeouts and subsequent rebounds, as well as the 'composition effect'—i.e. the increasing importance of the service sector whose growth, in turn, has been fed by the flexible supply of jobs. But the weakening of trade unions and their ability to bargain, the erosion of individual job rights, especially among the low paid, and a reduction in the level and coverage of social security, plus tougher eligibility rules, have clearly all played a major role in these developments (Brown 1990).

Major changes in the public sector have also contributed to the proliferation of poor quality, low-paid work. Labor restructuring before and after the privatization of nationalized industries and especially the contracting out to private firms of central government, local authority, and NHS services have contributed to a growing divide between a 'core' of secure professionals and a 'periphery' of non-professional staff. The scrapping of ILO fair wage resolutions and legislation outlawing the insertion of fair labor standard clauses in local authority contracts has removed a growing number of low-paid public sector workers from collective bargaining, depriving them of previous pay relativities plus entitlements and fringe benefits (Michie and Wilkinson 1992).

Growing income inequality has been linked with an increase in the relative importance of jobs at the two extremes of the earnings distribution and by a differential rate of change in high- and low-level earnings. Jobs lost in manufacturing and other non-service sectors were concentrated in the middle range of the earnings distribution. But the increase in employment has been concentrated in sectors like banking, finance, and business services where earnings are relatively high and in hotels, catering, and other services where pay is low (Michie and Wilkinson 1992). Meanwhile, earnings at the upper end of the spectrum have grown relative to those at the lower end since 1979.[5] Consequently, there was a rapid growth in the polarization of income distribution over 1978–92, with essentially no real wage growth for the 10th percentile and rapid growth at the 90th percentile (Machin 1996). By 1995, the share of income distribution for the 10th decile was eight times that of the first decile, compared with 4.5 times in 1979 (OECD 1998: 80). The increase in the number of working poor is the other side of Britain's apparent success in creating more jobs than its Continental counterparts. Between 1990 and 1995, the number of working families with children receiving means-tested Family Credit to top up low

---

[5] Figures for the period 1986–99 reveal that of the increase in service sector employment (of around 3.7 million), around 47% was in sectors where higher-paid workers predominate (financial services, research, computing and other business activities, and real estate), 20% in sectors where one-fifth to one-quarter of workers are low-paid (education, transport, and storage), and 33% in sectors where the low-paid account for one-third to two-thirds of all workers (community, social and personal activities, wholesale, retail and repairs, and hotels and restaurants) (see HMSO 1999; Michie and Wilkinson 1992; and, for a positive view of these developments, Robinson 1997).

pay almost doubled from 309,000 to 591,000 (Webb 1995: 14–15).

The poverty statistics are the most damning indictment of the failings of the British system in protecting and raising the incomes of the poor and of the further impoverishment of many people under the Conservatives. In the mid- to late 1990s, nearly 10 million people in 5.7 million families (20% of the population) were dependent on the means-tested Income Support, compared with 4.4 million in 2.9 million families receiving the equivalent Supplementary Benefit in 1979 (Johnson 1996; OECD 1998). Currently almost one-fifth of all working age households are jobless—a threefold increase since the late 1970s—while one-third of all children live in poor families, more than in any other EU country (OECD 1998: 80–81).

For a party that dislikes the impoverished (Lord Harris, a founder of the Thatcherite Institute of Economic Affairs, wrote a book in 1971 called *Down with the Poor*) the Conservatives did an excellent job in producing more of them—and boosting the welfare bill, which it also hates, in the process. Meanwhile, the capacity of the social security system to counterbalance these trends became much weaker. Although social security spending increased by more than 50 percent in real terms between 1979 and 1993–94, over the same period the number in poverty (those receiving less than half the average national income) more than doubled from 5 million to 10 million, and by 1997 there were 14 million people— a quarter of the population—officially classified as poor (Piachaud 1998, 1999).

2.3. The Emerging New 'Model': A 'Third Way' for British Welfare?

This article began by arguing that, the British welfare state has been the victim rather than the cause of the UK's economic problems. The industrial relations system, however, became closely caught up with the pathology of British industrial decline during the first three postwar decades, in part precisely because of the absence of a constructive link between the labor market and formal welfare provision via an institutionalized consensus on the social wage. The chaos and crisis of the mid- to late 1970s was very much the final culmination of a spiral of mini-crises, each of which confirmed the incapacity of the British state, rather than its oft-supposed power to act under the Westminster model. The loss of control over the macroeconomy and an inability to innovate effectively at the micro-level (in training policy, education, and industrial policy) were linked to the presence of fragmented yet powerful vested interests, capable of blocking and frustrating attempts at reform. Political debilitation has combined with economic decline to create welfare 'with the lid on', cost efficient but insufficient public services and a system of education and training that has failed to equip many individuals and firms to adapt and survive in a modern, internationalized economy.

Against this backdrop, both Thatcherism and New Labour's 'Third Way' should be understood as combining political and economic projects. The Conservatives under Thatcher were as determined to restore the power of the government to rule as they were to implement a neo-liberal agenda; indeed, by using the market to break the power of vested interests, aggressive neo-liberalism also empowered the state. Neither the Labour Party nor their Conservative counterparts had found an alternative means of establishing autonomy from either trade unions or producer groups (Marquand 1988; Wolfe 1991) or forging a consensus on distributional issues. Thus, distributional conflict fed into a vicious circle of industrial maladjustment, macroeconomic mismanagement, and social strife.

Only Thatcher's Conservatives succeeded in breaking this circle—and therein lies the power and profundity of their legacy. To rescue and transform British capitalism, the state itself had to be liberated and transformed. To recreate the market, the state itself had to be strong. It is a mistake to believe that Thatcher availed herself of a constitutional structure that empowered governments. She did not. To wield power as she saw fit, Margaret Thatcher had to demolish then rebuild. As she intended, this effectively destroyed social democracy as a political force and made its bearers, the British Labour Party, reinvent itself in her image.

Not that Thatcher's (even less so Major's) Conservatives were all-powerful or always successful in attaining their objectives. They were much less radical in practice than in rhetoric and the limits of retrenchment and continuity in welfare policy have often been emphasized (e.g. Pierson 1994; Atkinson, Hills, and Le Grand 1987). Thus, public spending on welfare changed little as a proportion of GDP over 1976–96, and spending on health, social services, and social security all increased (while education stagnated and the housing budget plummeted). The role of welfare in alleviating the otherwise disastrous impact of economic restructuring in the 1980s on income distribution and social stability has been hailed as its greatest achievement (Le Grand 1990: 359–60).

However, general spending totals conceal a great deal, including a considerable deterioration in the quality of certain programs, capital investment reductions (affecting especially public housing, infrastructure, and education—where it was halved over 1976–90), and a reduction of the public sector work force by over 10 percent. Moreover, the stability of spending to GDP since the late 1960s contrasts with significant increases in other countries. Britain over this period moved from being a relatively high spender and taxer to its current status as one of the lowest on both counts.

Most importantly, the 'continuity thesis' ignores the extent of socio-economic and political change. This includes the challenge to collectivism, the promotion of private provision, the long-term effect of cuts and the break in the linkage between earnings and benefits, the new managerialism in the NHS, the political and economic consequences of greater social divisions, and changes in citizenship rights as explicit and implicit disentitlement hit vulnerable sections of the population.[6] Then there is the long-term impact of these changes on the ideology of the left, producing an elected Labour government in the late 1990s bearing much more resemblance to the Conservatives in its policy priorities than to its predecessors (Wilding 1997). The Thatcherite project was based on a new 'neo-liberal' electoral coalition supporting its strong-state/free-economy strategy, while also catering to middle-class supporters of the welfare status quo. So successful was Thatcherism as a 'hegemonic' project that its anti-inflation, low tax, and liberal labor market policies have become socially and politically embedded. In making itself electable, Labour had therefore to embrace the same macro- and microeconomic policy orientation and engage with the 'Thatcherite' electoral coalition, while also striving to differentiate itself from Conservative neo-liberalism and bring its own traditional supporters on board (Gould 1998 provides an 'insider' account of this process).

As this concluding section argues, New Labour has thus made itself the heir to the Thatcher legacy, while repudiating strongly that of its own tradition and forebears—*faute de mieux*. Labour has not just inherited a completely different institutional structure from that it left behind in the late 1970s, but a welfare system reconfigured to match a new economic trajectory. It is this new configuration, rather than any simplistic notions of 'capitalist constraints on social democratic governments' or 'selling out to capitalist interests' that explains the nature and orientation of New Labour. If alongside tax reform one considers the combination of industrial relations law, labor market re-regulation and the restructuring and reorientation of social security one becomes aware of the formidable weight of the past twenty years now shaping the New Labour and the future of the country.

As King and Wood (1999) argue, those changes have arguably recreated a functional compatibility between the institutional infrastructure and essential individualism of a liberal market economy, after attempts in the past to build relationship capitalism so dismally failed (King 1999 argues

---

[6] While 'explicit' disentitlement is the consequence of purposive policy change, the 'implicit' variety occurs when new needs and risks are not met by the existing system of social protection (see Standing 1995).

further that 'illiberal' policies—such as 'coercive workfare'—are intrinsic to liberal democracies). Thus, Britain now has a welfare state that a country at the bottom of the G7 prosperity league can afford. Take the example of the broken link between pensions and earnings which New Labour has refused to restore. By breaking that link in 1980, and reducing expectations, the Conservatives have freed the current government from one of the most complex and difficult problems facing most of its European counterparts—coping with accumulated pensions liabilities. Thus, since the link was broken, the estimated pension cost increase between 1990–91 and 2030, compared with maintaining that link, has fallen by more than one-third (and by even more if 2050 is the benchmark). This will allow a decline in employer and employee National Insurance contributions over that period (from 19% to 14%) as against a 30 percent increase if earnings indexation had still been in place. At the same time, the value of the pension will fall considerably—from 21 percent to 12 percent of earnings for men and from 19 percent to 16 percent for women. Private provision and tax-financed, means-tested income supplements will of necessity fill the gap (OECD 1994: 97 ff.).

This provides the UK with a distinct source of competitive advantage—especially at its lower levels of productivity—and partly explains the current government's stance. The same argument can be made for the regulatory dilemmas posed in the labor market. Thus, if Conservative training policy gradually became a means of providing firms with temporary, low-cost labor, in-work means-tested social security benefits effectively subsidized employers so that they could create more low-wage employment (Grover and Stewart 1999). The consequent dovetailing of the social security system—as well as the deregulated labor market—with the demands of the large low-wage, low-skill sector of the economy, has become a powerful structural constraint on future policymaking. If we extend the analysis to taxation, we can posit the existence of a 'model' in which the supply of low-wage, low-skill (increasingly service sector) labor is met by demand sustained by relatively high levels of personal disposable income. In these circumstances, income polarization is not just a consequence of a deregulated employment system, but a key functional component of the current economic system. In the same vein, the internationalization strategy of the Conservatives has created considerable dependence on FDI for investment, employment, and exports, assisted by low corporation taxes and employers' social charges, and a compliant workforce. Thus, Britain's formal and informal welfare systems are now locked into an institutional ensemble sustaining a particular form of competitiveness and economic growth that is highly resistant to change.

Thus, to the extent that New Labour will innovate in welfare and employ-

ment policy it will of necessity have to build on the micro-foundations for
economic growth bequeathed it, while also playing on its new image as a fis-
cally responsible, low-tax party.[7] At the same time, the almost paranoid fear
of being identified in any way with the Labour Party of the 1970s (and the
debacle of the 'Winter of Discontent') or that of the 1980s (when it was
'hijacked by the loony left') dictates caution and stealth. 'Prudence' (a word
frequently uttered by Gordon Brown during his first two years as
Chancellor of the Exchequer) has also been counseled by the disastrous
experience of Conservative macro-mismanagement in the 1980s. A determination to avoid another boom–bust cycle has encouraged a tight monetary policy and awarding the central bank independence in setting interest
rates and inflation targets.

Within these constraints there appears to be little scope (or desire) for
traditional social democratic welfare policies. Indeed, as Freeden (1999)
argues, New Labour's conception of welfare appears to be purely instrumental. It is as determined as Thatcher's Conservatives to use social and
employment policy to liberate the citizen from undignifying and wasteful
welfare dependency and to empower him or her to participate in a fully
competitive market place. To New Labour's critics, this is a world of market citizenship not social citizenship.

For Freeden this philosophy is quite distinct from that of social democracy—or even traditional British liberalism—and much closer to an
older and more capitalist version of liberalism and one-nation, paternalis-
tic conservatism. But this is to ignore the complexity and more innovative
aspects of New Labour's program which, for all its neo-liberal conformi-
ties, does seek a genuine new departure. If there really is a 'Third Way', it
is one in which the harsh, uncompromising spirit of Thatcherism is given
a cloak of compassion and humanity by linking it not with collectivism
(New Labour targets the individual rather than categories and groups) but
with community and contractarianism. This may be neither a clear and
distinct alternative nor a balanced compromise between neo-liberalism
and social democracy (cf. Plant 1998); but it does contain elements of both
in a creative new amalgam (for a detailed analysis of the new Labour policies, see Powell 1999; Rhodes 2000 extends the present discussion).

In spending and taxation there has been much continuity. Labour came
to power pledging to hold public spending for the first two years to the
Conservatives' targets, with the exception of the 'New Deal' to be financed
by a £5.2 bn 'windfall tax' on the privatized public utilities. It also

---

[7] At the time of writing, the government is gradually trying to shift public opinion by
linking higher public spending since 1997 with the electorate's perceived support for
improvements in health, education, and transport. But the extreme caution with which
New Labour is proceeding in this direction demonstrates the possible perils in doing so.

promised not to raise income taxes—either from the low 23 percent or from the higher 40 percent rates—for the whole parliamentary term. The July 1998 spending review appealed to the financial markets, stressing spending responsibility. Overall spending was to rise by 2.8 percent per annum in real terms in the three years between 1998 and 2002, leaving total spending at 40.6 percent GDP in 2001–2 and below the 41.1 percent of the Conservative's last year in government (Hills 1998).

One analysis suggested New Labour would bring the ratio of public spending to GDP to its lowest level since Harold Macmillan (Travers 1999)—assisted, of course, by falling unemployment and a smaller number of social security claimants. Other efforts at budgetary consolidation made under the Conservatives have also been continued, including the controversial Private Finance Initiative (PFI) which brings the private sector and private sector management into public infrastructure projects via competitive tendering. This transfers the risk involved in such projects to the private sector and is designed to yield better value for money.

But at the same time, New Labour has engaged in a process of 'taxation and redistribution by stealth'. The increases in the health and education budgets may prove quite substantial with a combined increase of £5 bn per annum by 2002. This is equivalent to an increase in tax of 2p/£1 but will be raised from economies elsewhere—e.g. savings from the lower number of unemployed and higher alcohol and tobacco taxes. There is also a surreptitious 'guns to welfare' redistribution. In 1993/94, defense received £25 bn and the NHS £32 bn; but in 2001–2 defense will get £21 bn and health spending will rise to £41 bn (in 1997/98 prices) (Hills 1998).[8] In the March 1999 budget, the Chancellor introduced a lower tax band of 10 percent to benefit low-income earners and lowered the standard rate to 22 percent (reducing income tax to its lowest level for seventy years) while also increasing National Insurance contributions and announcing a budgetary surplus of £5 bn. It also cut taxes for the average family by over £1.00 per week, but given stealthily introduced tax rises in previous budgets, the average citizen now 'works for the government' for two days longer—until 25 May—than when it came to power.

'Stealth' taxes included a £5 bn per annum tax on pension funds and

---

[8] In health, there has been a step back from the quasi-market system introduced by the Conservatives and an attempt is being made to resurrect national health dentistry which has all but collapsed in recent years. New Labour will create local partnerships that consolidate family doctors and community nurses into Primary Care Groups to work with hospitals and care services (OECD 1998). In education, the aim is to raise standards by centralized initiatives and regulatory systems, including a major focus on literacy and numeracy, but here again reforms are cautious. A proposed new, more unified and inclusive 14–19 qualifications system has been quietly abandoned in favor of modest reforms to academic and vocational certification (Hodgson and Spours 1999).

future pension incomes and the abolition of mortgage tax relief and the married couple's tax allowance. 'Stealth spending' included the new working families tax credit (see below), presented as a £1.5 bn tax cut rather than an increase in expenditure, as it strictly was. The budget also awarded a guaranteed minimum income of £175 per week to unemployed older workers (aged 50 to 64) finding work and a £40 per week top-up to part-timers. They will also be offered a £750 grant if they find work to help with training and a personalized advice service if unemployed for more than six months. Child benefits were given above inflation increases. A new minimum income guarantee for pensioners of £75 a week for singles and £121 a week for couples adds £500 and £800, respectively to their annual incomes, and increases will be linked to earnings not inflation. These are all important innovations, although much less extensive than many welfare professionals and traditional Labour supporters would like. But then this is the 'Third Way', not the 'old way'.

As for the labor market and employment, Crouch (2000) draws attention to the 'social democratic' or mixed 'social/democratic neo-liberal' character of certain reforms. The most important 'mixed' policies are in the 'New Deal at Work' program, while the introduction of the minimum wage and new union recognition rights awarded under the 1999 Employment Relations Act both have social-democratic elements. New Labour's pensions policy also falls into the mixed 'social democratic/neo-liberal' category.

In a genuine departure from Conservative neo-liberalism, the minimum wage realizes an ambition first set out by the Labour Party as long ago as 1912. As a result of the introduction of the new £3.60 per hour minimum wage[9] in April 1999 (for adults aged 22 and over), more than two million workers have benefited from wage rises of up to 40 percent. There have been many implementation problems, with employers seeking ingenious methods of avoiding the minimum, but signs are that it is now being effectively enforced with apparently no detrimental effect—as long claimed by its opponents—on employment.

Trade union recognition was introduced after extensive negotiation with employers and trade unions, indicating a small step towards consultation with the social partners after two decades of marginalization. Workers in firms with more than twenty employees will be entitled by law to union representation if at least 40 percent of their number vote for it, while in firms where at least 50 percent of workers are already union members, recognition is awarded as of right. The Employment Relations Act

---

[9] This compares to minimum wages of £1.65 an hour in Portugal; £2.10 in Spain; £2.18 in Greece; £2.41 in Japan; £3.18 in New Zealand; £3.67 in the United States; £3.80 in Canada; £3.97 in France; £4.27 in Holland; £4.56 in Belgium; and £4.77 in Australia.

also extends protection against dismissal to all employees after twelve months' service and all employees involved in a grievance procedure will have a right to representation by a union official (Crouch 2000). At the same time, to help build trust and partnership in the workplace, £5 m has been made available for skills and innovation 'partnership projects in the workplace', while £2 m will be added to the Union Learning Fund (established in 1998 to promote union involvement in such projects) bringing its total endowment to over £10 m by 2002.

As Crouch (2000) argues, the New Deal and Welfare to Work initiatives bring together the inherited neo-liberal design and incentive structure (if anything making the latter more coercive) with elements of Swedish-style social-democratic active labor market policy. The New Deal moves people from social security benefits to work through new resources for training and subsidies for employers taking on workers for more than six months (or older people for two years). In another key departure from the Conservative workfare system, there is a commitment to guaranteeing work for all 18–24 year olds unemployed for six months or more (Grover and Stewart 1999). Young people have four options: training, subsidized private sector workforce, voluntary sector work, or work with the new Environmental Taskforce. There is no fifth option of benefit receipt for unemployed young people under 25 years of age beyond six months. 'Something for nothing' welfare is a thing of the past, replaced by a system of 'hand ups not hand outs' in which the 'something' is linked to a contract between the state and the individual in which the latter has no choice but to deliver. As for pensions, New Labour's reform adds a new second tier and a third tier to the existing flat-rate contributory pension (which is indexed to prices). The new State Second Pension provides those earning less than £9,000 per annum with state-funded contribution credits, while those earning between £9,000 and £18,500 receive tapered credits. A third tier of 'stake holder' pensions provides the market component in the form of privately administered income protection plans for retirement that will compete with other such schemes in the private pension market and rely on a new partnership with private pension companies (Hyde, Dixon, and Joyner 1999).

More generally, other benefit changes seek to reinforce the 'in-work' welfare initiatives of the Conservatives. Welfare payments to lone mothers without jobs have been reduced, and their workforce participation encouraged by the provision of both childcare and occupational training.[10] The Working Families Tax Credit (WFTC) is more generous than the

---

[10] The £200 m devoted to this scheme represents a 50% saving on the One-Parent Benefit that was abolished with its introduction.

Family Credit that preceded it. Including the new childcare tax credit—which will give a maximum amount of childcare support of £70 per week for a family with one child and £105 per week for a family with two or more children—WFTC will help to combat the unemployment trap. But as the OECD (1998) points out, as with all means-tested benefits, the clawback may mean that it is insufficient to get people out of poverty. A key difference from Family Credit is that it is paid to employees through the wage packet. As Hills (1998) argues, this aims to have the psychological effect of linking benefits paid to work carried out, which—as mentioned above—it has the presentational advantage of appearing in the public accounts as lower taxation rather than higher public spending.

Thus, if the Conservatives under John Major could be described as 'Thatcherism with a grey face', New Labour under Blair can be characterized as 'Thatcherism with a human face'. With its rapidly acquired reputation for running capitalism better than the British right, New Labour's greatest triumph may well be its ability to provide the 'new model' of British capitalism and welfare with the social shock absorbers and public legitimacy required to render it sustainable. But this will continue to be a mean welfare state, with wide disparities of income between individuals, families, and regions of the country and an ongoing crisis of poverty. For in this respect the legacy of Britain's transformation is massive and not susceptible to ready solutions.

Taking all relevant New Labour measures into account, Piachaud (1999) calculates that over the next five years only two million people will be taken out of poverty. This will leave a further 12 million—still double the number in 1979—living in appalling conditions, the majority in degraded housing estates and run-down inner city areas. Child poverty—which Blair has committed his party to eradicate over twenty years—will have been reduced some 800,000 or a sixth of the total. Moreover, an economic slump—and the large labor shakeout that a deregulated employment system may consequently generate—will quickly reverse these gains and undermine the current success of the New Deal and WFTC initiatives. Moreover, despite more money being spent on the major programs of health and education, dissatisfaction is mounting. An opinion poll at the end of 1999 revealed that 41 percent of the public believed the quality of NHS provision was deteriorating, while only 14 percent saw an improvement. As Travers (1999) remarks, New Labour will not easily escape one of the major paradoxes of the 'new British model': continuing demand for better public services in a system where both electoral support and the sustainability of a large consumer-driven, low-skill, low-wage, low productivity service economy depend on tax restraint not expansion.

To that extent, British welfare remains the victim not the cause, of the country's economic problems.

REFERENCES

ATKINSON, ANTHONY B., and MICKELWRIGHT, JOHN (1989). 'Turning the Screw: Benefits for the Unemployed 1979–1988', in Andrew Dilnot and Ian Walker (eds.), *The Economics of Social Security*. Oxford: Oxford University Press, 17–51.

—— HILLS, JOHN, and LE GRAND, JULIAN (1987). 'The Welfare State', in Rudiger Dornbusch and Richard Layard (eds.), *The Performance of the British Economy*. Oxford: Clarendon, 211–52.

BACON, ROBERT, and ELTIS, WALTER (1978). *Britain's Economic Problem: Too Few Producers*. New York: Macmillan.

BARNETT, CORELLI (1986). *The Audit of War: The Illusion and Reality of Britain as a Great Nation*. London: Macmillan.

Barr, Nicholas, and Fiona Coulter (1990). 'Social Security or Problem?', in John Hills (ed.), *The State of Welfare: The Welfare State in Britain since 1974*. Oxford: Clarendon Press, 274–337.

BEARDWELL, IAN (1996). ' "How Do We Know How It Really Is?": An Analysis of the New Industrial Relations', in Ian J. Beardwell (ed.), *Contemporary Industrial Relations: A Critical Analysis*. Oxford: Oxford University Press, 1–10.

BOSTON, JONATHAN (1985). 'Corporatist Incomes Policies: The Free-Rider Problem and the British Labour Government's Social Contract', in Alan Cawson (ed.), *Organized Interest and the State: Studies in Meso-Corporatism*. London: Sage, 65–84.

BROADBERRY, STEPHEN N. (1991). *Why Was Unemployment in Postwar Britain so Low?*. CEPR Discussion Paper No. 541. London: Centre for Economic Policy Research.

—— and CRAFTS, NICHOLAS (1996). *British Economic Policy and Industrial Performance in the Early Postwar Period*. CEP Discussion Paper No. 292. London: Centre for Economic Performance.

BROWN, RICHARD K. (1990). 'A Flexible Future in Europe?: Changing Patterns of Employment in the United Kingdom'. *British Journal of Sociology*, 41/3: 301–27.

BROWN, WILLIAM (1994). 'Incomes Policy in Britain: Lessons from Experience', in Ronald Dore, Robert Boyer, and Zoe Mars (eds.), *The Return to Incomes Policy*. London: Pinter, 31–46.

BURK, KATHLEEN, and CAIRNCROSS, ALEC (1982). *'Goodbye, Great Britain': The 1976 IMF Crisis*. London: Yale University Press.

CAIRNCROSS, ALEC, and EICHENGREEN, BARRY (1983). *Sterling in Decline: The Devaluations of 1931, 1949 and 1967*. Oxford: Blackwell.

CRAFTS, NICHOLAS F. R. (1995). ' "You've Never Had It So Good?": British Economic Policy and Performance, 1945–1960', in Barry J. Eichengreen (ed.),

Europe's Postwar Recovery. Cambridge: Cambridge University Press, 246–70.

CROUCH, COLIN (1999*a*). 'Employment, Industrial Relations and Social Policy: New Life in an Old Connection'. *Social Policy and Administration*, 33/4: 437–57.

CROUCH, COLIN (1999*b*). 'The Parabola of Working-Class Politics', in Andrew Gamble and Tony Wright (eds.), *The New Social Democracy*. Oxford: Blackwell, 69–83.

—— (2000), 'A Third Way in Industrial Relations?', in Stuart White (ed.), *Labour in Government: The 'Third Way' and the Future of Social Democracy*. Forthcoming.

CRUZ CASTRO, LAURA (1999). *Qualifications, Unemployment and Youth Training Policy in the United Kingdom*. Working Paper No. 131. Madrid: Instituto Juan March de estudios e investigaciones.

DILNOT, ANDREW, and STARK, GRAHAM (1989). 'The Poverty Trap, Tax Cuts and the Reform of Social Security', in Andrew Dilnot and Ian Walker (eds.), *The Economics of Social Security*. Oxford: Oxford University Press, 169–78.

—— and WEBB, STEVEN (1989). 'The 1988 Social Security Reforms', in Andrew Dilnot and Ian Walker (eds.), *The Economics of Social Security*. Oxford: Oxford University Press, 239–67.

DUNN, STEPHEN, and METCALF, DAVID (1996). 'Trade Union Law since 1979', in Ian Beardwell (ed.), *Contemporary Industrial Relations: A Critical Analysis*. Oxford: Oxford University Press, 66–98.

EICHENGREEN, BARRY J., and RITSCHL, ALBRECHT (1998). *Winning the War, Losing the Peace? Britain's Post-War Recovery in a West German Mirror*. CEPR Discussion Paper No. 1809. London: Centre for Economic Policy Research.

ELBAUM, BERNARD, and LAZONICK, WILLIAM (eds.) (1986). *The Decline of the British Economy*. Oxford: Clarendon Press.

ELTIS, WALTER, and HIGHAM, DAVID (1995), 'Closing the UK Competitiveness Gap'. *National Institute Economic Review*, Nov.: 71–84.

FINEGOLD, DAVID, and SOSKICE, DAVID (1988). 'The Failure of Training in Britain: Analysis and Prescription'. *Oxford Review of Economic Policy*, 4/3: 21–53.

FISHBEIN, WARREN H. (1984). *Wage Restraint by Consensus: Britain's Search for an Incomes Policy Agreement, 1965–79*. London: Routledge and Kegan Paul.

FLANAGAN, ROBERT J., SOSKICE, DAVID W., and ULMAN, LLOYD (1983). *Unionism, Economic Stabilization and Incomes Policy: European Experience*. Washington, DC: Brookings Institution.

FREEDEN, MICHAEL (1999). 'True Blood or False Genealogy: New Labour and British Social Democratic Thought', in Andrew Gamble and Tony Wright (eds.), *The New Social Democracy*. Oxford: Blackwell, 151–65.

GLENNERSTER, HOWARD (1990). 'Social Policy since the Second World War', in John Hills (ed.), *The State of Welfare: The Welfare State since 1974*. Oxford: Clarendon Press, 11–27.

—— (1998). 'Welfare with the Lid On', in Howard Glennerster and John Hills (eds.), *The State of Welfare: The Economics of Social Spending*. Oxford: Oxford

University Press, 308–44.

GLYN, ANDREW (1992). 'The "Productivity Miracle", Profits and Investment', in Jonathan Michie (ed.), *The Economic Legacy, 1979–1992*. London: Academic Press, 77–88.

GOULD, PHILIP (1998). *The Unfinished Revolution: How the Modernisers Saved the Labour Party*. London: Abacus.

GROVER, CHRIS, and STEWART, JOHN (1999). '"Market Workfare": Social Security, Social Regulation and Competitiveness in the 1990s'. *Journal of Social Policy*, 28/1: 73–96.

GRIFFITH, RACHEL (1999). *Productivity and Foreign Ownership in the UK Car Industry*. IFS Working Paper No. W99/11. London: Institute for Fiscal Studies.

HALL, PETER (1986). *Governing the Economy: The Politics of State Intervention in Britain and France*. Oxford: Oxford University Press.

HART, ROBERT A., and RUFFELL, ROBIN J. (1998). 'Labour Costs and Employment Policy'. *National Institute Economic Review*, 165: 99–108.

HILLS, JOHN (1995). 'Funding the Welfare State'. *Oxford Review of Economic Policy*, 11/3: 27–43.

——(1998). *Thatcherism, New Labour and the Welfare State*. CASE Paper No. 13. London: Centre for the Analysis of Social Exclusion, London School of Economics.

HMSO (1999). *Employment Trends*. London: HMSO.

HM Treasury (1979). *The Government's Expenditure Plans 1980–81*. Cmnd 7746. London: HMSO.

HODGSON, ANN, and SPOURS, KEN (1999). 'So when is the Revolution?'. *Guardian*, 25 May.

HOPKIN, BRYAN (1998). 'Freedom and Necessity in Economic Policy: Britain 1970–1979'. *Political Quarterly*, 305–18.

HYDE, MARK, DIXON, JOHN, and JOYNER, MELANIE (1999). '"Work for Those That Can, Security for Those that Cannot": The United Kingdom's New Social Security Reform Agenda'. *International Social Security Review*, 52/4: 77–78.

JENKINS, STEPHEN P. (1996). 'Recent Trends in the UK Income Distribution: What Happened and Why?'. *Oxford Review of Economic Policy*, 12/1: 29–46.

JOHNSON, PAUL (1996). 'The Assessment: Inequality'. *Oxford Review of Economic Policy*, 12/1: 1–14.

JONES, RUSSELL (1985). *Wages and Employment Policy, 1936–1985*. London: Allen & Unwin.

KING, DESMOND (1999). *In the Name of Liberalism: Illiberal Social Policy in the United States and Britain*. Oxford: Oxford University Press.

——and WOOD, STEWART (1999). 'The Political Economy of Neo-Liberalism: Britain and the United States in the 1980s', in Herbert Kitschelt, Peter Lange, Gary Marks, and John D. Stephens (eds.), *Continuity and Change in Contemporary Capitalism*. Cambridge: Cambridge University Press, 371–97.

LE GRAND, JULIAN (1990). 'The State of Welfare', in John Hills (ed.), *The State of Welfare: The Welfare State since 1974*. Oxford: Clarendon, 338–62.

LOWE, RODNEY (1993). *The Welfare State in Britain since 1945*. London: Macmillan.

MACHIN, STEPHEN (1996). 'Wage Inequality in the United Kingdom'. *Oxford Review of Economic Policy*, 12/1: 47–64.

MACHIN, STEPHEN and MANNING, ALAN (1992). *Minimum Wages, Wage Dispersion and Employment: Evidence from the UK Wage Councils*. CEP Discussion Paper No. 80. London: Centre for Economic Performance.

MARQUAND, DAVID (1998). *The Unprincipled Society: New Demands and Old Politics*. London: Fontana.

MAYNARD, GEOFFREY (1988). *The Economy under Mrs Thatcher*. Oxford: Blackwell.

MICHIE, JONATHAN, and WILKINSON, FRANK (1992). 'Inflation Policy and the Restructuring of Labour Markets', in Jonathan Michie (ed.), *The Economic Legacy, 1979–1992*. London: Academic Press, 195–217.

MIDDLEMAS, KEITH (1990). *Power, Competition and the State*, ii. *Threats to the Post-War Settlement: Britain, 1961–1974*. London: Macmillan.

——(1991). *Power, Competition and the State*, iii. *The End of the Post-War Era: Britain since 1974*. London: Macmillan.

MORGAN, JULIAN (1996). 'What Do Comparisons of the Last Two Economic Recoveries Tell Us About the UK Labour Market'. *National Institute Economic Review*, May: 80–91.

OECD (1982). *OECD Economic Surveys: United Kingdom*. Paris: OECD.

——(1983). *OECD Economic Surveys: United Kingdom*. Paris: OECD.

——(1986). *OECD Economic Surveys: United Kingdom*. Paris: OECD.

——(1993). *OECD Economic Surveys: United Kingdom*. Paris: OECD.

——(1994). *OECD Economic Surveys: United Kingdom*. Paris: OECD.

——(1995). *OECD Economic Surveys: United Kingdom*. Paris: OECD.

——(1996). *OECD Economic Surveys: United Kingdom*. Paris: OECD.

——(1998). *OECD Economic Surveys: United Kingdom*. Paris: OECD.

O'MAHONY, MARY (1995). 'International Differences in Manufacturing Unit Labour Costs'. *National Institute Economic Review*, Nov.:, 85–100.

OULTON, NICHOLAS (1995). 'Labour Productivity and Unit Labour Costs in Manufacturing: The UK and its Competitors'. *National Institute Economic Review*, Nov.: 49–60.

PARRY, R. (1986). 'United Kingdom', in Peter Flora (ed.), *Growth to Limits: The Western European Welfare States since World War II*. Berlin: De Gruyter, 155–240.

PIACHAUD, DAVID (1998). 'Changing Dimensions of Poverty', in N. Ellison and Christopher Pierson (eds.), *Developments in British Social Policy*. London: Macmillan, 233–46.

——(1999). 'Wealth by Stealth'. *Guardian*, 1 Sept.

PIERSON, CHRISTOPHER (1994). 'Continuity and Discontinuity in the Emergence of the "Post-Fordist" Welfare State', in Roger Burrows and Brian Loader (eds.), *Towards a Post-Fordist Welfare State*. London: Routledge, 95–113.

PIERSON, PAUL (1994). *Dismantling the Welfare State? Reagan, Thatcher and the Politics of Retrenchment*. Cambridge: Cambridge University Press.

PLANT, RAYMOND (1998). *The Third Way*. Working Paper 5/98. London: Friedrich-Ebert-Stiftung.

POLLARD, SIDNEY (1992). *The Development of the British Economy 1914–1990*. London: Arnold.

POWELL, MARTIN (ed.) (1999). *New Labour, New Welfare State?* Bristol: Policy Press.

PRAIS, SIG J. (1995). *Productivity, Education and Training: An International Perspective*. Cambridge: Cambridge University Press.

RHODES, MARTIN (1989). 'Whither Regulation?, "Disorganised Capitalism" and the West European Labour Market', in Leigh Hancher and Michael Moran (eds.), *Capitalism, Culture and Economic Regulation*. Oxford: Clarendon, 227–67.

——(2000). 'Desperately Seeking a Solution: Social Democracy, Thatcherism and the "Third Way" in British Welfare'. *West European Politics*, 23/2: 161–87 (special issue on 'Recasting European Welfare States', edited by Maurizio Ferrera and Martin Rhodes).

ROBINSON, PETER (1995). *The British Disease Overcome? Living Standards, Productivity and Education Attainment, 1979–94*. CEP Discussion Paper No. 260. London: Centre for Economic Performance.

——(1997). *Water under the Bridge: Changes in Employment in Britain and the OECD*. CEP Discussion Paper No. 325. London: Centre for Economic Performance.

ROWTHORN, ROBERT (1992). 'Government Spending and Taxation in the Thatcher Era', in Jonathan Michie (ed.), *The Economic Legacy, 1979–1992*. London: Academic Press, 261–95.

——(1999). 'The Political Economy of Full Employment in Modern Britain'. The Kalecki Memorial Lecture, Department of Economics, University of Oxford, 19 Oct.

SENTANCE, ANDREW (1998). 'UK Macroeconomic Policy and Economic Performance', in Tony Buxton, Paul Chapman, and Paul Temple (eds.), *Britain's Economic Performance*. London: Routledge, 38–40.

STANDING, GUY (1995), 'Labor Insecurity through Market Regulation: Legacy of the 1980s, Challenge for the 1990s', in Katherine McFate, Roger Lawson, and William J. Wilson (eds.), *Poverty, Inequality and the Future of Social Policy: Western States in the New World Order*. New York: Russell Sage Foundation, 153–96.

STEWART, MICHAEL (1977). *The Jekyll and Hyde Years: Politics and Economic Policy since 1964*. London: Dent.

TIRATSOO, NICK, and TOMLINSON, JIM (1998). *The Conservatives and Industrial Efficiency, 1951–1964: Thirteen Wasted Years?* London: Routledge.

TOFT, CHRISTIAN (1995). 'State Action, Trade Unions and Voluntary Unemployment Insurance in Great Britain, Germany and Scandinavia, 1900–1934'. *European Economic Review*, 39: 565–74.

TOMLINSON, JIM (1995). 'Welfare and the Economy: The Economic Impact of the Welfare State, 1945–51'. *Twentieth Century British History*, 6/2: 194–219.

——(1998). 'Why so Austere? The British Welfare State of the 1940s'. *Journal of Social Policy*, 27/1: 63–77.

TRAVERS, TONY (1999). 'Public Spending: Squaring the Circle'. *Guardian*, 22 Sept.

VICKERSTAFF, SARAH (1985). 'Industrial Training in Britain: The Dilemmas of a Neo-Corporatist Policy', in Alan Cawson (ed.), *Organized Interest and the State: Studies in Meso-Corporatism*. London: Sage, 45–64.

WEBB, STEVEN (1995). 'Social Security in a Changing Labour Market'. *Oxford Review of Economic Policy*, 11/3: 11–26.

WHITESIDE, NOEL (1996). 'Creating the Welfare State in Britain, 1945–1960'. *Journal of Social Policy*, 25/1: 83–103.

WILDING, PAUL (1997). 'The Welfare State and the Conservatives'. *Political Studies*, 45: 716–26.

WILLIAMS, DAVID (1999). 'Foreign Manufacturing Firms in the UK: Effects on Employment, Output and Supplier Linkages'. *European Business Review*, 99/6: 393–98.

WOLFE, JOEL (1991). 'State Power and Ideology in Britain: Mrs Thatcher's Privatization Programme'. *Political Studies*, 34: 237–52.

WOODWARD, NICHOLAS (1993). 'Labour's Economic Performance, 1964–1970', in Richard Cooper, Stephen Fielding, and Nick Tiratsoo (eds), *The Wilson Governments, 1964–1970*. London: Pinter, 72–101.

ZEITLIN, JONATHAN, and HERRIGEL, GARY (eds.) (2000) *Americanization and Its Limits: Reworking American Technology and Management in Post-war Europe*. Oxford: Oxford University Press.

ZYSMAN, JOHN (1983). *Governments, markets, and Growth: Financial Systems and the Politics of Industrial Change*. Ithaca, NY: Cornell University Press.

3

Internationalization and Two Liberal Welfare States
Australia and New Zealand

HERMAN SCHWARTZ

3.1. Introduction

Australia and New Zealand differ in four ways from the other cases here.[1] First, relatively weak manufacturing sectors rendered them vulnerable to international economic pressures earlier, necessitating 'stop–go' policies that constrained employment protection and the elaboration of social policy early in the postwar period. Second, their employment and social protection models are quite different from the typical European model, and they created dynamics that amplified those international vulnerabilities over time. Third, these dynamics created crises that led to earlier and more profound transformations of their employment and social protection models. A relatively high dependence on foreign investment inflows to spur growth and cover chronic current account deficits combined with relatively liquid share markets and early financial liberalization to amplify pressures for transformation of their models. In particular, chronic balance of payments deficits made politicians and financial bureaucracies sensitive to falling exchange rates (which increased the real cost of foreign currency denominated debt), to interest rate shocks (including credit rating downgrades), and to the distribution of risk between the public and private sectors. Fourth, both countries have Westminster systems of government that permit governments anchored in minority voter blocs to change things rapidly.

'Golden age' Australia and New Zealand turned common European patterns of social and employment policy upside down. Employment policy in the antipodes operated primarily through trade policy (protected import substitution industrialization [ISI]), while social policy operated

---

[1] Except where noted, all data here, including in the Figures, are from OECD, *Economic Outlook*, various dates.

primarily through judicial regulation of wages and the labor market. What we will here call the informal welfare state—the whole range of state policies supporting delivery of a socially defined wage in a full employment environment—was thus much more important than the formal welfare state—tax-financed, state-provided transfers and services. Australia's and New Zealand's common history as highly indebted primary product exporters explains social and employment strategies based on ISI and informal welfare (Mabbett 1995; Schwartz 1998). These strategies generated internal dynamics and faced external trends that threatened to price their largely primary product exports out of world markets. Social policy—that is, judicially regulated wages—reversed the usual Scandinavian dynamic and pushed up costs in the sheltered sector of the economy in order to shift rents out of the exposed sector. Employment policy—that is, ISI—constantly expanded the sheltered part of the economy. But because Australian and New Zealand primary product exports faced declining and volatile terms of trade, accompanied by slow volume growth, eventually the sheltered sector got too big for the exposed sector to support, necessitating some change in the model. Foreign direct investment largely financed ISI, while direct borrowing overseas financed recurrent current account deficits. This pattern of borrowing and investment simply shifted the locus of foreign pressures from one kind of burden to another, in two directions: away from volatile prices for primary goods and onto maintenance of the exchange rate, and away from the exchange rate onto wage developments in the sheltered sector. These dilemmas had already emerged in the late 1960s, but became acute in the 1970s.

Despite their similar 'golden age' models, these two countries displayed enough divergence in three critical variables so that their economies did not run along absolutely parallel lines after 1973. Australia's and New Zealand's different responses to the crisis of their respective 'golden age' models are best explained by divergence in the patterns of institutional representation for organized interests, in union structures (and thus in attitudes about the possibility of working within existing collective bargaining arrangements), and in notions about what constituted the social wage. Put simply, one combination of state structures, union structures, and the moral economy generated a Labour Party-led neo-liberalism that changed New Zealand more profoundly (in many respects) than Thatcher changed Britain, while a different combination of state structures, union structures, and moral economy allowed the Australian Labor Party (ALP) to produce a more gradual corporatist restructuring of labor markets and the state. The initial transformations sponsored by the left, in turn, structured even greater divergence in the intensity of change when right-wing governments replaced each labor party in 1990 and 1996, respectively.

State power in the collective bargaining arena was much more robust in Australia than in New Zealand, providing an institutional arena in which corporatist compromises could be enforced. Second, Australia's labor movement was much more centralized than New Zealand's, and the same is true of their respective business communities. Relatively greater organization for labor and business meant that a compromise program for adaptation could be negotiated and, conversely, that efforts to 'smash through and crash through' were much less likely to succeed. In New Zealand relatively fragmented manufacturing and labor communities were unable to articulate compelling compromise responses to international pressures. Finally the values underpinning unions' and voters' 'moral economy' determined whether compromise positions would find electoral support, giving parties with programs for adaptation time to reorganize employment and social policy.

Thus, in Australia the Labor Party was able to transform implicitly corporatist collective bargaining structures into open corporatist structures, to expand the social wage, and to redistribute an expanded employment base until a more neo-liberal coalition government came to power in 1996. The Labor Party also systematically introduced competitive pressures into most product and service markets. 1980s Australia thus most closely resembles the post-Wassenaar Netherlands or Belgium after the decision to tie wage increases to those in Belgium's seven largest trading partners. In New Zealand the Labour Party put forward similar policy proposals but could not make them stick, and eventually it turned to more radical attempts at replacing the old model of protected employment with pure market forms. Then the successor National Party government replaced socially defined wages with market wages. Both of these governments also systematically introduced market competition into most product and service markets. New Zealand thus resembles a more systematic and theoretically rigorous version of Thatcher's ad hoc reorganization of the British economy.

Differences between Australia's and New Zealand's Westminister systems of government also matter, but not much. Until 1996 New Zealand's system clearly gave electoral minorities with parliamentary majorities tremendous leeway to implement their agenda. Australia's version of proportional representation and its strong upper house tends to retard proposals for change, particularly when they emanate from a party representing only a plurality of voters. But this institutional difference only conditions the rate of change, not its direction. Table 3.1 presents a precis of electoral and constitutional structures.

The discussion below combines perspectives on Australia's and New Zealand's very similar 'golden age' models. The discussion then turns to

Table 3.1 *State institutional structures, c.1970*

	Australia	New Zealand
State	Federal; central government funds but state governments control tertiary education, health, and social assistance	Unitary; local government has no independent status
Legislature	Bicameral, effective upper house	Unicameral
Elections	Lower House: single transferable vote Senate: proportional representation, thus minority parties exist in Senate	First past the post, single-member districts, thus: majority parties from plurality vote shares
Parties	Labor Liberal (urban bourgeois) National[a] (rural bourgeois)	Labour (largely urban) National (largely rural) Social Credit (rural protest)
Typical government 1945–70	Coalition Liberal–National, majority in House with 40–50% of voters, minority in Senate	National Party majority, with 40–45 % of voters

[a]For simplicity's sake I will use National Party to designate its predecessors, the Country Party and National-Country Party.

serial consideration of their divergent responses to the shocks of the 1970s and 1980s, looking first at the unraveling of their models, then at their reconstruction. The conclusion illuminates the similarities and differences between the two countries.

3.2. 'Golden Age' Australia and New Zealand

Australia's and New Zealand's essentially similar employment and social policies worked differently from European models. In Australia and New Zealand, employment policy operated through trade policy. Both governments deliberately sheltered local manufacturing from world markets in order to encourage import substitution industrialization (ISI) and thus generate employment. Both governments shifted rents from efficient primary product exporters toward the protected parts of the economy to induce ISI. In Australia and New Zealand, social policy operated through judicially set wages (Castles 1989). Formal, state-run arbitration courts[2]

[2] For clarity's sake, I use 'arbitration court' to label Australian and New Zealand wage-setting institutions whose names have changed over time. (State-level arbitration systems in Australia are largely ignored.)

set wages at socially defined levels rather than leaving them to market forces or free collective bargaining. This created highly structured labor markets in which both unions and business organizations were often little more than appendages of the state. Consequently, in contrast to Europe, where taxes and transfers level out the unequal incomes labor markets produce, here incomes are leveled in the labor market itself, and taxes and transfers do minimal work. The typical worker receives around 90 percent of his or her income from wages, unlike the Scandinavian combination of 70 percent from market wages and 30 percent from government transfers.

Both countries thus had relatively limited formal welfare states (i.e. a European-style social policy) at the beginning of the 1970s, because both accommodated most new social demands by retooling the arbitration system rather than creating new welfare programs. For example, formal disparities between female and male wage levels were removed in the 1970s. Both countries thus had relatively little in the way of an active labor market policy, because they responded to rising unemployment with growing trade protection. So long as trade protection and robust raw materials exports generated full (male) employment, these small formal welfare systems adequately handled residual pockets of poverty. Relatively speaking, Australia relied more on high, socially defined wages and New Zealand more on an elaborate formal welfare state.

3.2.1. Employment Policy by Other Means

Australia and New Zealand used high tariffs and import licensing to generate local full employment. These trade policies, in turn, accommodated the relatively high direct and indirect wages in the manufacturing sector that arbitration created. In tandem, full employment and high wages obviated the need for many of the tax-funded transfers and services common in Europe. The effective rate of protection for manufactured goods—that is, the share of value added by tariffs—averaged between 60 and 70 percent in New Zealand and 46 percent in Australia, and reflected deliberate efforts to generate more employment (OECD 1972: 29–31, 1989: 39). In Australia, the Tariff Board literally told industrial firms, 'You make it and [we'll] protect it' (Capling and Galligan 1993: 105). The deliberate suppression of manufactured goods imports gave both economies relatively low levels of trade compared to similarly sized OECD economies (see Table 3.2).

Exports of foods and raw materials from their highly efficient primary sectors funded residual imports of manufactured goods. In New Zealand, dairy, meat, wool, and timber accounted for about 76 percent of exports, while in Australia coal and other ores, wool, meat, wheat, and dairy

Herman Schwartz

Table 3.2 *Trade structure, various indicators, 1961–1997*

	Australia			New Zealand		
	1963	1970	1996	1965	1970	1996
Trade (% of GDP)	31.8	32.0	40.4	36.6	47.8	60.4)
Compare	(Sweden	42.3	70.6)	(Denmark	49.5	64.0)
Exports (% of total)	1961	1970	1997	1960	1970	1992
Wool	41.4	13.8	7.2	33.0	18.8	6.0
Meat	9.2	10.3	3.2	24.2	33.5	16.8
Dairy, fruit, fish, sugar	13.3	11.7	2.9	25.3	23.1	28.7
Metals, ores, aluminum	7.3	10.0	17.1	0.0	0.0	3.7
Coal, oil, fuels	n.a.	5.8	19.3	0.0	0.6	2.7
Australia: cereals	9.4	12.1	7.5	—	—	—
NZ: Forestry						
(+ pulp, paper)	—	—	—	1.3	5.8	10.0
RAW MATERIALS SUBTOTAL	80.6	63.7	57.2	83.8	81.8	67.9
Manufactures						
Commodity based	18.3	11.0	9.7	19.4	11.0	7.3
Non-commodity						
manufactures	—	15.0	22.5	—	9.0	17.0
Export destinations	1961	1971	1995	1960	1970	1993
United Kingdom	23.9	11.2	3.5	53.0	35.9	6.4
Europe (exc. UK)	15.9	9.4	8.7	16.9	11.6	9.2
United States	7.5	11.9	8.1	13.1	16.1	11.9
Japan	16.7	27.1	22.9	2.9	9.8	14.7
Rest of world	36.0	40.7	56.8	14.1	26.6	57.8

n.a. = not available

Sources: OECD, *Economic Surveys, Australia* or *New Zealand* (Paris: OECD, various dates).

amounted to about 65 percent of exports. In 1970 both countries were still substantially oriented towards traditional European markets, but Australia's minerals exports were already diversifying its customer base towards Asia. The shift to minerals exports and toward Asia gave Australia much stronger growth, a better balance of payments situation, and higher average incomes than New Zealand in the 1960s and 1970s. Australia's and New Zealand's efficient primary sectors absorbed relatively little labor, and their employment share fell continuously after 1945. Only 6.5 percent of Australia's labor force farmed or mined (slightly more than in Sweden), and 8.6 percent of New Zealand's (again, slightly more than in Denmark). Both countries oriented their industrial policy around protecting manufacturing to generate employment growth, and both also used government ownership and regulation of services to absorb labor. In both, manufacturing and services contained considerable hidden unemployment.

Protection funded itself by inducing inflows of foreign investment (see Table 3.3). In New Zealand, foreign firms accounted for 20 percent of employment and, because their productivity typically exceeded that of local firms, 26 percent of value added by the end of the 1960s. Foreign firms dominated most of the durables sector and a substantial part of the non-durables, leaving light consumer durables and non-durables to local firms. New Zealand's small domestic market limited economies of scale and the incentive to use capital-intensive production processes, leaving most enterprises labor-intensive and inefficient. Firms with fewer than 100 employees generated over half of employment by the 1970s; the average firm had 30 employees. The 5 percent of firms employing over 100 people were typically capital-intensive export processing operations like meat packing or subsidiaries of multinational corporations (Gould 1982: 108; Hawke 1985: 258–59, 274; OECD 1975: 42).

By the end of the 1970s, foreign firms controlled about one-fourth of Australian manufacturing and half of mining as measured by value added (OECD 1972: 42; UNCTC 1988: 529). As in New Zealand, much of the employment that ISI generated was actually disguised unemployment. Australian firms achieved somewhat greater economies of scale than their New Zealand counterparts, but they remained uncompetitive and unable to export. In automobile manufacturing, Australian labor productivity was less than half the Japanese average. Similarly, consumer durables firms

Table 3.3 *Inward foreign direct investment, c.1980*[a]

	Australia	New Zealand
MNCs % share of manufacturing employment	26.7	n.a.
Profits of MNCs as % of profits of all firms	22.6	28.9
Book value, MNCs capital stock, as % of GDP	10.7	10.0
MNCs % share of employment (Australia) or assets (New Zealand), 1981 in		
Chemicals	59.6	86.4
Transport equipment	43.0	56.5 (metals)
Electrical equipment	37.1	55.5
Coal and/or petroleum	80.8	n.a.

n.a. = not available.
MNC = multinational corporations

[a]Dates vary, 1978 through 1982–83.

Source: Dunning and Cantwell 1987: 110, 117, 270, 277, 305.

had an estimated 25 percent cost disadvantage based on diseconomies of scale alone (BIE 1983).

3.2.2. Social Policy by Other Means

Australia and New Zealand have fairly minimal formal welfare states by European standards, because their arbitration courts achieve European social welfare goals by setting wages at high levels, mandating occupational welfare, and regulating work conditions, while tariff protection generates full employment. The arbitration system structures collective bargaining and, thereby, both employee and employer organizational patterns.

3.2.2.1. Australia

In Australia, for roughly a century, federal and state courts have set wages through judicial proceedings. Only labor and employer organizations may initiate proceedings; individuals have no standing. The courts hand down judicial decisions—'awards'—setting the 'basic' or minimum wage, additional skill-based wages for specific occupations, conditions of work, occupational benefits, and 'wage relativities' (i.e. the relationship or parities between wages in different occupations). After 1907 the federal court set a high basic wage, defined socially by reference to a decent standard of living for a family of four (originally presumed to be male-headed). Wage relativities were set by awarding additional wages—margins—for skills and enforced via a doctrine of comparative wage justice. The arbitration court defined comparative wage justice to mean that 'employees doing the same work for different employers or in different industries should by and large receive the same amount of pay irrespective of the capacity of their employer or industry' (CAR 1970: 165; Plowman 1980: 85). The ruling created an almost automatic transmission of wage gains from one sector to another. Women received 75 percent of the male basic wage until the early 1970s. Beginning in the 1930s awards covered roughly 85–90 percent of workers. In 1974 the basic wage was equal to US$12,650 (in 1998 dollars), or about half of Australia's per capita GDP at the time.

As in the Netherlands and Denmark, awards generally bind workers and employers who did not go to court themselves but who do operate in the industry governed by the award. De facto, this compels capital and labor to organize in order to participate in wage setting; de jure, registration before the court creates a monopoly of representation. Consequently, 'Australian unions are a part of the state, but in the sense of local governments with entrenched traditions of autonomy' (Scherer 1985: 92). In 1976, 322 unions covered 2.8 million Australian workers (versus 40 unions for 3.6 million Swedish workers), and over 50 percent of the labor force was unionized. Many awards provided for a closed shop, but there was not compulsory unionization across the board as in New Zealand. The union movement was divided between a few large industrial unions and many small crafts-based unions.

Public sector workers, roughly 25 percent of the workforce in 1970, were handled in a similar way. State tribunals governed most public sector workers (because the states did most service delivery) and typically awarded wage increases across the board. Across the board public sector wage increases meant that wage relativities among occupational groups there increasingly diverged from wage relativities in the private sector (Scherer 1980). But after 1962 occupational groups in the public sector began getting group awards based on private sector awards generated in the federal system, and so the metals award became the implicit standard for comparison.

The apparent lack of concentration in collective bargaining conceals two important axes of centralization. First, the Australian Confederation of Trade Unions (ACTU) represents the entire union movement in basic wage cases. By the 1970s the ACTU covered virtually the entire unionized private sector workforce, or roughly 75 percent of unionized workers. Within the ACTU five unions, each representing over 100,000 workers, were covering the metals industries, rural workers, the retail sector, clerks, and hospitality by 1971, and by the late 1970s the ACTU included most public sector unions. Second, the Australian Metal Workers Union (AMWU)[3] and its employer counterpart, the Metal Trades Industry Association (MTIA), typically have a decisive hand in shaping the Metal Trades Award. The MTIA covers over 10,000 firms, but its eight largest enterprise groups account for nearly 30 percent of employment and value added. The metals award covers about half of manufacturing labor, most skilled labor, and about 10 percent of all Australian workers. Until 1967 higher pay from the metals award spilled over into manufacturing, construction, and eventually white-collar jobs via well-established parities (Frenkel 1987: 100). The AMWU and MTIA thus had a decisive hand in shaping the wage differentials and working conditions that the federal arbitration court subsequently imposed on the majority of manufacturing workers.

Employers, by contrast, were more divided, spanning about 700 organizations which aggregated themselves into three broad confederations representing manufacturing in sheltered industries, primary production

---

[3] I use AMWU to label the Amalgamated Engineering Union and its successors after 1972; I use MTIA to designate the Metal Trades Employers Association and its successors.

and manufacturing for export, and multinational firms. In the early 1970s employers were split between the Associated Chambers of Manufacturing and the more primary product-oriented Australian Council of Employers Federations. These amalgamated as the Confederation of Australian Industry in 1978, but rancorous rifts continue to split this group (Plowman 1989). Meanwhile a separate, parallel, and powerful lobbying organization, the National Farmers Federation, represented 80 percent of farmers (Matthews 1991: 197), typically taking a harder line against unions than did the various manufacturers associations.

How did arbitration really work? Essentially, prior to the 1960s, Australian unions were so weak that most wage increases came only via basic wage claims organized by ACTU and brought before the arbitration courts. Industrial employers, aware that tariff protection would rise enough to compensate them for their increased wage bill, usually acquiesced. With full employment after 1967, bargaining on a second tier became more prevalent and a larger share of wage gains emerged from this more local bargaining. When the courts tried to enforce wage restraint in the late 1960s, unions struck and the court could not enforce any legal sanctions against them. Politicians ratified the courts' weakness by legislating away penalties. Employers counterattacked, revealing unions' fundamental weakness as unemployment rose after 1973. Unions thus spent the 1970s building the ACTU into a real federation with central powers, which helps explain why arbitration functioned as a de facto incomes policy in the 1970s and 1980s.

3.2.2.2. New Zealand

New Zealand's arbitration system pre-dates Australia's, but a socially defined living wage did not emerge until the 1920s. Collective bargaining occurs inside a set of state-run courts. Unlike Australia's courts, however, which were staffed by professional jurists, New Zealand's three-person arbitration panels were composed of a judge, an employer representative, and an employee representative. The two labor market actors were constantly tempted to cut out the middleman, forcing the state to intervene directly in pursuit of balance of payments and macroeconomic goals. The courts covered only about three-fifths of the labor market. This relative lack of coverage and institutionalization, together with the courts' lack of insulation from labor market actors, hurt their ability to discipline both capital and labor while remaining free of idiosyncratic political pressures.

The court set private sector wages and conditions across most industries and agriculture, fixing and adjusting the minimum wage with flat dollar or percentage increases under General Wage Orders, similar to Australian

Basic Wage increases. No formal, Australian-style principle of comparative wage justice existed, but the court refused to change established wage
parities. Sectorally, employer associations and unions usually bargained
over wages, and the court imposed binding arbitration only when talks
failed, much as in Denmark. The court ratified collective bargaining
through industry-specific awards, which bound firms and workers who
were not members of either the employer associations or unions in the
affected industry. In principle, employers and unions could sign limited
contracts approximating 'enterprise bargains' (i.e. plant-specific contracts). Prior to the 1990s, the enterprise bargains affected about 25 percent of workers, in contrast to the 40 percent covered by industry awards,
so that there was a significantly higher degree of decentralization than in
Australia (Boston 1984: 70).

Compulsory union membership from the mid-1930s through 1990 put
three-fifths of the labor force into largely craft-dominated, and thus fragmented, unions. In 1973 24 unions with more than 5,000 members represented only 60 percent of the unionized workforce (Deeks and Boxall
1989: 50). By the 1970s two broad but weak federations existed. The private sector Federation of Labour (FOL) covered about two-thirds of
unionized workers, while the public sector Combined State Unions covered one-third. On the other side, the similarly fragmented Employers
Federation covered 10,000 employers and 80 percent of the private sector
workforce. Until the 1980s, the Employers Federation supported the
existing collective bargaining system, although one current within the
Federation wanted more Scandinavian-style centralization and a different
current preferred more enterprise bargaining. Farmers presented a united
bargaining and lobbying front through Federated Farmers, which had
extensive ties to the National Party. As in Australia, retail, manufacturing,
and farming employers were divided against each other.

The award system tended to compress wages and preserve wage differentials, despite some wage drift. Wage drift had no legal standing, but in
the 1960s and 1970s roughly 25 percent of FOL workers enjoyed the benefits of drift above contractual wages (Boston 1984: 68, 81–82). Generally
wage increases tended to follow the gains made by the Engineers (i.e. metals) Union, the three electricians' unions and the General Drivers' Union.
Technically, strikes and lockouts were illegal during the tenure of any given
award. From 1946 onward, public sector wages were linked to private sector wages in principle, and statutorily after 1969. Though the state
intended public sector wages to follow private sector wage movements,
public sector employees were wage leaders in some bargaining rounds
during the 1970s. As in Australia, the basic female wage was initially set at
40 percent of the male wage but later normalized. Female public sector

workers gained wage equality in 1960, and female private sector workers gained equality in 1972.

The state used arbitration in its attempt to control the balance of payments and inflation during the full employment era of the 1950s and 1960s, typically arguing for a low General Wage Order when either inflation or the current account deficit grew. The court's awards in the 1960s held real wage growth below GDP growth (Boston 1984: 90). As in Australia, the court's ability to enforce awards disappeared in the late 1960s, when wage pressures were greatest, labor markets tightest, and labor militancy high.

3.2.3. The Formal Welfare State

Australia and New Zealand also had formal welfare states—state-funded services and transfers—though these were clearly secondary to trade protection and arbitrated wages. Before the 1980s welfare supplemented work, buffering against life cycle events and accidents. Generally, these formal welfare programs provided flat-rate benefits funded from general revenue (see Table 3.4). Universality varied, but tax abatements were common. In 1960 Australian social spending was about 25 percent lower than in the other small OECD economies, although it grew faster. While New Zealand started out at about OECD average levels, real expenditure grew more slowly in the 1960s (OECD 1985: 28).

3.2.3.1. Australia

Australia's welfare state is an adjunct to the system of full employment at a high minimum wage (Castles 1987, Castles 1989). Complex combinations of public and private funding characterized many sectors. In health care during the 1960s, for example, public funding provided roughly 90 percent of hospital costs, but private insurance favored by tax incentives funded most medical services. In 1974 the Whitlam Labor government passed a law creating Medibank, a public health insurance system financed out of an earmarked flat income tax. Old age pensions were flat, small, universal, tax-abated, and financed through general tax revenue. About half of all people had private, earnings-related pensions, but the bulk of these were males in large or public sector firms. Social assistance was essentially non-existent until Whitlam's Australian Assistance Plan in 1973 and its accompanying single-parent benefit. Spending on these roughly doubled in the 1970s, in line with a tripling of unemployment and a two-thirds increase in the number of single-parent families. Primary education, however, was free and universal, with substantial federal and state support for private and parochial schools; tertiary education was essen-

Table 3.4 *'Golden age' formal welfare states, 1970s*

	Australia	New Zealand	OECD–18 Average
Unemployment			
Average rate, 1960–73	2.0	0.2	2.2
UI replacement rates, 1971, % of average wage	19	38	40.5
Type	Flat, family related	Flat	Varies
Financing	Revenue	Revenue	Usually payroll
Participation			
Male	92.4	n.a.	89.7
Female	45.6	n.a.	48.3
Health			
Doctors	Private, fee for service	Private, fee for service	—
Population with private insurance coverage (%)	88	n.a.	n.a.
Public Funding (%)	56.7	80.3	73.8
Old age pension			
Replacement rate (married)	25	60	n.a.
Means test/Eligibility age	Yes/65	Yes/65	Rare/65
Financing	Revenue	Revenue	n.a.
Secondary pension	Private[a]	Public	Usually public
Coverage	ca. 50%	n.a.	n.a.
Social assistance			
Replacement rate	<25%	58%	n.a.
Means test?	Yes	Yes	n.a.
Outcomes (1980)			
Post-tax/transfer Gini	0.29	n.a.	0.25
Single mothers, % in poverty	44.5	n.a.	17.1

n.a. = not available.

[a]Publicly mandated, tax sheltered.

Sources: Compiled from OECD, *Economic Survey: Australia* and *Economic Survey: New Zealand* (Paris: OECD, various dates); Easton 1980; Kewley 1980.

tially free after 1975. Labor tried to create a national compensation scheme and a national superannuation (second-tier pension) scheme in 1972–75 but failed because the Liberal–Country Party coalition controlled the upper house, and because of potential constitutional objections to having the national government absorb activities traditionally reserved to the states.

3.2.3.2. New Zealand

During the 1930s the New Zealand Labour Party created a stable and generous formal welfare state that slowly decayed as inflation eroded benefits. Labour legislated universal, public, and free hospital care, free drugs, and medical payments to independent doctors. It replaced a means- and morality-tested old age pension with a universal flat rate (though income-tested) pension and added a second tier of voluntary earnings-related pensions. It subsidized mortgages for state housing. It made tertiary education free and provided a portion of students' living expenses. It passed a comprehensive social assistance package financed from general revenue. This basic architecture remained largely untouched until the 1970s, when two major changes occurred. First, in 1975, the National Party substituted a single generous flat-rate pension—universal but taxable, and financed from general revenue—for Labour's two pensions. Second, various forms of disability assistance (including workman's compensation) were homogenized into one Accident Compensation fund, financed by various user fees—wage levies and taxes on cars—and paying out tax-abated, contribution-based benefits at 80 percent of prior wages.

One final commonality between formal welfare in New Zealand and Australia that stems from arbitration wage awards which are normed against a four-person family is the use of universal child and family benefits to lift larger families out of poverty. The Australian system relied on a mix of tax expenditures and direct allowances. In the mid-1970s this combination was transformed into a direct cash benefit that was not indexed for inflation. In New Zealand a universal cash benefit was changed into a tax rebate in the 1970s.

3.3. Vulnerabilities

Australia's and New Zealand's arbitrated labor markets interacted with their export profile to create long-term vulnerabilities. Arbitration deliberately raised wage and input costs in sheltered sectors to squeeze economic rents out of the export sectors and fund an expansion of employment in the sheltered sectors. The arbitration courts awarded high wages in the manufacturing and service sectors. Manufacturing industry asked for and received high levels of tariff protection to stay competitive, despite low productivity. Employment grew because of Keynesian multiplier effects, as more workers got jobs at higher wages. Racist immigration laws kept the supply of labor low. The sheltered sector captured part of the rents generated by hugely competitive primary sectors because export firms passed on high domestic costs to foreign buyers. *In effect, Australia and New Zealand ran the Scandinavian EFO-inflation model, which prescribed that sheltered sectors wages should not rise faster than exposed sector wages, backwards. The sheltered manufacturing sector deliberately raised wage and input costs for the exposed primary sector to squeeze economic rents out of exposed sector production.*

This growth model worked as long as the export sectors generated enough foreign currency to fund imports of manufactured goods not locally produced, pay interest on foreign currency denominated debt, and repatriate profits for direct investors. But over the long term, the export sectors could not earn enough dollars to fund a volume of consumption and capital good imports consistent with the socially defined standard of living. Both governments addressed the symptomatic aspects of this problem without curing the underlying causes. They used a variety of standard policy routines, pressing on one side of the balloon only to see new symptoms bulging out elsewhere. They tried boosting the volume of primary exports to offset falling prices, diversifying among primary exports, substituting domestic manufactures for imported manufactures, and (eventually) exporting more manufactures. By 1975 the failure of both traditional strategies forced each country into addressing underlying dynamics by using incomes policy to moderate sheltered sector wage gains and by moving away from informal welfare and towards formal welfare. Australia institutionalized this shift, but the failure of incomes policy in New Zealand led it decisively in a neo-liberal direction. The discussion below examines both countries together until they begin to diverge in the 1970s.

This 'Antipodean' growth model had two fundamental problems generated by its domestic dynamics and one fundamental problem generated overseas by agricultural protectionism. First, arbitration plus protection led to diverging productivity levels between the stagnant sheltered sector and the more dynamic export sectors. Second, arbitration reduced the primary sector's long-term ability to export profitably. Third, European overproduction depressed global prices for food exports. This last threat was the easiest to understand, so politicians predictably responded to it first and only tried to reorganize the production model's internal dynamics after exhausting the easy responses. As changes in the international economy removed the export sector's ability to extract rents by the late 1970s, the old redistributive model could not long endure.

3.3.1. *Falling Terms of Trade: Four Responses 1945–1970*

Falling (and quite volatile) terms of trade, rising agricultural protection, and British entry into the European Union (EU) comprised the exogenous threat to the Antipodean model. Falling terms of trade after 1953 slowly eroded the generation of rents in the primary sector. Falling terms of trade meant that a given unit of exports bought fewer and fewer units of imports, and that real incomes in both countries would inexorably fall relative to more robust manufacturing economies. In fact, per capita income in both countries did slide relative to other OECD countries during the post-World War II period.

Alternately, if local consumption of imported goods did not fall as terms of trade fell, then both countries would have chronic current account deficits and rising foreign (though not necessarily foreign currency-denominated) debt. From 1949 to 1974, Australia ran a current account surplus in only four years, of which three occurred during the Korean War and 1972/73 commodities shocks. Interest on foreign debt and multinationals' profit repatriation tended to overwhelm Australia's merchandise trade surpluses. New Zealand, similarly, saw a 30 percent secular decline in the terms of trade for its three largest exports, meat, dairy, and wool products (1965–1982). As in Australia, repatriated profits and interest payments offset merchandise surpluses and accounted for 75 percent of New Zealand's current account deficit in the 1970s (Gould 1982: 144; Blondal 1986: 188–90; Reserve Bank 1986: 446, 1989: 155). In both countries, current account deficits and unemployment were the dominant macroeconomic concerns vying with each other for the attention of policymakers. Both countries accumulated modest new foreign debts through the early 1970s (see Figure 3.1 for trade and invisible deficits).

Finally, the volatility of export prices interacted with collective bargaining structures to create a tendency to overconsume imports. Australia's and New Zealand's exports from 1951 to 1971 had average annual price changes of roughly 7.5 percent, versus about 3 percent for Europe; including the chaotic 1971–74 period, boosts the average swing to 12 percent. Export volumes were similarly erratic, with the peak decline in New Zealand's exports at minus 10.0 and the peak gain at 13.8 (OECD 1976*b*: 6, 10). This volatility will be examined later.

There were four potential responses to falling terms of trade: increasing export volumes to offset price declines, shifting to new primary product exports, local production of manufactured goods to reduce import volumes and conserve foreign exchange, and exporting manufactured goods.

Both countries increased export volumes, and New Zealand subsidized dairy and meat exports in the 1970s. But agricultural protection and the EU's subsidized exports limited volume expansion. Britain's entry into the Common Market also reduced export volumes, although Australia weathered this better than New Zealand because it had already diversified towards minerals exports and Asian markets.

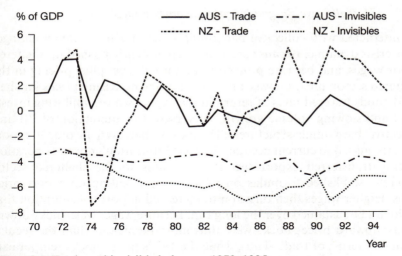

Figure 3.1 Trade and invisible balances, 1970–1995
Source: OECD, *Economic Outlook* (Paris: OECD, various dates).

What about diversification? Wool, grain, dairy, and meat had accounted for about 68 percent of Australian exports in the late 1950s, and minerals only 7 percent. By 1970 the former accounted for only about 32 percent of exports while minerals and fuels jumped to 40 percent (OYBCA, various dates). In New Zealand, wool's share of exports fell, while non-traditional exports like pulp and paper, fish and fruits rose in volume, but nothing like Australia's wholesale shift towards minerals occurred. Diversification occurred within product groups, as skim milk powder displaced other dairy exports and beef replaced sheepmeats. The really big shift into forestry and fruits did not occur until the 1980s. Finally, both began exporting modest volumes of non-traditional manufactured goods, that is, something other than processed foods.

Import substitution thus was the dominant policy response. This was politically easy: it simply continued explicit pre-World War II policy, generated the most employment quickly, and (given arbitration) also generated high wage employment. But ISI had a significant internal limit, because the more successful ISI was, the greater the burden on the primary sector. The volatility of primary sector exports interacted with collective bargaining structures to create persistent tendencies towards balance of payments deficits.

3.3.2. *ISI, Collective Bargaining, and Incomes Policy*

ISI interacted with collective bargaining structures to create an endogenous crisis dynamic. Because arbitration consistently pushed up sheltered sector wages, and because protection permitted 'cost plus' pricing in the sheltered sector, inflation was a persistent problem. Rising prices for sheltered goods lowered rates of return in the export sector, inhibiting investment and slowing volume growth. Perversely, the interaction of ISI and collective bargaining structures also meant that even favorable export price trends led to current account deficits. Arbitration's normal operation quickly transferred export sector wage gains to the sheltered sector through established formulas on relative wages, eating up export price gains. Higher wages then turned into increased import consumption that could not be sustained over the long run. Because wages were sticky downwards, upward price shocks were thus more pernicious than the secular decline in terms of trade. Thus, while the 1970s price shocks temporarily boosted export prices, they also led to large current account deficits and rising inflation. Politicians tried to use arbitration as an incomes policy tool to keep wages and inflation at sustainable levels. Arbitration and its associated incomes policy thus stood at the intersection of the domestic and international markets: the more successful ISI was, the greater the need to use incomes policy to contain inflation in order to keep the export sector profitable. Put differently, successful ISI in Australia and New Zealand exposed the inherent limits in running the EFO model backwards.

New Zealand's typical postwar economic cycle shows this well. In any given cycle, wool and/or dairy prices would revive temporarily. To prevent export receipts from being turned into unnaturally high levels of imports, the state would use its marketing boards or private stabilization schemes to try sequestering part of the additional export income. Sequestration worked well given the availability of effective capital controls. The Reserve (central) Bank captured roughly 40 percent of export revenue, and marketing boards much of the rest. But by the 1970s farmers discovered they could borrow against sequestered money and spend the money anyway, boosting imports. This forced the state into increasingly intrusive and futile controls over interest rates and credit allocation in the financial sector. Meanwhile the tight labor markets created by import substitution and booming exports led to growing militancy among meat workers. Rising wages in meat packing spread into the rest of the economy as the award system maintained parities across industries, also boosting imports. Meat-packing firms simultaneously passed their rising wage costs onto farmers as lower farm gate prices, inhibiting investment in agriculture and limiting further expansion in exports. The packers' behavior also shifted rents from exporters to sheltered firms. When export prices fell, import demand did not, starting a balance of payments crisis and the 'stop' part of the 'stop–go' cycle.

The strikes of the late 1960s aggravated this cycle by decisively shifting income away from capital, especially in farming, and towards workers. A 14 percent fall in farmers' share of the gross sales price in the 1960s depressed their investment. Despite subsidies amounting to 25 percent of net farm income, New Zealand's livestock herd barely grew between 1968 and 1979 (Gould 1982: 137–38, 161). While agricultural exports became less and less able to fund New Zealand's import bill, protected manufacturing could not generate enough exports to fund itself. The same dynamic occurred in Australia, although minerals exports eased the balance of payments problem. Australian rural debt-to-income ratios rose from dead even in 1960 to 2.4 to 1 by 1970 (OECD 1972: 33).

Efforts to change employment and social policy in Australia and New Zealand have to be understood in this context. When import substitution no longer generated new investment and growth at the end of the 1960s, inflation and current account deficits became prominent problems. The proximate causes for change were the essentially simultaneous collapse of wool prices and the arbitration rounds of 1967–69, wage explosions following the 1973 commodity shocks, and British entry to the EU. The shift to floating exchange rates as Bretton-Woods collapsed produced an exaggerated version of the usual routines. The Australian and New Zealand dollars both appreciated by roughly 30 percent from 1970 to 1974, making imports cheaper and increasing the socially necessary level of import consumption. When both dollars subsequently depreciated by the same amount from 1974 to 1977, the current account deficit increased substantially.

The parallel labor party (Whitlam in Australia and Rowling in New Zealand) governments of 1972–75 tried unsuccessfully to cope with these shocks by using incomes policy and more formal welfare to regulate class conflict and wage growth, and by decreasing trade protection. Australia's better institutionalized arbitration system preserved real wages and kept inflation at roughly the OECD average level in the 1970s, while Australian unions suffered increasing unemployment and import penetration in the manufactured goods markets. New Zealand, by contrast, had inflation one-third higher than the OECD average, as the government used overseas borrowing to finance a soft-money, full-employment policy constellation, while its relatively poorly institutionalized arbitration system could not enforce wage restraint. These differences had substantive consequences in the 1980s. Australian unions proved willing to trade a higher social wage and more employment for a gradual liberalization of the economy; New Zealand unions refused a social contract and got abrupt liberalization and a worsening social wage. Because the story diverges at this point, we consider each country separately.

3.4. New Zealand: Towards a New Model

3.4.1. Summary

The postwar model has been more thoroughly transformed in a market-oriented direction in New Zealand than in any other country considered in this volume, including Britain. The inability to run a well-institutionalized incomes policy led New Zealand governments in the late 1970s to combine a last, disastrous round of import substitution with a politicized wage policy. In turn this probably made an Australian- or Dutch-style incomes policy impossible in the 1980s, although the incoming Labour government of David Lange (1984–89) initially seemed inclined toward such a solution. Lacking an incomes policy, the Labour Party successively liberalized all parts of the economy except for labor markets. This rapid change split the Labour Party, and an openly neo-liberal National government (Bolger) was elected in 1990. This government completed the transformation to a full market model by replacing arbitration with purely private contracts between individuals and firms, and by replacing socially defined wages with market wages. These rapid changes proved to be just as politically unacceptable as Labour's reforms, creating a wave of popular support behind a referendum that introduced a German-style mixed member proportional representation (MMP) electoral system for the 1996 election. Subsequent center-right coalition governments have been riven by conflict over the degree to which markets should continue to be inserted into welfare and other state operations. The next three sections focus on incomes policy and the last spasm of the old model under National in the 1970s, Labour's response 1984–90, and National's neo-liberal spasm 1990–96.

3.4.2. Incomes Policy Fails in the 1970s

The Rowling Labour Party government (1972–75) and Muldoon's National Party governments (1975–84) persisted with the essential elements of the old model of the 1960s: ISI, efforts to increase export volumes, and control over finance to dampen import demand. All three governments ran a typical 'stop–go' cycle, responding first to inflation and current account deficits with a contractionary policy, shifting to an expansionary policy as unemployment rose, and then resorting to direct controls in order to maintain employment without also boosting inflation and the current account deficit. Both Labour and National governments borrowed overseas to sustain the old employment model, and in doing so they generated international financial obligations that the existing structure of production could not sustain. When this became apparent in 1984, the old model collapsed in the face of an unsustainable foreign debt burden, large fiscal and current account deficits, and a currency crisis.

The commodity price boom of the early 1970s reinforced the tendency toward inflation and a current account deficit despite a rise in New Zealand's overall terms of trade from 80 in 1971 to 124 in 1973. By using currency controls and wage and price freezes, both the outgoing National government and the new Labour government tried to prevent boom level imports from becoming endogenized in consumer habits. A successful incomes policy might have eased these problems. But New Zealand's arbitration system became increasingly politicized, personalized, and deinstitutionalized after 1968.

Arbitration collapsed in 1967/68 when the state tried make use of its traditional role as the enforcer of macroeconomic stability. The 1967/68 devaluation of the British pound and the simultaneous collapse of wool prices in 1967/68 motivated the arbitration court to protect the current account balance by denying workers a general wage increase (Boston 1984: 91). But in the tight labor markets of the 1960s some FOL unions had begun bargaining directly with employers and then allowing the court to ratify these private agreements. Confronted with rank and file anger about the zero wage order, both the Employers Federation and FOL had their representatives jointly vote to overrule the state's representative in a second ballot. But stronger unions—metalworkers and electricians—withdrew from arbitration anyway, striking for even higher wage gains. The number of workdays lost to strikes doubled in 1968 and then doubled again by 1970 (Deeks and Boxall 1989: 40). Without the arbitration system to maintain relative wages, unions engaged in wage leapfrogging, producing an 8.4 percent rise in real wages in 1972.

Politicians responding to the street compelled New Zealand's politically subservient central bank to ratify both these wage gains and the government's loose fiscal policy with an accommodating monetary policy (see Figures 3.2 and 3.3 for real interest rates and fiscal deficits). They also continued tariff protection and import licensing to ratify firms' ongoing practice of markup pricing. As in Britain, the state's lack of a credible threat to punish aggressive union wage demands with a restrictive monetary policy and the FOL's institutional inability to moderate its constituent unions'

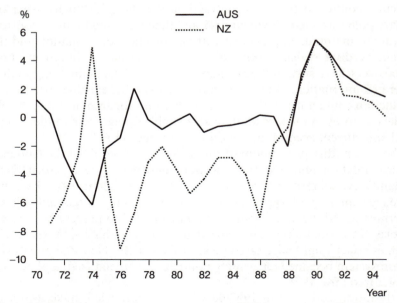

Figure 3.2 Real long-term interest rates, net of US interest rate, 1970–1995
Source: OECD, *Economic Outlook* (Paris: OECD, various dates).

wage demands led to high inflation and downward pressure on employment (Scharpf 1991).

At this point the state began searching for a new institutional framework to control wage growth and implement a formal incomes policy.
From 1970 to 1975 both National and Labour attempted to freeze wages
and reconstitute the arbitration system as the only bargaining arena. Both
governments legislated flat wage increases and prohibited reopening contracts to prevent wage 'leapfrogging'. Both efforts failed in the face of rising worker militancy and employer accommodation to the reality of
essentially zero unemployment through 1977. Unlike in Australia and
Britain, where strikes subsided after 1974, in New Zealand strike activity
rose 70 percent between 1975 and 1977.

The 1972–75 Labour government also used the temporary surge in
export receipts to repay New Zealand's foreign debt (a variation on the
sequestration theme), and it induced farmers to voluntarily sequester
NZ$83 m in 1973. It sharply increased welfare payments by restoring the
real value of a variety of means-tested benefits that had been eroded by
inflation. It introduced a contribution-linked national pension. Both of
these efforts at formal welfare made a European-style pact over the social
wage more likely if and when unions became a reliable bargaining partner.

Robert Muldoon's two follow-on National Party governments also failed at incomes policy, oscillating between outright wage freezes and free collective bargaining. The initial freezes combined with twelve-month contracts and flat wage increases to preserve the disturbed pattern of relative wages that had been driving the dynamic of continuous leapfrogging in wage demands by different unions. Muldoon intervened repeatedly to secure the outcomes he preferred, which further weakened the institutions of arbitration. Knowing full well that the government would eventually reverse moderate arbitration outcomes, export sector unions took to striking in the middle of wage freezes. This naturally provoked even more strikes in search of exceptional settlements. While free collective bargaining rounds went on, Muldoon also intervened to influence the trendsetting metalworkers' contract. Finally, Muldoon shifted the locus of wage determination from the arbitration court to the Remuneration Authority, which corresponded to a shift in procedure from formal legal precedent to easily amended regulations. All this soured the FOL on any notion of a formal incomes policy run by politicians.

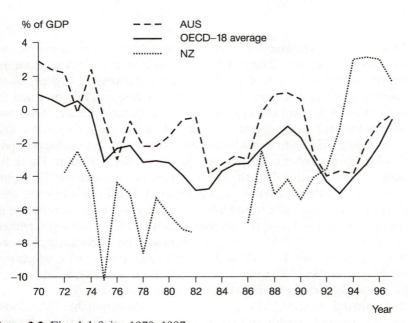

Figure 3.3 Fiscal deficits, 1970–1997
Source: OECD, *Economic Outlook* (Paris: OECD, various dates); OECD, *Economic Survey—New Zealand* (Paris: OECD, 1985).

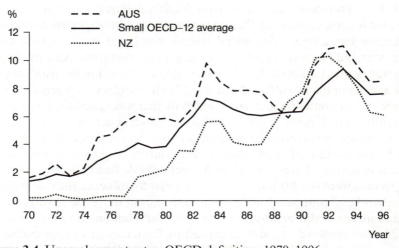

Figure 3.4 Unemployment rates, OECD definition, 1970–1996
Note: The 12 smaller OECD economies as opposed to the 6 or 7 big ones (G7): Austria, Australia, Belgium, Denmark, Finland, Ireland, Netherlands, New Zealand, Norway, Spain, Sweden, and Switzerland.
Source: OECD, *Statistical Compendium: Labour Force Statistics* (Paris: OECD, 1997).

Muldoon also resorted to price controls, interest rate controls, and direct credit allocation. These policies created as many macroeconomic problems as they solved (see Figure 3.3 for fiscal deficit, Figure 3.4 for unemployment, and Figure 3.5 for inflation rates). This, in turn, led Muldoon to try solving all his government's self-induced macroeconomic problems through an exaggerated version of the old ISI policy. After 1978 he borrowed NZ$5 bn to expand steel production, increase refinery capacity, and create a synthetic fuel plant in the 'Think Big' program. Think Big closely resembled the British Labour Party's 'Alternative Economic Strategy' of the 1980s. Partial monetization of Think Big's interest costs and subsidies for agriculture and manufactured exports drove inflation up to 16 percent by 1982, and the current account deficit to nearly 6 percent by 1984 (EMG 1984: 5–8). Muldoon essentially financed unemployment at below-average OECD levels with more foreign public debt, which rose from 5.3 percent in 1974 to 24.2 percent of GDP in 1984; total overseas debt was 45.8 percent of GDP (Reserve Bank 1986: 555).

This proved economically and politically unsustainable. Muldoon's electoral base had steadily shifted away from business and towards lower income New Zealanders. This change in Muldoon's constituency, combined with his steadily increasing interventionism, provoked a rising tide of pro-market opposition within the National Party that eventually spilled over into the formation of a new minor party, the neo-liberal New Zealand Party. In the 1984 election, this party attracted 12.5 percent of the electorate, giving Labour a plurality. Speculators, anticipating that Labour would win and devalue the dollar, had meanwhile exhausted the Reserve Bank's foreign exchange reserves, forcing the incoming Labour government under David Lange to devalue the New Zealand dollar 20 percent.

3.4.3. *New Zealand: Toward a Pure Market Model, Step One—Labour 1984–1990*

While Labour used the currency crisis to drive through significant change with the usual 'there is no alternative' rhetoric, the Lange government initially oscillated between two paths for change: either a corporatist bargain, like Australia's 1983 Accord, or the systematic introduction of markets into sheltered sectors. Labour had run on an anodyne platform that concealed conflicts between interventionist and market-oriented wings. A loose coalition of unions and politicians seeking to imitate the Australian Accord opposed another coalition of politicians (including the finance ministers), the Treasury, some unions, and internationally exposed businesses seeking to reverse Muldoon's excessive interventionism and introduce markets as widely as possible. The latter group won, partly because the currency crisis allowed it to liberalize financial markets immediately. It is important to note, however, that many actors in the liberalizing

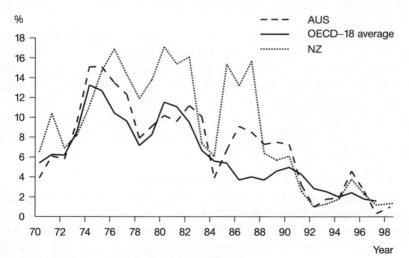

Figure 3.5 Consumer price inflation, 1970–1998
Source: OECD, *Economic Outlook* (Paris: OECD, various dates).

coalition sought to save the welfare state from itself, that formal welfare spending rose throughout both Labour terms in office, and thus that Labour was not openly imposing costs on its major constituencies until late into the 1980s.

The market faction's triumph pushed Labour to change the old model's core elements by introducing market principles into a wide range of formal and informal welfare state activities. Labour removed trade protection for manufacturing and commercial services, removed subsidies from agriculture and manufacturing, and privatized the bulk of state-owned enterprises (SOEs). This forced businesses newly exposed to competition and state agencies operating on business-like principles to shed excess labor. Because the old informal welfare state operated through systematic overmanning of all enterprises in order to assure low unemployment, Labour in this sense dismantled an important part of the welfare state. It did not, however, fully attack the wage regulation side of the old informal welfare state. Labour pursued a mix of policies intended to create a slightly more flexible labor market. This was not done at the expense of unions' bargaining power relative to employers or, even more significantly, at the expense of the notion that wages were to be set socially rather than by markets. Public sector collective bargaining was reformed along private sector lines. Finally Labour expanded and consolidated social assistance programs. We will primarily deal with these policy changes below. Marketization was at its most limited in the formal welfare state (health, education, and various pensions) and greatest in areas that were commercial operations by nature, like agencies producing easily marketed goods and services.

Labour also pursued four subsidiary policies designed to enforce market pressures. It liberalized the financial sector, institutionalized the world's most independent central bank, broadened and flattened taxes, and tried to privatize the public debt by the simultaneous privatizing SOEs. Labour privatized a greater proportion of the public sector than Thatcher, selling everything from the state's computer services to NZ Telecom. Figure 3.6 shows the falling share of public sector employment relative to the entire population.

3.4.3.1. Financial and Trade Liberalization

Labour concentrated on financial and trade liberalization and desubsidization in its first term, 1984–87. These reforms profoundly transformed New Zealand's welfare state by making disguised unemployment transparent and imposing market allocation of capital. Henceforth, instead of having the state create employment (indirectly, via protection, or directly, via SOEs and targeted capital allocation), jobs had to be self-sustaining in

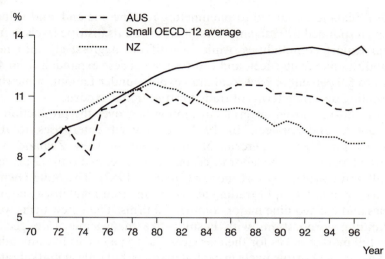

Figure 3.6 Public sector employment to population, 1970–1997
Source: OECD, *Statistical Compendium: Economic Outlook* (Paris: OECD, 1998);
own calculations.

open markets. Total substantive deregulation of financial markets removed capital allocation, interest rate controls, and barriers to foreign entry and domestic exit. Financial liberalization permitted aggressive local investors to use foreign capital in order to take over businesses, amalgamate them into large conglomerates, and shutter inefficient operations. Effective rates of assistance (the share of value added provided by subsidies and protection) for manufacturing fell from an average of 38 percent in 1984 to 19 percent in 1990 (OECD 1991: 63). Falling protection and high real interest rates cleared out inefficient, labor-intensive manufacturing enterprises and roughly 25 percent of manufacturing employment. Investment in manufacturing fell in real terms through 1989 (Reserve Bank 1988: J1, J2, 1989: 112–17). While productivity per employee increased, manufacturing employment has not. Manufacturing output returned to trend levels during the 1990s, but at a lower level of employment. Some new, 'non-traditional' manufactured and services exports have emerged, particularly where manufacturing has strong linkages to the major commodity exports.

In agriculture, similarly, effective rates of assistance fell from 49 percent in 1981/82 to negative 6 percent by 1989/90 (OECD 1991: 63). Farmers cut employment 15 percent between 1983/84 and 1987/88 (OECD 1989: 37). Desubsidization, rising interest rates, and the subsequent appreciation of the New Zealand dollar led to plummeting real income and land values. Farmers responded by reducing investment to half its historic levels in traditional export commodities, while diversifying aggressively into new commodities like fruits, deer, and eco-tourism. These expanded from 4.8 percent to 6.9 percent of New Zealand's exports under Labour, somewhat ameliorating declining terms of trade for traditional exports.

Labour also removed government monopolies over the production of many goods and services. In 1984 state-owned enterprises (SOEs) accounted for over 20 percent of investment in New Zealand and employed 5 percent of the labor force, but they generated only 12 percent of GDP and consistently lost money (Gregory 1987). The State Owned Enterprise Act (1986) split trading activities off from regulatory and line agencies and created nine major commercial firms. These new firms were self-standing corporations with business-like management, obliged to charge full market prices for their services and to pay taxes like any other firm. They could borrow freely in capital markets, but only at market rates, without government debt guarantees or subsidies. Management had to promulgate explicit performance targets using private sector notions of profit. They could only underprice services if parliament provided them with an explicit subsidy and policy mandate (Jennings and Cameron 1987). Market-based reforms reversed the situation for public enterprises. SOEs shed 18,000 workers, despite rising output, between 1984 and 1988. Market pricing of basic public services meant that SOEs' dividends, taxes, and interest payments to the state rose, providing nearly 6 percent of revenues in fiscal year 1987/88 and 8.7 percent a year later (Reserve Bank 1989: 124–26; Caygill 1989: 28–33). By 1993 all of the SOEs had been sold off, yielding receipts equal to 3.55 percent of New Zealand's average 1988–92 GDP, proportionately three times as much as Britain's privatization receipts (*Economist* 1993: 112).

3.4.3.2. Labor Markets

Labour's financial and trade policies had direct labor market consequences, driving official unemployment up 40 percent by 1990, to 7.7 percent (OECD basis). Participation dropped 2.6 percent, long-term (over six months) unemployment rose from 15 percent in 1986 to 45 percent in 1990, and part-time work increased from 14.9 percent to 20.0 percent of the labor force. Figures 3.7 and 3.8 show falling total labor market participation and a falling ratio of business sector employment to total population; for the former, the divergence between trends in New Zealand and in the smaller OECD countries is notable. Rising unemployment structured the politics surrounding Labour's cautious introduction of market forces into the system of socially defined wages during its second term, 1987–90.

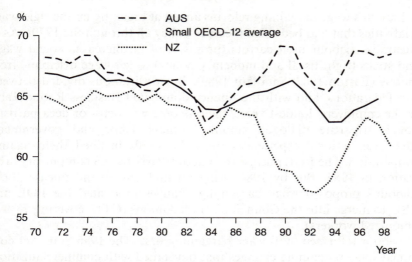

Figure 3.7 Employment to population rate, 1970–1998
Source: OECD, *Statistical Compendium: Economic Outlook* (Paris: OECD, 1999); own calculations.

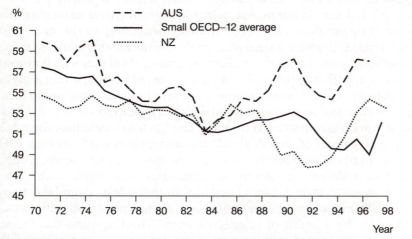

Figure 3.8 Business sector employment as a percentage of population, 1970–1997
Source: OECD, *Statistical Compendium: Business Sector Database* (Paris: OECD, 1999); OECD, *Statistical Compendium: Economic Outlook* (Paris: OECD, 1999); own calculations.

Labour's wage bargaining reforms aimed at breaking up the rigid wage relativities that had bedeviled incomes policy all through the 1970s. As in Australia, Labour used carrots (promises of an increased social wage) and sticks (tight fiscal and monetary policy) to get wage discipline from unions (Easton 1987; Sandlant 1989). But with unions divided between two federations, and with the finance-dominated Business Round Table as the employers' loudest voice, the outcome was octo- or deca-partism, not a tripartite dialogue among business, labor and government. Moreover, unions' experiences from the 1970s inclined them against cooperation. The FOL pushed the Labour Party to end compulsory arbitration in 1984. But by 1987 rising unemployment and unease about Labour's proposed wage bargaining changes motivated the FOL and CSU to merge into the Council of Trade Unions (CTU, covering 78% of unionized workers).

Labour reformed SOE wage bargaining first. The 1986 SOE Act contained wage bargaining changes that dovetailed with commercialization. Commercializing SOEs was pointless if wage bargaining practices blocked the reorganization of work, productivity-based remuneration, and redundancies. Before the Act, the State Services Commission set wages and conditions according to centrally determined job categories, without regard to a firm's individual needs, and enforced complex procedures for civil service tenure, appeals, and grievances. The 1986 Act harmonized SOE wage bargaining with existing private sector practices.

Labour then moved on to change private sector bargaining itself with the 1987 Labour Relations Act, which tried to increase unions' relative power while simultaneously decentralizing bargaining to the 'enterprise' (firm) level. Enterprise bargaining would break the automatic transmission of wage gains between the sheltered and exposed sectors, allow more variation in both wage levels and wage parities, and perhaps induce higher productivity. The Act simultaneously bolstered unions. Only union locals could initiate and sign contracts outside the arbitration system, and compulsory union membership continued. The Act also would have forced the roughly 60 percent of New Zealand's unions representing fewer than 1,000 workers (8.6% of all workers) to amalgamate with larger unions, without regard to traditional occupational boundaries. This would enable labor organizations to form a united front against individual or similar employers. Finally unions' right to monopolize worker representation was made contestable by a ballot of affected workers. The Engineers (i.e. metals) Union almost immediately employed the new regime to opt out of the national award and negotiate industry-specific awards with employers. Still, deviations from the first metals settlement were very small (the standard deviation of wage increases in 1988 was 2.9%), and greater wage dispersion awaited the National government's shift from enterprise to individual bargaining in 1991.

In two acts passed in 1988 and 1989 Labour finished the job of homogenizing public sector bargaining with private sector practices (Walsh 1991). The 1988 State Sector Act and the 1989 Public Finance Act created private sector-style wage and work disciplines in the traditional welfare state and in those 'non-commercial' agencies still overseen by the State Services Commission. Agency management gained the right to hire and fire at will, to reclassify and redeploy labor, and to set employee remuneration on an enterprise basis. Managers could cut separate deals with their workers on staffing levels, hours worked, productivity bonuses, etc. so long as they were in conformity with basic labor legislation. The State Services Commission became management's agent in agency-level collective bargaining. Managers thus could behave like private sector managers in their search for greater efficiency and productivity. This helped produce more customer-friendly service delivery in many instances.

Labour's industrial relations reforms addressed some of the dynamics underlying New Zealand's vulnerabilities. They exposed more people to market pressures and weakened socially determined wages. Was there a compensatory expansion of the formal welfare state based on tax-funded transfers and services?

3.4.3.3. Formal Welfare

Higher unemployment made the formal welfare state more important, and overall real social spending rose. Labour implemented the Guaranteed Minimum Family Income in 1986, a kind of negative income tax guaranteeing working families roughly 80 percent of the average post-tax wage. However, high effective marginal tax rates and rising unemployment limited the guaranteed income's impact on participation rates. From 1985/86 to 1988/89 health and education spending expanded 9.6 percent and 24 percent, respectively. Transfer spending also rose slightly as unemployment rose (OECD 1991: 39). In contrast to this partial expansion of the welfare state, Labour was also effectively slowing the growth of old age pension spending by (1) changing the basis for indexation from the CPI (consumer price index) to the average wage, a more slowly growing indicator, and (2) by increasing the eligibility age from 60 to 65. (See Figure 3.9 which shows the evolution of social spending.)

Labour increased social spending so it could buy acquiescence to institutional changes in the formal welfare state paralleling those changes taking place in the former SOE sector. Inquiries into health care and tertiary education promoted a more market-based governance structure. In tertiary education Labour imposed charges equaling 10 percent of tuition

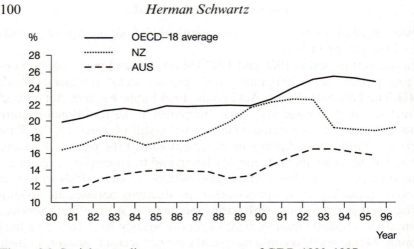

Figure 3.9 Social expenditures as a percentage of GDP, 1980–1997
Source: OECD, *Social Expenditure Data Base 1980–1996* (Paris: OECD, 1999);
own calculations.

costs and compensated low-income students with targeted allowances. Primary education began shifting towards a voucher-like system. These reforms combined with collective bargaining changes to put competitive pressures on schools.

Finally, Labour reformed taxes to attract foreign capital and reduce the relative cost of exporting. A broad goods and services tax (GST [i.e. VAT], currently 12%) replaced a miscellany of sales taxes. The GST was rebateable for exporters. Income tax reform also broadened and lowered brackets. The maximum income tax rate went from 48 percent to 33 percent.

3.4.3.4. Summary

While Labour opened the economy to international financial and goods markets, the Lange government also tried to reduce New Zealand's vulnerabilities. Labour intended liberalization, desubsidization, and currency stability to increase local firms' ability to export more and different goods profitably. Central bank autonomy, decentralization of wage bargaining, and repatriation of foreign currency public debt all aimed at producing currency stability. Net government debt rose slightly under Labour, from 41.4 percent to 45.6 percent of GDP 1984 to 1989, but the foreign currency-denominated share fell from 51 percent to 44 percent (OECD 1993: 124). Theoretically, at least, markets for traditional public goods like education meant increased productivity and thus, perhaps, future wage gains.

Politically, though, core Labour voters rejected all this. During its first term, 1984 to 1987, Labour had bought acquiescence to economic liberalization with a series of payoffs to its core constituencies: the 'no nuclear ship visit' policy for the peace movement, an environmental ministry for the greens, decriminalization of homosexuality for the gay movement, a women's ministry for feminists, reinstatement of the closed shop for private sector unions, ratification of Treaty rights for the indigenous Maori population, and expanded social service spending for public sector unions. But in Labour's second term, 1987 to 1990, reforms and events like privatization, the widespread introduction of user fees, and the stock market collapse alienated both traditional Labour voters and yuppies. In 1989 supporters of the old welfare/growth model split off from Labour and formed the NewLabour [*sic*] Party, helping the National Party to win a 38-seat majority in a 97-seat house in the 1990 election.

3.4.4. National from 1990 Onward: Build It and They Will Come

The National government finished dismantling the informal welfare state by attacking unions directly and individualizing wage bargaining. It finished privatizing and desubsidizing the economy. In the formal welfare state it fully marketized education and cut social assistance, but it failed to introduce real markets into health care and to privatize old age pensions. National basically bet that the natural operation of markets would ensure New Zealand's future prosperity and that no positive policy, aside from the introduction of markets, was needed to generate growth. But National hedged its bet by actively soliciting direct foreign investment, which jumped from about 5 percent of gross domestic capital formation in the 1980s to 25 percent by 1992. Exports increased 48 percent in volume between 1989 and 1996. This seemed to validate National's 'build it (the free market) and they (the investors) will come' policy stance. However, renewed economic expansion merely brought New Zealand back to its long-term trend rate of growth. By 1998 the chronic current account deficit re-emerged for the old reason—repatriation of investment income, which increased from 5.3 percent of GDP in 1988 to 9.1 percent in 1995. At that point this outflow was roughly twice the size of the current account deficit (OECD 1998: 178, 182, 184).

3.4.4.1. Informal Welfare and Collective Bargaining

National fundamentally changed the old informal welfare state mode with its Employment Contracts Act (ECA) 1991 (Dannin 1997). National argued that market-based, flexible wages would lead to higher productivity and growth. Under the ECA employers could contract freely with individuals, while unions could only represent individuals who explicitly delegated bargaining rights to the union. The ECA destroyed socially determined wages by limiting the arbitration court's jurisdiction to the interpretation of employment contracts, eliminating unions in sectors where workers were least able to organize themselves (e.g. hospitality and clerical work), eliminating automatic transmission of wage increases through general wage orders and clauses on relative wages, and allowing employers to avoid collective bargaining entirely.

After 1991 unions representing workers with weak labor market positions—like those in agriculture, construction, retail, wholesale, accommodation, and restaurants—simply collapsed. Union density fell from 45 percent to 20 percent by 1996, and the number of workers covered by union contracts fell 42 percent. Multi-employer contracts fell from 77 percent to 20 percent of all contracts, and individual contracts and wage scales became common even in the public sector. The collapse of weak unions lifted the 'market share' of the ten biggest unions from 45 percent to 77 percent of unionized workers. The labor movement split, as a minority of militant unions left the NZCTU to form the Trade Union Federation (TUF).

Deunionization drove unskilled workers' wages down and wage dispersion up every year after 1991. Productivity did not increase markedly, though profits did. The wage share of GDP is now back to its old levels from the 1960s, while rates of return have roughly doubled from where they were in the 1980s (see Figure 3.10). Unemployment fell from its recessionary high of 10.3 percent in 1990–91 to 6.7 percent by 1997, and labor market participation recovered to 1980s levels (Figures 3.4, 3.7, and 3.8) (Harbridge and Crawford 1997). 22.7 percent of employment was part-time work (OECD 1998: 187). So the ECA restored employment to its status quo ante level, but without unions.

Finally, National finished the job of exposing all sectors to international competition, cutting tariffs another third to 12 percent between 1993 and 1996. By 1998 falling tariffs forced all automobile assemblers to exit and most of New Zealand's clothing manufacturers to shift offshore to low-wage countries.

3.4.4.2. Formal Welfare

National's primary goal of eliminating the fiscal deficit and shrinking the state colored its policy towards the formal welfare state until the introduction of proportional representation in the 1996 election. After that, National's need to forge a coalition with the more centrist New Zealand First Party halted spending cuts. The threat of a credit rating downgrade linked to New Zealand's large foreign debt strongly influenced the general

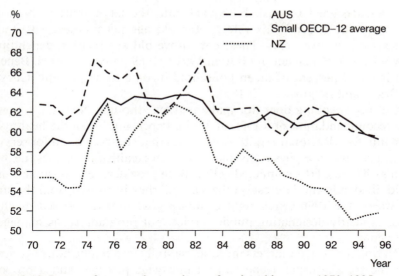

Figure 3.10 Income from work as a share of national income, 1970–1995
Source: OECD, *Economic Outlook* (Paris: OECD, various dates).

decision to cut nominal public spending by 7 percent, largely by cutting social assistance about 10 percent (Dalziel 1992; Rudd 1992). This sharp drop shows up in Figure 3.9. Total expenditure fell slightly in absolute terms over the course of the three National-led governments in the 1990s; in relative terms public spending thus dropped from 40.3 percent of GDP to 33.7 percent by 1997, in what amounted to yet another restoration (like the employment picture) of the pre-Labour status quo. Absolute revenues were also flat, falling to 35.7 percent of GDP. Fiscal surpluses after 1994 allowed the government to reduce gross public debt from 56.1 percent of GDP in 1994 to 37.5 percent in 1997, and to bring foreign-held public debt down from 42 percent of GDP in 1990 to 22 percent in 1997 (OECD 1998: 188).

National tried to reduce public involvement in the formal welfare state by getting more private money and private actors into newly created 'markets' for welfare services. In health care the public share of spending declined from 82 percent in 1991 to 76 percent by 1993. By 1995 about 40 percent of New Zealanders had some private health insurance (Kelsey 1995: 216). National's deepest cuts came in social assistance, where benefits were reduced on average by 10 percent and eligibility requirements were considerably tightened. The average reduction conceals a much sharper cut in social assistance for able-bodied males and childless females, designed to push both back into the labor market. National increased the effective tax rate on the old age pension and suspended indexation for two years. These cuts drove old age pension expenditure down from 7.84 percent of GDP in 1991 to 5.69 percent in 1996. Benefits fell from 72 percent of mean household income to 58 percent (Cheyne, O'Brien, and Belgrave 1997: 185).

Cutting spending does not make markets, though. National followed the recommendation of a Labour White Paper and broke the health system into four Regional Health Authorities that contracted out for services from primary care physicians and 25 Crown Health Enterprises (i.e. hospitals). These CHEs competed with private providers for 'consumers' and paid dividends and interest on the 'capital' they borrowed from the state. However, the 1996 center-right coalition government reversed much of this, explicitly designating public service, not profitability, as managers' core goal.

National inserted markets more successfully into public housing, dividing the state housing agency into a mortgage provider and a property management firm, raising rents to market levels, and partly compensating the poor with a housing benefit. In education National funded schools with a capitation-based block grant for both primary and tertiary education. Parent-dominated school boards and university administrations now compete for students, pay teachers individually calibrated wages, and offer services tailored to their 'market niche'. The state pays 75 percent of tuition costs for tertiary education (95% for those on social assistance), and universities charge students directly for the rest. Students are expected to borrow or earn that money.

National also introduced legislation that made it difficult to reverse their reforms. The Fiscal Responsibility Act 1994 mandated prompt publication of fiscal data based on generally accepted accounting practices, benchmarking so that the public can assess this data, and publication of budget statements well in advance of the actual budget in order to stimulate public debate over budget goals. The law forced diversion of operating surpluses into debt reduction and some balancing of the budget over the economic cycle.

3.5. Australia: Towards a New Model

3.5.1. Summary

Australia presents three contrasts with New Zealand: change in the model was negotiated rather than administered as shock therapy, change has been more gradual, and by most indicators economic performance has been better. The ease of the transition in Australia partly reflects the lingering benefits of a relatively 'hard money' policy stance in the 1970s as compared with New Zealand. It also reflects earlier conscious efforts to change the model by the Whitlam Labor government (1972–75) and the Fraser Liberal-National coalitions (1975–83). Both of these governments changed the ancillary elements of the old model. Change in the model's core—arbitrated wages—did not occur until the Hawke (1983–91) and Keating (1992–96) ALP governments successfully negotiated an incomes policy, the Accord. The Accord gave the ALP time to introduce markets into the service sector gradually, while liberalizing product markets to a greater extent than in New Zealand. The Hawke–Keating governments used the Accords to decentralize collective bargaining while still preserving minimum wages, to remove trade protection and encourage more manufactured exports, and to generate robust part-time employment as lower barriers to trade destroyed unsustainable full-time jobs. The ALP secured fairly broad public support for this policy shift, winning five straight elections through 1996.

The more classically neo-liberal Liberal–National coalition since 1996 and like-minded state-level governments continued privatizing and 'marketizing' the service sector. Despite the elimination of trade protection and the attenuation of wage relativities, substantial elements of the old social wage remain. The Howard Liberal-National coalition government since 1996 has continued decentralizing collective bargaining, but it failed to create something akin to New Zealand's Employment Contracts Act. The arbitration court still sets the basic wage. A severe reduction in the Liberal–National coalition's parliamentary majority in the 1998 federal election and the coalition's defeat in the 1999 election in the state of Victoria suggest political limits to further marketization. As in New Zealand's 1999 election, rural voters who have lost from the desubsidization of public services shifted their votes to Labor in Victoria.

3.5.2. *Incomes Policy and Monetarism in the 1970s*

As in New Zealand, the 1970s commodities shocks gave Australia sharply rising terms of trade that set off a wage explosion deleterious to the ISI model. The metals union (AMWU) and its employer counterpart, the Metal Trades Industry Association (MTIA), tried to get the arbitration court to limit wage increases to the CPI plus productivity gains. Both feared unsustainable wage gains that would raise unemployment. As in New Zealand, tight labor markets meant that rank and file workers demanded and employers conceded large second-tier wage increases.

These concessions ignited battles over wage parities, and strike levels doubled to nearly 600 lost days per 1,000 workers, three times New Zealand's rate and slightly higher than Britain's. Rising wages and Whitlam's tax increases shifted the wage share of GDP from 60 percent in 1974 to 66.7 percent in 1976, while the profit share collapsed from about 17 percent to 14 percent by 1976 (see Figure 3.10) (OECD 1976*a*: 24). Firms shed labor, pushing unemployment up to 4.5 percent by 1975 and 6.1 percent by 1978. Deteriorating terms of trade shifted the current account from surplus to a deficit of 3.3 percent of GDP by 1974. In short, wage dynamics in 1970–75 displayed all the model's pathologies.

The Whitlam ALP government and the Fraser Liberal–National coalitions both attacked different sides of the central dynamic while protecting their core constituencies. Whitlam lowered tariffs by 25 percent. He also built a formal welfare state with new public health and social assistance programs. Still, Whitlam maintained informal welfare by supporting the arbitration court's introduction of centralized wage indexation. Fraser (like his British contemporary British Dennis Healey) introduced a mild monetarism, targeting public sector wages and staffing in order to reduce inflation. Fraser undid Whitlam's tariff cuts, though. Like Muldoon, Fraser triggered one last spasm of the old model after 1979, abandoning his monetarism by increasing spending during a shortlived minerals export boom from 1979 to 1981.

Whitlam's and Fraser's efforts created the conditions essential to making the Hawke government's formal incomes policy work in the 1980s. Whitlam's ALP government tried to wean workers from the informal welfare state by creating a formal welfare state and to wean industry from protection and reorient it to export markets. Shifting from primary products to manufactured exports would ameliorate the problems caused by rigid wage relativities. Welfare spending came up to the OECD averages by 1975. The introduction of national health insurance (Medibank) drove public health spending from below to above the OECD average, and the public share of health spending increased 10 percentage points to 74 percent. Medibank reduced private insurance coverage from 80 percent to 60 percent of the population and private funding from roughly half to about one-quarter of spending (Scotton 1977: 7; Deeble 1978: 21). Whitlam substantially increased social assistance and old age pensions, doubling real spending in three years (see Figure 3.9). Public sector employment grew twice as fast as the OECD average between 1970 and 1975.

Whitlam cut tariffs across the board by 25 percent as a way of reminding the metals sector that insulation from world markets was a political choice; the assumption was that lower trade barriers would moderate wage militancy. Metalworkers learned this lesson right away, though other unions did not until the late 1970s. Whitlam's expansion of the formal welfare state increased public sector employment and thus the relative strength of public sector unions. Tight labor markets and even tighter wage parities generated inflation, which rose to 15.1 percent by 1974.

To control inflation (Figure 3.5), Whitlam proposed an explicit social contract with the ACTU in 1974. If the ACTU accepted flat dollar wage increases above a certain income level, the ALP would preserve real wages via tax indexation or an increased social wage. As then ACTU president Bob Hawke noted, this would gradually reduce the wage share of GDP if productivity grew. This early anticipation of the Accord failed because none of the partners could perform as expected. The ACTU did not include white-collar unions, and many of its blue-collar unions were still quite militant. The ALP lacked the Senate majority needed to deliver tax indexation and social wage increases. Business was still fragmented. Nonetheless, these tentative talks between the unions and the government revealed the ACTU's willingness to commit itself to centrally driven wage restraint (Plowman 1981: 20–24).

Fraser's conservative coalition governments, from 1975 to 1983, helped resolve these organizational problems, albeit inadvertently. Fraser anticipated classic 1980s monetarism by exercising greater fiscal restraint in the 1970s than happened in New Zealand, though not relative to OECD averages (Figure 3.3). Public sector employment grew in the states but not with the federal government (see Figure 3.6). Fraser cut public investment to keep spending growth below GDP growth. From a peak of 5 percent of GDP in calendar year 1975 the fiscal deficit fell to 0.3 percent in 1982, and the federal government's share of GDP fell from 30.7 percent in 1976 to 28.1 percent in 1981. Meanwhile inflation fell from 15.1 percent to 11.1 percent (Blondal 1986: 93–95). Fraser also shifted income to better off groups with tax changes, he de-indexed transfers, and he reduced Medibank funding.

Fraser's policy efforts limited but did not change the old model. First, the protected service sector continued to expand, especially the states' public enterprises and community services. These firms' losses increased the total public sector deficit to an average level of 5.3 percent of GDP and with no consistent trend across the 1970s (Treasury 1997: 7–16). Employment by state and local government community services increased 25 percent to total one million by mid-1979.

Second, Fraser was not able to weaken arbitration or the existing system of wage parities. White-collar workers unions proved difficult to control, and it was they who drove wage outcomes in the 1970s. White collar workers had become half the workforce by 1970, and their unions constantly struck to preserve wage parities with blue-collar workers (Plowman 1981: 14, 21–23).

Finally, Fraser yielded to the temptation to use traditional solutions, acquiescing in an exaggerated version of the standard policy response between 1979 and 1983. Rising commodity prices sparked a rough doubling of foreign direct investment into Australia, including a 35 percent increase in investment for minerals production in 1979. Tighter labor markets convinced both the government and the unions that prosperity was imminent, and strong unions in both sectors pressed for wage gains. Fraser made a pre-election wage concession well above the arbitration court's guidelines for public sector unions in 1980. This relaunched the battles over wage relativities and drove strike activity back up to 1974 levels. Unfortunately, recession hit in 1981, and by 1983 unemployment had nearly doubled to 10 percent. The ACTU and its manufacturing unions realized that declining manufacturing employment was a secular trend and signaled their preference for having the arbitration court restrain wages rather than for having to endure a government-imposed wage freeze (Singleton 1990: 61–64).

Why did the ACTU prefer arbitration? During the 1970s the arbitration court preserved real wages and contained inter-union rivalries. This experience convinced unions to exchange wage restraint for a managed expansion of the formal welfare state and employment in the 1980s. They hoped that wage restraint would allow them to reverse the job losses of the 1970s. Incomes policy worked in Australia but not in New Zealand (or Britain) for three reasons. First, Australia's professionally staffed arbitration court was committed to judicial autonomy, unlike New Zealand's tripartite court (Bray and Nielsen 1996). Arbitration jurists strove to preserve their role suppressing industrial conflict and defining wages, rather than simply steering a course between labor and business demands. This strong definition of the arbitrator's role created a shadow of hierarchy for enforcing a negotiated incomes policy. Second, the increased centralization and unity of both social partners in the 1970s meant they could actually bargain. The ACTU incorporated public sector and white-collar workers, and the ACTU's largest unions represented a greater share of ACTU workers. On the business side, manufacturing firms created a coherent organization. Finally, unemployment and tariff cuts motivated both manufacturing unions and firms, as well as public sector unions, to seek negotiated change. Rising import penetration made firms seek productivity increases from unions. Public sector unions preferred negotiated change to Fraser's open attacks on the public sector. With institutions, actors, and motives all present, the election of the Hawke ALP government provided an opportunity to try an incomes policy.

Substantively, during the 1970s and 1980s the arbitration court recentralized wage regulation and disciplined unions in their own interests. The court had consistently tried to reassert its control over wage determination after the breakdown of 1968, and rising unemployment in the 1970s motivated the ACTU to work with the court. The court's reintroduction of quarterly wage indexation facilitated a gradual reduction in the wage share of GDP. The ACTU itself sought this in order to protect employment and wages simultaneously: while real wages stayed flat, productivity gains would bolster profitability and investment. Over the 1970s indexation compensated for roughly 80 percent of the rise in the CPI. This gave the ACTU a more uniform outcome than it could have gotten from free collective bargaining, because battles over relative wages would have caused 'wage chasing' and higher unemployment (Carr 1979: 96; OECD 1980: 47). The court also created a legal loophole permitting a sustainable widening of wage parities: if individual unions could show that changes in 'work value' (productivity) had occurred, they could get wage increases above and beyond what indexation warranted. The court's maintenance of real wages also forced employers to cooperate with unions in seeking productivity growth. Productivity growth rates in Australian white goods, for example, were twice as high as in the USA during the 1970s. Improved productivity reduced employment by 30 percent but gave another 30 percent of the labor force 'work value'-based wage increases (BIE 1983). The arbitration court helped preserve the ACTU unions' internal unity because it moderated wage compression and allowed unions to externalize the blame for wage moderation. In contrast, the Danish and Swedish LOs had direct responsibility for both wage moderation and compression.

The court also helped centralize business organizations. Employers submerged their internal differences in order to cope with the wage indexation cases that came up every three months. The traditionally antagonistic Associated Chambers of Manufactures (protected industry) and Australian Council of Employers' Federations (export industry) merged into the Confederation of Australian Industry in 1976.

As in New Zealand, incomes policy became the focal point of efforts to balance employment, inflation, and current account deficits. During the mid- to late 1970s the Australian court, unlike its New Zealand counterpart, absorbed all the damaging political consequences that Danish and New Zealand unions experienced from directly legislated wages, that Swedish unions experienced from direct, centralized collective bargaining, and that British unions experienced from the failure of collective bargaining. Compared with unions in 1970s New Zealand, Australian unions endured higher unemployment, more import penetration, and a hostile government, while finding an ally in the institutions of arbitration. So Australian unions entered the 1980s willing to institutionalize wage restraint, and they made this public with the ACTU–ALP Accord that exchanged wage restraint for more employment and a higher social wage.

And as in New Zealand, the incumbent's mishandling of the economy put Labor in power, allowing it to try out the Accord.[4] The Liberal–National coalition took the blame for the widening of the current account deficit from 1.5 percent of GDP in 1979 to 5.2 percent in 1982, for unemployment running at 10 percent, and for a public sector borrowing requirement of 8.1 percent of GDP. The ALP won a 25-seat majority in the 125-seat lower House, and a working majority in the Senate.

3.5.3. Australia Reconstructed: The Accord, Markets, and Change in the 1980s

The ALP wanted to change the link between sectoral wages that generated current account deficits while preserving social equality and a decent society by retaining some social definition of wages and expanding the formal welfare state. The Accord was Labor's tool for breaking down the old horizontal pattern of wage parities responsible for pricing exports out of world markets. The Accord process aimed at freezing real private sector wages in order to generate more employment, at eroding sheltered sector wages in order to cheapen export prices, and at helping reorient manufacturing towards exports.

Simultaneously, the Accord explicitly and implicitly continued to provide basic social protection through a centrally set minimum wage. The Accord facilitated and rewarded productivity growth while still putting a floor under wages, and (as in the 1970s) the arbitration system helped the ACTU to externalize conflicts over greater wage differentiation. Meanwhile the ALP expanded the social wage in order to repay the ACTU for wage restraint. The ALP restored public financing for the health system, added a new second-tier pension and more social assistance, and created a negative income tax. Nonetheless, Australian social spending as a share of GDP was flat under Hawke and remained well below OECD and even New Zealand levels.

The Accord's macroeconomic side dovetailed with the ALP's liberalization and desubsidization of product markets. Decentralized collective bargaining and productivity-based wage increases rewarded competitive firms and cooperative unions. The ALP's microeconomic reforms—changes in trade and competition policy—forced firms to upgrade. The ALP reduced tariffs and non-tariff barriers across a wide range of industries. Though

---

[4] Bob Hawke, pressed in 1983 to explain the difference between the Australian and British Labour parties, said, 'We win.'

there was less outright privatization than in New Zealand, the institutionalization of competition in the public sector went further. However public sector employment did not decline as in New Zealand (see Figure 3.6).

During the 1980s Australia created jobs at roughly twice the OECD average rate even as labor force participation rose (Figure 3.7). The social wage grew in absolute terms through the ALP's first term and then stabilized for ten years. Australia's manufacturing and service sectors did increase their exports after sheltered sector costs were controlled. Here the ALP delivered to its silent business constituency, lowering the wage share from 62.3 percent in 1983 to 59.5 percent in 1995; relative unit labor costs fell from 117.8 in 1983 to 83.8 in 1987, before rising to 103 in 1989; and productivity grew twice as fast as wages between 1983 and 1995. By some estimates, the trend rate of productivity growth in Australia has increased sharply, from roughly 1 percent annually between 1975 and 1991 to 2.7 percent each year after 1991 (OECD 1999: 65). Australian export performance was well above OECD averages under Labor, rising at an annual average of 3.3 percent in 1984–96.

International shocks and pressure from domestic business shaped the evolution of specific policies, including the various Accords. As the economy recovered from the 1982/3 recession Australia's predominantly privately owed total foreign debt tripled to 28 percent of GDP and the current account deficit swelled to 5.5 percent of GDP. In response, the Hawke government committed itself to no increases in Federal taxation, spending, or deficits as shares of GDP. This so-called 'trilogy' promise severely constrained relative increases in the social wage. It also focused attention on attaining greater productivity in both the public and private sectors so as to boost GDP and thus the volume of spending permitted. Another constraint with an impact similar to Hawke's 'trilogy' promise, the 16 percent fall in the newly floated Australian dollar, also galvanized a series of changes: the devaluation led to the great push for a new kind of labor relations in the public sector, to a new style of public management, and to the corporatization of public enterprises. The 1990–92 recession sparked a new round of collective bargaining decentralization and a search for active labor market policies.

The next sections deal in turn with the Accord, incomes policy, and collective bargaining; trade protection and competitive policy; the formal welfare state; and public reactions.

3.5.3.1. The Renewal of Corporatism in Australia and the Evolution of Collective Bargaining

The ALP and ACTU tried to resolve the contradictions in the Australian model and stabilize that model through the Accord. (Here Accord refers to the basic ALP–ACTU compromise and Accord Mark II, III etc. to the eight specific Accords the two parties ultimately negotiated.) The Accord process had four aims. The first, tactical goal was to control any explosion in wages that might occur as Fraser's wage freeze came undone in 1983. This succeeded. A second, strategic aim was to reduce the wage share from its 1970s peak in order to stimulate employment. The wage share did fall from 64.6 percent of GDP in 1982/83 and stabilized at around 60 percent; investment rose from 22.8 percent of GDP in 1983 to 25.4 percent in 1989 before falling back to around 20 percent in the 1990s. Foreign debt financed much new investment. The third goal, articulated in Accord Mark III (1987–88), was to make wage gains in the sheltered sector contingent on productivity gains. Though harder to assess, the largest losses in real wages occurred in the public sector, while in the exposed sector (especially metals) real wages were stable. The fourth goal, hinted at in Accord Mark III and emphatically part of Accord Mark VI (1990–92), was to decentralize bargaining downward to the enterprise level, while still maintaining a decent, centrally set basic wage. This would permit successful exporters to pay high wages without the danger of automatically transmitting this higher pay to weaker sectors. By 1996 roughly one-third of all workers operated under enterprise-level contracts, one-third operated under centrally set awards, and one-third did not bargain collectively at all. Union density declined from 46 percent to about 31 percent during this period (Buchanan et al. 1997: 109).

The Accord process thus attacked the contradictions in the Australian model. With ISI exhausted as a development model, domestic demand alone could not make manufacturing output grow. Productivity had to grow in order to facilitate manufactured exports. The Accord linked productivity and wage growth, inducing unions to press employers for productivity-enhancing restructuring. The Accord rewarded cooperative unions and workers with legal second-tier wage increases. It also motivated employers to seek productivity gains and to invest. The combination of trade liberalization and persistently high basic wages meant that survival rested on productivity gains and investment. Firms that found acceptable productivity gains could raise workers' pay and attract more and better skilled workers, so firms needed to bargain with workers over acceptable productivity gains merely to compete in local labor markets, let alone compete with low-wage imports. Here the ALP tried to assure that the shift of income from labor to capital would not be frittered away in increased consumption, much like what befell the Swedish Rehn-Meidner model.

The centralization of business and (even more so) of labor made this strategy plausible. By 1980 the ACTU had incorporated the major public sector white-collar unions, bringing its coverage to 85 percent of union-ized workers. In the early 1980s business split into two peak associations, each with a credible claim to speak for an important segment of Australian industry. A third association, the AFE, represented the small-est (and thus politically less important) firms (Techritz and Hatcher 1981: 79). The Confederation of Australian Industry (CAI) represented SMEs (small and medium-sized enterprises) and local firms. In 1983 the Business Council of Australia (BCA) was formed by the fifty largest firms in Australia, each with 5,000 or more employees. Both participated in the 1983 National Economic Summit and in tripartite organizations created after 1983, but the CAI was more willing than its big business rival to accommodate the ALP. On collective bargaining, business presented a full spectrum of opinion: the AFE (the smallest employers) wanted to 'smash and crash' the whole arbitration system, the BCA wanted to replace arbi-tration with enterprise bargaining over a fifteen-year period, and the MTIA (representing the metal sector) wanted coordinated sectoral bar-gaining, while the CAI was content with the status quo supplemented by some enterprise level bargaining (Plowman 1987).

The ACTU and particularly its metal unions felt that business had to be led because, as then ACTU president, Bill Kelty put it: 'We have a man-agement class which is . . . incompetent . . . [and] incapable of generating the levels of investment and borrowing [needed] for this country' (*Sydney Morning Herald*, 30 Apr. 1986). The ALP and ACTU used corporatism to divide and neutralize business opposition. Each Accord involved a silent partnership between the ALP and one of these business organizations. The metals firms (MTIA) supported the early Accords, while the BCA was decisive in shifting the Accord process more in the direction of enterprise bargaining around the time of Accord Mark IV (1988–89). MTIA firms (like Danish metals firms) preferred to take wages out of competition for their sector, while the multinationals in the BCA wanted their own enter-prise bargains. So the evolution of the Accord was as much a political process as a rational response to Australia's structural problems.

Accord Mark III (1987), which supplemented award-based basic wage increases with productivity-based second-tier increases at the enterprise level, reflected the MTIA's influence. The arbitration court had to bless productivity-based increases to prevent cheating (and retain its institu-tional role). The metals sector stood to benefit the most from this arrange-ment, which permitted skills-intensive sectors of the economy to raise wages without fear that increases would spill over to stagnant parts of the economy (Thornthwaite and Sheldon 1993, 1996). Most of the metals sec-tor enterprise bargains were true supplements to the basic award, consis-tent with the MTIA's desire to keep wages out of competition in the metals sector. Private sector wages diverged strongly from public sector wages since, while public sector unions were motivated to seek enterprise bargains, they had fewer opportunities to actually increase productivity. Over time enterprise bargains became more common in the public sector.

The 1988 Industrial Relations Act formalized Accord Mark III, permitting enterprise bargains with the approval of the arbitration court. Enterprise bargains were not allowed to violate minimum standards, including the basic wage (Plowman 1992). As in New Zealand, the ALP used the new law to force smaller unions to merge or disappear, setting a 3,000-member minimum for union registration by 1991. By 1993, 98 percent of unionized workers were in nineteen unions, making coordination easier (Gahan 1993: 613).

In contrast, Accord Mark VI (1990), formalized in 1993 with the Industrial Relations Reform Act, reflected the BCA's influence. Accord VI extensively promoted enterprise bargaining as a real alternative to central awards (Reitano 1994). However the arbitration court continued to impose minimum wages and conditions on enterprise bargains. Furthermore, while non-unionized firms could sign an enterprise bargain, doing so exposed them to the possibility of union intervention. Most such awards granted through 1992 were generated by the metals industry, while small and medium industry outside of metals tended to avoid formal enterprise bargains. By 1995 over 60 percent of federal agreements were enterprise bargains (Buchanan et al. 1997: 109).

The Liberal–National coalition government elected in 1996 also tried to pass a bill very similar to the New Zealand Employment Contracts Act. This bill would have permitted unrestrained individual contracting, removed minimum conditions, banned industrial unions, and lowered the minimum size required for registration. However, lacking a majority in the Senate, the coalition was forced to retain an ongoing institutional role for the arbitration court. The court continued to impose minimum conditions (in the form of a 'no disadvantage' test) on enterprise bargains but lost its ability to do this for individual contracts (i.e. so-called 'Australian Workplace Agreements'). These individual contracts replaced the old non-union enterprise bargains of the 1993 Act and allowed small and medium-sized businesses to escape existing unions or prevent unionization. So far the new law has not significantly undermined either the award system or the ALP's version of enterprise bargaining, for two reasons. First, New South Wales' Labor government reversed similar state-level legislation. Second, unions in the waterfront and mining industries have successfully fought firms trying aggressively to move towards house unions.

3.5.3.2. Product Markets, Trade, and Competition

In trade policy both the ALP and Coalition government emulated New Zealand Labour, reducing effective rates of protection to industry and agriculture, albeit more slowly. Effective rates of assistance for manufacturing fell from 22 percent in 1983 to an estimated 13 percent in 1993 and were projected to fall to 5 percent by 2001 (OECD 1994: 78). Effective rates of assistance for agriculture fell from roughly 12 percent to 9 percent. These averages conceal wide variations in protection and also in the political modalities for reducing protection. Mirroring their core Accord bargain, the ALP showed a marked preference for corporatist solutions to problems in sensitive sectors.

In manufacturing, for example, the textiles, garments, footwear, automobile, and steel sectors were the most heavily protected, the last two for macroeconomic reasons and the first three because they accounted for 10 percent of manufacturing employment. The ALP made continued aid conditional on increased competitiveness and set up three tripartite fora for negotiating mutually acceptable transitions. Steel received the first such package in 1983, followed closely by autos and then by textiles, clothing, and footwear as a single group (Capling and Galligan 1993). These policies combined pre-announced and gradual market liberalization with penalties for firms if they did not comply with plan targets for upgrading quality and productivity.

Finally, in the single biggest signal of change, the ALP completely inverted the institutional apparatus for trade protection. The Industry Assistance Commission was relocated in the Treasury Department, combined with some of the tripartite fora, and ultimately renamed the Productivity Commission by the Coalition government. Rather than calculating the precise 'made to measure' tariff needed to support an industry, the Commission now churns out a whole range of international benchmark studies showing how far behind world market standards various Australian manufacturing and service industries are, so as to whip firms into higher productivity. As noted above, this new mission dovetailed nicely with the Accord's insistence that wage increases above and beyond the basic wage increase could only come from increased productivity. At the same time, all forms of export subsidy were grouped under one agency, Austrade, itself housed in an enlarged Department of Industry Trade and Commerce. Subsidies were used to promote exports rather than defend inefficient local production, and on this basis they rose to the highest level in the OECD (Capling and Galligan 1993: 141–44).

The ALP also deregulated finance and liberalized foreign entry in order to put pressure on domestic financial capital and make more foreign capital available (Perkins 1989). The postwar Australian state had used financial regulation and repression to manipulate the economy. But the utility of regulation had declined with the rise of non-bank financial enterprises in the postwar period. The Commercial banks' control of Australian financial assets fell from 52 percent to 39 percent between 1953 and 1979, while non-banks' share rose from 24 percent to 54 percent (Keating and Dixon 1989: 42). So the ALP viewed financial deregulation as an easy concession that might force down bank profits and benefit both real enterprises and workers. However, with the float of the Australian dollar, deregulation also subjected the government's ability to finance its fiscal deficit to approval or rejection by foreign financial markets. Given Australia's relatively low level of foreign currency-denominated debt, this was not an immediate constraint on the government. But financial deregulation and the floating dollar sent a strong signal to business and labor that the government would no longer guarantee full employment in the absence of reasonable relative unit labor costs. In this sense financial deregulation signaled to the ACTU that the ALP was bound either to the Accord or to an arbitration-imposed reduction in wage growth.

Finally, in the early 1990s the ALP set up the Hilmer commission on competition, which matured into the Australian Competition and Consumer Commission in 1995, and an intergovernmental National Competition Council (NCC). These organizations now oversee the introduction of competitive forces into various public and private sector markets. Hilmer and its follow-on organizations estimate that falling prices from the introduction of competition will stimulate a one-time gain of 5 percent in GDP, half of which will come from competition in core public utilities. While the NCC is a talking shop for ironing out differences between the federal and state governments, and while privatization is not a foregone conclusion of its policy deliberations, the introduction of market pressures is a certain outcome.

The federal and state governments also corporatized and privatized public enterprises. The federal government sold off its few but large holdings after 1990, including telephony. Formal privatization was more limited than in New Zealand, with both the ALP and some Liberal state governments preferring to retain public ownership but introduce competitive market pressures and full cost recovery. Only one neo-liberal Liberal Party government in Victoria privatized New Zealand-style. Essentially, though, full cost recovery, market pricing for capital, and product market competition had much the same effect that privatization would have had. By the mid-1990s, the government's business enterprises had shed labor, generated considerable income for all levels of government, halved their debt in proportion to GDP, and turned losses amounting to 2.1 percent of

Table 3.5 *Australia—utilities employment, 1985–1995*

	1985	1995
Employment, % of total employment		
Electricity, gas, and water	2.1	1.0
Transport, storage, and communications	7.5	6.6
	1985–90	1991–95
Productivity growth, annual average % change		
Electricity, gas, and water	11	6.9
Transport, storage, and communications	4	6.8

Source: OECD, *Economic Survey: Australia* (Paris: OECD, 1998), 175.

GDP (1985/86) into surpluses of 0.3 percent of GDP (1996/97) (Treasury 1997: ch. 7, pp. 27–31).

3.5.3.2. The Social Wage and Welfare

Formal welfare spending under the ALP was inextricably tied to the evolution of the Accords, because a rising social wage was part of the side payment to unions for acquiescing to a falling real wage. The increase in the per capita social wage was quite modest, 4.5 percent as compared with the 30 percent increase under Whitlam, but the raise reversed a 13 percent real decline under Fraser (Watts 1987). However, because the ACTU knew ALP trade policies would turn concealed into open unemployment, the bulk of the side payment to unions came as a result of increased employment. Unemployment fell by 2.8 percentage points from 1984 to 1989, despite a 5.1 percentage point increase in labor market participation. In addition, the practice of targeting made fewer dollars go further toward poverty reduction.

The ALP designed changes in the social wage to cushion the newly unemployed and to facilitate the entry of women into the workforce. The creation of dual or one-and-a-half income families and the topping up of single- or no-income families through social assistance would preserve families' disposable income during the transition to a more robust export economy. From 1985 to 1995 part-time employment rose from 18.2 percent to 24.5 percent of the labor force, and female participation rates rose from 45.7 to 53.8 percent (OECD 1997: 206).

Labor's social wage strategy had three elements: the restoration of a public health system (Medicare), more targeting of social assistance to those outside the labor market (especially single mothers), and the restructuring of universal entitlements in order to preserve public revenues for labor market losers.

In health care, the ALP reversed Fraser's privatization of Medibank. Fraser's reinstitution of private, voluntary health insurance had driven public share health spending from 72.8 percent to 62.9 percent. The ALP's 'Medicare' restored this to 71.5 percent by 1985, using a flat levy on taxable income (OECD 1995: 73). Because people paid whether they used the public system or not, this created an incentive to use the public system. Because the system was built on public payments to private providers, competition kept service quality high. Medicare's public approval rose from 44 percent to 68 percent in the 1980s, and the percentage of Australians buying private insurance fell from half to 31 percent in 1998. The system has survived Liberal–National efforts to shift people back towards private insurance with tax subsidies amounting to 30 percent of premia (Gray 1990: 238; OECD 1995: 76; Bagnall 1998: 19). Only 31 percent of the population used private health insurance in 1998. The ALP's restoration of public health detached health care access from employment access, easing fears about restructuring.

The ALP also used increases in social assistance to cushion the transition from covert to overt unemployment, and from full-time male to part-time and more female employment, using targeting to husband limited fiscal resources. Social assistance programs were redesigned to top up the wages of those now working for lower pay, and to train those who had fallen out of the labor market. After two years of large real increases in federal spending, total spending at both the federal and state level declined gradually and returned to their initial levels as a share of GDP during the 1980s. But the distribution of payments did change. The ALP shifted funding towards child benefits and single parents in order to offset falling real wages. The universal child benefit was changed into a means-tested family benefit (now Basic Family Benefit), but with a test that included roughly 60 percent of the population. The Family Allowance Supplement (now Additional Family Payment), which provided additional cash on a per-child basis to working families under a much lower threshold, also cushioned the working poor while providing an inducement to stay in the labor market. Both acted like negative income taxes. Rising transfer payments offset the decline in market wages for the three poorest deciles of Australians (Saunders 1994: 183–85). However, income inequality increased from 1975 to 1994; the gini coefficient for market income rose by 36.6 percent to 46.3 percent and for disposable income by 5.2 percent to 30.6 percent (OECD 1997: 49–59). Targeting characterized more universal programs too. In Accord II (1985), unions agreed to restrain wages in exchange for the creation of an employer funded mandatory second tier pension (supreannuation). This secured pension benefits without requiring government spending. Relatively highly paid skilled workers also preferred this defined pension benefit. Accord Mark VI (1990–92) institutionalized this ad hoc payment as the Superannuation Guarantee Charge, which committed employers to pay roughly 3 percent of wages into individual retirement accounts. The Liberal–National coalition has capped this at 9 percent of wages.

Finally, in May 1994 the Keating government launched a major active labor market policy called 'Working Nation'. Working Nation included a policy commitment to find public sector or subsidized private sector work lasting six to twelve months for anyone unemployed for more than eighteen months. Like similar Scandinavian programs, the idea was to keep the long-term unemployed from becoming permanently unemployable. Recipients had to choose between accepting a job offer or training. The Liberal–National government continued Working Nation as 'Jobstart'.

The ALP also introduced user fees in, among other things, higher education. Charging for access to tertiary education while providing a means-tested grant shifted resources from middle-class consumers to the poor. The Higher Education Services Charge (HESC), introduced in 1989, could be paid either up front as a discounted entry fee, or as a tax expressed as a straight percentage of income after graduation. Those without cash still had access to education; the amount they were obligated to pay back into the system was scaled against their actual income. From 1996 on, the HESC amounted to 23 percent of tuition costs for universities. Vocational educational venues traditionally used by poorer students either had no charge or a 10 percent charge. Efforts to bolster public primary education's share of the market for students failed when publicly funded, but private, Catholic schools fought successfully to retain their subsidies.

3.6. Institutional Capacity and Public Responses

Why and how did more radical change succeed in these two countries? The institutional and political capacities for change cannot be separated. Obviously, Westminster systems with fewer veto points make change easier, and (obviously) the easier it is for politicians to shift the costs of change onto politically weak sectors of society, the greater the potential for change in the face of international pressures. Like Britain, New Zealand had a pure Westminster system, 'first past the post' elections, single-member districts, a single-chamber legislature, and weak judicial oversight (Palmer 1979; Palmer and Palmer 1997). Determined minorities with parliamentary majorities could do as they pleased. In contrast, Australia has a two-chamber legislature, where the upper house is elected via proportional representation and federalism allows state governments to impede federal initiatives. But these institutional structures did not initiate change or determine the kinds of change; rather, they affected reformers' ability to make changes. Australia's strong upper house clearly blocks any policy blitzkrieg à la New Zealand. But the mere existence of a Senate was responsible neither for generating the Accord as a strategy nor for enforcing it. What the Australian Senate does is prevent well-organized minorities from using political parties to push policy in directions the majority does not favor.

So how did the institutional landscape help or hinder the changes actors desired? Three mutually reinforcing institutional factors answer this question: (1) the degree to which the electoral system and constitution created governing majorities; (2) bureaucrats' willingness to articulate and enact change; and (3) the degree to which politicians were sheltered from short-term political pressures. Put crudely, these factors answer a threefold question: (1) Did politicians have the votes? (2) Did they have a plan and bureaucratic instruments to carry out that plan? and (3) did they have the time to carry out the plan? 'First past the post' (FPTP) systems tend to create solid and durable majorities for reorganization-minded parties. FPTP limits the exit options for disaffected groups, making it relatively easy for governing parties to reorganize without high political costs. In turn, the more unitary the state, the larger the majority, and the more certain the government's tenure, the more bureaucrats were willing to help politicians craft and execute pre-emptive, comprehensive proposals for change that were difficult to oppose. And, finally, the more electoral breathing room politicians had, the easier it was for them to implement relatively comprehensive policies that would solidify their party's medium-term social base of support. Autonomy mattered because all the parties initiating reforms received significant electoral and financial support from actors threatened by change. Left parties experienced growing internal tensions along a fault line that separated unions representing workers in the exposed sector from those in the sheltered sector (with the public sector being the largest sheltered producer); right parties experienced tension along a fault line separating producers who were competitive in world markets from those relying on protected product or service markets.

3.6.1. New Zealand

New Zealand's state structures created considerable autonomy for both the Labour and National Parties, facilitating significant change. New Zealand's old FPTP single-member district system regularly gave minorities parliamentary majorities and great discretionary power. Labour's unqualified majority from 1984 to 1990 enabled it to ram legislation down the throats of the opposition both inside and outside parliament. National did exactly the same until the successful MMP (mixed member proportional representation) referendum in 1993 made it certain they would be a minority party after the 1996 election.

Certain of Labour's tenure and majority, Treasury bureaucrats provided politicians with detailed blueprints for deregulating and marketizing the public sector (Treasury 1984, 1987; Jesson 1987; Oliver 1989). The Reserve Bank was equally aggressive with regard to exchange rate and fiscal policy; a new organic statute eventually made it the OECD's most independent central bank.

With plans in hand, Labour politicians proved adept at dividing up opposition. As noted above, symbolic and real payoffs to core constituencies in unions and the intelligentsia distracted those groups from making fundamental changes to economic and administrative structures (Vowles 1990). Significant internal opposition only emerged after unemployment doubled from 1987 to 1989, and it was concentrated among those hardest hit, mainly unskilled and public sector workers. They and their unions eventually hived off the Labour Party in 1989 and formed the NewLabour [*sic*] Party, which arguably helped destroy Labour's chances for electoral victory in 1990 in at least eight seats. Solid majorities of voters either openly distrusted or were not sure about their preferred party by 1990 (Vowles and Aimer 1993: 148, 150, 153).

National's extension of Labour's policies into the labor market also created serious public opposition, which spilled over into two referenda on changing the electoral system. A non-binding vote in 1992 showed that 71 percent of the electorate preferred MMP to the status quo; a binding referendum in 1993 confirmed this. MMP, with a 5 percent threshold, came into effect for the 1996 election. The party system immediately fragmented into five serious parties. The center-right National–NZ First coalition government that ensued proved much less aggressive about change than its National-only predecessor. The 1999 election returned a center-left coalition government committed to a cautious expansion of the formal welfare state. Just as in the prior election in Victoria, Australia, rural losers from the marketization of public services decisively swung to left parties.

3.6.2. *Australia*

Australia has single-member districts and transferable votes for the lower federal house but quasi-proportional representation in the upper house. It is also a federal system. Unlike Labour in New Zealand, the ALP could not simply legislate change. Instead, the ALP used its control over the federal government to lead by example and used block grants to the states as bribes/threats. Though the ALP moved more cautiously than New Zealand Labour, co-opting opponents of reorganization, Australian Labor moved just as systematically.

As in New Zealand, bureaucrats played a crucial enabling role, despite being somewhat hostile to change. The Reserve Bank's head in 1983 favored fixed exchange rates, as did his immediate successor. But Treasury, under Keating, and Finance, under John Dawkins, strongly favored marketization. The Finance Ministry and the Department of Prime Minster and Cabinet originated plans for public sector reorganization only slightly less comprehensive than those in New Zealand.

The ALP also skillfully balanced the competing interests of public sector/unskilled workers and private sector/skilled workers. Strong employment gains and a more pragmatic approach to privatization prevented a split along the public–private and sheltered–exposed cleavages until union voter defections sank the ALP's electoral ship in 1996. Unionized workers also defected from unions, which lost about one-third of their share of the workforce from 1982 to 1996. Still, it is notable that the Liberal–National coalition in 1996 ran on a fairly moderate platform rather than on a program as overtly neo-liberal, and losing, as its 1993 platform. Like Labour and National in New Zealand, the Coalition surprised everyone with its radicalism in deregulating the labor market. Here, Australia's two-house legislature proved an impediment to the actual implementation of change. The coalition lacked a majority in the Senate and had to compromise with a minor centrist/greenish party.

Federalism has also impeded change. Both the ALP in the 1990s and the Liberal–National coalition after 1996 faced hostile state-level governments in some of the larger states. Moreover state elections have sent strong signals about voter resistance to change. The unexpected Labor Party victory in Victoria in September 1999 both eviscerated the most neo-liberal of the state governments and induced more moderation in the federal government's neo-liberalism.

3.7. Conclusions

Divergent politics and policy reforms in Australia and New Zealand, as well as the contrast with Britain, suggest that there is no common Anglo-Saxon path in response to fairly similar economic vulnerabilities. Different collective bargaining institutions, different experiences with incomes policy, and different moral economies produced quite different policy choices in the 1980s and 1990s. Australian workers and their unions had less to fear from entrusting wages and employment to central institutions. In the 1980s autonomous state wage-setting institutions in Australia made a 'Blairite' path possible and preferable to a 'Thatcherite' path. Arguably, Hawke's example made Blair possible. The outcome of reforms also strongly suggests that neo-liberal reforms are not particularly conducive to successful employment or social policy.

Ironically, both of the Australasian political strategies have returned to post-Thatcher Britain. Blair absorbed and campaigned on the policy messages and party discipline demonstrated first by the Hawke ALP governments. Conservative party leader Hague meanwhile has absorbed the policy messages first demonstrated in New Zealand and then refined in Alberta, Canada and Ontario, Canada; Hague even adopted the campaign slogan of a 'Common Sense Revolution' from Ontario's Conservative government.

Despite the substantial transformations of their postwar models, both economies remain vulnerable to the international economy. While some of the older dynamics that generated current account deficits are gone, they have been replaced by new ones. For Australia, and even more so New Zealand, high levels of foreign debt have become a substantial burden, requiring ever larger trade surpluses. While their successfully reorganized models mean that they are both better positioned to supply manufactured exports to world (and particularly Asian) markets, they remain hostage to growth in those markets, just as they were hostage to growth in their nineteenth-century markets for wool and foods.

At the same time, reorganization has clearly shifted the burden of market risks away from capital and onto workers. Both Australia and (even more so) New Zealand have replaced systems of informal welfare with formal welfare. Open unemployment and employment at market-defined wages have replaced hidden unemployment at socially defined wages. The hidden unemployment of the postwar model imposed a burden on profit levels, particularly for export producers. Wages and mandatory benefits had to be paid first, then shareholders. The displacement of covert by overt unemployment means that firms can more easily externalize world market pressures by firing workers. This has placed additional burdens on these countries' public treasuries as people turn to formal welfare to ameliorate those risks. In Australia this motivated the Liberals' politically costly, but successful effort to replace income taxes with an exporter-friendly GST (i.e. VAT). In New Zealand, legislation binds the state to low taxes, low inflation, and low deficits, significantly constraining any effort to expand formal welfare.

What about these countries in relation to each other and to the international environment? By the 1990s, subsequent—although perhaps not consequent—to their reforms and public sector reorganization, Australia and New Zealand were performing at or better than the OECD average in terms of fiscal deficits, inflation, unemployment, and GDP growth. Only their current account deficits were higher than the OECD average. Moreover, from 1981 through 1993, as Table 3.6 shows, Australia's and (to a lesser extent) New Zealand's export performance were well above OECD averages. This suggests that efforts to change the old models certainly undid some of the dynamics generating excessive import growth. And per capita GDP grew significantly faster in both Australia and New Zealand after 1990 compared to rates in both the OECD in general and OECD Europe. However, Australia clearly did much better than New Zealand, growing at an average of 3.0 percent annually from 1984 to 1992 and 4.2 percent from 1992 to 1998, whereas New Zealand only grew 0.4 percent and 3.3 percent per annum, respectively. If New Zealand had grown at Australian rates, its GDP would have been 20 percent higher in 1992 than it actually was (Dalziel 1999).

Table 3.6 *Export growth, annual percentage change, 1981–1993*

	Goods			Services		
	Exports	Imports	Net growth	Exports	Imports	Net growth
Australia	10.6	9.7	0.9	12.2	9.3	2.9
New Zealand	9.2	8.7	0.5	10.6	9.3	1.3
Smaller OECD[a]	6.5	5.6	0.9	7.6	7.5	0.1

[a]Non-G7 OECD.

Source: OECD 1994: 55.

3.7.1. New Zealand: The New Model

Labour's and (even more so) National's changes to the formal and informal welfare state finished the shift from a state-led economy to a foreign investor-led, market-based economy. National especially tried to construct a virtuous circle of falling spending, falling deficits, and falling interest rates, which in turn would attract rising foreign private investment to generate more employment etc. To date this strategy has only returned New Zealand to its trend rate of growth and employment levels after the 1989–92 recession. Labour's prior privatizations and National's fiscal surpluses have reduced New Zealand's vulnerability to publicly held, foreign currency-denominated debt and to fiscal shocks driven by devaluation. Product and labor market liberalization eliminated the old inflationary dynamic created by rapid transmission of wage gains across sectors via horizontal wage relativities. The formal welfare state is lean and mean. All this came at the cost of increased income inequality, rising crime, and deteriorating health services. Real per capita income for the five lowest deciles fell from 1984 to 1995/96, and the share of the seven lowest deciles also declined (Dalziel 1999). Finally, export diversification has reduced vulnerability to price shocks in specific commodities, though not to general price shocks like the Asian financial crisis. But terms of trade for New Zealand's major exports continue to be cyclically volatile and to fall in a secular trend; growth and employment are hostage to foreign investment. Foreign debt, while declining, remained well above OECD averages at 80.9 percent of GDP in 1997.

3.7.2. *Australia: The New Model*

The 'new' Australian model strongly resembles the old. Socially defined wage minima, the most distinctive feature of the old model, remain an important part of the institutional landscape. Market principles mark major parts of the welfare state, but without compromising equal access. The welfare state was rationalized by adjustments that accommodated the rising share of part-timers and women in the labor force, not by downsizing. Unlike New Zealand, public spending and revenues have been constant relative to GDP since 1985, although the introduction of a GST (VAT) in 1998 marked the beginning of a shift away from income taxes. But import substitution via 'protection all around' is clearly gone, as is comparative wage justice.

Has Australia discovered a viable version of the 'decent' competitive welfare state? Economically, the persistence of non-market wage setting under the ambit of the arbitration court(s) conflicts with liberal macroeconomic, trade, and industrial policies, although the arbitration courts' coverage has shrunk to roughly two-thirds of the workforce. Continued wage minima and pockets of resistance to increased productivity arguably explain why Australia's open unemployment rate remains higher than New Zealand's or Britain's (and high by Australian historical standards, although not by comparison to Continental Europe). But despite higher unemployment the model has avoided the extreme poverty seen in both places, where work has been redistributed between winners and losers. Despite the explicit link between wage and productivity gains, the arbitration court retains the ability to shift part of the productivity gain out of firms and into the rest of the economy, avoiding the widening income gyre seen in New Zealand. This ability precisely mirrors the capacity of European governments to redistribute income through taxation, and with about the same degree of opacity.

Consequently, the political burdens of adjustment to international economic pressures fall harder on Australian workers' organizations than on unions in either New Zealand or Britain. Arbitration and efforts to maintain a social wage mean that competitiveness rests on some workers' willingness to accept lower wages than their underlying productivity merits. As Sweden in the 1980s shows, this is difficult over the long term. By 1996 it became clear that union members did not find this deal acceptable; union density fell considerably and union members did not support the ALP in 1996 in numbers large enough to win the election. Still, the ALP and ACTU clearly did a better job of ameliorating those tensions than did New Zealand Labour, which split in 1989, or New Zealand unions, which split in 1991. While the defecting groups were small, factionalization in New Zealand and Britain gave parties on the right parliamentary majorities and power. Later in Britain, by contrast, Blair's Australianization of Labour returned it to power.

Economically, Australia continues to accumulate foreign debt, which now stands at over 40 percent of GDP. But most of this is private debt, and so falls on business. For some time it looked as if Australia was repeating New Zealand's error from the 1970s and delaying adjustment by borrowing. But New Zealand's ongoing and growing reliance on foreign investment indicates that both countries continue to rely on foreign capital for growth. In this respect, nothing has changed since the nineteenth century.

REFERENCES

BAGNALL, DIANA (1998). 'How to Cure a Sick System', *Bulletin*, 31 Mar. 1998, 19–21.

BIE (Bureau of Industry Economics) (1983). *Research Report No. 12, Structural Adjustment in the Australian White-Goods Industry.* Canberra: Australian Government Printing Service.

BLONDAL, GISLI (1986). *Fiscal Policy in the Smaller Industrial Countries.* Washington, DC: International Monetary Fund.

BOSTON, JONATHAN (1984). *Incomes Policy in New Zealand 1968–1984.* Wellington: Victoria University Press.

BRAY, MARK, and NIELSEN, DAVID (1996). 'Industrial Relations and the Relative Autonomy of the State', in Francis Castles, Rolf Gerritsen, and Jack Vowles (eds.), *The Great Experiment.* Sydney: Allen and Unwin, 68–87.

BUCHANAN, JOHN, VAN BARNEVELD, KRISTIN, O'LOUGHLIN, TONI, and PRAGNELL, BRAD (1997). 'Wages Policy and Wage Determination in 1996'. *Journal of Industrial Relations*, 39: 96–119.

CAPLING, ANN, and GALLIGAN, BRIAN (1993). *Beyond the Protective State.* Cambridge: Cambridge University Press.

CAR (Commonwealth Arbitration Reports) (1970). 'Engineering Oil Industry Case 1970'. No. 134. Canberra: Australian Government Publishing Service.

CARR, BOB (1979). 'Australian Trade Unionism in 1978'. *Journal of Industrial Relations,* 21: 97–109.

CASTLES, FRANCIS (1987). 'Thirty Wasted Years: Australian Social Security Development, 1950–1980, in Comparative Perspective'. *Australian Journal of Political Science,* 22: 67–74.

——(1989). *The Working Class and Welfare.* Sydney: Allen & Unwin.

CAYGILL, DAVID (1989). *Securing Economic Recovery: Budget Speech.* Wellington: Government Printing OECD.

CHEYNE, CHRISTINE, O'BRIEN, MIKE, and BELGRAVE, MICHAEL (1997). *Social Policy in Aotearoa New Zealand.* Auckland: Oxford University Press.

DALZIEL, PAUL (1992). 'National's Economic Strategy', in Jonathan Boston, and Paul Dalziel (eds.), *The Decent Society.* Auckland: Oxford University Press, 19–38.

——(1999). 'New Zealand's Economic Reform Programme was a Failure'. Unpublished MS. Christchurch, New Zealand: Lincoln University.

DANNIN, ELLEN (ed.) (1997). 'Symposium on New Zealand's Employment Contracts Act, 1991'. *California Western International Law Journal,* Fall 28: 1–340.

DEEBLE, JOHN (1978). *Health Expenditure in Australia 1960–61 to 1975–76.* Research Report No. 1. Canberra: Australian National University Health Research Project.

DEEKS, JOHN, and BOXALL, PETER (1989). *Labour Relations in New Zealand.* Auckland: Longman Paul.

DUNNING, JOHN, and CANTWELL, JOHN (1987). *IRM Directory of Statistics of International Investment and Production.* London: MacMillan.

EASTON, BRIAN (1980). *Social Policy and the Welfare State in new Zealand.* Auckland: G. Allen & Unwin.

——(1987). 'Labour's Economic Strategy', in Jonathon Boston and Martin Holland (eds.), *Fourth Labour Government.* Auckland: Oxford University Press, 134–50.

The Economist (1993). June 19: 112.

EMG (Economic Monitoring Group) (1984). *The Government Deficit and the Economy.* Wellington: Government Printing Office.

FRENKEL, STEPHEN (ed.) (1987). *Union Strategy and Industrial Change.* Kensington, NSW: New South Wales University Press.

GAHAN, PETER (1993). 'Solidarity Forever? The 1993 ACTU Congress'. *Journal of Industrial Relations,* 35: 607–25.

GOULD, JOHN (1982). *The Rake's Progress.* Auckland: Hodder and Stoughton.

GRAY, GWEN (1990). 'Health Policy', in Christine Jennett and Randal Stewart (eds.), *Hawke and Australian Public Policy: Consensus and Restructuring.* Melbourne: Macmillan, 223–44.

GREGORY, ROBERT (1987). 'Reorganization of the Public Sector', in Jonathan Boston and Martin Holland (eds.), *Fourth Labour Government*. Auckland: Oxford University Press, 111–33.

HARBRIDGE, RAYMOND, and CRAWFORD, AARON (1997). 'The Impact of New Zealand's ECA on Industrial Relations'. *California Western International Law Journal*, 28: 235–51.

HAWKE, GARY (1985). *Making of New Zealand*. New York: Cambridge University Press.

JENNINGS, STEPHEN, and CAMERON, ROBERT (1987). 'State-Owned Enterprise Reform in New Zealand', in Alan Bollard and Robert Buckle (eds.), *Economic Liberalisation in New Zealand*. Wellington: Allen & Unwin, 121–52.

JESSON, BRUCE (1987). *Behind the Mirror Glass*. Auckland: Penguin.

KEATING, MICHAEL, and DIXON, GEOFF (1989). *Making Economic Policy in Australia 1983–1988*. Melbourne: Longman Chesire.

KELSEY, JANE (1995). *Economic Fundamentalism*. London: Pluto Press.

KEWLEY, THOMAS H. (1980). *Australian Social Security Today: Major Developments from 1900 to 1978*. Sydney: Sydney University Press.

MABBETT, DEBORAH (1995). *Trade, Employment and Welfare*. Cambridge: Cambridge University Press.

MATTHEWS, TREVOR (1991). 'Interest Group Politics: Corporatism without Business?', in Francis Castles (ed.), *Australia Compared*. Sydney: Allen & Unwin, 191–218.

New Zealand Official Yearbook (1987/88).

OECD (Organisation for Economic Cooperation and Development) (1972). *Economic Survey: Australia, 1972*. Paris: OECD.

——(1975). *Economic Survey: New Zealand, 1975*. Paris: OECD.

——(1976a). *Economic Survey: Australia, 1976*. Paris: OECD.

——(1976b). *Economic Survey: New Zealand, 1976*. Paris: OECD.

——(1980). *Economic Survey: Australia, 1980*. Paris: OECD.

——(1985). *Social Expenditure, 1960–1990*. Paris: OECD.

——(1989). *Economic Survey: New Zealand, 1988/89*. Paris: OECD.

——(1991). *Economic Survey: New Zealand, 1990/91*. Paris: OECD.

——(1993). *Economic Survey: New Zealand, 1993*. Paris: OECD.

——(1994). *Economic Survey: Australia, 1994*. Paris: OECD.

——(1995). *Economic Survey: Australia, 1995*. Paris: OECD.

——(1997). 'Income Distribution and Poverty in Selected OECD Countries'. *OECD Economic Outlook*, 62: 49–59.

——(1998). *Economic Survey: New Zealand, 1998*. Paris: OECD.

——(1999). *Economic Survey: Australia*. Paris: OECD.

OYBCA (Official Yearbook of the Commonwealth of Australia) (various dates).

OLIVER, W. HUGH (1989). 'The Labour Caucus and Economic Policy Formation, 1981–1984', in Brian Easton (ed.), *The Making of Rogernomics*. Auckland: Auckland University Press, 11–52.

PALMER, GEOFFREY (1979). *Unbridled Power: An Interpretation of New Zealand's Constitution and Government*. Wellington: Oxford University Press.

——and PALMER, MICHAEL (1997). *Bridled Power: New Zealand Government under MMP*. Wellington: Oxford University Press.

PERKINS, J. O. N. (1989). *Deregulation of the Australian Financial System*. Carlton, Victoria: Melbourne University Press.

PLOWMAN, DAVID (1980). 'National Wage Determination in 1979'. *Journal of Industrial Relations*, 22: 79–97.

——(1981). *Wage Indexation: A Study of Australian Wage Issues 1975–1980*. Sydney: George Allen and Unwin.

——(1987). 'Economic Forces and the New Right'. *Journal of Industrial Relations*, 29: 84–91.

——(1989). *Holding the Line: Compulsory Arbitration and National Employer Coordination in Australia*. Cambridge: Cambridge University Press.

——(1992). 'An Uneasy Conjunction: Opting Out and the Arbitration System'. *Journal of Industrial Relations*, 34: 284–306.

REITANO, ROBERT (1994). 'Legislative Change in 1993'. *Journal of Industrial Relations*, 36: 57–73.

Reserve Bank (various dates). *Reserve Bank Bulletin*. Wellington: Government Printing Office.

RUDD, CHRIS (1992). 'Controlling and Restructuring Public Expenditure', in Jonathan Boston and Paul Dalziel (eds.), *The Decent Society*. Auckland: Oxford University Press, 39–58.

SANDLANT, RICHARD (1989). 'The Political Economy of Wage Restraint'. MA thesis. University of Auckland.

SAUNDERS, PETER (1994). *Welfare and Inequality*. Cambridge: Cambridge University Press.

SCHARPF, FRITZ W. (1991). *Crisis and Choice in European Social Democracy*. Ithaca, NY: Cornell University Press.

SCHWARTZ, HERMAN (1998). 'Social Democracy Going Down vs. Social Democracy Down Under?' *Comparative Politics*, 30: 253–72.

SCHERER, PETER (1980). 'Salary Restraint in a Bureaucratic Hierarchy: The Case of the Australian Public Service under Wage Indexation'. *Journal of Industrial Relations*, 22/1: 1–18.

——(1985). 'State Syndicalism', in John Hyde and John Nurick (eds.), *Wages Wasteland?* Sydney: Hale and Ironmonger, 75–94.

SCOTTON, RICHARD B. (1977). 'Health Costs and Health Policy'. *The Australian Quarterly*, 49/2: 5–16.

SINGLETON, GWYNNETH (1990). *The Accord and the Australian Labour Movement*. Melbourne: Melbourne University Press.

TECHRITZ, VIC, and HATCHER, GARRY (1981). 'Employer Matters 1980'. *Journal of Industrial Relations*, 23: 70–80.

THORNTHWAITE, LOUISE, and SHELDON, PETER (1993). 'Ex Parte Accord: The BCA and Industrial Relations Change'. *International Journal of Business Studies*, 1: 37–55.

————(1996). 'The MTIA, Bargaining Structures and the Accord'. *Journal of Industrial Relations*, 38: 171–95.

Treasury Department (1984). *Economic Management*. Wellington: Government Printer.

——(1987). *Government Management*. Wellington: Government Printer.

——(1997). *Budget 1997, Statement 7—The Public Sector*. Canberra: Australian Government Printing Service.

UNCTC (United Nations Centre on Transnational Corporations) (1988). *Transnational Corporations in World Development*. New York: UNCTC.

VOWLES, JACK (1990). 'Nuclear-free New Zealand and Rogernomics', *Politics*, 25: 81–91.

——and AIMER, PETER (1993). *Voters' Vengeance*. Auckland: Auckland University Press.

WALSH, PAT (1991). 'The State Sector', in Jonathan Boston, John Martin, June Pallot, and Pat Walsh (eds.), *Reshaping the State*. Auckland: Oxford University Press, 52–80.

WATTS, ROB (1987). *Foundations of the National Welfare State*. Sydney: Allen & Unwin.

4

Switzerland
Adjustment Politics within Institutional Constraints

GIULIANO BONOLI AND ANDRÉ MACH

For much of the twentieth century, Switzerland has been an exemplar of political and economic stability. The events that shattered people's lives in its European neighbors, like wars, recessions, or political unrest, affected this country only marginally. In the late 1990s, Switzerland was still displaying patterns of political stability and economic prosperity that were unusual by international standards. Nevertheless, the solidity of the Swiss political and economic model does seem to have suffered somewhat over the last decade. Several developments have combined to undermine the economic, political, and social underpinnings of Swiss stability: the emergence of unemployment, a social problem that was virtually unknown in postwar Switzerland before the early 1990s; an increase in public budget deficits; and the pressures induced by changes in the country's international environment.

The magnitude of social and economic problems that Switzerland is currently facing remains low by European standards. With an unemployment rate of less than 4 percent, the country ranks among the best in Europe. Even though social problems are on the rise, developments like large-scale social exclusion remain virtually unknown. The budget deficits of the 1990s, although they stand out in historical data series, are moderate by European standards, and Switzerland would have qualified for membership in the EMU. Moreover, unlike the way it was in other European countries earlier, the recession of the early 1990s and ongoing trends toward economic internationalization have not resulted in dramatic losses of business confidence.

Deteriorating socio-economic conditions have probably not been the most significant development of the 1990s. Instead, the landmark change has been a decline in the level of support for the traditional postwar model

We are grateful to Klaus Armingeon for comments and for access to his data on foreign workers, and to Franz-Xaver Kaufmann, Fritz W. Scharpf, and Vivien Schmidt.

by some economic and political actors. The most internationalized sections of the business community have shown increasing dissatisfaction with a number of socio-economic and political arrangements, some of which constituted the very cornerstones of the postwar model. Many of the social and economic policy reforms discussed in this chapter can be ascribed to a shift in the preferences of export-oriented business.

The postwar Swiss model was characterized by two important equilibria, or compromises, between the country's key social and political forces. The first pact, between labor and capital, was based on labor's acceptance of peaceful industrial relations, in exchange for high salaries and relatively generous occupational social protection. The second compromise, between export-oriented business and domestic producers, rested on a combination of economic openness, essential for a successful export sector, and tolerance for non-competitive arrangements in the internal market, which benefited domestic producers.

In the early 1990s these two equilibria were increasingly threatened. Export-oriented business expressed increasing dissatisfaction with both compromises, the pact with labor and the one with domestic producers. These are now portrayed as factors that penalize Swiss economic competitiveness in the global market. In the 1990s, this change of attitude on the part of a large and influential section of the business community was instrumental in generating a series of social and economic policy reforms, that aimed at redefining the equilibria on which the postwar model was based.

As in other countries, the position of export-oriented business in national politics was strengthened as a consequence of economic internationalization and the growing availability of an exit option for them. As a result, compromises once regarded as acceptable are no longer always seen this way. This interpretation is supported by an observable shift in the stated policy preferences of some sections of the business community, which occurred in the early 1990s and was illustrated by a series of highly publicized proposals to change policy.

Thus, the 1990s saw new pressures impinging on the postwar politico-economic model, pressures that prompted policymakers to change public policy. The overall direction of change is towards a more liberal model, characterized by a more deregulated labor market, a more competitive domestic market, and a slightly leaner welfare state. So far, nevertheless, change has been limited, particularly in social policy, largely because Switzerland has a political system that favors power sharing and political institutions that offer little scope for imposing losses on any important group (Armingeon 1998, 2000). Thus, the 'new' model seems to be a slightly revised version of the old one, with some of its more liberal features reinforced.

This chapter tries to account for these developments. It starts by high-lighting the key features of the postwar model, then asks why this model remained viable throughout the 1970s and 1980s, and finally looks at what changed in the early 1990s. The chapter concludes by focusing on the likely outcomes of the ongoing adjustment process.

4.1. The Postwar Model

Stability is probably the word that best describes Switzerland's postwar politico-economic model. A political system characterized by the inclu-sion of a wide range of interests was matched by a system of industrial relations in which a relatively weak and fragmented labor movement took a pragmatic line on most labor market issues. All this was comple-mented by a welfare state that, while not highly developed by inter-national standards, did focus on workers and provided them with generous protection against the most important social risks. Stability had a great deal to do with the model's inclusive character, based on power sharing in the political arena and wealth sharing in the economic one. However, stability was also facilitated by the exclusion of some groups from both arenas, especially foreigners and women. For much of the postwar period, these two groups did not have the right to vote, were neglected by the welfare state, and functioned as a buffer against cyclical shocks in the labor market.

The political system, the structure of economic and industrial relations and the welfare state, can be seen as the defining feature of the postwar model. Each of these components is now examined in turn.

4.1.1. *Political Institutions and Consensus Democracy*

The Swiss political system is structured by a set of institutions that reduce the potential for power to be concentrated and encourage the formation of large coalitions. The constitutional order is geared towards limiting the power of the federal government, whose authority can be challenged and decisions overruled at a number of points. The result is a political system where extremely broad agreement is needed to pass legislation. These institutional features, briefly reviewed below, combined with a social struc-ture characterized by multiple cleavages (socio-economic, religious, and linguistic), tend to diminish even further any likelihood of power being concentrated in the hands of a single group. This combination of institu-tional and socio-structural features has produced a political system known as 'consensus' or 'consociational' democracy, based on the integration of dissent and the inclusion of conflicting interests in the policymaking process (Lehmbruch 1993; Lijphart 1984; Linder 1994).

The Swiss political system has at least three institutional features that help reduce the amount of power concentration government can use: (1) de facto separation of powers between the executive and the legislative branches of government; (2) federalism with minority representation at the parliamentary level; and (3) a referendum system.

The relationship between the Swiss government (Federal Council) and parliament has been described as a hybrid between European parliamentarism and US-style separation of powers (Lijphart 1984). As in parliamentary regimes, the Federal Council is elected by the legislature. However, as in a system based on separation of powers, the Federal Council cannot be brought down by the legislature during its four-year term. Conversely, the Federal Council cannot dissolve parliament. Legislators are not under the same pressure to support government-sponsored legislation as is the case in parliamentary systems. The result is a system in which the government has relatively little control over parliament. As in the USA, the executive branch has to negotiate with the legislature; policy cannot be imposed on parliament.

The second element of power fragmentation is federalism, reinforced by the representation of the federated states (cantons) in the upper chamber of parliament. Swiss bicameralism is symmetrical (the two chambers have equal powers): in the lower chamber (National Council), territorial representation is proportional to the size of the population; in the upper chamber (Council of States) each canton is entitled to two representatives. The power of the numerous, but small, rural cantons is thus magnified.

Third, and perhaps most notably, Switzerland has a referendum system that allows voters to bring various issues to the polls.[1] According to Neidhart (1970) referendums are the key factor behind the development of a consensus-based political system. Governments, in order to reduce the vulnerability of their bills to the referendum challenge, adopted an inclusive policymaking strategy. By allowing the relevant actors to co-draft legislation, policymakers have been able to diffuse the threat potential of referendums.

---

[1] The Swiss constitution makes provision for various types of referendums. Both constitutional change and accession to a supranational organization are automatically subjected to referendum. Constitutional change can also be proposed by voters by means of a 'popular initiative', which requires 100,000 signatures. For these referendums to succeed, a double majority—voters and cantons—is needed. With 50,000 signatures, voters can also challenge at the polls any act passed by parliament. In this case, a simple majority of voters is sufficient for the referendum to succeed (see Kobach 1993 for a comprehensive account).

One of the most significant features of Swiss consociational democracy is an oversized coalition government. The Federal Council, which has had the same composition since 1959, consists of a four-party coalition that includes the Christian Democrats, the Social Democrats, the Free Democrats, and the Swiss People's Party (formerly a farmers' party). Together, these parties account for some 75 percent of the lower chamber of parliament, and a government could rule with the support of any three of these four parties. Since Federal Councillors are elected individually, they need the votes of other parties, and for this reason they tend to be selected among the more moderate individuals in each camp. This facilitates the consensual character of the government's operations, but it also reduces the Council's control over parliament and the electorate during referendums. Overall, the Federal Council's influence on policymaking is not comparable to that of governments in parliamentary systems.

A second important consociational practice is a policymaking process allowing interest groups to play a substantial role in defining policy (Papadopoulos 1997). Typically, legislative change is preceded by a lengthy and highly structured consultation procedure, which can be more or less encompassing depending on how much controversy the policy in question is likely to provoke. Legislation is often drafted by 'expert commissions', which normally include representatives of all the relevant interest groups. The expert commission usually produces a compromise that is acceptable to all parties concerned, since each group has de facto veto power, which it can wield by threatening a referendum challenge. During the 'golden age' of the consensus model (the 1950s and 1960s), the agreements reached this way were generally accepted by parliament with very few amendments, thanks also to the existence of an informal core of policymakers who made most of the decisions (Kriesi 1982; 1995). In more recent years, as will be seen below, parliament has become increasingly reluctant to ratify agreements reached by interest groups, and on various occasions the legislature has even imposed change by majority rule.

The Swiss consociational model guaranteed political inclusion to influential groups whose power resources were sufficient to make effective use of the veto points provided by the political system. Inclusion, thus, was not universal. Those left out included women, first granted the right to vote in 1971, and foreigners, who make up some 15 percent of the population and do not have the right to vote at the federal level. This pattern of inclusion and exclusion in decision making is, to a large extent, replicated in the two other major arenas of the Swiss politico-economic model: the labor market and social policy.

4.1.2. Economic Relations and the Labor Market

Four major features of the Swiss political economy are especially worth noting: (1) the weakness of the federal state, combined with strong organized interests; (2) peaceful and decentralized industrial relations; (3) a cleavage in the economy between a competitive export-oriented sector and a somewhat protected sector producing mainly for the domestic market; (4) an immigration policy that allowed the recruitment of a large number of foreigners with temporary work permits.

1. We need to underline the weakness of the federal state, which is associated with the power of organized interests. The end of the nineteenth century was a crucial period for the institutionalization of relations between the 'recent' federal state and strongly organized economic interests created very early in the second half of the nineteenth century and thus already accustomed to organizing social and economic life as well as providing collective goods to their members. In a variety of fields—such as vocational training, collecting statistics, and subsidizing specific economic sectors—the federal state had to cooperate with organized interests in order to define and implement economic policies. This historical background explains the strong influence of organized interests at every step of the policymaking process and the frequent use of the terms 'parastate' or 'militia system' (Germann et al. 1985). Despite the progressive extension of the federal state's responsibilities into the economy and social welfare during the twentieth century, the role of organized interests has remained central down to the present day (Mach 1999).

The relationship between the federal state and organized interests is institutionalized by way of non-parliamentary commissions and consultation procedures. However, this link between the state and interest groups remains highly fragmented. In contrast to more typical corporatist countries—where one finds a few highly encompassing institutions representing the state, trade unions, and employers associations—the Swiss system relies on a number of bodies, each of which focuses on a specific area only. As a result, arrangements between organized interests and the state are mainly sectoral in character, and coordination between social and economic policies is very rare. The absence of coordinated macroeconomic policies is also due to the autonomy of the Swiss National Bank (SNB) and the decentralization of industrial relations, both of which prevent the joint use of monetary, fiscal, and income policies as is the case in other corporatist countries.

2. Industrial relations are characterized by decentralization, flexibility, and the virtual absence of industrial conflicts. The federal state does not intervene in industrial relations, which have always been decentralized at

the sectoral, regional, and firm level. This decentralization is due to several factors: the spatial diversity of industrial structures, the fragmented structure of trade unions (and, to a lesser extent, of the employers associations), and the decentralization of political structures, which affects the organization of economic interests (Kriesi and Farago 1989). Employers, strongly attached to the principle of subsidiarity, have managed (to some extent with the support of unions) to keep a large portion of working conditions regulated by collective bargaining rather than governed by uniform legislation.

Swiss industrial relations are very stable and peaceful. Confrontation has been very rare since the years immediately following World War II, when numerous industrial disputes took place. A 'labor peace' clause, which is included in most collective agreements, prohibits the signatories from using confrontational measures such as lock-outs and strikes for as long as the collective agreement is in force. The labor peace clause has its origin in the 'labor peace agreements' signed in 1937 by employers and trade unions in two major industrial sectors (machine and watchmaking industries). After World War II, most collective agreements adopted this clause, and the number of industrial disputes has remained very low ever since.

Collective bargaining is very diverse and takes place mainly at the sectoral and company level. Collective agreements negotiated between trade unions and employers associations at the sectoral level generally lay down procedural rules, working conditions (working time, holidays), minimum wages, cost-of-living adjustments, and some private welfare agreements. Yet, only about 50 percent of employees in private firms (1.4 million) are covered by a collective agreement. Among the over one thousand existing collective agreements that have been negotiated, the ten major sectoral agreements (for export-oriented industries, hotel and catering, the banking sector, and construction) already cover more than 800,000 employees, the rest being covered by regional or company agreements (see Prince 1994; Lopreno 1995). Collective agreements are generally also binding for employees and firms that are not members of the organizations acting as signatories to a collective agreement, even though the agreements do not formally apply to non-union members and non-federated firms. It is possible to extend the terms of a collective agreement to all firms, but this provision is rarely used because of its strict legal conditions (Hotz and Fluder 1998).

3. The third aspect of Swiss politico-economic development is the cleavage between competitive export-oriented sectors (Switzerland's four major industries, as well as its financial and insurance services) and more or less sheltered sectors producing mainly for the domestic market

(agriculture, construction and retail trade—see Bernegger 1990; Knöpfel 1988). This cleavage is also reflected in the structure of organized interests.[2] Despite the high degree of openness in the Swiss economy, domestic-oriented producers managed to obtain some measures that protected them from strong international economic competition: this is particularly true in the case of agricultural policy, which provides some of the most generous subsidies dispensed by any OECD country (Sciarini 1994), of the especially soft anti-cartel legislation that mostly benefited the domestic sectors (Hotz 1979; Rentsch 1989), and of various public regulations and an immigration policy that mainly favored the construction and tourist industries. While full-scale protectionism was not an option for the overwhelmingly export-oriented Swiss economy, subsidies to agriculture and the acceptance of some non-competitive arrangements constituted a form of 'selective' protectionism mainly of concern to producers for the domestic market.

Thus, although Switzerland is an open economy, its exposure to international markets has been significantly mitigated by such measures as subsidies (for agriculture), regulations, and private cartels, all of which have facilitated non-competitive behavior while protecting domestic markets from the pressures of international competition. Several recent studies (Hauser and Bradke 1992; OECD various issues/1992: 68 ff.; IMF 1998) have emphasized how almost two-thirds of domestic prices are either administered, strongly regulated, or fixed by private cartels, which helps to explain the high level of domestic prices. Because of changes in the international environment during the early 1990s (GATT agreements and closer ties with the EU), and because of internal demands for more efficiency, heavy pressure was finally applied to a domestic sector increasingly regarded as a 'rent seeking', non-competitive, and structurally weak part of the economy.

4. The fourth important feature of the Swiss economy is its very high proportion of foreign workers. Through the mid-1960s, because of a tight labor market and liberal immigration policy, Swiss firms hired a large number of foreign workers, who often worked on seasonal, annual, or cross-border commuter permits. Despite restrictive measures taken since the mid-1960s in response to the pressure of xenophobic movements, the overall number of foreign workers actually increased between the 1960s and 1990s (see Figure 4.2). These are mainly unskilled workers employed

[2] The USCI (Swiss Federation of Commerce and Industry) better known as Vorort, the UCAPS (Central Union of Employers Associations), and the Swiss Bankers Association (ASB) represent the export-oriented and financial sectors. On the other side, the Swiss Farmers' Union (USP) and the Swiss Association of Small Business (USAM) represent the more domestic-oriented sectors.

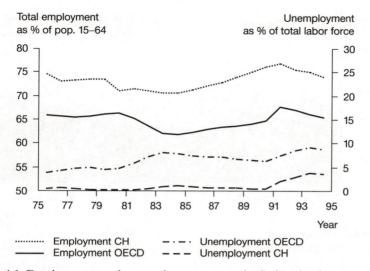

Figure 4.1 Employment and unemployment rates in Switzerland compared to OECD average, 1975–1995
Source: OECD, *Statistical Compendium: Labour Force Statistics* (Paris: OECD, 1997).

in the domestic sectors of the economy (construction, tourism, agriculture). The importance of the foreign workforce and the sectoral diversity of the Swiss economy explain the country's highly segmented labor market, in which working conditions and wages differ widely (depending on how strong unions and collective agreements are in each segment).

During the recession of the 1970s, a decline in total employment was largely absorbed by a reduction in the number of foreign workers and working women. Job losses were substantial: about eleven percent of total employment or 330,000 jobs were lost between 1973 and 1976, but this did not result in an increase in the unemployment rate (Figure 4.1). Over the same period, the female employment rate dropped by 3.3 percentage points to 50.8 percent, by far the biggest decline in female employment among OECD countries (OECD 1997*b*). Among foreign workers, the numbers dropped from just under 900,000 in 1973 to 650,000 in 1977 (see Figure 4.2). In his analysis of how the watch industry was restructured, Piotet (1987) convincingly characterizes Swiss industrial relations as 'selective corporatism': foreign and female workers bore the brunt of the recession's entire array of economic and social repercussions, whereas the core labor force (Swiss male workers) remained largely unaffected.

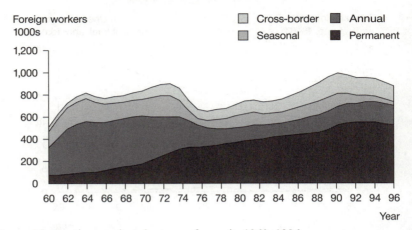

Figure 4.2 Foreign workers by type of permit, 1960–1996
Source: Armingeon 1999.

4.1.3. The Welfare State

The Swiss welfare state is generally described as relatively underdeveloped
in comparison with other European countries (Esping-Andersen 1990;
Huber, Ragin, and Stephens 1993). This view is certainly accurate, but it
conceals the existence of some 'peaks of generosity' for the core workforce: pensions (especially occupational pensions) and unemployment
insurance benefits. On the other hand, Switzerland is a clear welfare laggard in health insurance (not made compulsory until 1994), family policy,
and long-term unemployment compensation (still reliant on a locally
administered system of social assistance).

Until the 1980s, Switzerland fitted well into the conservative-corporatist[3] or occupational (Ferrera 1993) model of social protection.
Thereafter, however, a number of reforms were introduced, and occupational forms of protection were extended to the population as a whole. In
the early 1980s occupational pension coverage was made compulsory for
employees earning above a set limit, and unemployment insurance, which
up to then had only covered some occupational groups, was made universal. These reforms have allowed some of the more marginal sections of the

---

[3] In his classification of welfare regimes, Esping-Andersen (1990) puts Switzerland in the
liberal family. This is arguably a result of the focus on state programs. The strong reliance
on occupational welfare prior to the 1980s, however, makes Switzerland closer to the conservative-corporatist model. Occupational welfare, typically based on contributory, earnings-related benefits, resembles conservative-corporatist social programs because it is also
geared towards status maintenance.

workforce to profit from the most generous programs of the Swiss welfare state. However, social protection remains strongly connected to the labor market, both in terms of entitlements and of risks covered (Rossi and Sartoris 1995).

The Swiss system of pensions is based on a three-tiered structure. The first tier (AVS) provides universal coverage on a contributory basis. The scheme, introduced in 1948, is financed mainly through contributions paid by employers and employees (4.2% each) and by the self-employed (up to 7.8%). For those who do not have an income from work, contributions are based on their assets, with a minimum rate. While financing is entirely earnings-related, benefits can vary between a floor and a ceiling, the latter being twice as much as the former. The replacement rate for someone with average earnings and a full contribution record is 40 percent of gross earnings. Incomplete contribution records result in lower pensions, but since 1965 a means-tested pension supplement has raised the lowest pensions to a level just above social assistance. The scheme, which is relatively generous, offers a good illustration of the way social protection focuses on Swiss nationals and male employees: until the 1995 reform, married women were generally not entitled to a pension of their own, and entitlement to either insurance or means-tested benefits still requires a longer contribution record for foreigners (ten years) than for Swiss nationals (one year).[4]

The second tier of the Swiss pension system, pre-funded occupational pensions, was first granted tax concessions in 1916. These pensions developed substantially throughout the twentieth century, but coverage remained patchy. In 1970 some 50 percent of employees were covered by an occupational pension, though only 25 percent of women (OFAS 1995: 4). Since 1985, however, occupational pension coverage is compulsory for all employees earning at least twice the amount of the minimum AVS pension (about 35% of average earnings). Coverage is virtually universal among male employees, but only around 80 percent of female employees are covered (OFAS 1995: 10). Finally, the third tier of the pension system, private provision, consists mainly of tax concessions for personal pension schemes. These can be more substantial for people who are not covered by an occupational pension (self-employed, part-time, or temporary workers). In 1994, some one million people had personal pensions (OFAS 1995: 15).

Unemployment insurance was made universal in two stages: in 1977 through a temporary decree, and in 1982 with the adoption of an unemployment insurance law. Previously, unemployment compensation had

---

[4] For nationals of countries that have signed a social security convention with Switzerland, the minimum contribution period is also one year. These are mainly EU Member States.

been provided through a system run by the trade unions, which received federal subsidies. Coverage, however, remained low. In 1975 only some 22 percent of employees were covered by unemployment insurance (Gilliand 1988). The scheme grants benefits equal to 70 percent (80% for workers with dependent children) of gross earnings, with a ceiling set at around 150 percent of average earnings. Financing comes mainly from employer and employee contributions. Until the early 1990s, these were set at below 1 percent each.

The legislative framework for health insurance was introduced in 1910. It came after the government had been defeated in an attempt to set up a plan modeled on German social insurance (Immergut 1992). The 1910 scheme constituted a minimalist approach to public health care. Insurance coverage was (and still is) provided through a network of mutual funds that received state subsidies until 1994. Affiliation was not compulsory until the 1994 health insurance reform, and financing is based on individual, non-earnings-related premiums. The 1994 reform also replaced the subsidies mutual funds were receiving from the state with an income-tested health insurance grant (see Bonoli 1997).

Other areas of Switzerland's welfare state are much less developed than the ones reviewed so far. This is especially true in the case of provision for families and women. For instance, in spite of constitutional amendments adopted in the 1940s giving the federal government a mandate to pass legislation for family benefits and maternity insurance, there is still no national policy on either one of these. Income support, provided through a locally administered social assistance system, is regarded as highly stigmatizing and has a strong social control dimension (Eardley et al. 1996).[5] Social assistance is financed through general taxation, with participation from all three tiers of government: The federal government (16%), cantons (35%), and communes (49%). How expenditure is shared between the canton and the communes can also vary from one canton to another. For a single person, the monthly social assistance benefit amounts to about CHF 2,000, with small cantonal variations.

Because of the small size of its welfare state, Switzerland may seem an outlyer among small European countries, as these have tended to combine economic openness with public forms of domestic compensation (Katzenstein 1984, 1985). That pattern accurately reflects the situation in the Nordic countries and Austria, but in the Swiss case universal social policies, public sector employment, and labor market regulation never attained such a high degree. Compensation for economic openness, how-

---

[5] Since the early 1990s, a number of cantons (those with higher unemployment rates) have introduced new schemes for the long-term unemployed that include a reinsertion component and are perceived as less stigmatizing than traditional social assistance.

ever, took other forms, such as heavy subsidies for agriculture, soft anti-cartel legislation, an immigration policy that provided cheap labor for domestic producers, and an occupational welfare state for the core work-force. These and other forms of economic regulation can also be viewed as compensatory measures, benefiting mainly the domestic sectors of the economy. This aspect of the Swiss model has become increasingly visible as the international environment evolved since the end of the 1980s.

4.1.4. Macroeconomic and Policy Stability in the 1980s

Unlike other European countries, Switzerland saw little change in eco-nomic and social policies during the 1980s. Much of the adjustment undertaken by other European countries in that period, it could be argued, was not needed in Switzerland. Switzerland was already an exem-plar of a flexible labor market, a decentralized system of wage bargaining, a lean (welfare) state, and a low tax economy. More generally, Switzerland had never relied on Keynesian economic policies, so that unlike other European countries it was not forced to abandon a system of macroeco-nomic management. The 1980s can also be described as a period of sta-bility in terms of political confrontation, although opposition between left and right (or trade unions and employers) was slightly reinforced.

Overall employment performance remained positive throughout the decade. As seen above, job losses in the 1970s were absorbed by a reduc-tion in the number of foreign workers allowed into the country and by a withdrawal of women from the labor force. In the second half of the 1980s, thanks to an expansionary cycle, employment increased by 465,000 jobs (OFS, various issues/1996). Much of this increase occurred in the sheltered sector (construction, retail trade, personal, and social services). Between 1979 and 1989 the employment/working age population ratio for the con-struction industry increased from 5.13 percent to 7.4 percent (OECD 1997*b*). More generally, the proportion of employment provided by the sheltered sector (construction, retail trade, health and community ser-vices) increased throughout the 1980s (see Figure 4.3), which helps to account for the persistence of high employment rates throughout the 1980s in spite of losses in the exposed sectors.

The fact that Switzerland was not a member of the European Community might also account for the general climate of political stabil-ity and for the absence of policy changes in the 1980s. Until the end of the 1980s, European integration was not an issue in Swiss politics, and noth-ing was done to prepare for joining the EC. Only in 1989 did the govern-ment introduce a systematic check on the 'Euro-compatibility' of new legislation. Furthermore, all three levels of government achieved budget surpluses for most of the 1980s. As a result there were no external and financial pressures to reform social and economic policies.

At the beginning of the 1990s, however, the economic situation was to change dramatically: there was a sharp increase in the unemployment rate (Figure 4.1), and a new series of issues emerged surrounding European integration and the GATT's Uruguay Round. Within a very short period of time during the 1990s, several economic and social policy reforms were adopted, and the antagonism between left and right increased. Because of the country's generally favorable macroeconomic performance, its political isolation, and its comparatively large sheltered sector, Switzerland was able to delay the changes in social and economic policy during the 1980s. By the early 1990s, however, the combined effect of recession, economic internationalization, and European integration's heightened pace put new pressures on the country. These are reviewed in the next section.

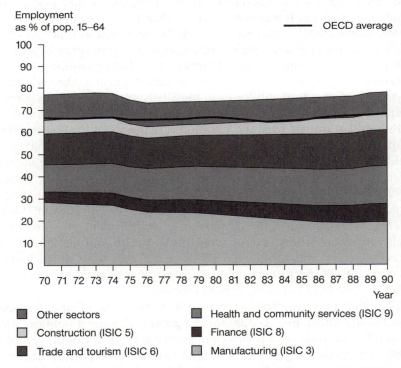

Figure 4.3 Sectoral composition of employment in Switzerland, 1970–1990
Source: OECD, *Statistical Compendium: Labour Force Statistics* (Paris: OECD, 1997).

4.2. Challenges to the Postwar Model

The beginning of the 1990s constituted a turning point for the stability of the Swiss politico-economic model. The two equilibria on which it rested, the balance between capital and labor and the compromise between export-oriented business and domestic producers, came under increased pressure. While criticism against various aspects of the model had been expressed before, the attack started to become stronger and more sustained in the early 1990s. Moreover, there was now a general perception in the country, promoted by the media and by various political and economic elites, that radical change was needed if the country was to maintain the high levels of prosperity it knew in the past. Three factors were crucial for this shift: first, the recession and sharp increase in unemployment; second, the issues surrounding the Uruguay Round and closer ties with the EU, which, despite Switzerland's failed attempt to join the EEA (the European Economic Area), stimulated major political debates and reforms; and third, pressures from some sections of the business community for a change in the orientation of social and economic policies. At the same time, however, it should be noted that, by international standards, Switzerland remained much less affected by social and economic problems than other European countries: its unemployment rate remained among the lowest in Europe, and developments like large-scale social exclusion remained virtually unknown.

Next we look at recent international and domestic economic developments and at the key challenges facing the Swiss model: lower employment, growing budget deficits, changing preferences among some sections of the business community, and the relationship with the European Union.

4.2.1. *International and Domestic Economic Trends*

Small countries like Switzerland can be expected to be comparatively less vulnerable to economic internationalization, as they have been used to high levels of exposure to international trade and competition, at least in product markets. In fact, Switzerland's export-oriented sector did rather well during the 1990s. The country's four big manufacturing industries, whose exports increased 10 percent between 1990 and 1996 (Table 4.1), remained competitive throughout the 1990s, as did financial services and the insurance business. The current account balance remained largely positive throughout the decade. In 1992, moreover, for the first time since the 1970s, the trade balance turned positive. This is even more significant when one considers that the Swiss franc appreciated against the other major currencies by 15 percent between 1991 and 1995 (OECD, various issues/1997: 30). The sharp appreciation of the Swiss franc is mainly due to the restrictive monetary policy pursued by the SNB following the introduction of the VAT, which the SNB feared would increase inflation, and to capital inflows from international investors worried about the instability of other European currencies.

Despite the Swiss franc's sharp appreciation, which damaged cost and price competitiveness by boosting relative unit labor costs about 20 percent (measured in common currency), Swiss exports actually increased during this period. The Swiss export industry's reliance on highly specialized market niches rather than price competition also helps account for this development. But this performance was only possible because of restructuring and rationalization in the major export sectors, and because profit margins in some companies decreased (Strahm 1997: 160 ff.). The 1990s were also characterized by spectacular mergers (Ciba and Sandoz into Novartis, UBS and SBS, various alliances between insurance companies and banks, etc.). Restructuring has often resulted in large-scale workforce reductions, including compulsory redundancies, which have contributed to the overall decline in employment (Table 4.3).

Arguably, restructuring was not only a response to increased competition in product markets; in fact, it might have been an answer to increased competition in the capital market. For, typically, returns on invested capital among Swiss firms have been lower than in the USA, and fears of hostile takeovers of some 'national champions' (like the big banks) were often mentioned as reasons for restructuring. The sharp increase in market capitalization since the beginning of the 1990s (from 69% of GDP in 1990 to 136% in 1996, OECD 1998) may thus also explain the process of restructuring. A related development is the increasing role of institutional investors (pension funds, insurance companies, investment funds, and banks), which was highlighted by the aggressive strategy of Martin Ebner's investment bank, BK Vision. More powerful institutional investors can be expected to play a greater role in the future, thereby putting greater pressure on managers to maximize the rate of return to capital (Anderson and Hertig 1992; Birchler 1995).

During the same period, export-oriented businesses in Switzerland invested heavily abroad, increasing employment by some 470,000 jobs (Table 4.2). These outcomes demonstrate significant changes in the strategies of multinational companies, who have increasingly relied on foreign locations for global outsourcing and proximity to markets. Between 1990 and 1996 the stock of foreign direct investment owned by Swiss companies more than doubled.

The restructuring of the export-oriented sector has also had an impact on the more sheltered sectors, which had enjoyed a relatively high degree of protection until the 1990s (thanks to the various forms of 'selective' protectionism discussed above). International firms, which rely on domestic producers for subcontracting, have put increasing pressure on them to reduce costs. The new pressure tactics have included favoring stronger competition and greater import penetration. Because of the Swiss franc's strength, imports are sometimes favored over local subcontracting (OECD 1997a). Demands for more competition in the domestic market were taken up by government. Deregulating and liberalizing the domestic sectors became key elements in the program to 'restart' the economy (see below).

The 1990s also saw a reversal in the big banks' role in the economy. Generous lending conditions in the 1980s favored a boom in some sectors, especially in the construction industry. But, with property prices declining since 1991 and numerous companies going bankrupt in this sector, large banks introduced more restrictive lending practices. Major deficits in this area of lending are increasingly forcing the big banks to withdraw from domestic markets and center their activities on more profitable sectors, like private and investment banking (OFDE 1998).

4.2.2. Employment

The structure of employment in Switzerland has been characterized by comparatively high employment/population ratios (Figure 4.1). To some extent, this is due to the presence of a comparatively large group of foreign workers, who participate in the labor force at rates higher than Swiss nationals and so help push up the employment/population ratio. Some groups of foreign workers (seasonal workers and cross-border commuters) have employment rates of 100 percent. Levels of employment were high throughout the postwar period, with significant declines on only two occasions: the mid-1970s and the early 1990s.

In contrast to the 1970s, the decline in the absolute number of employed persons provoked by the 1990s recession was accompanied by an increase in the unemployment rate. This time women did not withdraw from the labor market as female employment stagnated between 1990 and 1996. Similarly, the number of foreign workers decreased by around 30,000, a smaller decline than in the 1970s but not enough to compensate for the overall loss of male jobs. The labor market buffer traditionally provided by foreigners and women seems to have stopped working since the 1990s. This explains the emergence of unemployment in a country that had

Table 4.1 *Imports and exports, 1980–1996 (million CHF)*

	1980	1985	1990	1991	1992	1993	1994	1995	1996
Imports	60,859	74,756	96,611	95,032	92,330	89,830	92,608	94,483	96,664
Exports	49,608	66,624	88,257	87,947	92,142	93,289	95,827	96,236	98,589
Trade deficit or surplus	−11,251	−8,126	−8,354	−7,085	−0,189	3,459	3,219	1,753	1,925

Source: Office Fédéral de la Statistique, *Statistiques du commerce exterieur* (Berne: OFS, various issues).

Table 4.2 *Swiss foreign direct investment (stock) by region and employed persons, 1990–1996*

	1990	1991	1992	1993	1994	1995	1996
Swiss foreign direct investment (stock) by region (million CHF)							
EU	40,877	46,165	51,401	61,133	66,589	78,524	92,245
Other European countries	5,003	6,685	6,088	6,875	7,834	3,174	4,309
North America	19,298	23,534	23,163	30,488	36,967	43,936	52,646
Other industrialized countries	4,517	5,815	6,513	6,918	7,190	7,115	9,089
Emerging countries	5,155	6,312	7,562	10,560	12,188	12,477	14,987
Developing countries	10,304	13,605	12,750	19,506	16,890	19,310	21,611
TOTAL	85,154	102,116	107,477	135,479	147,656	164,536	194,887
Employed persons, thousands (end of year)							
EU	447,572	481,744	499,829	644,848	619,316	708,946	696,039
Other European countries	116,761	116,425	117,193	142,599	158,194	82,690	88,504
North America	183,636	210,041	209,389	241,743	257,472	245,891	238,016
Other industrialized countries	60,723	63,904	60,187	67,145	76,191	81,799	81,593
Emerging countries	97,721	104,247	105,756	150,813	182,286	197,204	205,514
Developing countries	64,773	71,753	86,236	89,572	102,188	120,021	142,170
TOTAL	971,186	1,048,114	1,078,590	1,336,720	1,395,647	1,436,551	1,451,836

previously managed to sustain full employment throughout the postwar years (Schmidt 1995).

Two major factors explain the abandonment of the buffer function played by women and foreign workers. (1) Where women are concerned, Switzerland seems to be abandoning the 'strong male breadwinner' model. A woman's job is no longer seen as an accessory occupation, and a massive withdrawal of women from the labor force now seems rather unlikely (the availability of unemployment benefits has also played a role). (2) Where foreign workers are concerned, the less secure types of work permits (seasonal, annual, and for cross-border commuters) are now used less (proportionally) than was the case during the 1970s and early 1980s (see Figure 4.2). To a large extent, this different frequency of usage is due to the conversion of temporary work permits into permanent residence permits after a number of years.

The 1990s also witnessed a shift in the relative importance of different types of work, notably a decline in full-time dependent employment. Part-time employment increased from 25 percent to 28 percent of total employment between 1991 and 1997, and during the same period the proportion of self-employed rose from 15 percent to 18 percent of the working population (OFS 1997).

Altogether, around 95,000 jobs (or 2.4% of total employment) were lost between 1991 and 1996 (OFS, various issues/1998:149). However, the drop in employment did not affect each economic sector the same way. The biggest job losses were experienced in the low-skill sheltered sector. Between 1991 and 1996, the construction industry lost around 39,000 jobs, wholesale and retail trade 39,000, and tourism 10,000. These job losses were not directly related to economic internationalization, but they were linked to the recession and, in the case of construction, to over-capacity in that industry (OFS, various issues/1998:141).

However, substantial job losses also occurred in the high-skill exposed sector, largely as a result of industrial restructuring. Over the same period, the machine industry (Switzerland's biggest export sector) lost around 28,000 jobs, the chemical industry 13,000, and the precision instruments industry 11,000, even though employment remained stable in the watch-making industry. Job losses were also incurred in the low-skill exposed sector (textile industry 7,000 and food industry 5,000).

Over the same period (1991–96) employment expanded mainly in the high-skill sheltered sector. Employment in health care and social services increased by 46,000 jobs, in telecommunications by 21,000, in auxiliary transport services (such as travel agencies) by 17,000, and in education by 7,000. In the banking and insurance sector, 6,000 jobs were lost, but over the same period Swiss banks sharply increased their employment abroad

(5,000). Banks no longer expand employment opportunities to compensate for job losses in industry, as used to be the case. In most other areas of economic activity, employment either stagnated or experienced relatively smaller changes (see Table 4.3).

The changes in the structure of employment discussed here constitute a challenge to the postwar Swiss model. For the first time since World War II, the country has fallen short of full employment. As will be seen below, this prompted at least two other developments that put pressure on the postwar settlement: first, unemployment has helped generate budget deficits, mainly because of increased expenditure on unemployment compensation, coupled with lower tax revenues. Second, the emergence of unemployment has tended to shatter the faith that various social groups had placed in the postwar model. Unemployment has also prompted some actors to seek a redefinition of the traditional model's defining equilibria.

From a comparative point of view, however, the job performance of the Swiss economy remains impressive. In 1996, the total employment/population ratio (79.8%) is still well above the OECD average (66.5%). Above OECD average levels of employment are found in particular in manufacturing (+3.4 percentage points), finance and real estate (+2.5), community and social services (+2.1), trade and tourist industry (+1.6), and construction (+1.3). Some of these outcomes can be explained by the vocation of the economy, which has always had a strong financial sector serving also foreign customers, or by the (expensive) system of private financing for health care. What is particularly striking, however, is the fact that Switzerland seems to be able to combine German levels of employment in manufacturing (17.3% for Germany and 16.3% for Switzerland), with American employment rates in the low-skill service sector (15.2% in Switzerland and 16.1% in the USA) (data for 1995, OECD 1997*b*). The segmentation in the labor market discussed above between a large manufacturing sector with a strong collective bargaining tradition and the more flexible service sector might help to account for this outcome, but it is notable that this is combined with moderate levels of earnings dispersion, much closer to the continental European average than to English-speaking economies.

4.2.3. Budget Deficits

Traditionally, the Swiss approach to public spending has been characterized by fiscal prudence. The combined budgets for all three levels of government—federal government, cantons, and communes—typically produced surpluses throughout the 1980s (see Figure 4.3). Things started to change with the recession of the 1990s. Since 1991 government outlays

Table 4.3 *Employment by sector, 1991–1996 (thousands)*

	1991	1992	1993	1994	1995	1996
Agriculture	166	162	165	157	163	175
Mining and quarrying	6	6	6	6	6	6
Manufacturing	825	771	744	736	747	728
Water, electricity	25	25	25	25	26	25
Construction	352	337	320	327	331	313
Trade and tourism	917	912	894	878	865	868
Transport, communications	249	248	255	250	265	269
Finance, real estate	513	509	518	524	522	531
Personal and social services	699	710	721	736	734	747
Public administration	145	146	146	146	142	143
TOTAL	3,898	3,827	3,793	3,785	3,802	3,803

Source: Recalculation of data from: Office Fédéral de la Statistique, *Statistique de la population active occupée* (Berne: OFS, various issues).

have exceeded receipts, and the resulting budget deficit peaked at around 3 percent of GDP in 1993–94. The general government budget deficit is mainly due to imbalances at the federal (48%) and cantonal (31%) levels, though there are substantial differences among cantons (OFS, various issues/1998).

Government budget deficits emerged just as the unemployment rate started climbing, in the early 1990s. In fact, much of the increase in the federal government budget deficit comes from the unemployment insurance fund deficit, which is compensated by federal (and cantonal) government(s) payments. The unemployment insurance fund went from producing a slight surplus in the late 1980s to making increasingly large deficits in the first half of the 1990s. The increase in the rate of unemployment accounts for the steep rise in expenditure and for the stagnation of receipts (Table 4.4). The deficit peaked in 1992, when it reached CHF 2.7 bn, or 0.8 percent of GDP. The deficit was dramatically reduced in 1995, thanks to an increase in the contribution rates for employer and employees, but started rising again as new active labor market policies (financed out of unemployment funds) were introduced in 1996 and 1997.

The increase in unemployment has had an impact on other areas of social expenditure, such as social assistance and disability benefits. Expenditure on social assistance increased sharply, from 0.6 percent of GDP in 1990 to 1.2 percent of GDP in 1996 (OFS, various issues/1998). A similar trend affected expenditure on disability benefits, as documented in Table 4.5, although this may be due to factors other than unemployment, since the number of beneficiaries had already started to increase before the rise in unemployment. Finally, in 1996, the basic pension scheme fund (AVS) also started to incur a slight deficit (CHF 29 m). This development, mainly due to population aging, was anticipated but expected to take place a few years later. The deficit showed up in 1996 mainly because unemployment and the underlying recession lowered revenues for the AVS scheme.

Swiss government budget deficits remain acceptable by international standards. Switzerland would have qualified for EMU according to the Maastricht Treaty criteria. Higher deficits, however, are generally regarded as unacceptable by the policymaking community. Since the early 1990s a number of plans to regain financial equilibrium have been adopted, but with only limited success. The debate on how to restore a balanced budget is currently high on the agenda, both at the federal level and in a number of cantons. The challenge facing policymakers is to balance budgets without abandoning current low rates of taxation, and do so in a way that can generate enough consensus to get a balanced budget proposal past the various veto points that characterize the Swiss political system.

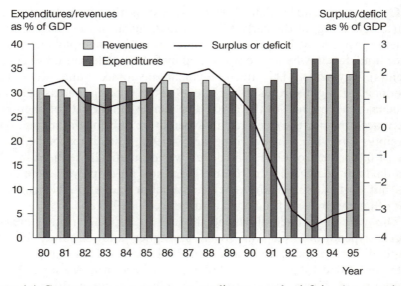

Figure 4.4 Government revenues, expenditures and deficit (or surplus), 1980–1995

Source: OECD, *Revenue Statistics* (Paris: OECD, various issues).

Table 4.4 *Receipts, outlays, and balance of the unemployment insurance fund, 1988–1997 (million CHF)*

	1988	1989	1990	1991	1992	1993	1994	1995	1996	1997
Receipts	907	976	787	866	805	3,556	3,680	5,488	5,955	5,745
Outlays	551	442	503	1,340	3,462	5,986	5,921	5,240	6,124	8,028
Balance	356	534	283	−474	−2,657	−2,430	−2,241	247	−168	−2,283

Source: Office Fédéral des Assurances Sociales, *Sécurité sociale* (Berne: OFS, various issues).

Table 4.5 *Beneficiaries (thousands), receipts, outlays, and balance of the disability insurance fund, 1988–1996 (million CHF)*

	1990	1991	1992	1993	1994	1995	1996
Beneficiaries	142	147	151	157	165	171	179
Receipts	4,412	4,841	5,262	5,567	5,771	6,483	6,886
Outlays	4,133	4,619	5,251	5,987	6,396	6,826	7,313
Balance	278	223	11	−420	−625	−343	−427

Source: Office Fédéral des Assurances Sociales, *Sécurité sociale* (Berne: OFS, various issues).

4.2.4. Employers' Changing Political Preferences

The early 1990s saw also a shift in the political orientation of the business community, especially its export-oriented sector. The change of attitude is well documented by a series of publications from the first half of the 1990s calling for radical change in social and economic policy. The first such document was a pamphlet published by an informal group of industrialists and representatives of the financial sector, who demanded the adoption of a 'more liberal order' (Leutwiler and Schmidheiny 1991). The business leaders claimed that, in order to preserve the competitiveness of the Swiss economy, some radical changes were needed, such as liberalizing domestic markets, privatizing the major public utilities, and reducing fiscal pressures. This publication became known as the first 'White Paper'. A second followed in 1995.

This initiative was unprecedented because it did not originate with one of the traditional business associations, but was instead the product of an informal group of fifteen to twenty representatives of Switzerland's largest companies along with several economists.[6] These leaders of the business community no longer felt adequately represented by the official business associations, which in their view were too inclined to negotiate and make

---

[6] On the 'neo-liberal' coalition, composed of leaders of the business community and economists, see Burkhalter, Petersen and Pini 1999. For publications by economists, see Borner, Brunetti, and Straubharr 1990 and Hauser 1993.

compromises with other political actors. Also novel was the heavy criticism expressed against several economic policies once widely accepted, such as agricultural policy, foreign workers policy, and competition policy, all of which benefited specific sectors while imposing costs on the national economy as a whole. Increasingly, export-oriented business argued, Switzerland's competitiveness was endangered by regulations and non-competitive arrangements making Swiss products and services too expensive. In a rapidly internationalizing economy, the cost of maintaining these arrangements was becoming unbearable.

After the publication of the first 'White Paper,' the Federal Council appointed a commission presided over by David de Pury, a former high-ranking civil servant then working as co-managing director of ABB, and co-author of the second 'White Paper'. The Commission's report (de Pury 1992) argued for the adoption of such measures as allowing female workers to work at night, prohibiting cartels, introducing a VAT to replace part of the federal direct tax, reducing the corporate income tax, and privatizing telecommunications and the postal service.

The Central Union of Employers Associations (UCAPS) called for a 'moratorium' on social policy. They argued that the welfare state had reached a point where further expansion would endanger the country's economic competitiveness. Proposals for social policy reform were also part of the second 'White Paper' (de Pury, Hauser, and Schmid 1995). These included introducing tighter targeting in social programs, privatizing unemployment insurance, and removing employers' obligation to provide occupational pensions for their employees. Proposals like these elicited numerous critical reactions from the left and from trade unions, but also from the media.

Thus, the 1990s signaled a change of attitude among some sections of the business community, particularly those better integrated into international markets. These sectors were expressing growing dissatisfaction with the Swiss model's two equilibria, to which (ironically) they had contributed since helping to establish the political foundations of the postwar economy. The compromise between export industries and domestic producers, based on the combination of economic openness and tolerance for non-competitive arrangements, was now increasingly seen as a burden by the export-oriented business. Similarly, the welfare state and labor market regulations, cornerstones of the compromise between capital and labor, came under attack.

4.2.5. The Relationship with the EU

In its 1988 report on European integration, the Federal Council did not seem particularly enthusiastic about joining the EC, largely because of concerns about the peculiarities of Switzerland's political system (neutrality, direct democracy, and federalism). It has been argued, however, that the major arguments against becoming an EC member were really economic: the tough impact on domestic-oriented producers, the already high penetration of export-oriented sectors in European markets, and (in case of membership) Swiss exporters' dependence on European trade policy (Freiburghaus 1989).

Things changed only at the beginning of the 1990s with the failed attempt to join the European Economic Area (EEA) and the federal government's articulation of full EU membership as its medium-term objective (Sciarini 1992). In 1992 the EEA Treaty was rejected by a slim majority of voters (though by a higher proportion of cantons). As a result, plans for full membership were shelved, and the decision was made to negotiate an association agreement. Negotiations were completed late in 1998. Throughout this period of wavering European aspirations, representatives of business, politicians, and commentators often complained that Switzerland was losing out on opportunities because of its self-imposed isolation. In some cases, the inability of federal authorities to make progress towards European integration prompted intense cross-border cooperation at the regional level (Ratti and Reichman 1993).

Full membership remains the long-term objective of the federal government, but direct democracy is likely to constitute a serious obstacle to any form of integration, including an association agreement (Riklin 1995). Opinion polls generally show narrow majorities in favor of membership, but there has not been a substantial swing in public opinion since the EEA Treaty was rejected in 1992. What is more, for a referendum on membership in any supranational organization to succeed, two majorities—voters and cantons—are required. Because a large number of small cantons represent rural Switzerland, which tends to oppose European integration, full membership might prove an extremely difficult target.

The European Union, however, is already exerting a strong influence on domestic policy, as a euro-compatibility check has been introduced for every new piece of legislation. In many areas, too, national regulations are being adapted to comply with European Union directives. In addition, many of the policies reviewed below (such as liberalizing the telecom market) can also be seen as moves toward preparing for EU membership, even though the government originally presented them as part of its program for restarting the economy. The adoption of a single EU currency in 1999 is also expected to have a substantial impact on the Swiss economy. The National Bank has even considered pegging the Swiss franc to the euro if currency fluctuations should threaten to undermine economic stability.

Isolation constitutes a disadvantage for the national economy, yet it does not seem to offer the country countervailing advantages such as protection against external influences on domestic policy. Non-EU membership means that Swiss producers do not have automatic access to the single market, which is a significant obstacle to a successful export strategy. The sharp increase in foreign direct investment to EU countries, particularly after the EEA Treaty was rejected, is an indication of the difficulty Swiss companies have experienced exporting to the single market (see Table 4.2). On the other hand, Switzerland is preparing for eventual membership by adapting its legislation to European norms (liberalizing public utilities, introducing a VAT, abolishing certain protectionist measures). In sum, Switzerland is in the awkward position of being subjected to many of the pressures affecting EU members without having the opportunity to profit fully from the single market.

4.3. Policy Responses

Where policymaking was concerned, the 1990s stood in sharp contrast to previous decades, which were characterized by slow, incremental, and generally limited policy change. The first half of the 1990s saw the introduction of some substantive reforms in fiscal and competition policy. The decade also witnessed some changes that were moderate (though notable by Swiss standards) in social and employment policy. Four areas have been particularly affected by policy change: labor market regulations, social policies, fiscal policy, the liberalization of the internal market and the major public monopolies.

4.3.1. Labor Market Regulation and Industrial Relations

In the early 1990s, in spite of a traditionally low level of regulation for Switzerland's labor market and a decentralized wage bargaining system, the country's main employers' associations began questioning the scope of employee protection, both with regard to federal labor legislation and collective agreements.

The centerpiece of labor legislation is the federal labor law, introduced in 1964. It provides a general framework of regulation with provisions for health and safety, maximum working hours, and special protection for women and young workers. In 1993 the federal labor commission, a consultative body composed of trade unionists, employers' representatives, and civil servants, prepared the first draft of a major reform of the labor law. After further consultation the proposal was accepted without significant changes by the government and presented to parliament. The labor commission seemed to have reached a compromise on the question of night work by female workers: this kind of work was to be authorized, but compensated by additional time off from work. At the same time, however, employers' associations were complaining that the burden of compensation was too heavy; they argued that a more genuine deregulatory reform was needed to improve the Swiss economy's competitiveness. Thus, during the parliamentary vote, a small right-wing majority supported by the employers' associations managed to remove the compensation measures from the government's proposal and introduce new measures of their own, such as an increase in authorized overtime hours and the option of working six Sundays per year in the retail sector. At this point, the trade unions, with the support of the Social Democratic Party, decided to call a referendum against the law as adopted by parliament. In December 1996, after a confrontational referendum campaign, voters rejected the bill by a huge majority (67%). Following this defeat, the government quickly relaunched a new reform process, this time leaving out the controversial deregulatory measures inserted by the parliamentary majority. A proposal much closer to what had been consensually decided by the federal labor commission in the early 1990s was finally adopted in November 1998.

Legislation, however, was never the chief instrument of labor market regulation in Switzerland. The most important rules have always been stipulated in collective agreements at the sectoral level, and that is where major changes occurred during the 1990s (see Fluder 1998; OECD 1996a; and Rieger 1994). In general, that decade was characterized by greater reluctance on the part of employers' associations to make substantial concessions to the trade unions. This unwillingness was also encouraged by some companies' defection from their employers' association, so as not to be constrained by collective agreements. Even though the number of industrial conflicts did not increase significantly, industrial relations are now characterized by stronger tensions, and negotiating each new collective agreement now tends to take longer than it used to. Despite the weak constraints that the 'institutional configuration' of labor market regulations imposed upon collective bargaining, the employers' associations deliberately picked a strategy aimed at decentralizing the norms contained in sectoral collective agreements to the firm level. The employers thereby hoped to facilitate flexibility and increase individual firms' room for maneuver. They suggested excluding bread-and-butter issues (wages, working time, and holidays) from collective agreements and transferring them to firm-level. Shifting wage bargaining to the firm level has been just one of collective bargaining's main trends in recent years. Other tendencies have been the recourse to individual, performance-based wage increases and increased flexibility in working time.

In the machine industry, where wages were always negotiated within individual firms and never at the sectoral level, both parties accepted a collective agreement in 1993 that introduced a 'crisis' clause allowing individual companies experiencing economic hardship to cancel the 'thirteenth month' salary and to increase working time without increasing wages rates. The latest example is the new collective agreement for the machine industry, signed in June 1998: in order to maximize the use of their machinery in periods of high demand, employers introduced greater flexibility by adopting working time limits on a one-year basis. Initially, the main trade union (FTMH) opposed this measure unless it was combined with an overall reduction of working time. Since the employers' association refused to make concessions, the FTMH finally accepted the new collective agreement. Similar developments occurred in the chemical and banking sectors. Wage bargaining, which had traditionally taken place at the sectoral level, was transferred to the firm level, with the approval of the banking employees' association but against strong opposition from the trade unions in the chemical sector (Sigrist 1996; Schaad 1997).

In a majority of cases, wage indexation is no longer fixed in the collective agreement but has to be negotiated every year. About 55 percent of workers covered by a collective agreement are subject to this renegotiation clause, and only 2 percent benefit from automatic indexation (Revaz 1993). During the 1990s wage increases were slow and simply kept up with inflation. Soskice (1990) has underlined how—despite a decentralized system of wage bargaining that should not be facilitating wage restraint according to models like that of Calmfors and Driffill (1988)—Swiss employers are still strong enough to coordinate and restrain wage increases.

In spite of relatively flexible labor market regulations and decentralized industrial relations—and in contrast to the trend in Anglo-Saxon countries—the recent evolution of earnings inequality in Switzerland (as measured by the difference between the first and ninth, or between the first and fifth, deciles) remained stable and very close to the OECD average. Relatively generous unemployment benefits and cantonal social assistance help account for this trend (see OECD 1996a: 91 ff.).

The employers' offensive on labor market regulation did not face strong opposition at the sectoral level, where we can observe a progressive erosion of the regulations contained in the major collective agreements. These changes occurred almost without open conflicts between employers and trade unions. In the most controversial cases, unions were generally the ones who backed down. On the other hand, the trade unions were much more successful in challenging deregulation at the polls, most notably by winning the referendum against the 1996 labor law. In the 1990s referendums seem to have been the unions' and the left's most effective weapon against labor market deregulation and, as we will see next, against retrenchment in social welfare policy.

4.3.2. Social Policies

Social policymaking in the early 1990s was characterized by a change in the direction of policy. Until the late 1980s, welfare reform generally meant expanding social programs' coverage (or their generosity). To some extent, the Swiss welfare state was catching up with its European counterparts in areas where it was still underdeveloped. It was in the 1980s that occupational pension coverage and unemployment insurance were made universal. Since the early 1990s, by contrast, the main theme of social policy reform has become retrenchment and the attempt to contain growth in public expenditure.

Given how a fragmented political system like Switzerland's requires broad agreement to pass legislation, one may expect welfare retrenchment there to be particularly difficult. Those who stand to lose out from welfare reform have numerous opportunities to challenge the government and prevent legislation they regard as unsatisfactory. In fact, as some of the few reforms that were successfully adopted recently have shown, Swiss policymakers trying to overcome the obstacle posed by institutional power fragmentation (especially the referendum) had to develop a two-pronged strategy for every measure of reform: within each single piece of legislation, reformers had to combine retrenchment with expansion. This combination was a key feature of two reforms adopted in the 1990s: the 1995 pension reform and the 1995 unemployment insurance reform.

The 1995 pension reform illustrates the shift in the direction of social policymaking since the early 1990s. Work on this reform started in 1979, with the intention of introducing gender equality into the basic pension scheme. Under the legislation in force at the time, pensions for married couples were generally calculated on the basis of the husband's contribution record only. Moreover, the scheme made no provision for contribution credits for informal carers (generally women), a common practice in most European countries.

The bill reached parliament in the early 1990s, and by then the political climate had changed. A series of gender equality measures were adopted, as planned, but it was also decided to raise the retirement age for women from 62 to 64 (for men, the retirement age is 65). This last-minute amendment on retirement was imposed by the right-of-center parliamentary majority, against the Social Democrats and against government (Bonoli 2000).

The pension reform was attacked by the trade unions, who collected the 50,000 signatures needed to have a referendum on the pension bill. Referendums, however, decide between adoption and rejection of a bill; voters cannot modify the law's content. Therefore the referendum called by the trade unions challenged not only the new retirement age, which organized labor opposed, but also the provisions for gender equality, which had long been advocated by trade unions and the left. For the left, this situation constituted a powerful dilemma. The decision on whether or not to support the referendum against the pension bill depended on what was seen as more important, the positive value of gender equality or the negative extension of women's retirement age. The result was that the Social Democrats declined to join the unions in supporting the referendum against the pension bill, thereby reducing their chances of defeating it at the polls. In fact, the bill survived the referendum obstacle and it is now law. The division within the left obviously played an important role in making its adoption possible. To a large extent, the way the bill was designed encouraged the division, as it combined elements of retrenchment with measures that were key priorities for the left.

A similar strategy made it possible to pass the 1995 unemployment insurance reform, adopted in response to a sharp increase in unemployment insurance outlays (see Table 4.4). The reform was drafted by a joint group of employers' representatives and trade unions and passed by parliament without major changes. Like the 1995 pension reform, the new unemployment insurance law included measures going in two diverging directions. On the one hand, contribution rates were increased and more funds were made available for active labor market programs, such as vocational training and job creation schemes. On the other hand, benefits were cut from 80 percent to 70 percent of salary, and the entitlement period was limited to two years, whereas previous legislation made it possible to draw benefits for a virtually indefinite period of time, since it was also possible to regain entitlement by participating in labor market programs.

The 1995 unemployment insurance reform was adopted by parliament and not later challenged by referendum. The left cared mainly about introducing the new labor market programs, whereas the right was satisfied with the two-year limit imposed on benefits. The 1995 unemployment insurance reform can thus be regarded as a legislative package that slipped a substantial element of retrenchment past the hurdles of the legislative process.

In 1997, because of a persistent deficit in the unemployment insurance fund, the government proposed an emergency decree to reduce benefit payments for the unemployed (a 1% or 3% cut, depending on the amount of the benefit and family obligations). After the right-wing majority in parliament adopted this proposal, a referendum was called by an association of unemployed people, later joined by the trade unions and Social Democrats. After a confrontational campaign, and to the surprise of many observers, the bill was rejected by a slim majority (50.8%) in September 1997. Unlike the 1995 unemployment insurance reform, the 1997 decree did not contain improvements in provisions or any measures capable of attracting support from labor and the left.

4.3.3. Fiscal and Financial Policies

Because of the Swiss state's federal structure, fiscal policy is made by three different tiers of government. Here we focus on the federal level only. However, one should bear in mind that the regional and local levels account for two-thirds of total public revenues and expenditures (excluding social expenditure). At the federal level, the main revenues come from custom duties, taxes on consumption (turnover tax, or TT, until 1996, when the TT was replaced by the VAT), the federal direct tax (FDT) on personal income and on corporate profits and capital, the withholding tax,[7] stamp duties, and the military tax. At the cantonal level, most taxation is on personal income and net wealth, on business profits and capital. Municipal taxes are usually levied in the form of tax supplements on cantonal direct taxes (for an overview, see Dafflon 1977 and OECD, various issues/1990). Levels of taxation are among the lowest in OECD countries (see Figure 4.5).

While the fiscal system remained largely untouched before the 1990s, that decade saw some important changes: the introduction of VAT, a reduction in stamp duties, a reform of business taxation, and various measures to contain expenditure. Political responses in this field have been strongly affected by two important factors: (1) the deterioration of public finance at all three levels of the state (Figure 4.4) and (2) demands to improve the country's economic attractiveness and maintain Switzerland's advantage over its European neighbors in the competition for mobile taxes resources. Strong pressure came from the business community to reduce levels of taxation in general and on some specific taxes (FDT, stamp duty, business taxation), as well as to introduce a VAT (see Guex 1998).

---

[7] The withholding tax (*impôt anticipé*) is a tax levied at source at a flat rate of 35% on the income of personal capital assets (interest, rent, dividends). This tax can be refunded when the taxpayer declares the relevant earnings in the framework of cantonal income and property taxes.

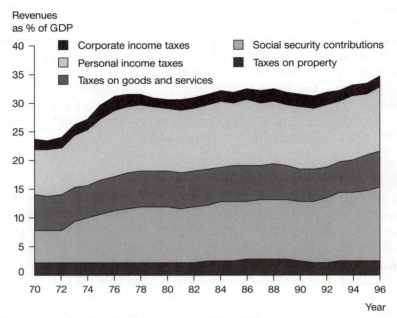

Figure 4.5 Switzerland's tax structure, 1970–1996
Source: OECD, *Revenue Statistics* (Paris: OECD, various issues).

Attempts to introduce a VAT were made (unsuccessfully) as early as the 1970s, when voters turned down the government's plans on two occasions (1977 and 1979). The 1990s saw a renewed interest in tax reform, partly because legislation governing the two main federal taxes at the time (TT and FDT) were temporary fiscal instruments that expired in 1994. Introducing a VAT was among the government's top priorities, and so two further attempts to replace the old turnover tax were made, in 1991 and in 1993, of which the latter succeeded.

The 1991 attempt to introduce VAT was part of a larger package of fiscal reforms in two stages. (1) First, the VAT was to replace the existing turnover tax (TT). In fact, going back to the mid-1970s, the TT had increasingly come to be seen as an inadequate form of taxation. The TT was a single-stage tax on final sales, but producers had to pay the TT on investment goods and equipment, which meant that final products were charged at a higher rate than the nominal TT rate ('hidden tax' or *taxe occulte*). With the introduction of VAT, this 'hidden tax' would have disappeared thanks to reimbursement for previous taxes. An additional problem was exemption of many services from the TT, which caused competition distortions. With the VAT, the tax base would have been enlarged to include the service sector. (2) A second measure, strongly advocated by the banking sector as a response to financial market deregulation, was the reduction of stamp duties affecting financial and capital transactions. These two measures benefited the business community exclusively. To obtain the support of the left, some compensatory measures were introduced: (*a*) the FDT (Switzerland's most progressive tax) was to be definitively inscribed in the Constitution; (*b*) legislation was to make it possible to raise the rate of the VAT from 6.5 percent to 7.5 percent, in order to finance the AVS pension scheme; and (*c*) there was a partial reform of business taxation.

On the whole, this 'fiscal package' was expected to increase government revenues by CHF 200 m. In contrast to what happened in the 1970s, this time the left favored the VAT, because of the compensatory measures attached to the reform. The business community was divided. The peak associations representing business (USCI and USAM) were against the proposal because they regarded the concessions made to the left as too important. By contrast, the Swiss Bankers Association and some associations representing export-oriented sector supported the reform. From their perspective, introducing VAT and reducing stamp duties was an urgent matter. In June 1991, however, 54 percent of voters rejected the 'fiscal package'. After this initial rejection, a new proposal to introduce VAT was adopted by parliament in June 1993. This second attempt, which contained only minor compensations for the left, was accepted by a majority of voters in November 1993.

After the first fiscal package was rejected, Parliament (under pressure from the business community) decided to reduce the stamp duties on new shares issues from 3 percent to 2 percent. But the left decided to call a referendum against this new package, since it did not include any measure compensating for the loss of revenue. However, the reduction of stamp duties (representing a loss of revenues of about CHF 500 m to the federal government) was accepted by a large majority of voters in 1992.

Even though rates of corporate taxation are among the lowest in OECD countries,[8] a partial reform of business taxation (Guex 1998: 242 ff.) was introduced in 1997 to improve the competitiveness of Swiss companies by lightening their tax bill (about CHF 320 m in reduced revenues). This reform consisted of five measures: (1) the replacement of progressive taxation (FDT) on business profits by a flat-rate tax of 8.5 percent; (2) a further reduction of the stamp duties on new shares issues from 2 percent to

---

[8] 2% of GDP against an average of 2.7% of GDP of OECD countries. This represents 5.7% of the total tax revenues in 1995.

1 percent; (3) the introduction of a new stamp duty on life insurance policies, which had become increasingly popular because of tax incentives encouraging individuals to provide pensions for themselves; (4) the alignment of taxation on capital gains from restructuring holding companies with EU rules (two new directives on merger-type transactions and parent–subsidiary relations between corporations), a measure meant to restore Switzerland's attractiveness as a location for holdings; (5) a more generous tax treatment for employees acquiring stock from their own companies.

Finally, the most recent measure taken in the field of fiscal policy was the adoption of the 'Consolidation plan 2001' by Parliament and its subsequent endorsement by voters in a referendum. Under this name, a new article was introduced into the Constitution stating that the deficit should not exceed CHF 5 bn in 1999, 2.5 bn in 2000, and 1 bn in 2001 (about 2% of total revenues). These results could only be reached by reducing expenditures. Should the economic situation worsen, however, Parliament can delay achieving this goal for two years. 'Consolidation plan 2001' did not impinge on referendum rights, which means that voters may still call for referendums on relevant pieces of legislation even if the laws they might reject are reforms needed to achieve the plan's stringent fiscal goals. Each year after 2001, the fiscal deficit should not exceed 2 percent of total revenues, and if it does, it needs to be corrected by the following year.

4.3.4. Liberalization and Deregulation Measures

In the 1990s, the high level of public and private regulation of the domestic market and the numerous impediments to competition favoring sheltered sectors were highlighted by public debates (on the EEA Treaty and the Uruguay Round of the GATT) as well as by the simultaneous publication of several economic studies (Borner, Brunetti, and Straubharr 1990; Hauser and Bradke 1992), administrative reports, and 'White Papers' put out by the major export-oriented sectors.

Over the last few years, a number of measures to liberalize and enhance competition in the domestic market have been adopted. Most of them were induced by pressures from the international environment (the Uruguay Round of the GATT and closer ties with the EU). After the negative result of the referendum on joining the EEA in December 1992, the government launched a program of 'economic revitalization', inspired by the report of the 'de Pury commission' (de Pury 1992). Its main objective was to liberalize the internal market (Sieber 1995). On that occasion, the government strongly underlined the need to introduce on its own accord the same structural economic reforms that EEA membership would have imposed. The leitmotiv of the 'revitalization program' was: 'Competitiveness abroad through increasing competition on domestic markets.'

One of the key elements of the revitalization program was the reform of the 'cartel law,' adopted in October 1995 by Parliament and clearly inspired by European regulations. Although the new law did not forbid cartels,[9] it provided clearer guidelines and gave the Competition Commission power to combat anti-competitive practices. It also introduced a merger control mechanism. This reform faced strong opposition from the Small Business Association, which initially threatened to challenge the new law with a referendum but eventually came to accept the changes (for a detailed analysis, see Mach 1998).

The revitalization program also included a new federal law on the internal market, based on the principle of 'mutual recognition' for qualifications and technical standards. The law is expected to facilitate the free movement of goods, services, and persons on Swiss territory, and thus to reduce market segmentation across cantons. A third measure removed the legal basis for technical barriers to trade, helping open up Swiss markets to greater foreign competition.

In the field of immigration policy, a first cautious step was taken toward free movement for foreign workers, though only if they were specialists or highly skilled workers. This measure was strongly advocated by the export-oriented and financial sectors, who had sharply criticized the old foreign workforce policy for only favoring the recruitment of low-skilled workers. The association agreement between Switzerland and the EU signed in 1998 contained a provision allowing for the free movement of persons to be introduced gradually.

Liberalization measures induced by the Uruguay Round certainly had a stronger impact on some Swiss policies than on policy in other countries, because liberalization implied reforms affecting economic sectors benefiting from high levels of protection. This was especially the case for agricultural policy (Sciarini 1994) and the regulation of public markets (Pravato 1995). The GATT agreements did generate some opposition among organized interests representing domestic economic sectors. However, the attempt by marginal farmers' organizations to launch a referendum did not succeed. On the whole, the GATT agreements were strongly supported by a large majority of the political and economic elite.

Like all other European states, although with some delay, Switzerland decided to liberalize its telecommunications sector (with a partial privatization—49%—of the public operator) and postal services before the first

---

[9] The prohibition of cartels would have necessitated a constitutional reform, which would have required more time and ratification by referendum.

of January 1998, when the European directive on liberalizing telecommunications went into force (Finger, Pravato, and Rey 1997; Syz and Odermatt 1997). Liberalizing reforms are also underway in other fields, such as electricity, air transport, and railways.

All of these reforms assumed a special place in the 'revitalization program of the Swiss economy'. Their main objective was to reduce production costs in the domestic sectors and enhance competition in the internal market. But it is still difficult to evaluate the effects of such liberalization/deregulation reforms, which were undertaken very recently and have impacts that are also difficult to measure.

4.3.5. Institutional Capacity

The fragmented character of the Swiss political system and the existence of a series of veto points in the legislative process mean that the federal government's capacity to control policy outcomes and steer the economy is often limited.

Institutional fragmentation among three distinct tiers of government, the delegation of monetary policy to an independent central bank, the important role played by the social partners in the regulation of the labor market, and the segmented character of state–society relationships—all these factors prevent the government from being able to coordinate initiatives undertaken in these different arenas of social and economic policy. Policy responses requiring intervention in a number of different areas are thus particularly difficult to implement. The result is that the degree of influence that politicians can hope to exert on the economy is more limited than in most other European countries.

The limits on policy control are not only due to institutional fragmentation, but also to the multiplicity of veto points in the legislative process, most notably referendums. As seen above, the main impact of referendums on the policy process has traditionally been to favor the inclusion of outside groups in decision making, so as to reduce the likelihood that they will resort to referendums. In the current phase of social and economic policy restructuring, referendums are arguably limiting the pace and extent of change, though to different degrees in different areas.

The impact of referendums is stronger when policy change imposes losses on large groups or on groups with a high capacity to mobilize support. This is demonstrated by the contrast between the slow pace of change in social policy, on the one hand, and the more far-reaching reforms deregulating the domestic market, on the other. Retrenchments in social programs, such as the increase in women's retirement age, have proved unpopular with large sections of the population, which has put pressure on policymakers not to take too radical a line in social policy reform. In competition policy, by contrast, reform did force some comparatively smaller groups (farmers, domestic producers) to lose out. As a result, change in this area has been more substantial. On occasion, losers tried to use referendums, though without success (for example, against the liberalization of the telecom market and the GATT agreement). In sum, referendums constitute a limit on loss imposition only when the group on which those losses are imposed is large enough, or influential enough, to pose a credible threat of winning a referendum against the relevant reform.

In this respect, it is striking that some reforms imposing losses did occur in social policy (pensions and unemployment insurance). However, if one looks at the details of retrenchment-oriented changes in social policy, one finds that the successful reforms combined cuts in existing programs with improvements or expanded benefits and services. The 1995 unemployment insurance reform, for example, combined the introduction of a time limit on benefits with increased spending on active labor market policies. Similarly, the 1995 pension reform combined an increase in women's retirement age with contribution credits for informal carers and other improvements. Both reforms became law. In contrast, the 1997 unemployment insurance decree and the 1996 labor law reform, neither of which included any expanded benefits, were rejected by voters. In sum, it seems that welfare reforms succeed in Switzerland only when they combine retrenchment with expansion as a way of getting past the referendum obstacle (see also Obinger 1998).

Ironically, in the Swiss case, pressures for retrenchment might facilitate the welfare state's modernization, or policy changes that respond to new needs and aspirations expressed by modern societies, like gender equality, reconciling work and family life, or help in (re-)entering the labor market. As Cattacin (1996) has argued, federal social policy in the past has tended to be reactive rather than proactive in responding to newly emerging needs and demands. Introducing innovative policy change has always proved problematic, and the federal government has typically lagged behind individual cantons. At present, however, the fact that retrenchment needs to be accompanied by expansion to gain voters' approval provides the federal government with an opportunity to take a more proactive approach and to 'squeeze' innovative policy solutions into otherwise retrenchment-oriented reform packages (Bonoli 2000).

Finally, policymakers have been less successful in securing change in the area of European integration. As seen above, the failed attempt in 1992 to join the EEA constituted a major blow to the government's European policy. To some extent, the contrast between European integration and welfare reform can be accounted for by the fact that integration does not allow much room for compromise or for combining policy changes that go in different directions. Issues concerning European integration are very much 'yes or no' questions, and the Swiss political system seems to have a problem accommodating them (Church 1995).

Institutional capacities, thus, seem to have different impacts in different policy areas. Change in competition policy has not been significantly affected by the Swiss system's multiple veto points. Attempts to challenge competition legislation at the polls failed, generally before reaching the referendum stage. In social policy, change seems to be possible, but the referendum option pushes policy in a very clear direction, which can be described as a combination of retrenchment and modernization. Finally, with regard to European integration, veto points are proving a more serious obstacle to the fulfillment of the government's objectives. This differential impact of political institutions, we argue, will substantially shape the new Swiss model now emerging.

4.4. The New Model

The 1990s stand out in the history of Swiss postwar public policy because the extent and pace of change over this period bear no comparison to previous decades. In the space of a few years, a whole series of social and economic policy reforms (many of which have been discussed above) were adopted. This stands in sharp contrast to the pre-1990 period, when legislative change on some contentious issues might typically have taken ten or fifteen years.

Notwithstanding this acceleration of policy change, the new politico-economic model is unlikely to look very different from what the country knew in previous decades. To a large extent, in fact, the first postwar Swiss model (with its low taxation, flexible labor market, and lean welfare state) was already well equipped to succeed in an internationalized global market. In comparison to most other European countries, what the model required was only minor adjustment.

Thus, the Swiss story is somewhat different from that of the other European countries. The changes in the international economy that pressured its neighbors into policy change did not have such a dramatic impact on Switzerland. First, the deregulation of financial markets did not constitute a problem, as these were never highly regulated. Second, the postwar Swiss model never relied on centralized macroeconomic management, with coordination among fiscal, monetary and incomes policy. As a result the country was not forced to abandon its traditional economic policy instruments.

Instead, international economic pressures had an impact on the political and distributional equilibria that underpinned the postwar model. Forms of 'hidden protectionism' that benefited domestic producers increasingly came under attack from the export-oriented sector, as did parts of the welfare state. Economic internationalization has affected the balance of power between political and economic actors. Those who are mobile (such as export-oriented businesses) have become more influential, since they can more credibly threaten to use the exit option if dissatisfied. By contrast, non-mobile actors, namely domestic economic sectors (farmers, small companies producing for domestic markets) and the trade unions, have been weakened. In the Swiss case, thus, the impact of internationalization on the national economy takes place through a redefinition of the key political equilibria.

The Swiss story is also different because of the peculiar set of political institutions that structure policymaking there. In particular, the referendum system has proved crucial in determining how the balance of power between political and economic actors has shifted. The labor movement, because of its capacity to mobilize support and the overall popularity of welfare arrangements, has been rather successful in defending postwar social programs. By contrast, interest groups representing domestic producers have failed to preserve advantages they had enjoyed throughout the postwar period.

Based on how Swiss exceptionalism has responded to economic internationalization, we can identify the key features of a possible new model. The policy changes adopted, as well as those planned for the near future, reveal some sort of coherent project, which can be described as a process of 'selective Europeanization'. By selective Europeanization we mean the adoption of those aspects of EU social and economic policy most friendly to business: liberalization of the domestic market; reduction of government budget deficits (to a large extent, through welfare reforms), and access to the single market. This process is unlikely to constitute a major overhaul, because Switzerland is rather close to these objectives.

However, given the government's limited steering capacity, Switzerland may not produce a coherent response to globalization. Even though there is a political majority in the country prepared to go along with a project of selective Europeanization, the institutional effects on policy reviewed above are likely to continue affecting the direction of adjustment, possibly in a substantive way. The left and the trade unions may decide to trade their support for this project against modernization of the welfare state. Access to the single market, obviously an important part of the project, may turn out to be politically unfeasible. Thus, depending on the degree of success the current adjustment strategy achieves within strict institutional constraints, that strategy might have to be redefined in the future.

REFERENCES

ANDERSON, MARTIN, and HERTIG, THIERRY (1992). *Institutional Investors in Switzerland: Their Behavior and Influence on Financial Markets and Public Companies*. Zurich: Schulthess Verlag.

ARMINGEON, KLAUS (1998). 'The Impact of Globalization on Swiss Policy Making: A Comment'. *Swiss Political Science Review*, 2: 104–11.

——(1999). 'Wirtschafts- und Finanzpolitik', in Ulrich Klöti, Peter Knoepfel, Hanspeter Kriesi, Wolf Linder, and Yannis Papadopoulos (eds.), *Handbuch der Schweizer Politik*. Zurich: NZZ-Verlag, 725–66.

——(2000). 'Renegotiating the Swiss Welfare State', forthcoming in Gerhard Lehmbruch, and Frans van Waarden (eds.), *Renegotiating the Welfare State*. London: Routledge.

BERNEGGER, MICHAEL (1990). 'Die Schweiz und die Weltwirtschaft: Etappen der Integration im 19. und 20. Jahrhundert', in Paul Bairoch and Martin Körner (eds.), *La Suisse dans l'économie mondiale*. Geneva: Droz, 429–64.

BIRCHLER, URS (1995). 'Aktionärsstruktur und Unternehmenspolitik— Bedeutung für die Sicherheit des Bankensystems'. *Quartalsheft der SNB*, 3: 265–77.

BONOLI, GIULIANO (1997). 'Switzerland: The Politics of Consensual Retrenchment', in Clasen Jochen (ed.), *Social Insurance in Europe*. Bristol: Policy Press, 107–29.

——(2000). *The Politics of Pension Reform: Institutions and Policy Change in Western Europe*. Cambridge: Cambridge University Press.

BORNER, SILVIO, BRUNETTI, AYMO, and STRAUBHARR, THOMAS (1990). *Schweiz AG: Vom Sonderfall zum Sanierungsfall?*. Zurich: NZZ-Verlag.

BURKHALTER, VÉRONIQUE, PETERSEN, ALEXANDER, and PINI, FABIENNE (1999). 'Le Néo-libéralisme comme revendication politique: Acteurs et discours dans la Suisse des années 1990', in André Mach (ed.), *Globalisation, néo-libéralisme et politiques publiques dans la Suisse des années 90*. Zurich: Seismo, 51–104.

CALMFORS, LARS, and DRIFFILL, JOHN (1988). 'Bargaining Structures, Corporatism and Macroeconomic Performance'. *Economic Policy*, 6: 14–61.

CATTACIN, SANDRO (1996). 'Die Transformation des Schweizer Sozialstaates'. *Swiss Political Science Review*, 1: 89–102.

——(1999). 'Les Politiques sociales', in Ulrich Klöti, Peter Knoepfel, Hanspeter Kriesi, Wolf Linder, and Yannis Papadopoulos (eds.), *Handbuch der Schweizer Politik*. Zurich: NZZ-Verlag, 807–38.

CHURCH, CLIVE (1995). *The Crisis of Konkordanz Democracy in Switzerland*. Paper presented at the workshop on 'Consociationalism, Parties and Party Systems', ECPR, Bordeaux.

DAFFLON, BERNARD (1977). *Federal Finance in Theory and Practice, with Special Reference to Switzerland.* Bern: Haupt.

DE PURY, DAVID (1992). *Rapport final du groupe de travail informel 'Ordnungspolitik'.* Berne: DFEP.

——HAUSER, HEINZ, and SCHMID, BEAT (eds.) (1995). *Mut zum Aufbruch: Eine wirtschaftspolitische Agenda für die Schweiz.* Zurich: Orell Füssli.

EARDLEY, TONY, BRADSHAW, JONATHAN, DITCH, JOHN, GOUGH, IAN, and WHITEFORD, PETER (1996). 'Switzerland', in Tony Eardley et al. (eds.), *Social Assistance in OECD Countries*, ii. London: HMSO, 369–78.

ESPING-ANDERSEN, GØSTA (1990). *The Three Worlds of Welfare Capitalism.* Cambridge: Polity Press.

FERRERA, MAURIZIO (1993). *Modelli di solidarietà.* Bologna: Il Mulino.

FINGER, MATTHIAS, PRAVATO, SERGE, and REY, JEAN-NOEL (eds.) (1997). *Du monopole à la concurrence: Analyse critique de l'évolution de six entreprises publiques.* Lausanne: LEP.

FLUDER, ROBERT (1998). *Politik und Strategien der schweizerischen Arbeitnehmerorganisationen.* Zurich: Rüegger.

FREIBURGHAUS, DIETER (1989). *Réflexions sur l'attitude de l'économie suisse face à l'intégration européenne.* Lausanne: Cahiers de l'IDHEAP No. 54.

GERMANN, RAIMUND, FRUTIGER, ANDREAS, MULLER, JEAN-DANIEL, POITRY, ALAIN-VALERY, and VON SURI, MONIKA (1985). *Experts et commissions de la Confédération.* Lausanne: Presses polytechniques romandes.

GILLIAND, PIERRE (1988). *Politique sociale en Suisse.* Lausanne: Réalités Sociales.

GUEX, SÉBASTIEN (1998). *L'Argent de l'État: Parcours des finances publiques au XXe siècle.* Lausanne: Réalités sociales.

HAUSER, HEINZ (1993). 'Die Ablehnung des EWR-Vertrags als Chance nutzen!'. *Aussenwirtschaft*, 1: 7–36.

——and BRADKE, SVEN (1992). *Traité sur l'EEE, Adhésion à la CE, Course en solitaire: Conséquences économiques pour la Suisse.* Zurich: Rüegger.

HOTZ, BEAT (1979). *Politik zwischen Staat und Wirtschaft.* Diessenhofen: Rüegger.

——and FLUDER, ROBERT (1998). 'Switzerland: Still as Smooth as Clock Work?', in Anthony Ferner and Richard Hyman (eds.), *Changing Industrial Relations in Europe.* Oxford: Blackwell, 262–82.

HUBER, EVELYN, RAGIN, CHARLES, and STEPHENS, JOHN (1993). 'Social Democracy, Christian Democracy, Constitutional Structure and the Welfare State'. *American Journal of Sociology,* 3: 711–49.

IMMERGUT, ELLEN (1992). *Health Politics: Interests and Institutions in Western Europe.* Cambridge: Cambridge University Press.

International Monetary Fund (1998). *Switzerland: Selected Issues and Statistical Appendix.* IMF Staff Country Report No. 98/43.

KATZENSTEIN, PETER (1984). *Corporatism and Change: Austria, Switzerland and the Politics of Change.* Ithaca, NY/London: Cornell University Press.

——(1985). *Small States in World Markets: Industrial Policy in Europe.* Ithaca, NY/London: Cornell University Press.

172   Giuliano Bonoli and André Mach

KNÖPFEL, CARLO (1988). *Der Einfluss der politischen Stabilität auf die internationale Wettbewerbsfähigkeit der Schweiz*. Grüsch: Rüegge.

KOBACH, KRIS (1993). *The Referendum: Direct Democracy in Switzerland*. Aldershot: Dartmouth.

KRIESI, HANSPETER (1982). 'The Structure of the Swiss Political System', in Gerhard Lehmbruch and Philippe Schmitter (eds.), *Patterns of Corporatist Policy Making*. London: Sage, 133–61.

——(1995). *Le Système politique suisse*. Paris: Economica.

——and FARAGO, PETER (1989). 'The Regional Differentiation of Business Interest Associations in Switzerland', in W. Coleman and H. J. Jacek, *Regionalism, Business Interests and Public Policy*. London: Sage, 153–72.

LEHMBRUCH, GERHARD (1993). 'Consociational Democracy and Corporatism in Switzerland'. *Publius: The Journal of Federalism*, 2: 43–60.

LEUTWILER, FRITZ, and SCHMIDHEINY, STEPHAN (1991). *La Politique économique de la Suisse face à la concurrence internationale: Programme pour un ordre plus libéral*. Zurich: Orell Füssli.

LIJPHART, AREND (1984). *Democracies: Pattern of Majoritarian and Consensus Government in Twenty-One Countries*. New Haven and London: Yale University Press.

LINDER, WOLF (1994). *Swiss Democracy: Possible Solutions to Conflict in Multicultural Societies*. London: Macmillan Press.

LOPRENO, DARIO (1995). 'Conventions collectives de travail en vigueur en Suisse au 1er mai 1994'. *La Vie économique*, 10: 62–68.

MACH, ANDRÉ (1998). 'Quelles réponses politiques face à la globalisation et à la construction européenne? Illustration à partir de la révision de la loi suisse sur les cartels'. *Swiss Political Science Review*, 2: 25–49.

——(1999). 'Associations d'intérêt', in Ulrich Klöti, Peter Knoepfel, Hanspeter Kriesi, Wolf Linder, and Yannis Papadopoulos (eds.), *Handbuch der Schweizer Politik*. Zurich: NZZ-Verlag, 299–335.

NEIDHART, LEONHARD (1970). *Plebiszit und pluralitäre Demokratie: Eine Analyse der Funktionen des schweizerischen Gesetzesreferendum*. Bern: Frank.

OBINGER, HERBERT (1998). *Politische Institutionen und Sozialpolitik in der Schweiz*. Frankfurt: Lang.

OECD (Organisation for Economic Co-operation and Development) (various issues). *Economic Surveys. Switzerland*. Paris: OECD.

——(1996a). *Labour Market Policies in Switzerland*. Paris: OECD.

——(1996b). *OECD Reviews of Foreign Direct Investment: Switzerland*. Paris: OECD.

——(1997a). *Globalisation and Small and Medium Enterprises*. Paris: OECD.

——(1997b). *Statistical Compendium (Labour Force Statistics)*. Paris: OECD.

——(1998). *Financial Market Trends, 69*. Paris, OECD.

OFAS (Office Fédéral des Assurances Sociales) (1995). *Rapport du Département fédéral de l'intérieur concernant la structure actuelle et le développement futur de la conception helvétique des trois piliers de la prévoyance vieillesse, survivants et invalidité*. Berne: OFAS.

OFDE (Office Fédéral du Développement Économique et de l'Emploi) (1998). *La Collaboration des PME avec les banques*. Berne: OFDE.

OFS (Office Fédéral de Statistique) (1997). *Le Travail à temps partiel et l'activité profiessionnelle indépendante poursuivent leur essor*. Berne: OFS.

——(various issues). *Annuaire Statistique de la Suisse*. Berne: OFS.

PAPADOPOULOS, YANNIS (1997). *Les processus de décision fédéraux en Suisse*. Paris: L'Harmattan.

PIOTET, GEORGES (1987). *Restructuration industrielle et corporatisme: Le Cas de l'horlogerie suisse 1974–1987*. Lausanne: Imprivite SA.

PRAVATO, SERGE (1995). *Influence du contexte international sur le fonctionnement du système politique suisse et sa capacité d'adaptation: Le Cas de la libéralisation des marchés publics*. Geneva: Études européennes No. 5.

PRINCE, JEAN-CLAUDE (1994). *L'Impact des conventions collectives de travail en Suisse*. Zurich: Schulthess Polygraphischer Verlag.

RATTI, REMIGIO, and REICHMAN, SALOMON (eds.) (1993). *Theory and Practice of Transborder Cooperation*. Basle/Frankfurt: Helbing and Lichtenhahn.

RENTSCH, HANS (1989). *Cartels and Wealth: A Paradox in the Swiss Economic System*. Zug: Forschungsinstitut für Wirtschafts- und Sozialpolitik.

REVAZ, FLORIAN (1993). 'La Flexibilité des salaires en Suisse'. *La Vie économique*, 10: 38–44.

RIEGER, ANDREAS (1994). 'Vertragspolitik am Wendepunkt? Geschichte und Perspektiven der Gesamtarbeitsverträge in der Schweiz'. *Widerspruch*, 3: 88–101.

RIKLIN, ALOIS (1995). 'Isolierte Schweiz. Eine europa- und innenpolitische Lagebeurteilung'. *Swiss Political Science Review*, 1/2–3: 11–34.

ROSSI, MARTINO, and SARTORIS, ELENA (1995). *Ripensare la solidarietà*. Locarno: Amado.

SCHAAD, NICOLE (1997). *Arbeitgeberverbände, kollektive Arbeitsbeziehungen und Lohnregulierungen in der chemischen Industrie*. Zurich: Institut für empirische Wirtschaftsforschung.

SCHMIDT, MANFRED (1995). 'Vollbeschäftigung und Arbeitslosigkeit in der Schweiz: Vom Sonderweg zum Normalfall'. *Politische Vierteljahresschrift*, 1: 35–48.

SCIARINI, PASCAL (1992). 'La Suisse dans la négociation sur l'Espace économique européen: De la rupture à l'apprentissage'. *Annuaire suisse de science politique*: 297–322.

——(1994). *Le Système politique suisse face à la Communauté européenne et au GATT: Le Cas-test de la politique agricole*. Geneva: Georg.

SIEBER, HANS (1995). 'La Régénération de l'économie de marché—meilleure que sa réputation? Du degré de réalisation des revendications du Groupe de travail "de Pury"'. *Cahiers des questions conjoncturelles*, 1: 3–9.

SIGRIST, DIETER (1996). 'Transfert des négociations salariales au niveau des établissements'. *Employeur suisse*, 18: 851–54.

SOSKICE, DAVID (1990). 'Wage Determination: The Changing Role of Institutions in Advanced Industrialized Societies'. *Oxford Review of Economic Policy*, 4: 36–61.

STRAHM, RUDOLF (1997). *Arbeit und Sozialstaat sind zu retten: Analysen und Grafiken zur schweizerischen Wirtschaft im Zeichen der Globalisierung.* Bern: Werdverlag.

SYZ, DIETER, and ODERMATT, JEAN (1997). *Histoire de la réforme des PTT.* Berne: PTT.

5

How Small Countries Negotiate Change
Twenty-Five Years of Policy Adjustment in
Austria, the Netherlands, and Belgium

ANTON HEMERIJCK, BRIGITTE UNGER, AND JELLE VISSER

5.1. Introduction: Birds of a Feather?

Austria, Belgium, and the Netherlands seem like 'birds of a feather', albeit with different colors (Alber 1998). They are small and open economies, each with a tradition of social partnership, Bismarckian-type welfare state, and consociational democracy based on political coalitions that bridge cleavages of class, religion, or language. Comparing these 'most similar cases' (Przeworski and Teune 1970) can potentially contribute to our understanding of the interaction among economic vulnerability, institutional capacity, policy legacies, and policy responses.

'Birds of a feather flock together,' says the Duchess in *Alice's Adventures in Wonderland*. But in our case, they did not. In response to the economic shocks of the 1970s, Austria, Belgium, and the Netherlands went different ways. Austria managed to keep unemployment low and was able to check inflation, whereas Belgium and the Netherlands accomplished neither. Why? Did policymakers perceive or approach the problems differently? Did they act under different external and internal constraints? Did they pursue different objectives? When the oil shock of 1979 and rising interest rates in the 1980s had to be addressed, imbalances were much more pronounced in Belgium and the Netherlands than in Austria. But crises do trigger learning processes and create political conditions for change. This is most clearly seen in the Dutch case, where reforms in the 1990s were more daring than in Austria. Did the Dutch learn their lesson better, or

Our joint paper has greatly benefited from comments and suggestions made by the directors of the 'adjustment' project, Fritz W. Scharpf and Vivien A. Schmidt. We thank Martin Schludi (MPIfG) and Friso Janssen (University of Amsterdam), who helped with preparing the tables and figures. We have divided our labor as follows: Brigitte Unger wrote Section 5.2 (Austria), Anton Hemerijck Section 5.3 (the Netherlands), and Jelle Visser Section 5.4 (Belgium). Section 5.1 (introduction) was written by Anton and Jelle; the conclusion by the three authors together. Jelle Visser did the final editing.

will they be just as vulnerable when another international shock hits? Why was learning of this kind blocked in Belgium, despite highly unsatisfactory labor market outcomes?

Our aim in this chapter is to present description and explanation. In this first section we offer a bird's-eye view of the similarities and variations among our three countries. In the following three sections we offer a dynamic, fine-grained account of each country's problems, perceptions, legacies, policies, and outcomes. The chapter ends with an attempt at explaining the diversity in policy responses and an assessment of vulnerabilities and capacities.

5.1.1. Small, Open Economies

Austria, the Netherlands, and Belgium are three small countries bordering on Germany, their main trading partner (see Table 5.1). Belgium and the Netherlands trade heavily with each other, Austria with Switzerland and Italy. As transit economies, with the two largest ports of mainland Europe, Belgium and the Netherlands are two very open European economies, with imports and exports making up 75 percent and more of their gross domestic product. Austria's share is 60 percent, still above average in Europe but not unusual for a small economy. With limited domestic markets, these countries are highly dependent upon access to foreign markets and have always given a great deal of attention to trade liberalization and competitiveness. Not surprisingly, they are advocates of European economic integration. Belgium and the Netherlands were among the six founding nations of the European Economic Community. Austria, a former member of the European Free Trade Association, joined the European Union in 1995. All three qualified for membership in the Economic and Monetary Union in 1999.

5.1.2. Different Industrial Profiles

Small domestic markets encourage open economies to seek competitive advantage through product specialization and economies of scale in export markets. For historical and geographical reasons, our three countries exhibit different patterns of specialization. As continental Europe's oldest industrial nation, Belgium developed a strong position in the production of raw materials, coal and steel, and related industrial products, until decline began in the 1960s. In the past forty years, the economic axis has shifted to light industry and services, with a strong impact on the port of Antwerp and domestic investment by multinational, mainly US, firms. The Netherlands industrialized late and never became a truly industrial

Table 5.1 *Austria, Belgium, and the Netherlands compared, 1994*

	Population (in 1000s)	GDP (in million ECU)	GDP/capita (ECU)	Germany's share of exports (%)	Openness of the economy[a] (%)
Austria	8,030	168,865	21,029	38.0	60.9
Netherlands	15,381	283,920	18,459	26.8	74.6
Belgium	10,116	193,610	19,139	19.4	81.4[b]
Flanders	5,857	113,740	19,420	—	—
Wallonia	3,538	50,538	15,274	—	—
Brussels	950	29,332	30,864	—	—

[a]Exports plus imports in percentage of GDP. See: OECD (1997) *Statistical Compendium (National Accounts)* (Paris: OECD, 1997); own calculations.
[b]Including Luxembourg.

Sources: Eurostat, 1997; MPIfG, Adjustment Database, 1999; OECD, *Economic Outlook 1999*; Belgian Statistical Office.

nation, despite its post-1945 efforts. The Dutch economy is specialized in transportation and logistics, international finance, business services, agro-industry, and foreign trade, a tradition that goes back to the seventeenth-century colonial ventures of the Dutch East-India Trading Company. The country is home to large indigenous and Anglo-Dutch multinational firms, like Philips, Unilever, Shell, Heineken, and some of Europe's largest banks. Postwar Austria lagged even further behind, and in 1970, 12.2 percent of its labor force was still employed in agriculture, compared with 3 percent in Belgium and the Netherlands. Today Austria has a larger industrial sector in terms of people employed or value added. Unlike Belgium and the Netherlands, Austria nationalized large parts of industry and the banking sector after 1945. In the 1970s nationalized industry comprised 70 percent of banking, credit, and insurance, 33 percent of industrial manufacturing, 23 percent of food distribution, and 40 percent of housing construction (Kurzer 1993: 38). The private sector used to be dominated by small and medium-sized firms, and none of the major multinational enterprises had its home base in Austria.

Neither the Netherlands nor Belgium has had a particularly happy or interesting experience with industrial policy. After 1945 both countries undertook large-scale industrialization programs for the purpose of recovering from war damage (Netherlands) or developing rural areas, especially in Dutch-speaking Flanders (Belgium). In the 1970s both also became increasingly immersed in hopeless rescue operations for ailing industries. At this time Austria showed fewer signs of strain, and its nationalized

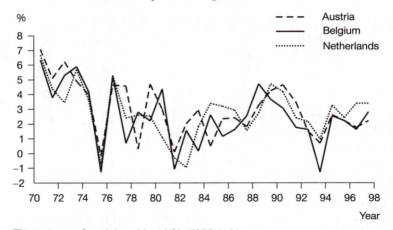

Figure 5.1 Annual real growth, 1970–1998
Source: OECD, *Economic Outlook* (Paris: OECD, various years).

industrial firms maintained high levels of employment. But problems arose in the mid-1980s, when the nationalized sector was restructured and privatized under both domestic and international pressure.

5.1.3. Growth, Employment, and Unemployment

On a cumulative basis, economic growth hardly differs among the three countries. All three experienced the slowdown in output and productivity growth that has characterized all advanced economies since 1973 (Figure 5.1). Until 1985 Austria did better. From 1986 to 1996 the economy grew at a rate of 21 percent in Belgium, 25 percent in Austria, and 26 percent (the OECD average) in the Netherlands. The number of people employed increased by 4 percent in Belgium, 6 percent in Austria (just above the OECD average), and 18 percent in the Netherlands. Labor force growth was much slower in Austria and Belgium, yet only in the Netherlands did employment growth outpace labor force growth. Hence the Netherlands was the only one of the three countries in which unemployment was lower in 1996 than it had been ten years earlier (Figure 5.2). It should be noted, though, that the Dutch unemployment rate had to come down from very high levels. This predicament was shared with Belgium but had been avoided in Austria, where unemployment never exceeded 4 percent of the labor force until quite recently. 1998 was the first year in two decades during which the Dutch unemployment rate dipped under 4 percent. In 1998 Belgium unemployment fell to 8.8 percent (OECD 1999).

Table 5.2 *Output, employment, labor force, and unemployment, 1970–1996*

Countries	Variability of output[a]	Employment responsiveness to output[b]	Labor force responsiveness to employment[c]	Variability of unemployment rates
Austria	1.79	0.47	0.83	0.35
Belgium	1.88	0.45	0.15	1.40
Netherlands	1.55	0.52	0.12	1.02

[a]Standard deviation of the first difference (in log and multiplied by 100) of output.
[b]The estimated coefficient b in the regression. (Employment deviation from trend) = a + b* (output deviation from trend), where the trends have been established using the Hodrick-Prescott filter, imposing identical smoothing factors for employment and output in each country.
[c]The estimated coefficient b in the regression. (Labor force deviation from trend) = a + b* (employment deviation from trend), where the trends have been established using the Hodrick-Prescott filter, imposing identical smoothing factors for employment and output in each country.
[d]Standard deviation of the first difference (in log and multiplied by 100) of unemployment.

Source: Pichelmann and Hofer 1999: 34; Belgium: own calculations.

Belgium and the Netherlands experienced very high levels of unemployment while Austria did not (Figure 5.2). How did this relate to the rather small difference in the (accumulated) growth of output? Figure 5.1 shows that the recession years of 1975 and 1993 were greater periods of setback in Belgium than in the Netherlands and that the Dutch fared worse than the Austrians until the mid-1980s. Yet the variability in Austria's output is not lower (Table 5.2). By means of labor hoarding and labor force withdrawals (foreign workers, women), however, Austria matches variability in output with considerable responsiveness in how the labor force reacts to employment opportunities, so that the overall result is a much lower, and hardly varying, unemployment rate (Pichelmann and Hofer 1999). This adjustment mechanism was not available in the Netherlands and Belgium. Foreign workers had obtained residential rights by 1975, and the Netherlands in particular experienced strong growth in the female labor supply, which was unresponsive to cyclical demand changes (Hartog and Theeuwes 1983). Overall, unemployment rates in Belgium and the Netherlands showed greater variation over the cycle (Table 5.2). Once unemployment is high and long-term unemployment is allowed to rise, joblessness tends to be persistent (Layard, Nickel, and Jackman 1991; OECD 1994).

How the Netherlands caught up is also shown in the employment/population ratios. Around 1970 the Netherlands, like Belgium, had one of the lowest employment rates in Europe. At the time this was entirely due to the fact that married women were not participating in the workforce. After a further decline lasting through the early 1980s, the Dutch employment ratio leaped from 50 percent in 1990 to 61 percent in 1998, almost level

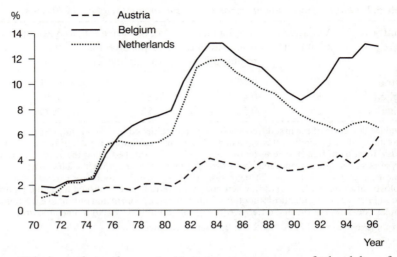

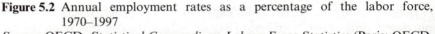

Figure 5.2 Annual employment rates as a percentage of the labor force, 1970–1997
Source: OECD, *Statistical Compendium: Labour Force Statistics* (Paris: OECD, 1997); own calculations.

with Austria and five points above the OECD average. From Figure 5.3, based on OECD Economic Outlook data, we learn that over a thirty-year period the Dutch got back to where they were in 1970, with employment rising after 1984. Austria has been unable to keep up its high level of employment from the 1970s; in the 1990s it experienced a jobs decline. Downward drift and stagnation characterize developments in Belgium, which started from the same position as the Dutch and had almost the same experience until the late 1980s. The difference with the Netherlands is to be found in the 1990s. Behind these trends there are significant shifts in female and male employment, a pattern of withdrawal from the labor market by older males, a unique rise in part-time employment in the Netherlands, and very different employment levels and trends in domestic private services.

5.1.4. Negotiated Economies

In *Small States in World Markets*, Katzenstein (1985) classifies our countries under the label of 'democratic corporatism'. In response to their dependence on exports, the imperative of competitiveness, and their inability to exert control over external events, small and open economies tend to develop tightly-knit organized networks of consultative bodies at

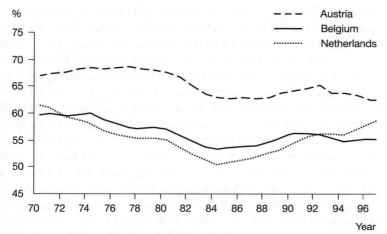

Figure 5.3 Employment as a percentage of the working age population (15–65), 1970–1997

Source: OECD, *Statistical Compendium: Economic Outlook* (Paris: OECD, 1999); own calculations.

the national level oriented toward advancing economic and social progress and preserving social peace. The Parity Commission and its various sub-committees in Austria, the Central Economic Council and National Labor Council in Belgium, and the Foundation of Labor and Social-Economic Council in the Netherlands are all postwar inventions. They embody the idea that organized capital and organized labor, together with representatives of the state and central bankers, share responsibility for the welfare of the nation.

In each country the umbrella organizations of employers and unions are involved in consultation, both with each other and the state. Overall,

Table 5.3 *Some characteristics of labor relations in the mid-1990s*

Countries	Union density rate (total and private sector) (%)	Employees in firms joining employers' associations[a] (%)	Employees covered by collective agreements[a] (%)	Extension of agreements through public law	National minimum wage
Belgium	53/40	80	82	Significant	Statutory
Austria	44/37	96	97	Significant	Agreement
Netherlands	28/20	80	79	Limited	Statutory

[a]Private sector.
Source: Visser 1996.

social partnership is more fully developed and stable in Austria (Tálos 1996; Traxler 1997) than in the Netherlands (Hemerijck 1995; Visser and Hemerijck 1997) and Belgium (Van Ruysseveldt and Visser 1996; Vilrokx and Van Leemput 1997). The state is weakest in Belgium, for reasons we will indicate later, while cooperation between unions and employers is most balanced in Austria. Belgian trade unions count among the strongest outside Scandinavia (Ebbinghaus and Visser 1999). Compared to the other two countries, they are more integrated with (and divided among) separate political parties, and they must constantly perform a delicate balancing act between Belgium's two main linguistic communities and regions. From a comparative perspective, Belgium's central organizations of unions and employers are rather weak, with little authority over affiliates and with pronounced regional divisions. Dutch trade unions weakened considerably between the mid-1970s and the mid-1980s, whereas Dutch capital and employers' associations remain well organized (Visser 1997). In all three countries collective bargaining is pervasive and primarily organized by economic sector. In each country there is intensive coordination by the umbrella organizations, but in Belgium agreement has been rare. Dutch wage negotiators operate under a 'shadow of hierarchy'. The opposite trend is found in Belgium. Here the state has taken over the role of wage bargainer and negotiates under a threat of dissent and implementation failure. Table 5.3 captures some features of current labor relations.

5.1.5. Economic Performance

Institutional variation is associated with variation in performance. Austria had much less trouble with inflation in the 1970s than the other two countries. The Dutch got inflation under control more quickly than the Belgians (Figure 5.4). Each of the three countries assigned monetary policy the task of fighting inflation, but Belgium and the Netherlands paid a high price in terms in terms of competitiveness. While the schilling and the gulden were pegged to the Deutschmark in an early stage, Belgium had to accept a major devaluation of the franc in 1982 and waited till 1990 before it tied its hands. The extent of continuity in Austria and policy reversal in Belgium and the Netherlands is well captured by the competitiveness indicator, based on unit labor costs in manufacturing (Figure 5.5).

In the wake of the 1973 oil-price shock, policymakers in each country tried to combine a hard currency policy with Keynesian demand stimulation. But only in Austria did congenial wage-setting policies help to avoid the negative outcome of cost-push inflation, a loss of competitiveness, and higher public debts. Austria (along with Switzerland) was among the few Continental European countries where levels of industrial and societal

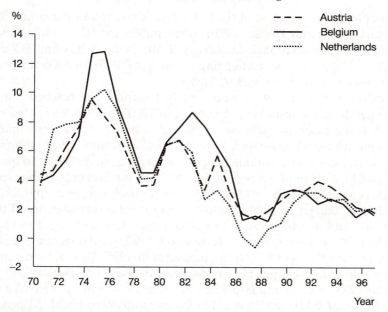

Figure 5.4 Annual percentage change of consumer prices, 1970–1997
Source: OECD, *Economic Outlook* (Paris: OECD, various years).

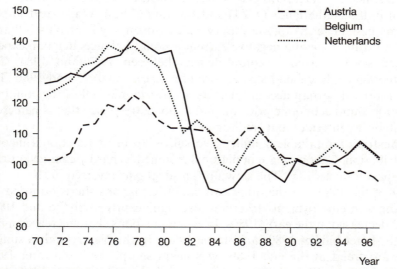

Figure 5.5 Index of unit labor costs, in real terms, relative to 1990 (= 100), 1970–1997
Source: OECD, *Statistical Compendium: Economic Outlook* (Paris: OECD, 1997); own calculations.

conflict had remained low in the late 1960s (Crouch and Pizzorno 1978). Lijphart (1968) and Huyse (1970), when publishing their studies on the wonders of consociational democracy in the Netherlands and Belgium, noted that 'the times were changing'. Steiniger (1975), in his comparative study, found no such changes in Austria.

Austria started the 1970s with a budget surplus and reached a maximum net deficit of just over −5 percent of GDP in 1995. The deficit varied with the business cycle but remained within a −5 percent margin. Belgium, where the net deficit peaked at −12 percent in 1981, shows the most extreme variation and managed only with great difficulty to qualify for the EMU norm of −3 percent in 1998. The Netherlands' public sector deficit peaked in 1982 at −6.6 percent and has declined since, approaching a balanced budget in 1999. The debt–output ratio increased in all three countries until the 1990s. Austria started with a low public debt of 19 percent in 1970, increasing to 69 percent in the 1990s until it recently declined to 64 percent thanks to austerity measures in 1995. Belgium entered the 1970s with a debt–output ratio of 64 percent, rising to a peak of 137 percent in 1993, and declining to 122 percent in 1998 with the help of a special 3 percent EMU surcharge. The Netherlands began with 52 percent, allowed the debt–output ratio to rise to 81 percent in 1993, and then managed a reversal to 71 percent. The debt problem is reflected in debt interest payments, which have been lower in Austria (3.5% of GDP in 1997) than in the Netherlands (4.3%) and Belgium (7.5%). While Austria performs best in terms of the misery index (unemployment plus inflation rate), it runs a slightly negative current account balance. Belgium experienced severe current account deficits between 1977 and 1984. The Netherlands always had strong surpluses, except in 1978 and 1980. The toleration of current account deficits in Austria may reflect the country's overall sound economic position and a monetary policy that is perceived as stable by international creditors.

Austria's remarkable stability also shows up in its functional income distribution. Labor's share in national income has hardly changed during the past four decades. The slow upward drift was reversed in the second half of the 1980s. In the other two countries, labor's share, adjusted for changes in employment structure, rose significantly after the mid-1960s and decreased in the early 1980s. In Belgium labor's share increased again in the latter half of 1980s and in the 1990s. In the Netherlands a similar upward trend in the late 1980s was again sharply reversed after 1993. Labor's share of Belgian national income is today still above its 1960s average and above the European average, whereas it has fallen under its 1960s level in the Netherlands (Table 5.4). Underneath these trends lie different wage policy experiences.

Table 5.4 *Labor's share in the national income, 1960–1997*

Country	1960–69	1970–79	1980–89	1990–97
Austria	68.5	69.6	71.4	69.9
Belgium	69.6	74.5	73.2	71.5
Netherlands	69.9	74.2	67.6	65.8
EU average	71.3	75.2	73.1	69.9

Source: European Commission, DG II, *European Economic Review* 4/1998; adjusted for changes in employment structure.

In terms of personal income distribution, Austria is the most unequal of our societies. In 1993 the D5/D1 earnings ratio was 2.00 in Austria, as opposed to 1.43 in Belgium and 1.54 in the Netherlands (OECD 1996: 61–62). In the upper earnings range Austria is the most, and Belgium the least, unequal. Inter-sectoral earnings differentials in Austria are particularly large on account of inequality between male and female workers (Pichelmann and Hofer 1999). The incidence of low pay, or the percentage of workers who earn less than two-thirds of the median, is higher in Austria (13.2%) and the Netherlands (11.9%) than in Belgium (7.2%) (OECD 1996: 72). Or should we say that wage compression at the lower end of the labor market is strongest in Belgium? The Belgian national minimum wage tends to be high by international standards. In 1993 medium wages in manufacturing were only 43 percent higher than the minimum wage, which is rather similar to the situation in German manufacturing. In the Netherlands, the distance between medium and minimum wage had risen to 56 percent, in France to 65 percent, and in the UK even to 80 percent (Roorda and Vogels 1997). In Austria minimum wages are contractual, vary by sector, and are much lower in most services than in manufacturing (Dolado et al. 1996). If measured in purchasing power parity, the Belgian minimum wage is estimated to be about 10–20 percent above the Dutch minimum wage, which stood at just over 2,000 guilders, or 1,120 euros in 1999. More Belgian (9%) than Dutch (3%) workers actually earn the minimum wage (Roorda and Vogels 1997).

5.1.6. Continental Welfare States

In the comparative literature on European welfare states, Austria, Belgium and the Netherlands are classified under the regime-types of Continental, 'Bismarckian', conservative, or Christian Democratic welfare states (Esping-Andersen 1990; Kersbergen 1995). Protection is based on employee insurance against occupational risks, financed by earmarked payroll contributions from employers and workers. Traditionally, trade unions and employers' associations are involved in the supervision and administration of social security provision. Programs revolve around income replacement and are targeted at the male breadwinner in order to preserve traditional family patterns. In contrast to the Nordic welfare-state model, social services are underdeveloped. Instead, the system is highly transfer-oriented. Active labor market policies are a recent discovery. In terms of resources spent on such policies in 1995, Belgian ranked fifth and the Netherlands sixth among fifteen European countries, after Sweden, Denmark, Finland, and Ireland. If recalculated as percentages of GDP per percentage point of unemployment, Belgium (0.14%) trails the Netherlands (0.21%) but is ahead of Austria (0.09%) (OECD 1997).

A comparison of policy provisions addressing the social risks of unemployment, sickness, disability, poverty, and old age renders a differentiated picture of the three countries' social security profiles. Here we present the state of affairs in the early 1980s (Flora 1986: vol. ii); in Sections 5.2–5.4 we narrate the most significant changes and reforms. Unemployment insurance is compulsory in all three countries and financed by contributions from employers and employees, often with additional state subsidies. In the event of unemployment, dependent workers must register as unemployed and be available for work. Entitlement to benefits requires a minimum record of 26 insurance weeks in the year preceding dismissal. Benefits are payable for 12 to 30 weeks in Austria; 26 weeks in the Netherlands, with an additional, lower but not means-tested provision for another two years; and without limitation but at a lower benefit level in Belgium. In all three countries insurance benefits are related to the level of wages last earned: the range extends from 58 percent for low-income workers to 40 percent for high-income workers in Austria, in the Netherlands the maximum is 80 percent of former earnings (70% after 1987), and in Belgium during the first year of unemployment benefits were fixed at 60 percent, then cut to 40 percent for single persons in the second year, and thereafter to a (non means-tested) flat rate of half the national minimum wage. Family supplements, up to 80 percent of prior wages for the lowest income groups, are granted on application in Austria. In the Netherlands people who are still unemployed after 2.5 years, have been entitled to means-tested flat-rate social assistance, guaranteeing 70 percent of the national minimum wage, with extra provisions in the case of breadwinners. Trade unions in all three countries are involved in the administration and supervision of sectoral insurance funds, but only Belgian unions have a role handling individual cases of unemployed workers. This is generally seen as a powerful incentive for workers to join the union and an explanation for the high unionization rate in Belgium during periods of high unemployment (Rothstein 1992; Ebbinghaus and Visser 1999).

All employees in these three welfare states are covered by sickness and disability insurance. In Austria, sickness benefits are payable from the fourth day of illness for a maximum of 78 weeks. Legally guaranteed benefits range from 50 percent to 75 percent of wages last earned, depending on the length of illness, the degree of incapacity to work, and family circumstances. Disability benefits vary from 60 percent of wages last earned for single persons to 100 percent for breadwinners. In Belgium and the Netherlands sickness benefits are payable from the first day up to a maximum of one year, at a legally guaranteed level of compensation of 60 percent in Belgium and 80 percent (now 70%) in the Netherlands, though in most collective agreements this is topped up to 100 percent. After one year Dutch workers qualify for a disability benefit, which is payable until the legal retirement age of 65 at a maximum of 80 percent (70% after 1987) of last-earned wages. The actual benefit level corresponds to the degree of claimant's incapacity. After one year of sickness leave, Belgian workers may claim a disability benefit equal to 65 percent of their last wages in the case of workers with dependent relatives and to 43.5 percent for single persons (subject to income ceilings). In Austria and Belgium disability coverage is restricted to accidents at the workplace or going to and from work, whereas in the Dutch disability program entitlement is unrelated to the cause of the incapacity.

Social assistance provides the public safety net for citizens who no longer have other entitlements or means of subsistence. Assistance programs are financed by general revenue, administered by municipal social service agencies, and subject to means testing. In the Netherlands, benefits are set at the so-called social minimum, pegged since 1974 at 70 percent of the national minimum wage for a single adult, 90 percent for a single-parent household, and 100 percent for a married or cohabitant couple. In 1974 a national 'right to a subsistence minimum' was promulgated in Belgium, with maximum social assistance amounting to 28 percent of a single industrial worker's average monthly wages and 40 percent in the case of married couples. In Austria social assistance falls within the jurisdiction of the provinces, which administer their own social assistance provisions, with significant regional variation.

The prior employment record is the main criterion for entitlement to old-age pensions in Austria and Belgium. Pension schemes are financed on a pay-as-you-go basis. In Austria, benefits can add up to about 80 percent of wages last earned. There is no public basic pension in Austria and Belgium. In Austria older citizens in need must seek support from the family, voluntary organizations, and social assistance. Since 1969 there has been a minimum guaranteed income for the elderly in Belgium, providing a safety net for all senior citizens who are insufficiently covered by occupational pension schemes. Benefits levels of this scheme are flat rate, rather low, and means-tested. The Dutch pension system has three tiers. The first tier is a basic public pension, which guarantees everybody over the age of 65 a (non means-tested) flat-rate basic income of 1,400 guilders (660 euros). This part is financed out of general taxation and financed on a pay-as-you-go basis. The second tier provides for obligatory additional pensions, up to 70 percent of last earned wages. In contrast to Austrian and Belgian pensions, this second tier is funded. The third tier consists of personal equity plans and other voluntary private pensions, many of which are tax-deductible.

In the 1970s and 1980s each of the three countries used different social policy provisions to subsidize exit from the labor market and discourage entry. While early retirement and the repatriation of foreign workers provided for the main exit routes in Austria, in Belgium extended unemployment benefits performed similar functions, and generous and lenient sickness and disability pensions became the main 'escape route' in the Netherlands.

The three countries reveal similar trends in terms of total government outlays, resources spent on social expenditure, the share of social transfers, the financial basis of the welfare state, and taxation. In all these areas Austria was a laggard but has meanwhile caught up. The data show that total government outlays have continued to increase in Austria while declining in Belgium since 1993 and in the Netherlands since 1988. Total government outlays were 53.2 percent of GDP in Austria, 55.3 percent in Belgium, and 54.5 percent in the Netherlands in 1995. Social transfers as a percentage of GDP were 22 percent in Austria, 24.3 percent in Belgium, and 25.1 percent in the Netherlands. This share has been growing since the 1980s in Austria, whereas it has been rather stable in Belgium and the Netherlands. Almost three-fifths is paid out of employers' and workers' social security contributions. In 1995 social security contributions covered about 57 percent of expenditure in Austria, 58.6 percent in Belgium, and 59.5 percent in the Netherlands. The non-wage share of total labor costs is around the average of all OECD countries.

5.1.7. *Segmented Pluralism: Class, Religion, and Language*

Austria, Belgium, and the Netherlands have long been considered 'segmented' or 'pillarized' societies (Huyse 1970; Lorwin 1971; Lijphart 1968). In Austria, the two opposing sides reflected the class-divide between workers and owners, the latter including the self-employed, small business, and farmers. Before the war they had behaved like two separate societies or *Lager* (literally, 'camps'), each with its own set of parties, unions, newspapers, sport associations, and para-military organizations, which clashed in the 1934 civil war. After 1945, with memories of civil war and Nazi barbarism still fresh, they invested a great deal in mutual cooperation.

The Reformation and Counter-Reformation had divided the Netherlands into Protestants and Catholics who (alongside Socialists and Liberals) emerged as self-contained communities or vertical 'pillars' during the development of mass democracy and worker mobilization, each camp with its own set of parties, associations, unions, mass media, and clubs. Following the school pact of 1917, those at the top of these pillars learned to compromise and cooperate, each leadership safeguarding a large degree of autonomy and control within its own pillar (Daalder 1966; Lijphart 1968). This system witnessed its maximum strength in the 1950s but began to disintegrate with astonishing speed after the mid-1960s. Religious attendance and voting declined, Catholic or Protestant associations and parties disappeared or merged, the ties between interest groups and parties loosened, and elite control over society and in associations was diminished.

The class-division in Belgium was cross-cut by other divisions, between Catholics (on the one hand) and anti-clerical Liberals and Socialists (on the other) over the role of Church and State in education, and by the language conflict between Dutch- and French-speaking Belgians (Lorwin 1966). The school issue was finally put to rest in 1958, but the language conflict intensified. Within a hundred years of Belgium's founding as an independent state in 1830, hopes for French as its sole, unifying language had vanished. The majority of the population spoke various local variants of Dutch, or Flemish, and many were alienated from a state that had been ruled by foreigners most of the time and long refused the use of Dutch in its laws, courts, and in secondary education. Since French-speaking Belgians never had to learn Dutch, there was no basis for generalized bilingualism. Eventually Belgium became divided in three linguistic territories: a Dutch one, a French one, and a bilingual one, taking into account the reality of Brussels, a former Dutch-speaking city that was located in Flanders but had gradually expanded and become Frenchified throughout the nineteenth and twentieth centuries.

The linguistic conflict was always contaminated by differences of class and economic fortune between the regions. Ever since the decline of the manufacturing and trading towns of Flanders, this province and other Dutch-speaking regions had been the backwaters of the Low Countries, whereas the mines and steel mills of Wallonia became the champions of nineteenth-century railway capitalism. In the 1960s the economic position of the two regions began to reverse. Mutual distrust in the Belgian state channeled the preference of each community towards a federal solution: whereas Flemish nationalists wanted more cultural autonomy, Wallonia's Socialists and union leaders hoped to gain more economic power against what they saw as flawed policies from Brussels' *haute finance* and American capital. The Brussels conundrum ruled out a simple solution (Van Parijs 1998). The Flemish side defended devolution to language communities, Wallonia demanded regional autonomy, and the French-speaking majority in Brussels feared Flemish domination since Brussels is the capital of Flanders. The solution eventually found was a double feder-ation, i.e. a devolution into two, and later three (taking into account the small German-speaking minority within Wallonia) language communities and three regions, yielding five sub-national parliaments and governments (the Flemish community has merged with the Flanders region). The pow-ers and responsibilities of these entities have been defined in extremely complex negotiations, beginning with fixing the language border in 1963 (which had previously depended on a census in which people were asked what language they spoke). In 1993 Belgium was formally declared a fed-eral state and, henceforth, all parliamentary bodies of the communities and regions have been elected directly. The federation remains responsible for defense, justice, security, social security, labor law, and fiscal and mon-etary policy. Foreign and European affairs are shared depending on the policy issue at stake.

5.1.8. Consociational Democracies

The political systems of Austria, Belgium, and the Netherlands, along with Switzerland, have been regarded as the clearest examples of consoci-ational democracies (Lipset and Rokkan 1967; Lehmbruch 1967; Lijphart 1968). In such democracies party elites are encouraged to cooperate in a spirit of non-competitive power sharing. In his seminal theoretical case study of Dutch politics, Lijphart sums up the ideal-typical consociational democracy as an alternative to the majoritarian Westminster model by cit-ing four institutional characteristics: proportional representation, coali-tion governments, mutual veto rights, and cleavage autonomy. How well party elites are able to accommodate divergent world views in broad coali-tion governments depends as much on institutional features as upon the various political actors' preferences, strategic goals, power resources, and control over their respective constituencies. How policy choices affect pol-icy performance cannot, therefore, be answered by merely focusing on institutional characteristics (Scharpf 1997). Only when grand coalitions adhere to common objectives and elites have control over their supporters does consociationalism yield the institutional advantage of quick or consistent policy implementation. If, however, coalition partners adopt divergent policy goals or are faced with non-compliance and internal competition, they tend to engage in counterproductive political interactions, ending in policy immobilism. This was the fate of the divided governments in Dutch politics in 1970s and of the many large but unstable coalitions that ruled Belgium in that decade.

The Austrian variant of *Proporzdemokratie* is rather unique, inasmuch as its cleavage structure between the two prewar *Lager* has translated into two large parties, each with a potential majority (SPÖ and ÖVP). From 1945 through 1966 they formed grand coalitions; in 1966 the ÖVP formed a single-party majority that lasted until 1970, when the SPÖ won the first of several general elections, allowing it to govern on its own until 1983, at which point the Socialists lost their absolute majority. In 1986 the SPÖ returned to a grand coalition with the ÖVP, which continued into the 1990s. The size of the two major parties' combined electoral support has, however, decreased and this decline, together with the strong showing of the Free Democrats (FPÖ), a nationalist, anti-establishment party on the right, tends to threaten the continuity of Austria's consociationalist-corporatist polity (Table 5.5).

Table 5.5 *Electoral results of Social Democrats and Christian Democrats, 1975–1999[a] (%)*

| Year | Austria (%) | | Belgium | | | | Netherlands | |
| | | | Flanders | | Wallonia | | | |
	SPÖ	ÖVP	SP	CVP	PS	PSC	PvdA	CDA
1976–80[b]	50.4	42.9	12.4	26.1	13.0	10.0	33.8	31.4
1981–85	51.9	41.9	13.5	20.5	13.2	7.4	29.1	32.0
1986–90	43.1	41.3	14.9	19.5	14.6	8.0	32.6	35.0
1991–95	42.8	32.1	12.3	17.0	12.7	7.7	24.0	22.2
1996–99	35.6	22.6	10.1	14.5	10.0	6.3	29.0	18.4

SPÖ: Sozialistische Partei Österreichs; ÖVP: Österreichische Volkspartei; SP: Socialistische Partij; CVP: Christelijke Volkspartij; PS: Parti Socialiste; PSC: Parti Social Chrétien; PvdA: Partij van de Arbeid; CDA: Christen Democratisch Appèl.

[a]Share of valid votes in percentage of total, in general elections for the national parliaments.
[b]Results are averaged for each interval in case of more than one election.

In the Netherlands coalition governments are the rule. The three main parties are, from left to right, PvdA, CDA (before 1977 divided between a Catholic and two Protestant parties), and VVD, the conservative Liberal Party, which draws its support from the middle classes, white-collar workers, and the business elite. Between 1945 and 1958 the government was built round the alliance between PvdA and the Catholic Party. From 1958 to 1973, with a brief interruption, the three Christian parties allied with the Liberals. From 1973 to 1977, around the time of the first oil shock, the PvdA dominated a center-left coalition with two small left-of-center parties and two of the Christian parties. From 1977 to 1989, with an interruption of only nine months, the government was formed by a CDA–VVD coalition, with the CDA dominating. In 1989 it changed partners and allied with Labor. Since 1994 the government has been run by a unique Labor–Liberal coalition, forcing the Christian Democrats into opposition for the first time since 1917. Electoral support for the traditional backers of the welfare state and Dutch corporatism, the PvdA and CDA, has meanwhile dropped below 50 percent, as more voters shift their preference to the Greens on the left and the Liberals on the right.

The Belgian political landscape is more complicated and has recently undergone major changes. Between 1968 and 1978, the three mainstays of Belgian politics, the Christian Democrats (CVP/PSC), Socialists (PSB/BSP), and Liberals (PVV/PLP), split into regional parties that have had to compete with local rivals. However, the religious-ideological segments of like-minded political parties and trade unions, especially the alliances between the CVP and the dominant Christian federation (ACV) in Flanders and between the PS and the socialist federation (FGTB) in Wallonia, have survived. The last all-Catholic cabinet dates from the 1950s, followed by a Socialist–Liberal coalition that put the school issue to rest in 1958. Over the next forty years, Christian Democrats ruled in alternating coalitions with Socialists (1972–74; 1977–81, and 1988–99) and Liberals (1974–77 and 1982–87). Some of these Cabinets were enlarged by regional parties or have been based on grand coalitions of all the major parties for the purpose of constitutional reform. Support for the Socialists and Christian Democrats has declined and even fell under 50 percent in the most recent general elections of June 1999. Belgium's federal government, and four of its five regional or community governments are now based on a coalition of Liberals, Socialists, and Greens.

5.1.9. Negotiated Change under Domestic Constraints

In small countries like Austria, Belgium, and the Netherlands a sense of vulnerability is usually engraved in the minds of policymakers. External shocks induce policy actors to play down divisions, though it may take time to understand the nature and implications of such challenges. Policymaking in the three countries under study is critically dependent upon the consent of different coalition parties and on support from social partners. None of the actors is autonomous and free to choose its most-favored response to new conditions or external pressures. This is particularly true for the government, whose role under the rules of corporatism and consociationalism is constrained both from without and from within. By incorporating multiple parties in coalition governments and integrating the social partners into the administrative structures of public policy-making, the state can mobilize more resources and rally support for policy change. But consociationalism and corporatism can also inhibit change, precisely because of the need for extensive compromises and coalition formation. All negotiated systems are vulnerable to so-called 'joint-decision traps' (Scharpf 1988). Where the state is weak and its powers are 'hollowed out', this may create prolonged policy stalemates.

In the sections that follow we observe varying configurations of the relationships between the state and social partners, ranging from a very stable, uncontested, and consensual pattern in Austria, through a narrower, and variable though (in major areas) renewed cooperative style in the Netherlands, to a troubled and conflictual mode in Belgium. We will argue that these configurations matter for the formation and implementation of policies affecting wages, employment, and social security, since outcomes do depend on cooperation, at different levels, among a variety of actors with veto power.

5.2. Austria: The Rewards of Slowness

Austria entered the 1970s with full employment and a sound macroeconomic performance. Its postwar economic policy profile was strongly influenced by the fact that all interested national actors shared the goal of freeing Austria from the surveillance of foreign occupation forces and re-establishing a sovereign nation. This feeling of 'sitting in the same boat' explains the highly consensual style and the involvement of social partners in many policy areas. The cornerstone of Austrian social partnership is the tripartite Parity Commission with its subdivisions for Wages and Prices. It was founded in 1957, one year after the Hungarian uprising, under the threat of an influx of immigrants. The subcommittee for prices controlled about 80 percent of all consumer goods. Though the effectiveness of price regulation was contested and imported goods were beyond its scope, the committee did have a dampening effect on price developments and gave Austrian trade unions a unique position to influence wages and prices, i.e. to negotiate over real rather than nominal wages.

Austria's postwar model of cooperation among organized labor, capital, and the state was embedded in a climate of consensus, based on shared preferences for growth, exports, full employment, stability, social peace, and on a deep fear of inflation. From the start, Austria's economic policy model included demand-side as well as supply-side elements, such as interest rate subsidies, export subsidies and guarantees, subsidies to tourism, and, above all, tax exemptions. The creation of the Beirat für Wirtschafts- und Sozialfragen in 1963, with representatives of the social partners and ministries along with academic experts, reinforced the 'expert' quality of Austrian social partnership. This Advisory Board issued policy recommendations on a purportedly scientific basis and became an instrument for orchestrating a policy consensus on the basis of a common understanding of the problems at hand. Implicitly, it was understood that the shared interests were those of Austrian male breadwinners. Negative effects, like the benign neglect of consumer interests and a bias against women and foreigners, were ignored most of the time by the social partners and government officials. Austrian unions also had no explicit goal of narrowing income inequalities. Full employment, they argued, is the most effective incomes policy (Guger 1998), while redistributive policies are best left to the state.

Collective bargaining in Austria essentially takes place at the sectoral level, but is highly coordinated via preparatory talks at the central headquarters of the social partners. The sectoral affiliates of the Austrian Confederation of Trade Unions (ÖGB, Österreichische Gewerkschaftsbund) and the Austrian Economic Chamber (WKÖ, Wirtschaftskammer Österreichs, formerly the BWK) negotiate over the wage level for each industry, but under strict supervision about when and how. Compulsory membership in the Chamber and the unitary structure of the ÖGB produce an extraordinarily degree of discipline and membership (100% in the case of employers, 43% in the case of workers, down from 60% in 1970) (Ebbinghaus and Visser 1999; Traxler 1997). From the outset the peak associations were keen to prevent inflationary pressure emanating from competition among their affiliates. The ÖGB always wanted to be involved in all areas of social and economic policymaking and not just be a 'wage machine'.

This encompassing view of trade unions was enhanced by the fact that the unions had a strong foundation in Austria's unusually large public sector. After the war large firms were mostly nationalized, since indigenous big businesses were scarce and the Austrian government tried to save them from the Soviet army's confiscation of German property. Nationalized industries in Austria accounted for about 20 percent of manufacturing employment, one-third of these jobs in the two main nationalized steel firms. The three leading banks and the mining, chemical, and engineering industries were also practically under state control. Consequently, many of Austria's key industries were strongly unionized and in the mire of domestic policies, and they offered a useful tool for sheltering employment if need be. In 1970 almost 80 percent of all employees in the public sector—nationalized industries, rail and postal services, and government employees—were unionized. This compared with 54 percent in the private sector (Guger 1998).

Macroeconomic policy during the era of postwar reconstruction emphasized cheap money, a balanced budget, and a strong currency in order to dampen imported inflation. The Austrian central bank (ÖNB, Österreichische National Bank) was partly owned by the social partners and the political parties, with a government share of 50 percent. This set the stage for a consensual and negotiated monetary and exchange rate policy. The ÖNB pegged the schilling first to the US dollar and then to a currency basket of its main trading partners before finally joining the European currency 'snake' in 1971. Low interest rates set by the ÖNB encouraged private investment by making loans cheaper. Savings were heavily subsidized in order to dampen consumption and encourage private investment. At the time, stable exchange rates with interest rate differentials between Austria and Germany could still exist, because capital controls prevented excessive and sudden capital movements. In case of inflationary pressures, the ÖNB put up credit ceilings. And as long as there was full employment, the budget was balanced or even in surplus.

5.2.1. Collective Mistakes 'Jointly Corrected' in the 1970s

When it was confronted with the first OPEC oil-price shock, Austria appeared to have had the luck of the innocent. It had everything in place for an economic policy model that matched the requirements of fighting stagflation. The oil shock hit unexpectedly, as it did in other countries. With an expected inflation rate of 10 percent, unions and employers had agreed to a 14 percent wage rise for 1975. When, contrary to the expected growth rate of 3.5 percent, a −2 percent contraction occurred, the social partners jointly 'corrected' their mistake (Scharpf 1991: 56). The unions and the government assigned priority to full employment over real wage increases, redistributive objectives, or budgetary restrictions. This even applied to the conservative opposition. The SPÖ government pursued an expansionary budget policy, including public investment programs and indirect subsidies to industry, in order to stabilize demand, while (as a way of curtailing inflationary pressures from abroad) the ÖNB kept interest rates low and tied the schilling to an appreciating Deutschmark. This 'unusual mix' (Guger 1998) of policies proved extremely successful in countering the dilemma of stagflation. It could only work if every actor played its part and the social partners were able to control inflationary pressures and prevent the erosion of competitiveness through wage moderation. Austria's social partners were able to do just that because of their organizational strengths, consensus, and the all-encompassing corporatist framework. Keynesian ideas had reached the Austria economic policy-making community only late (Rothschild 1993: 137), but in the 1970s the interaction of budget, monetary, and wage policies provided a good fit with the prescriptions of Keynesian demand management.

This combination of deficit spending, hard currency, and incomes policy was later coined 'Austro-Keynesianism'. It essentially revolved around five demand- and supply-side instruments aiming at full employment and growth: deficit spending in order to stimulate demand, an accommodating monetary policy of low interest rates in order to stimulate private investment, labor hoarding in the nationalized industries, a hard currency policy, and an incomes policy. Austro-Keynesianism differed from traditional demand management in that it was not confined to anti-cyclical policies, but rather represented a long-term device to stabilize business expectations with the help of incomes and exchange rate policies, encouraging growth and investment (Tichy 1985). Employment-stimulating budget measures were supported by cheap loans promoting private investment and allowing labor hoarding in the public sector. Inflation was held down by means of a hard currency and wage restraint. The commitment to fixed exchange rates necessitated that current account deficits resulting from such a policy had to be dealt with separately through export subsidies and taxes on imports.

Inflation came down from its 1974 peak of 9.5 percent. The increases in real wages during the recession of 1975 were compensated by subsidies to firms out of the budget and corrected in the bargaining rounds for the next year. Since business could rely on moderate wage claims in the future, it did not need to increase prices. The hard currency choice helped keep the price of imported goods low. Consequently, Austrian inflation fell rapidly in line with Germany's. A comfortable budgetary position allowed enough room for maneuvering in macroeconomic policy. 1975 was an election year and the SPÖ, aiming at maintaining its absolute majority, gave priority to full employment and was willing to experiment with Keynesian deficit spending in a way that overruled the traditional commitment to a balanced budget. The government allowed the deficit to increase from 1.5 percent of GDP in 1974 to 4.5 percent a year later. Since the budget deficit was largely financed abroad, the domestic money supply increased and crowding out private investment through higher interest rates was avoided.

It has been argued that Austria's exchange rate policy in the mid-1970s was hard, whereas its monetary and labor market policies were soft (Breuss 1978: 6). The currency policy of the early 1970s was quite flexible, and there were still visible signs of an autonomous exchange rate policy. Having depreciated by an accumulated −13 percent between 1968 and 1973, the schilling next appreciated 2.9 percent against the dollar from 1974 to 1977, which helped keep the price of imported oil down (Tichy 1985: 500). Within the SPÖ Party, the unions emphasized the importance of stable exchange rates as a bulwark against inflation and the loss of purchasing power. As an alternative to depreciation, massive export subsidies helped ease the burden on industry, and they also help explain why Austrian exports (−3.5%) declined less than in Germany (−6.1%) (Uher 1993: 86 f.). Trade unions did not take advantage of labor hoarding in the nationalized industries by pressing real wage increases, demonstrating that full employment was their true priority. Between 1973 and 1983, redundancies in the state sector were half of what they were in the private sector—indicating that the public sector did in fact shelter employment. It was a political decision that turned out to be an advantage once the crisis had passed. Nationalized industries were eager to exploit new market opportunities, whereas comparable German firms were reluctant to hire new workers after they had gone through the experience of costly layoffs. The number of workers employed in Austrian industry fell only slightly in 1975–76 and increased immediately afterwards. An additional source of support for employment came from the service sector. Tourism, retailing, and public sector jobs in municipalities, police departments, and post offices soaked up those industrial workers who had been laid off (Scharpf 1991: 58).

The demand-side success of Austro-Keynesianism was supported by fairly effective supply-side measures. First, like other European countries in the mid-1970s, Austria implemented a previously negotiated reduction of the working week to 40 hours. Second, the government and the social partners jointly decided to implement a more restrictive quota on foreign laborers. The influx of foreign workers had played an important role in postwar Austria, helping to overcome the labor shortage during the period of reconstruction. Immigrant labor served as a buffer during the 1970s, when policymakers agreed to restrict immigration and encouraged repatriation, although not as extensively as in Switzerland. A limit on work permits resulted in a reduction of 52,000 foreign workers (−20%) between 1973 and 1978, equaling a 2 percent reduction in the labor force (Scharpf 1991: 58). The combined effect of all these measures showed up in low open unemployment and a rising employment/population ratio, despite the slight decline in employment (−56,000) in 1975.

Chancellor Kreisky received a political bonus for his economic management in the elections of 1975 and, again, in 1979. Hence, the SPÖ maintained its absolute majority throughout the crisis-ridden 1970s. Inflation was contained thanks to trade union wage moderation and a strong currency. Full employment was preserved because the SPÖ privileged job creation, labor hoarding in nationalized sectors, and repatriation of foreign workers over the goal of budget consolidation. Unemployment remained below 2 percent in the second half of the 1970s. The price of the hard currency option was a deteriorating external balance, but this seems not to have been a major constraint. The problem was addressed with an increase in the VAT rate on luxury goods and cars, intended to restrict imports, and through special investment and export-promoting measures in the context of the Association Treaty with the European Community (Lehner 1991: 474). In contrast to later periods, confidence in the ability of national crisis management was high (Kienzl 1993: 71). By virtue of the outstanding macroeconomic performance it achieved—maintaining full employment in the face of the 1970s dilemma of stagflation—the policy-mix of Austro-Keynesianism was raised to the status of an effective crisis management model.

5.2.2. The Policy of 'Diving Through' in the Early 1980s

The oil shock of 1979, in combination with the financial constraints of 1981's high interest rates and increased international capital mobility, posed a new challenge to Austrian policymakers. This time they managed less well. Their anticipated policy response of 'diving through' this second crisis in a manner that was tried and familiar underestimated changes in the international environment. Financing the US current account deficit had absorbed 10 percent of world savings, and the resulting high interest rates spilled over into Europe. The effectiveness of capital controls had eroded, and international financial markets had become less predictable. This became evident in 1979, when the ÖNB set interest rates below the German level.

The negative trade balance, due to the increased cost of oil imports in combination with low interest rates, resulted in a massive withdrawal of capital. The ÖNB lost about one-third of its reserves. This effectively caused the central bank to give up its active nominal interest policy (Winckler 1980). The schilling depreciated 2.3 percent against the Deutschmark in 1979 (Tichy 1985: 500) and inflation increased from 3.7 percent in 1978 to 6.8 percent in 1981. Since all Austrian actors were afraid of depreciation and its inflationary consequences, the schilling was officially pegged to the Deutschmark in 1980. By tying its hands, the ÖNB sacrificed monetary policy in order to concentrate on exchange rate stability (Hochreiter and Winckler 1996). The dramatic loss of currency reserves had persuaded the central bank to abandon one crucial pillar of Austro-Keynesianism.

The budget deficit came under increased pressure from rising interest rates. In principle, the government applied a formula, which prescribed that the annual net deficit should not exceed −2.5 percent. Fiscal policy did not allow heavy deficit spending. But, as in 1974–75, the recession of 1981–82 was fought with the help of expansionary employment programs, letting the deficit slip to −4 percent in 1983. Employment in the exposed sector was kept relatively constant, due to continued labor hoarding by the nationalized industries. Elderly workers were allowed to take early retirement. If unemployed, they received special allowances. Sending foreign workers home by withdrawing work permits, however, proved more difficult now, since many immigrants had applied for Austrian citizenship after an uninterrupted stay of ten years. Still, banking on its successes from the 1970s, Austria managed to keep unemployment down at 3.5 percent in 1982. Full employment policy was not maintained, however. Using national rather than OECD or ILO statistics (the latter being more restrictive since they measure readiness to accept a job), unemployment rates had more than doubled within four years (from 2% in 1979 to 4.5% in 1983). The employment/population ratio fell from 68 percent in 1979 to 63 percent in 1983, reflecting early retirement and discouragement. Active labor market policies were hardly used. Favorable developments in the 1970s had induced Austrian policymakers to continue without major changes, applying the rule: 'If it ain't broke, don't fix it' (March and Olsen 1989).

Restricting the labor supply was a major policy response to the labor market problems of the 1980s. Giving in to union demands for a new round of working time reduction, employers granted two extra holidays in 1985, and a year later the minimum vacation was increased to five weeks, six weeks for workers with twenty-five years of service (Hauth 1989: 19). Negotiations over working hours were later moved from the national to the sectoral level, a practice adopted for wage bargaining since 1982. By the end of the 1980s the average working week was 38 or 38.5 hours. Eligibility criteria for receiving disability pensions were eased, and special allowances were made available to redundant workers too young for early retirement but deemed too old to find a new job. These arrangements, targeting firms in difficulties, were supported with public money and became very expensive in due course. Between 1975 and 1985 the number of older workers fell dramatically: while 98 percent of men and 47 percent of women between 55–59 participated in the labor force in 1975, these percentages had dropped to 70 percent and 30 percent in 1985. Participation rate for males aged 60–64 were halved from 38 percent to 18 percent; female rates in this age group decreased from 13 percent to 8 percent (Walterskirchen 1997). The SPÖ paid the price for its diminished success in managing the 1981–82 recession with disappointing results in the 1983 general elections. The Social Democrats lost their absolute majority and turned to the FPÖ (then still quite liberal) to form a new coalition. In 1985 'Austro-Keynesianism', already dead for some years, was officially buried by the new SPÖ Chancellor, Sinowatz, when he observed that it had been a policy of 'diving through', which could only bring temporary relief and never work in the long run (Seidel 1993: 146). It had helped to retard the consequences of internationalization and prevented a rise in unemployment rates.

5.2.3. 'Stepping on the Brake' in the Later 1980s

The new SPÖ–FPÖ coalition gave budget consolidation priority over full employment. Labor hoarding in the nationalized sector was increasingly seen as a burden on the public budget. The crisis of the steel industry became a factor in Austrian politics in the 1980s (more than ten years after Belgium or Germany). Between 1981 and 1985 the two major steel firms, Voest-Alpine and VEW, had received 25 bn ATS (3.6 bn DM) in subsidies. In 1985 Voest needed another 16 bn ATS while, for the first time, it announced plans for a mass layoff of between 25,000 and 34,500 people to be completed by 1990. At the same time, Voest Intertrading announced enormous losses from speculating on international financial markets. Consequently, the issue of privatization stopped being taboo in Austria's negotiated economy, and labor hoarding in the nationalized industries was gradually abandoned. Finally, Austrian corporatism was willing and ready to open up to the outside world, though at a slow pace, as summed up in a famous quote by ÖGB President Verzetnitsch: 'The most important person in a bob-sled is the one who handles the brake.'

The 1980s were marked by changes in policies, politics, and perceptions. Nationalized industries were increasingly perceived as rent seekers. When the right-wing populist Haider took over the FPÖ, the SPÖ ended its coalition with the ostensibly liberal party. After the elections of 1986, Social and Christian Democrats formed a grand coalition. The new SPÖ Chancellor, Vranitzky, came from the banking sector and was committed to a modernizing course. Both parties set their sights on membership in the European Union. They agreed on an extended program of privatization in 1986–87. Begrudgingly, an internally divided ÖGB went along, its member unions squeezed between the never-ending claims of the protected sector and a private sector that was less willing to foot the bill. The WKÖ wanted privatization and deregulation, but slowly. 'Let up on the brakes but don't step on the gas' was the slogan of its general secretary (Teufelsbauer 1986). The privatization program for 1987 left 51 percent of the shares of the public sector, including banking, Austrian airlines, and energy firms, in public hands (Feuchtmüller 1987). Privatization proceeded in steps, and the impact was cushioned with social plans elaborated by the social partners. This helped keep unemployment stable at 3–4 percent. Yet the abandonment of labor hoarding and the restructuring of the nationalized industries—the country's most unionized sector and home to the Socialists' most stable electorate—led to a decrease in ÖGB and SPÖ membership. Under threat of losing their jobs, the frustrated workers became the ideal constituency for an increasingly right-wing FPÖ.

In 1987, later than in most other countries, capital controls were abandoned. Now international evaluation of Austria's economic performance became even more important. A sound budget figures high in international country ratings, which governments cannot afford to ignore. One convenient way to create revenue is to sell off the 'silverware' of state-owned enterprises. Once again, this gave Austria time to postpone substantial social policy reforms. By the end of the decade, when privatization and industrial restructuring were well under way, the government finally succeeded in its consolidation effort. Helped by the expansionary effect of German unification, the budget deficit fell from 4.4 percent of GDP in 1987 to 1.8 percent in 1992. The tax reform of 1988 played a minor role in consolidation; it was mainly seen as a step to adjust Austria to international standards. The employment effects were very modest (one calculation put them at a 0.2 percentage point cut in the unemployment rate). Taking its cue from examples in the USA, Germany, and Sweden, the reform was meant to increase the Austrian tax system's efficiency and transparency by reducing exemptions in exchange for lower rates and a broader tax base (Nowotny 1989). It was a political signal to capital that tax subsidies could no longer be expected (Lehner 1991: 475). The corporation tax rate was reduced from 55 percent to 30 percent, later raised to 34 percent again (comparable to Belgium at 39% and the Netherlands at 35%). Going against the international trend, the progressive element in the income tax system was strengthened (Guger 1998), and the SPÖ and unions continued to favor lenient treatment for small investors and savings accounts, many held by their members. The tax reform of 1993 abolished the inheritance tax and the tax on artisan enterprises. Austria appears to have the lowest property tax in the OECD (Farny 1996: 74). As was discussed in the introduction, overall levels of taxation are slightly above the OECD average, though slightly lower than in Belgium and the Netherlands. The overall tax burden rose in the period up to the early 1980s but has been constant since, hiding a shift in the composition of revenues towards social security charges, now just over one-third of all revenues. Again, at this point there are hardly differences with Belgium and the Netherlands. The Austrian tax reforms of 1988 and 1993 shifted the tax burden from capital to labor. The effective tax rate on labor in Austria (43% in 1995) lies now between Belgium (40%) and the Netherlands (46%) and is not greatly out of line with other European continental welfare states (OECD 1998: 60).

While reducing employment in the nationalized industries, Austria increased public sector employment, going against an international trend that even included Scandinavia. Government employment increased steadily from 8.9 percent of total employment in 1970 to 11.6 percent in 1980, 13.3 percent in 1990, and 14.3 percent in 1994. Between 1987 and 1996, the public sector, including education and health services, contributed toward easing the labor market situation by adding 140,000 jobs, equal to two-thirds of total employment growth (Walterskirchen 1997: 7). Most of these public service jobs went to Austrians, whereas foreign workers found jobs mainly in construction, retail, restaurants, and manufacturing. In 1995 the federal government imposed an employment stop, and all new jobs now have to come from the regions and municipalities, responsible for education and health. Social Security and related public services expanded employment. By separating the post office and Austrian railways (now independent corporations) from the state budget, the government was able to generate new revenue.

5.2.4. The 1990s: Going Europe

The end of the Cold War and the opening of borders led to a revival of an old Austrian fear—to be left in the isolated corner where its capital lies geographically: East of Prague. Until 1989 Austria's place in the West had been assured by the Iron Curtain. To join the EU became now a matter of utmost urgency. Back in the 1960s Austria had already applied for membership, but the USSR had vetoed this. Its robust economic position, based on a hard currency, low inflation, low unemployment, and close trade links with Europe and Germany, made Austria a sure candidate for EU membership. The budget deficit was the only cause for worry. Entry into the EU in 1995 and the austerity measures required to meet EMU membership criteria became two showpieces for the resurgence of Austrian corporatism in the 1990s.

In the early 1990s Austria's relative growth performance had improved and public finances were in good shape again. Though small by international comparison, Austria's labor market problems had however increased. Austria was strongly affected by the crisis in Yugoslavia. In 1991 an inflow from the traditional immigrant countries Yugoslavia and

Turkey added 7 percent to Austria's labor force. Unemployment increased steadily, to 4.4 percent according to OECD and ILO statistics, 7.8 percent according to national statistics. This is still modest by European standards of today, but high if judged in the light of Austria's postwar accomplishments. Increased public sector employment and the effects of introducing the second year of a maternity allowance helped keep unemployment down, but at the cost of higher budget deficits. Under the impact of lower growth rates, the deficit rose to 5 percent in 1995, despite consolidation efforts. No alleviation was to be expected from tax policy or the sale of state enterprises. Substantial expenditure cuts became unavoidable. In order to divert blame from this unpleasant policy problem, domestic politicians welcomed the use of Brussels as a most convenient scapegoat.

In the late 1980s the SPÖ and ÖVP had presented their ideas on joining the EU and, after some massaging, managed to convince their respective social partners. This had been more difficult for the SPÖ than for the ÖVP. Initially, the unions received Vranitzky's liberal pro-European ideas with a great deal of skepticism. The ÖGB was split between two wings, one in favor led by the powerful metalworkers union representing mainly members from export industries, and one against led by the union of white-collar staff in industry and services, now the ÖGB's largest affiliates. The ÖVP had to appease the opposition from small artisans and farmers. Farmers were induced to vote in favor of EU membership by the promise from industrialists to support liberalization of trade regulations, enabling farmers to earn money outside their traditional tasks. Later business reneged under pressures from tourism and retailing, and ÖVP had to orchestrate a new compromise, less favorable to farmers (Tálos and Kittel 2000). In the end, Austria's social partners 'went Europe' and joined the grand coalition in support of EU membership. In 1992 unions and employers negotiated an agreement in which they codified the switch from a closed to an open economy. A subcommittee for international affairs was founded and the long obsolete subcommittee for prices was changed into a subcommittee for competition (Nowotny 1998). The hope of being able to meet future shocks of internationalization under an EU umbrella, with closer ties to Austria's big German neighbor, had outweighed fears about a loss of sovereignty and lower social standards. After they had convinced themselves, the social partners played a leading role in persuading the public, and in the 1994 referendum 66 percent of the Austrian electorate voted in favor of EU membership, leaving only Haider's FPÖ and the Green Party opposed. Austria became a member of the European Union in January 1995, together with Sweden and Finland.

With EU membership Austria had set its sights on joining the EMU as well. It effortlessly fulfilled all the membership criteria, except the 3 percent norm for budget deficits and the 60 percent norm for the public debt ratio. A consolidation package of rather unpopular fiscal authority measures would have to be implemented. The social partners had been involved in virtually every major economic policy decision since the late 1950s. However, for the first time in forty years, the government decided after initial negotiations in November 1994 to go ahead with its austerity plan without asking the prior consent of the social partners. Vranitzky was the banker-technocrat type of politician who had no close ties with the union leadership, and even within his own party he was not fully supported. The ÖVP was split among the different interests of big industry, farmers, small business, and artisans. Perhaps the idea was that some demonstration of political power or public leadership was called for. The trade unions denounced the procedure as intolerable and stepped up resistance. Their substantive criticism was that the package, including cuts in maternity and early retirement allowances, family assistance, unemployment benefits, and civil servants pay, as well as higher contributions for health insurance, schoolbooks, and public school transport, was socially unbalanced. This led to fierce tension between unions and the party. The SPÖ was dependent on union support in parliament, and the austerity measures that were ultimately presented and adopted did not go as far as originally planned.

The unions had demonstrated their veto position but they were no longer gatekeepers. They could not avoid accepting the government's agenda and be drawn into negotiations over stronger austerity measures. But its failed show of political resolve had taught the government the lesson that it could not go against the social partners when making painful decisions. Yet the conditions for cooperation had changed. The government now decided the issues and the social partners worked them out (Tálos, interview, Sept. 1998). The second austerity package of September 1995 was negotiated with the social partners but was also far more severe than the first one. It included expenditure cuts of 34.5 bn ATS (2.5 bn euros), including a cut in family assistance and in birth assistance allowances, a cap on health care expenditure, and stricter regulations on unemployment benefits. Furthermore, the Structural Adjustment Acts of 1995 and 1996 raised the threshold for early retirement, subjected disability pensions to stricter criteria, and phased out the special early retirement schemes. Paradoxically, the social partners had gone much further than the government would ever have dared (Tálos, interview, Sept. 1998). The measures were implemented without protest—a unique feat in Europe.

5.2.5. Social Policy: A Pensioners' State

As discussed in the introduction, Austria's social security has developed along lines typical for Continental welfare states. It relies heavily on gainful employment and joint family coverage. This is reflected in the fact that about 95 percent of benefits are devoted to health, pensions, and unemployment insurance (plus family benefits), and only 5 percent to social assistance. Austria's policy of keeping overt unemployment low through the early retirement is clearly visible in the structure of social expenditures. In 1995, 49 percent of social spending went to old age pensions, which is significantly above the EU-12 average of 44 percent. On the other hand and for the same reason, expenditure on unemployment (6%) is below the EU average (9%).

The 1995 restrictions on unemployment insurance increased the reference period from 20 to 26 weeks; benefits now end after 20 weeks, though under certain conditions they may be extended to one year. Net replacement rates have been lowered from 58 percent to 56 percent of net wages. When unemployment insurance benefits expire, a means-tested allowance, up to a maximum of 92 percent of the prior unemployment insurance benefit, is available under more restrictive conditions. The extended benefits introduced in 1990 for older workers or workers in crisis regions have been abandoned again. Some local authorities responsible for social assistance have made payment contingent upon the willingness to work, introduced sanctions in cases of abuse, and reduced benefits for asylum seekers (Alber 1998: 18; Tálos and Wörister 1998: 273–79). In the health system small user charges were introduced in 1989 for hospital care, and in 1996 for ambulant care (Tálos and Wörister 1998: 230).

Austria's main problem, so far unsolved, is the pension system. The 1980s and 1990s transformed the Austrian welfare state into a 'state of pensioners' (Esping Andersen 1996: 74). Since 1975 the average retirement age for the dependent labor force has declined by roughly three years. In 1996 it averaged 58 years for men and 56.5 years for women (Pichelmann and Hofer 1999: 9). In 1993, 2.2 times the amount of transfers going to young people were spent on the aged. Only Italy beats Austria in this respect. The 1997 Pension Reform raised the assessment base of pension benefits from fifteen years of highest earnings to eighteen so as to harmonize the private sector scheme with pensions for civil servants (Tálos and Wörister 1998: 262). This change will be gradually phased in through 2003 and will make it harder for people with a short employment record, especially women, to draw a full pension (Alber 1998: 14). Early retirement was made financially less attractive by cutting the replacement rate and terminating allowances for the elderly unemployed who go into 'pre-early' retirement. This has resulted in a curtailment of premature pensions, drawn after only thirty years of work, by an estimated 7 percent (Alber 1998: 15). The Constitutional Court has ruled against the unequal pension age for men and women, and women's pensions will now be raised from 60 to 65 years, to be fully phased in by 2024. Under pressure from the European Court of Justice, foreigners must be granted access to emergency aid. This is one of the few exceptions to the restrictive trend in social policy during the 1990s. The others are the introduction of health care benefits for the old and sick, demanded by the SPÖ, and the extension of maternity allowances (to 18 months) and two years of unemployment insurance for employees who become self-employed, a benefit demanded by the ÖVP and business groups. We agree with Alber (1998: 19) that the Austrian welfare state is still intact and that no major shift towards a new welfare mix strengthening private provisions ever occurred.

5.2.6. The Alpine Model: Success or Failure?

Austria's overall macroeconomic performance is quite good. Unemployment rates have been among the lowest in Europe (4.4% in 1999), though higher than what they used to be. Inflation is low, and the current account improved owing to the international recovery and unusually high receipts from tourism. Income inequality is significant and growing, but not a major issue. Social peace and stability are still as solid as the Alps.

Schettkat (1999) used ILO data and called Austria one of the four European tigers, along with the Netherlands, Denmark, and Ireland, on account of these countries' growing employment/population ratios. However, our OECD Economic Outlook data, shown in Figure 5.3, suggest that Austria was more like a paper tiger. Employment has been on a downward trend since the 1970s. There are not enough new jobs to absorb the increase in the labor supply due to more women (re-)entering the labor market and immigrants seeking work. Employment ratios for those over 55 are extremely low. Roughly four-fifths of job creation comes from the public sector, the major pillar of employment policy in the 1980s and the 1990s. Between 1980 and 1996 50,000 new jobs were created in the private sector and 208,000 in the public sector. It is more than likely that this public job machine will not continue to work, owing to additional consolidation efforts. Recently a trend towards more part-time employment is observed. In 1998 15 percent of all new jobs had less then 10 weekly hours, and these were mainly held by women. But part-time jobs for women are often of inferior quality, involuntary (Muehlberger 1998), and socially unacceptable to men.

What is left, then, of Austro-Keynesianism? We have argued that this peculiar but successful combination of policies was abandoned in the early

1980s. Fifteen years later, upon joining the EMU, Austria delegated monetary and exchange rate policy to the European Central Bank. The nationalized industries have progressively been sold off and privatization has been practically completed. Industrial policy is busy applying EU standards. In order to fulfill the criteria for the Growth and Stability Pact of the Amsterdam Treaty, additional budget cuts have been proposed. These have to come out of the expenditure side, since the near future is unlikely to bring any new increase in receipts. The tax reform for the year 2000 is forecast to result in a reduction of 30 bn ATS in government receipts. Trade unions wanted lower tax rates as compensation for real income losses over the last fifteen years, and the remainder of the lost receipts derives from tax deductions of families demanded by the ÖVP. The original reform goal, as announced in the National Action Plan for employment submitted to the European Union, was to improve Austria's competitive position by reducing taxes and duties on labor costs, especially through a reduction of payroll taxes in low-wage sectors. But this was not realized. The employment effects will therefore be modest, and budgetary concerns paramount.

Wage moderation is the only instrument remaining from the traditional Austro-Keynesian toolkit. Throughout the turmoil of the late 1980s and early 1990s, the Austrian wage bargaining system remained a beacon of stability. Bargaining practices remained firmly entrenched at the sectoral level, with the metalworkers assuming wage leadership (Traxler 1997). But what if unemployment keeps creeping up? Will disillusioned trade unions demand higher wages for insiders? Will passive labor market policies be abandoned? Access to the EU Social Cohesion Fund has increased the attractiveness of active policies. Supervised by a tripartite board, the Austrian public employment service is managed by the social partners. The revised National Action Plan (1999) foresees a drop in the unemployment rate from 4.4 percent in 1999 to 3.5 percent by 2003 and the creation of 100,000 additional jobs. The emphasis is on reducing youth unemployment. There are doubts as to whether these measures will be enough to make up for expected job losses in textiles and clothing ($-23,000$ jobs), food manufacturing ($-5,000$ jobs), and building materials ($-15,000$ jobs). Employment in services picked up, but only slowly. In 1998 30,000 additional jobs, many of them part-time, were created, mainly in the business-related service sector and in retail. Working time flexibility appears to be rather limited; compared with Belgium and the Netherlands, fewer Austrians work in shifts, at night, or during weekends. After considerable pressure from the government and heavy resistance from trade unions against amending the working time law in 1997, the power to regulate these matters has been devolved to sectoral level collective agreement.

In short, the Alpine model is rather old-fashioned. Despite the rhetoric of modernization, it is an example of 'defensive corporatism'. It continues to rely on compromise by the social partners reached by unanimous decision between comprehensively organized peak associations based on compulsory membership for employers and a union monopoly on representing workers. Economically, the model has not escaped the 'welfare without work' logic of Continental welfare states. Exit from work has been the main strategy to keep overt unemployment low. Public employment has been the most important instrument for confronting the shortage of jobs. Job creation in private services has been lackluster. Politically, the two big coalition parties have succeeded in retaining their exclusive hold on political power, but the challenge of Haider's right-wing populism has become stronger and now poses a major obstacle to social partnership. In 2000 the new coalition between ÖVP and FPÖ meant an end to forty years of SPÖ government. Most social changes have come from abroad. Equal rights and affirmative action for women were pushed onto the Austrian agenda by the European Union and became law in 1995 after an impressive showing in a referendum. A European Court decision required that Austria stop excluding foreigners from receiving social assistance. The Austrian paradox seems to be that, even with a high level of female labor market participation (higher, in any case, than in Belgium and the Netherlands), this society is still very male oriented.

The Alpine model has its drawbacks, but is it a failure? Is it a dinosaur, incapable of adjustment to the needs of post-modern society (Crepaz 1995)? We prefer to speak of a midlife crisis for a 42-year-old social partnership, based on fears of faltering potency, a perception that the best years may be over, and sudden engagement to a younger bride in Brussels (Unger 1996). If there are signs of modernization, they essentially come from without—Europe—rather than from within. But a midlife crisis eventually passes, even if the best years are over. Union density has fallen by one-third during these twenty-five years, and compulsory membership in the Chambers has been challenged, but the ÖGB and WKÖ are still formidable powers. Recent efforts of the new coalition to exclude labor from policy reform negotiations and to split the social partners might change this drastically. In 1997, 60 percent of Austrians (in 1983 it was 69%) agreed that social partnership was an advantage for Austria, whereas only a small minority of 12 percent expressed the opposite view (Tálos and Kittel 2000). Referenda among members of the Economic Chamber and the Chamber of Labor produced a large turnout and considerable majorities in favor of continuing compulsory membership.

Adjustment towards a flexible deregulated labor market progresses faster than the public debate likes to admit. Many plant-level agreements have flexible working time schemes, hardship clauses are used, and troubled firms are exempted from sectoral collective agreements. In the retailing and building industry, in tourism and business services, there is greater regulatory flexibility than before (BMAGS 1999). This is part of Austria's social partnership culture, which accepts internal flexibility, especially when demanded by works councils, which are interested above all in their firms' survival. Typically, they defend internal flexibility and deviance from the rules while simultaneously sticking up for strong external constraints as fixed in collective agreements and law. In the process, Austrian social partnership has witnessed some devolution towards sectoral negotiations and agreements. This implies some loss of central coordination capacities. Associational self-regulation is primarily confined to wage bargaining and vocational training. In short, the social partners no longer decide which issue should be on the public policy agenda. Rather they must deal with issues presented by the government, which itself is increasingly borrowing from the EU agenda. As the story of the consolidation package has so clearly demonstrated, the social partners are, however, still perfectly able to defend their institutional veto powers.

Of the three countries, Austria was both last and least exposed to the challenges of international trade. In combination with the country's extremely slow pattern of adjustment, this may have helped Austria avoid extreme fluctuations in output and employment. Being a laggard with roughly ten years of retarded development has its advantages. In Nadolny's novel *The Discovery of Slowness*, the captain prevents his ship from being lost in the driving ice precisely because his innate slowness prevents him from reacting at once. Austria entered the 1990s with lower unemployment rates and fewer fiscal problems compared to most other welfare states. Incremental or defensive corporatism was able to absorb external shocks and avoid internal upheaval by successfully shifting some problems ahead and solving only others that were most urgent. The transformation of the welfare state has only just started. But Austrian corporatism's still strong institutional capacity, demonstrated by a successful accession to the European Union and the austerity measures of 1995, means that implementing difficult changes can happen quickly, once the actors have decided on a course of adjustment.

5.3. The Netherlands: Reinventing Itself

A distinctive feature of Dutch postwar economic policy was its stringent wage policy. Between 1945 and 1963, longer than any other Western democracy, the Netherlands ran a statutory wage policy (Windmuller

1969). Collective agreements needed prior approval from a Board of State Mediators, which was bound by wage guidelines issued by the Minister of Social Affairs. These annual guidelines were subject to central negotiations and intense consultation with the central organizations of unions and employers, which kept affiliates under strict hierarchical control. Statutory wage policy disintegrated in the 1960s under the pressure of tight labor markets and considerable wage drift.

After a failed experiment with self-regulation and intermittent state intervention, the new Wage Act of 1970 handed the responsibility for wage setting back to unions and employers. The government retained the power to order a temporary wage stop or impose a ceiling on wages if the economic situation did in its view warrant such a step. The unions opposed the law and temporarily left the main advisory body, the Social Economic Council (SER), in protest. Experience had told the Dutch unions that government controls placed them in the impossible position of having to defend low wages while profitable firms repeatedly broke the rules under pressure and paid higher wages. Without control over the works councils or some other kind of presence within individual firms, government controls tended to 'hollow out' unions' bargaining role and make members disaffected (Visser 1995). Distrusting the works councils and the government, the trade unions defended central wage negotiations, at a distance from the firm but also without government involvement. Dutch employers likewise ruled out decentralization, since they feared that company bargaining would only help a radicalizing union movement gain entry into the firm. Small and medium-sized firms lobbied for the continuation of government controls. Large and multinational firms might easily have done without government interference, which they increasingly resented, but they did not break ranks with other employers.

By the late 1960s Dutch wage policy, the distinctive element of postwar economic growth and industrialization, was in shambles. Unions and employers were increasingly divided, even within their own ranks, over how to conduct a responsible wage policy and over the role of the government. They still maintained (and would continue to maintain until 1982) that wages should be determined centrally, with annual guidelines fixed by their peak associations represented in the Foundation of Labor. This disarray resulted in only one agreement, in 1972, but that accord was overshadowed by a leadership crisis in the Dutch Federation of Trade Unions and a strike in the metal industry over extra compensation for low-paid workers.

Comparing the Netherlands with Austria on the eve of the first oil shock, we find a completely different institutional setting. While both countries had a legacy of centrally coordinated wage bargaining, this had broken down in the Netherlands, and there was still no agreement on an alternative.

Institutional failure was aggravated by the rise in social conflict and break-down of elite control that accompanied 'depillarization'. This proved all the more serious because postwar industrialization, helped by low wages and rich natural gas finds, had relied upon labor- and energy-intensive export products. By the 1970s the Netherlands had become a high wage economy as a result of large wage hikes from the 1960s—a formalization, in effect, of what some large firms were already paying out as 'black wages' (Visser and Hemerijck 1997). It proved impossible to sustain industries like coal min-ing, textiles and clothing, and shipyards, and we observe that these indus-tries' decline began earlier (before the currency appreciation of the 1970s) and was more intense than in Austria or Belgium (earlier, in fact, than in every European country except Britain). This would have been less of a problem had the Netherlands managed to match its industries' decline with growth in services, private or public. But services did not step into the breach, and the entire 1970s were marked by a decline in manufacturing employment and a stagnation of private services.

5.3.1. The Dutch Disease

When the Bretton-Wood system collapsed, the Netherlands joined the 'snake'. There seems to have been agreement on this move among policy actors, reflecting a tradition of defending a strong currency and of placing financial before industrial interests. This choice meant that competitive-ness would decline if Dutch unions proved unable to enforce wage restraint while the currency was appreciating. This is exactly what hap-pened, especially when Denmark, Italy, France, and the UK defected from the 'snake'. Breaking the wage-price spiral became the key issue of the 1970s. Since labor costs in manufacturing were rising faster than in com-peting countries, all relevant policy actors agreed on the desirability of some form of incomes policy to combat cost-push inflation, but there was no consensus. On the eve of the first oil crisis, a left-of-center government led by Den Uyl (PvdA) had taken office. Impressed by the recession but expecting the crisis to be short-lived, he opted for a Keynesian strategy of fiscal stimulation. The stage was set for a corporatist policy package, along the lines of the Austrian example, exchanging fiscal reflation for voluntary wage restraint. But the radicalized Dutch unions wanted more reforms in economic policy than this government, with weak support from its Christian Democratic coalition partners in Parliament, could offer. In 1974 the government imposed a wage and income freeze, but its effect was undone as soon as the ban on higher wages was lifted.

Thanks to its gas exports, the Netherlands did not experience balance of payments problems after the oil-price hike (the country itself was targeted by OPEC's embargo). Hence, an expansionary course seemed feasible and appropriate. There were various sizeable employment programs, but the main rise in government spending came from expanding welfare programs. This was partly the result of more people becoming unemployed or reaching the limits of their insurance and partly a concession to the egalitarian and solidaristic preferences of the unions. In 1974 the minimum wage and, indirectly, public sector salaries and social security benefits were 'linked' to private sector wage increases. Youth minimum wages increased sharply and were also indexed. Most collective agreements contained automatic price escalators. The result was that pay increases in the private sector automatically translated into higher public sector outlays. The escalators made the government hostage to the outcome of negotiations in the private sector and an interested party in wage bargaining that unavoidably became tripartite (Hemerijck 1995).

From 1960 to 1980 the public sector's claim on national income doubled. Between 1961 and 1971 the share of government outlays increased from 30 percent to 46 percent of GDP, compared to an OECD average jump from 30 percent to 37 percent (OECD 1974). The share rose further to 60 percent by the end of the decade. This expansion was almost exclusively caused by sharply higher transfer payments to households and, in later years, rising interest payments (Kam 1996: 263). The rapid growth of the public sector was only partly matched by higher taxes and social security charges. Price indexation via semi-annual automatic cost-of-living adjustments in wages and benefits remained the main sticking point. An employer offensive to revise the system in 1977 was badly prepared. After a brief but massive strike, the unions claimed victory. As a result, indexation became the litmus test for solidarity between high- and low-paid workers, and between those with and without jobs. It was hard to convince union members that they should give up this instrument at a time of high inflation, when indexation was most needed. Unlike their Austrian counterparts, Dutch unions were in the dark about pricing decisions for common consumer goods. The rational expectation game of achieving lower prices and wages by anticipating lower wages and prices could not be played. The penalty paid by the unions for their defense of indexation was government intervention and an ever smaller space for negotiated nominal wage increases (Visser 1990).

Indexation limits the room for maneuver in case of external shocks. International comparative data show that the short-term and long-term responsiveness of wage rates to changes in unemployment was much smaller in the Netherlands (and Belgium) than in Austria. Thus a much larger rise in unemployment was needed to induce wage moderation. Indexation tends to increase real wage stickiness. Indexation 'tends to make inflation less painful and socially disruptive, but faster and more difficult to brake' (Braun 1976: 235). Since firms in the sheltered sector and government services do not have to fear a loss in market share, they can compensate higher wages by raising prices with impunity. Higher prices in the sheltered sector, much like rising non-wage labor costs, end up stimulating wage increases throughout the economy, undermining the competitiveness of the exposed sector. Indexation is associated with a higher overall wage level, since the 'power of less favored groups to insure that their wages rise more closely in line with other wages will probably not be offset by the reduction in the power of the most favored groups to secure above average wage increases' (Braun 1976: 234). Dutch unions tried to negotiate lower increases for higher-paid employees, but this backfired when senior white-collar staff founded their own unions in the 1970s.

Natural gas turned out to be a mixed blessing, contributing ultimately to the infamous 'Dutch disease'. The embargo aside, OPEC's oil-price hike should not have caused major problems for a country that had its own energy resources. Export revenues and import savings from natural gas resulted in a current account surplus, which put upward pressure on the guilder. The Dutch Central Bank (DNB) pursued its hard-currency policy with the utmost of zeal when it realized that the government was losing control over wage setting and public finances. The guilder's effective exchange rate increased by 30 percent between 1973 and 1977. Profits, real investment, net exports (excluding natural gas), and private sector employment all came under pressure. The inconsistencies in the Dutch policy mix grew to self-defeating proportions (OECD 1980). In hindsight, one might have thought policy actors would have been aware that the combination of an appreciating currency, fiscal reflation, and wage (cost) growth was bound to worsen the stagflation dilemma. In 1976 some prominent Labor Party economists called for a return to the statutory incomes policy and stronger public sector expansion. But the unions rejected the proposal without so much as a thought. Employers did not want any additional state influence and stepped up their attack against what they called 'anti-business' policies. In an unprecedented open letter addressed to the prime minister in 1976, CEO's from the nine largest multinational corporations demanded a change of policy. A massive outflow of capital, from 2.3 bn to 7.5 bn guilders between 1972 and 1982 (Kurzer 1993), was widely seen as a vote of no confidence at the time.

In 1976 Finance Minister Duisenberg put on the brakes. Public expenditure was not to rise by more than 1 percent of net national income per annum (Zanden and Griffiths 1989). By moderating public sector growth the government hoped to make room for private sector investment. Den

Uyl resigned the next year over the issue of land ownership, then won the largest victory for his party in any general election, but failed to form a new governing coalition. Van Agt, the leader of the newly formed Christian Democratic Party (CDA), brokered a coalition with the conservative Liberals (VVD). Like its predecessor, this government tried to talk the trade unions into restraint, but it had even less to offer. Unable to bring public finances under control, the new government felt obliged (against its own intentions) to intervene in wage setting in 1979, 1980, and 1981. The government's wavering position was epitomized by internal conflict between two of the government's CDA ministers, for Social Affairs and Finance (Toirkens 1988; Hemerijck 1995; Snels 1997). Albeda, responsible for Social Affairs, stressed the importance of cooperating with the social partners in order to fight rising unemployment. Cuts in government expenditures and wage restraint were necessary but had to be made acceptable to the unions through compensating policies. Albeda rightly perceived a change in opinion within the trade union movement after 1978. Worried by the continued decline in manufacturing jobs and the collapse of shipbuilding, the major industrial union made a U-turn and defended wage moderation in combination with working time reduction. The union won support from the Federation of Dutch Trade Unions (FNV), and late in 1979 there was even a draft central agreement at the Labor Foundation. But FNV leader Kok withdrew his signature at the last minute when affiliates opposed to the agreement threatened with revolt (Nobelen 1983). Following this failed accord, so carefully arranged by Albeda, his Finance Minister Andriessen wanted an extended wage freeze for two years. Since even VVD regarded this demand as outlandish, Andriessen decided to resign. The commitment to concertation had triumphed over the objective of fiscal restraint, but not for long. When the second oil crisis hit, the Social Affairs Minister had no choice but to impose another wage freeze.

5.3.2. The Crossroads at Wassenaar

The restrictive macroeconomic policies of the USA, UK, and Germany in the wake of the second oil shock made more problems for the Dutch. Higher interest rates exacerbated firms' financial liabilities, squeezed profits, and caused a spate of bankruptcies and factory closures. Unemployment soared at a rate of 10,000 to 15,000 per month, to a record 800,000 in 1984 (14% according to national statistics, later revised to 12% in accordance with ILO and OECD standards). Against the background of strong labor force growth, forecasts were extremely gloomy. Within five years trade unions lost 17 percent of their members, and of the remaining membership nearly one-quarter was out of work, on social benefits, or in retirement. The public deficit peaked at 6.6 percent in 1982.

Slowly but surely the relevant policy actors in the Dutch political economy came to understand the economic and social implications of the perverse spillover effects linking high real wages and indexation to low profits, unemployment, and fiscal crisis. In 1980 the Scientific Council for Government Policy issued a devastating report on the state of Dutch manufacturing and industrial policy, with a biting rebuke of the 'waiting for corporatism' attitude (WRR 1980). Alarmed by its conclusion, Van Agt installed an ad hoc commission, chaired by the president-director of Royal Dutch Shell and members selected on personal merits (from the main industrial trade union, among others). Not wasting any time, this commission recommended lowering wage costs to boost profitability, introducing greater flexibility and decentralization into wage negotiations, boosting wage differentials, and disconnecting public sector wages from the private sector (Dellen 1984).

The general elections of 1981 had resulted in a patched-up coalition between the Christian and Social Democrats, but the new administration immediately fell back into a deadlock and lasted only nine months. New elections in 1982 brought an austerity coalition of the CDA and VVD to power, thanks to gains for the Liberals. This 'no-nonsense' coalition, led by Lubbers (CDA), committed itself to a three-track strategy of (1) economic recovery through improved business profitability, lower wage costs, industrial restructuring, and less regulation; (2) reorganization of public finances and fiscal consolidation; and (3) cost-neutral work-sharing in order to alleviate the unemployment problem. Unveiling its plans on 22 November 1982, the new cabinet declared that 'it is there to govern' with or without the consent of the social partners. Two days later the leaders of the main union and employers' confederation, Kok and Van Veen, announced that they had struck a deal. They had started preparing this deal in the Labor Foundation over the summer, but now the social partners were in a hurry to prevent another intervention. The government had already announced that it would suspend indexation in 1983, and its Minister of Social Affairs, De Koning, bluffed that he might have to impose mandatory work-sharing if voluntary measures were not forthcoming.

With unemployment running into the double digits, 14 percent of the working age population receiving disability or early retirement benefits, and 6 percent on sickness leave, the trade union movement was in no position to fight over wages. Employers saw a chance to rid themselves from recurrent state intervention (van Bottenberg 1995). The Wassenaar agreement was only a recommendation, but one that carried authority. The opposition to the agreement—from the food and services union, through Philips, to the metal employers' federation—was defeated and isolated. To help investment and employment, negotiators in sectors and firms were advised to forsake price indexation and use the savings for a cost-neutral reduction of working hours. With this agreement Dutch unions acknowledged that higher profits were required for the higher level of investment essential to job growth (Visser and Hemerijck 1997). Like the government, employers recognized that working-time reduction was a small price to be paid for this concession. The response to the Wassenaar agreement was swift. Although negotiations over shorter hours proved cumbersome, in less than a year two-thirds of all collective agreements were renewed, mostly for two years, during which the payment of price compensation was suspended and a 5 percent reduction of working hours took place. By 1985 cost-of-living clauses had virtually disappeared; average real wages fell by 9 percent in real terms (Visser 1990). The adjusted share of income from dependent employment, which had risen from an average 69.9 percent in the 1960s to 74.2 percent in the 1970s, fell to 67.6 percent in the course of a few years.

Assured of restraint, the government had its hands free to regain control over public sector finance. Between 1983 and 1986, a 3 percent decline in the public sector deficit was achieved through a small drop in employment (−1%) and salaries (−3%). In 1983 salaries, minimum wages, and related benefits were frozen, and for 1984 the government cut public sector wages by 3 percent. This pushed the public sector unions to the barricades, but after a strike of three weeks they found themselves isolated. Formally, the government had ended the mechanism that had assured public employees' salary rises in line with private sector wages since 1962. Henceforth, unions and employers could no longer shift the costs of stagflation onto the government, but were forced instead to internalize the external effects of wage inflation and unemployment (CPB 1997: 165). Private sector unions could no longer be held hostage by public sector unions (and benefit recipients). Years later, the unions would accept another 'binding' principle, tying their wage demands to increased labor force participation (see below).

Social Affairs Minister De Koning took care of the human face of 'no-nonsense' government. Special measures were taken for the poor and families living on just one income at the social minimum. As the most influential CDA power broker after Lubbers, De Koning had convinced the prime minister, against the advice of the DNB and the Finance Ministry, not to follow the Germans in the EMS currency realignment of 1983. The guilder was devalued by 2 percent against the Deutschmark—a decision that was soon regretted when financial markets demanded an extra risk premium. In March 1983 Dutch monetary authorities announced that henceforth the gulden would be pegged to the Deutschmark. There would no longer be an independent exchange rate policy.

Helped by the international economic upswing, investments and jobs benefited from the recovery of profits in the second half of the decade. The reduction of working hours had an additional work-sharing effect, but the largest boost to jobs came from the rapid expansion of part-time jobs, mainly for married women and young people (Visser 1999). The initial growth in part-time jobs during the early and mid-1980s did not result from policy changes, but rather from behavioral changes by women and employers. In the early 1980s, employers presented part-time work as the flexible and individual alternative to the campaign for a 36-hour work week employers were bent on resisting. Dutch mothers once used to withdraw from the labor market upon childbirth, but this habit was rapidly changing under the impact of better education, higher female wages, smaller families, and changing social norms. Faced with high risks of unemployment for themselves or for their husbands and partners, withdrawal from the labor market was becoming more costly and risky. More women decided to stay employed and ask for reduced working hours instead of quitting their jobs. In the absence of childcare facilities, part-time work became the dominant 'coping' strategy for working mothers. Employers in sectors and firms with overcapacity saw part-time work as a welcome form of voluntary layoffs with little cost to themselves. In health, education, and social services, but also in central and local government, part-time employment was the least painful means of adjusting to budget restrictions. Hiring young people was often limited to 32-hour entry jobs.

Lubbers's austerity policy paid off politically. In 1986 the center-right coalition was re-elected with gains for his CDA party. Two governments of the same persuasion meant a clear break with the immobilism of the 1970s. Inflation declined to near zero in the mid-1980s and has disappeared from the country's worries, until recently. The strict exchange rate policy exerted discipline on wage developments, while wage moderation, in turn, enabled the DNB to stick credibly to its non-inflationary policy. Low inflation allowed unions to forget about indexation. The new mix of macroeconomic policy and wage setting also changed the institutional relations among unions, employers, and the state (Visser 1998). The new pattern became a central dialogue about a wide range of policy issues combined with sectoral wage bargaining, based on the primacy of industrial self-regulation. The role of the central organizations was confined to redirecting sectoral contracting towards tacit, economywide wage restraint and public-regarding behavior (Toren 1996). These new principles have been recognized politically. The 1970 Wage Act was revised in 1986, and the possibility of intervention was narrowed to situations of extreme economic distress.

Since 1982 there has been no political intervention in wage setting. This is not to say the state has lost all leverage over Dutch wage setting. There is no unlimited *Tarifautonomie*, not even under the revised Wage Act (which has not been tested yet). Moreover, a 1937 law authorizes the Social Affairs Minister to declare collective bargaining agreements legally binding for all workers and employers in a certain branch of industry. This provision was routinely applied till the early 1990s but has since been used as a bargaining chip to obtain certain 'public-regarding' objectives from wage negotiators, especially lower entry wages just above the statutory minimum wage for people with low skills, little experience, or a history of unemployment. The government, no longer dependent on the social partners for its own finances, is now in a stronger, more independent position from which it has been able to drive unions and employers closer together.

5.3.3. Trapped in a Spiral of 'Welfare Without Work'

The second Lubbers administration promised to reduce the deficit even further, stop increasing taxes and social premiums, and lower unemployment to under 500,000 people. The new policy challenge was to curtail the costs of social security and reduce the number of welfare recipients, which had continued to rise throughout the 1980s. Cost reduction did take place, mainly through a 1983 freeze (in nominal terms) on the minimum wage and all related benefits, followed by a 3 percent cut in 1984, and the delinking of benefits from wages. The gap between employed workers' average earnings and the minimum wage increased by 12 percent between 1983 and 1989. Since the minimum wage is the basis for calculating state-guaranteed minimum levels for all benefits, social assistance, and basic old age pensions, the freeze reduced the state's liabilities. Youth minimum wages were reduced even more drastically (Salverda 1997). At the same time, fewer adult workers remained at the minimum—so that the proportion of adult workers earning the minimum wage went down from 10 percent to 3 percent between 1983 and 1995.

Under the growing competitive pressures of the 1980s, firms in the high-wage Dutch economy could only survive if they were able to increase labor productivity. Many embarked on a strategy of channeling less productive and more expensive (mostly older) workers out of the labor market into unemployment or onto disability. Here there was a clear moral hazard, since the insurance costs were borne by all firms and (in case funds should run out) by the taxpayer. Rising insurance premiums resulted in higher social security contributions, while the wedge between total (wage and non-wage) labor costs and take-home pay increased. The result was a vicious cycle of job destruction, layoffs caused by firms seeking to match rising costs through increased productivity, leading to higher costs, and so forth. The high average and marginal wedge created clear disincentives for workers to seek a job and threatened the continuation of wage restraint.

It became increasingly obvious that firms, with the complicity of social security administrators, were reducing slack while externalizing costs, leading to an ever-growing volume of claimants. The so-called 'system reforms' in social security, implemented in 1987, had tightened eligibility and lowered guaranteed benefits from 80 percent to 70 percent of last-earned wages in case of unemployment, disability, and sickness, but the reforms had not altered the bipartite governance structure. After the reforms, Lubbers had promised 'peace on the social security front', but it was not to be. The contest over the rise in disability claimants could no longer be avoided and came to a head in 1991. When it came, Lubbers was fortunate enough to have traded his Liberal coalition partners for the Social Democrats, after a break in the old coalition (over environmental policy) and new elections in 1989.

Already in 1986, workers in the age group 55–64 who received a disability benefit outnumbered those with a job (Aarts and de Jong 1992). These authors list four features that may explain the Dutch disability crisis (Aarts and de Jong 1996). First, disability risks were defined as social rather than occupational, and the scheme did not make a distinction between different causes of disability. Second, until it was corrected in 1987 entitlement was based on an assessment of a worker's particular incapacity to find a job similar to his former job. Third, administration for the sickness and disability schemes was kept separate; workers could first spend a year on sickness leave, virtually unsupervised, and than move on to disability. Fourth, under collective agreements, most firms topped up sickness benefits to 100 percent of previous earnings and supplemented disability benefits to 100 percent for a year or longer. Workers drawing full-time disability pensions were not required to be available for hire on the labor market.

Legislation regulating dismissals under the 1945 Extraordinary Decree, originally meant to address postwar chaos but still on the statute books four decades later, was another factor. The Decree had instituted preventive controls and required employers who wanted to end an employment contract to ask permission from the regional labor office director. Procedures could drag on for months, with uncertain outcomes, and no permission could be legally granted when workers were sick or pregnant. The route through sickness and disability became the path of least resistance for many employers. Finally, administration and supervision of the system was in the hands of the social partners through so-called Industry Boards. These Boards were responsible for the medical service that assessed the degree of disability of claimants. As it happened, there was an extraordinary lack of transparency in these assessments. All these factors conspired to bring about a seemingly unstoppable rise in the number of claimants. The Disability Program was expected to support no more than 200,000 people when it was inaugurated in 1967, but was coping with almost 900,000 beneficiaries by 1990. Estimates at the time suggested that between 30 percent and 50 percent of all recipients really were full-time or part-time unemployed. The scheme also was a harsh welfare trap: once officially recognized as (partially) disabled, workers acquired a permanent labor market handicap, often combined with social isolation.

5.3.4. The Political Risks of Welfare Reform

The third Lubbers administration (1989–94), now including a PvdA led by ex-union leader and Wassenaar negotiator Kok as Finance Minister, began in an optimistic mood. Union decline had stopped and unions were regaining confidence, demonstrated by a series of strikes in industry, transport, education, and health services. For the first time in a decade, real wages increased (Visser 1998). Economic recovery allowed for a partial restoration of the suspended 'index linking' that tied the minimum wage and benefits to wage developments. This had been one of PvdA's demands in its coalition negotiations with the CDA. Top civil servants at the Ministry of Social Affairs designed a new system of linking, which became operative in 1992. Index linking of minimum wages and benefits would henceforth depend on the volume of benefit claims in relation to employment measured by the so-called I/A (inactive/active) ratio. If this ratio exceeded a given reference level, fixed at its 1990 value (82.8), the government would be entitled to suspend linking, fully or partially. In 1990, 1991, and 1992 linking was fully applied, but in 1993, 1994, and the first half of 1995 linking was suspended, since the I/A ratio had exceeded its reference value. In recent years the I/A ratio has rapidly fallen and linking has been applied every year since 1995. The new conditional linking mechanism gave the unions, whose (aging) members care much about linking of benefits to wages, a direct incentive to take account of the employment effects of wage bargaining.

Soon after the formation of the Lubbers–Kok cabinet in 1989, an unusual tripartite Common Policy Framework promising growth, employment, tax relief, and wage moderation was concluded between the government and the social partners. Employers signed an agreement with the unions to create 60,000 additional jobs for ethnic minorities, among whom the unemployment rate is three times the national average. This agreement was not implemented, however, and local employers and unions hardly seemed aware of it (Heertum-Lemmen and Wilthagen 1996). In 1994 the agreement was renewed, but employers made sure that no precise target was mentioned. Early in 1991 members of the central employer federation withdrew their signature from the tripartite Policy Framework and stepped up their campaign for tax relief, lower non-wage labor costs, and a cap on government spending. To drive home their point, employers decided to stay away from the customary spring meeting of the Labor Foundation with core Cabinet ministers. They preferred one-to-one exchanges with the unions or with the government, rather than tricky tripartism.

At around this time German unification boosted economic growth, but soon high interest rates dampened economic activity. Although the downturn of 1992–93 was not as bad as in other countries, the decline in unemployment was immediately halted and reversed. The government was preoccupied with the lack of a quick response from wage negotiators and prepared to intervene on the basis of the 1986 law. The pressure worked, and early in 1993 the Labor Foundation recommended a two-month 'breathing space' in order to absorb the new facts of the international recession. Later in the year, after lengthy negotiations, a new agreement called the 'New Course' was reached, a true follow-up of Wassenaar, with more organized decentralization and negotiated flexibility (Visser 1998). Employers gave up their blanket resistance against shorter working hours. Both parties agreed to work together to improve the unfavorable employment/population ratio and recommended flexible working time patterns and part-time work as a solution. There was a separate agreement to abolish residual differences in rights and fringe benefits between full-time and part-time workers. This was backed up in 1994 by legislation forbidding all discrimination on the basis of working hours. In the course of the third Lubbers administration, the exchange logic behind organized wage restraint changed character. Increasingly, wage moderation was matched by lower taxes for workers and lower social contributions for employers, made possible by improved public finances and a broader tax base. This was supported by the tax reform of 1990, which integrated taxes and social security charges, lowered the overall and highest rate, while limiting deductions. Since the national social security contributions were integrated, the first band (37.3%) is mainly (32.3%) a social security charge, while the second (50%) and third (60%) bands are exclusively income taxes. (Payment for each of the three kinds of employee insurance—disability, sickness, and unemployment—is collected collaterally, based on a fifty-fifty division between employees and employers.) By absorbing social security into the lowest band and eliminating deductibility for social insurance contributions (the single largest item before 1990), the tax base was broadened by almost two-thirds. The motive behind the 1990 tax reform, adopted in order to bring about a cost-neutral rationalization of the Dutch tax system, was largely administrative. However, since the reform was sugared with a tax break for most households, consumer spending surged by 4 percent in real terms, while private savings also picked up (Kam 1996). As a consequence, the tax reform had unintended but highly favorable employment effects.

Lubbers I and II had exhausted the 'price' policy of bringing social expenditures under control by freezing and lowering benefits. The PvdA opposed any further measures of this kind. The emphasis therefore shifted to a so-called 'volume' policy aimed at reducing the number of social security recipients. Unavoidably, the political crisis of the Dutch welfare state came to revolve around disability pensions. The number of people receiving disability benefits seemed to approach the magic number of one million in a working age population of seven million. In a well-played *cri de coeur*, in September 1990, Lubbers shocked viewers of the TV evening news by saying that the country was 'sick' and required 'tough medication'. The next summer, after long agony, the government decided to restructure the sickness and disability programs. In response, the unions organized the largest postwar protest march in The Hague. This episode had far-reaching political consequences. The PvdA went through a very deep crisis and Kok, its leader, nearly resigned. Notwithstanding popular resistance, the reforms were enacted. They included a reduction of replacement rates for all workers under 50, including those who were already disabled (and could not take extra insurance). After some time, benefits would decrease to 70 percent of the statutory minimum wage plus an additional age-related allowance. Anyone under the age of 50 in the system would furthermore be subjected to a new medical examination based on stricter rules. In 1993 re-examination affected 43,000 people under the age of 35, of whom 30 percent lost their benefits and 18 percent saw their benefits reduced. (Under pressure from Parliament, the regime has recently softened again.) The legal requirement for partially disabled workers to accept alternative employment was tightened. Under the new sickness law of 1994, the first six weeks in which a worker on sick leave continues to receive wages were charged directly to the employer (later this was extended to the first year). In response to lower legal disability benefits, the unions negotiated extra-legal supplementary benefits in their collective agreements for 1995 and 1996, at the expense of wage increases. As a result, the costs of sickness and disability have been internalized by the bargaining parties to a greater extent.

The 1994 election was a vote of popular discontent. The Lubbers–Kok coalition was effectively voted out of power, losing 32 of its 103 seats in Parliament, just four short of a majority. This amounted to a political earthquake (Koole 1995): no single Dutch coalition had ever lost as much support in one election. The CDA's extraordinary decline (from 54 seats to 34 seats) was caused by a leadership crisis and the untimely publication of a party document suggesting that future retrenchment might include a freeze on the basic Dutch pension scheme. Social democratic voters punished the PvdA for its part in the attack on hard-won social rights. Ironically, however, the PvdA became the largest party after losing 12 of its 49 seats. A restored PvdA–CDA coalition was now only possible with the help of the progressive Liberals (Democrats 66). This party convinced historical enemies, the PvdA and VVD, to form the first coalition government since 1917 without a confessional party. The new 'purple' coalition did not slow down the reform effort, but the PvdA had a bottom line condition for its cooperation: the level and duration of social benefits would not be tampered with. Kok had conceded that this position might have to be reviewed after two years if developments should turn out unfavorably regarding public sector deficits, inactivity on the labor market, and employment. From this very defensive position, the party was entirely committed to the 'job, jobs, and more jobs' approach as the only way out. This explains its support for reforms aiming at improvements in efficiency by introducing financial incentives through partial re-privatization of social risks and managed liberalization of social policy administration.

The common thread running through many legislative changes in social security system is placing greater financial responsibility on employers and employees. This applies to privatization of sickness benefits, differentiation in invalidity benefit premiums, and lengthening the number of reference days required before workers receive a benefit under the new Unemployment Benefit Act. Under the new Disability Act of 1997, employers can 'opt out' and take full responsibility for the first five years of occupational disability, while legally obliged to pay at least 70 percent of the disabled employee's most recent earnings. If they remain in the public system, they have to bear the risk of rising costs if the incidence of disability in the industry rises. This reform allows differentiation among employers' contributions and encourages firms to invest in health and safety at work. Employers can re-insure risks, but may have to pay higher premiums if rates are higher than average.

The welfare reforms of the 1990s were helped, politically, by the results of some alarming inquiries into the causes of the social security crisis. A Parliamentary Inquiry in 1993 revealed what was already common knowledge, namely that the social partners had made 'very liberal use' of social security for purposes of industrial restructuring. The inquiry established that the Industrial Boards had no intrinsic interest in getting people off welfare and that the social partners had all along known that the system was being abused. The government limited the self-governing autonomy of the social partners and set up an independent Supervisory Board. A separate National Institute for Social Insurance was set up with responsibility for contracting out social security's administration to privatized delivery agencies. Trade unions and employers' associations have retained an advisory status only. A final string of measures concentrated on introducing or intensifying 'activation' obligations for the long-term unemployed, fortified by penalties since 1996. For young people, entitlement to benefits was replaced by the entitlement to a job under the Youth Work Guarantee scheme. Single parents with children older than 5 (no longer 12, as before) must be prepared to take a part-time job. The standard for 'appropriate' work was broadened, and benefit recipients are now expected to accept jobs lower than their former job in terms of earnings. Municipal social services are required to draw up so-called reintegration plans and training programs, in collaboration with regional employment services. In line with the Luxembourg employment guidelines, the government is spending an extra 500 m guilders for a so-called 'integral approach' in which every unemployed worker will be offered a job or an education within the first year of unemployment.

Unlike Austrians and Belgians, Dutch citizens are entitled to a flat basic public pension when they reach the age of 65. In the face of a rapidly greying population, which is expected to reach a peak round 2020–30, nearly all parties have agreed to put aside extra tax revenue from the current successful growth spurt for a special fund to meet future obligations in this universal tier of the pension system. With respect to the obligatory, occupational-based and earnings-related, second tier of Dutch pensions, unions and employers are quietly negotiating a change from a final to a middle wage system, and the replacement of collective early retirement schemes (financed out of the wage sum and adding up to 8% in some industries) with a funded time-saving system. Finally, with regard to the private non-compulsory tier, there is a move towards restricting the tax deductibility of private equity plans because of how they narrow the tax base. Owing to its three-tiered make-up, the Dutch pension system appears better adapted to flexible, interrupted, or part-time working careers than most continental European systems (Alber 1998).

5.3.5. From Fighting Unemployment to Increasing Participation

In the late 1980s, policymakers became aware that the low level of labor market participation was the Achilles' heel of the extensive but passive Dutch system of social protection. In 1990 the Netherlands' Scientific Council for Government Policy proposed breaking with the past and advocated a policy of maximizing the rate of labor market participation as the single most important labor market policy goal of any sustainable welfare state (WRR 1990). Gradually the message, though not the policy recommendation to lower the statutory minimum wage, was adopted by the government. In 1993 the social partners followed suit by embracing higher levels of participation in the New Course agreement (Visser and Hemerijck 1997).

The new policy priority made its imprint on all kinds of policy initiatives, beginning with using the I/A ratio as the basis for linking benefits and wages. There was a new focus on active labor market policies, an underdeveloped area in postwar policymaking. The public employment service was reorganized. It had long been run in a highly bureaucratic fashion from the Ministry, held a monopoly on job placement, was avoided by employers, and was swamped by unemployed people with no chances on the open labor market. It was estimated that one-third of those registered as unemployed were not available for work or were already working. Around 1980, the idea of involving the social partners was placed on the policy agenda. Minister De Koning believed that a tripartite organization would condemn the social partners and the government to mutual cooperation in the fight against unemployment. After lengthy preparations, the 1991 reform brought the service under tripartite control, financed by the government but run independently. There was also a strong element of devolution of responsibility to regional employment boards. A critical evaluation after four years led to another overhaul in 1996 and provided a policy window for issue linkage between labor market and welfare policy. As a result of strengthening 'activating' measures in unemployment insurance and social assistance, municipalities and social insurance organizations have allocated a budget to buy placement and training activities from the employment service. Beginning in 2000 the employment service is expected to compete with private providers like the temporary work agencies. Cooperation between social security organizations, the municipal assistance offices, and the employment service is further enhanced by the 1998 Mobilization of Unemployed Persons Act. As new Centers for Work and Income, they are expected to work together in one location. New government plans are bringing all the various kinds of insurance into a single public service, whereas job placement services will be privatized, possibly within minimum requirements established by collective agreement. Unions, supported by employers, oppose these plans, which would further reduce the social partners' involvement, but the Lib–Lab coalition appears determined to have its way.

Beginning in the early 1990s, the Lubbers–Kok administration and the two purple coalitions government had started to redress the imbalance between active and passive policies. Under the Youth Guarantee Plan and with the so-called 'Melkert-jobs' (named after the PvdA Minister of Social Affairs and Employment), permanent jobs in the public sector for unemployed youth and the long-term unemployed were created. These jobs are usually for 32 hours a week at a maximum of 120 percent of the hourly minimum wage. Additional job programs based on these schemes have been expanded and now absorb around 1.5 percent of total employment. The majority of these programs are carried out by the municipalities. With the introduction of the Jobseekers Integration Act, local authorities have been granted more resources to target projects for the long-term unemployed. In addition to job creation in the public sector, the government has introduced several kinds of employment subsidy schemes based on reducing the social security contributions paid by employers. Subsidy schemes cover as many as one million workers. The first initiatives were directed at the long-term unemployed, women, ethnic minorities, and low-skilled groups. Because of a disappointing take-up, more recent schemes cover all jobs with an hourly wage of up to 115 percent of the minimum wage. The majority of these jobs go to new entrants. Employment subsidies can add up to 25 percent of the annual wage. First evaluations of these schemes suggest that they accelerate employment creation and the reintegration of unemployed workers (SZW 1998; NEI 1999).

Labor market flexibility is an integral part of the new Dutch labor market policies. Legislation removing constraints on shop hours, business licenses, temporary job agencies, working time, and on dismissals consolidate this development. Following the 'New Course' agreement of 1993, unions and employers in decentralized bargaining rounds have concentrated on exchanging shorter working hours, more leave arrangements, and income stability throughout the year for the annualization of working hours, more opportunities for working evenings or on Saturday, and lower overtime rates (Tijdens 1998). The new Working Time Act of 1996, which allowed negotiated contracts to deviate from legally defined maximum working hours or minimum rest periods, supports this trend. In 1993 the Labor Foundation recommended that employers grant workers' requests to work part-time unless there are compelling business reasons for rejection. A right to part-time work is currently under parliamentary review. Temporary work agencies provided employment for over 200,000 person years in 1997. Almost half of the workers in a flexible job are under the age of 25; among adult workers the share of tenured contracts has been stable at 90 percent during the past ten years. In 1995 unions and employers signed the first collective agreement for temp workers, introducing a right of continued employment and pension insurance after four consecutive contracts or 24 months of service. It prepared the ground for the central agreement on 'Flexibility and Security' of 1996, which, in turn, paved the way for an overhaul in 1999 of Dutch law on protection against dismissals . This 'flexicurity' law (Wilthagen 1998) is a compromise, not just between employers and employees, but also within the unions between workers with and without stable jobs. A relaxation of statutory dismissal protection for regular employment contracts (more opportunities for negotiated termination of employment) is exchanged for an improvement in the rights of temporary workers and the introduction of a 'presumption of an employment relation' in the case of freelance work. Temporary employment agencies no longer need a license, but the law assumes their responsibility as employer.

The incremental individualization of the tax system since 1984, improved opportunities for switching from full-time to part-time jobs, and the removal of all remaining elements of discrimination based on working hours have all contributed to a 'normalization' of part-time employment (Visser 1999). The differences in hourly wages between full-time and part-time workers is 7 percent in the private sector, but much smaller in the public sector where almost half of all part-timers work. Dutch social security legislation is especially friendly to part-time employment, since the main principle for coverage (for health insurance too) is the employment contract, irrespective of hours worked (SZW 1995). The current government has introduced a Framework Bill on Employment and Care into Parliament, which is intended to harmonize different forms of leave and create a framework to save time or money for leave. Employers are lobbying hard to defeat this bill; their alternative is a proposal to have the unions sign a Framework Agreement containing greater sectoral flexibility. A tax reform, coined the 'Tax Plan of the 21st Century', was proposed in September 1999. It includes lower tax rates on labor and capital, financed by the broadening and 'greening' of the tax base. Capital asset taxes will be replaced by a fixed capital revenue tax. VAT will be raised, with an exemption for labor-intensive services, for which the VAT rate will be lowered. The Central Planning Bureau expects the new tax system to boost job growth considerably so long as there is wage restraint. But unions deny any relationship and have already twice stepped up their demands for 2000, clearly in response to pressure from a tight labor market. Help on the tax side is still needed to get more low-skilled workers employed. But one might question whether it would not be wiser, under the current circumstances of a balanced budget and full employment, to increase public investment in education, technology, infrastructure, innovation, and stress prevention, rather than heaping more money on house owners and consumers.

5.3.6. The Record: Wage Restraint, Flexibility, Part-Time Jobs, Services, and Welfare Reform

Since 1982 a new mix of macroeconomic policy and wage setting emerged that generated a virtuous cycle of price stability, fiscal consolidation, restored profitability, and strong (part-time) job creation in private services. Subsequently supported by welfare and labor market reforms, this virtuous cycle has had important positive feedback effects on female employment and domestic demand, leading in turn to a slow but solid decline in labor market inactivity without having to sacrifice basic social security. According to the Central Planning Bureau, wage moderation has been the single most important weapon in the Dutch adjustment strategy. CPB (1997) estimates that two-thirds of job growth between 1983 to 1996 should be attributed to wage moderation. Unit wage costs in 1996 were at the same level as they were in 1981. Over the same period they increased by 40 percent in Germany and 15 percent on average in the EU. The return to wage moderation contributed to job-intensive growth in three ways. First, by restoring profitability, it created a necessary condition for investment and job growth. Second, by lowering the external exchange rate, it supported export growth and employment in the exposed sectors of the economy. Third, wage moderation kept more people on the payroll and, in combination with lower taxes, had a favorable effect on employment in domestic services. As a corollary of the shift to services, growth in labor productivity per hour, although already very high by European and American standards, was smaller than in other countries.

Sectoral employment trends in the Netherlands went in almost opposite directions before and after 1984. In the 1970s the subsidized sector (health, education) and government employment witnessed the strongest growth, whereas private sector employment stagnated. Employment levels in industry fell steeply and employment growth in private services (trade and transport, financial and personnel services, hotels and restaurants) was faint. After 1984, job decline in industry and agriculture stopped. Employment growth is now strongest in private services, 3 percent per year, four times as much as in the public and subsidized sector. The public sector absorbs only 13 percent of total employment, which is low in comparison with most European countries. The reason is that health services and social welfare in the Netherlands are often organized by formerly pillarized voluntary associations with support from public subsidies. Together with these semi-public activities, the public absorbs 25 percent of total employment.

Next to wage restraint, labor time reduction and higher labor time flexibility have played a key role in job growth. Over time policy preferences shifted from across-the-board reductions in the working week towards the enhancement of part-time work and annualization of working time. Two-thirds of the jobs created since 1982 have been part-time jobs. The surge in part-time employment and the shift to services coincided with the rapid increase in labor force participation of women, from 29 percent to 60 percent between 1971 and 1996, the strongest rise in any OECD country. While the labor force increased by one-fifth between 1970 and 1997, the female labor force more than doubled (SCP 1998).

By taking wage moderation, the proliferation of part-time work, the shift to services, and increased female participation together, the following picture emerges (Hartog 1999). Between 1987 and 1996, value added in the total economy grew by 31 percent. However, employment volume (in hours) declined by 7 percent in the exposed sector and increased by 33 percent in the sheltered sector. Because private consumption is more service-intensive, and services are more employment-intensive, job growth really took off in the service sector. Private consumption has made a major contribution to economic growth and was boosted by a 'feel good' factor related to the labor market's steady improvement and rising housing prices (with most double income families owning their house). Strong domestic growth has allowed the Netherlands to be relatively unaffected by the recession in Germany. The positive interaction effects among wage moderation, part-time work, the shift to services, and increasing female participation have been supported by social security reform and innovations in labor market policy since the early 1990s. Transfers to households in GDP terms came down from 31 percent to 26 percent, and government expenditure's share of GDP declined from 62 percent to 52 percent from 1983 to 1998. Relative to the size of the labor force, there are fewer people on disability and sickness benefits. Today's discussions center on the wisdom of further privatization and on incentives for employers to invest in preventing sickness and reintegrating inactive workers. The reform of the employment service, the strengthening of activation requirements in social security, additional job programs in the public sector, wage subsidies to encourage employers hiring low-skilled workers, tax reduction for those in work, negotiated flexibility in working hours, statutes and pensions, and policies to enhance the growth of part-time work—are all components of the Dutch job miracle. However remarkable that miracle is, it should be emphasized that inactivity, especially in the form of disability, is still high and that the present success story is no more than a game of catch-up from a truly dismal situation in the recent past.

5.4. Belgium's *sur place*

The international monetary crisis, the oil-price shock, and the international recession of the 1970s had a powerfully disturbing influence on the Belgian economy. During the recession unemployment doubled from 100,000 in mid-1974 to 228,000 two years later. By the end of the decade Belgium had the highest unemployment rate and the fastest increase of unemployment in Europe with the exception of Spain. Employment contracted by almost 6 percent between 1974 and 1983. In the private sector (not counting subsidized employment programs and the self-employed) the decline was 15 percent. In manufacturing employment declined by 29.8 percent and, taking into account the fact that average hours were reduced by 11 percent, we find that total labor input in manufacturing fell by 37.5 percent, a sharper contraction than in any other European country in this period.

Sneessens and Drèze (1986), from whom these figures are taken, present a broader picture of the Belgian economy using time series data from 1962 to 1983 showing national income shares for labor, unemployment, inflation, balance of payments, and budget deficits. The striking feature of these data is the sharp break after 1973, indicating a deep transformation and severe imbalance in the Belgian economy. During the 1960s the Belgian economy had performed as well as its neighbors. In the early 1970s inflation and wage growth was above the trend in Germany or the Netherlands, unemployment was slightly higher, the overall employment/population rate was among the lowest in the OECD (as in the Netherlands), and the debt–output ratio was near the 60 percent limit that would become the EMU norm thirty years later. Belgium had found it difficult to adjust to the loss of its African colony in 1960. Unlike the Netherlands, there was no compensation from gas resources. Thus, Belgium had less leeway when confronted with the new realities of the 1970s.

Comparing the period 1968–73 with 1973–80, we find that GDP growth was halved, export growth fell from 11 percent to 3 percent per annum, and inflation rose to 8%, whereas unemployment increased from 2.4 percent in 1973 to 7.9 percent in 1980. Public sector debt, fueled by costly settlements of Belgium's linguistic conflicts and by steeply rising deficits in the social security funds, reached alarming proportions by the end of the decade and would necessitate perennial austerity in the next. In 1981 the public deficit stood at −12.7 percent of GDP, which was the record in the OECD. Debt servicing alone had risen to almost 20 percent of government revenue. Deficit spending, which had helped to boost domestic demand in excess of supply in the 1970s, had as its counterpart an external deficit equivalent to −12 percent of GDP on a cumulative basis in 1981. This had to be financed by increased public borrowing, crowding out private investment. At the end of 1981 net external liabilities were larger than the foreign exchange reserves of the Belgian National Bank (BNB). In that year the economy contracted by more than a full percentage point, and unemployment, already high by the end of the 1970s, rose to 500,000 (10.2%), or 700,000 (16%) if people in various early retirement schemes are included. In sum, when the second oil crisis hit Belgium, its economic imbalances 'were more marked than in the majority of member countries and were tending to become self-perpetuating' (OECD 1983: 2).

5.4.1. *Contradictory Responses: Hard Currency and Keynesianism*

When the Bretton-Woods system collapsed, Belgium joined the 'snake'. It stayed in till the very end, despite the defection of France and other participants of the first hour. It did so for broadly the same reason as the Netherlands: with wage negotiators unwilling or unable to control cost-push inflation, a hard currency policy was Belgium's main protection against imported inflation. As explained in the case of the Netherlands, this came at the tremendous cost of lost competitiveness in foreign markets. Jobs in the exposed sector were disappearing at an alarming rate. The index of unit labor costs in manufacturing, relative to the OECD average, shows that by 1975 Belgium had slipped to one of the worst positions. The so-called 'wage gap', or difference in wage costs between Belgium and its five main trading partners (Germany, France, the Netherlands, Italy, and the UK), widened from 100 to 113 index points (1970 = 100) between 1972 and 1975, and then to 129 points by 1979 (Goubert and Heylen 1999).

Exchange rate stability had long been a priority in Belgian monetary policy and was not contested by the unions. The experience of the 1949 devaluation had taught them that, in a small economy where most goods are imported, devaluation hurts workers' purchasing power (Kurzer 1993). Difficulties in obtaining voluntary wage restraint posed a dilemma for policymakers, and all governments after 1974 were caught between the brake of a hard currency policy and the engine of a reflationary course for which there were insufficient resources (Jones 1995). The immediate government response to the oil crisis and the recession of 1974–75 had been to rescue troubled industries with subsidies, job creation in the public sector, and demand-stimulating measures. Another response consisted of various measures aimed at reducing the labor supply: a recruitment ban on foreign workers, which was largely ignored; early retirement of older workers; and an additional year of education for young people. Policy did not change much in 1974 when the Christian Democrats shifted coalition partners, from left to right, or when they welcomed back the Social Democrats in 1977. All governments till 1982 were wedded to a Keynesian approach.

If civil servants for both central and local government are counted together with employees in the nationalized industries, public employment increased by 35.5 percent between 1970 and 1984; there was a spurt of 123,000 jobs in the direct aftermath of the 1974–75 recession and another expansion in 1978–79. The share of public jobs in total employment rose from 23 percent in 1970 to 32 percent in 1982 (OECD 1986). It was not enough. The recession accelerated the decline in the very industries that had been the mainstays of employment: steel, metal processing, chemicals, cars, and transport equipment. Until 1975 heavy industry had absorbed redundant workers from labor-intensive industries such as textiles, clothing, and leather, as well as coal mining, but this was no longer the case. Overall, the employment ratio in manufacturing fell by more than four percentage points between 1973 and 1980, from 18.6 percent to 14.3 percent. This contraction was twice as strong as in the Netherlands, not to mention Austria where industrial labor was hoarded.

The BNB estimated that total aid to business in the form of subsidies, capital transfers, loans, and government equity investment, averaged 5.5 percent of GDP per year in the second half of the 1970s, peaking at 8.9 percent in 1982. This equaled 13 percent of government expenditure at the time and was unsustainable. In later years it would fall to around 7 percent (OECD 1986). The largest items in the budget were subsidies to traditional sectors and large firms, which compensated for the hard currency policy but hampered innovation at the same time as they slowed down job losses. In the 1980s attempts were made to target government aid to start-up firms and innovative projects in new technology. This coincided with the devolution of industrial policy to the regions, as part of the institutional reforms of 1980. However, the so-called 'national industries' (steel, coal, ceramics, and glass, mainly located in Wallonia, and textiles and shipbuilding, mainly in Flanders) remained under the responsibility of the central government.

Before 1973 Belgium's main difficulties had been related to its outdated industrial structure and the shifting economic balance between the two regions. As the first industrial country on the Continent, the country had inherited a large manufacturing base, concentrated in Wallonia. The decline in the demand for steel and coal began to hurt Wallonia as early as 1960. Postwar industrialization programs and accommodating tax treaties had helped to attract foreign (mainly American) investment (oil and chemical industry near the coast and the port of Antwerp, light metal engineering and transport industry around Ghent) and solve the age-old problem of underemployment in rural Flanders. With Belgian and foreign capital shifting their weight towards expanding Flanders, Wallonia fell behind. Unemployment had always been much higher in Flanders, but in 1970 unemployment in Wallonia (5.1%) was almost double the rate in Flanders (2.8%). By 1980 unemployment rates in both regions had slipped into double digits. However, unemployment has persisted in Wallonia, where rates are currently three times higher than in Flanders.

5.4.2. Divided Employers and Strong Unions

In the 1970s wage negotiators failed to take account of the country's deteriorating external position (Goubert and Heylen 1999), and Belgium ended the decade with the highest manufacturing wage costs in the European Community (De Grauwe 1994: 67). The unions continued to negotiate real wage gains in spite of the sharp rise in unemployment. This may be thought to reflect their continued strength (Hancké 1993; Ebbinghaus and Visser 1999) and is consistent with our hypothesis that Belgian trade union leaders continued to believe that wage restraint would not help but only depress demand and therefore aggravate the crisis.

With corporate profits under pressure, employers screamed for wage restraint and lower taxes every year since 1975. But they were internally divided and unable to attract the unions to a deal. In 1974 they signed what would turn out to be the last central agreement for a long time. Building on the 1944 Draft Agreement on Social Security and the 1954 Productivity Agreement, the unions had committed themselves to the maintenance of social peace and the promotion of productivity in exchange for giving workers a share in the proceeds of economic progress. In this spirit seven central agreements had been reached between 1960 and 1975. These had expanded workers' rights and benefits, including old age pensions (1971), paid holidays (1960, 1963, 1966, 1973, and 1975), shorter working hours (1969, 1971, and 1973), national minimum wage (1975), equal pay (1975), as well as union representation rights in firms (1971). In this 'Golden Age of Planning and Growth' (Dancet 1988: 217), parliaments had signed into law and governments had executed what the social partners wanted.

Until 1974 wage setting was entirely a matter for unions and employers, with no role for the government. Actual wage bargaining took place at the sectoral level and has been characterized as rather uncoordinated (Van Ruysseveldt and Visser 1996; Vilrokx and Van Leemput 1997). In comparison with Austria and the Netherlands, the role of the central organizations is limited. Internally divided among sectors, regions, and ideological currents, the central organizations carry little authority over their member organizations. This has proven to be a problem, especially in the Socialist union federation (FGTB), but also in the Belgian Federation of Employers (FBE), which faces a strong contender in a Flemish organization (VEV). The central organizations do meet in direct consultation within the National Labor Council (CNT), where they have had the right since 1968 to negotiate binding agreements. At the sectoral level, collective agreements are negotiated in some 130 parity commissions that meet under an independent chairperson and are assigned the task of negotiating (binding) agreements, settling and preventing disputes, and advising the government. With the major exception of the chemical industry, company bargaining is secondary and mainly concerned with non-wage issues.

In 1975 the central employers' organization pulled the brake and recommended a small wage increase, but according to FBE chairman Puellinx his advice went unheeded and most sectors negotiated a real wage increase of 5 percent or more (interview, SWAV 1995: 5). Similar attempts in later years failed, and until 1982 gross wages and wage costs outpaced productivity growth by a wide margin, with the result that unit labor costs increased (see Table 5.6 for a comparison with the Netherlands). The result of uncoordinated wage bargaining was, as in a prisoners' dilemma, a higher cost for society in the form of rising unemployment and social security expenditures. The bargaining parties maintain an interest in demanding social protection (unions) and subsidies (firms), the costs of which are shouldered by the community at large. Unavoidably, this development led to government involvement in wage bargaining and a change from bipartism to tripartism (Slomp 1983). Until 1981, however, all attempts at encouraging unions and employers to accept restraint failed. Each side had a sticking point: employers refused to discuss working time reduction, unions ruled out real wage restraint, and governments could not afford to give up the strong currency (De Swert 1989). But the government was not in a position to stand aside. It needed wage restraint, if only to limit the rising claims and costs of social security and the growing deficit in public spending. After 1981 the government took an authoritarian line, and from 1982 to 1986 autonomous wage setting through negotiations between unions and employers was suspended.

The central organizations not only lacked control over their members, they also disagreed over policies. As in many other European countries after 1968, Belgium witnessed a period of worker militancy and radicalization of union demands (Molitor 1978) and Belgian employers felt under attack ideologically (Moden and Sloover 1980). With the slowdown of economic growth, it became less easy to find compromise solutions. In 1976 Fabrimetal, FBE's powerful affiliate in the steel and metal industry, alarmed by the rapid deterioration of its members' competitive position, demanded the abolishment of the indexation system. Established in the immediate postwar years, this system guaranteed that wages were fully adjusted to price increases, making wages inflation-proof. The technique was for each point rise in the consumer price index to be translated, after two months, into a similar rise in wages. Coverage was nearly complete and in 1975, the system was extended to the national minimum wage and social benefits. Fabrimetal's attack received insufficient backing in other sectors, and employers were forced to retreat under pressure from strikes. Indexation became a 'holy cow' and remained a sticking point in Belgian industrial relations over the next several decades. The arguments for or against indexation and the deleterious effects on bargaining discussed in the preceding section on the Netherlands apply with equal force to Belgium. Unlike Dutch (and later Italian) union leaders, however, Belgian union leaders remained steadfast in their defense. Their behavior contradicts the hypothesis that union leaders in a continuous low inflation environment lose interest in an automatic cost-of-living adjustment wage, since it constricts their role and autonomy in collective bargaining (Braun 1976). The unions countered employers' pressure for wage restraint with demands for working-time reduction. In 1976 Belgian unions, beginning in the troubled steel industry, were the first in Europe to raise the demand

Table 5.6 *Average annual growth of real (gross) wages and productivity (%)*

	Real (gross) wage growth[a]		Productivity growth[b]	
	Belgium	Netherlands	Belgium	Netherlands
1971–82	4.14	2.72	2.80	2.28
1983–85	−0.75	−0.91	1.35	2.53
1985–89	0.70	0.70	2.02	0.79
1990–95	2.20	0.31	1.73	0.72

[a]Annual change in wage, in percentage, averaged per period.
[b]Annual change in productivity, in percentage, averaged per period.

Note: Real (gross) wage is calculated as the sum of all (nominal) compensations to wage and salary earners divided by the total number of wage and salary earners employed, deflated by the consumer price index. Labor productivity is calculated per person (rather than per hour, explaining the low figure after 1985 in the Netherlands, due to part-time employment).

Source: Conseil Central Économique, report on the Belgian economy in 1997.

for shorter working hours as a work-sharing measure, but negotiations proved fruitless.

The first of many state interventions in wage bargaining came at the end of 1976 when Belgian's outgoing center-right government imposed a 'special levy' of 50 percent on all contractual pay increases above those linked to indexation in order to finance a special fund for older unemployed workers who were allowed to stay outside the labor market on a transitory pension till legal retirement age. This decision provoked a national strike, jointly organized by the socialist and Christian unions, the first-ever strike of the latter against the government (including their own ministers). The incoming center-left government boosted public sector employment and tried to win unions and private sector employers over to a package deal based on wage restraint, working time reduction, and job targets equivalent to 2 percent of the workforce. This attempt at political exchange failed. Unions wanted more assurances that there would be additional jobs, whereas employers rejected the targets as 'bad therapy' and interference with management. When the government dropped the targets and offered a voluntary scheme for subsidized working time reduction, employers in some sectors, mainly those with overcapacity, did accept negotiations over working time reduction. The moderating effect on wages was small. The unions were disappointed that the job targets were dropped, and the subsidies lowered the employers' resistance to wage demands.

5.4.3. The 1980s: International Pressure and Recovery

In the early 1980s, Belgium earned 'the dubious distinction of being the first and only Member State to receive an official recommendation of the European Commission to address its growing public deficits and rapidly growing wages' (Kurzer 1997: 118). At the European Summit of 1980, Belgium was 'advised in strong terms' to modify its 'prejudicial system of wage indexation if it wants to stay in the EMS' (Dancet 1988: 211). Impressed, Prime Minister Martens proposed a temporary suspension of indexation, apparently without consulting his socialist coalition partners, whose ministers resigned. The next government, again with the socialists, asked special powers of Parliament, and only 48 hours before a wage stop would have taken effect, unions and employers agreed to seek voluntary restraint, packaged with some working time reduction for 1981–82. Unlike the Dutch agreement of Wassenaar, this agreement was not the dawn of a new era in industrial relations. It was too obvious a dictate. Intellectually, union leaders had not come around to the idea that profitability and competitiveness had to rise in order to prevent further job losses, as had Dutch union leaders by this time. Moreover, in addition to Belgian negotiators' low mutual trust, there was no stable government that might have protected a compromise between the social partners against defection or abuse. Indeed, within weeks the government fell (over the federalization issue), provoking the fourth crisis in two years. In an unusual speech King Baudouin reminded politicians that the time had come 'to put our differences aside' and 'give priority to survival', as one 'would do if we were at war . . . war for the preservation of our economy' (Deweerdt and Smits 1982: 262). But the next government did no more than solve another piece in the federalization puzzle and postpone what Belgian employers now called 'the self-evident decision', by which they meant the suspension of wage indexation. Instead, the government bought time and offered employers a flat-rate reduction in social security contributions for manual workers in struggling manufacturing firms (Maribel, Law of 29 June 1981).

The general elections of 1981 resulted in losses for the Christian Democrats in Flanders and gains for the Liberals. Forming his fifth cabinet, CVP leader Martens chose the Liberals as his coalition partner. Despite its narrow majority in Parliament, this coalition would stay in office the full four years and continue unchanged after the elections of 1985. Martens V more or less ruled by decree, seeking special enabling powers from Parliament in an annual vote of confidence. This silenced not only the Socialist opposition but also the prime minister's critics inside his own CVP, especially from the party's Christian union wing. This 'less democracy for a better economy' approach (Smits 1983) was defended by Martens as 'an unavoidable step in the recovery of our country' (Bastian 1994: 92). Not only Parliament but also the collective wage negotiators were placed in 'preventive custody' (Vilrokx and Van Leemput 1997: 336–37).

The recovery began with a large devaluation of the franc. Early in 1982, after negotiations within the IMF and Ecofin, an 8.5 percent devaluation was obtained, the largest since the start of the EMS (Gros and Thygesen 1994: 76). The liberals had wanted more, the unions (like the Bundesbank) less (Kurzer 1993). Devaluation could only restore the competitiveness of Belgian firms if combined with foolproof wage restraint. Hence, a standstill on wages (till May 1982) and a suspension of indexation for the entire year were crucial. Martens and his aides had secretly negotiated the recovery plan with the veteran leader of the Christian workers' association, who used his influence to assure cooperation from the Christian unions. They consented on condition that suspension of indexation would be temporary and special income protection be given to low-paid workers and large families. The Socialist unions were left in the dark, but their strikes changed nothing about government policy. During the next four years, until the end of 1986, the government decreed that three index jumps, each amounting to a price increase of 2 percent, would not be translated into wages and that any wage increase above inflation was prohibited. In combination with the devaluation, these draconian measures did indeed lead to a sharp turnaround in competitiveness. Real wages fell between 1982 and 1986, and all productivity gains were captured by firms, leading to a sharp decline in labor's share in enterprise income. At the same time, however, the government raised the employers' contributions for social security in order to meet its second objective of fiscal consolidation. Hence, non-wage labor costs decreased much less than wages, and the wedge between labor costs and take-home pay rose sharply. Since the government had agreed to exempt minimum wages and heads of (large) families from its measures, or to offer them compensation, the distance between minimum and average wages narrowed, and the overall wage structure compressed.

There are similarities, in background and content, between the Belgium recovery plan of 1982 and the 'no nonsense' approach that started later the same year in the Netherlands. Both were responses to a very severe crisis, implemented by center-right governments with a strong electorate mandate for the conservative Liberals. In both countries, as in Germany or in Britain two years earlier, the Social Democrats had exhausted themselves as partners in government by their failure to tame or convince the unions (as well as by their antagonism toward permitting a new generation of nuclear weapons on Dutch and Belgian soil). In both countries the recovery plans aimed at restoring private sector profitability, consolidating the budget, and using job sharing to slow down (if not reverse) the upward trend in unemployment. The overall package was deflationary in both countries and initially increased unemployment. It implied a shift of incomes from households to enterprises, showing up as a fall in labor's share of net national income. The main difference, however, was that recovery in the Netherlands was consolidated by a major agreement between the unions and the employers. As was argued in the preceding section, this allowed the Dutch government to concentrate on fiscal consolidation and uncouple public sector pay from private sector wage negotiations. In Belgium there was no such agreement, leaving the government in a more vulnerable position, with many risks of implementation failure and political horse-trading.

The Belgian government's choices were constrained by the fact that it started the decade with a huge public debt and social security costs that had risen spectacularly. There was no money to lower taxes on employers or workers or boost consumer demand through tax reform. While the cost crisis in social security was probably more severe, the austerity measures were rather piecemeal and drawn out over a longer period than in the Netherlands, possibly because opposition from the more powerful Belgian unions and within the Christian Democratic Party was stronger. Social security for workers in Belgium is contributions-based, but premiums in 1983 covered only 62 percent of total expenditures, as against 84 percent in 1970 (Peeters 1989: 202). Many funds had fallen into debt. The deficit in social security (all programs combined) had increased nearly tenfold, from 26 bn Belgian francs in 1970 to 254 bn francs in 1980, with the rise in unemployment benefits as the largest contributing factor. The number of unemployed receiving full compensation from the insurance funds had trebled between 1974 and 1980, while expenditure on unemployment rose from 0.7 percent of GNP in 1970 to 5 percent in 1985. In 1980, as part of an initial austerity package, the beneficiaries receiving unemployment insurance entitlements had been differentiated among principle breadwinners with dependent families, single households, and persons earning a second household income. For the latter two categories, benefits were lowered and phased out earlier. In later reforms, an extended 'waiting time' of 150 days has been applied to school-leavers before they may claim a reduced benefit. After 1982 benefits no longer followed wage increases (a principle only introduced in 1975), but breadwinners and large families received compensation.

Another cost explosion concerned the various early retirement schemes. Faced with the explosive growth in youth unemployment, which had risen to 25 percent in 1980, and with the structural crisis in coal mining, steel, ceramics, textiles, and shipbuilding, Belgian governments believed they had no choice but to encourage the 'pre-pensioning' of workers. It was, moreover, the only policy response on which there was agreement between the social partners (Bastian 1994). The appeal of this approach shows up in the sharp fall of the employment ratio for older males between age 60 and 65, from just over 60 percent in 1970 to 32 percent in 1981. By 1983, the first year for which we have internationally comparable data, the employment/population ratio in this age group was lower in Belgium than in all other countries except Luxembourg. Older workers received an early pension until legal retirement age in case of unemployment, and public subsidies were made available for early retirement in case a young worker was hired as a replacement. The costs were initially fully borne by public funds, like the unemployment insurance fund, but after 1982 the government introduced special levies.

Work sharing was the third plank of the 1982 recovery plan. Under the so-called 5 + 3 + 3 operation, initiated in 1982, unions and employers were encouraged to negotiate a 5 percent reduction in working hours in exchange for a 3 percent wage sacrifice and a 3 percent increase in employment or, failing that, an obligatory employer contribution to the National Employment Fund. Attempts to negotiate a central agreement along these lines came to naught. Employers, once assured of government-imposed wage restraint, needed to make no further concessions. Unions felt that they had been robbed of an instrument—wage pressure—to wrest concessions from employers on labor time reduction and job creation. Yet in sectors and firms with overcapacity, employers and unions did reach agreement for about 1.3 of the two million employees in the private sector (Béguin 1985: 37). With an average working time reduction of 1.4 percent and a net employment effect of 52,100 jobs (Werner and König 1987: 62), about half of the government's target was reached. The Federal Minister of Labor defended state intervention on the grounds that he had no choice but to 'oblige the labor market organizations to negotiate amidst a web of constraints, which both sides had refused in previous years' (Hansenne 1985: 56). This approach was also applied in the so-called 'Hansenne working-time experiments', in which the state offered to suspend legal norms on maximum daily or weekly hours and overtime rules if firms could show positive effects on investment and employment and sign an agreement with the unions and the Ministry. Fifty-five plant agreements of this kind were signed between 1983 and 1986, in total affecting 26,000 employees (Denys, Hedebouw, and Lambertl 1985), nearly all in large manufacturing firms, including Siemens, Phillips, Samsonite, and General Motors, all of which were interested in increased flexibility and located in Flanders. The Socialist unions in Wallonia would have nothing of it (Bastian 1994: 101; Colpaert 1987: 41).

5.4.4. *Safeguarding EMU Participation*

In 1990 the monetary authorities, anxious to quell the occasional speculative frenzies against the franc, promised to preserve parity with the Deutschmark in the event of a realignment, while the BNB gained the same degree of independence as the German and Dutch central banks. Having signed the Maastricht Treaty on Economic and Monetary Union, Belgium set itself the objective of belonging to the first group of EMU members. It had much to gain from borrowing the Deutschmark's reputation (Dyson 1994: 207) and, as a transit economy, it had much to lose should it be excluded. But on at least two major indicators among the EMU convergence criteria—the public sector deficit and the debt–output ratio—Belgium was way off target.

With the entrance of the Socialists into Martens's seventh cabinet (1988–91), fiscal control had been relaxed and the links among price indexation, wages, and benefits restored. From 1987 to 1993 wage bargaining was again in the hands of unions and employers, albeit under a 'shadow of hierarchy', as defined by the 1989 Law on Safeguarding Competitiveness of Enterprises. This law authorized the government to intervene, *ex post*, if wages in Belgium had risen faster than the average trend among its five major trading partners (Michel 1994). Twice a year, the Conseil Central Économique (CCÉ), with bipartite representation by unions and employers joined by economic experts each side gets to appoint, issues a report on the state of the economy. If it sees fit, the CCÉ may recommend wage guidelines and other measures. The balance sheet on this period of limited 'free' wage bargaining (1987–93) is mixed. The central organizations were able to conclude (biennial) central agreements, but 'devoid of content and largely dictated by government' (Vilrokx and Van Leemput 1997: 341). The fact of the matter is that these agreements did not uncouple, or differentiate, collective bargaining in different sectors, as was by now the case in the Netherlands (and would keep happening there even more intensely in the 1990s), and as had always been the case (under strict supervision) in Austria. In Belgium, instead, wages in high productivity sectors like manufacturing kept setting the norm for wage increases in low productivity sectors like domestic services. By their very nature, statutory interventions are unable to differentiate by sector, because of asymmetrical information and monitoring problems. (The Dutch had already tried this, and failed miserably, in the early 1960s.) Between 1987 and 1989, and again in 1993, but not in other years, growth in gross wages did stay within the boundaries of overall productivity growth. In all years, however, wage increases exceeded the productivity gains in both private and public services (which were about four times lower than in manufacturing according to figures of the Belgian Planning Bureau). Moreover, responsiveness to unemployment and to economic shocks was limited. Regressions over the full period from 1970 to 1993 showed that in the case of Belgium a rise in unemployment by 2 percent was needed to obtain a 1 percent decline in real wages (less than half the elasticity of Austria, for example) (Heylen and Van Poeck 1995).

In the 1990s the old competitiveness problem resurfaced. One reason was that Belgium suffered more from the EMS troubles of 1992 and 1993 than Austria or the Netherlands. The new round of federalization in 1988 had not encouraged 'the kind of fiscal behavior associated with restricted monetarism' (Kurzer 1997: 120). International confidence in the franc remained low (in 1993 the BNB had to accept wider margins between the franc and Deutschmark). The other cause was wage growth. The CCÉ report for 1994 stated that Belgium had again developed a handicap of 6 percent vis-à-vis its trading partners. This figure was disputed by the unions, who called the statistics unreliable and blamed the recession on the deflationary policies of the Bundesbank and the restrictive EMU membership criteria agreed upon in Maastricht (Serroyen and Delcroix 1996: 36). Formalized in its so-called EMU convergence plan of 1992, the government had ushered in a fiscal consolidation package aiming at reducing the deficit from 7 percent to 3 percent of GDP by 1997 (OECD 1995: 7). Later a 3 percent EMU tax surcharge was introduced (abolished in 1999). During the EMS crisis a group of prominent Belgian economists called for unpegging the franc, abolishing indexation, and overhauling the social security system which they described as 'wasteful' and 'inefficient' (Kurzer 1997: 120). The proposal was hardly echoed in the press. Some unions might have favored a softer currency but not at the price of giving up indexation or lowering social security. Employers, choking under high costs, might have favored a softer franc, but they did not trust the unions to give up on indexation and deliver restraint. Instead, their primary objective was to lower government expenditure, taxes, and social security charges. The BNB was adamant in its defense of a *franc fort*; devaluation would mean higher imported inflation, diminished fiscal discipline, a rising public debt, and probably goodbye to EMU-membership.

In comparison to the Netherlands, where a temporary wage stop was implemented early in 1993, followed by a new central agreement later that same year, Belgian wage negotiators were slow to adjust. The renewed Christian–Socialist coalition, led by the CVP's new leader Dehaene (1992–95), was unable to coax the unions into signing a similar pact for competitiveness and employment. Alarmed by sharply rising unemployment, the government had proposed a 'Global Pact' early in 1993. On the basis of a grim report on the Belgian economy, prepared under guidance of the National Bank, negotiations started in October. Infuriated by the proposal to trim the cost-of-living index, the socialist federation FGTB, under pressure from its powerful affiliates, walked out (Van Ruysseveldt and Visser 1996: 215). The government, including its socialist ministers, went ahead and excluded tobacco, alcohol, petrol, and diesel fuel from the calculation of the cost-of-living index. The new so-called 'health index' lowered the adjustment of wages and benefits projected for 1994 and 1995 by 1.3 percentage points (with a projected 2% annual rate of inflation) (OECD 1995: 10). When the government's Global Plan became law in 1994, the eight-year interlude of limited freedom in wage setting had ended (Blaise and Beaupain 1996). From now on, wage bargainers were placed under 'house arrest' (Vilrockx and Van Leemput 1997). Nominal wage increases, beyond the watered down price indexation, remained banned until the end of 1996.

The second Dehaene government (1995–99), again a Christian–Socialist coalition, started off proposing a 'Pact for the Future of

Employment' in pursuit of three objectives: to halve the current unemployment level of 12 percent by 2002, improve the sluggish rate of GDP growth (1.5%–2%), and secure the 3 percent budget deficit target required for EMU membership. The new government was under pressure from Europe and the regions. In Flanders in particular, employers and the regional government were showing impatience with the national government. Consultations over the Future Pact continued until April 1996, when the VEB reached a draft agreement with the unions. Its contents were (once again) wage moderation, a legal maximum working week of 39 hours in 1998, improved rights for leaves of absence without pay, part-time retirement at age 58, and full-time retirement at age 60, annualization of working time, and lowering of employers' social security contributions through the expansion of the Maribel subsidy schemes. The agreement failed, however, when the socialist union federation FGTB was unable to gain approval from its affiliates. The leadership of the Christian federation ACV slipped through with a slight majority (Van Ruysseveldt and Visser 1996: 217).

The government went ahead anyway, selectively borrowing from the failed agreement. The central wage standard was given a legal status with a new framework law. This 1996 Law on Safeguarding the Competitiveness of Enterprises prescribes that wage increase in Belgium must remain below the average wage increases of its three neighbors Germany, France, and the Netherlands. This was a clear tightening of the old law of 1989, which had entitled the government to intervene *ex post*. The new law introduced an *ex ante* maximum wage norm based on predicted wage increases in Germany, France, and the Netherlands. Under the law, industries and firms are punishable if they exceed the norm; they may settle for lower wage increases, for example, in exchange for extra job measures. The (revised) indexation mechanism remained in place. The Act also stipulates that multi-industrial bargaining must take place every two years, on the basis of the CCÉ's technical report, and lead to an agreement on the precise margin for sectoral bargaining and additional job creation or working time matters. If no agreement is reached, as was the case in 1996, the government unilaterally sets the margin. For 1997 and 1998 it specified a maximum increase of 6.1 percent over two years, including a predicted 3.6 percent rise in consumer prices, 1 percent seniority related wage increases, and a real across-the-board improvement of 0.75 percent per year (Vilrokx and Van Leemput 1997: 339–40). Unlike the stalemate of 1996, a second round of bargaining for 1999–2000 did produce an agreement. This was eased by the government's decision to reduce social security contributions by 108 bn francs (2.5 bn euros) in five years and bring social charges down to the average level of Belgium's three neighbors. The FBE was under pressure from its Flemish regional partner, which had announced that it would 'go alone' should no national agreement be reached. This time the federal leadership of the unions gained its member unions' consent. The deal itself was complex and linked future reductions in social insurance contributions to compliance with the wage norm or, failing that, extra spending on vocational training. Companies and sectors paying above the norm will not be penalized (as they should have been for exceeding the norm in 1997 and 1998) if they can show that there are no negative employment effects. Not only has this been extremely difficult to monitor, but it requires types of sectoral, regional, and company data on investment and employment that are not available.

5.4.5. Lackluster Growth in the 1990s

In the 1990s Belgium exemplified Europe's main illness: high structural unemployment and a lack of productivity and employment growth in private services. As elsewhere, the problem was magnified by the slowdown in international economic growth and restrictive policies in the run-up to EMU. But this cannot explain the difference between Belgium and the two other countries discussed in this chapter. The causes of Belgium's low employment growth are probably a cluster of factors relating to problematic wage setting, a high tax and social security wedge, various unemployment traps, and inefficient active labor market policies, to mention just a few of the factors (Elmeskov, Martin, and Scarpetta 1998; Goubert and Heylen 1999). Past culprits were an aging industrial structure, full wage indexation, and excessive real wage growth. Once unemployment became high and persistent, social policies and labor market measures had to be expensive, even after various retrenchments. The weak social consensus and capacity for compromise delayed and weakened responses. The job leak due to deteriorating international competitiveness was only mended by placing wage negotiators under direct government control. But in international comparisons of wage costs, Belgium still comes up very high, second only to Germany. The OECD (1997: 1) maintains that 'improving the wage formation process remains a largely unresolved issue'. This is also the view of the government's own advisers, like the newly established High Council for Employment, even though the Council's 1998 report on the matter was largely ignored.

Pattern bargaining has negative consequences, especially when productivity trends diverge. In Belgium differences in productivity gains across sectors are very large; from 1970 to 1996 average annual productivity gains were 4.7 percent in manufacturing industry, as against 1.0 percent in services (BFB 1998: 108), a gap that is almost twice as high as the European average. If wages exceed the very small productivity margin, and wage bargaining is in real terms, profits and investments will decline. Consequently, job losses in manufacturing (between 1970 and 1994: −463,000) were hardly compensated by job increases in services (+682,000, of which only +114,000 were in non-market services). With further declines in agriculture, energy, and construction, overall growth was just +35,000 jobs.

Another reason for concern is the compressed wage structure, especially at the lower end, with little variation across sectors, regions, and skill levels, despite very large differences in unemployment, labor demand, or productivity. Together with the strong bias towards passive labor market policies and an earnings-compensating role for social security, this may explain why job turnover and labor mobility in Belgium is low, especially in Wallonia (De Grauwe 1998; Goubert and Heylen 1999; Marx 1999). There are a number of unemployment traps, related to the length rather than to the level of unemployment benefits. Net replacement rates for single parents and breadwinners, measured against the minimum wage for full-time workers, are estimated at 107 percent and 91 percent respectively. For part-time workers at 50 percent of the minimum wage, net replacement rates vary around 90 percent and 96 percent for breadwinners and unemployed spouses (Cantillon and Thirron 1997). Married women receive a small unemployment benefit, which often serves as a second income in the family. They have little monetary incentive to accept a job if it is not full-time. This applies particularly to low-income families. Moreover, the strong family bias in unemployment benefits discourages spouses of unemployed workers from seeking or holding on to part-time jobs. Already in 1975 the female rate was twice the male unemployment rate, and in 1980 the ratio had increased to 3:1. This was partly determined by faster labor force growth for women, but unlimited unemployment insurance is another part of the story. In the 1990s the female/male disadvantage returned to its old ratio of 2:1, partly because of withdrawals from the labor market. Since 1987 administrators have been entitled to suspend unemployment benefits for second earners whenever unemployment spells were exceptionally long (i.e. 1.5 to 2 times the average for the industry or occupation).

Effective minimum wages, as defined by collective agreements, lie 20–30 percent above the statutory minimum. This would suggest that unemployment traps may be not as bad as they seem (Jadot 1998). However, the high level of wages at the lower end of the Belgian labor market, combined with a high level of wage costs and low profits, discourages job creation in services. This situation disadvantages workers with low levels of education, those with long spells of unemployment, or women who try to re-enter the labor market. For exactly this reason, Dutch governments since 1993 have successfully exerted pressure on unions and employers to lower negotiated minimum wage levels and provided wage cost subsidies for the low paid.

Wage cost subsidies to employers have remained the only answer, but until recently they were only targeted to industry. During the 1992–93 EMS crisis there was a rapid expansion, from 15 bn BEF in 1993 to 60 bn BEF in 1996 (there are roughly forty francs to the euro). As in the original Maribel scheme of 1981, subsidies were intended to compensate exporting firms for the hard currency policy and to slow down the decline of manual work jobs in manufacturing. On precisely these grounds the European Commission repeatedly criticized the subsidies as a distortion of competition, since they were not open to all firms. In response, the program was widened in 1997 and now lets all private firms, including services, reduce social insurance contributions proportionate to 'labor intensity'. The revised Maribel scheme is valid until the year 2000 and applies to about 770,000 workers, as against 431,000 in the old program. Unions have criticized the subsidy as a handout to employers (Serroyen and Delcroix 1996: 37). But the proposal of Socialist ministers to make the subsidies contingent on explicit job targets was not implemented. Studies of the Belgian Planning Bureau suggest that a selective subsidy program, targeting workers with low earnings, would create more jobs but prove costlier and more difficult to monitor (CNT 1998). In 1995, however, the federal government phased in an additional 'low earnings' subsidy scheme, which applied to 782,000 workers at or around the minimum wage who get to have their social security charges lowered by between 2 percent and 12 percent of total wage costs. In 1996, 36 percent of total expenditures on tax- and charge-reducing subsidies went to Maribel, 24 percent to the low earnings scheme, and 20 percent to special job creation plans for the long-term unemployed (De Lathouwer 1999: 199). The remainder was set aside for contingency plans, negotiable with trade unions and employers.

As was mentioned in the introduction, Belgium spends more on 'active' labor market policies than either Austria or the Netherlands. Total expenditure nearly doubled from 64 bn BEF in 1985 to 112 bn BEF in 1994. Against the background of a rise in long-term unemployment amounting to 6 percent of the active labor force, the spending increase is less impressive than it sounds and the effectiveness of policies more questionable. Placement offices and employment services are extremely overburdened, and in 1990 it took an average of 20 months before an unemployed person was contacted by a case officer (OECD 1994). Non-participation in job placement programs is rarely penalized. Only 20 percent of total expenditure concerns training and education, and just 6 percent of the unemployed participate in training or work experience programs (De Lathouwer 1999: 200). Subsidies absorb most costs. Although there is perhaps no other government in Europe with so many job plans, many quite creative, Belgium's top civil servant in the Ministry of Labor described his government's job policies in a recent policy review as 'plainly unrealistic' (Jadot 1998).

Many of the schemes are along the lines of the 5 + 3 + 3 schemes of the early 1980s. The government makes subsidies available, or lifts certain legal restrictions on work or working-time regulation, if employers create extra jobs, and unions sign on to extra wage restraint and greater flexibility. Some of these schemes are specifically designed for young workers, the long-term unemployed, small firms, or the non-profit sector of charitable work. The take-up for subsidy schemes, to be negotiated under company or plant-level agreements, has been disappointing (Serroyen and Delcroix 1996: 43) and control over implementation is extremely difficult. A possible explanation is that Belgian unions and employers are not ready for the kind of decentralized bargaining required (Vilrokx and Van Leemput 1997: 341). Internally divided between their regional wings, Belgian employers' associations fear the strength of the union delegate system at the local level and the militant stance of the union rank-and-file in Wallonia. The Socialist union confederation dislikes decentralization for opposite reasons; left to their own devices, Flemish representatives would go along with more flexibility than the FGTB and Christian unions presently do, whereas Wallonian union representatives would probably accept even less change. Sectoral plans, negotiated under a central agreement of 1994, have been more numerous, but they mainly focused on early retirement. Once again, the agreement widened the opportunities for early retirement from age 58 to 55, under certain conditions. Many agreements allow workers who have been contributing for a minimum of 33 years to leave at age 55, and nearly all permit older workers to continue working half-time and receive a supplementary unemployment benefit until they reach the legal retirement age of 65.

Part-time employment has remained unpopular with the unions. Unlike in the Netherlands, it has not been (or become) the dominant choice of working mothers. The full-time employment/population ratio of Belgian women is almost double that of the Netherlands, whereas the part-time employment/population ratio is nearly three times lower (Visser 1999). Historically, a much larger number of Belgian married women continued to work full-time, and childcare facilities, especially for very young children, have generally been available on a much wider scale (Daly, this volume). In Belgium married women used to stop working if their husbands earned enough, while in the Netherlands women continue working if they can buy or obtain private childcare. Hence the relationship among family income, women's work, and working hours is quite opposite in the two countries (Henkens, Siegers, and van den Bosch 1992).

The policies of Belgian governments concerning part-time work have been hesitant and inconsistent. Around 1980, part-time work was encouraged. Combining part-time work with part-time unemployment benefits made it a very popular option at the time (Casey 1983). The program became too expensive and was stopped in 1982 because of its success. In recent years, the government has reinstated the possibility of combining part-time work with benefits, especially for older workers. These options also exist in the case of part-time career breaks. The regional government of Flanders has introduced additional incentive schemes for part-time jobs and career breaks whose purpose is caring for young children or taking vocational training (Serroyen and Delcroix 1996: 47).

Part-time work is treated with ambivalence in labor law and social security, as well as in statistics. Until 1987 anyone working two hours per week or less was not counted and remained outside the social security system. When the two-hours rule was abolished, employment rose by 55,000 extra jobs. Many workers became self-employed for tax and social security purposes (De Swert 1999: 44). In Belgium, mock self-employment is the equivalent of small part-time jobs amounting to less than 12 weekly hours in the Netherlands, except that since the 1990s the latter are covered by tax and social security. In Belgium, employment protection and minimum wage and vacation rights apply only to part-time jobs that have at least one-third of the hours of full-time jobs, with a minimum of three hours per day. In the Netherlands the opposite move took place, to raise the status, rights, and popularity of small part-time jobs, especially important in domestic services (Visser 1999).

5.4.6. *The Efforts of a* sur place

In professional cycling there is a game in which you have to work hard to stay in the same place and then leap to victory. This *sur place* appears to be a pertinent description of the Belgian case. There is no other country where governments have designed so many pacts, proposals, plans, and schemes to coax unions into accepting wage restraint and employers into creating jobs, and with so little success. There is also no other country where five Ministers of Labor, at the federal, regional, and communal levels, compete for attention and resources. The unanswered question is whether the new political situation will break the immobilism of Belgian politics —the Lib–Lab–Green coalition that gained power in 1999 has a clear mandate for change after the string of scandals in recent years and disastrous electoral results for the Christian and Social Democrats, especially in Flanders. In conjunction with the 1998 central agreement, this may be the time for a new start. One promising proposal by the new government is to expand 'social Maribel' in 2000 and substantially reduce non-wage labor costs by about 32,000 BEF per year per employee for 'entry'-level wages. In sum, the government wants to lower the 'tax on labor' by 50 bn BEF, to be financed with a tax reform announced for 2002 (but with a content yet unknown, except for the detail that the VAT on labor-intensive services will be lowered from 21% to 6%).

Like the Netherlands, Belgium entered the 1970s with one of the lowest employment/population ratios in Europe. Thirty years later, unlike the Netherlands, the situation has deteriorated (Figure 5.3). Cutting the labor supply is still accepted as an alternative to overt unemployment, and governments have gone along with subsidizing early retirement for lack of alternatives. Unemployment remains high, hides large regional variations (with Flanders approaching full employment), and includes a large structural component, with the highest share of long-term and youth unemployment in Europe outside Italy and Spain. Like its northern neighbor, Belgium went through a very difficult phase in the 1970s and sought to redress a rather desperate situation through a combination of wage restraint, fiscal consolidation, and job sharing. While some of this worked and Belgium's external competitiveness was restored, the outcome in terms of employment was less favorable. Despite a large amount of job sharing and job creation plans, employment growth remained sluggish. There was nothing compared to the growth in domestic services and part-time jobs experienced later in the Netherlands. In contrast to the Dutch economy in the 1990s, the Belgian economy, in spite of its exposed sector's recovery, suffered from lackluster consumer spending, The savings rate of households reached an all-time high and remained high in 1995–97. The OECD (1995: 7) speaks of a 'healthy financial position of households' and a show of 'low confidence'.

The various subsidy schemes have mainly affected the distribution of jobs rather than their overall number. Unions criticize how many of the schemes targeted at low-experience workers fail to requalify workers and instead trap them in dead-end jobs. Economists have raised the criticism that subsidizing firms exposed to international competition has lowered employer resistance to union wage demands and slowed down the rate of innovation. There are remarkably few hard facts or impartial studies on these issues. The only observations that can be made with certainty are these: that there were many plans and schemes, that nearly all of them were contested, that many of these plans were designed to obtain cooperation from unions and employers but very hard to monitor, that many were short-lived and depended upon complex implementation procedures, and finally that the actual job creation rate was disappointing. The narrow employment base of Belgium's economy and the absence of a jointly held view on how that might be changed suggest continued vulnerability for this otherwise very wealthy country.

One may ask why there was not more policy change in response to stagnation and failure. Our main hypothesis is that organized actors in Belgium—inside and outside the government—failed to agree on the causes of the job crisis and its therapies, and that they continued to work at cross-purposes. Hence, the kind of contrast in policies before and after 1982 found in the Netherlands is much less apparent in Belgium. Both countries suffered from a lack of consensus and coordination in the 1970s and went through a deep crisis in the early 1980s. In addition to a massive rise in unemployment, Belgium experienced a depletion of its national reserves, a crisis of international confidence, and currency devaluation. Yet Belgian trade unions did not accept that wage restraint and a recovery of profits were necessary conditions for economic recovery and job growth, as did the Dutch unions at the time. Was this a reflection of the continued strength of the Belgian economy? Did Dutch unions learn faster, and even shift paradigms, because they were so much weaker? The upshot was that Belgian governments had to impose conditions on trade unions and firms that were mutually negotiated in the Netherlands. In the Belgian case, this restricted decentralization and the flexibility of wage bargaining made linkages with other policies (especially to work-sharing) more difficult, and rendered implementation-failure more likely. Moreover, their ongoing attempts at begging for support of policy measures made successive Belgian governments far more vulnerable to various pressures (like having to repackage wage policies with subsidies to firms or promulgate protective measures for the low paid), and pleading for constituency support also compromised attempts at fiscal consolidation and welfare reform.

It is tempting to shift some blame onto the linguistic conflict and the cumbersome federalization process, discussed in the introduction to this chapter. The linguistic-federal dimension overshadowed other pressing problems, like industrial decline, unemployment, public administration, justice, or environmental decline (Swyngedouw and Martiniello 1998). Michel Albert observed that the Belgians 'were amusing themselves with their linguistic squabbles' while the 'ship was sinking' (introduction in Hansenne 1985). The conflict was germane to government instability and produced a kind of 'crisis consociationalism' in which problems were combined until they became so big, numerous, or pressing as to require a large coalition in which each of the parties was allowed to deal with its particular clientele (Deschouwer 1998). The average tenure of postwar Belgian governments has been exceedingly short; in the ten crucial years between 1972 and 1982, when two major economic shocks needed a response,

Belgium had no less than thirteen governments (compared to five in the Netherlands and only three in Austria). The weakening of the state was compounded by the partisan use of the state, with recruitment practices not based on merit but on party membership and the right combination of language and region (Swyngedouw and Martiniello 1998; Dewachter 1989).

5.5. Conclusions

In the introduction we characterized Austria, Belgium, and the Netherlands as 'birds of a feather', albeit of different colors. Why did they not 'flock together'? For the answer we have examined the external and internal conditions, perceptions of problems, policy choices, and any spillover from unsolved problems and unhelpful choices.

The Austrian economy was hit less severely by the oil shocks because it was (and is) less exposed to internationalization than the other two countries. Multinational firms were (and still are) lacking. Financial and stock markets were (and are) less developed, whereas Belgium hosts a number of very powerful financial holdings and the Netherlands traditionally had a highly developed stock market and a number of MNCs operating worldwide. For a much longer time and to a far greater degree, Austria has relied on all kinds of regulations, such as controls on prices, exports, and capital. Domestic-oriented policies were maintained longer than they were abroad, and the public sector played a greater role in buffering external shocks. With the passing of time, however, Austrian exceptionalism subsided. But the country's geopolitical location and particular history help explain why political actors shared the same fears and the same perception of what the problems were: avoiding both mass unemployment and hyperinflation and restoring growth to an export-oriented economy. The homogeneity of policy priorities is most prominently demonstrated by the amazing fact that income inequality was never a major topic in Austria, while wage moderation proved much easier to maintain than in Belgium and the Netherlands.

The reasons for the poor performance of the Belgian and Dutch economy in the 1970s were not dissimilar. High exposure to foreign trade was certainly a factor and meant that external shocks had a huge impact, but this was compounded by domestic factors, especially by a problematic method of wage setting fraught with diverging objectives and insufficient coordination. The result was that corporate incomes had to bear the brunt of adjustment in the terms of trade after the oil crises of 1973 (for both countries) and 1979 (for Belgium). In the Netherlands real wage growth stopped in 1979, whereas between 1978 and 1982 Belgium was alone 'among the seven small countries of Scandinavia, the Low Countries, Austria, and Switzerland, in having a real wage increase' (Therborn 1986: 150). Since small countries are price-takers in the international economy and the authorities maintained a fixed exchange rate policy, the export sector was unable to pass on the higher costs. The fixed exchange rate policy came at the price of very high real interest rates in the Belgium case. This worsened business conditions but did not attract sufficient foreign capital to offset the public sector's borrowing requirements. The export sector could only stay competitive through above-average productivity growth and had to accept lower profit margins, which in turn led to a decline in investment. The combination of real wage growth, rising non-wage labor costs and strong external constraints explains the large drop in manufacturing employment. The deterioration of public finances alarmed both countries' governments by 1976 at the latest, but attempts at reversing the trend were difficult in light of unstable and internally divided coalitions and growing compulsory expenditures to pay for rising unemployment and service the public debt. In the Belgian case we may add expensive solutions to linguistic conflict as well as the absence of any fundamental review of institutional mechanisms for manpower deployment and wage determination in the public sector.

Looking back on twenty-five years of policy adjustment, one is struck by the ongoing importance of wage restraint for maintaining competitiveness and of a hard currency for fighting imported inflation. Apparently there were no alternative policy options in economies exposed to international competition, not even in Austria. Debate over alternative tools has been rare in each of the three countries. The contrast between Austria and the other two countries shows that the hard currency option, however unavoidable, is very harmful if not combined with wage restraint. The Austrian example also shows that wage restraint, if organized in cooperation with the social partners, facilitated opportunities for fiscal expansion and fighting unemployment that the other countries did not have.

In negotiated political systems like Austrian, Belgium, and the Netherlands, policy change is critically dependent upon the agreement of ruling coalition parties and support from the social partners. These systems may suffer from what Fritz Scharpf calls a 'negotiator's dilemma'. Negotiators must simultaneously search for effective policy responses in terms of policy content while resolving distributive conflict, i.e. finding a 'fair' distribution of the social costs of adjustment between and among ruling coalition parties and the social partners (Scharpf 1997). Perhaps because Austria's problems were less pressing, but more likely because social partnership there was not as challenged from within, Vienna's governments and social partners had little difficulty resolving the 'negotiator's dilemma' in the 1970s. All the relevant actors, in both the political and industrial arenas, agreed on a Keynesian definition of the crisis, a definition that was contested by key actors in Belgian and Dutch economic policymaking. Because of the conservative bias in Austrian society, there was no opposition to using foreign workers as a buffer by sending them home. This was not possible in the Netherlands and Belgium, and by the time of the second oil crisis it was also ruled out in Austria. Austrian unions were rather unique in giving priority to full employment over income redistribution. This amounted to an unfaltering policy choice for restraint. In the face of a much weaker Keynesian political consensus, Dutch and Belgian unions, partly as a result of union radicalization in the 1970s, were unprepared to forsake income redistribution for employment. The internal cohesion of the Austrian model was strikingly different from the situation in Belgium and the Netherlands, where the postwar consensus had in fact ended and was to be renegotiated within and between the different segments of society. Austria's legacy of a civil war between labor and capital in the 1930s and its position on the frontline between the communist East and the capitalist West bolstered the conviction that social conflict should be avoided at all costs. Moreover, Austrian social and economic policymaking—more encompassing, with fewer actors, and more informal in style—appeared easier to coordinate than in the other two countries (Unger 1998*a*). There are very few checks and balances in the Austrian political system. Institutional arrangements such as a weak bipartite system, modest federalism, and grand coalitions allow each governments to push through its agenda, provided the government has somehow engineered an agreement with the social partners. As demonstrated by numerous examples from the section on Austria—actions like privatizing the steel sector in the mid-1980s, the 1988 tax reforms, joining the European Union, or the 1995 austerity package—agreements can be swiftly reached and promptly implemented. By comparison, the much more pluriform systems in the Netherlands and especially Belgium make for more cumbersome bargaining practices.

Lack of agreement in a negotiated policy system is very costly. The more the Belgian and Dutch social partners proved unable to organize restraint, the more important each country's hard currency stance became. The resultant negative side of declining competitiveness led to soaring unemployment in the 1970s and early 1980s, which in turn exacerbated the cost explosion in social security and the attendant potential for a damaging cycle of higher non-wage costs, productivity hikes, unemployment, and a fiscal crisis. Austria experienced neither one of these two dire straits and was therefore in much better shape to stick to its incrementalist pattern of corporatist adjustment. Before 1987 Austria maintained virtually full employment, thanks to a joint consensus between the political parties and social partners on the merits of Austro-Keynesianism.

In the face of the acute unemployment crisis, a severe challenge to their power and pent-up frustrations over recurrent government intervention, the Dutch unions finally conceded to the new realities of the world economy and returned to a strategy of wage moderation. Rather than continuing the prisoners' dilemma game, in which third party intervention would have become unavoidable, they redefined their position in terms of a 'battle of the sexes', preferring a coordinated policy over distributive privilege. From 1982 on, Dutch unions have consistently placed jobs before income. This learning process on the part of the trade unions led to a revitalization of social partnership in the Netherlands during the 1980s. Over time, wage restraint allowed for a rather smooth interplay between wage setting and fiscal policy, stimulating economic growth while keeping inflation down.

This painful learning experience did not occur in Belgium, where the social partners remained stuck in a prisoners' dilemma and, moreover, suffered from internal fragmentation. Consequently, the government had to replace, and repay, the unions in the organization of wage restraint, accepting bargains with employers and unions over compensation through subsidies, make-work programs, and measures for the low paid. Whereas the Austrian and Dutch social partners were successful in combining moderate wage increases with a high level of flexibility at the micro level, the Belgian strategy of imposed wage restraint sacrificed micro-flexibility in the labor market for the purpose of macro-adjustment. In addition, Belgian governments were faced with much larger implementation failures. Finally, they ran a much larger risk of being taken hostage and being forced to renegotiate their preferred policies of austerity and social security reform, policies that repeatedly overran their targets. Of course, the options of Belgian governments were also limited by the fact that more money had to be spent on interests and repayment of debts and that less was available for lowering taxes or propping up the purchasing power of workers and their families. Unlike the Netherlands, Belgium was unable to support wage moderation in the 1990s with tax rebates. Under conditions of permanent austerity the slightest of setbacks to economic growth had extremely disheveling consequences for the country's public finances.

Austria's welfare state demonstrates the highest degree of continuity but also some signs of obsolescence. So far, however, the political and institutional capacity for incremental reform and fast policy implementation has been high, and overall performance is good, though not as good as it was. The flexibilization of the labor market progresses slowly. Pressures for changes towards a more liberal society and equal rights tend to come from abroad. The elections of 1999, turning the FPÖ into the second strongest party, demonstrate the persistence of Austrian conservatism and xenophobia, as well as some popular disenchantment with Austria's closed backroom politics. Austria's problems as a welfare state seem much less urgent than its difficulties transforming itself into a modern and open society. Belgium's welfare state reforms are much more severe because of larger and unsolved financial burdens, the federal conundrum, less homogeneity of preferences, and few learning experiences (so far) with successful, piecemeal reform. The Dutch welfare state certainly has experienced the greatest transformation and shown considerable capacity for reform and innovation. However, it now stands again at the crossroad of deciding how to spend its newly gained resources and reassess the balance between public and private investment and responsibilities.

REFERENCES

AARTS, LEO, and DE JONG, PHILIP (1992). *Economic Aspects of Disability Behaviour*. Amsterdam: North-Holland.

——— (1996). *Curing the Dutch Disease*. Aldershot: Avebury.

ALBER, JENS (1998). *Recent Developments in Continental European Welfare States: Do Austria, Germany and the Netherlands Prove to be Birds of a Feather?*. Paper for the 14th World Congress of Sociology, Montreal, 29 July 1998.

BASTIAN, JENS (1994). *A Matter of Time: From Worksharing to Temporal Flexibility in Belgium, France and Britain*. Aldershot: Avebury.

BÉGUIN, J. M. (1985). *Les Politiques d'emploi menées en Belgique de 1972 à 1984*. Mimeo. Brussels: Vrije Universiteit.

BFP (Bureau Fédérale du Plan) (1998). *L'Économie belge dans 1998*. Brussels: BFP.

BLAISE, PIERRE, and BEAUPAIN, THÉRÈSE (1996). 'La Concertation sociale 1993–95'. *Courier hebdomaire du CRISP*, No. 1497–98.

BMAGS (Bundesministerium für Arbeit, Gesundheit und Soziales) (1999). *Der Arbeitsmarkt im Jahre 1998*. Vienna: BMAGS.

BOTTENBURG, MAARTEN VAN (1995). *Aan den Arbeid! In de wandelgangen van de Stichting van de Arbeid, 1945–1995*. Amsterdam: Bert Bakker.

BRAUN, ANNE ROMANIS (1976). 'Indexation of Wages and Salaries in Developed Economies'. *IMF Staff Papers*, 23/1: 226–71.

BREUSS, FRITZ (1978). 'Die Konjunktur 1978 im Zeichen des österreichischen Experiments der Zahlungsbilanzsanierung'. *Wirtschaftspolitische Blätter*, 4: 5–15.

CANTILLON, BEA, and THIRRON, A. (1997). *Wegen naar een activerende verzorgingsstaat. Tussentijdse evaluatie van het BWA experiment*. Paper voor Jaarboek Armoede en Sociale Uitsluiting, Brussels, Nov.

CASEY, BERNARD (1983). 'Staatliche Maßnahmen zur Förderung der Teilzeit-arbeit: Erfahrungen in Belgien, Frankreich, Großbrittannien, den Niederlanden und der Bundesrepublik Deutschland'. *Mitteilungen aus der Arbeitsmarkt und Berufsforschung*, 16/4: 414–17.

CNT (Conseil National du Travail) (1998). *Le Marché du travail dans 1998*. Brussels: CNT.

COLPAERT, TOM (1987). 'Requiem voor de 32 uren week?'. *Socialistische Standpunten*, 17: 41–43.

CPB (Centraal Planbureau) (1997). *Macro-economische Verkenningen*. The Hague: Centraal Planbureau.

CREPAZ, MARKUS (1995). 'An Institutional Dinosaur: Austrian Corporatism in the Post-industrial Age'. *West European Politics*, 18/4: 64–88.

CROUCH, COLIN J., and PIZZORNO, ALESSANDRO (eds.) (1978). *The Resurgence of Class Conflict in Western Europe since 1968*. London: Macmillan.

DAALDER, HANS (1966). 'The Netherlands: Opposition in a Segmented Society', in Robert A. Dahl (ed.), *Political Opposition in Western Societies*. New Haven: Yale University Press, 188–236.

DANCET, GUY (1988). 'Wage Regulation and Complexity: The Belgian Experience', in Robert Boyer (ed.), *The Search for Labour Market Flexibility*. Oxford: Clarendon Press, 212–37.

DE GRAUWE, PAUL (1994). *Onze schuld: Ontstaan en toekomst van werkloosheid en staatsschuld*. Tielt: Lannoo.

——(1998). *Euro and Work*. Paper presented at AIAS Workshop on Economic and Monetary Union, 1 July. Amsterdam: University of Amsterdam.

DE LATHOUWER, LIEVE (1999). 'Het Belgisch werkloosheidsstelsel: een evaluatie vanuit sociaal zekerheids- en arbeidsmarktperspectief', in J. J. van Hoof and J. Mevissen (eds.), *Loonvorming en werking van de arbeidsmarkt in België*. Amsterdam: Elsevier, 185–210.

DELLEN, H. VAN (1984). *Een nieuw elan, de marktsector van de jaren tachtig*. Deventer: Kluwer.

DENYS, J., HEDEBOUW, G., and LAMBERTL, M. (1985). *Nieuwe vormen van arbeidstijdregeling: De experimenten Hansenne*. Mimeo. Louvain: KUL/Hoger Instituut voor de Arbeid.

DESCHOUWER, KRIS (1998). *Falling Apart Together: The Changing Nature of Belgian Consociationalism, 1961–1998*. Paper delivered at conference 'The Fate of Consociationalism in Western Europe, 1968–1998', 29–31 May. Harvard University: Minda de Gunzberg Center for European Studies.

DE SWERT, GILBERT (1989). 'Samen apart', in BVVA Belgische Vereniging voor Arbeidsverhoudingen (ed.), *Vijftig jaar Arbeidsverhoudingen*. Bruges: De Keure and BVVA, 3–16.

——(1999). 'België in oude banen gebleven? Tien om te herzien', in J. J. van Hoof and J. Mevissen (eds.), *Loonvorming en werking van de arbeidsmarkt in België*. Amsterdam: Elsevier, 43–54.

DEWACHTER, WILFRIED (1996). 'La Belgique d'aujourd'hui comme société poli-tique', in A. Dieckhoff (ed.), *La Belgique: La Force de la désunion*. Brussels: Complexe, 105–42.

DEWEERDT, M., and SMITS, J. (1982). 'Belgian Politics in 1981: Continuity and change in the crisis'. *Res Publica*, 24/2: 261–72.

DOLADO, J., KRAMARZ, F., MACHIN, S., MANNING, A., MARGOLIS, D., and TEULINGS, C. N. (1996). 'Minimum Wages: The European Experience'. *Economic Policy*, 23: 319–72.

DYSON, KEN (1994). *Elusive Union*. New York: Longman.

EBBINGHAUS, BERNHARD, and VISSER, JELLE (1999). 'When Institutions Matter: Union Growth and Decline in Western Europe, 1950–1995'. *European Sociological Review*, 15/2: 135–58.

ELMESKOV, J., MARTIN, J. P., and SCARPETTA, S. (1998). 'Key Lessons for Labour Market Reform: Evidence from OECD Countries' Experiences'. *Swedish Economic Policy Review*, 2/2: 205–51.

ESPING-ANDERSEN, GØSTA (1990). *The Three Worlds of Welfare Capitalism*. Princeton: Princeton University Press.

——(1996). 'Welfare States without Work: The Impasse of Labor Shedding en Familialism in Continental European Social Policy', in Gøsta Esping-Andersen (ed.), *Welfare States in Transition*. London: Sage, 66–87.

FARNY, OTTO (1996). 'Analyse des Gewinnsteueraufkommens 1988–96'. *Wirtschaft und Gesellschaft*, 22/1: 39–55 (Orac publisher, Vienna).

FEUCHTMÜLLER, WOLFGANG (1987). 'Der österreichische Kapitalmarkt und die Privatisierung'. *Wirtschaftspolitische Blätter*, 5–6: 564–74.

FLORA, PETER (ed.) (1986). *Growth to Limits: The Western European Welfare States since World War II*, 4 vols. Berlin: De Gruyter.

GOUBERT, LUCIA, and HEYLEN, FREDDY (1999). 'Loonvorming en de werking van de arbeidsmarkt in België', in J. J. van Hoof and J. Mevissen (eds.), *Loonvorming en werking van de arbeidsmarkt in België*. Amsterdam: Elsevier, 87–110.

GROS, DAVID, and THYGESEN, NIELS (1994). *European Monetary Integration*. London: Macmillan.

GUGER, ALOIS (1998). 'Economic Policy and Social Democracy: The Austrian Experience'. *Oxford Review of Economic Policy*, 14/1: 40–58.

HANCKÉ, BOB (1993). 'Trade Union Membership in Europe 1960–90: Rediscovering Local Unions'. *British Journal of Industrial Relations*, 31/4: 593–613.

HANSENNE, MICHEL (1985). *Emploi: Les Scénarios du possible*. Paris: Duculot.

HARTOG, JOOP (1999). *Country Employment Policy Review: The Netherlands*. Report Symposium on 'Social Dialogue and Employment Success', 2–3 March. Geneva: ILO.

——and THEEUWES, JULES (1983). 'De onstuitbare opkomst van de werkende gehuwde vrouw'. *Economisch-Statistische Berichten*, 68: 1152–1157.

HAUTH, ANTON (1989). 'Die Arbeitszeit der österreichischen Wirtschaft'. *Wirtschaftspolitische Blätter*, 1: 18–29.

HEERTUM-LEMMEN, ANKIE, and WILTHAGEN, TON (1996). *De doorwerking van de aanbevelingen van de Stichting van de Arbeid*. Den Haag: SDU.

HEMERIJCK, ANTON (1995). 'Corporatist Immobility in the Netherlands', in Colin J. Crouch and Franz Traxler (eds.), *Organized Industrial Relations in Europe: What Future?* Aldershot: Avebury: 183–226.

HENKENS, PAUL, SIEGERS, JACQUES, and VAN DEN BOSCH, KAREL (1992). 'Married Women on the Labor Market: A Comparative Study of Belgium and the Netherlands'. *Bevolking en gezin*, 24/1: 77–100.

HEYLEN, FREDDY, and VAN POECK, ANDRÉ (1995). 'National Labour Market Institutions and the European Economic and Monetary Integration Process'. *Journal of Common Market Studies*, 33/4: 573–95.

HOCHREITER, EDUARD, and WINCKLER, GEORG (1996). 'Advantages of Tying Austria's Hands: The Success of the Hard Currency Strategy'. *European Journal of Political Economy*, 11: 83–111.

HUYSE, LUC (1970). *Passiviteit, pacificatie en verzuiling in de Belgische politiek.* Antwerp/Utrecht: Standaard.

JADOT, M. (1998). 'La Politique fédérale de l'emploi, rapport d'évaluation 1998'. Brussels: Ministère Fédéral de l'Emploi, 13–28.

JONES, ERIK (1995). 'Changing the Political Formula: Economic Adjustment and Political Transformation in Belgium and the Netherlands'. Diss. Paul H. Nitze School of Advanced International Studies of the Johns Hopkins University, Baltimore.

KAM, FLIP DE (1996). 'Tax policies in the 1980s and the 1990s: The Case of the Netherlands', in Anthonie Knoester (ed.), *Taxation in the United States and Europe.* London: Macmillan, 259–301.

KATZENSTEIN, PETER J. (1985). *Small States in World Markets: Industrial Policy in Europe.* Ithaca, NY: Cornell University Press.

KERSBERGEN, KEES VAN (1995). *Social Capitalism: A Study of Christian Democracy and the Welfare State.* Londen/New York: Routledge.

KIENZL, HEINZ (1993). 'Gesamtstabilität, der Weg und das Ziel—Einkommenspolitik und Währungspolitik seit 1951', in F. Weber and Th. Venus (eds.), *Austro-Keynesianismus in Theorie und Praxis.* Vienna: Stiftung Bruno Kreisky Archiv and Dachs-Verlag, i. 63–72.

KOOLE, RUDY A. (1995). *Politieke partijen in Nederland: Ontstaan en ontwikkeling van partijen en partijstelsel.* Utrecht: Het Spectrum.

KURZER, PAULETTE (1993). *Business and Banking: Political Change and European Integration in Western Europe.* Ithaca, NY: Cornell University Press.

——(1997). 'Placed in Europe: The Low Countries and Germany in the European Union', in Peter J. Katzenstein (ed.), *Tamed Power: Germany in Europe.* Ithaca, NY: Cornell University Press, 108–41.

LAYARD, RICHARD, NICKEL, STEVE, and JACKMAN, RICHARD (1991). *Unemployment: Macroeconomic Performance and the Labour Market.* Oxford: Oxford University Press.

LEHMBRUCH, GERHARD (1967). *Proporzdemokratie: Politisches System und politische Kultur in der Schweiz und Österreich.* Tübingen: Mohr.

LEHNER, GERHARD (1991). 'Die steuerliche Wirtschaftsförderung'. *Wirtschaftspolitische Blätter*, 4: 472–81.

LIJPHART, AREND (1968). *The Politics of Accommodation: Pluralism and Democracy in the Netherlands.* Berkeley: University of California Press.

LIPSET, SEYMOUR-MARTIN, and ROKKAN, STEIN (1967). *Party Systems and Voter Alignments.* New York: Free Press.

LORWIN, VAL R. (1966). 'Belgium: Religion, Class and Language in National Politics', in Robert A. Dahl (ed.), *Political Opposition in Western Democracies*. New Haven: Yale University Press.

——(1971). 'Segmented Pluralism: Ideological Cleavages and Political Cohesion in the Smaller European Democracies'. *Comparative Politics*, 3/2: 141–75.

MARCH, JIM, and OLSEN, JOHAN P. (1989). *Rediscovering Institutions: The Organizational Basis of Politics*. New York: Free Press.

MARX, IVO (1999). *OESO-recept voor meer werk: Is de weerstand echt gerechtsvaardigd?*. Mimeo. Antwerp: Centrum voor Sociaal beleid.

MICHEL, E. (1994). 'La Loi sur la compétitivité: Évaluation et proposition'. *Reflets et Perspectives de la vie économique*, XXXIII-5: 395–417.

MODEN, JACQUES, and SLOOVER, JEAN (1980) *Le patronat belge. Discours et idéologie 1973–1980*. Brussels: Centre de recherche et d'information socio-politiques (CRISP).

MOLITOR, MICHEL (1978) 'Social Conflict in Belgium', in Colin J. Crouch and Alessandro Pizzorno (eds.), *The Resurgence of Class Conflict*, i. *National Studies*. London: Macmillan, 20–51.

MUEHLBERGER, ULRIKE (1998). 'Atypische Beschärtigung in Österreich, sozial- und arbeitsmarktpolitische Implikationen atypischer Beschärtigungsver-hältnisse'. Diplomawork, Vienna University of Economics and Business Administration.

NEI (Nederlands Economisch Instituut) (1999). *Wordt succes bepaald door de vorm? Onderzoek naar de doorstroom van gesusidieerderde naar reguliere arbeid*. Rotterdam: Nederlands Economisch Instituut

NOBELEN, PAUL W. M. (1983). 'Nederland: Kwijnend corporatisme en stag-nerende verzorgingsstaat', in T. Akkermans and Paul W. M. Nobelen (eds.), *Corporatism en Verzorgingsstaat*. Leyden: Stenfert Kroese, 99–142.

NOWOTNY, EWALD (1989). 'Die grosse Steuerreform 1988—Analyse und Bewertung', in Andreas Khol (ed.), *Oesterreichisches Jahrbuch für Politik 1988*. Munich: Oldenburg, 571–89.

——(1998). 'Privatization, Deregulation, Reregulation: Experiences and Policy Issues in Austria'. *IB Review, Journal for Institutional Innovation, Development and Transition*, 2 (Slovenia): 35–48.

OECD (Organisation for Economic Co-operation and Development) (1974). *Economic Surveys 1973: The Netherlands*. Paris: OECD.

——(1980). *Economic Surveys 1979: The Netherlands*. Paris: OECD.

——(1983). *Economic Surveys 1981–82: Belgium*. Paris: OECD.

——(1986). *Economic Surveys 1985: Belgium*. Paris: OECD.

——(1994). *Employment Outlook 1994*. Paris: OECD.

——(1995). *Economic Surveys 1994–1995: Belgium*. Paris: OECD.

——(1996). *Employment Outlook 1996*. Paris: OECD.

——(1997). *Economic Surveys 1996–1997: Belgium*. Paris: OECD.

——(1998). 'Key Employment Policy Challenges Faced by OECD Countries', in *Labour Market and Social Policy Occasional Papers*, 31. Paris: OECD.

——(1999). *Economics Outlook 1999*. Paris: OECD.

PEETERS, JAN (1989). 'De sociale zekerheid tien jaar later: Naar een crisismanagement', in BVA (Belgische Vereniging voor Arbeidsverhoudingen) (ed.), *Vijftig jaar Arbeidsverhoudingen*. Bruges: De Keure and BVA, 197–228.

PICHELMANN, KARL, and HOFER, HELMUT (1999). *Country Employment Policy Reviews: Austria*. Report Symposium on 'Social Dialogue and Employment Success', 2–3 Mar. Geneva: ILO.

PRZEWORSKI, ADAM, and TEUNE, HENRY (1970). *The Logic of Comparative Social Inquiry*. New York: Wiley.

RENAN, PAUL (1990). *La Sécurité sociale: Histoire, développement et perspectives*. Brussels: *Dossiers du Crisp*, No. 38.

ROORDA, WOUTER, and VOGELS, ELS (1997). 'Arbeidsmarkt: Bescherming en prestaties'. *Economisch-Statistische Berichten*, 4099: 245–48.

ROTHSCHILD, KURT (1993), 'Austro-Keynesianismus aus ökonomischer Sicht', in F. Weber, and Th. Venus (eds.), *Austro-Keynesianismus in Theorie und Praxis*. Vienna: Stiftung Bruno Kreisky Archiv and Dachs-Verlag, i. 135–45.

ROTHSTEIN, BO (1992). 'Labor-Market Institutions and Working-Class Strength', in Sven Steinmo, Kathleen Thelen, and Frank Longstreth (eds.), *Structuring Politics. Historical Institutionalism in Comparative Analysis*. Cambridge: Cambridge University Press, 33–56.

SALVERDA, WIEMER (1997). 'Verdringing en arbeidsmarktbeleid voor de onderkant', in F. Bergman, Joop Hartog, P. Hiemstra, Robert C. Kloosterman, Wiemer Salverda, and Jules Theeuwes, *Creëren van werk aan de onderkant*. Amsterdam: Welboom: 55–74.

SCHARPF, FRITZ W. (1988). 'The Joint-Decision Trap: Lessons from German Federalism and European Integration'. *Public Administration*, 66: 239–78.

——(1991). *Crisis and Choice in European Social Democracy*. Ithaca, NY: Cornell University Press.

——(1997). *Games Real Actors Play*. Boulder Colo.: Westview Press.

SCHETTKAT, ROLAND (1999). 'Small Economy Macroeconomics: The Economic Success of Ireland, Denmark, Austria and the Netherlands Compared'. *Intereconomics*, 34/4: 7–19 (Hamburg Institute for Economic Research: Review of International Trade and Development).

SCP (Sociaal Cultureel Planbureau) (1998). *Sociaal Cultureel Plan 1998*. Rijswijk: SCP.

SEIDEL, HANS (1993). 'Austro-Keynesianismus–Revisited', in F. Weber and Th. Venus (eds.), *Austro-Keynesianismus in Theorie und Praxis*. Vienna: Stiftung Bruno Kreisky Archiv and Dachs-Verlag, i. 145–49.

SERROYEN, CHRIS, and DELCROIX, JEAN-PAUL (1996). 'Belgium', in Giuseppe Fajertag (ed.), *Collective Bargaining in Western Europe 1995–96*. Brussels: European Trade Union Institute, 31–56.

SLOMP, HANS (1983). 'België: Naar "Nederlandse toestanden"?', in T. Akkermans and Paul W. M. Nobelen (eds.), *Corporatisme en verzorgingsstaat*. Deventer: Stenfert Kroese, 143–69.

SMITS, J. (1983). 'Belgian Politics in 1982: Less Democracy for a Better Economy'. *Res Publica*, 25/2–3: 181–217.

SNEESSENS, HENRI R., and DRÈZE, JACQUES H. (1986). 'A Discussion of Belgian

Unemployment Combining Traditional Concepts and Disequilibrium Economics', in C. Bean, Richard Layard, and Stephen Nickell (eds.), *The Rise in Unemployments*. Oxford: Blackwell, 89–120.

SNELS, BERT (1997). *Political Mechanisms and Institutional Interaction: Politics in the Dutch Economy*. Utrecht: Dissertation University of Utrecht.

STEINIGER, RUDOLF (1975). *Polarisierung und Intergration: Eine vergleichende Untersuchung der strukturellen Versäulung der Gesellschaft in den Niederlanden und Österreich*. Meidenheim a/G.: Anton Hain.

SWAV (Stweunpunbt Werkgelegenheid, Arbeid en Vorming) (1995). *De arbeidsmarktonderzoekersdag 1995*. Verslagboek, Louvain: SWAV, dossier 12.

SWYNGEDOUW, MARC, and MARTINIELLO, MARCO (eds.) (1998). *Belgische Toestanden: De lotgevallen van een kleine bi-culturele demoncratie*. Antwerp: Standaard.

SZW (Sociale Zaken en Werkgelegenheid)(1995). *Sociale Nota 1996*. The Hague: Ministerie van of SZW.

——(1998). *Evaluatie van het gebruik van de afdrachtskorting lage lonen, eindrapport*. The Hague: Ministerie van of Sociale Zaken en Werkgelegenheid.

TÁLOS, EMMERICH (1996). 'Gewerkschaften und Sozialpartnerschaft'. *Kurswechsel 4, Beirat für Gesellschafts-, Wirtschafts- und Umweltpolitische Alternativen* (Vienna), 59–72.

——and KITTEL, BERNHARD (2000). 'Austrocorporatism in the 1990s', in Stefan Berger and Hugh Compston (eds.), *Social Partnership in Europe*. Oxford: Berghahn.

——and WÖRISTER, KARL (1998). 'Soziale Sicherung in Österreich', in Emmerich Tálos (ed.), *Soziale Sicherung im Wande. Österreich und seine Nachbarstaaten. Ein Vergleich*. Vienna: Böhlau Verlag, 209–88.

TEUFELSBAUER, WERNER (1986). 'Bremsen lockern statt Gasgeben!—Ein Plädoyer für eine seriöse Regulierungsdiskussion in Österreich'. *Wirtschaftspolitische Blätter*, 6: 708–20.

THERBORN, GØRAN (1986). *Why Some Peoples Are More Unemployed Than Others*. London: Verso.

TICHY, GUNTHER (1985). 'Wie funktioniert die österreichische Wechselkurspolitik? Konzept, Voraussetzung und Handhabung'. *Wirtschaftspolitische Blätter*, 5: 493–506.

TIJDENS, KEA (1998). 'De balans van twee ronden arbeidsduurverkorting, 1982–85 en 1994–97'. *Tijdschrift voor Arbeidsvraagstukken*, 14/3: 212–25.

TOIRKENS, JOSE (1988). *Schijn en werkelijkheid van het bezuinigingsbeleid 1975–1986*. Deventer: Kluwer.

TOREN, JAN-PETER VAN DEN (1996). *Achter gesloten deuren? CAO-overleg in de jaren negentig*. Amsterdam: Welboom.

TRAXLER, FRANZ (1997). 'Austria: Still the Country of Corporatism', in Anthony Ferner and Richard Hyman (eds.), *Changing Industrial Relations in Europe*, Oxford: Basil Blackwell, 239–62.

UHER, JULIAN (1993). 'Fortschritt und Machtspiel', in F. Weber and Th. Venus (eds.), *Austro-Keynesianismus in Theorie und Praxis*. Vienna: Stiftung Bruno Kreisky Archiv and Dachs-Verlag, i. 78–100.

UNGER, BRIGITTE (1996). 'Sozialpartnerschaft in der Midlife Crisis'. *Kurswechsel 4, Beirat für Gesellschafts-, Wirtschafts- und Umweltpolitische Alternativen.* Vienna, 73–94.

——(1998a). *Beschäftigungspolitik in der Europäischen Union.* Informationen zur Politischen Bildung, No. 15. Vienna: Forum für politische Bildung.

——(1998b). *Room for Manoeuvre. Choices Left for National Economic Policy.* Vienna: Habilitationsschrift der Wirtschaftsuniversität.

VAN PARIJS, PHILIPPE (1998). *Should Europe be Belgian?.* Paper presented at the Conference 'The Historical Perspective of Republicanism and the Future of the European Union', Siena, 23–27 Sept.

VAN RUYSSEVELDT, JORIS, and VISSER, JELLE (1996). 'Weak Corporatisms Going Different Ways? Industrial Relations in the Netherlands and Belgium', in Joris Van Ruysseveldt and Jelle Visser (eds.), *Industrial Relations in Europe: Traditions and transitions.* London: Sage, 205–64.

VILROKX, JACQUES, and VAN LEEMPUT, JIM (1997). 'Belgium: The Great Transformation', in Anthony Ferner and Richard Hyman (eds.), *Changing Industrial Relations in Europe.* Oxford: Basil Blackwell, 315–47.

VISSER, JELLE (1990). 'Continuity and Change in Dutch Industrial Relations', in Baglioni Guido and Colin J. Crouch (eds.), *European Industrial Relations: The Challenge of Flexibility.* London: Sage: 199–240.

——(1995). 'The Netherlands: From Paternalism to Representation', in Joel Rogers and Wolfgang Streeck (eds.), *Works Councils: Consultation, Representation, and Cooperation in Industrial Relations.* Chicago: Chicago University Press, 79–114.

——(1996). *Trends and Variations in European Collective Bargaining.* Amsterdam: CESAR Research Paper 96/2.

——(1997). 'The Netherlands: The Return of Responsive Corporatism', in Anthony Ferner and Richard Hyman (eds.), *Changing Industrial Relations in Europe.* Oxford: Basil Blackwell, 283–314.

——(1998). 'Two Cheers for Corporatism, One for the Market: Industrial Relations, Unions, Wages, and Labour Markets in the Netherlands'. *British Journal of Industrial Relations,* 36/2: 269–82.

——(1999). *The First Part-Time Economy in the World. Does it Work?.* Paper presented at Euro-Japan Symposium on the Development of Atypical Employment and Transformation of Labour Markets, Japan Productivity Center for Socio-Economic Development, Tokyo, 24–25 Mar.

——and HEMERIJCK, ANTON (1997). *A Dutch Miracle: Job Growth, Welfare Reform and Corporatism in the Netherlands.* Amsterdam: Amsterdam University Press.

WALTERSKIRCHEN, EWALD (1997). *Austria's Road to Full Employment.* WIFO Working Papers, 89. Vienna: Österreichisches Institut für Wirtschaftsforschung.

WERNER, HEINZ, and KÖNIG, INGEBORG (1987). *Maßnahmen zur Förderung der Beschäftigung und zur Bekämpfung der Arbeitslosigkeit in Belgien.* Beiträge zur Arbeitsmarkt- und Berufsforschung, Nürnberg: IAB, 33–72.

WILTHAGEN, TON (1998). *Flexicurity: A New Paradigm for Labour Market Policy Reform?*. Discussion Paper FS 1 98–202. Berlin: Wissenschaftszentrum.

WINCKLER, GEORG (1980). 'Das Ende der aktiven Nominalzinspolitik in Österreich', *Wirtschaftsanalysen*, 4: 14–28.

WINDMULLER, JOHN P. (1969). *Labor Relations in the Netherlands*. Ithaca, NY: Cornell University Press.

WRR (Wetenschappelijke Raad voor het Regeringsbeleid) (1980). *Plaats en Toekomst van de Nederlandse Industrie*. The Hague: WRR.

——(1990). *Een Werkend Perspectief: Arbeidsparticipatie in the jaren '90*. The Hague: WRR.

ZANDEN, JAN-LUITEN VAN, and GRIFFITHS, RICHARD T. (1989). *Economische geschiedenis van Nederland in de 20e eeuw*. Utrecht: Het Spectrum.

6

Adjusting Badly
The German Welfare State, Structural Change,
and the Open Economy

PHILIP MANOW AND ERIC SEILS

6.1. Introduction

At first glance Germany does not seem to fit the conventional view of the impact economic globalization has on national economies. According to the conventional wisdom, intensified competition within a liberal international trade regime has put the industrialized countries of the West and their mature welfare states under intensified pressure. Year after year, as one of the world's most successful exporting nations, Germany seems to be gaining rather than suffering from trade liberalization. Moreover, German industry's outstanding export performance has apparently not been hurt by the generous German welfare state's high spending levels. At the same time, Germany's present economic problems, such as persistent mass unemployment, seem to owe more to poor job growth in those sectors of the economy usually perceived as sheltered from international competition, i.e. private and public services (Scharpf 1997). A widespread alternative interpretation of the Federal Republic's current economic troubles attributes these primarily to an historical singularity—German unification—rather than to secular changes in the world economy or fundamental malfunctions in the German model (Czada 1998). Thus, the political debate about the problems of Germany as a business location, the notorious *Standortdebatte*, is said to use dramatic changes in the international economy as the scapegoat for a much more mundane kind of economic stress, namely the enormous costs of unification.

We gratefully acknowledge valuable comments from the participants of the EUI/MPI workshop in Florence, Oct. 1998, the Adjustment workshop at Ringberg Castle, Feb. 1999, from Jens Alber, Peter Hall, Evelyne Huber, Gregory Jackson, Jim Mosher, Fritz Scharpf, Vivien Schmidt, Helmut Voelzkow, and Jörg Wiese. We would also like to thank Hans-Uwe Bach and Eugen Spitznagel from the IAB for data on early retirement and the Federal Statistical Office for various data.

In this paper we will argue that Germany's problems cannot be attributed solely to unification (although the German political economy was not, of course, entirely unaffected by this major 'shock to the system'—see Carlin and Soskice 1997); the problems are more fundamental. German unification and every economic slump since the early 1970s triggered a routine response pattern from the economic and political system, resulting each time in a higher level of unemployment, a lower level of total employment, and steadily increasing non-wage labor costs (especially for social insurance contributions), which adversely affected long-term job growth in the low-productivity service sector. We hold that the lack of job growth in private services is the most characteristic and problematic outcome of the strategic interplay among unions, employers, the central bank, and the government within the German political and economic system.

Central to the working of the German political economy is the interplay among a federal government with a restricted capacity for active economic steering, a highly independent German central bank, autonomous 'social partners', and a welfare state primarily contribution-based and committed to status maintenance. In our view the transition to the service economy is what is at the heart of the problem of the German model. Problems of structural change become acute at times of external shocks, such as the oil price increases of the 1970s or German unification in 1989/90. In such cases the independence of the German central bank prohibits the use of strategic depreciation or massive public spending as instruments to counteract an economic slump and maintain high levels of employment (Scharpf 1991). Another inhibiting factor is the fragmentation of public finances into numerous autonomous state budgets in a federal system that makes coordinated counter-cyclical spending unlikely (Busch 1995). Moreover, since unions are strong and employment protection is generous, wages are not downwardly flexible enough and labor shedding is very costly. As a consequence, the welfare state becomes the main instrument of economic adjustment.

The primary response to unfavorable economic conditions or to the secular decline of employment in manufacturing is to reduce the labor supply with the help of various welfare state programs. Because the German system of social protection is primarily financed by payroll taxes, this forces contribution rates up, and therefore it increases wage costs. At the same time, the Bundesbank's tight monetary course forces the government to observe strict fiscal discipline. Since Germany's social insurance schemes have fiscal autonomy and are primarily financed out of contributions levied on wages, the government has an incentive to shift financial obligations out of the general budget and into the special budgets of the insurance schemes, or to use employer and employee contributions as the primary source for financing new social policy commitments. Hence, the German welfare state comes under pressure from two sides, from firms that seek to externalize their adjustment costs onto the welfare state, and from a government that tries to ease budgetary pressures by reducing its own share of welfare finance. Since the German welfare state closes gaps between revenue and spending through quasi-automatic social insurance contribution hikes, the social costs imposed on labor increase steadily— making labor more expensive and so impeding job growth in the low-productivity service sector. Low employment, in turn, is fateful to a social policy model that relies almost exclusively on revenue stemming from dependent employment. The tendency to externalize costs at the expense of the German welfare state became especially salient in the wake of German unification, but it was already a well-established adjustment routine in the mid-1970s.

The paper proceeds as follows: in Section 6.2 we will give a brief account of Germany during the postwar 'economic miracle'. The end of the economic miracle, when the dominant policy response was to combine a tight money policy with an effort to consolidate the budget, will be briefly discussed in Section 6.3. In Section 6.4 it will be argued that, once industrial employment dramatically declined again as a consequence of the second oil crisis, political actors intensified their strategies of externalization instead of coping with the underlying problems of structural change and a high social wage. Obviously, the most pervasive external shock to affect Germany in the past thirty years was unification. Nevertheless, the political system responded in much the same way to the job loss and fiscal strain caused by unification as it had to the second OPEC crisis a decade earlier. Externalizing costs, both by the state and firms, became the routine response to a non-routine situation, as will be elaborated in Section 6.5. In the last section we will show in more detail the adverse employment effects of high social insurance contributions combined with a high level of social assistance.

6.2. The Postwar Equilibrium

6.2.1. Germany During the Economic Miracle

Central to the German postwar equilibrium, often described as the 'social market economy' (*Soziale Marktwirtschaft*), is a high degree of autonomy for the Bundesbank, strong unions, and employers' associations that need not fear government interference in collective bargaining (*Tarifautonomie*), a central state with only limited capacities for active economic steering and little more than 'semi-sovereignty' in many policy areas, and a 'Continental' welfare state focusing on occupational status and the 'insurance principle' (i.e. a strict correspondence between contributions and benefits). In the following we will describe the role of the central actors—state, central bank, social partners—within this framework, and how Germany's 'golden age equilibrium' worked in greater detail.

Postwar Germany is a federalist system. The federal states (Länder) are represented in federal decision making through the upper house (Bundesrat). They participate directly in the federal legislative process. This is usually—and somehow euphemistically—labeled cooperative federalism (Scharpf 1985; Lehmbruch 1998). At the same time, most taxes are shared between the federal government and the states. As a result, negotiation is the dominant mode of decision making and conflict resolution within the federal German system. The need for constant political compromise even increased with the introduction of joint (financial) responsibilities for certain policy domains (*Gemeinschaftsaufgaben*) and the expansion of joint taxes in the late 1960s (Ellwein and Hesse 1987: 79–80; Renzsch 1991). Blockages and political stalemate occur frequently due to intertwined jurisdictions and responsibilities, the Länder's strong legislative veto position in the upper house, and the interaction between federalism and party competition (the 'joint-decision trap'—see Scharpf 1985).

While federalism requires that policies command a broad consensus among the German polity's numerous veto players, the party system is competitive in character. The Christian Democrats and Social Democrats compete for hegemony, while the small liberal party (FDP) has often occupied a pivotal position between those two mass parties (Schmidt 1987: 162–70). The unique combination of consensual and competitive elements in the German political system is especially salient when there are opposing majorities facing off against each other in the upper and lower house. This kind of standoff, which first occurred between 1972 and 1982 and then again between 1991 and 1998, demands an even broader consensus, encompassing both political parties and federal-state relations.

The German federal government usually refrains from highly interventionist macroeconomic management. One reason is collective bargaining's fairly smooth functioning. Over the last fifty years unions and employers were quite successful in securing a low strike rate. Collective agreements' coverage of industrial relations has remained broad and stable—despite medium and (since the 1980s) steadily declining union density (OECD 1994: 173). Only during the first years of the 1950s and in the late 1960s did the state assume a more active role in smoothing out the business cycle. In 1966/67 the government managed to overcome the first major postwar recession by coordinating expansionary measures with the central bank.

Despite this one success, the capacity for counter-cyclical fiscal policy has been limited because of public finances' fragmentation into numerous state budgets and the central bank's exceptionally high degree of autonomy. Since there was a change of course in favor of strict monetary policy as early as 1973, Keynesian demand management therefore never really took hold in Germany (Allen 1989). Public debt was low throughout the 1960s and 1970s by international standards, since high deficits were regarded as unconstitutional until 1969 (Sturm 1997: 643). In other policy domains the role of government is relatively minor as well. There was no large stock of government enterprises as in other European countries, and privatization had already begun in the 1950s (Owen Smith 1994: 467–68).

The Bundesbank is one of the most independent central banks in the world. Its main role is as guardian of price stability. Central bank independence as a means of safeguarding monetary stability is a key feature of the German political economy (Streeck 1994; Hall 1994). In the absence of capital controls, however, the bank had to accept some imported inflation under the Bretton-Woods system of fixed exchange rates. The strength of 'non-majoritarian institutions' in Germany is further accentuated by the country's 'activist' Constitutional Court and (to a lesser degree) its independent Federal Cartel Office (*Kartellamt*).

The industrial arena is dominated by unions and employers' associations. They are granted the right to free collective bargaining without any kind of government intervention. Unions and employers are organized by industry and sector. Although collective bargaining is only moderately centralized, it is highly coordinated between regions and sectors (pattern bargaining). Collective agreements have broad coverage. The extension rule that authorizes the government to declare collective agreements generally binding for an entire industrial sector (*erga omnes* rule), however, is rarely invoked (OECD 1994: 178). The strong binding power of collective agreements is due to three factors: (1) the high degree of organization among employers; (2) legal provisions that grant a quasi-authoritative status to voluntary agreements reached between unions and employers;[1] and (3) the employers' interest in preventing wage competition.

The German system of industrial governance can be labelled corporatist. German corporatism, however, does not mean central corporatist concertation of the Austrian, Swedish, or Dutch variety. German industrial relations represent a more autonomous or horizontal variant of

---

[1] For example, unemployment insurance regulations include 'acceptibility criteria' allowing unemployed persons to refuse jobs whose pay falls below the level that has been agreed upon by unions and employers in collective bargaining (Paqué 1996; see also van der Willigen 1995: 28).

corporatism, not tripartite but mainly bilateral in character. Usually it is the metalworkers' union, IG Metall, that takes the lead in annual wage rounds. These wage rounds follow the principle 'that intra- and inter-sectoral wage differentials should not be allowed to change dramatically' (Streeck 1994: 127). Both unions and employers have usually opposed what are known as 'opening clauses'—special provisions allowing individual companies to opt out of collective agreements—so that neither side loses control over wage bargaining (Streeck 1994: 135–36). Wage bargaining is the sole prerogative of unions and employers' associations. Work councils representing employees at the level of the firm are prohibited from negotiating contractual wages.

In postwar Germany, the Bismarckian welfare state was reconstructed during the second half of the 1950s. It became an integral element of the postwar economic order. The welfare state facilitated corporatist cooperation between capital and labor, and it helped stabilize the German high-skill/high-wage production model that was on the verge of such remarkable success in world markets (Manow 1997). The Bismarckian welfare state initially had been designed to deal with the 'social question' (*Arbeiterfrage*), i.e. the social and political challenge posed by the rising industrial working class to the old order of the Wilhelmine Empire. Hence, to this day the German welfare state primarily covers risks associated with loss of income by male industrial wage earners, such as sickness, industrial accident, old age, and unemployment. Each risk is dealt with by a separate social insurance scheme with its own fund. In the following, we provide a short description of these schemes, in order of their historical evolution.

Health insurance was established early, in 1883. Today it is mainly financed by equal contributions from employers and employees, and it has never received major subsidies out of the central government's budget. The scheme is managed by several hundred funds separated according to region, occupation, and status. Full financial autonomy means that these funds have to raise contribution levels whenever a deficit appears. Health insurance covers the cost of medical treatment and compensates for the loss of earnings due to illness (up to a limit of 80% of net earnings after the first six weeks, during which employers are obligated to offer sick pay).

Industrial accident insurance, dating from 1884, is by far the smallest branch of social insurance and fully financed by employers. The scheme, which is run by liability associations (*Berufsgenossenschaften*), provides compensation in case of industrial accident or occupational disease. Here, too, benefit levels are linked to prior earnings. The system covers employees as well as university students and school pupils.

The pension scheme, originally established in 1889, was the first to receive a subsidy from the government. Nevertheless, the lion's share is financed by contributions from employees and employers. The share financed out of the government's budget declined from 35.6 percent in 1957 to 17.5 percent in 1977 (Mörschel 1978: 342). Contributions rose from 14 percent to 18 percent of gross wages in the same period. Whenever contributions and the state subsidy (as a fixed share linked to revenue, not outlays) were not sufficient to meet the expected expenditures, contribution rates had to be raised. In 1957 the system was adjusted to the postwar period's rapidly rising living standards with a formula that linked pensions to gross wages. The individual benefit level was determined by the size of contributions and the length of contribution periods. Benefits thus became dependent on earnings. Computed as the relative income position of the wage earner during his or her period of dependent employment, each pension entitlement was fixed in proportion to the prevailing level of wages at retirement and then adjusted yearly to changes in gross wages. Because of a rising tax burden and employees' growing social insurance contributions, pensioners' relative benefit levels increased faster than earnings. At the same time, all elements of a basic pension were eliminated from the system. Thus, pension benefits were made strictly dependent on individual performance in the labor market. Only in 1972 was something resembling a basic pension reintroduced. This was the 'pension according to minimum income' (*Rente nach Mindesteinkommen*), which topped up pensions of those who had a long contribution period but only low earnings. By the mid-1970s, pension insurance covered virtually all employees other than civil servants and those in 'atypical employment' (*geringfügige Beschäftigung*).

Unemployment insurance, introduced in the inter-war period (1927), is also a subsidized program. In 1969 unemployment insurance was integrated into the Employment Promotion Act (Arbeitsförderungsgesetz, AFG). The system is run by the Federal Employment Office (Bundesanstalt für Arbeit) and, like the other programs, mainly financed by a payroll tax. Contributions to unemployment insurance amounted to 1.3 percent of gross wages in 1970. However, the scheme's deficits have to be covered by the federal budget. Unemployment insurance provides compensation in case of unemployment and it is also used to finance training and active labor market policies. However, active labor market policies did not play an important role before the 1970s. Usually beneficiaries are entitled to unemployment benefits and turn to unemployment assistance only after they have exhausted their claims. The length of entitlement for unemployment benefits depends on the length of the contribution period and on the age of the recipient. While unemployment benefits are financed by the Federal Office, unemployment assistance, with its less generous means-tested benefits, is financed entirely out of the federal budget. Unemployment insurance covers employees except for civil servants

(*Beamte*) and those working less than 18 hours a week.

Means-tested social assistance is the last tier of the German safety net. It is run and financed by local authorities implementing national legislation. The old public assistance system was reformed in 1961 in order to adjust it to the needs of the affluent postwar society. The reform defined social assistance as a right rather than charity.

6.2.2. The Dynamics of the German Political Economy

The German economic miracle took place in an international environment governed by the Bretton-Woods system of fixed but adjustable exchange rates and characterized by a strong demand for investment goods as well as cheap raw material prices. This 'golden age' lasting through the early 1970s witnessed unprecedented economic growth and the triumph of mass consumption throughout the Western world. Unemployment was low almost everywhere. Germany shared these features of mass prosperity with the rest of the industrialized West. Yet under the institutional setting of the social market economy, the major actors in Germany's political economy produced outcomes that set the Federal Republic somewhat apart from many of the other countries studied in this project. In our explanation of these outcomes, we will focus on the interplay of three key actors and their goals: the Bundesbank with its insistence on price stability, moderate unions, and governments trying to maintain balanced budgets.

As a result of the Bundesbank's policy and the unions' moderate wage demands, Germany became noted for price stability. However, under the Bretton-Woods system, an inflation rate consistently lower than America's combined with rising demand for high-quality German manufactures to make the Deutschmark chronically undervalued. The German government's reluctance to revalue its currency ensured that German exports would continue to sweep European and world markets. At the heart of the German 'export machine' were, of course, its manufacturing products. To be sure, other factors like specialization in investment goods also supported the industrial sector's dominance. All this contributed to the German economy's export orientation (Kreile 1978) and an extremely high share of employment in manufacturing. In fact, employment in manufacturing kept growing in Germany long after it had markedly declined in other Western countries (Ambrosius 1989: 35). The high employment/population ratio in manufacturing combined with overall full employment and the unions' solidaristic wage policy to give low-skilled workers a chance to earn decent wages as well. Partly as a result, earnings inequality was quite low in comparative perspective (Mosher 1999: 13).

By contrast, employment in services was low by international standards. This is not to say that the service sector was not gaining ground in the 1960s, but rather that Germany was clearly a laggard in this area. Given the minor role played by the state, public employment was also low. Public employment as a share of the working age population in 1970 was at 7.7 percent. This was lower than in most OECD countries for which data are available. Female labor force participation was average in the same period. Many of these traits of the German model were challenged after the onset of the first oil shock.

6.3. The End of the Economic Miracle

It has often been said that the year 1973 marked a watershed in the postwar economic history of the West. This is certainly true for the German case. On a global level, the main changes associated with that year were the final breakdown of the Bretton-Woods system and the steep rise in the price of oil.

In May 1971 the Deutschmark was allowed to float against the US dollar. This event had a dual impact on the domestic political economy. First, it freed the Bundesbank from the obligation to support the dollar (Buchheim 1989: 192) and allowed it to cope with domestic inflation. The central bank switched almost immediately to a very tight monetary policy until the economy was in the midst of a recession. As early as 1973, the Bundesbank had begun to use instruments targeting the volume of central bank money rather than bank reserves (OECD 1983: 30). In 1974, when it announced that growth in the volume of money had become its new guideline, the Bundesbank shifted officially to monetarism. It thereby created credibility for its anti-inflationary stance and established itself as a powerful actor whose signals neither governments nor unions dare ignore. Second, floating the Deutschmark led to a substantial appreciation of the currency over the next two decades, creating additional risks and cost pressures for Germany's export-oriented industries.

The first oil shock was the most obvious sign that the 'golden age' had come to an end. Germany was hit hard by the recession. Economic activity had already slowed down in 1974, not least of all because of the Bundesbank's policy. However, in 1975 things got worse. With growth turning negative, unemployment rose above one million, while industrial employment declined dramatically. This loss was not made up when the economy finally recovered. The permanent decline in industrial jobs contrasted with developments in the service sector, where the only impact of recessions was to retard, not stop, job growth. However, growth in service employment still proved insufficient to absorb industries' job losses. The overall result was therefore a drop in the total employment/population ratio to a point below the international average, in spite of a shrinking working age population. It goes without saying that the decline in employment created a problem for a welfare state largely financed out of social insurance contributions levied on labor.

The government, acting in Keynesian style, switched from a restrictive stabilization course to policies fostering investment (BMF 1974: 9–10, 1975: 7–8). But their expansionary measures were increasingly counteracted by a central bank more committed than ever to strict monetary rigor. The Bundesbank kept sticking to a tight monetary policy until its battle against inflation had pushed the Federal Republic into a deep recession (Scharpf 1991: 132). Faith in Keynesian macroeconomic steering faded gradually. This triggered a policy shift by the SPD/FDP government. In 1976 fiscal policy tightened considerably as a result of the Social Democratic-led government's measures to consolidate the budget (as in its Haushaltsstrukturgesetz or 'budgetary structure law'). Public investments were severely curtailed. Expenditure cuts in pensions and health insurance (combined with major contribution rate hikes) were also significant. In the last years of the 1970s, public spending rose again, along with measures to promote housing construction, lower taxes, and provide additional incentives for investment. Not least of all, this brief Keynesian revival was due to growing international pressures. At the Bonn G-7 summit in the summer of 1978 the Schmidt government was urged to undertake a more expansionary fiscal policy. Germany—together with Japan—was supposed to function as the locomotive that would pull the Western world into a new period of growth and prosperity. Tax cuts and additional measures adopted as a result of the conference amounted to about 1 percent of GNP (BMF 1978: 7). By the time the Federal Republic entered another recession in the early 1980s, fiscal policy was clearly on an expansionary course again.

In labor market policy, an immediate response to the recession of the 1970s was stopping the inflow of migrant workers. The notion that reducing the size of the foreign workforce (so indispensable in the 1960s) represented a 'solution' to German labor market problems was part of a broader approach emphasizing overall reduction in the 'labor supply'. It is here that we witness, for the first time, the enlistment of social insurance schemes as an instrument of 'negative labor supply policy' (Claus Offe). To be sure, even in the heyday of the economic miracle, unemployment and pension schemes had been used to channel older workers out of the labor market and so avoid the appearance of open unemployment in declining sectors like mining and steel. But after the severe recession of the mid-1970s this supply-reduction strategy became more widely used.

There are three major routes out of the labor market for older workers below the regular retirement age of 65. Only months before the onset of the crisis, the pension reform of 1972 had opened up the possibility of 'flexible retirement' at 63 without any actuarial reductions in benefits. Although this measure was introduced for reasons completely unrelated to labor market considerations, deteriorating employment prospects for older workers made the flexible retirement option seem increasingly attractive.

Flexible retirement's implementation had an immediate impact on a second pathway to early retirement, disability pensions for those completely unable to work (*Erwerbsunfähigkeitsrenten*). The two paths intersected because it proved easier for those handicapped workers who had fulfilled the specified waiting period to leave the labor market by way of flexible retirement rather than through the cumbersome procedures of the disability scheme. As a result, there was a sharp decline in the number of those entering the disability scheme. In the years following the recession, however, the number of entrants increased again. This was also due to two important court rulings (in 1969 and 1976) holding that the definition of '*Erwerbsunfähigkeit*' ('inability to work') must also take into account the situation on the labor market, that is, the prospects for a person who was less than fully employable but not completely disabled to find adequate part-time employment in his or her respective profession.

The third path to early retirement is the so-called 59 rule. This provision was used above all by personnel departments in large companies as a means to reduce staff whenever business got slack. The practice makes use of a regulation establishing the right to claim a pension at the age of 60 after just one year of unemployment. Companies usually offer workers 59 or even younger the opportunity to top up their unemployment benefits to the level of their last net earnings until such time as the employee can draw a pension. In large firms this became the most important strategy (after overtime reduction) for cutting staff (Russig 1982: 263). It was a policy that met with broad acceptance among workers.

The government also undertook a few more active measures to fight unemployment using instruments already available in the Employment Promotion Act, a law originally designed to deal with labor scarcity rather than mass unemployment. Bonn initiated work creation programs, mostly in construction, though later on in social services as well (Schmid 1990: 403). The number of workers employed under these programs rose from 16,000 in 1975 to 51,000 in 1979. Vocational training had already been at the heart of the 1969 Employment Promotion Act. It was seen as an instrument for facilitating structural change and avoiding job losses. The scope and funding for these measures were considerably increased during the recession of 1975, but they soon fell victim to the austerity-minded Budget Act mentioned above (Garlichs and Maier 1982: 95–96).

After 1974 the unions began responding to the deteriorating labor market situation with more moderate wage demands. This is apparent from the slow growth in unit labor costs for manufacturing, matched only by Switzerland and Austria at the time and probably conducive to maintaining employment in the German economy's exposed sectors.

6.4. Policy Responses and their Effect: 1980–1990

At the start of the 1980s, the international economic situation deteriorated again. Another oil price hike depressed demand and fueled inflation in the industrialized countries. In the second half of the 1980s, however, prospects became brighter again. Energy prices fell steeply in 1986 and inflation was under control almost everywhere. Germany was the anchor of a stable European monetary system in which realignments became an exception after 1987 (Collignon et al. 1994: 36–37).

With respect to employment, history seemed to repeat itself after the second oil price shock. Once again there was a precipitous decline in manufacturing employment from which the German economy never really recovered, while growth in service employment was not sufficient to absorb all the redundant labor. This time, however, the job losses were accompanied by strong growth in the working age population. As depicted in the Figure 6.1, the result was another million unemployed and another drop in the employment/population ratio.

A subsequent upturn was too weak to reduce unemployment significantly until 1986. Thereafter the recovery gained momentum and developed into a boom that peaked around 1990. Strong aggregate employment growth even led to a rise in the employment/population ratio for manufacturing. Since the German welfare state is largely financed by social insurance contributions, the surge in unemployment at the beginning of the 1980s quickly threatened to turn into a fiscal crisis of the welfare state. We shall now discuss (1) responses to these fiscal difficulties and (2) reactions to rising mass unemployment.

6.4.1. *A Hard Currency, a Balanced Budget, and Rising Social Insurance Contributions*

How did the central bank and the federal government respond to the economic downturn in the early 1980s? The Bundesbank stuck to its hard

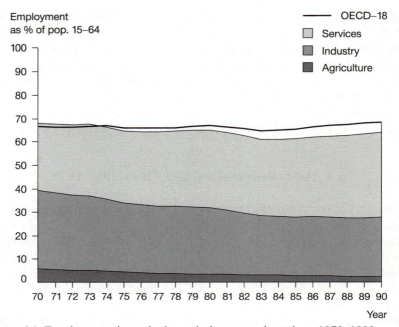

Figure 6.1 Employment in agriculture, industry, and services, 1970–1990
Source: OECD, *Statistical Compendium: Labour Force Statistics* (Paris: OECD, 1999); own calculations.

currency policy and urged the federal government to consolidate its budget. The Kohl government that took power late in 1982 sought to fight the public deficit, privatize state-owned companies, and reduce the level of taxation. Since revenue from privatization was not enough to achieve both goals, lower taxes and a balanced budget, at the same time, the government sought to cut spending in two ways—through 'real' cuts and through cost-shifting at the expense of the social insurance schemes and their beneficiaries. As a consequence, contribution rates to the social insurance schemes grew steadily, even after the economy had pulled through the recession.

In 1980 the fiscal stimulus that resulted from the G-7 Bonn summit two years earlier combined with the growing energy bill from the second oil crisis to produce Germany's first current account deficit in fourteen years. The central bank soon came to regard the 'locomotive experiment' as a failure and resolved to maintain a strong external value for the Deutschmark. In order to achieve this goal and fight inflation, the bank had already adopted a tight monetary policy back in 1980 (Sachverständigenrat 1980: 97–102). The central bank stuck to its restrictive policy until the trough of the recession had been passed in 1983. The fiscal expansion prior to the recession also left its mark on the federal budget. It went into deficit. The central bank made it clear that it was not willing to accept persistent budget deficits, since these would strengthen inflationary pressures and undermine confidence in the Deutschmark (Franz 1990: 25). Given that the Bundesbank's restrictive policy contributed to high real interest rates, this monetary stringency compelled the government to follow a course of budgetary consolidation. The rising opportunity costs of any spending program contemplated by the Schmidt government led to major tensions within the Social Democratic/Liberal coalition. Ultimately, the government fell over irreconcilable differences within the coalition about the proper budgetary policy and the necessity of further social spending cuts. Nevertheless, it was the Social Democratic-led Schmidt government that initiated the shift to a more restrictive fiscal policy (Schmidt 1990: 53–55, 60). The best known package of cuts was the so-called 'Budget Operation 82' (Sachverständigenrat 1982: 98).

When the Kohl government came to power, it shelved expansive policies altogether and embarked upon a policy of budgetary consolidation with the aim of reducing taxes afterward. It intended to do so mainly by curbing public, and especially social welfare, expenditure. The Kohl government further declared that it would reduce public ownership in industry and deregulate labor markets. This moderate supply-side policy was finally in line with the Bundesbank's monetarism and the views of the independent Council of Economic Experts. In the 1980s, the Kohl government was clearly successful in reducing the deficit. The general government deficit of −3.3 percent of GDP in 1982 was converted into a slight surplus of 0.1 percent of GDP in 1989.

How was this achieved? First, the economic recovery after 1983 reduced budgetary pressures. Second, the government increased revenue by raising the VAT from 12 percent to 13 percent in June 1983. A third factor that eased the task of balancing the budget was the Bundesbank's profits, which had been negligible in the 1970s but turned out to be quite substantial after 1982. From 1986 onward, privatization also proved to be a rich source of revenue.

In the course of this program, the federal state sold its shares in several hundred companies, including VEBA, VIAG, and the car manufacturer VW (OECD 1989: 55–57, 1990: 40–41). While revenues from the Bundesbank and later from privatization clearly helped the government achieve its goals, the CDU/CSU/FDP coalition also undertook efforts to curb expenditures (mainly transfer payments and public investment). Towards the end of the government's first term, a two-stage tax reform became a priority, for which the Finance Minister Stoltenberg was prepared to accept somewhat higher deficits (Sturm 1998: 186). In 1985 the Bundestag approved the Act on the Reduction of Taxes to Promote Performance and to Ease the Burden on Families, which provided taxpayers with aggregate tax relief of DM 19.4 bn in two stages (1986 and 1988). A 'third stage' to be implemented in 1990 involved the biggest cuts. All in all, the tax cuts amounted to around 2.25 percent of GDP. Unfortunately, the revenue losses from the last stage occurred exactly at the time when additional lay-outs for incorporating the former GDR into a united Germany became necessary (Sachverständigenrat 1990: 136–37). As will be discussed in detail below, it was during the drive to unification that the Kohl government finally departed from the consolidation policy it had embarked on in the 1980s.

In its effort to balance the budget so as to provide voters with tax relief later on, the government tried to control growing welfare expenditures caused by high unemployment and rising health care costs. At first the government relied mainly on ad hoc measures that raised revenues and curbed expenditures. The 1983 and 1984 budget laws raised contribution rates and broadened the insurance system's tax base beyond regular wages to include other forms of renumeration like vacation allowances and the annual Christmas bonus. Among the measures preventing additional increases in the cost of welfare were temporary suspensions or delays in the adjustment of pensions to gross wages. The 1984 cuts in benefit levels for the unemployment insurance (from 68% to 63%) and assistance scheme (from 58% to 56% of the previous net wage) for single persons had more of a long-term impact. It should be noted that these schemes involved substantial financial involvement by the federal government. The sickness funds, by contrast, were burdened with the obligation to pay con-tributions to the pension and unemployment insurance on sickness pay and other transfers from the health insurance. This lowered the cost bur-den for schemes with a financial involvement of the federal government while schemes without a state subsidy had to bear an even larger burden. The same was true of cuts in transfer payments from old age insurance to health insurance for pensioners (Berg 1986: 29–30). In fact, the same pat-tern of burden-shifting can be detected throughout the 1980s.

The 1985 and 1986 increases in contribution rates forced the govern-ment to engage in a more profound reform of the social insurance system following its electoral victory in 1987, if it did not want to jeopardize the positive political and economic benefits it expected from its tax reform (Webber 1989: 269–70). Health and pension insurance were to be reformed in Kohl's second term. When the Health Reform Act was passed after tremendous fights with pressure groups and tension within the gov-erning coalition, the outcome fell far short of what had been touted as the 'reform of the century'. There were some cutbacks in benefits, and co-payments were raised, while spending for pharmaceuticals was efficiently capped. In order to assure the support of the Christian Democratic Party's left wing, the party's market-oriented liberals and right wing had to accept a government commitment to introduce a new branch of social insurance for frail and elderly people later on (Long-Term Care Insurance).

On the very same day the Berlin Wall came down, the pension reform scheme passed the Bundestag with a broad majority from the governing parties and the opposition Social Democrats. The law changed the long-standing basis for indexing pensions from gross to net wages. Further-more, a gradual scaleback in early retirement was planned for the period after 2001 (Rüb and Nullmeier 1991: 451–54). Again, the immediate financial effects were rather modest. The change in the pension indexation for-mula did not lead to a drop in the replacement ratio but simply prevented that ratio from accelerating further.

Thus, the 1980s were not a time of simple retrenchment. Under condi-tions where neither federal nor state government was obligated to pay the welfare bill, the door was even open for increased benefits or expanded entitlements (Alber 1996). After a few years of cutbacks in social assis-tance benefits, leading to a real decline in the 'standard benefit' (*Regelsatz*) until it had reverted to its 1970 level (Buhr et al. 1991: 514–24), the losses were made up in 1985, when the indexation mechanism was reformed. From that year until after unification, the 'standard benefit' rose consid-erably. In the 1980s the level of social assistance, including expenditures on rent, rose not only in real terms, but also in relation to average wages (Boss 1999: 38–40). The Länder, who initially had been worried about higher costs, did not oppose the reform, instead they demanded compensation. They were finally compensated by way of higher transfers out of the cen-tral budget within the 'federal financial equalization scheme' (*Föderaler Finanzausgleich*; Renzsch 1991: 269–73).

Later cuts in the health and pension schemes could not prevent contri-bution rates to the social insurance schemes from rising further, even though the economic situation had become much brighter in the second half of the 1980s. It is important to note that cuts in entitlements hardly affected the various paths into subsidized non-employment. In the next section we shall discuss responses to the deteriorating employment situa-tion after the second oil shock.

6.4.2. *Reducing the Supply of Labor*

Growing labor market problems in the 1980s could not be solved by gov-ernment alone. Here union and employer strategies were also important.

We shall first consider the impact of social and labor market policies on employment and then turn to the strategies of the social partners.

At first sight, the Kohl government's labor market and social policies during the 1980s appeared to be highly incoherent. Measures that were introduced in order to restrict early exit from the labor market were soon followed by measures that made early retirement even more attractive. The contradictory course of politics can only be understood by taking into consideration how the government was simultaneously trying to achieve two partly conflicting goals, namely containing social spending and helping firms cope with the economic crisis by offering them the opportunity to lay off workers 'painlessly' with the assistance of the welfare state. The tradeoff between these two objectives was partly solved by 'policy sequencing,' which led to the same pro-cyclical policy profile we may also observe in active labor market policy (see below): cutbacks during economic slumps were followed by considerable expansion of entitlements and eligibility during booms. The latter became especially important when the next crisis came around in the early 1990s.

Similarly, it was social entitlements granted earlier, when economic prospects were brighter, that came to be crucial for the German welfare state's response to the recession in the first half of the 1980s. Among the more restrictive measures, the 1983 reduction in unemployment benefits (see above) deserves special mention. Where early retirement was concerned, the budget law tightened eligibility criteria for disability pensions as of 1984, a restriction that particularly affected women, who tend to have more uneven working careers. As a result we find a steep decline (of about 50%) in the take-up rate for women's disability pensions from 1984 to 1985 (VDR 1997: 53). At the same time, however, obtaining a standard old age pension for women at age 60 was made considerably easier. Hence, the decline in disability pensions was partly offset by a significant rise in the take-up rate for the standard old age pension scheme. In 1984 the government introduced the Pre-Retirement Act (Vorruhestandsgesetz). The Act was meant to be a substitute for the more costly 59er rule, i.e. for pensions owing to long-term unemployment (Mares, forthcoming). The Pre-Retirement Act gave employers a chance to let workers go at age 58 (so-called 58er rule) and pay them between two (women's retirement age: 60) and five years' ('flexible retirement' age for men: 63) incomes equal to at least 65 percent of their last net wage. At the same time, the law provided a public subsidy of up to 35 percent of the retirement wage in case a vacant position should be filled for at least two years by a registered unemployed person or trainee. However, pre-retirement did not stir up a lot of excitement among employers and workers, since it proved more costly to employers and offered less generous benefits to workers. The take-up rate was rather modest, at about 165,000 workers between 1984 and 1988, when the Act expired. The substitution rate has been estimated to have been about 80 percent, leading to a maximum of 135,000 new jobs (cf. Jacobs, Kohli, and Rein 1991; see Frerich and Frey 1993 for even lower numbers). This is a rather low number, especially since the government simultaneously tried to discourage employers from continuing to use the unemployment route to early retirement. As early as 1982 the government had forced firms using the 59er rule to pay back unemployment benefits for former long-term workers dismissed at age 59. Two years later employers were also forced to repay pension and health insurance contributions paid out by the labor office on behalf of the unemployed. However, firms were quick to challenge this new provision in court. After protracted legal battles, the employers' repayments turned out to be rather insignificant in the end. Thus, while the 59er rule is still frequently used as a pathway into retirement, the Pre-Retirement Act expired in 1988 (and was succeeded by an even less successful program with a negligible impact). The employers' obligation to pay back social insurance contributions made by the labor offices was abolished altogether in 1991. The number of unemployment pensions steadily increased since the mid-1980s and skyrocketed in the wake of the unification crisis in the early 1990s (see Section 6.5). While these attempts to counteract the tendency towards an ever earlier exit from the labor market did not add up to much, there was a greater impact from the extension of entitlements introduced after the crisis seemed to be over and social insurance had gone into surplus again.

Thus, in the second half of the 1980s, when economic growth had picked up again, one of the more important expansionary measures taken was certainly the major extension of the period for paying out unemployment benefits, especially to workers 54 and over. Since 1987 these workers have been able to receive the standard unemployment benefit (*Arbeitslosengeld*) for up to 32 months. From 1927 until as late as 1985, the maximum period for drawing this benefit had been 12 months. This significant extension was enacted at a time when economic prospects seemed to be turning brighter and social insurance budgets had moved into surplus.[2] Given the longer period of eligibility for unemployment benefits, workers could now leave the labor market as early as 57 and then go on to draw a long-term unemployment pension at age 60. The 59er rule effectively became a 57er rule (cf. Jacobs, Kohli, and Rein 1991: 203). This measure's focus on the long-term unemployed with only the dimmest prospects of re-employment was underlined by the way the government (in addition to prolonging

---

[2] The Federal Office of Labor had a budget surplus of 3.1 and 2.3 bn DM in 1984 and 1985, respectively, and a marginal deficit of 0.2 bn DM in 1986. Between 1983 and 1988 the government did not need to cover deficits of the Federal Office with state subsidies.

unemployment benefits for the elderly) freed workers 58 and older from any obligation to remain on call at labor offices. As a pleasant side-effect, these hard-to-employ persons (many of them jobless since the last crisis) no longer even appear in the unemployment statistics.

The overall effect of these various measures on labor force participation for the age group 55 to 65 is depicted in Figure 6.2.

However, there were also more active attempts to deal with the labor market problems of the 1980s. Participation in active labor market policies generally increased from the late 1970s through the 1980s, albeit with temporary reversals. Variation in spending was not due to anti-cyclical policies but (quite to the contrary) followed a pro-cyclical logic dictated by the

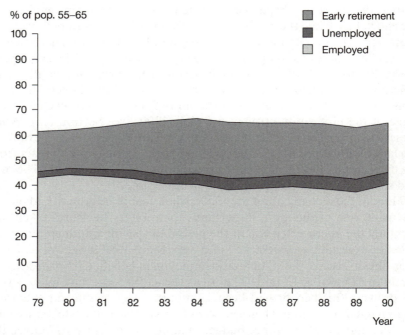

Figure 6.2 Early retirement and labor force participation, 1979–1990

Notes: The diagram displays the employed, unemployed, and retirees in the age group between 55 and 65 as percentage of total population of that age group. The retirees include those on disability pensions (*Erwerbsunfähigkeitsrenten*), pensions because of unemployment, early retirement because of disability, flexible retirement at age 63, the pre-retirement scheme, and persons leaving the labor market via §105c AfG.

Sources: Data on employment were provided by the Federal Statistical Office from various Mikrozensus 1957–1997; other data are from Autorengemeinschaft 1994: 296; BMA various years; IAB 1997: 99; own calculations.

mode of financing for active labor market measures (Scharpf 1982: 18–19). Unlike Sweden, where active labor market policy is financed out of the general budget, Germany has paid for active labor market policies out of unemployment insurance contributions. In a recession, the unemployment fund quickly runs into financial difficulties when the legal entitlements to benefits increase at the same time that the system's tax base is eroding. Politicians are then faced with the choice of either subsidizing the insurance fund from the federal budget or cutting expenditures. Since there is no general entitlement to training or job creation measures, these programs become an easy first target for cuts. This was clearly the case when the Social Democrats curbed spending in the 1975 Budget Act. Once a recession is over, the insurance fund's financial situation improves again and those who are still unemployed and have exhausted their benefits have to rely on unemployment assistance paid out of the federal budget. This turns the incentive structure around, since the government can shift part of the financial burden back into the insurance fund by introducing new work creation schemes. Such was the case after 1978. After the next recession hit, the government felt the need to restore the insurance fund's balance by saving on active measures. It did so by amending the Employment Promotion Act in 1981. By 1985, after the insurance fund had gone back into surplus, the cuts were partly reversed. In spite of these institutional impediments, active labor market policy did make a contribution toward lowering official unemployment. In international comparison, Germany had an unemployment policy that was quite active. It must, however, be left open to debate whether training measures were effective in providing participants with the right skills. There is uncertainty, for example, about the extent to which these measures have reached the low-skilled (Schmid 1990: 399).

Given the principle of *Tarifautonomie*, the social partners (i.e. employers' associations and the unions) hold major responsibility for the labor market. The unions in particular wanted to fight unemployment by reducing working time. They had been struggling for shorter hours for some time, though mainly for reasons of social welfare rather than as a way of preventing unemployment. Unions were able to reduce working time (i.e. labor supply) in two ways: (1) a minority in the trade union confederation DGB, including the powerful chemical workers' union (IG Chemie), opted for early retirement as a means of reducing the labor supply, (2) but a majority of the DGB, led by the largest union, the metalworker union (IG Metall), was in favor of a shorter working week. In this situation the conservative government tried to drive a wedge in the union movement by introducing the Pre-Retirement Act of 1984 mentioned above (Naegele 1987: 753). The government sided with the employers and IG Chemie at the same time that *IG Metall* was engaged in one of the longest and fiercest strikes in West German history, with the 35-hour week as their battle cry. In the end, the metalworkers' union got a reduction in the work week from 40 hours to 38.5, effective as of April 1985, in exchange for the more flexible working time arrangements employers had demanded (Keller 1999: 196). In spite of considerable tensions in German industrial relations following the controversial and complex 'Paragraph 116' dispute (the government's attempt to weaken unions by using a clause in the Employment Promotion Act to deny workers unemployment benefits after layoffs indirectly caused by strikes at other firms), the next step towards the 35-hour week occurred peacefully in 1987. IG Metall's 1990 settlement finally stated that the 35-hour week would be reached in the metalworking and printing industries by 1995. There is disagreement about how effective this strategy of reducing the labor supply has been in fighting unemployment. While there are many studies that find virtually no positive effects (Franz 1997: 21), others are more optimistic (Seifert 1991).

The issue of regulating working hours should not conceal the importance of wages. Here German unions were very moderate throughout the decade. From 1983 onward, the ratio of income from dependent work fell as a share of national income, down to its level from the period of full employment (Sachverständigenrat 1998: 289). This was accompanied by a rise in the rate of return on capital and investment (Sachverständigenrat 1996: 62). Some observers have concluded that this, rather than the redistribution of available work, was the reason for strong job growth in the 1980s (Lapp and Lehment 1997). While this is still open to debate (von der Vring 1998), there is still reason to think that the decade's moderate wage increases helped foster investment and thereby stimulated job creation. At the end of the 1980s the recovery gained momentum and developed into a powerful boom, as employment grew and social insurance funds went into surplus. In the following section we shall investigate the impact of unification on the German political economy.

6.5. A Routine Response to a Non-routine Situation: German Reunification

Needless to say, the most exceptional challenge Germany faced in the past thirty years was unification, which officially took place in October 1990. The integration of the other German state into the Federal Republic was mainly achieved by transferring western institutions to the new eastern Länder. In the course of this process, the interplay among the government, Bundesbank, and social partners was temporarily disturbed, producing some atypical policy outcomes like inflation, wage increases out of synch with productivity growth, and rising budget deficits. While the traditional balance of power has now largely been restored in the Federal Republic's western half, the situation in the east still differs greatly from what prevails in the old Länder. As in pre-1990 Germany, unification's devastating outcomes for fiscal policy and labor markets were merely buffered by the welfare state. In this section we shall investigate the dramatic events more closely.

In the late 1980s the planned economy of the GDR fell even further behind its western counterpart, and it also suffered from new competition in the Far East. As political change swept the entire Soviet bloc, East Germany's Communist government increasingly came under pressure. In the fall of 1989, dramatic protest marches every Monday in major cities combined with large-scale emigration to the west to topple the government. Along with demands for free elections and freedom of travel, calls for unification were soon voiced. Clearly, people from the east expected a lot from unification, not least a quick improvement in living standards. In order to have access to western consumer goods, they needed German marks and wages at western levels. Convergence toward western levels, rather than productivity increases, became the yardstick for wage demands. Once the border to the west was opened, east German workers could credibly threaten to go to the Deutschmark if the mark did not come to them; this logic compelled the introduction of the western Deutschmark into the east (Hoffmann 1993: 9).

In the last section it was pointed out that West Germany experienced a particularly strong boom in the late 1980s. The general government deficit had fallen to zero by 1989, and durable wage restraint led to substantial gains in employment. Resources seemed abundant. In spite of the economic upturn, the popularity of the governing coalition was very low. German unification became an issue that promised to enhance the Christian Democrats' electoral fortunes considerably. This proved salient during the GDR's first free elections in March 1990, where opinion polls predicted easy victory for the Social Democrats. The picture changed altogether when Chancellor Kohl promised to introduce the Deutschmark as early as July of that year. Politically, this move proved to be decisive. The Christian Democrats won the elections and Prime Minister de Maizière was able to form the GDR's first, last, and only freely elected government. The rate at which the East German marks were to be converted into Deutschmarks was also politically determined (Streit 1998: 698–99), while the Bundesbank's suggestions were simply ignored. Interestingly, the powerful Bundesbank was excluded from the decision-making process; it simply lacked legal authority to participate. The president of the Bundesbank,

Pöhl, resigned in protest on this issue but had no influence. Major economic research institutes predicted that a conversion rate as proposed by the two governments would immediately render east German export industries uncompetitive. In spite of this advice and the resistance of the Bundesbank, political logic prevailed and the treaty on 'Economic, Monetary and Social Union' was ratified in May 1990. When the currency merger went into force in July of that year, Chancellor Kohl promised that nobody would be worse off because of unification.

It was the same unwarranted optimism that favored the choice of a high-tech/high-wage strategy for rebuilding the east German economy, a strategy favored by politicians, capitalists, and unions alike. East Germany was supposed to catch up with western standards quickly, instead of turning into an Italian-style Mezzogiorno with low wages and low productivity. The same shock therapy that characterized the monetary union was now applied to the wage bargaining system. As early as a month prior to unification, demands for quick improvements in living standards had already resulted in wage increases of around 17 percent (Sinn and Sinn 1991: 145). In March 1991, when anyone could see the steep rise in unemployment just by looking at the daily mass layoffs, the metalworkers' union and the employers negotiated an agreement that would have closed the gap between eastern and western wages by 1994. Unlike what happened with wage negotiations in the 'old' Federal Republic, it was not productivity increases but the gap with western wages that became the guideline for collective bargaining in the east. There was little to prevent the unions from getting what they wanted. In the west neither organized labor nor capital was interested in competition from cheap labor in their home market. In addition, eastern employers were much weaker than their opponents. Since there was no way in which productivity could be increased in line with wages, unit labor costs skyrocketed above western levels, as can be seen in Table 6.1.

Thus, labor shedding in the eastern economy continued. Overall employment in the GDR had always been much higher than in the west, even if at the cost of incredible overstaffing. In the second half of 1990 overall employment began to decline sharply. Between 1991 and 1993 total

Table 6.1 *Unit labor costs by sector in East Germany, 1991–1997 (%, West Germany = 100%)*

Year	1991	1992	1993	1994	1995	1996	1997
Manufacturing	190.9	166.1	131.0	126.4	120.1	115.9	111.7
Total economy	150.6	139.4	128.0	126.0	126.5	124.0	123.2

Source: Sachverständigenrat (1997): p. 92, table 36 and 1998: p. 80, table 28.

employment shrank by 15 percent and manufacturing employment fell by some 45 percent. Employment in the latter sector even kept on shrinking, until quite recently. In some sectors employment did pick up after the trough of the depression had been passed. These exceptions were construction and services, such as retail trade, security, and sanitary services. More recently the picture changed yet again. Starting in 1996, construction ran into difficulty, and low-productivity services soon followed suit. Manufacturing, by contrast, has gained market share, and labor shedding has abated accordingly (Sachverständigenrat 1998: 90–97).

Another consequence of the failures of wage bargaining in the east has been that many employers have left their bargaining associations, as they are unwilling or unable to pay the rates set by industry-wide agreements (DIW 1999: 436–38). Many disappointed workers have also left their unions. Contractual coverage by collective agreement is much less widespread in the east than in the west.

The regions of the former Federal Republic initially benefited from unification. Massive financial transfers to the east stimulated demand for western consumer goods. The tax cuts involved in the third step of the tax reform further fueled the boom. In the wake of unification the federal government believed that the resulting costs would be covered by a new economic miracle in the east and by the sale of the 'Treuhand'[3] companies (Czada 1995: 5). It firmly promised the electorate not to raise any additional taxes. Facing the first all-German elections in December 1990, few politicians were prepared to dampen expectations. The SPD's candidate for Chancellor, Oskar Lafontaine, predicted the catastrophe that developed in the east and quite accurately described the financial implications of the unification process. Politically this was clearly a mistake; the Christian Democrats handily won this landmark election.

In any event, things did not quite turn out as expected. Instead of a renewed economic miracle, a depression devastated the east. The privatization of the 'Treuhand' companies became a burden on the federal budget (Deutsche Bundesbank 1994*a*: 22–31). In 1991 it was still possible to cover many expenses by raising additional tax revenues from the ongoing boom in the west. The remaining costs were financed out of rising deficits.

In view of steeply rising profits, the unions were no longer prepared to pursue a policy of wage moderation. Starting in 1990 they pushed for wage increases outstripping growth in labor productivity (Sachverständigenrat 1991: 200–201). Along with budget deficits resulting partly from the third stage of the Kohl government's tax reform, this wage push was one of the factors fueling inflation.

---

[3] A federally owned public agency holding a large part of the GDR's economy in trust.

Even in the face of such an extraordinary challenge as unification, the Bundesbank continued to follow its hard money policy. It made clear from the very beginning that it would not accept deficit financing of the unification process beyond a level that could be justified by initial 'unexpected burdens' (Deutsche Bundesbank 1991*c*: 21). Furthermore, the bank was also impatient with the high wage increases and explicitly signaled the federal government and the unions that it was unwilling to accommodate their expansionary policies (Deutsche Bundesbank 1991*b*: 17). In the months following unification it raised the bank rate to record postwar levels (Deutsche Bundesbank 1992). As manager of an anchor currency within the European Monetary System (EMS), the Bundesbank's monetary policy had wider European implications. Other EMS member countries had to follow the Bundesbank's policy if they wanted to stay within the system. High interest rates not only reduced demand for German exports in major European markets, but also caused turmoil in the EMS. Eventually, several major European countries were forced to leave the system, at least temporarily. Hence, the Deutschmark appreciated even further. High wage increases aggravated the competitiveness problem of German industry. Since the Bundesbank waited until September 1992 to begin lowering interest rates, the West German economy slumped into a deep recession in 1993. With the onset of the recession a decline in employment set in that did not really stop until 1997. To some extent one can recognize the same pattern already observed in postwar Germany's earlier recessions. Employment in industries (i.e. mainly manufacturing) declined, and the service sector was unable to absorb dismissed workers. Interestingly, employment in manufacturing had already dropped in 1992, when service employment was still on the rise. Although the economy recovered quickly in 1994, overall employment continued to fall. By and large, the economic situation had improved considerably by 1995. Wage negotiations that year were, however, unusually confrontational. Employers in the metal industry did not offer any wage increases at all, while radicalized union leaders again asked for large wage increases despite soaring unemployment. The metalworkers called a strike limited to a prosperous area in Bavaria and eventually managed to push through a wage increase of 5 percent. At the same time another surge in the exchange rate aggravated exporters' cost competitiveness problems (Lindlar and Scheremet 1998). Labor shedding continued until recently, despite the return to wage moderation in 1996 and 1997 and the Deutschmark's simultaneous depreciation.

To summarize: the economic integration of the former GDR into the Federal Republic initially followed a political logic leading to suboptimal labor market outcomes in both parts of unified Germany. This went hand in hand with severe fiscal problems. In the following two sections we shall discern the same pattern of cost-shifting already observed in the 1980s. Social insurance was used to cope with the financial and labor market implications of unification.

6.5.1. Financing Unification

By mid-1991 it had become clear to everyone that the Bundesbank's policy would force the government to increase taxes in order to reduce deficits. How could this be achieved? To what extent did international factors constrain political actors' choices? In the pages that follow we argue that while the government did raise some taxes, it responded to international constraints by turning to the old device of shifting financial burdens onto the insurance funds. As a result of this policy, social insurance contributions and other taxes on labor rose even further after 1990.

The 'Solidarity Law' and 'Tax Amendment Act' were among the first consolidation measures passed in June 1991. The former introduced a temporary 7.5 percent surcharge on personal and corporate income taxes and raised some excise taxes; the latter gave the new eastern *Länder* temporary tax allowances for special expenditures. These allowances were supposed to promote investment in the new Länder. However, they also reduced the price of capital in relation to labor. As a result, western companies placed highly capital-intensive production in the new Länder, which did not bring much relief to the unemployment crisis. As it turned out, the tax allowances (BMF 1991: 103–10) developed into a major fiscal loophole that lowered revenue from income taxation.

In spite of additional ad hoc measures, such as increases in the value-added tax (from 14% to 15%) and tobacco tax, the public deficit rose again to 3.2 percent of GDP in 1993 as economic growth turned negative. Meanwhile the Federal Constitutional Court had ruled that incomes lower than the level for social assistance had to be tax-exempt. Fearing fiscal strain, the federal government implemented this ruling only in a preliminary way. With the Standortsicherungsgesetz, an Act designed to make Germany more attractive as a business location, the Kohl government attempted to respond to international competition for investments. The Act essentially reduced taxes on business and so brought corporate taxation rates, quite high by international standards, closer to the average (BMF 1993: 127–33). In order to make up the loss in revenue, the government closed tax loopholes. This supposedly revenue-neutral tax reform exemplified the difficulties of financing German unification in a world with free capital movements.

The following years were marked by a general weakness of tax revenue and especially by a decline in the yield from direct taxes, i.e. corporate and income tax. Economic recovery in 1994 was quicker than expected, but tax revenue did not keep pace with growth. In 1994 this shortfall could still be traced to the effects of the recession on the intake from the income tax and to the consequences of the Standortsicherungsgesetz, which led to more revenue losses than expected. An increase in the mineral oil tax, by contrast, brought additional revenue. It was only in 1995 that the underlying erosion of the tax base became obvious. Even though the solidarity surcharge went into effect, tax revenue grew more slowly than nominal GDP (Deutsche Bundesbank 1997: 87). In 1996 preliminary legislation on the taxation of low incomes had to be replaced by a more permanent regulation in line with the Constitutional Court's 1993 decision. The new legislation raised the basic personal income tax allowance to the level of social assistance. In order to cover the revenue foregone, the initial scale of progression on income above the tax-exempt base was made steeper up to a certain threshold (BMF 1996: 115–17). This and other social reforms exacerbated the decline in direct taxes, but they were not at the root of the fiscal crisis. In fact, the underlying problem was the rapid decrease in the receipts from income and corporate taxes. The former declined from DM 41.5 bn in 1992 to DM 11.5 bn in 1996! This was mainly due to the generous tax exemptions for investments in the new Länder mentioned above. The decline in corporate income taxes was less pronounced, though rather conspicuous against a background of increased company profits. In this case, tax competition may well have played a role (Deutsche Bundesbank 1997: 92–93). The trend toward an eroding tax base continued in 1997 and gave rise to an urgent need for general tax reform. Tax amendments, however, need the approval of both houses. Since the Bundestag was dominated by the CDU/CSU/FDP coalition while the upper house was dominated by the major opposition party (SPD), the reform got stuck. Nevertheless, tax revenue stabilized even before 1998, when the newly elected Social Democratic-led government increased taxes on energy and lowered taxes on labor.

At a time when the government had to rule out higher deficits, could not rely on corporate and personal income taxes, and found it impossible to reduce expenditures for the east, it was tempting to finance unification via social insurance. This is exactly what happened. The social insurance schemes were in good shape financially at the beginning of the 1990s, so initially they were able to support the growing burden of unification without running up deficits of their own. Unemployment insurance was directly hit by the collapse of the labor market in the former GDR. The government raised the unemployment insurance contribution rate by 2.5 percentage points in 1991. Additional expenditures for the east that year amounted to some DM 30 bn, of which only 5 bn could be met out of the federal subsidy. The remaining deficit of 25 bn had to be financed by contribution payers from the west (Deutsche Bundesbank 1991*a*: 34).

Health insurance was also used, albeit indirectly, to cover expenditures that would otherwise have had to be paid out of the federal budget. This was achieved in 1995 by reducing transfers from general unemployment insurance to the dedicated sickness funds providing health insurance to the unemployed. Since the federal government is not involved in financing the health insurance scheme, but does have to cover upcoming deficits in unemployment insurance, this also helped save the government money. Finally, the government shifted some burdens onto the pension scheme. In 1992 the GDR's old pension scheme was integrated into the western system, two years in advance of the date initially planned. This meant that special pension deficits in the east resulting from the gap between revenues and expenditures were now covered in an all-German pension scheme including contributions from west Germans.[4] It has been calculated that the West German pension schemes would have run surpluses and even allowed for a reduction in contribution rates had the money not been spent to cover the revenue gap in the east (DIW 1997*a*: 433–34). In fact, similar things may be said about unemployment insurance (DIW 1997*b*: 729). The consequence of cost-shifting to the disadvantage of the social insurance schemes were rapidly rising contribution rates as is depicted in Figure 6.3.

This trend was not really counteracted by additional cost-cutting in areas like health care (Health Reform Act of 1993), which at best could have prevented further growth in expenditures and contribution rates. However, despite the precarious state of public finance and poor labor market performance, some expansion of social policy proved possible. The introduction of long-term care insurance in 1994 seemed to go against the tide of cutting back on welfare spending, lowering entitlements, and reducing welfare programs' coverage. These expansionary measures, however, reimposed the main financial burden of social policy on contribution payers and led to further cost-shifting from the 'public' to the 'para-public purse' in those instances where long-term care insurance ended up replacing social assistance payments to the old and frail once covered by local authorities (Alber 1994). While long-term care insurance had some positive employment effects (an estimated 67,000 new jobs, BMA 1997: 38; see also Pabst 1999), it is questionable how far these were able to

---

[4] Moreover, in some cases the recalculating of east German pensions to conform with west German law led to pensions lower than the old entitlements from the GDR. The difference was then made up by an additional transfer (*Auffüllbetrag*) until 1995. Initially it added up to DM 6 bn a year (Deutsche Bundesbank 1995: 22). This amount, in turn, had to be covered largely by contributions.

% of gross wages

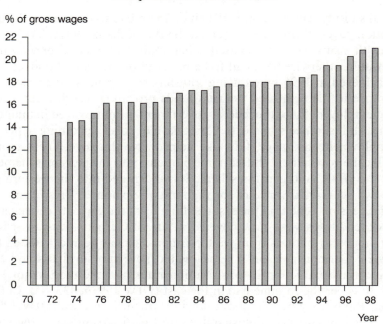

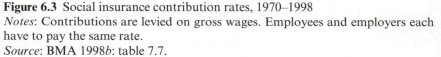

Figure 6.3 Social insurance contribution rates, 1970–1998
Notes: Contributions are levied on gross wages. Employees and employers each
have to pay the same rate.
Source: BMA 1998*b*: table 7.7.

offset the detrimental effects of higher non-wage labor costs on private service sector employment.

The next section shows how the various branches of social insurance
were used to relieve the unemployment situation, especially in the east.

6.5.2. *The Social and Economic Unification of Germany*

The failure of proper coordination among fiscal, monetary, and wage policy resulted in a labor market catastrophe for eastern Germany and a dramatic decline in employment in the west. At the end of the day, the brunt
of adjustment had to be borne by the welfare state.

It is clear that the kind of shock therapy applied to the east could not
have been carried out had not the huge west German welfare state acted
as buffer cushioning the impact of unemployment in the east (Seibel 1998).
When the collapse of the eastern labor market began, a functioning labor
market administration did not exist. A special provision for the eastern

Länder treated those who had lost their jobs in all but name as if they were simply working fewer hours. These unemployed people officially disguised as underemployed workers had to claim a special reduced-hours benefit (*Kurzarbeitergeld*), since this was administratively easier to handle (Brinkmann et al. 1995: 62–63). After 1991 early retirement became widely used. One pre-retirement provision had already been introduced by the last Communist government but was superceded by the Unification Treaty. If an older worker was eligible in the period between February and October 1990, (s)he could draw a pre-retirement pension. About 400,000 older workers in post-Communist, pre-unification East Germany left the labor market in this way. The Unification Treaty replaced this scheme, which had to be financed out of the federal budget, by a 'transition allowance' (*Altersübergangsgeld*) financed by the Federal Employment Office. For unemployed workers 55 or older the benefit amounted to 65 percent of their last net income and was granted for five years or until the claimant could draw a regular pension. This scheme was used by around 600,000 workers.

As can be seen from Figure 6.4, these and other early retirement programs substantially reduced labor force participation by older eastern workers even though the schemes were restricted to those seeking to enter these programs by the end of 1992.

In view of the overall disaster characterizing the east German labor market, early retirement programs could do little to relieve the unemployment crisis on their own. Active labor market policy was therefore expanded to unprecedented levels. Employment in work creation schemes was at least twice as high in the east as in the west for every year beginning 1991, even though the working-age population in the new Länder is only about one-fifth of the west's. In contrast to what had been going on in the old Länder, active labor market measures in the east were often used to improve infrastructure. Since such investments can be quite expensive, the federal government subsidized these schemes in 1991 and 1992. When budgetary pressures intensified, the government curbed spending. Consequently, employment in work creation schemes went down by 60 percent in the following years despite a short-lived upturn just before the 1998 elections. Training measures were initially also used extensively, but training also fell victim to the kind of competition between active and passive labor market policies (Schmid and Wiebe 1999: 389) we have already observed from previous decades.

In the west we find the same basic adjustment pattern that existed in the previous two decades. New cohorts of older workers continued to leave the labor market. After 1992 the pension reform of 1989 started to take effect. Workers who wished to retire early had to accept a somewhat smaller

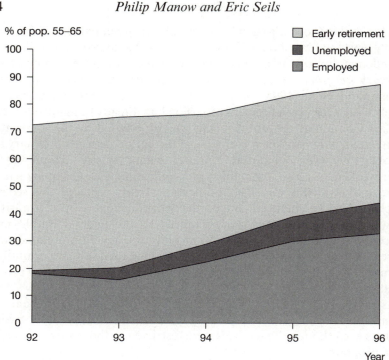

Figure 6.4 Early retirement and labor force participation in East Germany, 1992–1996

Notes: The figure displays the employed, unemployed, and retirees between 55 and 65 years of age as percentage of total population of that age group in the area of the former German Democratic Republic. Data for years before 1992 are not available.

Sources: Employment data were provided by the Federal Statistical Office from various Mikrozensus 1957–1997; other data are from BA 1998; Autorengemeinschaft 1999: 35: BMA various years; IAB 1997: 170; own calculations.

pension. Since this reduction was less than actuarial calculations would have predicted, the effects are not at all dramatic, as shown by Figure 6.5.

In the west, job creation programs never regained the importance they had in the late 1980s, in spite of worsening unemployment during the recession of the 1990s. This seems to have been a consequence of the large shift in resources to the east. Vocational training, by contrast, has remained rather stable in the old Federal Republic.

Of course, most of these labor market policies came at the cost of rapidly rising social insurance contributions. In the following section, we

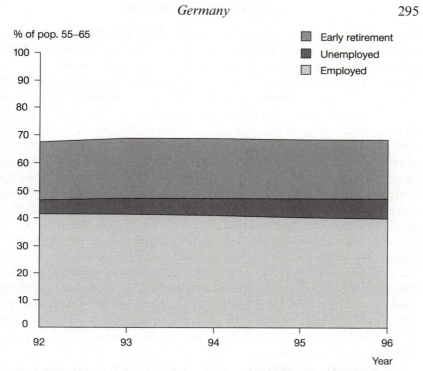

Figure 6.5 Early retirement and labor force participation in West Germany, 1992–1996

Notes: The figure displays the employed, unemployed, and retirees between 55 and 65 years of age as percentage of total population of that age group in the area of former West Germany.

Sources: Employment data were provided by the Federal Statistical Office from various Mikrozensus 1957–1997; other data are from BA 1998; Autorengemein-schaft 1999: 34; BMA various years; IAB 1997: 170; own calculations.

shall discuss the feedback effects of rising non-wage labor costs on labor market performance.

6.6. The Effects of 'Dual Externalization'

Where does the German employment problem come from? According to the conventional wisdom, unemployment has its roots in Germany's lack of international competitiveness as a business location. An overblown welfare state (the argument goes) has raised labor costs to levels that priced

German products out of world markets. The same high level of social expenditure has supposedly created strong incentives for companies to invest abroad. By contrast, and in light of German manufacturing's high productivity, we would argue that too much has been made of non-wage labor costs as a factor influencing the viability of Germany's exposed sectors. While unit labor costs did increase significantly during the 1990s, this increase had only a minor impact on Germany's share of world exports. One explanation for wage costs' negligible effect on competitiveness is that German firms have maintained a high capacity for successful innovation (Carlin and Soskice 1997: 57–61).[5] There is also little evidence pointing to a large-scale shift of production facilities abroad, although deteriorating price competitiveness may have played a role here as well. After all, the level of manufacturing employment is still very high in Germany.

As an alternative explanation for poor employment performance, we would like to draw attention to the impact of high non-wage labor costs on structural change. As long as the economy is growing, structural change happens smoothly. But unemployment in recessions does result when low-skilled workers in particular are dismissed from their jobs in the high-wage and high-productivity manufacturing sector and cannot immediately find employment elsewhere. Instead of moving into service sector jobs with low productivity and consequently lower pay, they fill the ranks of the long-term unemployed. While unemployment lasting longer than a year rose to 52.2 percent of total unemployment in 1998 (OECD 1999*a*: 242), private service employment is still underdeveloped in Germany compared against the OECD average.

At the same time (in the 1980s), labor productivity growth in services is said to have outpaced comparable growth for manufacturing (OECD 1988: 68; Grömling and Lichtblau 1997: 11). This aggregate effect may point to the relatively small size of a low-productivity sector within services. Note, that the categories ISIC 6 (which includes trade, restaurants, and services) and ISIC 9 (community and social services)[6] are especially low in comparison to the OECD average. Both sectors tend to include

---

[5] The increase in unit labor costs in Germany is partially due to the greater role played by in-firm provision of business services. Lower productivity gains in services may lead to higher unit labor costs in manufacturing without an adverse effect on competitiveness—since other firms will have to buy these services at correspondingly higher prices (see Deutsche Bundesbank 1994*b*). However, the data suggest that the relatively stable export market share cannot be explained by a low price elasticity of the demand for Germany's high-quality export goods or by a corresponding decline in profitability (Carlin and Soskice 1997: 59–60).

[6] Real estate and business services are included in ISIC 9 rather than ISIC 8; in the German case the size of community and social services is probably grossly overstated. For ISIC 8 accounts, of course, the opposite is true. Real estate and business services make up around three-quarters of ISIC 8 employment in the USA.

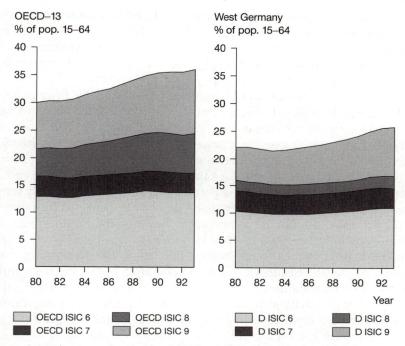

OECD–13
% of pop. 15–64

West Germany
% of pop. 15–64

Year

☐ OECD ISIC 6 ■ OECD ISIC 8 ☐ D ISIC 6 ■ D ISIC 8
■ OECD ISIC 7 ☐ OECD ISIC 9 ■ D ISIC 7 ☐ D ISIC 9

Figure 6.6 Private services in the OECD and West Germany, 1980–1993
Notes: The figure compares the employment/population ratios of private service
employment in the OECD (left-hand side) with West Germany. The OECD average is weighted and includes Australia, Austria, Belgium, Canada, Denmark,
Finland, France, Japan, Norway, Sweden, United Kingdom, the USA, and West
Germany. ISIC 6: wholesale and retail trade, restaurants and hotels; ISIC 7:
transport, storage, and communication; ISIC 8: financing, insurance, real estate,
and business services; ISIC 9: community, social, and personal services. Data are
partly estimated.
Sources: OECD, *Statistical Compendium: National Accounts* (Paris: OECD,
1999); Statistisches Bundesamt 1995: 62; IW 1994: table 15; own calculations.

'embodied' personal services with few opportunities for capital investment
and associated productivity gains (Klodt 1997: 17–19). These statistics on
productivity and services imply a striking conclusion: the largest share of
the total gap in service employment is due to the small size of the low-wage
sector (Klös 1997). In fact, this seems to be at the core of the German
employment problem.

It is often claimed that the absence of a regular low-wage sector is due
to generous social benefits that make it unrewarding to accept low-paid
work. A related claim is that beneficiaries trying to work themselves out of

welfare dependency face implicit marginal effective tax rates that are very high (Deutsche Bundesbank 1996: 61–66). While this argument can explain why certain groups, especially social assistance beneficiaries with children, might not accept low paying jobs, it only sheds light on one side of the problem.

This is where another line of argument developed by Fritz Scharpf (1997) comes into play. It starts from the fact that a large group of west European countries combines high reservation wages defined by unemployment and social assistance schemes with high social contribution rates. The latter drive a wedge between gross labor costs which are relevant for labor demand and the net wage that determines supply. In the case of average or high wages an increase in the wedge does not necessarily translate into higher labor costs, given that it can be compensated by a decline of the net wage.[7] In the case of low wages, however, the employer actually has no possibility to pass increasing non-wage labor costs over to the employee, since net earnings cannot fall below the reservation wage defined by social assistance.[8] Thus, the employer has to bear the entire burden of social insurance contributions. One can conclude from this that many low productivity jobs are not viable in Germany since they cannot support the gross labor costs that have to be paid for them. Figure 6.7 provides some justification for both views: the work disincentive argument and the tax wedge thesis.

Figure 6.7 shows that the level of social assistance has risen considerably in real terms since the early 1970s. As pointed out above, this implies that benefits have been getting closer to average net wages. Thus the gap between low wages and social assistance would have narrowed even if social insurance contributions had remained stable. However, gross labor costs have risen even faster due to the increase in non-wage labor costs. It is obvious that both the rise in contribution rates and the increased level of social assistance have contributed to the size of the wedge between net and gross wages and thus to the level of the gross labor cost at low earn-

---

[7] To which extent the tax burden can be shifted to workers in the industrial sector remains a matter of controversy. Bauer and Riphahn (1998) found some negative employment effects of social security contributions in 32 West German industries between 1977 and 1994.

[8] In fact, wages usually cannot fall below the level set by collective bargaining for the lowest wage groups. This 'reservation wage' is even higher than the social assistance level. Wage agreements between unions and employers' associations define the reservation wage also for those firms and workers not formally covered by collective bargaining, since unemployment insurance defines 'acceptable' jobs as those with a wage not below the reference wage agreed upon by unions and employers (cf. Paqué 1996). Hence, a firm cannot hope to hire a worker below the wage on which unions and employers' associations were able to agree, even if the firm is not covered by a collective agreement (i.e. is not member of an employer association).

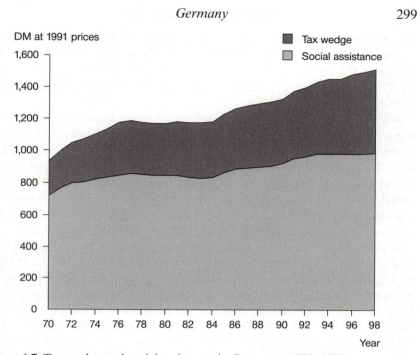

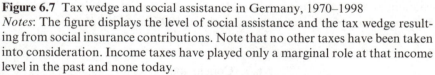

Figure 6.7 Tax wedge and social assistance in Germany, 1970–1998
Notes: The figure displays the level of social assistance and the tax wedge result-
ing from social insurance contributions. Note that no other taxes have been taken
into consideration. Income taxes have played only a marginal role at that income
level in the past and none today.
Sources: Data on social assistance were provided by the Ministry of Labor and
Social Affairs; other data come from BMA 1998*b*: tables 6.9, 7.7; Statistisches
Bundesamt 1999; own calculations.

ings. This makes it more difficult for low-skilled industrial workers who
have been fired or for new entrants into the labor market who have only
low skills to get service sector jobs. This difficulty is also reflected in figures on earnings dispersion for lower deciles in Germany, which has
declined considerably in Germany since 1983 (OECD 1996: 65). It should,
however, be noted that indirect taxes, especially VAT, have had a very similar impact on the price of labor in the low-wage sector. Since the combined effects of social assistance and taxes levied on labor have impeded
the growth of a regular low-wage sector, this kind of work is nowadays
often done under the rules governing atypical employment, not traditionally covered by social insurance. While estimates of the total number of
these kind of jobs vary widely, between two and six million, it seems clear

that the real number lies somewhere in between these extremes, though much closer to the upper boundary. A study commissioned by the Minister of Labor found 5.63 million persons in atypical employment in 1997. This represents an increase of 26.5 percent in only five years (BMA 1998*a*: 17).

Why is it that Germany has raised social insurance contributions and the level of social assistance? As was shown in more detail above, the rise in contribution rates resulted mainly from the process of dual externalization. We argue that the rise in the level of social assistance is best explained by looking at the regulatory responsibilities and financing structure of social assistance. The federal government regulates social assistance by legislation (the enabling statute is the Bundessozialhilfegesetz) but is not required to finance it. Hence, the government has little incentive to contain costs. The rules of the game, however, may have been changed by a recent ruling of the Constitutional Court. As noted before, the court ruled that the basic level of tax-exempt income has to be at least the size of social assistance. This ruling established an inverse link between federal revenue from income tax and the level of social assistance. The German judiciary thereby provided the federal government with its first incentive to lower social assistance levels or prevent them from increasing further. As a consequence, social assistance was indexed to the rise in pensions (which, in turn, were coupled to net wage growth) in 1997 and 1998.[9]

6.7. Conclusion

How has Germany fared in an increasingly open economy? How did the German model cope with the more unfavorable economic environment of the 1980s and 1990s? If one takes export market shares as a first rough indicator of German firms' ability to compete on world markets, nothing points to a significant deterioration of competitiveness, despite the fact that relative unit labor costs did rise sharply in 1986/87 and again in the early 1990s (Carlin and Soskice 1997: 58). Still, a liberal international market is a blessing, not a curse, to Germany and its export-oriented industry.

We have argued in this paper that Germany's main problem is not a lack of international competitiveness but poor job growth in services. External shocks regularly trigger adjustment in the German political and economic system, with adverse effects on overall employment in the long run, espe-

---

[9] Since mid-1993 the level of social assistance for households with four or more members has to remain below the average net income of low-wage groups. Since 1994 this also applies to families of up to five members.

cially in services with low productivity. It is here that the reason for the German system's poor labor market performance lies. We have described the interplay among the Bundesbank, state actors, and the social partners—within an institutional and legal setting comprising *Tarifautonomie* between strong and encompassing social partners, substantial central bank autonomy, fragmented public budgets, and an encompassing and generous welfare state—as the interaction responsible for Germany's low employment equilibrium. In the era of the economic miracle, full employment and the rising affluence were dependent on the manufacturing sector. Structural change has reduced the importance of industry for employment in all developed countries. German industrial employment shrank especially dramatically in the two oil crises. Industrial workers who lost their jobs tended to move into early retirement or unemployment schemes rather than into low-paid employment in the service sector. At the same time, the Bundesbank urged budgetary consolidation on the federal government as a way of keeping inflation low. The government's fiscal austerity in the service of monetary rigor came partly at the expense of social insurance, where contribution rates were forced up even higher. All this put a heavy burden on social insurance, both with respect to spending and revenue. High contributions to the German welfare state, which is primarily financed out of payroll taxes, add to the problem of high labor costs. As a consequence, the German employment ratio is low, job growth in low-productivity employment is poor, and older workers' labor force participation has fallen constantly since the mid-1970s.

German unification posed an unprecedented challenge, but the response of the key economic actors strongly resembled their behavior in earlier crises. The Bundesbank again insisted on price stability. The government, as in previous recessions, massively shifted the costs of crisis management onto the social partners' insurance schemes. Older workers, especially in the east, moved into special programs for early retirement. This process of dual externalization led to a considerable rise in contribution rates, itself a major obstacle to smoother structural change.

REFERENCES

ALBER, JENS (1994). *Paying for Long-Term Care in a Social Insurance System: The Example of Germany*. Paper presented at a meeting on caring for frail elderly people: policies for the future. Château de la Muette, Paris, 5–6 July: OECD, DEELSA/ELSA/FE, 94/7.
——(1996). 'Wohlfahrtsstaatliche Entwicklungen in Deutschland und den USA:

Zum Modellcharakter residualer Sozialpolitik in der Kürzungsphase des Sozialstaats'. Konstanz: unpublished manuscript.

ALBER, JENS (1998). *Recent Developments in Continental European Welfare States: Do Austria, Germany, and the Netherlands Prove to be Birds of a Feather?*. Paper presented at the 14th World Congress of Sociology, 29 July, Montreal.

ALLEN, CHRISTOPHER S. (1989). 'The Underdevelopment of Keynesianism in the Federal Republic of Germany', in Peter A. Hall (ed.), *The Political Power of Economic Ideas*. Princeton: Princeton University Press, 264–89.

AMBROSIUS, GEROLD (1989). 'Das Wirtschaftssystem', in Wolfgang Benz (ed.), *Die Geschichte der Bundesrepublik Deutschland*, ii. *Wirtschaft*. Frankfurt: Fischer Taschenbuch Verlag, 11–81.

Autorengemeinschaft (1994). 'Der Arbeitsmarkt 1994 und 1995 in der Bundesrepublik Deutschland', in *Mitteilungen aus der Arbeitsmarkt- und Berufsforschung*, 27/1: 269–99.

——(1999). 'Der Arbeitsmarkt in der Bundesrepublik Deutschland in den Jahren 1998 und 1999', in *Mitteilungen aus der Arbeitsmarkt- und Berufsforschung*, 32/1: 5–40.

BA (Bundesanstalt für Arbeit) (1998). *Strukturanalyse 1997. Sondernummer der Amtlichen Nachrichten der Bundesanstalt für Arbeit*. Nürnberg: BA.

BAUER, THOMAS, and RIPHAHN, REGINA T. (1998). *Employment Effects of Payroll Taxes—An Empirical Test for Germany*. IZA Discussion Paper No. 11. Bonn: Institute for the Study of Labor.

BERG, HEINZ (1986). *Bilanz der Kostendämpfungspolitik im Gesundheitswesen 1977–1984*. Bonn: Asgard.

BMA (Bundesministerium für Arbeit und Sozialordnung) (1994). *Sozialbericht 1993*. Bonn: BMA.

——(1997). 'Erster Bericht zur Lage der Pflegeversicherung'. *Bundestags-Drucksache* 13/9528.

——(1998a). *Sozialbericht 1997*. Bonn: BMA.

——(1998b). *Statistisches Taschenbuch: Arbeits- und Sozialstatistik*. Bonn: BMA.

——(various years). *Die Rentenbestände in der gesetzlichen Rentenversicherung in der Bundesrepublik Deutschland*. Bonn: BMA.

BMF (Bundesministerium der Finanzen) (various years). *Finanzbericht*. Bonn: BMF.

BÖRSCH-SUPAN, AXEL H. (1999). 'Das deutsche Rentenversicherungssystem: Probleme und Perspektiven', in Eberhard Wille (ed.), *Entwicklung und Perspektiven der Sozialversicherung*. Baden-Baden: Nomos, 21–67.

BOSS, ALFRED (1999). *Sozialhilfe, Lohnabstand und Leistungsanreize*. Kieler Arbeitspapier No. 912. Kiel: Institute of World Economics.

BRINKMANN, CHRISTIAN, EMMERICH, KNUT, GOTTSLEBEN, VOLKMAR, MÜLLER, KARIN, and VÖLKEL, BRIGITTE (1995). 'Arbeitsmarktpolitik in den neuen Bundesländern', in Hartmut Seifert (ed.), *Reform der Arbeitsmarktpolitik: Herausforderung für Politik und Wirtschaft*. Cologne: Bund-Verlag, 59–87.

BUCHHEIM, CHRISTOPH (1989). 'Die Bundesrepublik in der Weltwirtschaft', in Wolfgang Benz (ed.), *Die Geschichte der Bundesrepublik Deutschland*, ii. *Wirtschaft*. Frankfurt: Fischer Taschenbuch Verlag, 169–209.

BUHR, PETRA, LEISERING, LUTZ, LUDWIG, MONIKA, and ZWICK, MICHAEL (1991). 'Armutspolitik und Sozialhilfe in vier Jahrzehnten', in Bernhard Blanke and Hellmut Wollmann (eds.), *Die alte Bundesrepublik. Kontinuität und Wandel.* Opladen: Westdeutscher Verlag, 503–46.

BUSCH, ANDREAS (1995). *Preisstabilitätspolitik: Politik und Inflationsraten im internationalen Vergleich.* Opladen: Leske + Budrich.

CARLIN, WENDY, and SOSKICE, DAVID (1997). 'Shocks to the System: The German Political Economy under Stress'. *National Economic Institute Review*, 159: 57–76.

COLLIGNON, STEFAN, BOFINGER, PETER, JOHNSON, PETER, and MAIGRET, BERTRAND DE (1994). *Europe's Monetary Future.* Rutherford, NJ: Fairleigh Dickinson University Press.

CZADA, ROLAND (1995). *Der Kampf um die Finanzierung der deutschen Einheit.* MPIFG Discussion Paper 95/1. Cologne: Max Planck Institute for the Study of Societies.

——(1998). 'Vereinigungskrise und Standortdebatte: Der Beitrag der Wiedervereinigung zur Krise des westdeutschen Modells'. *Leviathan*, 26/1: 24–59.

Deutsche Bundesbank (1991a). 'Aktuelle Finanzentwicklung der Sozialversicherung'. *Monatsbericht der Deutschen Bundesbank*, 43/11: 30–39.

——(1991b). 'Überprüfung des Geldmengenziels 1991'. *Monatsbericht der Deutschen Bundesbank*, 43/7: 14–17.

——(1991c). 'Die westdeutsche Wirtschaft unter dem Einfluß der Vereinigung Deutschlands'. *Monatsbericht der Deutschen Bundesbank*, 43/10: 15–21.

——(1992). 'Überprüfung des Geldmengenziels 1992 und Anhebung des Diskontsatzes'. *Monatsbericht der Deutschen Bundesbank*, 44/8: 15–21.

——(1994a). 'Die Finanzen der Treuhandanstalt'. *Monatsbericht der Deutschen Bundesbank*, 46/4: 17–31.

——(1994b). 'Reale Wechselkurse als Indikatoren der internationalen Wettbewerbsfähigkeit'. *Monatsbericht der Deutschen Bundesbank*, 46/5: 47–60.

——(1995). 'Die Finanzentwicklung der gesetzlichen Rentenversicherung seit Beginn der neunziger Jahre'. *Monatsbericht der Deutschen Bundesbank*, 47/3: 17–31.

——(1996). 'Fiskalische Hemmnisse bei der Aufnahme einer regulären Erwerbstätigkeit im unteren Lohnsegment'. *Monatsbericht der Deutschen Bundesbank*, 48/2: 61–66.

——(1997). 'Neuere Entwicklungen der Steuereinnahmen'. *Monatsbericht der Deutschen Bundesbank*, 49/8: 83–103.

DIW (Deutsches Institut für Wirtschaftsforschung) (1993). 'Deutsche Geldpolitik wirkt prozyklisch'. *Wochenbericht*, 60/10: 93–97.

——(1997a). 'Gesetzliche Rentenversicherung: Senkung des Rentenniveaus nicht der richtige Weg'. *Wochenbericht*, 64/24–25: 433–42.

——(1997b). 'Vereinigungsfolgen belasten Sozialversicherung'. *Wochenbericht*, 64/40: 725–29.

——(1999). 'Gesamtwirtschaftliche und unternehmerische Anpassungsfortschritte in Ostdeutschland. Neunzehnter Bericht'. *Wochenbericht*, 66/23: 419–45.

ELLWEIN, THOMAS, and HESSE, JOACHIM JENS (1987). *Das Regierungssystem der Bundesrepublik Deutschland*. Opladen: Westdeutscher Verlag.

FRANZ, WOLFGANG (1990). 'Fiscal Policy in the Federal Republic of Germany'. *Empirical Economics*, 15/1: 17–54.

——(1997). *Wettbewerbsfähige Beschäftigung schaffen statt Arbeitslosigkeit umverteilen*. Gütersloh: Verlag Bertelsmann Stiftung.

FRERICH, JOHANNES, and FREY, MARTIN (1993). *Handbuch der Geschichte der Sozialpolitik in Deutschland*, iii. *Sozialpolitik in der Bundesrepublik Deutschland bis zur Herstellung der deutschen Einheit*. Munich: Oldenbourg.

GARLICHS, DIETRICH, and MAIER, FRIEDERIKE (1982). 'Die arbeitsmarktpolitische Wirksamkeit der beruflichen Weiterbildung', in Fritz W. Scharpf, Marlene Brockmann, Manfred Groser, Friedhart Hegner, and Günther Schmid (eds.), *Aktive Arbeitsmarktpolitik: Erfahrungen und neue Wege*. Frankfurt: Campus, 89–118.

GRÖMLING, MICHAEL, and LICHTBLAU, KARL (1997). *Technologie, Produktivität und Strukturwandel*. Cologne: Deutscher Instituts Verlag.

GRÜTZ, JENS, and FAIK, JÜRGEN (1998). 'Gesetzliche Rentenversicherung und Arbeitsmarkt—Eine ökonomische Betrachtungsweise'. *Deutsche Rentenversicherung*, 1998/5: 292–314.

HALL, PETER A. (1994). 'Central Bank Independence and Coordinated Wage Bargaining: Their Interaction in Germany and Europe'. *German Politics and Society*, 1994: 1–23.

HOFFMANN, LUTZ (1993). '*Warten auf den Aufschwung: Eine ostdeutsche Bilanz*'. Regensburg: Transfer Verlag.

IAB (Institut für Arbeitsmarkt- und Berufsforschung) (ed.) (1997). *Zahlen-Fibel: Ergebnisse der Arbeitsmarkt- und Berufsforschung in Tabellen*. Nürnberg: Institut für Arbeitsmarkt- und Berufsforschung der Bundesanstalt für Arbeit.

IW (Institut der deutschen Wirtschaft) (1994). *Zahlen zur wirtschaftlichen Entwicklung der Bundesrepublik Deutschland*. Cologne: Deutscher Instituts Verlag.

JACOBS, KLAUS, KOHLI, MARTIN, and REIN, MARTIN (1991). 'Germany: The Diversity of Pathways', in Martin Kohli, Martin Rein, Anne-Marie Guillemard, and Herman van Gunsteren (eds.), *Time for Retirement: Comparative Studies of Early Exit from the Labor Force*. New York: Cambridge University Press, 181–221.

KELLER, BERNDT (1999). *Einführung in die Arbeitspolitik: Arbeitsbeziehungen und Arbeitsmarkt in sozialwissenschaftlicher Perspektive*. Munich: Oldenbourg.

KLODT, HENNING (1997). *The Transition to the Service Society: Prospects for Growth, Productivity, and Employment*. Kiel Working Papers. Kiel: Institute of World Economics.

KLÖS, HANS-PETER (1997). 'Analyse: Dienstleistungslücke und Niedriglohnsektor in Deutschland', in *IW-Trends*, 24/3 <http://www.Iwkoeln.de/trends/tr3-97/tr3-2-01.html>.

KREILE, MICHAEL (1978). 'West Germany: The Dynamics of Expansion', in Peter J. Katzenstein (ed.), *Between Power and Plenty: Foreign Economic Policies of Advanced Industrial States*. Madison: University of Wisconsin Press, 191–224.

LAPP, SUSANNE, and LEHMENT, HARMEN (1997). 'Lohnzurückhaltung und Beschäftigung in Deutschland und in den Vereinigten Staaten'. *Die Weltwirtschaft*, 1: 67–83.

LEHMBRUCH, GERHARD (1998). *Parteienwettbewerb im Bundesstaat: Regelsysteme und Spannungslagen im Institutionengefüge der Bundesrepublik Deutschland.* Opladen: Westdeutscher Verlag.

LINDLAR, LUDGER, and SCHEREMET, WOLFGANG (1998). *Germany's Slump: Explaining the Unemployment Crisis of the 1990s.* Amsterdam: Universiteit van Amsterdam, Duitsland Instituut.

MANOW, PHILIP (1997). *Social Insurance and the German Political Economy.* MPIfG Discussion Paper 97/2. Cologne: Max Planck Institute for the Study of Societies.

MARES, ISABELA (forthcoming). 'Business (Non-)Coordination and Social Policy Development: The Case of Early Retirement', in Peter Hall and David Soskice (eds.), *Varieties of Capitalism.*

MÖRSCHEL, RICHARD (1978). 'Die Zuschüsse des Staates zu den gesetzlichen Rentenversicherungen der Arbeiter und Angestellten'. *Die Deutsche Rentenversicherung* 78: 332–49.

MOSHER, JIM (1999). *The Institutional Origins of Wage Equality: Labor Unions and their Wage Policies.* Paper. Cologne: Max Planck Institute for the Study of Societies.

NAEGELE, GERHARD (1987). 'Zwischenbilanz des Vorruhestands—Eine sozialpolitische Wirkungsanalyse nach über 3 Jahren Vorruhestand'. *WSI-Mitteilungen*, 40/12: 752–63.

OECD (Organisation for Economic Co-operation and Development) (1983). *OECD Economic Surveys: Germany.* Paris: OECD.

——(1988): *OECD Economic Surveys: Germany.* Paris: OECD.

——(1989). *OECD Economic Surveys: Germany.* Paris: OECD.

——(1990). *OECD Economic Surveys: Germany.* Paris: OECD.

——(1994). 'Collective Bargaining: Levels and Coverage', in OECD, *Employment Outlook 1994.* Paris: OECD, 167–94.

——(1996). *OECD Employment Outlook 1996.* Paris: OECD.

——(1999a). *Employment Outlook 1999.* Paris: OECD.

——(1999b). *Statistical Compendium 1999.* Paris: OECD.

OWEN SMITH, ERIC (1994). *The German Economy.* London: Routledge.

PABST, STEFAN (1999). 'Mehr Arbeitsplätze für Geringqualifizierte nach Einführung der Pflegeversicherung?' *WSI-Mitteilungen*, 52/4: 234–40.

PAQUÉ, KARL-HEINZ (1996). 'Unemployment and the Crisis of the German Model: A Long-Term-Interpretation', in Herbert Giersch (ed.), *Fighting Europe's Unemployment in the 1990s.* Berlin: Springer, 123–55.

RENZSCH, WOLFGANG (1991). *Finanzverfassung und Finanzausgleich: Die Auseinandersetzungen um ihre politische Gestaltung in der Bundesrepublik zwischen Währungsreform und deutscher Vereinigung 1948–1990.* Bonn: Dietz.

RÜB, FRIEDBERT W., and NULLMEIER, FRANK (1991). 'Alterssicherungspolitik in der Bundesrepublik Deutschland', in Bernhard Blanke and Hellmut Wollmann (eds.), *Die alte Bundesrepublik: Kontinuität und Wandel.* Opladen: West-deutscher Verlag, 437–62.

RUSSIG, HARALD (1982). 'Sozialversicherungs- und arbeitsrechtliche Rahmen-bedingungen für die Ausgliederung älterer und/oder leistungsgeminderter Arbeitnehmer aus dem Betrieb', in Knuth Dohse, Ulrich Jürgens, and Harald Russig (eds.), *Ältere Arbeitnehmer zwischen Unternehmensinteressen und Sozialpolitik*. Frankfurt: Campus, 237–82.

Sachverständigenrat zur Begutachtung der gesamtwirtschaftlichen Entwicklung (various years). Stuttgart: Metzler-Poeschel.

SCHARPF, FRITZ W. (1982). 'Optionen der Arbeitsmarktpolitik in den achtziger Jahren', in Fritz W. Scharpf, Marlene Brockmann, Manfred Groser, Friedhart Hegner, and Günther Schmid (eds.), *Aktive Arbeitsmarktpolitik: Erfahrungen und neue Wege*. Frankfurt: Campus, 12–28.

——(1985). 'Die Politikverflechtungs-Falle: Europäische Integration und deutscher Föderalismus im Vergleich'. *Politische Vierteljahresschrift*, 26/4: 323–56.

——(1991). *Crisis and Choice in European Social Democracy*. Ithaca, NY: Cornell University Press.

——(1997). *Employment and the Welfare State: A Continental Dilemma*. MPIfG Working Paper 97/7. Cologne: Max Planck Institute for the Study of Societies.

SCHMID, GÜNTHER (1990). 'Was tut das Arbeitsamt? Kooperative Arbeits-marktpolitik im Wandel der Arbeitswelt', in Helmut König, Bodo von Greiff, and Helmut Schauer (eds.), *Sozialphilosophie der industriellen Arbeit*. Opladen: Westdeutscher Verlag, 388–413.

——and WIEBE, NICOLA (1999). 'Die Politik der Vollbeschäftigung im Wandel: Von der passiven zur interaktiven Arbeitsmarktpolitik', in Max Kaase and Günther Schmid (eds.), *Eine lernende Demokratie: 50 Jahre Bundesrepublik Deutschland*. Berlin: Edition Sigma, 357–96.

SCHMIDT, MANFRED G. (1987). 'West Germany: The Policy of the Middle Way'. *Journal of Public Policy*, 7/2: 135–77.

——(1990). 'Staatsfinanzen', in Klaus von Beyme and Manfred G. Schmidt (eds.), *Politik in der Bundesrepublik Deutschland*. Opladen: Westdeutscher Verlag, 36–73.

SEIBEL, WOLFGANG (1998). 'An Unavoidable Disaster? The German Currency Union of 1990', in Pat Gray and Paul Hart (eds.), *Public Policy Disasters in Western Europe*. London: Routledge, 96–112.

SEIFERT, HARTMUT (1991). 'Employment Effects of Working Time Reductions in the Former Republic of Germany'. *International Labour Review*, 130/4: 495–510.

SINN, GERLINDE, and SINN, HANS-WERNER (1991). *Kaltstart: Volkswirtschaftliche Aspekte der deutschen Vereinigung*. Tübingen: J. C. B. Mohr (Paul Siebeck).

Statistisches Bundesamt (1999). *Wirtschaft und Statistik 1*. Wiesbaden: Statistisches Bundesamt.

——(various years). *Statistisches Jahrbuch für die Bundesrepublik Deutschland*. Wiesbaden: Statistisches Bundesamt.

STREECK, WOLFGANG (1994). 'Pay Restraint without Incomes Policy: Institutionalized Monetarism and Industrial Unionism in Germany', in Ronald Dore, Robert Boyer, and Zoe Marn (eds.), *The Return of Incomes Policy*. London: Pinter, 118–40.

STREIT, MANFRED (1998). 'Die deutsche Währungsunion', in Deutsche Bundesbank (ed.), *Fünfzig Jahre Deutsche Mark: Notenbank und Währung seit 1948*. Munich: C. H. Beck, 675–719.

STURM, ROLAND (1997). 'Aufgabenstrukturen, Kompetenzen und Finanzierung', in Oscar W. Gabriel, Eberhard Holtmann, and Katja Ahlstisch (eds.), *Handbuch politisches System der Bundesrepublik Deutschland*. Munich: Oldenbourg, 619–58.

——(1998). 'Die Wende im Stolperschritt—eine finanzpolitische Bilanz', in Göttrik Wewer (ed.), *Bilanz der Ära Kohl: Christlich-liberale Politik in Deutschland 1982–1998*. Opladen: Leske + Budrich, 183–200.

VAN DER WILLIGEN, TESSA (1995). 'Unemployment, Wages, and the Wage Structure', in Robert Corker, Robert A. Feldman, Karl Habermeier, Haris Vittas, Tessa van der Willigen (eds.), *United Germany: The First Five Years: Performance and Policy Issues*. Occasional Papers 125. Washington, DC: IMF, 21–40.

VDR (Verband Deutscher Rentenversicherungsträger) (1997). *Rentenversicherung in Zeitreihen*. Frankfurt: Verband Deutscher Rentenversicherungsträger.

VON DER VRING, THOMAS (1998). 'Lohnzurückhaltung als Mittel der Beschäftigungspolitik: Kritische Bemerkungen zu einer empirischen Beweisführung Harmen Lehments'. *WSI-Mitteilungen*, 51/12: 832–36.

WEBBER, DOUGLAS (1989). 'Zur Geschichte der Gesundheitsreformen in Deutschland—ii. Teil: Norbert Blüms Gesundheitsreform und die Lobby'. *Leviathan*, 17/2: 262–300.

7

France
Directing Adjustment?

JONAH D. LEVY

For much of the postwar period, the French welfare state operated in the shadow of the state-led or *dirigiste* model of economic development. The predominance of *dirigisme* could be observed in both the academic and policymaking arenas. The French case attracted widespread academic interest because it was seen as offering a particularly pure incarnation of state direction of the economy. Indeed the very vocabulary for describing state economic leadership is peppered with French expressions: *dirigisme*, from the French verb 'to direct'; *étatisme*, from the French word for 'state'; and *Colbertisme*, in reference to the French statesman, Jean-Baptiste Colbert, one of the early practitioners of mercantilism under Louis XIV. French social policy, by contrast, made few contributions to the vocabulary of comparative welfare scholarship. The prevailing typologies— Gøsta Esping-Andersen's 'three worlds of welfare capitalism' and the Bismarck–Beveridge distinction—were inspired by the experiences of Sweden, Britain, and Germany, rather than France. Far from a welfare ideal-type, the French case fell between two stools and tended to be either passed over completely in comparative studies or else appended awkwardly to a welfare model that it did not fit.

The French welfare state was overshadowed by the *dirigiste* model in a substantive as well as academic sense. France's postwar growth strategy aimed to accelerate the pace of modernization and economic restructuring by channeling resources to critical industrial sectors. From the perspective of the state technocrats, social spending represented a cost to be contained, a drain on 'productive' investment. Throughout the 'golden age', then, *dirigisme* tended to act as a brake on welfare state development.

I wish to thank the following people, in addition to the members of the working group, for their helpful comments and criticisms: Susan Giaimo, Peter Hall, François-Xavier Merrien, Bruno Palier, Paul Pierson, and John Stephens. An earlier version of this paper was presented to the French Study Group and Study Group on Policy Reform in the Advanced Industrial Studies, Harvard Center for European Studies, Cambridge, Mass., 23 Nov. 1998.

During the past decade-and-one-half, France's welfare state has emerged from the shadows of *dirigisme*. In 1983 a combination of tightening external pressures and growing internal dysfunctions prompted French leadership to begin dismantling the *dirigiste* system. Simultaneously, the authorities expanded social spending to help protect workers from dislocation and to undercut resistance to measures of economic liberalization. In short, just as the creation of the *dirigiste* state had helped define the contours of the welfare state, a redirection and expansion of the welfare state would underpin the movement away from *dirigisme*.

In the 1990s, while voluntarist industrial policy receded into the background, many of the hopes and aspirations associated with *dirigisme* were transferred to the social policy arena. Both the 1995 presidential election and the 1997 legislative elections were waged over social policy, with victorious candidates in each instance pledging to use the welfare state to reduce unemployment and heal social divisions. From a brake on social spending, then, *dirigisme*—or, more accurately, the passing of *dirigisme*—has evolved into a motor, one that is periodically revved into high gear by the dynamics of party competition.

The interplay of *dirigisme* and the welfare state has lent an uneven, contradictory quality to France's response to globalization and to new forms of economic competition. On the one hand, the institutions and practices associated with *dirigiste* economic policy have been dismantled with astonishing speed and thoroughness. On the other hand, France's welfare state has expanded relentlessly. Social spending rose from 23.5 percent of GDP in 1980, to 26.7 percent in 1990, to 30.1 percent in 1995 (OECD, various years). The increase of 6.6 percent of GDP between 1980 and 1995 was second only to that of Switzerland among the countries examined in this volume. As a result, by 1995, France had become the heaviest social spender outside Scandinavia, surpassing even Germany, laboring under the burdens of unification. Thus, seventeen years after the repudiation of *dirigisme*, the French state absorbs a greater share of the national product than at any time in the postwar period.

This chapter examines the relationship between France's *dirigiste* system and its welfare system from the 'golden age' to the global age. The chapter is organized into six sections. Section 7.1 identifies the main features of France's 'golden age' welfare regime. Section 7.2 traces these features to the logic of the postwar *dirigiste* growth model and to the shifting character of French politics, notably on the right (1945–68). Section 7.3 describes the erosion and breakdown of the *dirigiste* model in the wake of a near-revolution of 1968 and the emergence of a powerful 'Union of the Left' (1968–83). Section 7.4 relates how welfare policy was used to accompany the dismantling of *dirigisme* in the 1980s and early 1990s. Section 7.5

compares recent reform efforts by the governments of Édouard Balladur (1993–95), Alain Juppé (1995–97), and Lionel Jospin (1997–present) respectively, a comparison that highlights the enduring salience of *dirigiste* legacies and partisan competition. Section 7.6 concludes with thoughts on the role of *dirigisme* in France's ongoing process of adjustment.

7.1. Contours of the French Welfare Model: A Snapshot and a Movie

In France, perhaps more than any other country, there is no single, dominant image of the 'postwar welfare model'. The 'golden age' itself is argued to have ended variously in 1968, 1974, 1979, 1981, or 1983, and the welfare state has looked different at each of these moments. To help sort through the contrasting depictions, this section offers both a 'snapshot', describing some of the relatively stable features of the postwar system, and a 'movie', pointing to the regime's evolving, dynamic character.

A snapshot taken of the French regime in 1970 (or perhaps a bit later) would have revealed several unusual characteristics. First, as David Cameron has demonstrated, the level of French welfare spending was far higher than predicted by any kind of 'power resources' interpretation (Cameron 1991). France's labor movement has always been among the weakest in the advanced industrial world: union density peaked at under 25 percent in the 1970s, and this meager membership was divided among five trade unions, who seemed more interested in fighting each other than in joining forces to confront French employers. French labor was deficient in political as well as organizational 'power resources'. The Communist Party had been evicted from the government in 1947 and would not return to office until 1981. With the Communists garnering a steady 20 to 25 percent of the vote every election, Socialist or center-left elements possessed limited leverage over government policy under the Fourth Republic (1946–58) and were confined to the opposition during the first twenty-three years of the Fifth Republic (1958–81). Yet during this period of uninterrupted conservative rule, French social spending grew rapidly, attaining a level roughly comparable to that of neighboring countries with more influential left parties and trade unions (Figure 7.1). What is more, French spending significantly exceeded that of Italy (25.1% of GDP versus 19.8%), the one neighboring nation in which the left was similarly marginalized.

In many countries, high-spending welfare states have been constructed by Christian Democratic parties of the center-right, as opposed to Social Democratic parties of the left (Huber, Ragin, and Stephens 1993; Wilensky 1981). In France, however, the Christian Democratic Mouvement Républicain Populaire (MRP) tended to resist the expansion of the

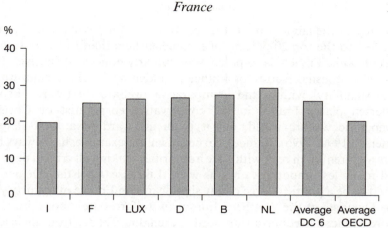

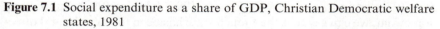

Figure 7.1 Social expenditure as a share of GDP, Christian Democratic welfare states, 1981
Source: OECD, *Social Expenditure Database 1980–1996* (Paris: OECD, 1999); own calculations.

welfare state. What is more, Christian Democracy essentially disappeared from the political scene under the Fifth Republic, when the MRP was supplanted by the Gaullist movement. Thus, the French welfare state was constructed not only in the absence of significant labor 'power resources', but also in the absence of a German-style, social-market-oriented Christian Democratic party.

A second unusual feature of the 'golden age' French welfare state was its limited impact on income inequality. Scholars of the Christian Democratic welfare regime observe that this system tends to be 'transfer-heavy' and 'status-preserving', as opposed to redistributive (Esping-Andersen 1990, 1996; Huber, Ragin, and Stephens 1993; Kersbergen 1995). Still, even when compared to other conservative Continental welfare states, France appeared as an outlier. A high-profile OECD study of income distribution in the early 1970s showed France to have the greatest level of income inequality of any member country, including the United States (Sawyer 1976).[1] Nor could the outcome be attributed solely to the

---

[1] The OECD study has been criticized on methodological grounds. Data from the Luxembourg Income Studies (LIS) paint a slightly less gloomy picture (Atkinson, Rainwater, and Smeeding 1985). France's income distribution still ranks among the most unequal in the OECD, but is roughly comparable to levels prevailing in Italy, Switzerland, Ireland, and the United States. The LIS data also cover a more recent period, 1980 instead of 1970, so that some of the improvement in the French performance may be due to shifts in French policy during the 1970s. I wish to thank John Stephens for drawing my attention to the LIS data and to the limits of the OECD study.

workings of the labor market. France stood out for paying more in social transfers to the top 20 percent of income earners than to the bottom 20 percent, while French fiscal policy was similarly non-redistributive.

A third unusual feature of France's 'golden age' welfare state was its unclassifiability within the comparative welfare literature. Esping-Andersen places France in the conservative corporatist or Christian Democratic welfare world, but it is an awkward fit at best (Esping-Andersen 1990, 1996). France's corporatism, for example, has always been more apparent than real, with state authorities making all critical decisions (and many less important ones as well). Likewise, Christian Democracy ceased to be a political force of any significance in France over thirty years ago. Theorists of the 'southern European welfare state', more prudently, ignore France's Mediterranean border, excluding France from their ideal-type (Castles and Ferrera 1996; Ferrera 1996; Rhodes 1997). Simplifying somewhat, we can say that the French state has been too activist and directive to fall within northern European models and too insulated and pro-fessionalized to belong to the southern European model. The French case is also problematic for the so-called 'Bismarck–Beveridge' typology (Bonoli 1997; Intignano 1993; Join-Lambert et al. 1997). As Table 7.1 sum-marizes, the French system combines elements of Bismarck and Beveridge, of categorical privilege and the universal rights of citizenship.

Shifting from a static perspective to a dynamic perspective, from a snap-shot to a movie, we uncover a fourth unusual feature of the French welfare state—its fundamental instability. Not only is the overall character of the regime unclear, but basic elements have changed over time. Such instabil-ity can be observed across all of the major dimensions of social policy, including labor market regulation, family allowances, pensions, health insurance, and welfare financing.

In the area of labor market regulation, prior to the late 1960s, French authorities pursued a low-wage, labor-exclusionary development strategy, making little effort to promote collective bargaining or, for that matter, to enforce statutory guarantees of the right to unionize. In the 1970s, by con-trast, state authorities placed considerable upward pressure on wages through sharp increases in the minimum wage and the use of the so-called 'extension' procedure to generalize wage hikes from the lead sector to the rest of the economy. The government also mandated that economically motivated layoffs of ten or more workers receive the approval of a state labor inspector. Since the mid-1980s, these restrictions on layoffs have been lifted; indeed, the government has facilitated labor shedding through extensive early retirement programs. Restrictions on part-time and tem-porary employment have also been eased, as has the use of the extension procedure and the minimum wage to boost worker purchasing power.

Table 7.1 *The French welfare mix: A combination of Bismarckian and Beveridgean features*

	Bismarck	Beveridge
Objective	Income maintenance – Unemployment benefits – Contributory pensions	Prevention of poverty – Minimum income (RMI) – Minimum social pension – Means-tested family allowances
Eligibility	Contribution record – Unemployment benefits – Contributory pensions	Citizenship – Basic family allowances – Anti-poverty programs
Coverage	Employees – Supplementary health insurance	Entire population – Basic health insurance

Financing	Contributions
	– Wage-based social security
	  charges
		Taxation
		– Taxes on all sources of
		  earnings, wages, property,
		  equity, etc. (CSG, RGDS)

Program management	Corporatist
	– Self-governing structure of
	  basic social security funds:
	  health, family allowances,
	  pensions
	– Ostensibly paritary programs
	  (unions and employers, no state):
	  unemployment insurance
	  (UNEDIC), supplementary
	  pensions (AGIRC, ARCCO)
		Statist
		– De facto state control of
		  program parameters: eligibility,
		  contribution and benefit rates,
		  retirement age, etc.
		– Government nomination of
		  general directors of social
		  security funds
		– Global budgeting in health care

France's family allowance program has likewise experienced sweeping changes. One change has been relative decline. Whereas family allowances constituted more than 30 percent of social spending as recently as 1960, today the figure is less than 15 percent. Another important change concerns the vocation of family allowances. In the French parlance, family policy has been redirected from 'horizontal redistribution' between childless workers and families with children toward 'vertical redistribution' between the wealthy and the poor (Join-Lambert et al. 1997; Lenoir 1990). The original natalist objective of boosting procreation and keeping women at home has given way to a more social orientation, emphasizing poverty prevention. Correspondingly, the share of benefits subject to means-testing has surged from 12 percent in 1970 to over 60 percent today (Commaille 1998: 21).

French pension policy has been in flux since its inception. The architects of France's social security system intended to provide a basic, Beveridge-style, universal pension to all citizens. In the face of violent protests and dissension within the government's ranks, however, the founding legislation was never implemented. Instead, prewar inequalities were restored and amplified, with separate systems created for blue-collars workers, white-collar workers, independent professionals, farmers, artisans, civil servants, coal miners, students, performing artists, and the list goes on. Furthermore, what was expected to constitute a meager, residual safety net, of limited cost to the national collectivity, soon became France's most expensive social program. Over the postwar period, the basic pension system has been partially 'unified', as certain social categories (generally, those in declining demographic pools) have adhered to the national system. Against this trend, however, liberal professional groups established an independent, second-tier pension system (the Association Générale des Institutions de Retraites des Cadres, AGIRC). Additional fragmentation has arisen as a result of a growing cleavage between workers in the public and private sectors. Not only do civil servants enjoy favorable pension terms—a variety of so-called *régimes spéciaux*, allowing for earlier retirement (in many cases, at age 50) and employing a more generous method of benefit calculations—but they have been spared recent austerity measures imposed on the private sector.

French health insurance has also been marked by instability. Liberation-era reformers intended for health insurance to cover 80 percent of medical treatment costs, with patients shouldering the remaining 20 percent. The French medical profession was able to block the imposition of binding fee schedules, however. As a result, on the eve of the Fifth Republic, de facto reimbursement rates were less than 50 percent of costs, placing non-emergency medical treatment beyond the reach of ordinary French citizens. During the 1960s, Gaullist authorities cajoled the medical profession into accepting binding fees, and for a decade or so, health care became more or less universally accessible. Since the late 1970s, however, a combination of government austerity measures and rapid health care inflation has generated new gaps in coverage. Social Security reimbursement rates remain high for hospitalization (90%), but have plummeted to 57 percent for ambulatory care and 58 percent for prescriptions, leading to problems of access (Huteau and Le Bont 1997: 140).

The financing of the French welfare state, like its expenditures, has shifted over time. In the early 1970s, as described above, French taxation was among the least redistributive in the OECD. Since then, however, the left has introduced two sets of reforms to enhance progressivity. During the 1980s, the government lifted caps on contributions for a number of social programs (widows' pensions, workplace accident insurance, health insurance, etc.). As a result, high-wage workers are no longer exempted from payroll taxes on the top portion of their earnings. Having shifted some of the fiscal burden from low-wage to high-wage workers in the 1980s, the left began shifting the burden from wages to other sources of income in the 1990s. A new tax was created in 1991, the *contribution sociale généralisée* (CSG), which is levied on all sources of earnings, including earnings from property and capital, as well as wages. The CSG has grown from 1.1 percent of earnings when it was established to 7.5 percent of earnings today, permitting corresponding reductions in more regressive payroll taxes. The latter have declined to less than 37 percent of government revenues, as opposed to 44 percent in 1990.

In many respects, the French welfare state is a social scientist's worst nightmare. It has been constructed in the absence of what are supposed to be fundamental preconditions: a strong labor movement, a hegemonic left, or at least a powerful Christian Democratic party. It does not engage in much redistribution (at least not toward the poor), even by the much-diminished expectations of recent welfare scholarship. It refuses to fit itself into any of the various ingenious analytical typologies devised by welfare comparativists. And like a hyperactive child, it will not sit still long enough for scholars to paint a clear portrait.

For all its peculiarities, the French welfare state does not lay beyond the pale of social science theory. Rather, what is needed is a proper specification of the factors that have structured its contours and evolution. Following the approach of the other country chapters in this volume, this essay places considerable emphasis on the role of the postwar economic growth model. Here, France is clearly an outlier. Alone among West European nations, France pursued a growth strategy centered on the voluntarist initiatives of a *dirigiste* state. Because France's postwar growth strategy was unique in Western Europe, we should not be surprised to find that its postwar welfare model was distinctive as well.

The second explanatory factor emphasized in this essay is the character of French politics. Once again, France appears as an outlier. In the postwar period, France has experienced not one, but two constitutional regimes. The movement from the Fourth Republic to the Fifth Republic in 1958 produced a fundamental shift in French governance, which carried over to welfare policy. The French party system was also changed beyond recognition, particularly among the parties of the right that would rule France during the first twenty-three years of the Fifth Republic. In the early 1960s, the newly established Gaullist movement supplanted the previously dominant conservative and Christian Democratic parties. Searching across the postwar European landscape, only Italy in the 1990s offers a comparable case of institutional and party transformation. As we will see, the unusual character of French politics, like the unusual character of its economics, has imparted a distinctive trajectory to French welfare state development.

7.2. Economic and Social Policy during the 'Golden Age' (1945–1968)

France's 'golden age' growth model was loosely coupled with its welfare system. *Dirigiste* or state-led modernization revolved around two sets of strategies–a strategy toward business and a strategy toward labor. Simplifying somewhat, we can say that welfare policy was largely tangential to the first strategy, to state efforts to structure the behavior of business, and that it was antithetical to the second strategy, to state efforts to shift resources from consumption to investment. Let us consider each of these strategies in turn.

France's *dirigiste* model was conceived as a way of creating a modern capitalist economy in the absence of a modern capitalist class (Bloch-Lainé and Bouvier 1986; Hoffmann 1963; Kuisel 1981; Zysman 1983). The French bourgeoisie had been sullied by its wartime collaboration with the Nazi occupiers, but also by its prewar economic behavior. The 'Malthusianism' of French employers, their preference for stability over growth and aversion to risk-taking, was widely blamed for having left France ill-equipped to face the Nazi war machine. In the postwar period, therefore, a directive, interventionist state would take the economy where timorous employers feared to tread.

State efforts to steer the strategies of business were backed by an arsenal of resources, starting with personnel. Following selection through rigorous, meritocratic exams, France's best and brightest students were trained in the *grandes écoles* (notably the École Polytechnique and the newly established École Nationale d'Administration or ENA), then 'parachuted' into key positions within the French state (Birnbaum 1977, 1978; Suleiman 1974, 1978). During the initial postwar period, state technocrats intervened primarily through the celebrated planning process, which channeled resources and guidance to priority heavy industrial sectors, like coal, steel, and electricity (Bauchet 1986; S. Cohen 1977; Hall 1986; Massé 1965; Rousso 1986; Shonfield 1965). In the 1960s and 1970s, planning was relayed by the so-called *grands projets*—a combination of subsidies, captive markets, and the transfer of technologies developed in public research labs, which catapulted French industry to positions of global leadership in such sectors as nuclear power, high-speed trains, and digital telephone switches (E. Cohen 1992; Cohen and Bauer 1985). Both the planning process and the *grands projets* were facilitated by the existence of a large public sector, a legacy of Liberation-era nationalizations, which was then expanded by the Mitterrand government in 1982.

The reach of French technocrats extended well beyond the public sector, however. Authorities mobilized a panoply of selective incentives to shape the behavior of private actors: protection from foreign competition, exemption from price controls, and subsidized credit. State officials not only 'chose winners' in the private sector; they often created these so-called 'national champions' in the first place through state-sponsored mergers and takeovers. Such intervention had a profound impact on the structure of French industry. Whereas France's 100 largest firms accounted for 20 percent of the nation's industrial output in 1950, by the mid-1970s, the proportion had increased to 50 percent (Cahiers Français 1992: 76).

Alongside the various mechanisms for steering business decisions, *dirigiste* policymaking arbitrated between capital and labor. From the perspective of the planners, wages and welfare spending were to be contained, lest they drain resources from industrial investment. Social spending was held in check for many years, increasing by only 2 percent of GDP between 1950 and 1960 (Cameron 1991). Industrial relations policy also operated in favor of business. Government authorities deployed a variety of techniques to hold down wages: turning a blind eye to systematic employer violations of the right to unionize; importing immigrant workers from former French colonies to preserve slack in the labor market; and neutralizing nominal wage increases by accommodating rapid inflation and by undertaking periodic 'aggressive' devaluations of the franc designed not only to restore competitiveness in international markets, but to confer a temporary price advantage on French producers (Hall 1986).

The 'golden age' welfare state was fashioned by more than the imperatives of *dirigiste* accumulation. It was also the product of political calculations. Indeed, France's welfare regime is perhaps best understood as a sedimentation of different welfare agendas, with successive layers imposed and blended in response to shifts in the political context. Struggles between left and right, a fundamental transformation of the identity of the French right, and the movement from the Fourth Republic to the Fifth Republic all left their mark.

At its origin in 1945, the French welfare state was conceived in Beveridgean terms. The founder of the French social security system, Pierre Laroque (often referred to as the 'French Beveridge'), lived in London for much of the war and brought back a blueprint for a universal welfare state, encompassing all citizens, and united in a single administrative agency (Laroque 1985a, 1985b, 1993). Laroque's plan was supported by the Liberation-era coalition encompassing de Gaulle, the Communist

Party, the Socialist Party, and (more reluctantly) the Christian Democratic MRP. Together, they enacted the basic framework of the French social security system in 1945—but they did not stay together long.

In 1946, de Gaulle quit the government, criticizing the excessive influence of self-serving political parties. The following year, policy and Cold War divergences led to the ouster of the Communist Party. As a result, for the duration of the Fourth Republic (1946–58), the center of gravity for most governments would be the Christian Democratic MRP. The Beveridgean aspirations of the 1945 Ordinance soon gave way to fragmentation and corporatization, as a combination of MRP resistance and protests and non-compliance by non-salaried groups (shopkeepers, independent professionals, peasants) blocked the unification of the social security system (Dupeyroux 1969; Gallant 1955). Christian Democratic influence also shaped the composition of social spending: as late as 1960, 30 percent of the social security budget went to family policy, designed to keep mothers at home with their (many) children. Thus, the Fourth Republic gave France a fragmented, Catholic welfare state much in the image of Esping-Andersen's Germanic welfare world.

The evolution of French welfare policy did not end with the Fourth Republic, however. De Gaulle's return to power in 1958 and the creation of the Fifth Republic introduced two critical changes. First, in contrast to the weak and unstable Fourth Republic, which experienced twenty-five governments in twelve years, the institutions of the Fifth Republic allowed for stable, strategic governance. As Ellen Immergut demonstrates, the decline in the number of 'veto points' in the French system allowed the government to push through controversial reforms, notably state regulation of medical fees and the introduction of full-time salaried practice for hospital physicians (Immergut 1992).

The second change in the wake of de Gaulle's return is that the dominant party of the right was no longer the Christian Democrats, who were essentially wiped off the electoral map, but rather the Gaullists. The Gaullist vision combined elements of Jacobinism, republicanism, nationalism, and *dirigisme*. De Gaulle saw the state as the agent of modernization and the general will, overriding parochial, self-serving traditional elites in order to restore France to greatness. An enlightened, interventionist state was essential to economic and geopolitical recovery. It was also essential for transcending class conflict: the French working class would be wooed away from leftist politics and political unionism by a more elaborate and better financed welfare system as well as expanded opportunities for upward social mobility.

The Gaullist era added a statist layer to the Beveridgean and Christian Democratic encrustations. The rate of growth of welfare spending (measured as a share of GDP) increased by 70 percent under de Gaulle, as compared to the Fourth Republic (Cameron 1991). Gaullist initiatives were particularly significant in the areas of health care and unemployment insurance. Gaullism also reshaped the administration of social security, reducing the number of insurance funds and tightening state controls.

Taken together, the logic of *dirigisme* and the character of French politics help to explain the peculiar features of the 'golden age' welfare regime described in Section 7.1. The French welfare state spent heavily, despite the hegemony of the right, because the basic social security system had been put into place prior to the breakdown of left unity in 1947 and because the Gaullist right, unlike the Christian Democratic right, expanded these protections as part of its vision of economic and social modernization. The French welfare state was non-redistributive or even regressive because the Christian Democrats were able to entrench status differentials and because their Gaullist successors believed in equality of opportunity or citizenship, as opposed to equality of outcome. Furthermore, to the extent that conservative leaders were interested in redistribution, under the logic of *dirigisme*, such redistribution operated from consumption to investment, rather than from high-income groups to low-income groups. The French welfare state was heterogeneous and unstable because it was transformed on at least three occasions by fundamental shifts in the political and institutional context. It was marked, as Esping-Andersen notes, by conservative Catholicism, but also by Beveridgean universalism and by Gaullism. Finally, the French welfare state was decoupled from the French growth model because *dirigiste* policymaking was erected upon worker exclusion, not incorporation. Although social spending was expanded for various political reasons, such extensions had little to do with the growth strategy. Put another way, France may have had welfare spending, but it did not have 'welfare capitalism'.

7.3. Pressures from Without, Erosion from Within: The Breakdown of *Dirigisme*

Beginning in the late 1960s, France's *dirigiste* model confronted a less hospitable political and social environment (Levy 1999*a*). Two developments, in particular, undermined the *dirigiste* system: the near-revolution of May 1968 and the emergence in the 1970s of a powerful Socialist–Communist alliance, the 'Union of the Left'. Although France's break with *dirigisme* was ultimately precipitated by international pressures, the stage for the 1983 U-turn was set by the growing domestically driven dysfunctions of the 1970s and early 1980s.

The events of May 1968 sent a shock wave throughout the French political establishment. General de Gaulle, who had dominated French politics
for a decade, was no longer the unquestioned leader. Indeed, one year
later, de Gaulle resigned from office when a referendum designed to re-
legitimate his rule failed to secure a majority. May 1968 not only broke de
Gaulle's hegemony; it also broke the labor-exclusionary premise of the
dirigiste model. On the heels of 1968, the marginalization of the French
working class would give way to attempts at incorporation. Furthermore,
in a country with a relatively new and contested constitution and a long
tradition of revolutionary politics, the unrest of 1968 left deep psychological scars. Henceforth, French leaders would become extraordinarily
conflict-averse, often backing down at the first sign of street resistance—
whether from shopkeepers, farmers, or workers.

The emergence of a powerful Socialist–Communist alliance in the
1970s, the 'Union of the Left', posed a further challenge to *dirigiste* policymaking. With the left no longer divided, governments of the right found
themselves under constant electoral threat. In 1974 the center-right candidate for President, Valéry Giscard d'Estaing, outpolled his Socialist rival,
François Mitterrand, by a mere 50.8 percent to 49.2 percent. The left
swept nationwide municipal elections in 1977 and was widely expected to
triumph in the 1978 parliamentary elections. Although Giscard weathered
this challenge, his popularity quickly began to sink, and he would be
ousted by Mitterrand in the 1981 presidential election.

The period from 1968 to 1983 brought an attenuation or even reversal
of the traditional pro-business orientation of French policy (Adam,
Reynaud, and Verdier 1972; Howell 1992*b*; Lipietz 1984). Workers benefited from rapid increases in the minimum wage and the use of the so-
called 'extension procedure' to make settlements reached in labor
strongholds legally binding throughout the economy. Labor registered
additional gains through national agreements (*conventions*) that were formally negotiated by the social partners, but in fact largely drafted and
imposed by the government. Two such *conventions* were especially significant: the one providing unemployment benefits equal to 90 percent of previous wages for up to one year; the other requiring the approval by a
Ministry of Labor inspector of layoffs conducted for economic reasons
(the administrative authorization for layoffs). The 1970s were also a time
of vigorous growth in social spending, particularly under the Giscard
presidency. Between 1974 and 1981, social transfers surged from 19.4 percent of GDP to 25.3 percent (Palier 1999: 255). The rate of increase relative to GDP under Giscard was more than one-and-one-half times that of
the de Gaulle presidency and two-and-one-half times that of the Fourth
Republic (Cameron 1991). Thanks to these and other changes, labor's

share of value added expanded from 61 percent in 1967 to 69 percent in 1981 (INSEE 1998: 65).

The contested political environment of the 1970s affected not only social policy, but also the operation of *dirigiste* economic policy. More accurately, political pressures diverted *dirigisme* from its postwar modernizing mission (Berger 1981; E. Cohen 1989). Anxious conservative leaders had no stomach for painful, if much-needed, rationalization of declining or uncompetitive enterprises. Indeed, their initiatives often ran in the opposite direction. While embracing a rhetoric of liberalization and market-driven adjustment, the Giscard administration nationalized the bankrupt French steel industry and created a special agency, the Comité interministériel de l'aménagement des structures industrielles (CIASI), to bail out companies in difficulty. In 1978 a government-commissioned report revealed that fewer than one dozen firms, most of them uncompetitive and many in declining sectors, were receiving more than 75 percent of all public aid to industry (Cahiers Français 1983: 16). Worse still, these resources tended to be used, not to undertake much-needed restructuring and positioning in viable market niches, but to delay layoffs and adjustment.

Giscard's rather timid brand of liberalism yielded dismal results— aggravated, of course, by the effects of the OPEC oil shocks. Unemployment nearly tripled during his presidency, from 2.4 percent in 1974 to 7.3 percent in 1981 (*Le Monde* 1981), while corporate profitability dropped from 15–16 percent of value added in the early 1970s to 9.3 percent in 1981 (Faugère and Voisin 1994: 32). When Giscard confronted Mitterrand again at the polls in 1981, the economy was growing at an anemic 1.5 percent rate, inflation exceeded 13 percent, and the trade deficit topped 50 billion francs (*Le Monde* 1981).[2] Mitterrand hammered the incumbent for being too liberal, too market-oriented. The way to restore growth, competitiveness, and employment, the left argued, was by running a 'real industrial policy'. Campaigning on a pledge to take *dirigiste* intervention to new heights, Mitterrand and his allies swept to victory.

The initial years of the Mitterrand administration marked the revival of *dirigiste* policymaking on a grand scale. The left enacted a sweeping program of nationalizations, covering twelve leading industrial conglomerates and some 38 banks. When combined with the Liberation-era nationalizations carried out by General de Gaulle, this latest program, costing 47 bn francs, placed thirteen of France's twenty largest firms and virtually the entire banking sector in state hands (Stoffaës 1984). Public enterprises would also receive over 60 bn francs in subsidies between 1982 and 1986 (Hall 1990: 177).

---

[2] One US dollar equals approximately six French francs.

The left's industrial policy objectives were more than a match for these resources. President Mitterrand captured the voluntarist spirit of his new administration with the oft-repeated declaration: 'There are no condemned sectors; there are only excessively old factories and equipment' (Cahiers Français 1983: 26). Sectoral plans to 'reconquer domestic markets' were announced in all manner of troubled French industries, including coal, steel, chemicals, textiles, machine tools, furniture, leather goods, and toys. Such voluntarism was by no means confined to traditional or declining sectors. In the electronics industry, the government's five-year 'Programme d'Action Filière Électronique' pledged to mobilize some 140 bn francs (55 bn from the government), create 80,000 jobs, boost the annual rate of growth of production from 3 percent to 9 percent, and transform a 19 bn franc balance of payments deficit into a 14 bn franc surplus (Barreau and Mouline 1987: 169–70).

The limits of the Socialist strategy were felt first, not in microeconomic policy, but in macroeconomic management. Gambling on a US-led global recovery beginning in 1982, the government had sought to launch France upon a fast-growth track by priming the pump. The minimum wage was increased by 15 percent in real terms and social transfers (pensions, family allowances, etc.) by over 12 percent (Hall 1986: 194). This policy of 'redistributive Keynesianism' held the further advantage of rewarding working-class constituents. Instead of recovery, however, 1982 brought the worst recession since the war. What is more, while French authorities were priming the pump, France's trading partners were slamming on the brakes in order to combat inflation. The predictable result was a surge in France's budget and trade deficits—the former rose from 0.4 percent of GDP in 1981 to 3.0 percent in 1982 and the latter from 56 bn francs to 93 bn francs (Hall 1986: 198)—bringing pressure on the franc.

For much of 1982 and 1983, President Mitterrand and his inner circle agonized over how to respond to the growing macroeconomic crisis (Bauchard 1986; Cameron 1996; Favier and Martin-Roland 1996; Hall 1986). Mitterrand's advisers were divided into two basic camps. One side advocated a fortress France strategy, encompassing withdrawal from the European Monetary System (EMS), a sharp devaluation of the franc, and tightened exchange and trade controls. The other side favored European solidarity, backed by a severe austerity program to eradicate inflation once and for all and stabilize the franc's position within the EMS.

Mitterrand chose the path of austerity for a variety of reasons. A loyal Europeanist, he balked at pulling France out of the EMS. Advisers also feared that a sharp depreciation of the franc, by raising the price of imports, notably oil, would feed back into domestic inflation. Perhaps of greatest importance, although technically a macroeconomic policy decision, Mitterrand's choice reflected a disenchantment with the microeconomic dimensions of Socialist policy. Those favoring withdrawal from the EMS argued that a relaxation of international constraints would provide the breathing room needed for *dirigiste* measures to work effectively. Once French industry had been restructured, recapitalized, and revived, France could rejoin the international community on a stronger footing. Such a strategy was predicated upon the assumption that *dirigiste* measures were improving the competitive position of French industry.

It was becoming increasingly evident that Socialist *dirigisme* was not producing the desired results, however. French firms were falling well short of the ambitious targets enshrined in the various sectoral plans. Even the newly nationalized enterprises, the linchpin (*fer de lance*) of the left's strategy, could not meet their investment targets. In 1982 and 1983 vast capital grants to these companies were offset by equally large losses (Stoffaës 1985: 159). As a result, their investment levels increased not by 50 percent, as planned, but by a mere 5 percent. Disappointing as this result might have been, it was a far better performance than that of the private sector, where investment decreased every year from 1981 to 1984 (*Le Monde* 1989).

Like Giscard, the left found it difficult to shift resources from traditional to emerging sectors. Given its claim that there were no declining sectors, only outmoded technologies, the government was obliged to attempt to turn around lame ducks. Supporting industries like shipbuilding or coal deprived the authorities of resources needed for more promising sectors, however. The electronics industry, for example, received less than one-third the public aid pledged under the '*filière électronique*' program (Le Bolloc'h-Puges 1991: 203–7).

Finally, Mitterrand—like Giscard before him—proved unable to resist pressures to protect jobs at all costs. Indeed, having pledged that *dirigiste* policies would enable industry to create jobs, rather than eliminating them, Mitterrand was trapped by his own campaign rhetoric. Furthermore, job cuts would strike at the core of the left's electorate—unskilled and semi-skilled blue-collar workers in heavy industry. The government, therefore, opted to buy social peace. But this strategy yielded increasingly untenable economic outcomes. By 1983 a number of firms were so heavily subsidized that it would have been far cheaper for the government to pay workers not to produce. In shipbuilding, for example, it was estimated that each job paying 100,000 francs in annual wages cost the government 150,000 to 450,000 francs in subsidies (E. Cohen 1989: 230–31). Taken together, these many dysfunctions raised the question of whether *dirigisme* was worth defending.

The left's break with *dirigisme* is commonly attributed to international and especially European pressures (Hall 1990; Loriaux 1991). The pressures of the European Monetary System could have been escaped in 1983, however, by allowing the currency to float, just as Giscard had done during the 1970s (twice) and a number of other countries—including Italy, Britain, Spain, Portugal, and Sweden—would do in the 1990s. Mitterrand was not compelled to remain within the EMS; he chose to do so, and this choice cannot be explained without reference to the growing dysfunctions of *dirigisme*. The same holds true of the extent of change following the 1983 U-turn. The left and its successors did not confine themselves to the kinds of austerity measures necessary for the defense of the franc and membership in good standing in the EMS. They did not simply tighten fiscal and monetary policy. Rather, as described in the next section, successive governments launched an across-the-board assault on the *dirigiste* model, with reforms extending to policies and practices that had little or no bearing on the value of the franc. Thus, if international pressures crystallized the debate over *dirigisme*, the outcome of that debate was determined by domestic pressures that had transformed *dirigisme* over the years from an agent of modernization into a hostage to the status quo.

7.4. Welfare Policy as an Instrument of Economic Policy: The Dismantling of *Dirigisme* (1983–1993)

The 1983 U-turn touched off a range of reforms that struck at the core of the *dirigiste* model. These changes, inaugurated cautiously by the Socialists from 1983 to 1986, were amplified when the right returned to power under a neo-liberal banner from 1986 to 1988, and confirmed and completed by subsequent governments on both sides of the political spectrum. Four sets of changes have figured most prominently.

The first change concerned macroeconomic policy. French authorities accepted the logic of the EMS with a vengeance. Under the so-called *franc fort* policy, the French franc was informally anchored to the Deutschmark. Since devaluations were no longer an option (let alone 'aggressive' devaluations), France would gain the edge through 'competitive disinflation', that is, by running a rate of inflation lower than that of its trading partners. Toward this end, redistributive Keynesianism gave way to austerity budgets, wage indexation was abandoned, and most important, monetary policy was tightened, with real interest rates ranging from 5 percent to 8 percent for over a decade (Fitoussi 1995). These measures reduced French inflation from 9.6 percent in 1983 to 2.7 percent in 1986, but at the price of several years of growth below 2 percent and an increase in unemployment from 8.3 percent to 10.4 percent (OECD 1992). Since the early 1990s, the French inflation rate has been among the lowest in Western Europe, while the balance of trade, after nearly twenty years in the red, has registered steady surpluses.

The second set of reforms pertained to France's public enterprises. In 1983 the Minister of Industry released the nationalized companies from their planning targets, instructing them to focus instead on profitability. While slashing capital grants and subsidies, the Ministry offered no resistance when public enterprises closed factories and withdrew from businesses formerly deemed strategic. This shift in public sector management set the stage for the right to launch a campaign of privatizations upon its return to power in 1986.[3] Before the privatization process was interrupted by the 1987 stock market crash, thirteen financial and industrial groups had been sold off, netting 84.1 bn francs to the French treasury (Zerah 1993: 183). Since 1993, a second round of privatizations has been conducted by governments of both the right and the left, reducing the once-vast holdings of the French state to little more than energy production, public transportation, and some weapons manufactures.

The third major policy shift was the abandonment of state efforts to steer private industry. The guiding spirit of this change was that firms would receive less government assistance, but would be subject to fewer restrictions, so that they could raise the necessary resources by their own means. The budgets for CIASI-sponsored bail-outs, industrial policy programs, and loan subsidies quickly dried up, triggering a wave of bankruptcies. As a counterpoint, however, French business gained a number of new freedoms. The deregulation of financial markets, initiated in 1985, enabled firms to raise funds by issuing equity, reducing their dependence on state-allocated credit. The removal of price controls in 1986 allowed companies to reap the full benefits of successful competitive strategies. The elimination of capital controls in the late 1980s facilitated the expansion of production abroad and gave managers an 'exit' option if domestic conditions were not to their liking. Taken together, these and other reforms helped boost corporate profitability from 9.8 percent of value added in 1982 to 17.3 percent in 1989 (Faugère and Voisin 1994: 32).

The revival of corporate profits was also fueled by a fourth set of developments, the reform of France's system of industrial relations (Groux and Mouriaux 1990; Howell 1992*a*, 1992*b*; Labbé and Croisat 1992). State authorities lifted a number of restrictions limiting managerial prerogatives,

[3] In the time-honored French tradition, the government tried to insulate the privatized companies from hostile takeovers and demanding stockholders (i.e. from the sanction of the marketplace) by creating a system of interlocking directorates (Bauer 1988; Schmidt 1996). This method of privatization held the further advantage of allowing the right to give its allies in the business community control over the heart of French industry and finance at low cost. The system of interlocking directorates proved fragile, however, and broke apart in the 1990s (Levy 1999*a*).

most significantly, the administrative authorization for layoffs. The left's expectation was that rigid, centralized statutes limiting working hours and part-time and temporary employment would be replaced by firm-level agreements better suited to the needs of workers and managers in each enterprise. A 1982 initiative, the Auroux laws, had expanded opportunities for plant-level bargaining. French unions were in no position to exploit these opportunities, however. Battered by the recession and high unemployment, organized labor lost half its membership during the 1980s, and the French unionization rate dropped below 10 percent of the workforce (5% in the private sector), the lowest figure in the OECD.

With the unions in free fall, French employers were able to use plant-level bargaining to impose flexibility on their own terms. Studies of initial firm-level deals revealed that most accorded no compensation to employees in return for acceptance of greater flexibility and that up to one-third of these agreements actually violated French labor law. Not surprisingly, much of capital's gain in the post-1983 period would come at labor's expense. From 1982 to 1989, the share of value added received by capital increased from 24.0 percent to 31.7 percent, surpassing the levels of the early 1970s (Faugère and Voisin 1994: 28–29).

Welfare policy played a critical role in France's move away from *dirigisme*. In a logic first articulated by Karl Polanyi, the extension of market forces was softened, made politically acceptable through the expansion of social protections for those most affected by liberalization (Polanyi 1944). On the one hand, beginning in 1983, state authorities made a market, imposing liberalization from above. Austerity, privatization, deregulation, and labor market flexibility all heightened the vulnerability of French workers. On the other hand, successive governments, especially those on the left, expanded the welfare state in number of ways, so as to cushion the blow to the working class and, equally important, to undercut the possibilities for union mobilization (Daley 1996; Levy 1999). This compensatory strategy centered on two sets of policies.

The first compensatory strategy was the creation of some fifteen 'conversion poles' in geographic areas that were especially hard-hit by the industrial restructuring launched in 1983. The government made no effort to hide the link between industrial restructuring and strategies of territorial and worker compensation: the creation of the conversion poles was announced the same day as retrenchment plans in the coal, steel, and shipbuilding sectors. The conversion poles received sizeable subsidies to help clean up unsightly abandoned factories, retrain workers, modernize infrastructure, and support new technologies and emerging high-tech start-ups. From the perspective of displaced workers, the biggest advantage of the conversion pole program was the possibility of retiring on full pension as early as age 50 (as opposed to age 60 or 65 under normal conditions).

This points to a second dimension of the state's compensatory strategy—a huge expansion of the possibilities for early retirement, not just in the conversion poles, but in every troubled industrial agglomeration. The use of generous early retirement provisions to blunt resistance to industrial restructuring had begun under Giscard. From 1974 to 1980, the number of early retirees more than tripled from 59,000 to 190,400 (DARES 1996: 100). The Socialists would triple the figure again, with the number of early retirees rising to 705,500 in 1984; since then, it has ranged between 450,000 and 600,000 every year.[4] Not surprisingly, since 1974, France has experienced an unusually sharp drop in labor force participation rates. As Figure 7.2 reveals, the French participation rate for males between the ages of 55 and 64 is now well below that of such paragons of passive labor market policy as Germany and Italy. Even the Netherlands boasts a higher activity rate among this category of workers (43.1 percent versus 42.3 percent in 1996).

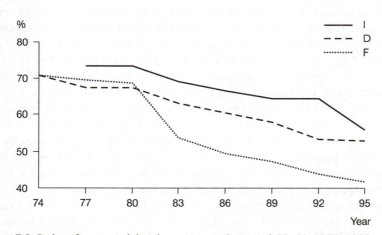

Figure 7.2 Labor force participation rates, males, aged 55–64, 1974–1995
Source: OECD, *Labour Force Statistics* (Paris: OECD, various issues).

[4] Official figures actually understate the number of early retirees because in 1982, the government lowered the minimum retirement age from 65 to 60. In other words, whereas in Giscard's final year in office, 190,400 workers between the ages of 55 and 64 took early retirement, in 1984, 705,500 workers below the age of 60 took early retirement, with retirees aged 60 to 64 no longer included in the early retirement figures (as they had been under Giscard).

Beyond salving the left's guilty conscience, the widespread recourse to early retirement served a more strategic purpose—demobilizing France's working class and undercutting trade union capacity to mount resistance to industrial restructuring. The vast majority of French workers were more than willing to quit smelly, physically taxing, alienating jobs, to receive 90 percent of their previous wages without having to report to work. In such a context, France's already anemic trade unions were completely incapable of mobilizing their members to fight industrial restructuring.

Welfare policy was deployed not only to facilitate the liberalization of economic policy, but also to palliate the perceived limits or failings of economic liberalization. This logic figured especially prominently when the left returned to power in 1988, following François Mitterrand's re-election as president (Daley 1990). Given that five years of austerity had barely dented France's sky-high rate of unemployment and that the problem of poverty and homelessness was reaching alarming proportions, the left felt compelled to take action. The new Socialist government headed by Michel Rocard launched two important initiatives.

The first initiative was the creation of a national social safety net, the *revenu minimum d'insertion* (RMI). The RMI replaced a patchwork of local and targeted social assistance programs that had left large segments of the population uncovered, notably the long-term unemployed and persons suffering from psychological problems, alcoholism, and/or chemical dependency. Benefits are available on a means-tested basis to all citizens and long-term residents over the age of 25. The RMI provides a monthly allowance of 2,500 francs along with the promise of support services to help 'insert' (the 'I' in 'RMI') recipients back into society and, in some cases, into a job.[5] Claimants are also eligible for housing allowances and free health insurance. Although the 'insertion' dimension of the RMI remains underdeveloped, the program does provide non-negligible financial assistance to some 1 million of France's neediest citizens.

The second initiative taken by the Rocard government was to expand active labor market policies, notably training programs, public internships, and subsidies for hard-to-place youths and the long-term unemployed. Once again, government intervention was deemed necessary to palliate the deficiencies of a liberalized labor market, a market that was failing to pro-

---

[5] While job placement is one of the objectives of the RMI, the program has no employment search requirement. For many recipients—older, unskilled workers or persons suffering from psychological problems, alcoholism, and/or chemical dependency— employment is a remote possibility, at best. In addition, the RMI has been criticized for creating poverty traps. A claimant who accepts a low-wage, part-time job can lose as much in benefits as s/he earns in wages. Even for a full-time, minimum-wage position, the effective tax rate is estimated to exceed 60% (Bourguignon and Bureau 1999).

duce sufficient jobs to prevent the spread of unemployment and social exclusion. The number of beneficiaries of government measures had already risen from 450,000 in 1984 to 850,000 in 1989, but it would more than double during the next five years, reaching 1,900,000 in 1994 (DARES 1996: 100). In the latter year, while France counted 3.1 million workers officially unemployed, another 2.5 million citizens benefited from some kind of labor market measure (early retirement, subsidized employ-ment, training programs, and public internships).

Thus, France's break with *dirigisme* in the 1980s provided a dual impe-tus to welfare state expansion. The promise of liberalization induced authorities to commit vast resources to the transition process, to the alle-viation of social pain and political resistance, in the expectation that a more flexible labor market would quickly generate enough jobs make such costly transitional measures unnecessary (or, at least, much less neces-sary). The disappointments of liberalization, the continuing high levels of unemployment not only made it impossible to wind down supposedly transitional early retirement measures, but drove new spending in the form of active labor market programs and a guaranteed minimum income. In short, 'de-*dirigisation*' and welfare state expansion were two sides of the same (very expensive) coin.

7.5. Beyond *Dirigisme*: Welfare Reform as the Core Issue of Economic Policy (1993–present)

In the 1990s, the French welfare state, like welfare states everywhere, has come under intense fiscal pressure. Although the instruments and practices associated with *dirigisme* have been largely dismantled, the French state is spending more than ever. In 1999, government taxation, at 45.3 percent of GDP, reached a postwar high, exceeding by several percentage points the figure in 1983, at the peak moment of Socialo-Communist voluntarism. The same held true of budget deficits, which attained 5 to 6 percent of GDP in the mid-1990s, double the 1983 level. Much of the blame lies with social spending, which surpassed 30 percent of GDP in 1995, while from 1991 to 1997, the French social security system ran a cumulative deficit of almost 300 bn francs (*Le Monde* 1999). Given that government expenditures and deficits continued to grow, even though French authorities were no longer pouring hundreds of billions of francs into voluntarist industrial projects, efforts to slow or reverse the trend—at least long enough to qualify for Maastricht—have tended to focus on the welfare state.

High unemployment has likewise placed pressure on the French welfare state. Despite the proliferation of early-retirement and make-work programs, the official unemployment rate has remained above 11 percent for almost a decade. France's minimum wage is fairly generous (6,900 francs or approximately $1,100 per month), and social security charges can add as much as 50 percent to the wage bill. Critics charge that this combination of high statutory wages and payroll taxes is pricing French workers out of the labor market. In order to generate low-skill, low-productivity jobs in sufficient number to bring down unemployment, France must loosen its social protections (Minc 1994).

French social policy is not made by economic pressures alone, however. In the 1990s, as in earlier periods, two other factors have figured prominently: the logic of *dirigisme* and the dynamics of domestic political competition. Although the *dirigiste* model has passed from the scene, it continues to cast a long shadow on French social policy. Three legacies of *dirigisme* have proven especially salient.

The first legacy is experiential. The experience of de-*dirigisation* has led many in France to feel that they have already been subjected to retrenchment—and have little to show for it. Since 1983, French citizens have reluctantly accepted a series of painful liberalizing measures. Each time, they were told that the reforms in question would relaunch growth and bring down unemployment: if French inflation were held below that of Germany or Italy, then French workers would get the jobs that were going to German and Italian workers; if the state spent less on uncompetitive firms, then fast-growing start-ups would arise to take their place; if wages gave way to profits, then investment and jobs would follow; if French employers were given the right to fire, then they would be more inclined to hire. The reforms were implemented one after the other, yet economic growth remains anemic, and unemployment is higher than ever. Given these disappointments, the idea that what is needed is another turn of the neo-liberal screw, welfare retrenchment on top of *dirigiste* retrenchment, does not elicit great popular enthusiasm. In a sense, rather than spilling over sequentially from economic policy to social policy, the bitter experience of de-*dirigisation* has stiffened resistance to further liberalizing measures.

The second legacy of *dirigisme* is aspirational. France's 'golden age' growth model was erected upon the premise that enlightened state intervention could better serve the nation's economic interests than the anarchic play of market forces. With the dismantling of *dirigiste* industrial policy, these aspirations for state direction and misgivings about the market have not necessarily disappeared from the scene. Rather, much of the rhetoric and imagery associated with *dirigiste* economic policy has been transferred to social policy. Although the French state is no longer called upon to promote industrial development, it is increasingly solicited to preserve 'social cohesion', combat 'social exclusion', and heal the 'social fracture'. As in the earlier *dirigiste* era, the perceived threat comes from a free-market jungle associated with US hegemony: instead of predatory American multinationals, the enemy is US-led 'globalization' and homogenizing 'Anglo-Saxon liberalism'. Seen from this perspective, the expansion of state intervention is not merely a social imperative, but a measure of France's capacity to preserve its sovereignty and identity in an increasingly integrated, interdependent world.

The third legacy of *dirigisme* is institutional. *Dirigiste* policymaking concentrated power in a 'strong', centralized state at the expense of societal and local associations that were deemed too self-serving and particularistic to be trusted. Such policymaking tended to reinforce the weakness and irresponsibility of France's intermediary institutions, since ultimately, all power rested with Paris. One consequence is that as state authorities grapple with reform in the 1990s, they often stand alone (Levy 1999*a*). Organized interests that were largely excluded from policymaking during the heroic age of welfare expansion are less than eager to jump aboard in the age of retrenchment. Even if one particular trade union or physician association is willing to cooperate, the fragmentation of interest groups means that five or six rival organizations immediately denounce the collaborator for 'selling out', and successful implementation of the reforms is anything but guaranteed. The relative isolation of policymakers has lent a peculiar character to French welfare reform: the plight of proposed changes is determined less by bargaining among political and corporatist elites than by unmediated exchanges between state and citizen, either through the ballot box or in the streets. In this state-centric context, the success or failure of social reforms hinges to a considerable extent on techniques of communication and legitimization, on the capacity of leaders to persuade the man in the street (quite literally) that the government's aims are both appropriate and just (Vail 1999).

Along with the weight of economy and *dirigiste* history, French social policy has been fashioned by the dynamics of political competition. In recent years, the welfare state has moved to the center stage of French politics. Both the 1995 presidential election and the 1997 legislative elections were waged explicitly over social policy. Although it has become fashionable to dismiss the effects of partisanship on social and economic policy, the behavior of French authorities in the 1990s suggests otherwise. Successive governments have gone to great lengths to define a welfare agenda that is both consistent with their ideology and distinct from the offerings of predecessors and rivals. As we will see, the evolution of the French welfare state, if pressured and in some ways constrained by the economic forces associated with 'globalization', has been driven primarily by the *dirigiste* policies of the past and the partisan politics of the present.

Since 1993, three different prime ministers have grappled with welfare reform: Édouard Balladur (1993–95), Alain Juppé (1995–97), and Lionel Jospin (1997–present). Simplifying somewhat, we can say that Balladur and Juppé, as Gaullists on the right of the political spectrum, have pursued roughly similar economic objectives, but have diverged sharply in their style of reform. The current prime minister, Lionel Jospin, a Socialist, has sought to articulate a distinct leftist approach to reform, one that differs in both style and especially substance from its Gaullist predecessors.

7.5.1. The Balladur Method: Welfare Reform Negotiated with the Streets

Édouard Balladur pursued a fairly conventional conservative economic agenda while serving as prime minister from 1993 to 1995. Balladur's chief goal was to balance the budget by reducing social spending. He did not wish to increase taxes, but if forced to do so, his preference ran toward taxing wage earners, rather than capital. In point of fact, during his two-year tenure, Balladur would both trim benefits and impose regressive tax hikes.

Shortly after taking office, Balladur introduced limited austerity measures into the health care system, reducing patient reimbursement rates and cutting the budget for public hospitals (Hassenteufel 1997). In the fall of 1993, he implemented probably the most significant retrenchment measure in France this decade, a reform of the private sector pension system. The changes made by Balladur reduced the generosity of pensions in three ways: shifting the calculation of the reference salary for private pensions from the average of the best 10 years of earnings to the average of the best 25 years; indexing pensions to prices instead of wages; and requiring employees to work for a minimum of 40 years before retiring, as opposed to 37.5 years previously (Join-Lambert et al. 1997). By confining these changes to the private sector, Balladur avoided the potentially explosive (and considerably more expensive) problem of public sector pensions. Still, the reform will generate considerable savings over time: twenty years down the line, private pension expenditures will be reduced by an estimated 33 percent (Palier 1999: 397).

Alongside benefit cuts in health care and private pensions, Balladur passed a variety of regressive tax increases. Consumption taxes were raised on gasoline and alcohol. Balladur also gave a regressive twist to a recent fiscal innovation of the left. In 1991, the Rocard government had created a new tax, the *contribution sociale généralisée* (CSG) which, in contrast to social security charges, is imposed on all earnings, including those of capital and property. The idea behind the CSG was to spread the costs of social policy more equitably across French society by taxing all sources of income and not simply wages. The establishment of the CSG had been accompanied by a reduction in other social security charges, making it revenue neutral. In 1993 Balladur increased the CSG from 1.1 percent of earnings to 2.4 percent as a straightforward revenue-raising measure. Worse, he made the additional 1.3 percent increment tax-deductible, transforming the CSG into a highly regressive tax. Deductibility meant that whereas a minimum-wage worker had to pay the full 1.3 percent increase in the CSG, a wage earner in the top income tax bracket (with a 56% tax rate) would pay only 44 percent of the increase.[6]

Balladur was also inclined toward regressive measures in the labor market. In early 1994, he attempted to create a so-called 'insertion wage' for youths. The 'insertion wage' was, in fact, a sub-minimum wage for youths. Under Balladur's proposal, employers would be allowed to pay young people 80 percent of the minimum wage, without any obligation to provide training and regardless of employee qualifications. This *SMIC-jeunes* (youth minimum wage),[7] as it was more accurately relabeled by critics, triggered massive protests among French youths, supported by their concerned parents. In response, Balladur withdrew his proposal.

Balladur's retreat from the *SMIC-jeunes* points to the principal novelty of his reform agenda—its strategy, as opposed to its substance. Balladur argued that French society was too traumatized by persistent high unemployment to tolerate scorched earth, confrontational, Thatcherite methods. While sharing Thatcher's belief that neo-liberal reform offered the only viable solution, that there was no 'third-way' alternative, Balladur maintained that in France, it was necessary to proceed gradually and cautiously. The 'Balladur method', as it was officially designated, was also part of Balladur's effort to position himself for the 1995 presidential campaign, to project a moderate reassuring image to the French electorate. Whereas Balladur's chief rival for the presidency, fellow Gaullist, Jacques Chirac, was impetuous and unpredictable, Balladur would be more careful. He believed in liberal economic principles, but he would not destabilize French society for the sake of a grand ideological vision.

In practice, the Balladur method encompassed a kind of direct negotiation between the state and the streets. On occasion, Balladur would attempt to give the appearance of conferring with concerned interests groups, meeting with them prior to the announcement of reforms and offering small, largely symbolic concessions. More often, though, Balladur did not even engage in symbolic consultation. Rather, he would

---

[6] One year later, Balladur repealed the tax break, but his conservative successor as prime minister, Alain Juppé repeated the maneuver in 1995, adding a 1%, tax-deductible increment to the CSG.

[7] SMIC stands for *Salaire Minimum Interprofessionnel de Croissance*, or Interprofessional Growth-Based Minimum Wage.

announce an initiative with no prior warning. The outcome of the initiative would then depend upon the level of popular protest. If the streets remained quiet following his announcement, Balladur would implement the reform. By contrast, if there were large-scale or violent protests, then Balladur would retract his initiative.

Although the Balladur method presented the singular advantage of allowing the prime minister to make a virtue of his defeats, to present them as a sign of his sensitivity and reasonableness, over time, these virtuous setbacks tended to multiply. The French people quickly learned how the Balladur method operated and were soon protesting—and blocking—his every initiative. The saga of the *SMIC-jeunes* became the rule, rather than the exception. French fishermen set fire to a prefecture to block a reduction in subsidies; employees of Air France compelled the government to repeal a proposed restructuring plan and to dismiss the CEO (who had been ordered by the government to implement the plan against his better judgment); and supporters of public schools forced Balladur to not only repeal proposed aid to private (mostly religious) schools, but to significantly increase spending on public schools.

Over time, what had seemed like an ingenious strategy for implementing sensitive reforms and allowing the prime minister to position himself to become president lapsed into immobilism and destroyed Balladur's popularity. On the one hand, by proposing controversial, often regressive reforms, Balladur made many enemies. On the other hand, by backing down at the first hint of resistance, he allowed pressing problems to fester. Air France plunged further into the red, eventually requiring a 20 bn franc bailout from French taxpayers. The Crédit Lyonnais bank, France's largest, was insolvent when Balladur took office, but continued to operate as before, while the government covered the losses: as a result, a rescue that had been estimated initially at 20 bn francs would ultimately cost over 100 bn francs. On an aggregate level, state spending, the budget deficit, and the social security deficit all increased under Balladur's watch (not just in absolute terms, but as a share of GDP). The Balladur method proved to be not only ineffective as a social and economic reform strategy, but disastrous as a presidential campaign strategy. It would allow Jacques Chirac to rally from far behind in the polls by denouncing Balladur for the somewhat contradictory sins of subservience to neo-liberalism (Balladur's proposals) and immobilism (Balladur's practice).

7.5.2. *Welfare Reform under Juppé: A Return to Technocratic Gaullism*

Balladur's successor as prime minister was also a Gaullist, Alain Juppé. Like Balladur, Juppé pursued a relatively regressive social and economic agenda. Although Jacques Chirac was elected president in May 1995 on a pledge to intensify state intervention in order to heal the country's 'social fracture', he quickly (and, in the minds of many, cynically) reversed course. In October 1995 Chirac announced that his top priority was to reduce France's budget deficit in order to qualify for EMU. Thus, Chirac's prime minister, Alain Juppé, like Balladur before him, would focus on curbing social spending. Also like Balladur, if forced to raise taxes, Juppé would do so in a regressive manner.

Less than one month after Chirac's policy declaration, Juppé presented a 'social security plan' to Parliament that was, in many respects, an extension of the changes enacted by Balladur. Where Balladur had raised the retirement age and reduced the pension benefits of private sector employees, Juppé would do the same to civil servants. Public employees, like their private sector counterparts, would be required to work for 40 years, instead of 37.5 years, in order to qualify for a pension. What is more, Juppé proposed to eliminate the various *régimes spéciaux* that allowed some civil servants to retire as early as age 50; henceforth, no public employee could retire before age 60. Juppé also followed in Balladur's footsteps by enacting a number of regressive tax hikes, notably an increase in the general value-added tax from 18.6 percent to 20.6 percent and a tax-deductible increase of the CSG from 2.4 percent to 3.4 percent.

Some elements of the Juppé plan went well beyond earlier initiatives. Juppé attempted to change the mechanisms of welfare policy, so as to attack runaway social spending at its roots. At the aggregate level, Juppé proposed and enacted a constitutional amendment subjecting the social security budget to a parliamentary vote. His hope was that by imposing an annual budget from above, rather than accommodating a series of autonomous spending decisions below, the government would be better able to limit social spending. This provision greatly angered France's trade unions, since it threatened their historic role in co-managing the social security system. At a programmatic level, Juppé sought to clamp down on health care spending by tightening controls on both hospitals and physicians. Of particular note, he proposed to reward or punish physicians by adjusting fees annually, from one region to the next, according to each region's success in meeting government spending targets.

In terms of economic substance, then, the Juppé plan constituted an extension and intensification of the earlier undertakings by Balladur. Once again, the government would combine spending cuts with regressive tax increases. That said, as the 'nationalization' of social security spending and the proposed changes to the health care system indicate, the Chirac–Juppé tandem embraced a very different style of reform. Indeed, the Juppé plan was in no small part a reaction against the perceived failings of the Balladur method. The lesson of the Balladur administration seemed to be that attempting to please everyone pleases no one. Governments are elected to govern, to make hard choices. Chirac's presidential campaign had emphasized activist leadership in contrast to Balladurian immobilism. Although the substance of Chirac's policy had shifted from healing the social fracture to healing the budget deficit, the style remained resolutely activist.

The Chirac–Juppé style was also something of a throwback to the insular, technocratic Gaullism methods of the 1960s. The government's role was to modernize the country, to pursue the general will, not to cater to the particularistic concerns of self-serving interest groups. The Juppé plan was conceived in this spirit—prepared in complete secrecy, lest it be contaminated by special pleading. The prime minister openly bragged that not ten people had seen his plan prior to its presentation to Parliament. Whereas under the Balladur method, the legitimacy of a reform stemmed from the absence of popular protest, under the neo-Gaullist approach of Juppé, the legitimating principle was one of 'equality of sacrifice'. The Juppé plan spared no one. Taxpayers, doctors, civil servants, pharmaceutical companies—everyone had to contribute their fair share. The Juppé government would prove its mettle by being right, not by being popular.

That said, as in the case of Balladur, tactical and electoral considerations were by no means absent. With legislative elections due by 1998 at the latest, Chirac and Juppé reasoned that it was best to implement a thoroughgoing austerity program immediately. In this way, France could qualify for EMU in 1997, and the economy would begin to recover in time for the elections in 1998. A go-slow approach, by contrast, while perhaps more appealing in the short term, would jeopardize both of these critical objectives.

If Balladur sinned by his timidity, the Chirac–Juppé tandem sinned by its ambition and hubris. French voters were not about to forget the promises of candidate Chirac. They had elected their president in order to avert Balladurian austerity, not to intensify it. Furthermore, the secretive, technocratic methods of Juppé smacked of arrogance, especially when the prime minister refused to compromise or even negotiate any elements of his program. Finally, by pursuing the 'equality of sacrifice', Juppé ensured the equality of enmity toward his government and its objectives. Groups that normally had little in common, such as doctors and civil servants, found themselves united in their opposition to the Juppé plan.

The response to Juppé's initiative was a six-week strike by civil servants and transportation workers that paralyzed the country. What is more, French public opinion ran resolutely in favor of the strikers and against the government. In order to end the strike, Juppé was forced to abandon his public sector pension reform. Although he maintained a tougher line toward the physicians, ultimately, this part of the reform also unraveled. The system of penalties lacked effective enforcement mechanisms, and after a brief pause, medical spending was again increasing at two to three times the level of inflation. To add insult to injury, in the summer of 1998, France's administrative courts struck down the implementing agreements signed with the medical profession, forcing Juppé's successors to begin anew.

The Juppé plan not only failed on its own terms. More fundamentally, it delegitimized the government. Henceforth, every remotely controversial initiative launched by Juppé, notably in the area of privatizations and fiscal policy, was hotly contested. After eighteen months of stalemate, Juppé finally convinced President Chirac to dissolve Parliament and hold early elections, in an effort to renew his mandate and press forward with the difficult measures needed to qualify for Maastricht. Instead, in June 1997, the French electorate repudiated Chirac and Juppé, ushering into office a shaky Socialist–Green–Communist coalition headed by Lionel Jospin.

7.5.3. The Jospin Government: A Welfare Reform of the Left?

The Balladur and Juppé governments offered two variants on a roughly comparable set of policy objectives. As conservatives, both sought to rein in social spending and, to the extent that balancing the budget required raising taxes, both targeted wage earners, rather than capital. Balladur and Juppé differed greatly in their policy style, with the former seeking to assuage public opinion, while the latter seemed to go out of his way to disregard public opinion. But as for the substance of their proposed reforms, Balladur and Juppé were not very far apart.

Lionel Jospin is seeking to make a more fundamental break, to show that even in an age of globalization, the left can govern differently from the right. Part of the difference is stylistic. As against the insular, technocratic approach of Juppé, Jospin professes a desire to negotiate with societal actors, to engage in genuine concertation. Moreover, in contrast to the post facto concertation of Balladur, Jospin has solicited input during the process of policy formulation. A favorite technique has been the commissioning of expert reports, which are then used as trial balloons, allowing the government to elicit feedback before moving ahead (or not moving ahead) with controversial reforms. Jospin is also trying to open a space for collective bargaining. In many instances, the government will set a broad objective, such as shortening the work week from 39 hours to 35 hours or keeping the increase in medical spending below a certain figure, while encouraging the relevant interest groups to work out the best way (or ways) to meet this objective.

Still, Jospin is well aware that his government cannot succeed on style alone. In order to retain the support of his constituents, Jospin must offer a different product from the right, not simply a different process. Toward this end, he has deployed a two-pronged strategy to anchor his government's actions on the left: (1) launching high-profile initiatives that demonstrate commitment to a progressive agenda; (2) giving a leftist turn to necessary measures of austerity and liberalization.

7.5.3.1. New Programs that Demonstrate the Government's Commitment to a Leftist Agenda

Jospin has launched three high-profile initiatives designed to placate the leftist faithful, to show that his government is genuinely committed to social progress. The first reform is the *couverture maladie universelle* (CMU), inaugurated at the beginning of 2000, which makes health care available to low-income groups free of charge. The CMU originated with a pledge by the Juppé government to extend public health insurance to the 200,000 French citizens (0.3% of the population) who lack such coverage. The Jospin government is honoring this pledge, but also taking aim at the far greater problem of access among those who actually have health insurance. France's public health insurance reimburses just 70 percent of the costs of medical treatment on average (Join-Lambert et al. 1997). Although 85 percent of the population reduces co-payments by subscribing to a supplementary insurance, for the remaining 15 percent, low reimbursement rates have tended to place all but emergency medical treatment out of reach. The CMU seeks to alleviate this problem of access by providing free supplementary health insurance on a means-tested basis to an estimated 6 million people (those living on less than 3,500 francs per month for a single individual, 7,700 francs for a family of four).

The second major initiative has been a youth employment program, the *Programme Emploi Jeunes* (PEJ), which is expected to create 350,000 positions by the year 2002. The PEJ is targeted at young people with no significant work experience. Under its highly generous terms, the state pays 80 percent of the minimum wage and all social security contributions, leaving only 20 percent of the SMIC to the charge of the employer. In order to avoid substitution effects in the private sector, the program is confined to non-profit and public organizations. In contrast to previous state-sponsored, make-work projects, the PEJ provides full-time employment for an extended period (five years). The government hopes that this extended tenure will enable participants to acquire the skills and experience necessary to secure permanent employment once the subsidies run out. As of November 1999, some 221,000 PEJ contracts had been signed, with about one-half the participants serving as educational aids or security guards.

The third and probably most significant initiative of the Jospin government is the slated reduction of the work week from 39 hours to 35 hours. Although conservative critics and the national employer association have denounced the reform as a job-killer that will force companies to lay off workers as a result of higher labor costs, the government has taken a number of measures to assuage business concerns. The reform is being phased in gradually: announced in 1997, the 35-hour rule began to take effect in the year 2000 for companies employing more than 20 workers and will not apply to small firms until 2002.[8] The government is also allowing businesses to reorganize work time as part of the move toward 35 hours, notably through the annualization of working hours. Instead of working 39 hours every week, as in the past, employees will work an average of 35 hours, but at moments of peak demand, they may be called upon to put in as many as 42 hours per week—an arrangement of particular benefit to companies engaged in seasonal activities. Finally, the government is partially funding the transition to the 35-hour week. Significant subsidies are available to companies that sign agreements with the unions reducing work time and resulting in the 'creation or preservation' of jobs. The latter criterion means that employers need not hire additional workers, but merely forego planned layoffs.[9] The subsidies are greatest at the bottom of the pay scale (21,500 francs per year for a minimum-wage hire), then decline gradually to 4,000 francs for jobs paying more than 1.8 times the minimum wage.

Jospin's initiatives carry a hefty price tag: 9 bn francs for health insurance, 35 bn francs for youth employment, and 110 bn francs for the 35-hour week. That said, they do not mark as sharp a departure, either substantively or financially, as it might at first appear. The French state was already subsidizing local authorities to provide health care to the indigent, so that the net cost of its reform is closer to 2 bn francs than to 9 bn. Similarly, as the PEJ expands, a number of existing programs for unemployed youths, which have been deemed less effective, are being wound down. Even the 35-hour reform treads upon familiar policy ground. Jospin did not invent the practice of paying employers to shorten the work week while 'creating or preserving' jobs; the Juppé government passed the

[8] In addition, in year one of the 35-hour law, companies will be authorized to pay the 36th and 37th hour worked at 10% above hourly wages, as opposed to the standard 25% overtime premium. In year two, the provision will apply to the 36th hour only. Thus, the 35-hour limit does not become fully effective until 2002 for large firms and 2004 for small ones.

[9] As of January 2000, 23,269 work time reduction agreements had been signed: 21,958 so-called 'offensive' agreements, adding 137,239 new jobs, and 1,311 'defensive' agreements, 'preserving' 22,276 jobs (Ministry of Employment and Solidarity website, www.35h.travail.gouv.fr/actualite/bilan/index.html).

Robien law in 1996 for just that purpose. Nor did Jospin pioneer assistance for low-wage hires: Balladur exempted employers from family allowance contributions, while the so-called 'Juppé refund' (*ristourne Juppé*) provided subsidies of 5,000 to 15,000 francs for jobs paying less than 1.3 times the minimum wage. According to the Jospin government's calculations, by using the funds from these programs and curbing subsidies for early retirement, the net cost of the 35-hour law will be around 25 bn francs, as opposed to 110 bn francs (*Le Monde*, 1 June 1999). Thus, Jospin is managing to earn his leftist credentials, enacting highly visible social reforms, without breaking the bank in the process.

The Jospin government has applied the same kind of cost-shuffling approach to more modest initiatives (Levy 1999*b*). In his inaugural budget (for the year 1998), Jospin wanted to provide some kind of benefit to the left's constituents, but hemmed in by Maastricht deficit criteria, he could neither boost spending nor cut taxes. The government's solution was to enact a revenue-neutral reform that shifted the tax burden from low-income groups to high-income groups (leaving business unaffected). The 1998 budget increased the CSG—applied to all earnings and not just wages—from 3.4 percent to 7.5 percent, while decreasing worker contributions to health insurance from 5.5 percent to 0.75 percent. Although the fiscal yield was unchanged, the reform provided the average worker with a 1.1 percent gain in purchasing power; conversely, it added to the tax bill of those (primarily, the affluent) who derive earnings from property or capital.

7.5.3.2. Liberalization and Austerity of the Left

The Jospin government has not avoided measures of austerity and economic liberalization. Despite a campaign pledge to place domestic reflation ahead of qualification for EMU, Jospin presided over a reduction of the French budget deficit from 4.2 percent of GDP in 1996 to 3.0 percent in 1997 and 2.9 percent 1998 (OFCE 1998: 17), thereby meeting the Maastricht criteria.[10] Jospin also ignored his campaign promise to put a halt to privatizations. Indeed, once in office, his government sold off more companies than its predecessors. While operating on the ideological terrain of the right, however, Jospin has gone to great lengths to show that his actions are consistent with the ideals of the left. Three principles have guided this strategy.

---

[10] The Jospin government has maintained its commitment to deficit reduction subsequent to France's qualification for EMU. The budget deficit declined from 2.9% of GDP in 1998 to 2.1% of GDP in 1999. According to the government's 'Multi-Year Finance Program', the deficit is to be reduced by 0.4% of GDP annually from 2000 to 2003, with French public finances edging into the black in 2004.

The first principle is that if government spending must be reduced, the cuts should be targeted at the affluent. One of the first initiatives of the Jospin government was to de-universalize family allowances by introducing income-testing to exclude the well-to-do (Levy 1999*b*). The 1998 budget eliminated family allowances to those households with an income of more than 350,000 francs and also halved the tax deduction for families who hire domestic childcare (a 'nanny tax deduction' affecting only 0.25 percent of French families). In response to criticism from pro-family organizations, Jospin restored the family allowance the following year, but he retrieved the increased expenditure from the wealthy by reducing the maximum child income tax credit from 16,380 francs to 11,000 francs. Actions such as these are designed to show that cutting benefits need not be synonymous with slashing the protections of society's most vulnerable citizens—at least, not under a government of the left.

The second policy principle is that structural welfare reform should take aim at constituents of the right, rather than the left. The clearest illustration is the emerging reform for the health care system. With the collapse of the Juppé plan and continued, rapid health care inflation, the Jospin government was forced to go back to the drawing board. In March 1999, the newly appointed director of the national health insurance fund, Gilles Johanet presented a four-year 'strategic plan' to the government. The Johanet plan, which aims for annual savings of 62 bn francs by the year 2002 (roughly 10% of public health care expenditures), centered around three proposals. First, French patients would be encouraged to choose a primary care physician who would act as a gatekeeper. Under the current system, patients can self-refer to specialists, see as many doctors as they choose, and cumulate prescriptions from different doctors. Under the new system, they could continue to do so, but would be reimbursed at a lower rate than if they went through their primary care physician. Second, the (often excessive) prices paid by the social security system for prescription medications and physician services would be re-examined in light of both therapeutic value and prevailing prices in neighboring countries. Third, public hospitals would no longer receive a fixed budget, but rather be funded on a fee-for-service basis at the same rate as private hospitals.

Minister of Labor and Social Solidarity, Martine Aubry, who is in charge of health care policy, was quite satisfied with Johanet's first two proposals. Taking on affluent doctors and price-gouging pharmaceutical companies, traditional constituents of the right, is grist to the mill for a government of the left. Aubry herself has engaged in a number of high-profile showdowns with these groups, levying heavy fines on medical specialists, such as radiologists and cardiologists, as well as on the pharmaceutical industry, for exceeding government spending targets. By contrast, Johanet's third recommendation, to save 30 bn francs by making public hospitals operate in the same manner as private hospitals, met with an icy reception from Aubry. France's public hospitals were already reorganizing, she argued, and Johanet's provocative proposals threatened to upset delicate, ongoing negotiations. What went unsaid by Aubry is that public hospitals are staffed by employees who are heavily unionized, militant, and loyal to the left. Notwithstanding the potential savings of the Johanet plan, a government of the left had no intention of attempting to impose hundreds of hospital closings and tens of thousands of layoffs on its own constituents. Indeed, in February 2000, in response to hospital worker protests denouncing inadequate funding, staffing, and equipment levels, Aubry committed an extra 10 bn francs over the next three years to the public hospitals.

The third principle of Jospin's reform is that even when pursuing policies associated with the right and with neo-liberalism, these policies should be redirected to the maximum extent possible along left-progressive lines. Privatizations offer a case in point. While going back on his promise to halt the sale of public enterprises, Jospin has sought to demonstrate salient differences between privatizations of the left and privatizations of the right. Whereas Juppé's privatizations were essentially financial transactions, designed to raise money and unload state responsibility for critical sectors, Jospin's privatizations have reflected a genuine industrial strategy. Operations in the defense, aeronautics, and financial sectors have paired public enterprises with private French firms engaged in complementary lines of business, in the hope of creating strong European players. Jospin's privatizations have also been more sensitive to social considerations than those of his predecessor. In most instances, managers and unions have been involved in the selection of the acquiring firm, and the government has included guarantees of employment and investment as part of the privatization agreements.

A similar tale could be told with respect to the creation of private pension funds. In March 1997, the Juppé government passed a law authorizing individual companies to establish and operate pension funds on behalf of their employees. Jospin denounced the move as a threat to the state-run, pay-as-you-go pension system and pledged to repeal the legislation if elected. Instead of stamping out pension funds, however, the government is designing an alternative system more in line with its preferences. As against the pension funds of the right, the pension funds of the left will be managed collectively, by employer and union organizations, rather than by private companies. Furthermore, contributions to pension funds will not be deductible from contributions to the public, pay-as-you-go system, thereby eliminating the risk that the former would cannibalize the later.

Jospin has also promised not to authorize the creation of pension funds until first implementing reforms to guarantee the long-term viability of the public pension system.

7.5.3.3. Limits and Uncertainties

It is too early to judge whether the Jospin government will prove able to implement a welfare reform of the left. Much hard work still lies ahead. Indeed, if there is one point on which the left is vulnerable, it is that the government's creative energies have focused on the extension of benefits (health care for the indigent, jobs for youths, the 35-hour work week), rather than the correction of existing difficulties and imbalances. Jospin has yet to enact the kinds of structural changes needed to restore the financial equilibrium of the social security system. Health care reform is in its incipient stages, and already political considerations have narrowed its scope. In the meantime, contrary to government promises, the health insurance program remains heavily in the red.

France's pay-as-you-go pension system also awaits government action. Despite the changes introduced by the Balladur government, the Planning Commissariat forecasts that the pension system will become insolvent in the year 2005, then register massive deficits (between 4 and 6% of GDP annually) during the years 2015 to 2040 (Charpin 1999). Public sector pensions account for more than one-half of this deficit, making the task of reform especially dicey for a government of the left. Jospin's team is understandably unenthusiastic about the Planning Commissariat's recommendation to raise the minimum years of contributions from 40 to 42.5 years in the private sector and from 37.5 to 42.5 years in the public sector. That said, the government has not proposed an alternative solution to the pension problem.

The task of welfare reform is further complicated by the open antagonism between the government and the national employer association, the Conseil National du Patronat Français (CNPF). The conflict has grown out of the 35-hour reform, to which the CNPF is viscerally opposed. In October 1997, when Jospin announced his intention to enact legislation mandating the 35-hour work week, the head of the CNPF resigned in protest, declaring that his organization needed a 'killer', rather than a 'negotiator'. The new CNPF president, Ernest-Antoine Seillère, renamed the organization Mouvement des Entreprises de France (MEDEF) and called upon members to 'destabilize' the government. At Seillère's urging, several employer associations pushed through agreements that essentially emptied the 35-hour reform of its substance—generally, by increasing the annual ceiling on overtime hours, while allowing employers to pay regular rates (as opposed to the standard 25% overtime premium) for the 36th through 39th hours worked. The government countered by declaring that these agreements failed to meet the 35-hour standard, since they did not reduce the number of hours actually worked, and that they were, therefore, ineligible for subsidies. Subsequently, most French employers have fallen into line, bargaining in earnest to implement a 35-hour reform that they could not prevent—and reaping the accompanying subsidies before these disappear. That said, MEDEF continues to denounce the reform (along with the government) in the harshest terms, and the association's confrontational stance extends to other issues as well. In particular, MEDEF has taken a hard line on both pension and health care reform, arguing that the minimum number of years of contributions for a pension should be raised to 45, rather than the (already ambitious) 42.5 years proposed by the Planning Commissariat, and threatening to withdraw from the public health insurance fund unless the Johanet plan is implemented in its entirety. This radicalization of MEDEF's aims and tactics does not bode well for a negotiated, concertational approach to welfare adjustment.

Despite the difficulties and uncertainties surrounding welfare reform, Prime Minister Jospin can be reasonably satisfied with his record to date. His government has responded to popular aspirations for expanded social protections, broadening health care coverage for the indigent and launching ambitious initiatives to shorten the workweek and to provide jobs for unemployed youths. At the same time, the left has managed to bring down France's budget deficit, and to do so in ways that reduce, rather than aggravate, inequality (shifting health care contributions to the CSG, curtailing the nanny and child benefit tax credits enjoyed by the affluent, etc). Jospin has also navigated the ideological minefields of privatizations and pension funds, conceiving reforms that are consonant with left principles as well as market principles. Through it all, investment and employment growth have exceeded expectations, not to mention the levels attained previously under the right. If no one is ready to anoint France as the next European 'third way', the Jospin government has done a credible job of reconciling equity and efficiency, the pursuit of profits with the pursuit of progressive politics.

7.6. Conclusion: *Dirigisme* and Social Policy

Seventeen years after the 1983 U-turn, virtually nothing remains of the institutions and practices associated with France's *dirigiste* growth model. Sectoral industrial policies and ambitious *grands projets* have been abandoned; the vast majority of nationalized companies have been privatized; credit, price, and capital controls have been lifted; restrictions on layoffs and temporary and part-time employment have been eased; and inflationary growth has given way to competitive disinflation. Looking across the advanced industrial democracies, one would be hard-pressed to find any country that has moved so far away from its postwar economic strategy as the France of François Mitterrand and Jacques Chirac.

While France's *dirigiste* state has retreated over the past decade-and-one-half, its welfare state has continued to expand. Many of the most significant initiatives since the early 1980s have entailed new spending commitments: a reduction in the retirement age from 65 to 60 (in practice, much closer to 55); the creation of a universal guaranteed minimum income (RMI); and under the current administration of Socialist Prime Minister Lionel Jospin, the provision of health insurance to the indigent, the youth employment plan, and the 35-hour work week. At the same time, France has been slow to grapple with runaway spending in existing programs, notably pensions and health care. On an aggregate level, the steady increase in social spending since 1983 has lifted public expenditures to an all-time high, despite the decline of industrial policy. Moreover, in the last two elections, presidential in 1995 and legislative in 1997, French voters sent a clear message that they want more state intervention in the social arena, not less. Thus, the end of *dirigiste* economic policy has by no means marked the end of state activism—nor of the popular expectations that nurture such activism.

The contradictory evolution of French economic and social policy since 1983 lends itself to two divergent interpretations, both of which revolve around the role of *dirigisme*. The first interpretation sees France as a case of late and reluctant welfare state adjustment. Just as France was slow to establish a comprehensive welfare state in the postwar period, it has lagged in rationalizing the welfare state in the contemporary period. The culprit, in both instances, is *dirigisme*. The postwar *dirigiste* model was erected upon a pattern of labor exclusion, aborting the promising Liberation-era movement toward a universalist, Beveridgean welfare regime. Monnet trumped Laroque. During the past two decades, the reorganization and downsizing of the French welfare state has been delayed by the need to first dismantle *dirigisme*. Polanyi has trumped Thatcher. France is lagging, however, not diverging. With the winding down of *dirigisme* and the winding up of international and employment pressures, welfare reform can be avoided no longer. In the coming years, therefore, France can be expected to accept the logic of international integration and to pare back its free-spending ways—in short, to put some Thatcherite water in its post-*dirigiste* wine. Barring such adjustment, France's future will be bleak indeed.

The alternative interpretation casts France as the harbinger of a more promising set of welfare developments. Once again, *dirigisme* figures prominently. At its most basic level, *dirigisme* stands for the primacy of politics, for the belief that through purposive state action, it is possible to create a social and economic order that is superior to that produced by the anarchic play of market mechanisms and individual interests. With the dismantling of *dirigiste* industrial policy, the aspiration to impose political sovereignty upon the market has been displaced from the economic to the social arena. Such an aspiration is not necessarily a bad thing, however, even in a world of quicksilver capital. Although international economic and institutional conditions have certainly changed, in many cases, the proper response is to redeploy welfare state intervention, as opposed to rolling it back. Seen from this perspective, it would be wrong to dismiss recent French reforms—attempts to find new resources in old places, to spread the costs of social protection more evenly across society, and to inject a social logic into liberalizing measures like privatizations—as a fit of Gallic pique, a last gasp of a dying, *dirigiste* dinosaur. Rather, such initiatives reflect an entirely salutary effort to reconcile globalization with governance, markets with mores—an undertaking whose significance extends well beyond France's borders, to the wider world of welfare capitalism in the twenty-first century.

REFERENCES

ADAM, GÉRARD, REYNAUD, JEAN-DANIEL, and VERDIER, JEAN-MAURICE (1972). *La Négociation collective en France*. Paris: Éditions Ouvrières.

ATKINSON, ANTHONY, RAINWATER, LEE, and SMEEDING, TIMOTHY (1985). *Income Distribution in OECD Countries: Evidence from Luxembourg Income Study*. OECD Social Policy Studies, No. 18. Paris: OECD.

BARREAU, JOCELYNE, and MOULINE, ABDELAZIZ (1987). *L'Industrie électronique française: 29 ans de relations État-groupes industriels, 1958–1986*. Paris: Librairie générale de droit et de jurisprudence.

BAUCHARD, PIERRE (1986). *La Guerre des deux roses: Du rêve à la réalité, 1981–1985*. Paris: Bernard Grasset.

BAUCHET, PIERRE (1986). *Le Plan dans l'économie française*. Paris: FNSP.

BAUER, MICHEL (1988). 'The Politics of State-Directed Privatisation: The Case of France, 1986–1988'. *West European Politics*, 11/4: 49–60.

BERGER, SUZANNE (1981). 'Lame Ducks and National Champions: Industrial Policy in the Fifth Republic', in William Andrews and Stanley Hoffmann (eds.), *The Fifth Republic at Twenty*. Albany, NY: SUNY Press, 160–78.

BIRNBAUM, PIERRE (1977). *Les Sommets de l'État: Essai sur l'élite du pouvoir en France*. Paris: Seuil.

——(1978). *La Classe dirigeante française: Dissociation, interpénétration, intégration*. Paris: PUF.

BLOCH-LAINÉ, FRANÇOIS, and BOUVIER, JEAN (1986). *La France restaurée, 1944–1954: Dialogue sur les choix d'une modernisation*. Paris: Fayard.

BONOLI, GIULIANO (1997). 'Classifying Welfare States: A Two-Dimension Approach'. *Journal of Social Policy*, 26/3: 351–72.

BOURGUIGNON, FRANÇOIS, and BUREAU, DOMINIQUE (1999). *L'Architecture des prélèvements en France: État des lieux et voies de réforme*. Paris: La Documentation Française.

Cahiers Français (1983). *La Politique industrielle*. No. 212.

——(1992). *Histoire économique de la France au XXe siècle*. No. 255.

CAMERON, DAVID (1991). 'Continuity and Change in French Social Policy: The Welfare State under Gaullism, Liberalism, and Socialism', in John Ambler (ed.), *The French Welfare State: Surviving Social and Ideological Change*. New York: New York University Press, 58–93.

——(1996). 'Exchange Rate Politics in France, 1981–1983: The Regime-Defining Choices of the Mitterrand Presidency', in Anthony Daley (ed.), *The Mitterrand Era: Policy Alternatives and Political Mobilization in France*. New York: NYU Press, 56–82.

CASTLES, FRANCIS, and FERRERA, MAURIZIO (1996). 'Home Ownership and the Welfare State: Is Southern Europe Different?'. *South European Society and Politics*, 1/2: 163–85.

CHARPIN, JEAN-MICHEL (1999). *L'Avenir de nos retraites*. Report submitted by the General Planning Commissariat to the Prime Minister, Apr. 1999. Paris: La Documentation Française.

COHEN, ELIE (1989). *L'État brancardier: Politiques du déclin industriel (1974–1984)*. Paris: Calmann-Lévy.

——(1992). *Le Colbertisme 'high tech': Économie des telecom et du grand projet*. Paris: Hachette.

——and BAUER, MICHEL (1985). *Les Grandes manoeuvres industrielles*. Paris: Belfond.

COHEN, STEPHEN (1977). *Modern Capitalist Planning: The French Model*. Berkeley: University of California Press.

COMMAILLE, JACQUES (1998). 'La Politique française à l'égard de la famille'. *Regards sur l'actualité*, Jan.: 12–24.

DALEY, ANTHONY (1990). *All Worked Up Again: Employment Policy under Mitterrand II*. Paper presented at the American Political Science Association, San Francisco, 1 Sept. 1990.

——(1996). *Steel, State, and Labor: Mobilization and Adjustment in France*. Pittsburgh: University of Pittsburgh Press.

DARES (Direction de l'Animation de la Recherche, des Études et des Statistiques) (1996). *40 ans de politique de l'emploi*. Report to the Ministry of Labor. Paris: La Documentation Française.

DUPEYROUX, JEAN-JACQUES (1969). *Sécurité sociale*, 3rd edn. Paris: Dalloz.

ESPING-ANDERSEN, GØSTA (1990). *The Three Worlds of Welfare Capitalism*. Princeton: Princeton University Press.

——(1996). 'Welfare States without Work: The Impasse of Labour Shedding and Familialism in Continental European Social Policy', in Gøsta Esping-

Andersen (ed.), *Welfare States in Transition: National Adaptations in a Global Economy*. Thousand Oaks, Calif.: Sage Publications, 66–87.

FAUGÈRE, JEAN-PIERRE, and VOISIN, COLETTE (1994). *Le Système financier français: Crises et mutations*, 2nd edn. Collection CIRCA. Luçon: Nathan.

FAVIER, PIERRE, and MARTIN-ROLAND, MICHEL (1996). *La Décennie Mitterrand*, 3 vols. Paris: Seuil.

FERRERA, MAURIZIO (1996). 'The "Southern Model" of Welfare in Social Europe'. *Journal of European Social Policy*, 6/1: 17–37.

FITOUSSI, JEAN-PAUL (1995). *Le Débat interdit: Monnaie, Europe, pauvreté*. Paris: Arléa.

GALLANT, HENRY (1955). *Histoire politique de la sécurité sociale, 1945–1952*. Cahiers de la Fondation nationale des sciences politiques, No. 76. Paris: Fondation nationale des sciences politiques.

GROUX, GUY, and MOURIAUX, RENÉ (1990). 'Le Cas français', in Geneviève Bibes and René Mouriaux (eds.), *Les Syndicats européens à l'épreuve*. Paris: FNSP, 49–68.

HALL, PETER (1986). *Governing the Economy: The Politics of State Intervention in Britain and France*. New York: Oxford University Press.

——(1990). 'The State and the Market', in Peter Hall, Jack Hayward, and Howard Machin (eds.), *Developments in French Politics*. London: Macmillan, 171–87.

HASSENTEUFEL, PATRICK (1997). *Les Médecins face à l'État: Une comparaison internationale*. Paris: Presses de la Fondation nationale des sciences politiques.

HOFFMANN, STANLEY (ed.) (1963). *In Search of France: The Economy, Society, & Political System in the Twentieth Century*. Cambridge, Mass.: Harvard University Press.

HOWELL, CHRIS (1992*a*). 'The Dilemmas of Post-Fordism: Socialists, Flexibility, and Labor Market Deregulation in France'. *Politics & Society*, 20/1: 71–99.

——(1992*b*). *Regulating Labor: The State and Industrial Relations Reform in Postwar France*. Princeton: Princeton University Press.

HUBER, EVELYN, RAGIN, CHARLES, and STEPHENS, JOHN (1993). 'Social Democracy, Christian Democracy, Constitutional Structure, and the Welfare State'. *American Journal of Sociology*, 99/3: 711–49.

HUTEAU, GILLE, and LE BONT, ERIC (1997). *Sécurité sociale et politiques sociales*, 2nd edn. Collection Concours Droit. Paris: Armand Colin.

IMMERGUT, ELLEN (1992). 'The Rules of the Game: The Logic of Health Policy-Making in France, Switzerland, and Sweden', in Sven Steinmo, Kathleen Thelen, and Frank Longstreth (eds.), *Structuring Politics: Historical Institutionalism in Comparative Analysis*. Cambridge: Cambridge University Press, 57–89.

INSEE (Institut National de la Statistique et des Études Économiques) (1998). *L'Économie française, Édition 1998–1999*. Paris: INSEE.

INTIGNANO, BÉATRICE MAJNONI DE (1993). *La Protection sociale*. Paris: Éditions de Fallois.

JOIN-LAMBERT, MARIE-THÉRÈSE, BOLOT-GITTLER, ANNE, DANIEL, CHRISTINE, LENOIR, DANIEL, and MÉDA, DOMINIQUE (1997). *Politiques sociales*, 2nd edn. Paris: Presses de la Fondation nationale des sciences politiques.

KERSBERGEN, KEES VAN (1995). *Social Capitalism: A Study of Christian Democracy and the Welfare State*. New York: Routledge.

KUISEL, RICHARD (1981). *Capitalism and the State in Modern France*. Cambridge: Cambridge University Press.

LABBÉ, DOMINIQUE, and CROISAT, MAURICE (1992). *La Fin des syndicats?* Paris: L'Harmattan.

LAROQUE, PIERRE (1985*b*). 'Quarante ans de sécurité sociale'. *Revue française des affaires sociales*, July–Sept.: 7–35.

——(1985*a*). 'La Sécurité sociale de 1945 à 1951'. *Revue française des affaires sociales*, July–Sept.: 11–26.

——(1993). *Au service de l'homme et du droit: Souvenirs et réflexions*. Paris: Association pour l'étude de l'histoire de la sécurité sociale.

LE BOLLOC'H-PUGES, CHANTAL (1991). *La Politique industrielle française dans l'électronique*. Paris: L'Harmattan.

Le Monde (1981). *L'Élection présidentielle, 26 avril–10 mai 1981: La Victoire de M. Mitterrand*. Collection 'Dossiers et Documents'. Paris: Le Monde.

——(1989). *L'Économie française: Mutations, 1975–1990*. Paris: Le Monde.

——(1999). *Bilan du Monde: L'Année économique et sociale 1998*. Paris: Le Monde.

LENOIR, RÉMI (1990). 'Family Policy in France since 1938', in John Ambler (ed.), *The French Welfare State: Surviving Social and Ideological Change*. New York: NYU Press, 144–86.

LEVY, JONAH (1999*a*). *Tocqueville's Revenge: State, Society, and Economy in Contemporary France*. Cambridge, Mass.: Harvard University Press.

——(1999*b*). 'Vice into Virtue? Progressive Politics and Welfare Reform in Continental Europe'. *Politics and Society*, 27/2: 239–73.

LIPIETZ, ALAIN (1984). *L'Audace ou l'enlisement: Sur les politiques économiques de la gauche*. Paris: La Découverte.

LORIAUX, MICHAEL (1991). *France after Hegemony: International Change and Financial Reform*. Ithaca, NY: Cornell University Press.

MASSÉ, PIERRE (1965). *Le Plan ou l'anti-hasard*. Paris: Gallimard.

MINC, ALAIN (1994). *La France de l'an 2000*. Report to the Prime Minister, Paris: La Documentation Française.

OECD (Organisation for Economic Co-operation and Development) (1992). *Historical Statistics, 1960–1990*. Paris: OECD.

——(various years). *Social Expenditure Statistics of OECD Member Countries*. Paris: OECD.

OFCE (Observatoire Français des Conjonctures Économiques) (1998). *L'Économie française 1998*. Paris: La Découverte.

PALIER, BRUNO (1999). *Réformer la Sécurité Sociale: Les Interventions gouverne-mentales en matière de protection sociale depuis 1945, la France en perspective comparative*. Doctoral thesis, Institut d'Études Politiques de Paris.

POLANYI, KARL (1944). *The Great Transformation*. Boston: Beacon.

RHODES, MARTIN (1997). 'Southern European Welfare States: Identity, Problems, and Prospects for Reform', in Martin Rhodes (ed.), *Southern European Welfare States: Between Crisis and Reform*. Portland: Frank Cass, 1–22.

ROUSSO, HENRI (ed.) (1986). *De Monnet à Massé: Enjeux politiques et objectifs économiques dans le cadre des quatre premiers plans (1945–1965)*. Paris: CNRS.

SAWYER, MALCOLM (1976). *Income Distribution in OECD Countries*. Paris: OECD.

SCHMIDT, VIVIEN (1996). *From State to Market? The Transformation of French Business and Government*. New York: Cambridge University Press.

SHONFIELD, ANDREW (1965). *Modern Capitalism: The Changing Balance of Public and Private Power*. Oxford: Oxford University Press.

STOFFAËS, CHRISTIAN (1984). *Politique industrielle*. Paris: Les Cours de Droit.

——(1985). 'The Nationalizations: An Initial Assessment, 1981–1984', in Howard Machin and Vincent Wright (eds.), *Economic Policy and Policy-Making under the Mitterrand Presidency*. New York: St Martin's, 144–69.

SULEIMAN, EZRA (1974). *Politics, Power and Bureaucracy in France: The Administrative Elite*. Princeton: Princeton University Press.

——(1978). *Elites in French Society: The Politics of Survival*. Princeton: Princeton University Press.

VAIL, MARK (1999). 'The Better Part of Valour: The Politics of French Welfare Reform'. *Journal of European Social Policy*, 9/4: 311–29.

WILENSKY, HAROLD (1981). 'Leftism, Catholicism, and Democratic Corporatism: The Role of Political Parties in Recent Welfare State Development', in Peter Flora and Arnold J. Heidenheimer (eds.), *The Development of Welfare States in Europe and America*. New Brunswick, NJ: Transaction Books, 345–92.

ZERAH, DOV (1993). *Le Système financier français: Dix ans de mutations*. Paris: La Documentation Française.

ZYSMAN, JOHN (1983). *Governments, Markets, and Growth: Financial Systems and the Politics of Industrial Change*. Ithaca, NY: Cornell University Press.

8

Italy
Rescue from Without?

MAURIZIO FERRERA AND ELISABETTA GUALMINI

For much of the postwar period Italy was regarded as the sick man of
Europe. The Italian disease had both political and economic components:
harsh ideological divisions, chronic governmental instability, an inefficient
bureaucracy, uneven socio-economic development, organized crime, and
unbalanced public finances—just to mention the most classical stereo-
types. In the course of the 1990s, however, some encouraging signs of a
healing process appeared on the scene. The most visible and relevant indicator of this was certainly Italy's entry into the Economic and Monetary
Union by the established deadline of 1998, at the same moment as the
other 'core' European countries. Only a few years back this event seemed
almost unimaginable to any realistic observer. Respecting the Maastricht
criteria would, in fact, have required a massive effort of macroeconomic
adjustment, which would in turn have required both stable politics and
coherent policies: two goods that had always been in very scarce supply
South of the Alps. But entry into the EMU is only the tip of the iceberg.
In addition to macroeconomic adjustment, the 1990s witnessed a multitude of other innovations—some quite big, some small but nevertheless
significant—which have slowly redesigned the country's institutional fab-
ric, greatly enhancing its political and policy capabilities.

'Internationalization'—but especially the dynamics of European integration—has played a major role in fostering these positive developments.
In the specialized literature, internationalization is often portrayed as a
threat to domestic employment and welfare state regimes. Equally often,
it is suggested that these regimes can be preserved (or successfully

This paper is based on common work by the two authors. Sections 8.1.1, 8.1.3, 8.1.4, 8.1.5,
8.2.1.4, 8.2.2.2, 8.3, and the introduction have been written by Maurizio Ferrera; sections
8.1.2, 8.2.1, 8.2.1.1, 8.2.1.2, 8.2.1.3, 8.2.2.1, 8.2.3, 8.2.3.1, and 8.2.3.2 have been written by
Elisabetta Gualmini. The authors are grateful to all the MPI project participants, as well as
to Miriam Golden and Jonathan Zeitlin for the comments received. They also thank Paolo
Graziano for the precious research assistance. A longer and much more detailed version of
this chapter has appeared as a book in Italian (Ferrera and Gualmini 1999).

adjusted) by mobilizing existing state capabilities in order to neutralize or attenuate exogenous challenges and shocks. With respect to this line of argument, the Italian experience seems to go in exactly the opposite direction. First, the Italian disease (including structural unemployment and an unbalanced welfare system) was there long before the winds of globalization started to blow. Second, the new dynamics of economic internationalization that started to unfold in Italy during the 1980s did not produce those harmful effects on employment and income distribution that made their sinister appearance elsewhere in the OECD. Quite to the contrary, what seems to emerge from the available empirical literature on the issue is that, if anything, the process of internationalization probably benefited the average Italian worker. Third, combined with internal developments, the process of internationalization stimulated a real 'quantum leap' in terms of institutional capabilities: in other words, it triggered a sequence of changes that is transforming Italy into a proper state, finally able to act on a par with its political allies and economic competitors in inter-state arenas (including, obviously, the EU). The transformation is not complete. And there are worries that Italy's vulnerability to exogenous challenges may dramatically increase in the new phase that the international economy is now entering. But the path to 'virtuous statehood' is still visible and open. The sick man can get well—if he so chooses.

This chapter is organized in two parts. Section 8.1 will illustrate the start-up constellation and discuss the endogenous and original problems of 'welfare capitalism Italian style' as they were manifested in the 1970s. Section 8.2 will reconstruct the circuitous process of adjustment from its early (and largely unsuccessful) steps in the 1980s to the turning points of the 1990s. The conclusion will present the challenges ahead and the emerging profile of the new Italy—an Italy 'European style'.

8.1. The Scene in the 1970s: Lights, Shadows, and Thunders

8.1.1. The Lights: The Rise of Keynesian Welfare . . .

In the first two and a half decades after World War II, the Italian economy underwent a process of remarkable growth, which enabled the country to gain a quite respectable position among the top industrialized powers. Average per capita income grew some 2.5 times between 1950 and 1970. GDP skyrocketed in 1955–69, mainly as a result of international trade and the successful penetration of foreign markets.

This long 'economic miracle' was accompanied by a gradual consolidation and articulation of the state apparatus, putting in place and fine-tuning the fairly complex institutional framework designed by the 1948 constitution. Perhaps the major accomplishment on this front was the creation of the regions, completed by 1970. The national executive remained firmly in the hands of the Christian Democrats (Democrazia cristiana— DC), but during the 1960s this party struck a new alliance with the Socialists (the so-called Center Left, formed in 1962), which was to last for the next thirty years. The opposition remained monopolized by a Communist Party with a strong Marxist-Leninist orientation. Though highly combative in the electoral arena, the PCI was de facto involved in shaping the most important domestic policies, especially in the economic and social fields.

The economic miracle and the coming together of the DC and PSI offered a fertile background for the expansion of the welfare state. The institutional framework inherited by the new Republican regime born in 1948 divided social protection into three separate parts: social insurance (*previdenza*), health and sanitation (*sanità*), and assistance (*assistenza*). Social insurance included six major schemes (for pensions, unemployment, TB, family allowances, sickness and maternity, occupational injuries and diseases), administered by a number of separate agencies and funds for selected occupational categories, often with diverse eligibility and benefit regulations. Insurance coverage was limited to employees, thus excluding the self-employed; most benefits were flat rate or related to previous contributions. The provision of health services relied heavily on the private sector. Finally, a plethora of public and semi-public agencies provided social assistance for the needy at both the national and local levels, paralleled by private and church charities.

This institutional setting witnessed only a few alterations during the 1950s and 1960s. The latter decade was one of ambitious reforms plans, promoted by the new Center-Left coalition. But—as Table 8.1 shows—the record of actual reforms was quite poor until the end of the decade. From 1968 onwards, however, the institutional profile of the Italian welfare state started to change rapidly in the wake of new and heated social conflicts and under popular and union pressures.

Thus, in the second half of the 1970s the Italian welfare state emerged as a relatively distinct and coherent institutional configuration. Though still largely centered on the Bismarckian principles of social insurance typical of all Continental, conservative-corporatist welfare regimes, this configuration now added an explicitly 'Beveridgean' element—or at least a Beveridgean aspiration—to the field of health care. The Bismarckian transfer schemes provided relatively generous benefits, most of which were earnings-related and fully indexed. The formerly dispersed health care and social services had been replaced by a relatively unitary—though highly

Table 8.1 *Social policy reforms, 1950–1980*

Social Insurance

1952	Pension reform: improvement of pension formula and establishment of pension minimums
1955	Family allowances reform
1958–67	Pension insurance extended to farmers, artisans, and traders
1968	Unemployment insurance improved
1969	Pension reform: introduction of earnings-related and social pensions; cost of living indexation
1974	Reform of invalidity pensions
1975	Wage indexation of pensions

Health

1968	Reform of administrative and financial regulations for hospitals
1974	Hospital care transferred to regions
1978	Establishment of the National Health Service

Education

1962	School leaving age raised to 14; introduction of unified post-elementary curriculum
1969	Access to higher education greatly expanded
1974	Creation of parent/student representative boards

Social Assistance

1972	Jurisdiction over social assistance and services transferred to the regions
1977	Social assistance 'categorical' funds abolished; jurisdiction transferred to local authorities

decentralized—national and universal service, based on citizenship rights; education had been reformed and greatly expanded, and housing services broadly decentralized.

The institutional maturation of the welfare state was paralleled by a rapid and substantial quantitative expansion. In the mid-1950s, total social expenditure (including income maintenance, health care, and social assistance) absorbed around 10 percent of GDP—a relatively low level by international standards (Flora 1983, 1986/87; Ferrera 1987). In 1970 this percentage had risen to 17.4 percent, reaching 22.6 percent in 1975—a level in line with that of France or Belgium and higher than that of Britain (EC 1993).

8.1.2. . . . and of a 'Guaranteed' Labor Market

The long economic miracle caused profound modifications in the employment structure. At the beginning of the 1950s Italy was to a large extent still an agrarian country: more than 40 percent of the labor force was occupied in the primary sector, with a large number of independent farmers and sharecroppers. By 1970 this proportion had fallen to under 20 percent, with the secondary and tertiary sector at about 40 percent each. Although certainly more modern by the early 1970s, Italy's labor force continued to have a profile displaying some peculiar traits, such as the high incidence of self-employment (about 20%) and a very low female participation rate (at about 30%).

In the 1970s a generous system of *ammortizzatori sociali* (social shock absorbers) was completed for unemployment policy. These mechanisms were 'passive policies', that is they were mainly addressed to the workers who had lost their job and who had come out from the labor market (and not to those who entered it): these ex-employed were in addition the regular adult workers who constituted the core of the employment structure. Three different but intertwined phenomena contributed toward improving social protection against the risk of unemployment: the extension and improvement of cash benefits, the overall institutionalization of labor relations through the Workers' Statute, and the rise in union power.

After the war, state regulation of the labor market rested on three main pillars: a general unemployment insurance scheme, a scheme for short-term earnings replacement in case of temporary redundancies (*Cassa integrazione guadagni ordinaria*), and centralized employment services. The insurance scheme was addressed to private sector workers remaining without work, and eligibility required at least two years of contributions. The allowance was very low and based on a flat-rate daily amount. The *Cassa Integrazione* allowance was still based on contributions, but it was related to previous earnings (60%–65%) and aimed at protecting those workers who had been temporarily hit by working time reductions and whose re-entry into the firm was thought to be certain. Finally, in 1949 the state monopoly on employment services was established. The unemployed had to register onto compulsory lists, where their positions depended on pre-defined criteria; employers had to notify the placement office about the kinds of workers they needed to hire, and each worker was automatically assigned to a firm.

From the 1950s to the 1970s these three pillars mutually reinforced each other. The amount of the unemployment insurance benefit was adjusted several times, but since it did not keep up with the cost of living, the benefit eroded in real terms. By contrast, the *Cassa Integrazione* scheme literally boomed and started to function as a substitute for the general unemployment pillar.

The unemployment insurance schemes were integrated by new legislation on workers' rights in 1970. That year's Workers' Statute, the result of a heated political debate, strongly limited employers' power by imposing constraints and sanctions in case union activities were repressed. Individual and collective workers' rights in the factories were acknowledged and widened. The law was to be applied in enterprises with more than fifteen employees. It included rules for the protection of the dignity and freedom of the worker, for the defense of union political activities, and for the exercise of a rich set of social rights connected to working life. It also severely restricted the possibility of individual firings.

In addition, the Workers' Statute reinforced the presence of trade unions in the workplace. This was also a result of the changed political and social climate at the end of the 1960s. The explosion of conflicts and strikes during the 1969 'hot autumn' allowed the unions to take on a primary role in the battle for reforms (for pensions, housing, taxes) and higher wages. Union demands were unanimous: greater control over income policies, active participation in the management of the firm, and 'egalitarianism' (i.e. the reduction of wage differentials based on sex, job category, and skill) (Cella and Treu 1989, 1998). The rise in power of national trade unions was reflected in a parallel rise of union membership. Between 1968 and 1975 the members of the CISL, the Catholic-oriented union, rose from 1 million to 2.5 million, while those of the CGIL, the Communist-oriented union, grew from 2.5 million to 4.5 million (Ricciardi 1986). From 1970 to 1980 overall union membership in Italy rate rose from 33.4 percent to 44.1 percent, overtaking the Dutch (33.8%), German (34.3%), and EC average rates of union growth (38.1%) (Carrieri 1995: 149).

Table 8.2 *Labor policies, 1950–1980: A summary*

1919	General unemployment insurance
1945–47	Regular short-term earnings replacement benefits (*Cassa Integrazione ordinaria*)
1945	Wage indexation (*scala mobile*)
1949	State employment services
1955	Apprenticeship
1966	Law on individual dismissals
1968	Special short-term earnings replacement benefits (*Cassa Integrazione estraordinaria*)
1970	Workers' statute
1975	Improvement of wage indexation and unification of the regular and special *Cassa integrazione* scheme to 80% of the previous earnings
1977	Law on youth employment
1977	Law on industrial mobility and restructuring
1978	Law on vocational training

8.1.3. The Shadows: An Internally Flawed Constellation

The socio-economic and institutional dynamics illustrated thus far undoubtedly contributed in a major way to Italy's overall modernization. However, they left a number of structural questions unresolved. Moreover, these changes planted some new, dangerous seeds causing additional problems to emerge. As stated at the outset of this section, the 1970s witnessed the appearance of an endogenous crisis, the most visible symptoms of which were concentrated in the welfare state's financing.

The Italian welfare state's unresolved structural questions essentially had to do with the persistence of the country's historical divisions: the socio-economic division between a rapidly industrializing North and a deeply backward South, and the ideological and political division between a moderate, largely Catholic 'white' subculture and a radical, largely Communist 'red' subculture.

Despite the huge flows of resources channeled into the Mezzogiorno by the central government, the Southern economy was still lagging far behind at the beginning of the 1970s. The North–South divide was especially dramatic in occupational terms. In 1970 the unemployment rate was 4.9 percent in the South, as against 2.3 percent in the Center-North. By 1979 these figures had risen to 10.9 percent and 6.2 percent respectively (Gualmini 1998). In the early 1970s the first statistics on the 'black' economy brought to light almost three million underground workers, mainly concentrated in the Southern regions (Census 1976).

The North–South dualism was only one of the deep and persisting domestic tensions of the hot 1970s. That decade also witnessed a dramatic intensification of the traditional political divisions within the country. Growing competition between the Communist Party and the governing coalitions, widespread and heated social conflicts, and the rise of terrorism were the most visible symptoms.

The persistence (and, in some respects, even the aggravation) of these perennial questions was not the only shadow hovering over the political stage during the 1970s. New problems were, in fact, opening up in the wake of the social policy and labor market regimes built during the previous two decades. Using summary formulas, we can say that those two regimes had laid the groundwork for the five 'original sins' of welfare capitalism Italian-style, which have been (and still largely are) the object of debates and policies in the 1980s and 1990s.

8.1.4. Five 'Original Sins' of Welfare Capitalism Italian-Style

The first two sins can be characterized as 'distortions'. The social insurance reforms listed in Table 8.1 initiated, first of all, an allocative distortion, clearly favoring certain risks or functions of social policy (most notably, old age and survival) at the expense of certain others (most notably, family benefits and services, total lack of employment or income, and relief from poverty). The 1969 pension reform introduced what probably was, at the time, the most generous 'defined benefit' formula in the Western world (70% of previous wages after 35 years of work with no age threshold, or 80% at age 60 for men and age 55 for women). On the other hand, those schemes aimed at catering to the needs of large and poor families remained underdeveloped and underfunded. At the beginning of the 1950s, pensions and family benefits absorbed roughly equal shares of GDP (Ferrera 1987). By 1980 pension expenditure was almost seven time higher than that on family benefits, the highest ratio in the EC except for Greece (EC 1993). The 1969 reform set the country on the road to becoming a 'pension state' rather than a balanced and articulated welfare state.

The second distortion was of a distributive nature. Centered as they are on occupational status, all Bismarckian systems give rise to some disparity of treatment across sectors and categories. However, the fragmented development of Italy's social insurance initiated a true 'labyrinth' of categorical privileges that has very few counterparts in other countries (Ferrera 1996). The main cleavage (which had already become easy to see by the 1970s) pitted workers located in the core sectors of the (industrial) labor market against those located in the more peripheral sectors (semi-regular and unemployed). As this strong dualism has persisted as one of the Italian employment regime's most important features, it may be useful to discuss it in some detail.

The dualism finds its roots in two distinct phenomena: the institutional design of unemployment programs and the dynamics of wage policies. The system of social shock absorbers illustrated above was mainly centered on insurance mechanisms. The eligible workers were those who had paid contributions for at least two years of regular work. In other words, the main beneficiaries were industrial workers belonging to the primary labor market (so-called 'insiders'). The two major instruments of labor policy, unemployment insurance and the *Cassa Integrazione* schemes, had adopted this kind of contributory logic. By the same token, the procedures for placement were based on two different trajectories, one for the formerly employed 'insiders' (eligible for insurance benefits) and another for the unemployed 'outsiders' (young people in search of first jobs, women, peripheral and underground workers, etc.). The former could move from one firm to another without respecting the rule of the 'call by lot' (i.e. the numerical order of the list), but simply responding to the employers' 'nominative call' (i.e. a job offer *ad personam*); the latter were instead subjected to the rule of the 'call by lot'—which meant no freedom of choice for the employers and automatic placement for workers. The most immediate effect was a propensity on the part of employers to hire the previously employed 'insiders', to the detriment of the unemployed 'outsiders'.

Such a distortion in the distribution of benefits was also reinforced by union strategies on wage policy. The social conflicts of the 1970s gave rise to significant improvements in real wages and the indexation regime. Earnings were transformed into an 'independent variable' (independent of inflation and the economy in general), and the immediate beneficiaries of this kind of policy, which has become notorious as an 'income policy in reverse' (Rossi 1998), were (of course) members of the unions—'insiders' again.

During the 'hot autumn' of 1969, union wage demands had numerous objectives: to extend union control over wage dynamics, to increase the wage scale, to reduce differentials among the various categories of workers, to fill the gap between the less protected workers and the more protected ones and to abolish most of the productivity- and performance-related wage components (Somaini 1989). An impetuous rise in earnings and a higher 'egalitarianism' were, in fact, achieved during that period.[1] Of particular importance was the reduction of wage differentials, resulting from the elimination of the so-called 'wage cages' in 1969. This system was based on a list of geographic areas characterized by different wage minimums. Strikes to dismantle the 'cages', thought to be the most tangible sign of the Italy's non-democratic backwardness, began in 1968, both in the public and private sectors. Opposition from employers, who favored the 'cages' as instruments of flexibility, was strong. The first to surrender were the employers in public firms, followed by the associations representing small and medium-sized firms, and finally by Confindustria (representing big business) (Turone 1988). The suppression of the 'wage cages' opened the way for nationally centralized collective bargaining, still regarded as one of the main rigidities in the Italian labor market (Faini, Falzoni, and Galeotti 1998).

In 1975 the national trade unions and Confindustria signed an agreement establishing a new system of wage indexation for industrial workers.[2] For each percentage point increase in consumer prices, all wages were to increase by a single flat-rate amount (the so-called *punto unico di contingenza*). This meant that lower wages were more strongly protected than higher wages, leading to a gradual 'egalitarian' ironing out of the earnings

[1] In the period 1970–71 nominal wages increased by 19.9% and in the 1973–75 period by 22.7% (compared to 6.8% in 1968–69). In 1970 real wages rose by 15% (Rossi 1998).
[2] The so-called *scala mobile* had been introduced early in 1945 to safeguard wages against inflation. The level of wages was periodically anchored to the level of the cost of living which was measured on the basis of a pre-defined 'basket of goods'.

pyramid. But the new *scala mobile* concealed many countervailing effects: it was simultaneously a powerful barrier against the inflationary erosion of wages and a powerful incentive for the wage–price spiral (and thus a spur to inflation).[3]

The third original sin that characterized the initial 'Keynesian' constellation had to do with the financing of public, and especially social, expenditure. In 1950–64 Italy's public finances witnessed a phase of relatively balanced growth, in which the expansion of outlays was matched by a parallel expansion of revenues. However, the subsequent decade was marked by a new pattern of unbalanced growth, in which outlays continued to rise while revenues stagnated at around 30 percent of GDP.[4] This stagnation was the effect of two distinct phenomena: the official conversion to deficit spending (through a Keynesian reinterpretation of Article 81 of the Italian Constitution) which weakened the pressure to raise real revenues (as opposed to public borrowing) even in the presence of mounting outlays; the political obstacles to passing a tax reform capable of extending the tax base and the effectiveness of the tax system (this reform only arrived in 1973). The 'flat decade' on the revenue side created an 'original hole' in Italy's public finances, which made things much worse when the exogenous shocks hit in the mid-1970s (Gerelli and Majocchi 1984).

Developments over the next decade, however, did not correspond to the intentions and expectations of Keynesian doctrine. It was not public investment that grew, but current expenditure (transfers and subsidies in particular), leading to a rapid erosion of public saving. General government net lending rose from 0.8 percent of GDP in 1964 (the last 'virtuous' year) to 7.0 percent in 1974 and 11.4 percent in 1975—at the peak of the first oil shock slump. And public deficits largely served to finance the growth of the welfare state. From the mid-1960s onward, the aggregate balance between statutory contributions and benefits turned negative for many pension and most sickness funds: contribution rates were, in fact, kept artificially low, in the hope of stimulating job creation, but also to please social constituencies who were crucial for political stability. Despite repeated doses of ad hoc financial aid from the Treasury, the budgetary situation in the social security sector continued to deteriorate, and in 1974/75

---

[3] The indexation dynamic was not in fact perfectly aligned with the consumer prices trend. If in the period 'A' the inflation had risen, wages would have grown in the period immediately following, that is in period 'B', when inflation had probably diminished. And if wages had risen, this was an occasion for firms to push up prices; employers had no hesitations in doing this, since they could rely on the lira devaluation mechanism. The 1975 agreement ended up by offering the basis for an uncontrollable wage-inflation rise.

[4] From 1965 to 1975 the total outlays of government rose from 34.2% of GDP to 43.4%; in the same decade total revenues remained basically unchanged moving from 30% of the GDP to 31.2% (ISTAT, various issues).

the government had to launch an extraordinary operation to repay enormous debts accumulated by the funds, amounting to 5.2 percent of GDP.

The remaining two original sins had to do with legality and efficiency. Though highly structured from a legislative and organizational viewpoint, the social policy configuration built between the 1950s and the 1970s was marked by a high degree of institutional 'softness'. Especially in some sectors and areas, the degree of compliance with the rules disciplining access to benefits and payment of contributions remained very low, not only on the part of the social programs' various clienteles, but also on the part of public authorities. This syndrome assumed inordinate proportions with respect to disability pensions, which became the privileged currency of an extended clientelistic market: between 1960 and 1980 the total number of disability pensions rose almost five times, and in the mid-1970s (following an expansive reform) it came to surpass the total number of old age pensions, an unparalleled record in the OECD area (Ferrera 1984, 1987, 1996).

As to the efficiency of public services (in virtually all areas of public intervention), the situation in the 1970s fell short of all the Keynesian modernizers' expectations from the 1960s. The lack of a pragmatic culture, the partisan colonization of the administrative apparatus, the opportunistic use of public employment by the patronage system, the failure to design rational systems of incentives—these and other factors gave rise to an oversized bureaucracy with very low levels of performance (Cassese 1974).

These five original sins of 'welfare capitalism Italian-style' were partly the result of specific policy choices (or non-choices) made in the formative decades (1950–70), choices that in turn reflected quite closely the overall 'political logic' of what is currently called Italy's First Republic (1948–92). This is especially true for the aforementioned distortions: for example, the development of a pension-heavy welfare state, financially unsound and inclined towards particularistic-clientelistic manipulations, was highly congruent with the competitive mechanics of polarized pluralism (Sartori 1982) in Italy and, more particularly, with the interests of the three major parties (DC, PCI, and PSI). The emphasis on pensions as 'deferred wages' and the neglect of family policy actually mirrored the social doctrines of both Marxism and Catholicism.[5] More crucially, the expansion of a highly fragmented social insurance system offered ample opportunities for

---

[5] At least in the Italian tradition, both doctrines saw pension insurance as an extension of the wage relationship. For Catholics, this meant that there was no violation of the subsidiarity principle, even with generous public benefits, while for Marxists it meant that pensions were to be a crucial target of the class struggle between workers and employers. On the contrary, the family was regarded as an 'off-limits' area for the state by Catholics, and as only a secondary objective for public policy by Marxists.

distributing differentiated entitlements to selected party clienteles. To some extent, though, it should not be forgotten that the distinctive elements of *welfare all'italiana* (Ascoli 1984) find their roots in some of Italian society's broader historical features, such as the traditional 'uncivicness' of political culture, the aforementioned 'historical divisions' (of an economic and ideological nature) and ensuing deficit of 'normative' integration, and the failure to create a Weberian administration.

Whatever their historical origins, and however congruent with the overall complexion of post-war Italy, the internal flaws and malfunctioning of the Keynesian-Fordist constellation of the 1970s rendered the country structurally vulnerable to the external shocks that appeared on stage at the beginning of that decade. Hitting brittle ground, the storm produced more serious damage in this country than elsewhere in Europe.

8.1.5. Enter the External Challenges: From Miracles to Thunderstorms

Italy's political economy stepped into the 1970s with the wrong foot. In the wake of the wage hikes of 1969, the Bank of Italy and the Treasury decided on a monetary squeeze in 1970, which provoked a recession in 1971. This prompted the government to shift back to an expansionist policy in both monetary and budgetary terms. The cycle turned swiftly upwards, but so did inflation, while the balance of payments witnessed increasing strains. With the collapse of the dollar standard (and as a consequence of strong speculative attacks), the lira was devalued in 1973. This move did not compromise the upward trend of the cycle, but devaluation did reinforce already existing domestic inflationary pressures by making imported raw materials more expensive. Severe administrative controls were also introduced on capital movements, in order to discourage an alarming rise in capital flight. In 1974 the rate of inflation had risen to 19 percent, up from 2 percent in 1968. The first oil shock produced a dramatic slump in 1975; in that year GDP fell by almost 4 percent. Inflation went down too. But in 1975 the aforementioned *scala mobile* agreement created what we can now see (with hindsight) as an infernal stagflation-multiplier, whose consequences were to be seriously felt for many years to come. By guaranteeing an immediate adjustment of wages to prices, the new *scala mobile* not only contributed to the spread of inflation throughout all branches of the economy; it also fostered an overall climate of self-sustaining inflationary expectations. At the end of 1975 the government lowered interest rates and created new liquidity in order to get out of the recession and support a severely ailing industrial sector. However, a massive new speculative attack was launched against the lira, and in the winter of 1976 the national currency's official rate had to be suspended for forty days. When the exchange rate market reopened, the lira had suffered a heavy new devaluation. The vicious circle of devaluation-inflation-indexation brought the rate of inflation up to 21 percent by 1980. In the same year, public debt had mounted to 58.1 percent of GDP (1970 = 38.1%) and public deficit to 8.6 percent (1970 = 4%).

The macroeconomic policies pursued by the Treasury and the Bank of Italy in the 1970s have been severely criticized as inadequate responses to the new international context, and thus largely responsible for the ailing state of Italy's economy and public finances at the end of the decade.[6] This indictment must be tempered by at least two considerations: (1) initial conditions were characterized by a high degree of vulnerability; (2) the social and political situation placed severe constraints on policymakers. To some extent, inflation and deficits were the most viable instruments available for spreading the costs of adjustment in a context that allowed very little room to define policy priorities ex ante and impose explicit sacrifices.

Indeed, a deliberate attempt at macroeconomic stabilization was made in the second half of the decade. In 1976, following an outstanding electoral success of the Communists, a 'national solidarity' majority was formed in Parliament, including the PCI. This coalition made significant decisions in many policy domains (e.g. the fight against terrorism). More specifically, it tried to pursue an explicit policy of 'real' macroeconomic adjustment.

The point of departure for this attempt was a fully-fledged neo-corporatist agreement—the first ever experienced in Italy. This agreement had a precise date and a precise venue: February 1978, during the so-called 'EUR' union assembly (from the name of the neighborhood in Rome where it took place). The implicit pact was for the government to commit itself to protecting existing employment levels and to finding innovative solutions for combating youth unemployment while the unions promised to restrain wages. A number of fiscal measures followed, with positive effects on labor costs and productivity. More significantly, some innovative industrial and labor policies were introduced (cf. Table 8.2): the new climate of social cooperation between the unions and the government offered a fertile ground for the development of active labor market policies.

The 'real' adjustment policy of the national solidarity coalition was not very effective. The attempt was short-lived (1976–79) and collapsed over continuing political and ideological strains between its main protagonists.

However, the 1970s closed with a political *coup de reins*, which was to have significant repercussions in the period to follow: this coup was the

---

[6] For a discussion, cf. esp. Salvati 1981, 1984.

decision to adhere to the newly created European monetary system (EMS). The issue was quite hot for Italy, since it involved the abandonment of the old (and basically successful) devaluation-centered monetary policy in favor of a new (and thus more uncertain) monetary policy. The PCI was firmly against the adhesion, which in its view risked tying Italy's hands with countries that were 'cruelly classist'. Thus, Prime Minister Giulio Andreotti opted for a bold game. Initially, he said no in Brussels when the EMS was officially launched on 5 December 1978. But back in Rome, he crafted a new political majority excluding the PCI and including the right. On 13 December the Italian Parliament voted the lira's entry into the EMS. On this vote, the 'national solidarity' coalitions broke down, with the PCI joining again the ranks of the opposition. Why did Andreotti do this? He was definitely convinced that an exogenous spur was beneficial for Italy's battered economy. But he also seized a good opportunity for severing the link between the DC and the PCI that was becoming increasingly suffocating for his own party in electoral terms and increasingly costly in terms of Italy's credibility abroad. In the last months of 1979 the lira finally entered the EMS, though with a larger fluctuation band (6% instead of 2.25%) than the monetary system's core currencies. Joining the EMS marked the beginning of a new phase in Italy's EC membership, which was bound to affect most policy sectors. But in order to analyze the important impact of this new phase, we need to turn another page.

8.2. The Winding Road to Adjustment

8.2.1. The Impact of Economic Internationalization

Entry into the EMS represented the first stage in a long process of adjustment to exogenous challenges; the second stage coincided with the completion of the internal market in the late 1980s; and the third with Italy's convergence towards the Maastricht criteria during the 1990s. The adjustment pressures for all three stages had different relative weights, however, since each process was filtered by domestic dynamics of the policy and political change. Already in the first half of the 1980s some important preconditions for an effective adjustment of both the economy and public finances were posed. But policymakers—disturbed as they were by high political instability, the persisting challenge of terrorism, and the inflationary effects of the second oil shock—did not seem prepared to undertake a process of change. So instead they persevered with the expansionary and distributive policy strategies of the past. The pressures stemming from internationalization became more visible beginning with the Maastricht Treaty, when the process of 'restoring to health' (*risanamento*) public finances (and hence economic and social policy) became more a necessity than a virtue. Moreover, in the early 1990s, international pressures to adjust intertwined with the deep institutional changes following the fall of the 'First Republic'. The rapid transformation of the most familiar rules and ingredients of both the domestic political system and of the international economic environment forced Italian politicians to modify their strategies substantially and introduce important policy innovations.

8.2.1.1. The Contradictory 1980s: Testing Adjustment while Accumulating a Huge Public Debt

As far as the real economy was concerned, the 1980s were characterized by contradictory trends. On the one hand, entry into the EMS and the reforms in the governance of the central bank made it possible to pursue a rigorous monetary policy whose main goals were deflation, currency stability, and regaining national credibility after the gloomy performance of the 1970s. On the other hand, the Center-Left coalitions (revived under the novel name of penta-party governments) that remained in power for the entire decade were not able to take advantage of changed economic conditions (a significant GDP recovery that started in 1983 and even outlasted the 1986 oil counter-shock). Instead, the penta-party governments (like their Center-Left predecessors from the 1960s and early 1970s) kept on playing their traditional distributive games based on easy spending.

Participating in the EMS proved to be particularly important for the Italian economy, since it involved a radical transformation in monetary policy. The lira's entry into a fixed band of currency oscillation, though wider than the standard one, forced abandonment of those traditional devaluation strategies that had allowed Italian competitiveness to be safeguarded without implementing strategies of real adjustment. Two years after entering the EMS, in 1981, a 'divorce' between the Treasury and the Bank of Italy was finalized: under the new regime the latter ceased to be the last-resort buyer of unsold government bonds, and the instruments of monetary and credit policy were modified by dismantling direct controls on credit and removing administrative obligations, in favor of a more market-oriented regulation (Addis 1987; Epstein and Shor 1987). The most immediate aim after the 'divorce' was to curb inflation through a smaller emission of currency. In addition, the new Governor Ciampi began to call for a substantial reform of the budgetary process and for a new bargaining regime in order to keep wages and productivity under control. Ciampi's repeated pleas opened the way for the 1988 reform, which introduced new rules and instruments for the planning and control of public accounts (Verzichelli 1999). As for wages and productivity, a broad political agreement among the government, trade unions, and employers' associations was signed in 1983.

The restrictive monetary policy carried out by the central bank had a series of interrelated effects: inflation began to decline, but the trade balance progressively deteriorated both for goods and services, since competitive devaluation could no longer be used to boost exports.

But in the second half of the 1980s, in the wake of the oil counter-shock, real economic indicators improved significantly. GDP growth rate surpassed 3 percent, while the inflation rate fell below 6 percent. The trade balance showed a surplus, investments rose (from 18.8% in 1986 to 20.3% in 1990), and exports boomed.[7] The Single European Act (1986), soon followed by liberalization of the market for financial capital (1988), encouraged further mobility of goods and capital outside national boundaries. Thus, for example, in the period 1981–90 direct foreign investment (FDI) in Italy amounted to $28,707 m, compared to $3,597 m in the previous decade.

However, these positive economic conditions did not stimulate national policymakers to take incisive measures in order to contain expenditure growth—despite frequent lip-service paid to this objective. Despite a notable increase of revenues, the balances of public accounts thus continued to deteriorate.

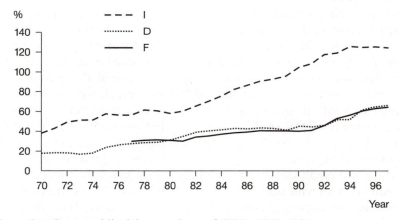

Figure 8.1 Gross public debt as a share of GDP, 1970–1997
Source: OECD, *Economic Outlook* (Paris: OECD, various issues).

---

[7] In 1990, 58.2% of the exports were addressed to EC countries, 4.9% to Eastern Europe, and 14.7% to development countries (Onida 1993: 192). The Italian share of world export also increased (from 3.8% in 1980 to 4.7% in 1989).

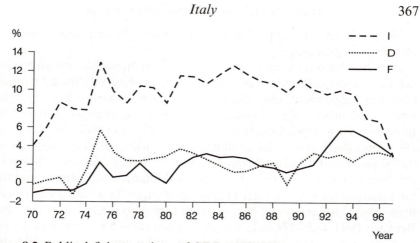

Figure 8.2 Public deficits as a share of GDP, 1970–1997
Source: OECD, *Economic Outlook* (Paris: OECD, various issues).

8.2.1.2. 1992–1998: A Copernican Revolution?

There were other symptoms of crisis making an appearance in the early 1990s aside from the alarming conditions of public finances: these included a decline in production, the rapid acceleration of labor costs, and the declining employment in the tertiary sector—especially in tertiary self-employment, as a result of both the recession and the process of structural adjustment initiated in this sector. In such a difficult situation, Italy's signature on the European Union Treaty in February 1992 could be seen (and actually was viewed by many national and international commentators) as an act of temerity or even folly. The immediate aftermath of the EU Treaty signing seemed to confirm this view. As a matter of fact, after the negative result of the Danish referendum on EMU in the summer of 1992, a massive speculative attack was launched against the lira. The central bank tried to counterattack by drawing down currency reserves and by virtually risking a financial collapse. It proved possible to avoid this risk, however, because of some interrelated circumstances that jointly produced a sudden and rather extraordinary virtuous adjustment. The strong devaluation of the lira (by 30%) and its consequent exit from the EMS laid the foundation for a sizeable increase in exports, allowing Italy to catch up with competitors and establish a remarkable foothold in international trade. In the meantime, the last government of the First Republic, led by Andreotti, was swept away by the investigations of Tangentopoli, and the 'technical' government of Giuliano Amato entered the scene. Amato undertook a portentous budgetary manoeuvre (equal to 6% of the GDP), which was the first truly effective step taken to correct public finance imbalances after fifty years of profligacy.

1992 has become a sort of *annus fatalis* in the scholarly and public debate, usually referred to as a watershed dividing the 'maladjustment' from the 'adjustment' era. Some authors have spoken of a 'Copernican revolution', others of a 'big turn' or at least a 'big change' (Salvati 1997; Bodo and Viesti 1997; Graziani 1998). In fact it can hardly be denied that 1992 witnessed a successful combination of various positive events; it was the beginning of a rather fortunate chain of 'policy windows' (Kingdom 1984) opening up conditions for continued financial adjustment and thus for a positive response to international challenges. This view is clearly confirmed by Italy's economic performance throughout the rest of the 1990s. Between 1992 and 1998 inflation went down from 5.6 percent to 2.5 percent, the public deficit from 9.6 percent to 2.6 percent, and public debt started a slow but visible decline (1997 = 121.7%) after peaking at 125 percent of GDP in 1994. In 1996 the lira went back into the EMS. Interest rates started to go down, and hopes for investments were revived. Between 1996 and 1997 the number of privatizations in Italy was the highest in Europe: one year later, in May 1998, under the Prodi government, Italy finally entered the ranks of the first group of countries joining the EMU, by virtue of satisfying the Maastricht criteria. As mentioned above, some preconditions for the post-1992 virtuous circle had already been posed in the previous decade; and several shadows still spoil the picture, as will be shown later. But the fact remains that the 1990s will be remembered as a crucial decade for Italy's firm and irreversible 'anchoring' to the European core—one of the few grand objectives unifying the nation since the 1950s.

Italy's remarkable macroeconomic adjustment has been accompanied by significant changes in this country's international economic profile, especially as regards exports, alliances and partnerships with foreign companies, and foreign direct investment. Big firms that traditionally specialized in exports have been joined as exporters by small- and medium-sized firms. From 1992 to 1995 the measure for the whole economy's openness jumped from 35.5 percent to 45.2 percent. From 1985 to 1995 the stock of Italian FDI grew from 3.8 percent to 8.7 percent of GDP (Faini, Falzoni, and Galeotti 1998). As clearly shown in Figure 8.3, Italy began to catch up in the early 1990s, even though its considerable progress was not sufficient to reach the levels of its European partners.

This process of internationalization has not, however, fully alleviated Italy's historic problems. Exports have indeed increased, but the 'specialized polarization' of Italian industry has intensified: a high volume of exports from the traditional sectors (shoes, clothes, textile, ceramic, furnishing), but very few from other sectors (especially high-tech). In addi-

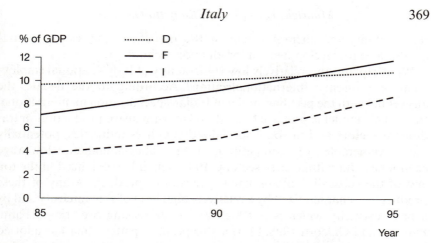

Figure 8.3 Foreign direct investment outward stock, 1985–1995
Source: Faini, Falzoni, and Galeotti 1998: 53.

tion, Italy has remained a poor attraction for foreign investors, given the unreliability of the state bureaucracy, public services, and communication systems. R & D expenditure is still among the lowest in the OECD countries. More seriously, the social and economic gap between a highly industrialized North and a backward South has widened.

8.2.1.3. Internationalization and National Employment: A Many-Sided Italy

According to the most recent economic literature, Italian employment has not suffered much from the growing openness of markets.[8] In the Italian case there is no evidence of those trends typically associated with internationalization in other industrial countries, such as growing unemployment among low-skilled and uneducated workers and/or a shift of wages in favor of skilled employees. Moreover, there appears to be no significant correlation across time between the standard set of trade indicators—such as the trade balance or the degree of import penetration—and labor market conditions. In fact, the data thus far indicate that Italy has experienced a relatively low degree of import penetration from low-wage countries (potentially harmful for national employment) and that the growing internationalization of Italian firms (including the growing number of employees in foreign affiliates of Italian multinationals) bears much less

---

[8] The main arguments of the debate can be found in: Barca and Visco 1992; Bodo and Viesti 1997; Micossi and Visco 1993; Onida 1993; Lawrence 1996; De Nardis and Galli 1997; Cominotti and Mariotti 1997; Deaglio 1998.

responsibility for unemployment in the manufacturing sector than is attributable to developments in production technology.

What explains this relatively low vulnerability of Italy's national employment to economic internationalization? According to the debate, the answer lies with the peculiar model of Italian specialization in international trade. This model is primarily based on labor-intensive production in traditional sectors and in some specialized suppliers industries, potentially quite vulnerable to competition from labor-abundant, low-wage economies. But within these sectors, 'Italy is mainly specialized in the top end of the vertically differentiated spectrum of products. Many of these products are characterized by a relatively high level of skill intensity and by a price elasticity which is not high and is decreasing over time' (Faini, Falzoni, and Galeotti 1998: 8). It is this peculiar pattern that has allowed Italy to survive well—in aggregate terms—in the new environment, and to take advantage of profitable niches in a trading system that is growing and becoming more open. This favorable match may not last forever. In fact, as will be discussed later, the Italian producers' profitable niches are increasingly at risk from some impending developments in world trade. Thanks to these niches, however, the Italian economy has been able to withstand the dangerous winds of globalization during the 1980s and (especially) the 1990s. Italy's unemployment problems thus appear to be primarily connected to domestic rather than exogenous factors.

This relatively optimistic assessment must be qualified, however, by geographical area. The intensification of international trade has actually thrown new light on Italy's regional and sectoral cleavages. First and foremost, it is necessary to distinguish among 'three different Italies': the industrialized North, and especially the historical industrial triangle of Piedmont, Lombardy, and Liguria (first Italy); the 'classical' Mezzogiorno, characterized by backwardness and underdevelopment (second Italy); and the so-called 'third Italy', comprising the North-East, Emilia-Romagna, Tuscany, Umbria, and the central Adriatic rim (Marche, Abruzzi). The sectoral composition of the three Italies is also divergent. In the North companies are mainly large and specialized in manufacturing and services. Third Italy is mainly based on family-led small firms and on industrial districts specializing in those products that are on the cutting edge of Italy's competitiveness: textiles and apparel, footwear, ceramics, precision mechanics. Southern regions, hardly to be regarded as homogeneous territory, are characterized by a mixed production profile: large (and declining) firms in the chemical, iron, and steel industries (the aging traditional sectors launched by state-assisted industrial development in the 1950s), small firms mainly operating in the (backward) construction and tertiary sectors, and large public bureaucracies.

Thus, the growth of employment in small firms has not been adversely affected or slowed down by international competition. Compared to Northern and Southern companies, the small and medium-sized companies of the 'Third Italy' have responded in a remarkably positive way to international pressures. Thanks to small firms' high level of product specialization, on the one hand, and to the outstanding entrepreneurship and innovativeness traditionally associated with the 'industrial districts' culture, on the other, small firms seem to have successfully exploited the new opportunities offered by internationalization, which these firms perceived as a stimulus to expansion and change.

There has been greater variation in the response of large firms, mainly operating in the North of Italy, to international challenges. The statement that globalization has had positive effects on employment holds true in general terms, but the exact meaning of this generalization depends on the time period. The available data on employment in manufacturing reveal that vulnerability to economic openness can both contract and expand employment at different times. Two different periods can be identified: the first lasting from 1985 to 1992 and the second starting after 1992. In the first phase the big rise in imports, which was the main result of the export strategies of the 'early internationalizing countries' (US, Japan, Germany, etc.), reduced the growth in the Italian demand for labor (from +9% to +5%). After the devaluation of 1992, however, the trend reversed, and export growth was able to compensate for past losses and so have a significant impact on the demand for labor (De Nardis and Galli 1997). In fact, it is in 1992 that Italy, undoubtedly a 'late internationalizer', begins to catch up and the nexus between internationalization and employment performance becomes very loose. This is especially well illustrated by Table 8.3 (drawn from the aforementioned analysis by Faini, Falzoni, and Galeotti 1998), which links changes in sectoral import penetration between 1992 and 1996 to employment dynamics. The growth of import penetration, which is particularly remarkable for footwear, leather goods (11.5%), and electrical machinery (8.4%), does not produce a corresponding reduction in employment. The decrease is limited (-1.3% and -0.3%, respectively) and lower than the one referred to total manufacturing (-1.7%).

International challenges thus combined with domestic economic dynamics in a way that affected employment only indirectly. Large Italian firms, with a preference for sticking to domestic markets, did not seem able to counter the import boom with expansionary strategies prior to 1992; only later did devaluation and economic recovery encourage them to explore European and world markets more fully. The export boom was so intense that it pushed employers to enlarge and diversify production, with positive repercussions on employment levels.

Table 8.3 *Employment and imports: sectoral trends*

1992–96	Change in employment (%)	Change in import penetration level (%)	Import penetration level (%, average value)
Mineral and non-mineral products	−1.8	4.2	35.68
Non-metallic mineral products	−2.4	1.2	10.83
Chemical products	−3.7	3.8	35.43
Metal products	−2.1	2.7	8.10
Agricultural and industrial machinery	−0.8	3.4	31.53
Office machinery	−1.5	−0.8	79.33
Electrical apparatus	−0.3	8.4	14.75
Motor vehicles	−3.3	4.2	57.75
Food, beverages and tobacco	−1.7	1.5	17.83
Textiles and apparel	−1.1	3.6	19.68
Footwear and leather goods	−1.3	11.5	31.65
Wood and wood products	−1.9	1.1	11.23
Paper, paper products, and painting	−2.0	2.1	11.78
Rubber and plastic products	−0.4	2.2	19.03
Total manufacturing	−1.7	4.2	26.45

Source: Faini, Falzoni, and Galeotti 1998: 58.

Still different is the picture of the Mezzogiorno, which at first sight may appear as the only loser from globalization. And, in fact, the major recession of 1991, the termination of state-aid legislation in 1992, the reform of EU structural funds, and the association agreements between the European Union and Eastern European countries all contributed to make the 'old' problems of Southern unemployment and poverty even worse (Cafiero 1997). In particular, de-industrialization and the end of state subsidies, the result of national legislation from the 1990s, were behind the employment collapse observable in this area of the country. Between 1991 and 1996, 600,000 jobs were lost. In 1996 less than 38 out of 100 Southern working age people had a job (52 in the Center-North) (Bodo and Viesti 1997: 73). Marked by such a low employment rate and high concentration of long-term unemployment, the Mezzogiorno stands out as one of the most backward regions of the EU. In the short run, at least, EMU cannot but aggravate this ailing region's problems: the disappearance of the exchange rate as a mechanism of adjustment will require higher factor mobility and greater price and wage flexibility—elements that remain quite foreign to the political and economic tradition of the Mezzogiorno.

The sectoral connection between internationalization and employment is even weaker than the regional link, mainly because of the increase of employment in the sheltered sectors. From 1980 to 1994, employment in the exposed sectors employment decreased substantially from 33 percent in 1980 to 27.3 percent in 1994, remaining below the OECD average (cf. Figure 8.4). By contrast, employment in the sheltered sectors rose from 21.7 percent in 1980 to 24.1 percent in 1994. In addition, public sector employment increased from 8.6 percent in 1980 to 9.2 percent in 1994. In combination, employment in these two sectors is higher than in the exposed sectors.

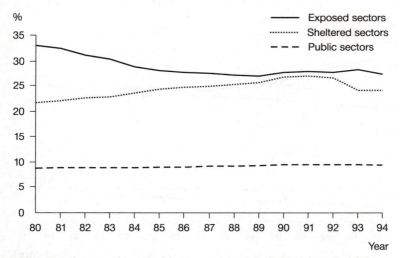

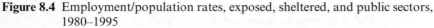

Figure 8.4 Employment/population rates, exposed, sheltered, and public sectors, 1980–1995
Source: OECD, *Statistical Compendium: Labour Force Statistics* (Paris: OECD, 1997).

As is shown in Figure 8.5, however, the employment rates in ISIC 6 (trade, restaurants, and hotels) and ISIC 9 (social and personal services) diminished significantly in the period 1992–94. In ISIC 6, the joint effect of the 1992 recession and of the restructuring of small companies seem to be the main causes. Employment in the social and personal services seems also to have suffered from a recruitment stop in schools and in the health care and from the 'disappearance' of part of this employment in the black economy.[9] But these losses, which were made up again in 1995–96, have

---

[9] It is however interesting to remark that these significant losses in the tertiary sector have not been discussed a lot in the Italian public debate; neither its causes nor its consequences. And it is not by any chance that the European Commission—with reference to the

not affected the general robustness of the sheltered, as compared to the
exposed sector, where the demand of labor has fallen in the advanced services (such as transport and communication—ISIC 7) as well. The
increase of employment in financing and insurance (ISIC 8), was not sufficient to close the gap to the OECD average. In 1994 communications and
transport absorbed 2.9 percent of the working age population as against
4.3 percent on average in the OECD area. In financing and insurance, the
employment rate amounted to 3.9 percent as against 6.7 percent on average in the OECD countries. Similar conditions can be found in some other
Southern European countries, such as Portugal, Spain, and Turkey.

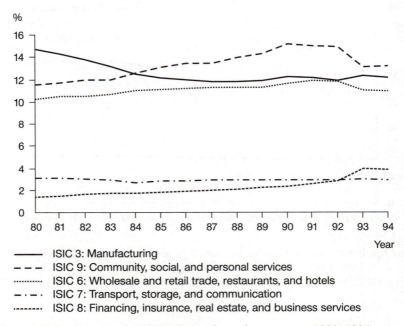

—— ISIC 3: Manufacturing
– – – ISIC 9: Community, social, and personal services
·········· ISIC 6: Wholesale and retail trade, restaurants, and hotels
– · – · ISIC 7: Transport, storage, and communication
········ ISIC 8: Financing, insurance, real estate, and business services

Figure 8.5 Employment/population rate in various sectors, 1980–1994
Source: OECD, *Statistical Compendium: Labour Force Statistics* (Paris: OECD,
1997).

Let us now look at unemployment. As mentioned several times, this is
particularly concentrated in the South and in some specific categories of
the labor force (women and youth). From 1980 to 1995 unemployment in
the Center-North increased from 5.8 percent to 7.8 percent, in the
Mezzogiorno from 11.5 percent to 21 percent (Gualmini 1998). In the

1999 National Action Plan—has recently underlined the weaknesses of the Italian employment situation within the service sector.

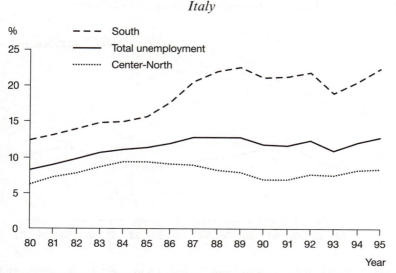

Figure 8.6 Total, Center-Northern, and Southern unemployment rates, 1980–1995
Source: Gualmini 1998: 271–73

same period, female unemployment rose from 13.2 percent to 16.2 percent, while male unemployment rose from 4.8 percent to 9.3 percent. The 1980s were characterized by a rapid increase of female entry into the labor market (also due to the 'baby boom' of the 1960s), but the demand for labor was not sufficient to absorb the increased supply. As for youth unemployment, Italy holds a record: it increased from 25.2 percent in 1980 to 32 percent in 1995 (while the OECD average is about 15%).

In addition to mass unemployment (12.5% in 1998), Italy has seen a significant spread of the black market economy—to 22.3 percent by 1996 (18% in the North and 33.9% in the South) (ISTAT 1998)—and the slowest diffusion of part-time work in Europe (5.1% in 1980 and 6.6% in 1996). As will be shown in the next section, opening international markets (and, what is related, higher mobility among citizens and workers) has shaken rigid and protected labor markets, like the Italian one, at their roots. And the adjustment of the Italian labor market and labor legislation has been slow, partial, and in many respects ineffective.

8.2.1.4. Internationalization and Social Policy

The impact of internationalization on social policy has been more straightforward—at least in institutional terms. The *vincolo esterno* (i.e. the constraint imposed directly or indirectly by international regimes and

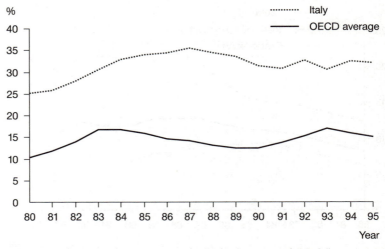

Figure 8.7 Youth unemployment rate in Italy (pop. aged 15–24), compared to
OECD average, 1980–1995
Source: OECD, *Labour Force Statistics* (Paris: OECD, various issues).

especially by the EU) has in fact become an increasingly powerful stimulus for pushing through measures of welfare retrenchment and rationalization on the part of the national executive.

In order to fulfill the criteria set by the Maastricht Treaty, Italy had to seriously tackle its public debt and deficit. The pressing need to reduce both, with a view to joining EMU along with the first group of countries, fostered a climate of permanent financial emergency. The margin of manoeuver for tax increases was extremely narrow. Public revenues had been growing quite rapidly since the early 1980s, turning Italy into a relatively big taxer by international standards. In the early 1990s both the high level of taxation (clearly shown by Figure 8.8) and its uneven distribution (because of significant cheating by some taxpayers) clearly started to provoke a tax revolt, especially among Northern taxpayers.

In such an environment, spending cutbacks appeared as the only viable strategy for containing public deficits and debt: Social benefits immediately became the prime target for the new policy of *risanamento.*

In comparative perspective, it is true, the Italian welfare system was not (and still is not) disproportionally large, as demonstrated by Figures 8.9 and 8.10.

Yet in public debates inside Italy, welfare programs were commonly indicted as the main culprit for the country's severe financial problems and, more generally, for its serious politico-institutional predicament.

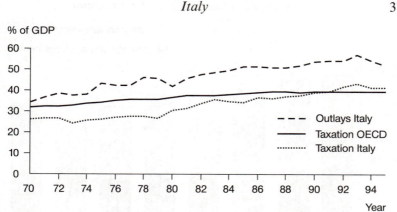

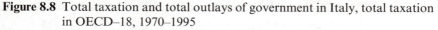

Figure 8.8 Total taxation and total outlays of government in Italy, total taxation in OECD–18, 1970–1995
Source: OECD, *Historical Statistics* (Paris: OECD, various issues).

Why this paradox—in the absence of a 'New Right' coalition? There were a number of factors explaining this phenomenon from the early 1990s: first, despite its comparatively modest aggregate size, social expenditure was still the largest item by far among total government outlays. Second, both the pension and health care systems were on a rather shaky financial and (in, the case of health care, organizational) footing. Demographic

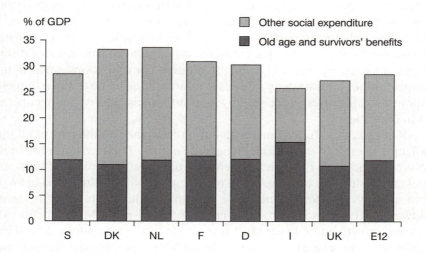

Figure 8.9 Old age and survivors' benefits as part of total social expenditure, 1993
Source: EC 1995: ch. 3, p. 67.

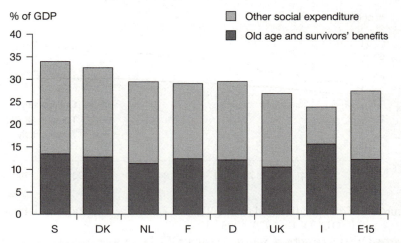

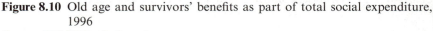

Figure 8.10 Old age and survivors' benefits as part of total social expenditure, 1996
Source: EC 1997: ch. 3, p. 6.

projections pointed toward alarming scenarios for the future: without any change in legislation, pension expenditure was expected to increase from *c.* 14 percent to *c.* 16 percent of GDP between the early 1990s and the year 2000, then surpass 20 percent by the 2020s, and finally reach 23.2 percent by the year 2040 (cf. Figure 8.11). Third, the 'sins' of legality and efficiency (described above in Section 8.1.4) had fostered a mounting 'negativism' against the *stato assistenziale* (a rather pejorative term for state assistance) in public debates, imparting a sense of legitimization to retrenchment measures. In other words, the combination of fiscal constraints—of discipline imposed by the EU—and qualitative contradictions opened up opportunities for a strategy of welfare reform in the name of three (largely apolitical) objectives: *risanamento finanziario*, social equity, and recuperation of efficiency.

Of course, this strategy met with strong resistance on the part of all the affected interests—most notably the trade unions. This resistance has been overcome not only through an open style of negotiation offering substantial concessions on the phasing-in of reform (as will be illustrated below), but also by an effort to persuade the unions that there are long-term advantages connected with *risanamento* and entry into EMU: benefits like revived growth and a lower burden from the interest on public debt. This latter point has played a crucial role in the reform process: the *risanamento* could actually be presented as a 'fight against rent', with possible gains for all workers. With interest rates at 9.5%, a relatively modest bank deposit of Lit 260 m (*c.*135,000 euros) invested in state bonds during the early 1990s would produce a 'rent' equal to a metalworker's annual wage (Pennacchi 1998). Thus, the 'bet' proposed by the government to the social partners (and repeatedly explained publicly and privately by such figures as Amato, Ciampi, Dini, and Prodi) was for workers to accept sacrifices (especially benefit cuts and wage restraint) with a view toward abating a huge and unproductive debt service, diverting the resources thus liberated to more productive purposes, and thereby triggering a virtuous circle of revived growth, new public investment, and 'healthier' redistribution (Ciampi 1998). In retrospect, we know that this bet has paid off: between 1992 and 1998 the interest on public debt declined from 10.2 percent to 6.4 percent of GDP. The downward trend is expected to continue for several years to come, thanks to the convergence of Italian and German interest rates and the gradual restructuring of the debt stock (a sort of EMU 'dividend' for Italy's public finances).

At first the trade unions were somewhat reluctant to accept the bet. The turning point in this respect was 1995. In the winter of that year, as a consequence of the political crisis and the ensuing loss of credibility, interest rates soared and the lira witnessed an alarming fall as against the German mark. Thus, the unions understood that rejecting reform was not equivalent to maintaining the status quo but to making things much worse. In other words, negative reinforcement got the unions to appreciate that the arguments of the government and Bank of Italy were well grounded and their 'bet' worth accepting. Throughout the 1990s (and especially in 1992 and 1995), international financial markets were a powerful force in the domestic dynamics of policymaking (and learning).

8.2.2. Policy Responses and their Effects: The Influence of Embedded Institutions

8.2.2.1. The Labor Market: The Uncertain Deregulation of the 1980s and the Reforms of the 1990s

The evolution of labor policies in the 1980s followed two distinct directions, corresponding to the periods 1981–83 and 1984–89. In the first years of the new decade, the government responded to recession and loss of employment in large firms accompanying the second oil shock defensively, by expanding already existing income support programs and introducing burdensome new passive policies, such as pre-retirement benefits. In the second half of the decade, in a more favorable economic environment, active labor market policies and a broad dejuridification of the labor market regime started being promoted. In a new consensual social climate, both the government and organized interests agreed to introduce 'atypical' labor contracts (e.g. for part-time and temporary work), work sharing, and a reform of employment services. However, implementing these measures did not meet up to their original expectations.

The decade opened with a severe crisis for large firms and a concomitant job hemorrhage (of which the 1980 Fiat crisis was the most alarming). Like the French, German, and Spanish governments, Italy's penta-party coalition tried to face the consequences of growing unemployment in large companies by encouraging a subsidized exodus from work through pre-retirement benefits (Law 155/1981). But while Germany and France established pre-retirement schemes to encourage generational turnover, in Italy and in Spain these soon turned into instruments for avoiding dismissals, with no positive impact on workers' mobility.

But in a context of massive unemployment, also linked with the accelerated participation of women in the labor market, it was no longer possible to rely on medium-term interventions and income support subsidies. Especially in the Mezzogiorno, there was a need for radical change in the overall strategy of labor policy, so as to expand the productive capacity of firms and foster job creation. To pursue such an ambitious goal, the idea of a new social agreement with economic interest groups was launched, and the word 'deregulation' officially entered the political discourse. In 1983 the national trade unions, the national employers' associations, and the Minister of Labor signed an important social pact. The negotiation was actually a complex political exchange involving income policies, fiscal policies, and incentives. Where labor policy was concerned, the agreement introduced a set of new instruments favoring greater flexibility in the labor market (Law 863/1984).

Law 863 of 1984 introduced three new instruments, all belonging to the family of deregulative policies: work-sharing agreements (the so-called solidarity contracts), work and training contracts, and part-time work. Work and training contracts were an immediate and remarkable success. But the other two instruments, part-time, for example, were not very successful: it was rarely used, mainly because the non-wage costs of part-time work were too high.

A few other active policies were introduced in the second half of the decade. In 1986 Law 44 established a set of financial incentives for young employers creating new firms and cooperatives. In 1987 Law 56 reorganized the structure of the Labor Ministry, established new regional agencies to promote 'active' employment and modified placement procedures. Though rather innovative, the new policies of the 1980s did not seem sufficient to have an impact on the structural factors affecting unemployment.

As the new decade opened, conditions in the labor market were alarming. From 1992 to 1995, the employment rate fell continuously. It was, moreover, accompanied by an increase in unemployment surpassing 12 percent by 1995. The gap between Northern and Southern regions widened, and a new record appeared: in 1995 long-term unemployment reached 63.2 percent of total employment, the highest ratio in Europe. In the Mezzogiorno it amounted to 69.8 percent (55.5% in the North) (Pugliese and Rebeggiani 1997).

In this context, the evolution of labor policies in the 1990s again proceeded along two different paths: (1) the revival of concerted action and income policies and (2) the implementation of a substantial labor market reform introducing greater decentralization and privatization.

Between 1992 and 1993 the technical governments led by Amato and Ciampi undertook a series of non-stop negotiations with the unions under growing pressures from Confindustria, which saw high labor costs not only a cause for inflation but also as the main culprit for high unemployment. The negotiations resulted in two different agreements: the 'Amato agreement' in July 1992 and (exactly one year later) the 'Ciampi agreement', which completed the reform. The solutions identified for fighting inflation and unemployment were quite tough: abolition of the wage indexation mechanism (the *scala mobile*), the reform of collective bargaining, and the introduction of income policies.

The *scala mobile* was abolished fifty years after it was established. This was perceived as a big victory for employers, who had been fighting for wages to cool down ever since the labor cost agreement of 1983. Especially important was the reform of collective bargaining. The new structure was organized around two levels of negotiation: the national level (*contratto nazionale di categoria*) for the regulation of wages in connection with the dynamics of inflation and the firm or territorial level (*contratto aziendale o territoriale*) for the regulation of wage differentials and for the compensation of productivity hikes in strict connection with the company profitability. Finally, a new kind of incomes policy based on a 'virtuous cycle' of flexible adjustment to the expected inflation rate was established. Two tripartite 'meeting sessions' were set up to coincide with the different phases of macroeconomic and budgetary planning: one session met in May–June to help define budgetary objectives and another in September to plan income policies in connection with the financial law. In December 1998, the structure of income policies, as foreseen by the Ciampi agreement, was completed and fortified by the so-called 'Social Pact for Economic Development', which the new Prime Minister D'Alema and more than thirty interest groups signed. That agreement ratified the work done by the two incomes policy sessions and the two tiers of collective bargaining. The pact also lent further formality and discipline to the new cooperative-corporatist style of policymaking.

The Ciampi agreement also included a complex and coherent reform of labor market policies, which subsequently resulted in the 'Pact for Work' signed by the unions, employers, and the Prodi government in September 1996. The Pact was centered around a strategy of active policy, but the role of passive policies was not reduced. The strategy of the dual track continued. In the 1990s, public utilities works were the most widespread kind of labor program. The so-called 'Treu law' (from the name of the Labor Ministry) of June 1997 contained the most important part of the September pact: it introduced temporary work and laid the groundwork for a reform of the training system. The introduction of temporary work is particularly worth mentioning, since it meant the end of the state monopoly on employment services. Italy, along with Greece, was the last country to legalize temporary work. Six months after the Treu law, Decree No. 469/1997 (following the so-called 'Bassanini laws' that reformed, and above all decentralized, public administration) abolished the public monopoly on job placement offices, transferred related administrative responsibilities to the regions, and allowed private agencies to set up placement offices. The law has rightly been perceived as a sort of revolution: the regions have since become the most powerful actors of labor market regulation, and the old ministerial institutions have been fully redesigned. Only responsibility for the *ammortizzatori sociali* has remained under the purview of the central government; but parliament has now charged the government with broader reform.

The 'Pact for Work' also established the so-called policies for local development. This broad menu of innovative measures includes such important new instruments as territorial and area contracts. They are specifically addressed to the most depressed regions and are already rather widespread in the Mezzogiorno. The contracts are negotiated agreements aimed at developing business, cooperatives, and employability in a particular territory, exploiting its social and economic resources.

The D'Alema government formed in October 1998 reaffirmed its strong commitment to the new, active policies of employment promotion. The aforementioned 'social pact for development', signed in December 1998, aimed at relaunching public and private investments (especially in the South), giving training programs a new impulse, and reforming the traditional system of passive policies.

8.2.2.2. The Welfare State: The Chaotic Restructuring of the 1980s and the Breakthroughs of the 1990s

Despite their unremitting lip service to the exigencies of financial adjustment, the various penta-party governments that held office during the 1980s did not accomplish much in the way of structural measures. Since the beginning of the decade, new proposals of reform pensions and health care started being discussed in Parliament and getting included in the agenda of different cabinets. All these proposals pointed in the same, austerity-minded direction: rationalizing the pension system, raising the age of retirement, and trimming old-age benefit formulas in order to restore financial balances, reorganizing the structure and financing mechanisms of the Health Service (as part of the so-called 'reform of the health reform'). Neither the pension reform nor the Health Service reform made much progress until the early 1990s. What the 1980s did see were some first 'cuts' in both sectors: relatively peripheral and not very effective in the case of pensions, more substantial in the case of health.

From 1983 onward, a number of measures were taken aimed at subordinating some pension entitlements to recipients' actual incomes and at controlling abuses. Income ceilings were established for maintaining the right to minimum pensions and to multiple benefits (e.g. an old age, as well as a survivor's pension). The rules concerning disability pensions were completely revised, medical criteria tightened, and periodical reviews of the beneficiaries' physical conditions introduced. Though important in symbolic terms, these steps taken toward greater 'targeting' of Italy's social insurance were only modestly effective in financial terms.

Cutbacks were more substantial and more effective in the field of health care. Alarmed by post-reform expenditure increases, and aware that a new 'reform of the reform' would take its time, the penta-party government inaugurated a policy of 'financial management' for the health system aimed at curbing the demand for services by imposing expenditure ceilings on regions and making users contribute co-payments. The annual budget bill became the instrument par excellence for controlling health care from the center. Allocations were set on the basis of available public funds, to be shared out among the regions. The savings deemed necessary to remain in line with the ceiling were created by co-payments (what the Italians call *tickets*) and other cuts (reduction of facilities, staff, investments).

If the 1980s were an ambiguous decade on the expenditure side (combining ongoing expansion with chaotic retrenchment), the dominant trend on the revenue side was much clearer: increases on all fronts. Contributory rates were repeatedly raised, especially for the self-employed. The effectiveness of the tax system vis-à-vis such categories was also greatly improved throughout the decade, which also witnessed the abolition of many existing loopholes to elude taxes on the side of higher incomes. Thus, the general government's total tax take grew extremely rapidly.

By increasing taxes rapidly and intensely in the 1980s, Italy completed its march to catch up with its European partners, thereby narrowing the distance created by the 'flat decade' (1965–75). But this remarkable tax adjustment did not suffice to cure the structural imbalance in the national accounts. As already mentioned, the deterioration was largely due to the self-sustaining dynamic of the 'debt spiral' in an unfavorable international conjuncture. But the internal imbalances of the welfare system (especially pensions) did play a part in the story.[10]

These imbalances were targeted by a series of reforms in the following decade, starting in 1992 with pensions. While maintaining the overall architecture of the system established in 1969 (occupational schemes and earnings-related formulas), the 1992 Amato reform introduced a number of significant restrictive changes after decades of incremental and expansive ameliorations. The main provisions of this reform can be summarized as follows: elevation of the retirement age from 55 to 60 for females and from 60 to 65 for males (private employees), to be phased in by the year 2002; gradual elevation of the minimum contribution requirement for old age benefits from 15 to 20 years; gradual extension of the reference period for pensionable earnings from the last 5 years to the last 10 years (and to the whole career for new entrants in the labor market); elevation of the contribution requirement for seniority (early retirement) pensions to 36 years for all workers (including a gradual phase-in for civil servants, who previously enjoyed the privilege of a much lower 20-year requirement); a new increase in contribution rates; and replacement of wage indexation for benefits with a cost of living indexation.[11]

As a follow-up to the reform, new provisions for supplementary pensions were passed in 1993. They introduced a coordinated legal framework and fiscal incentives for the establishment of supplementary occupational funds. The Ciampi government decided to put a temporary freeze on seniority pensions as well as controls on disability benefits, in order to contain fraud. However, the persistent crisis of public finances, the upward trend in pension expenditure (in spite of the 'cuts'), and pressure from international agencies like the IMF, OECD, and EU all convinced the government that more decisive reform was needed. In May 1995 the Dini government succeeded in striking the agreement with the trade unions. At least three factors explain the attitude of the trade unions. One was the concertational style of Dini ('technically' also supported by the left in Parliament), as opposed to the adversarial style adopted by Berlusconi, who had failed at negotiating with the unions during his shortlived gov-

---

[10] In spite of the huge increase of contributions, the transfer of the central government to finance social protection rose by 76% in real terms between 1980 and 1990, passing from 5.0% to 7.1% of GDP.

[11] According to long-term projections, as a consequence of the Amato reform pension expenditure will be *c.*1% of GDP lower than expected in the absence of reform by the year 2000 and *c.*4% of GDP lower by the year 2035. These figures are inferred from *Ministero del Tesoro* (1998).

ernment in 1994. Second, there were the spurs of 'international markets' (cf. above, Section 8.2.1.4). Third, there were the concessions that Dini made on the phasing in of the reform: for example all workers with more than 18 years of contributions were exempted from the new rules.

The main innovations of the Dini reform were: the shift from the old earnings-related formula to a new contribution-related formula, to be phased in by 2013; the introduction of a flexible retirement age (57–65); the introduction of an age threshold for seniority pensions (57 years) for all workers, to be phased in by 2008; the gradual standardization of rules for public and private employees; the graduation of survivor benefits according to income; and, finally, stricter rules on the ability to accumulate disability benefits and incomes from work, as well as tighter controls on beneficiaries. In addition to changes on the benefits side, the Dini reform also rationalized and raised contribution rates, and it widened the contribution base by extending compulsory pension insurance to special categories of self-employed workers.[12]

The autumn of 1992 also marked an important turning point for health care: the 'reform of the reform' was finally approved (with additional fine-tuning provisions in 1993). This reform transformed the local health units (USL, the basic structure of the National Health Service) into 'public enterprises' with ample organizational autonomy and responsibility. Larger hospitals, formerly acting as branches of the USL, can now establish themselves as independent public hospitals agencies, with autonomous organization and administration. The reform also brought changes in the regulations governing health finance. The central government maintains overall planning responsibilities; that is, it pays for a standard set of services that must be guaranteed to each citizen in each region. In this way, each region continues to receive a predetermined amount of resources (based on population, though corrected for other factors) from the center. However, additional payments to a region over and above its standard yearly endowment must be covered by regional resources (higher co-payments or taxes).

The 1992–95 reforms represented major breakthroughs with respect to the institutional legacies of the past. They were also, however, the result of social and political compromises in which the government had to make a number of concessions (e.g. on the phasing in of the reforms). But the approach of the EMU deadlines kept Italian authorities under acute and constant budgetary pressures. Soon after each new compromise was

---

[12] Such as freelance workers and other semi-autonomous workers (*lavoro para-subordinato*). This type of self-employment started to grow very rapidly during the early 1990s, esp. among young people. This growth obfuscated in the debate the possible adverse effects in terms of employment of introducing compulsory contributions.

struck, the government relaunched its efforts, thus widening the scope of its reformist ambitions even further. In this spirit, the new center-left 'Olive-Tree' coalition led by Romano Prodi and voted into office in the spring of 1996 made comprehensive reform of the *stato sociale* one of its highest priorities. In January 1997 Mr. Prodi appointed a Commission of experts to draft a broad plan for reform. A highly structured report was submitted by this Commission (known as the Onofri Commission, after the name of its chairperson, a Bologna economist). The report focused on the idea of re-equilibrating and containing (though not reducing in the aggregate) social expenditure.

The Onofri report was the object of a rather heated debate in the summer and fall of 1997. In the budget law for 1997, the Prodi government tried to adopt many of the Commission's recommendations. However, fierce opposition from the Refounded Communists (whose votes were crucial for obtaining a majority in Parliament) and difficult negotiations with the social partners forced the government to scale down its ambitions substantially. On pensions, Prodi was able to make some cuts in seniority pensions, especially for public employees: the minimum years of contributions required to get a pension were aligned with those of private employees. Contributions for the self-employed were raised, a temporary freeze on the indexation of higher pensions was introduced, and some steps were taken on the 'harmonization' front. However modest as measured against the government's original ambitions, these cuts had the advantage of going into effect immediately and thus making a small contribution (0.2% of GDP) toward achieving budgetary targets for 1998. The most important recommendation of the Onofri plan, a much faster phasing in of the new pension formula introduced in 1995, could not be adopted. By fomenting a cabinet crisis, the Refounded Communists were able to exempt blue-collar workers from the cuts in seniority pensions.[13] The government was also able to push through some important innovations in social assistance and selectivity: most notably, it introduced a new device (*indicatore della situazione economica* or ISE) for conducting the means test on claimants of certain benefits and it introduced an experimental scheme of guaranteed minimum income (*reddito minimo di inserimento* or RMI).[14]

This series of reforms has not fully eliminated the distributive and allocative distortions of the Italian welfare state described in Section 8.1. But the reforms have made significant steps in this direction. On the one hand, setting more transparent and clear-cut boundaries between social

---

[13] For a full review of the 1997 pension reform and its financial impact, cf. Mira d'Ercole and Terribile 1998.

[14] A more detailed discussion of these new developments is contained in Ferrera 2000.

insurance and social assistance and consolidating new instruments like the ISE and RMI are bound to strengthen that safety net of means-tested and need-based benefits and services historically lacking in Italy. On the other hand, the new architecture of the pension system will work to gradually downsize a sector that has been historically hypertrophic. At the end of the 1990s and in spite of the reforms, it is true, Italy still has one of the highest ratios of pension expenditure to GDP in the entire OECD area, and that the situation is going to get worse. But the significance of the 1992/1995/1997 reforms must be appreciated by contrast with the status quo. As Figure 8.11 shows, without reforms spending on pensions peaked at an impressive 23.2 percent of GDP by 2040 before starting to decline. With reform, the peak is expected to reach 'only' 15.8 percent of GDP by 2032. The virtual stabilization of pension expenditure may not have been enough to fully cure the long-standing disease of Italy's unbalanced welfare state. But it has certainly contained its fatal worsening.

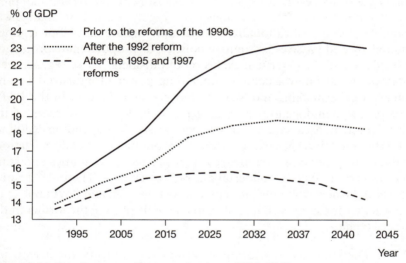

Figure 8.11 Pension expenditure projections, 1995–2045

8.2.3. *Institutional Capabilities: The Slow Beginning of a Learning Process*

The adjustment of national economies to internationalization can be regarded as a process of institutional change, a highly complex phenomenon combining two levels of change, in public policy and the broader politico-institutional framework. It is not only the specific goals, instruments, and techniques of public policy that change, but also the structures and rules in which policymaking is embedded. Institutional change takes place via a delicate learning process, in which policymakers learn how to implement new programs or solve specific problems on the basis of a changing external environment, of newly available knowledge and information, or by trying to emulate successful models from abroad.[15] But learning processes are particularly difficult, since they involve the restructuring of the norms, strategies, and routines that were successful in the past and that commanded widespread trust and loyalty. What is necessary to break out of the loop and bring about institutional change? Historical contingencies, major technological changes, and the (more or less) fortuitous combination of exogenous and endogenous challenges can all interrupt the process of institutionalization and release energy and resources for new activities and experiments.

Institutional theory seems particularly well-suited to describe and explain the Italian economy's process of adjustment to international pressures.[16] Up until the 1980s, a vicious circle highly resistant to change was created by highly institutionalized Keynesian welfare and labor regimes, centered around passive-distributive policies, disproportionate protection for insiders, and the persistent exclusion of outsiders. These regimes were sustained by an interest coalition including powerful industrial unions, center-left governments, and weak employers' associations. In the 1990s, however, some endogenous and exogenous challenges (the crisis of the political system, fiscal strains, the currency crisis, the impending deadlines of EMU, and more general pressure of economic internationalization) combined to produce a 'virtuous' cycle of positive externalities and stimulate decision makers to undertake a radical change. The old, 'vicious' circle and the new 'virtuous' one still co-exist, in part, and it remains to be seen whether the latter will be fully capable of displacing the former in the years to come.

8.2.3.1. The Vicious Circle: Spoils-Sharing Governments, Inefficient Bureaucracy and Distributive Policies

Why did this (distorted) 'welfare capitalism Italian-style' survive (indeed, become consolidated) during the 1980s, in spite of its numerous perverse effects on allocation and distribution as well as the growing mismatch between the welfare state and rapid socio-economic transformation? As

---

[15] The literature on policy learning and policy change is quite vast. In particular, cf. Heclo 1974; Hall 1993; Sabatier and Jenkins-Smith 1993; Haas 1992. For a discussion Gualmini 1995, 1997.

[16] For a discussion of this literature, cf. Hall and Taylor 1996; Immergut 1998.

already mentioned in Section 8.1, the answer lies primarily with the 'political logic' of the 'First Republic', and especially with four interrelated ingredients of that regime: a spoils-centered model of party government, a weak and inefficient public administration, a highly institutionalized system of political exchanges between government and organized interests, and the distributive nature of labor and social policies. In the 1980s some efforts to modify these ingredients were attempted, but they were not very effective, owing to strong resistance from supporters (and, needless to say, major beneficiaries) of the status quo.

As is well known, the Italian political system was characterized—at least until the end of the First Republic—by high party fragmentation and an absence of competition (Sartori 1982; D'Alimonte 1978; Cotta 1987). Multi-party coalition cabinets were not based on clearly defined and shared programs, but rather on the proportional distribution of offices and spoils. These unstable executives were led by prime ministers with a weak coordinating role, while cabinet ministers who derived their legitimization directly from political parties enjoyed substantial autonomy. The best survival strategy for the government was to respond in two ways to all the inputs and micro-demands coming from social and political groups: on the one hand, governments survived by formulating broad, ambiguous, and therefore ineffective public policies. On the other hand, they also held on to power by proliferating particularistic laws and regulations that distributed incentives and benefits to social constituencies whose electoral support seemed especially important.

This micro-sectional style of policymaking, characterized by a very low degree of overall substantive coherence, intersected with a system of public administration marked by high centralization, a top-down, hierarchical implementation style, and weak problem-solving capacity.

Another important factor for the institutionalization of welfare capitalism Italian-style was the very nature of social and labor policy. Both kinds of policy are inherently micro-distributive: their benefits are highly concentrated and their costs widely dispersed. Distributive policies were the major outcome of the 1960s economic miracle and the political strategies pursued by center-left governments then and in the 1970s, when governments inclined toward incorporating a growing number of social groups into the welfare edifice. Distributive policies are very particularistic; in contrast to universalistic policies, they encourage fiscal irresponsibility, create loyalty, and foster growing expectations among their beneficiaries (Pierson 1993, 1994; Ferrera 1998). They generate incentives for client groups to organize and mobilize in defense of their entitlements.

It is important to remember that the vicious circle we have described so far—'vicious' because it assured the perpetuation of the same policy path and hindered every attempt at reform—was a perfectly coherent (a 'tightly coupled') system, when viewed from inside. Beneficiaries were keen on supporting it, unions agreed to its distributive policies, employers got attractive incentives, and the Centro-sinistra or Pentapartito governments could meet their voters' demands and distribute spoils among the various coalition partners. But in the 1990s the whole castle began to crumble under the growing pressure of demands from citizens left out of the system, the explosion of costs, and the radical transformation of the external economic environment.

8.2.3.2. The Virtuous Circle: Government Stability, Economic Integration, and Policy Reforms

In the early 1990s the old model of welfare capitalism Italian-style was shaken to its roots by domestic developments known as 'the transition from the First to the Second Republic' and by stringent pressures to meet EMU deadlines. These two dynamics combined to initiate a virtuous cycle of policy reforms.

In the first half of the 1990s, the Italian party system underwent dramatic, sudden change. The discovery of an intricate, pervasive system of political corruption involving prominent figures on the economic and political scene quickly discredited the established elite. The investigations of the 'Clean Hands' (*Mani pulite*, as the magistrates of the Milan team came to be known) brought to light widespread illegal practices (party financing and tax fraud) implicating both politicians and famous entrepreneurs and exposing a web of hidden connections between politics and business. Under the axe of 'Tangentopoli' (Milan as 'Bribesville'), several businessmen and political leaders were convicted, and most of the First Republic's ruling elite retired to private life.

Tangentopoli had a dramatic impact in combination with other major changes in the political system. In 1993 a new electoral system based on single-member districts was introduced. A year later, for the first time in Italy, two large coalitions of parties faced off against each other in a direct bid for electoral support. This bipolarization of political competition marked the end of the so-called *conventio ad excludendum,* i.e. the unwritten rule according to which the Communists were to be kept outside the national executive. This was also a consequence of the end of the Cold War, symbolized by the fall of the Berlin Wall. The cleavage 'pro-system vs. anti-system' on which postwar Italian party government had been born and consolidated began to lose legitimacy, and opposition parties gained greater credibility as candidates for governing responsibility.

But let us look in more detail at the profound transformations of the political system. In the first place, the old parties precipitated an irreversible electoral crisis after the elections of 1994. The pillars of the *Pentapartito*—i.e. the Christian Democrats, Socialists, Social Democrats, the Republicans, and Liberals—virtually disappeared. Second, the crisis of the old parties brought about a related crisis in some aspects of the party system as a whole: Its polycentric structure, lack of competition, bias toward center-based coalitions, and low capacity for leadership. In the third place, the crisis of the old party government marked the turnover of an entire political class. In 1994, 71 percent of the deputies were elected for the first time. The old political elite dissolved for a number of reasons in addition to 'Tangentopoli': the explosion of internal conflicts within the parties, loss of control over the executive, an inability to change, and the entry of new actors into the political arena (Cotta and Verzichelli 1996). Fourth, the demise of the First Republic changed the nature of the relationships among the different political institutions. The executive-presidency relationship shifted in favor of the latter, the executive-parliament relationship in favor of the former, and the relationship between the judiciary and the overall political system in favor of the judges. The national executive has therefore gained more power. The technical cabinets of Amato, Ciampi, and Dini, which were somehow detached from strict party control, could enjoy greater autonomy and exercise more direct leadership over policymaking. The final relevant factor was the entry into the political arena of new parties and movements. After the electoral success (as early as 1992) of the Lega Nord, whose main claims were against centralization and Rome's 'suffocating' system of taxation, a new political movement led by Berlusconi, 'Forza Italia', organized itself within a space of four months and gained power. Berlusconi's center-right government did not last long, however, due to harsh conflicts with its ally, the Lega Nord, and so was replaced by Dini's technical executive just a year later. The government led by Prodi, which was formed after the April 1996 elections, lasted longer (not falling until October 1998); it also had a higher political (center-left) profile.

In such a changed political environment, the style and resources of policymaking significantly changed, posing the conditions for the cycle of reforms illustrated in the previous section.

All the reforms were marked by a high level of policy integration and cohesion. All of them seem to be inspired by a culture of 'managerialism' and 'professionalism' (and not merely in rhetorical terms), which meant greater efficiency, effectiveness in achieving policy goals, and a higher quality of service. The institutional capacity essential to implementing these reforms greatly improved thanks to tighter horizontal coordination between the ministries and vertical cooperation between the prime minister and his ministers. Strengthening the executive has enhanced the prime minister's capacity for leadership and assured major cohesion inside the government, thus also lending coherence to policy projects and encouraging cross-sectoral policy initiatives.

Another important feature of the reform cycle is the strongly negotiated character of innovations: almost all reforms were introduced via consensual concertation between the government and organized interests. Prime ministers have played a stronger role than in the past and have actually coordinated actions by individual cabinet ministers. The search for cooperation and consent on the part of trade unions and employers' associations was a major consequence of this negotiating style. The agreements of 1992 and 1993, the 1992 reform of both pension and health care, and the new pension reform of 1997 were outcomes of that strategy. With Prodi's 1996 'Pact for Work' and D'Alema's 1998 'Social Pact', concertation became a quasi-permanent strategy.

8.3. Conclusion: A New Model, but How Stable?

The turbulent 1990s were a successful decade for Italy. An impressive series of reforms allowed this country to put its battered public finances in order and start decisively modernizing its backward bureaucratic apparatus, rigid labor market, and unbalanced welfare state, without jeopardizing social peace or the economy's overall competitiveness. The dynamics of internationalization and (especially) European integration have been crucial in instigating this quantum leap in institutional capabilities: indeed, the Italian experience shows that internationalization may well be a solution rather than a problem. As illustrated in Section 8.1, a major handicap in Italy's start-up constellation was the very weakness and 'softness' of the state (its paucity of legality, efficiency, and normative integration). In fact, the 1970s and early 1980s were the decades of a syndrome in which the Italian state acted primarily as a machine for the generation of spoils and as an arena for the predation of such spoils by different socio-political groups. Solving collective problems through some sort of rational solution was only a secondary function of the state. What exogenous shocks and the Maastricht process did to Italy's politico-institutional system was to encourage the state's 'hardening', the strengthening of its capacities: the state's (but also society's) elites learned that 'puzzling about problems' and finding effective solutions to these problems were more important than (or, at least, a prerequisite for) 'powering about spoils'.[17]

---

[17] For recent interpretations of the Italian experience in similar veins, cf. also Della Sala 1997; Dyson and Featherstone 1996; Walsh 1999. The puzzling/powering contrast is borrowed from Heclo 1974.

Of course, we are not arguing that internationalization and European integration have been the only spurs to this process of institutional modernization. Other factors have played a role as well: the sudden waning of endogenous obstacles to change (the demise of the First Republic), the rapid de-ideologization of the political culture (in the wake of the fall of the Berlin Wall), as well as Italy's traditional pro-European-integration leanings, the emergence of new actors (fresh political faces, experts, a new 'technocratic' elite), new styles of policymaking (the *concertazione*), and— as a result of all this—an accelerated dynamic of social and institutional learning.

The notion of 'learning' (both cognitive and socio-political learning) is particularly helpful, we submit, for capturing the nature of change in Italy, and especially that transformation's internal dynamic. The first stage of the learning process was emergence of a diagnosis asserting that Italy needed a decisive *risanamento* of its public finances in order to resume a healthy course of economic growth and social modernization, and anchoring the country firmly to the European Community was the best (perhaps the only) way to achieve this.[18] This diagnosis matured into a project for change during the 1980s, when its various institutional implications (all pointing toward a wide-ranging reform agenda) unfolded. The project came to be fully shared and supported by technocratic circles inside the Bank of Italy and Treasury, and it also made headway within some sector-specific policy networks. The monetary crisis of 1992 convinced all these circles that a failure of the project '*risanamento* in the name of Europe' would have had disastrous consequences. Thus a campaign started to persuade the social partners (and especially the unions) about the long-term advantages of the *risanamento*: revived growth and a lower debt burden from interest payments. As shown in Section 8.2.1.4, the campaign was successful. For the leaders (*condottieri*) of this campaign (Amato, Ciampi, Dini, Prodi, etc.), but also for their opposing players (the leadership of the social partners), the celebrations of May 1998, when Italy was formally admitted into EMU, were thus well deserved.

To be sure, our positive assessment is predicated on recognizing what bad shape Italy was in, not just from 1975 to 1990, but even at the height of the so-called 'golden age'. Measured against this domestic historical standard, the whole process of *risanamento* leading up to EMU membership's final seal of approval can only appear as a remarkable achievement. The picture would obviously change if we were to take other reference points. In comparison with the pioneers of structural adjustment (e.g. the

---

[18] For a reconstruction of the debates that nurtured this diagnosis and a presentation of its main proponents, cf. Ferrera 1992. For a detailed reconstruction of the *risanamento* as an institutional project, cf. Verzichelli 1999.

Netherlands), Italy still appears to be lagging far behind. Moreover, the reforms of the 1990s have not fully eradicated the old vices. In national public debates it is widely recognized that the institutional transition is not over yet and that the innovative dynamics that emerged during the 1990s have not reached a stable political or economic equilibrium.

What are the prospects for reaching such an equilibrium and thus bringing *la transizione* to a positive conclusion? It is obviously very hard to say. By way of conclusion, we would like to suggest two conditions that are likely to play a crucial role in this respect.

The first condition has to do with the labor market and the Southern question (which are two sides of the same coin). Unemployment and the North/South dualism are still national emergencies, and there are signs that developments in world trade and investment will seriously hurt Italian employment over the next several years.[19] Thus, prompt decisive actions must be taken, both to overcome the endogenous causes of unemployment and to anticipate future endogenous shocks. The dividends of the *risanamento* and EMU membership offer a unique opportunity to push through vital reforms in Italy's wage-setting mechanisms and *ammortizzatori sociali*. As mentioned above, the *risanamento* was partly a 'bet' from which substantial savings were expected, thanks to a decline in interest rates. The bet has now been won and the savings are there. If appropriately mobilized in the right direction (public and private productive investments, education and training, incentives to attract mobile capital, especially in the Mezzogiorno, reducing taxes and especially social charges, etc.), this dividend can facilitate the kind of reforms and spur the kind of employment (creating 'jobs, jobs, and even more jobs') that paved the way for the Dutch miracle. Responding to the unemployment and 'Southern' emergencies is crucial not only for the sake of the jobless and the Mezzogiorno, but also in order to reinforce the dynamics of positive learning on the part of social and political actors: institutional change 'pays' (the lesson goes); it delivers the goods and must therefore be continued. The 'Social Pact' signed in December 1998 by the government and the social partners seems to rest on this logic: its aim was precisely to channel resources towards investment, employment, and training. But it remains to be seen whether the Pact's provisions will actually be imple-

---

[19] This is esp. true for the implementation of the Uruguay Round and most notably the phase-out of the MFA. This process will gradually remove barriers to trade from which Italian producers have so far benefited. More generally, the increased supply of LDCs manufacturers in the wake of global trade liberalization will have a greater impact on Italy's terms of trade compared to other industrialized countries (Faini, Falzoni, and Galeotti 1998). The 'niche advantages' enjoyed by Italy in the international economy (cf. 8.2.1.3) will in other words be gradually lost.

mented, and whether social behaviors will really follow the expected directions.

The second condition has to do with politics. The so-called Second Republic has witnessed the emergence of new political actors, of a new unwritten equilibrium among the executive, legislative, and the judicial powers, and of new electoral rules. But despite repeated and grand efforts (such as the establishment of a bicameral commission chaired by D'Alema), the basic constitutional framework has remained unaltered. This means that the old (and 'vicious cycle-oriented') political logic of the First Republic may easily resurrect itself—even if disguised or tamed. True, the new macroeconomic regime put in place during the 1990s is politically much less manipulable than the previous one. As a matter of fact, it contains a number of 'institutional stabilizers' capable of making semi-automatic corrections in crucial policies (e.g. pensions or healthcare) and macroeconomic variables (e.g. inflation, public deficits, and debt). But the margins of discretion are still wide: the return of an unstable, irresponsible, and purely distributive politics could seriously jeopardize the effective functioning of the new regime (as well as obstructing progresses on the labor market and 'Southern question'). If this is true, then only intelligent constitutional reforms will be able to complete the transition, initiating and anchoring a new politico-economic equilibrium. Unfortunately, the road toward this destination is still long and rugged.

REFERENCES

ADDIS, ELISABETTA (1987). 'Banca d'Italia e politica monetaria: La riallocazione del potere fra Stato, Mercato e Banca centrale'. *Stato e mercato*, 19: 73–95.

AMENDOLA, ADALGISO, CAROLEO FLORO, ERNESTO, and ROSARIA GAROFALO, MARIA (1997). 'Labour Market and Decentralized Decision-Making: An Institutional Approach'. *Labour*, 3: 497–516.

ASCOLI, UGO (ed.) (1984). *Welfare state all'italiana*. Bologna: Il Mulino.

BARCA, FABRIZIO, and VISCO, IGNAZIO (1992). *L'economia italiana nella prospettiva europea: Terziario protetto e dinamica dei redditi*. Rome: Banca d'Italia.

BODO, GIORGIO, and VIESTI, GIANFRANCO (1997). *La grande svolta*. Rome: Donzelli.

BRUSCO, SEBASTIANO, and PABA, SERGIO (1997). 'Per una storia dei distretti industriali dal secondo dopoguerra agli anni novanta', in Fabrizio Barca (ed.), *La storia del capitalismo italiano*. Rome: Donzelli, 265–333.

CAFIERO, SALVATORE (1997). 'La questione meridionale nella prospettiva dell'UE'. *Rivista economica del Mezzogiorno*, 4: 815–21.

CARRIERI, MIMMO (1995). *L'incerta rappresentanza*. Bologna: Il Mulino.

CASSESE, SABINO (1974). *L'amministrazione pubblica in Italia*. Bologna: Il Mulino.
CELLA, GIAN PRIMO, and TREU, TIZIANO (eds.) (1989). *Relazioni industriali: Manuale per l'analisi dell'esperienza italiana*. Bologna: Il Mulino.
————(eds.) (1998). *Le nuove relazioni industriali: L'esperienza italiana nella prospettiva europea*. Bologna: Il Mulino.
Censis (1976). *L'occupazione occulta: Caratteristiche della partecipazione al lavoro*. Rome.
——(1995). *Rapporto sull'occupazione*. Rome.
CIAMPI, CARLO AZEGLIO (1998). 'Risanamento e sviluppo, due momenti inscindibili della stessa politica'. *Info/Quaderni, special issue on L'Euro e le politiche per lo sviluppo e l'occupazione*: 198–203.
COMINOTTI, RUGGERO, and MARIOTTI, SERGIO (1997). *Italia multinazionale: Tendenze e protagonisti dell'internazionalizzazione*. Milan: F. Angeli.
COSSENTINO, FRANCESCO, PYKE, FRANK, and SENGENBERGER, WERNER (1997). *Le risposte locali e regionali alla pressione globale: Il caso dell'Italia e dei suoi distretti industriali*. Bologna: Il Mulino.
COTTA, MAURIZIO (1987). 'Il sottosistema governo-parlamento'. *Rivista italiana di scienza politica*, 2: 241–43.
——and VERZICHELLI, LUCA (1996). 'La classe politica: Cronaca di una morte annunciata?', in Maurizio Cotta and Pierangelo Isernia (eds.), *Il gigante dai piedi di argilla*. Bologna: Il Mulino, 373–408.
D'ALIMONTE, ROBERTO (1978). 'Competizione elettorale e rendimento politico: Il caso italiano'. *Rivista italiana di scienza politica*, 3: 457–93.
DEAGLIO, MARIO (1998). *L'Italia paga il conto*. Milan: Guerrini & Associati.
DELLA SALA, VINCENT (1997). 'Hollowing Out and Hardening the State: European Integration and the Italian Economy'. *West European Politics,* 20: 14–33.
DE NARDIS, SERGIO, and GALLI, GIAMPAOLO (eds.) (1997). *La disoccupazione italiana*. Bologna: Il Mulino.
DYSON, KENNETH H. F., and FEATHERSTONE, KEVIN (1996). 'Italy and EMU as Vincolo Esterno: Empowering the Technocrats, Transforming the State'. *South European Society and Politics*, 1: 272–99.
EC (European Commission) (1993, 1995, and 1997). *Social Protection in Europe*. Brussels.
EPSTEIN, GERARD A., and SCHOR, JULIET B. (1987). 'Il divorzio tra Banca d'Italia e Tesoro: Un caso di indipendenza delle banche centrali', in Peter Lange and Marino Regini (eds.), *Stato e regolazione sociale*. Bologna: Il Mulino, 177–202.
FAINI, RICCARDO, FALZONI, ANNA MARIA, and GALEOTTI, MARZIO (1998). *Importing Jobs or Exporting Firms? A Close Look at the Labour Market Implications of Italy's Trade and Foreign Direct Investment Flows*. Discussion Paper No. 2033. CEPR.
FERRERA, MAURIZIO (1984). *Il welfare state in Italia*. Bologna: Il Mulino.
——(1987). 'Italy', in Peter Flora (ed.), *Growth to Limits*. Berlin: De Gruyter, ii. 385–499.
——(1992). 'Italian Political Science and Public Policies: A Late but Promising Encounter'. *European Journal of Political Research*, Annual Review: 469–81.

——(1996). 'The Southern Model of Welfare in Social Europe'. *Journal of European Social Policy*, 1: 17–37.

——(1998). *Le trappole del welfare.* Bologna: Il Mulino.

——(2000). 'Targeting Welfare in a Soft State', forthcoming in Neil Gilbert (ed.), *Targeting Social Benefits.* New Brunswick: Transaction.

——and GUALMINI, ELISABETTA (1999). *Salvati dall'Europa.* Bologna: Il Mulino.

FLORA, PETER (ed.) (1983). *State, Economy and Society in Western Europe.* London: Macmillan.

——(1986/87). *Growth to Limits: The Western Welfare States since World War II.* Berlin: De Gruyter.

GERELLI, EMILIO, and MAJOCCHI, ALBERTO (1984). *Il deficit pubblico: Origine e problemi.* Milan: F. Angeli.

GRAZIANI, AUGUSTO (1998). 'L'Italia nella crisi economica internazionale', in Augusto Graziani and Anna Maria Nassisi (eds.), *L'economia mondiale in trasformazione.* Rome: Manifestolibri, 297–329.

GUALMINI, ELISABETTA (1995). 'Apprendimento e cambiamento nelle politiche pubbliche: Il ruolo delle idee e della conoscenza'. *Rivista Italiana di Scienza Politica*, 2: 343–370.

——(1997). *Le rendite del neo-corporativismo.* Soveria Mannelli: Rubbettino.

——(1998). *La politica del lavoro.* Bologna: Il Mulino.

HAAS, PETER M. (1992). 'Introduction: Epistemic Communities and International Policy Coordination'. *International Organization*, 1: 1–35.

HALL, PETER A. (1993). 'Policy Paradigm, Social Learning and the State: The Case of Economic Policy-Making in Britain'. *Comparative Politics*, 25: 275–96.

——and TAYLOR, ROSEMARY C. R. (1996). 'Political Science and the Three New Institutionalisms'. *Political Studies*, 5: 936–57.

HECLO, HUGH (1974). *Modern Social Politics in Britain and in Sweden.* New York: Yale University Press.

IMMERGUT, ELLEN M. (1998). 'The Theoretical Core of the New Institutionalism'. *Politics and Society*, 1: 5–34.

ISTAT (Istituto nazionale di statistica). *Annuari statistici, 1966–1976.* Rome: ISTAT.

——(1998). *Forze di lavoro.* Rome: Media.

KINGDOM, JOHN W. (1984). *Agendas, Alternatives and Public Policy.* Boston: Little Brown.

LAWRENCE, ROBERT (1996). *Regionalism, Multilateralism, and Deeper Economic Integration.* Washington, DC: Brookings Institution.

MICOSSI, STEFANO, and VISCO, IGNAZIO (1993). *Inflazione, concorrenza e sviluppo: L'economia italiana e la sfida dell'integrazione europea.* Bologna: Il Mulino.

Ministero del Tesoro (1998). *Convergenze dell'Italia verso l'UEM.* Rome.

MIRA D'ERCOLE, MARCO, and TERRIBILE, FLAVIA (1998). 'Pension Spending: Developments in 1996 and 1997', in Luciano Bardi and Martin Rhodes (eds.), *Italian Politics. Mapping the Future.* Boulder, colo.: Westview, 187–207.

OECD (Organisation for Economic Co-operation and Development) (1998). *Social Expenditure of Statistics of OECD Members Countries.* Paris.

ONIDA, FABRIZIO (1993). 'Collocazione internazionale e fattori di competitività dell'industria italiana', in Stefano Micossi and Ignazio Visco (eds.), *Inflazione, concorrenza e sviluppo*. Bologna: Il Mulino, 171–213.

PENNACCHI, LAURA (1998). 'La moneta unica europea fra risanamento, sviluppo e crescita dell'occupazione'. *Info/Quaderni, special issue on L'Euro e le politiche per lo sviluppo e l'occupazione*: 8–30

PIERSON, PAUL (1993). 'When Effect Becomes Cause: Policy Feedback and Political Change'. *World Politics*, 45: 595–628.

——(1994). *Dismantling the Welfare State? Reagan, Thatcher and the Politics of Retrenchment*. Cambridge: Cambridge University Press.

PUGLIESE, ENRICO, and REBEGGIANI, ENRICO (1997). *Occupazione e disoccupazione in Italia (1945–1995)*. Rome: Edizioni Lavoro.

RICCIARDI, MARIO (1986). *Lezioni di storia sindacale. Italia, 1945–1985*. Bologna: Clueb.

ROSSI, SALVATORE (1998). *La politica economica italiana 1968–1998*. Bari: Laterza.

SABATIER, PAUL A., and JENKINS-SMITH, HANK C. (1993). *Policy Change and Learning: An Advocacy Coalition Approach*. Boulder, Colo.: Westview Press.

SALVATI, MICHELE (1981). *Alle origini dell'inflazione italiana*. Bologna: Il Mulino.

——(1984). *Economia e politica in Italia dal dopoguerra ad oggi*. Milan: Garzanti.

——(1997). 'Moneta unica, rivoluzione copernicana'. *Il Mulino*, 1: 5–23.

SARTORI, GIOVANNI (1982). *Teoria dei partiti e caso italiano*. Milan: Sugarco.

SOMAINI, EUGENIO (1989). 'Politica salariale e politica economica', in Gian Primo Cella and Tiziano Treu (eds.), *Relazioni industriali*. Bologna: Il Mulino, 307–44.

TURONE, SERGIO (1988). *Storia del sindacato in Italia dal 1943 ad oggi*. Bari: Laterza.

VERZICHELLI, LUCA (1999). *La politica di bilancio*. Bologna: Il Mulino.

WALSH, JAMES I. (1999). 'Political Bases of Macroeconomic Adjustment: Evidence from the Italian Experience'. *Journal of European Public Policy*, 6: 66–84.

9

Sweden and Denmark
Defending the Welfare State

MATS BENNER AND TORBEN BUNDGAARD VAD

9.1. Introduction

Although, at first glance, Sweden and Denmark almost seem like identical countries, they represent an odd couple in comparative studies of political economies. Both share a commitment to income equality and high levels of services (mostly financed out of taxes) that are universal in character. But they differ in most other respects, including social structure and political system, commitment to full employment, industrial structure, organization of industrial relations, and economic policy.

Postwar employment and redistribution rested on a more stable institutional foundation in Sweden than in Denmark. Sweden built upon an economic tradition of large industries, concentration of ownership, and well-organized employers. With the advent of social democracy and a centralized union structure, organized labor market relations gradually emerged, along with policies combining economic growth, full employment, and improved social protection. The Swedish policy mix was based on a productive entente between labor and capital, who agreed to rationalize production and institutionalize full employment out of mutual interest.

Denmark never experienced a 'golden age' to the same extent. The postwar economy got off to a poor start, with high unemployment and low growth, and the modernization of Danish industry came much later than in Sweden. Denmark, with its strong rural tradition and agricultural industry, did not develop the kind of heavy industry structure and centralized industrial relations system that Sweden did. Industrial development was also less regulated by the state. Thus, while the labor movement and big business jointly forged the Swedish path to development, rural interests and small industries were just as important as social democracy in shaping Denmark's social and economic development.

Through the 1970s and 1980s, Sweden still clung to the social democratic tradition of full employment, while Denmark's more weakly institutionalized model strayed from the path of full employment as early as the mid-1970s. From the early 1990s through mid-decade, however, unemployment in Sweden suddenly increased as public deficits verged on the uncontrollable. Equally interesting, the Danish economy started to appear quite healthy at the same time, which we attribute to a particularly fortunate sequencing of policy choices beginning in the early 1980s.

This chapter describes the problems of the 'Swedish model' in the 1990s and the development of a 'Danish miracle' in the same period. Our conclusion is that institutional stability in Sweden makes a dramatic increase in employment less likely, although growth and employment have returned to more normal levels following the profound crisis of the early 1990s. Denmark, on the other hand, has so far been able to develop a workable response to the bedeviling problems of the internationalized economy, where much depends on the ability to keep wage increases under control and simultaneously encourage structural change in the economy. An important issue that remains, however, is whether Denmark's decentralized industrial relations system can ensure wage restraint in the future.

We proceed along two tracks. We begin with a comparison of the original Swedish and Danish welfare constellations as they appeared during the 'golden age'. We then analyze the impact of internationalization and the separate adjustment processes of the two countries, from the 1970s to the present. The last section contains a comparative discussion of the functional and normative implications, as well as of the differences and similarities between the Swedish and Danish economic and social policy regimes.

9.2. The Postwar Swedish Model

9.2.1. Size of Industry and Sectoral Employment Structure

Agriculture shrunk rapidly as a source of employment in postwar Sweden. The decline of farm work was compensated by a massive growth of jobs in capital-intensive, high-wage industries like engineering, forestry, paper and pulp, mining, iron and steel (Larsson 1991). This development was triggered both by the home market (e.g. for autos and construction) and by economic expansion outside Sweden. The Swedish economy had been highly internationalized from the beginning of industrialization in the latter half of the nineteenth century, and this pattern continued after the War (Jörberg 1982). The economy performed well during the 1950s and 1960s, with high growth rates (up to 7% annually), large productivity increases, and low unemployment (ranging between 1 and 2%).

In the mid-1960s, industrial jobs still represented about 40 percent of total employment. Engineering accounted for almost half of industrial employment. Other important sectors were paper and pulp, forestry, chemistry, iron and metals, food and textiles (SOU 1971-5). The structural trend in Swedish industry was toward gradual concentration into ever larger firms; companies with more than ten employees accounted for over 80 percent of employment in industry (SOU 1971-5: 79). Agriculture went through a process of rapid modernization after the war until it only accounted for about 10 percent of employment by the 1960s, while private services became an expanding sector making up about a quarter of total employment. The public sector first became an important employer towards the end of the 'golden age,' especially after 1965, when it employed about 700,000 people, or about 20 percent of the total labor force at this time (Furåker 1987). Labor market participation rates for men in the 1960s were very high, at over 80 percent of full-time employment, while comparable rates for women in the same period were only near 40 percent (Erixon 1985; SOU 1979-24).

9.2.2. Macroeconomic Policy Priorities

The macroeconomic policy of the postwar period is often referred to as the Rehn–Meidner model, after Gösta Rehn and Rudolf Meidner, two influential economists from the trade unions confederation LO. The model was first outlined in a report to the LO congress in 1951 (LO 1951). It represented a coherent and integrated approach toward achieving full employment, structural change, and industrial rationalization without inflation. Rehn and Meidner proposed combining restrictive monetary and fiscal policies with a 'solidaristic' wage policy oriented around average productivity increases (rather than toward the profitability of individual firms or sectors) and an 'active' labor market policy facilitating the transfer of labor from declining regions and companies to expanding ones.

Macroeconomic policy also assisted the transformation of the industrial structure by maintaining low interest rates and imposing high taxes on any profits that were not reinvested. Short-term regulation also played a role in the macroeconomic policy mix, however, since taxes and fees for individuals and companies were actively used as countercyclical instruments to balance national and international demand. In international upswings they were meant to contain extra domestic liquidity and demand, whereas international downturns were dampened through tax cuts and other demand stimuli (SOU 1961-42; Werin 1993).

'Active' labor market policy had been introduced in the 1930s to support the unemployed through public relief work at wages slightly lower than what the market paid. Despite low unemployment, the active labor market policy remained important throughout the 1950s and 1960s, enlisting a wide variety of measures such as job mobility assistance, retraining programs, government home buying, vocational guidance, etc. The policy had the aim of securing a supply of labor for expanding sectors and industries while reducing the negative social side effects of industrial rationalization and structural change (SOU 1965-1).

The postwar tax system was based on three major principles: consolidating profitable companies by promoting reinvestment of profits; increasing the redistributive effects of taxation by sharpening progressivity in the personal income tax and increasing taxes on capital, wealth, and inheritance; and increasing the use of payroll taxes and indirect taxation to finance social policy expansion. In the late 1930s and 1940s, taxes on higher incomes, wealth, and inheritance were increased, a move motivated by the need to balance budgets and pay for higher social expenditures then being proposed. Corporate taxation was also increased, though with generous deductions for investment. In the 1950s payroll taxes were introduced to finance general health insurance, maternity leave, supplementary pensions, and job injury insurance. A sales tax was introduced in the late 1950s, and a tax on capital gains from housing and stocks in the mid-1960s (Elvander 1970). In 1970 joint taxation for married couples was abolished. Hailed as 'the greatest equality reform ever', this was intended to increase the supply of female labor power, but also to support equality between men and women. Personal taxation for low-income groups was also lowered in 1970, whereas taxes on capital, wealth, and inheritances were increased. Thus, towards the end of the 'golden age', tax policy was increasingly employed to support redistribution and equality.

9.2.3. The Role of the Capital Market

Since capital transfers could be strictly controlled during the 'golden age', the domestic Swedish capital market could also be effectively regulated to serve two functions, namely, to finance budget deficits and stimulate housing construction. Public regulation was able to allocate credit, while the tax system stimulated the reinvestment of profits to keep investments at a high level. The role of the stock market was quite limited. Instead, the capital market was dominated by corporate owners like the Wallenberg family and large banks associated with investment companies (Glete 1994). The banks and the owner families had long-term commitments to their companies—many of which had been originally founded by these groups (Larsson 1998).

9.2.4. Government–Business Relations

Industrial policy was never an important element in the structural transformation of Swedish industry during the 'golden age'. The debate during the first postwar years on a state-led reorganization of sectors and industries and expansion of public enterprises resulted in a very bitter conflict between the Social Democrats and industry ('the resistance to the planned economy'). Eventually, planned interventions were discarded (Lewin 1967). After this ideological confrontation, the labor movement chose a less controversial strategy, seeking to increase the pressure for adaptation through a combination of the solidaristic wage policy (irrespective of differences in corporate profitability), a tight macroeconomic policy, state procurement of technology for both civilian infrastructure and the military, and (not least) the 'active' labor market policy (Benner 1997).

9.2.5. Labor Market Policy Priorities

The Swedish employment regime was based on full employment and labor market mobility. The general goal was to achieve a high-wage economy, move labor into expanding sectors and regions, avoid inflationary bottlenecks, and (last of all) avoid the formation of low-wage/low-productivity coalitions between unprofitable companies and their workers (Erixon 1997). The cornerstone of this policy was the Rehn–Meidner model of egalitarian wage formation and active labor market policy. It was critically dependent on the centralization of wage bargaining, which began (at least between the LO trade union confederation and the SAF employers' federation) in 1956. This, in turn, depended on an internal structure for each partner to collective bargaining (first among the employers, later within the blue-collar unions) that was equally centralized (LO 1941). Both white- and blue-collar workers, as well as employers, were well organized, with union density reaching 80 percent for blue-collar workers and 60 percent for white-collar workers at the end of the 1960s (Kjellberg 1983). In a similar fashion, the employers' top-level organization, SAF, organized companies employing around 90 percent of the total workforce in the private sector. These patterns of industrial relations, in which the state played only an indirect and facilitating role, emerged from the 1938 Saltsjöbaden agreement, a landmark central agreement on conflict resolution and negotiating principles.

Postwar industrial relations operated within a multi-level structure of central, industrywide, and local wage bargaining. Agreements on the general level of wage increases were struck centrally. Hourly wages and overtime allowances were negotiated at the industry level, while local negotiations determined piecework rates (Kjellberg 1983: 79). Industry-wide and local negotiations were coordinated at the top of the SAF and LO organizations through various sanctions such as fines and warnings (A. Olsson 1989). Nevertheless, the level of wage increases was not prede-termined by the central and industrywide agreements. Local wage drift, often reflecting labor shortages, was an important if 'unauthorized' source of wage increases, sometimes accounting for up to 50 percent of total wage increases (A. Olsson 1989: 36). As a response to wage drift's unevenness, a number of compensation clauses for groups with little or no wage drift were included in bargaining after 1966 (A. Olsson 1989: 67).

There was a clear demarcation between the unions and employers on issues of corporate management and work organization. The unions gen-erally avoided attempts to influence local managerial decisions by claim-ing that a separation of power and interests was necessary to prevent unions and employers from forming unproductive coalitions locally. Wage compression, the argument went, would instead become the main tool forcing local firms to accept rationalization of production (LO 1961).

Wage leadership by export industries was generally accepted and even formed the basis for a joint initiative taken by unions and employers to formulate general rules on wage formation (Edgren, Faxén, and Odhner 1970). Public sector employees were only given the right to collective bar-gaining in the mid-1960s and thus played a limited role in industrial rela-tions. Until the late 1960s, the wage bargaining system was dominated by the LO–SAF axis. Negotiations began along this axis, and bargaining for the white-collar sectors followed the pattern of the LO–SAF agreements. Wage bargaining became more complicated towards the end of the 1960s, as compensation clauses made central and industrywide bargaining more conflictual and public sector wage bargaining challenged the hegemony of the export sector. These tensions were beginning to show in the mid-1960s but did not explode until the 1970s.

9.2.6. Social Security Priorities

Swedish social policy in this 'golden age' focused on the expansion and centralization of work-related benefits. The most important reform was the introduction of supplementary pensions in 1959 (ATP). There was also a general health insurance system (established in 1946, expanded in 1955) that replaced several fragmented, voluntary insurance plans and included all employees along with their spouses and children. In terms of expenditure or coverage, Swedish social policy was not radically different from comparable systems in Continental or Anglo-Saxon countries (Esping-Andersen 1990). It focused on work-related welfare financed by payroll taxes (especially for the elderly), while social services financed out of taxes were relatively underdeveloped and replacement rates rather limited (at 50 to 60%, roughly equal to the Continental countries). Accordingly, the effort to expand social insurance focused on the full-time employed.

9.2.6.1. Unemployment and Work Injury Insurance

Unemployment insurance, based on the income replacement principle and financed by a combination of contributions and government assistance, has been run by the trade unions since the 1930s (Edebalk 1975). Insurance was limited to six months, and the replacement rate was about two-thirds of previous income, with lower nominal support for non-bread-winners (Elmér 1971). A new kind of work injury insurance was established in 1955 to coincide with the new health insurance plan. It covered all public and private employees and was financed out of payroll taxes.

9.2.6.2. Family Policy

Family support was expanded through the universal child allowance in 1948. Childcare, organized by the municipalities, was supported by state subsidies from the 1940s onward, though on a limited scale. It expanded in the 1960s along with the growing demand for women on the labor market, although even by the late 1960s few children were in public daycare (Elmér 1971). Care for the elderly was also organized by the municipalities, although it was regulated and supported by the state. As late as the 1960s, however, it remained in the tradition of poor relief (Elmér 1971).

9.2.6.3. Health Care

Health care was primarily organized on a local basis, with self-employed district medical officers at the center until the late 1960s. The main site for providing services was therefore not the hospital, where only additional specialized care was provided. In other words, service provision remained primarily private, though almost all health care was financed by public health care insurance (which de facto covered all Swedish citizens following a 1955 reform) and by taxes. Health care insurance was funded by income-related contributions and payroll taxes, and it covered about three-quarters of the costs for medical services.

Health care was reformed in the 1960s (Berg 1980). Both general and more specialized health care was centralized to the hospitals. Most physicians are now publicly employed. Health care continues to be paid for on a fee-for-service basis, with huge public subsidies.

9.2.6.4. Pensions

The postwar pensions system comprises four pillars. The first is the basic pension, virtually unchanged since 1948. It is the same for all citizens, originally tax-financed (payroll taxes today), regulated by law, and indexed to inflation. Until 1975 the retirement age was 67. A general supplement for pensioners with little or nothing in the way of supplementary pensions was established in 1969. The second pillar is the supplementary ATP system itself, (introduced in 1960). It is based on labor market performance, with benefits calculated on the basis of the fifteen most favorable work years out of a maximum of thirty. The system is benefit-defined and financed through payroll taxes. Since the 1970s it has been based not only on regular labor market incomes, but also on sickness, unemployment, and parental insurance payments. The third pillar is the labor market pension, negotiated by the parties to collective bargaining. It includes four different systems for public and private employees, which collectively cover all employees on the labor market. The fourth pillar is private pension insurance. This pillar, established in the interwar period, was usually either a fringe benefit for corporate executives or the main type of pension for small company owners during the 'golden age' (Larsson 1998).

9.2.6.5. Housing

'Social housing policy', which controlled rents and housing construction by promoting public financing and regulating credit, was another important element of postwar social policy. This policy was expanded during the housing shortage of the late 1960s, when a program was launched to build one million dwellings in ten years (Bengtsson 1995).

9.2.6.6. The Welfare State as an Employer

There was a massive increase in public employment beginning in the late 1960s. Although there had been a gradual rise in public employment after World War II, the period between 1965 and 1980, when the public payroll doubled (from 700,000 to 1,400,000 employees), was exceptional. The main share of this increase was in public services provided by municipalities and county councils such as health care, childcare, care for the elderly, and education. The increase was reflected in higher female labor market participation, with no fewer than 500,000 housewives entering the labor market in this period (Axelsson 1992).

One important explanation of this increase was the radicalization of the Social Democratic Party in the late 1960s, which resulted in pledges to improve conditions for women on the labor market as a way of increasing gender equality. This reflected an ideological change within the LO, which used to be skeptical about the effect of more female labor market particip-ation on the viability of the 'solidaristic wage policy' (Hirdman 1998). In the 1970s leading Social Democrats argued that an expanded public sec-tor could improve public services and prevent growing unemployment (Hellström 1975). In a general way, if not explicitly, this conviction also guided the bourgeois governments holding power after 1976. Thus, our explanation of the expansion of public sector employment emphasizes three factors: the gradual increase in public sector employment through-out the postwar period, demands for improved conditions for women in the latter half of the 1960s, and greater public sector employment as one measure employed to keep unemployment low in the 1970s.

9.2.7. Institutional Capabilities

The institutional capacity of the 'Swedish model' rested on a number of pillars: the strength of the Social Democratic government and the hege-mony of the labor movement in Swedish politics, the discursively harmo-nized interests of the partners to collective bargaining on the labor market, the forums for consensus-formation in policymaking, and the ideological and normative stability of the 'work society'.

Sweden's multi-party political system was long dominated by the Social Democratic Party (SAP). It was capable of forming stable governments—most often alone, though sometimes in coalition with one or more of the bourgeois parties—on the basis of a constitution that caused the largest party to be overrepresented in the bicameral parliament (Ruin 1981). The agrarian, conservative, and liberal parties formed a non-socialist political bloc. The bourgeois bloc was weakened by cleavages caused, among other things, by the participation of the agrarian party in a coalition government with the SAP during the 1950s. In addition, links between the non-socialist parties and employers were weak, since the latter had chosen to cooperate with the unions and the Social Democratic government in shaping eco-nomic and labor market policies (Elvander 1966).

The role of the social partners in policy formation was very important throughout this period, especially in economic and labor market policy. Together with strong administrative bodies like the AMS (the Labor Market Board), unions and employers set priorities for labor market pol-icy (Rothstein 1996). What emerged was therefore a consensual and hier-archical system, with close links integrating policy fields and many forums for establishing consensus among the most important actors.

On the whole, the logic of the regulatory system and the need for struc-tural change and economic rationalization (regardless of interregional disparities) were widely accepted, as were the norms of cooperation and government by mutual agreement. The values of the 'work society' were also central to the stability of the Swedish model: it was widely held that full employment and labor market security were the things allowing men (and, to some extent, women) to achieve human dignity, and that full employment depended upon labor peace and labor force mobility (LO 1961).

9.3. The Postwar Danish Model

9.3.1. *Economic Profile and Structure of Industry*

Denmark never had a large base of raw materials for export. Nor was engineering a major engine of growth. Instead, agricultural, textiles, and clothing dominated the Danish economy during its 'golden age'.

Danish growth rates, at an average of 4 percent per year in the 1960s, were well below Sweden's. Similarly, productivity increased at a slower pace and unemployment was somewhere in between Sweden's low rates and the OECD average. Trouble in financing an ongoing current account deficit frequently forced Danish governments to dampen economic activity by increasing taxes and interest rates.

Denmark's level of market capitalization was slightly higher than Sweden's during the postwar period. The stock market played the same minor role as in Sweden, and for much the same reason. Very few of the international-oriented Danish companies were characterized by diversified ownership (Katzenstein 1985: 175–76; Lønroth, Nørreklit, and Sørensen 1997: 6). The vast majority of firms were family-owned, which prevented the stock market from assuming any central position in the Danish capital market.

In addition, Danish banks rarely appeared as dominant owners of companies. Directors of financial institutions are not allowed to own or participate in the management of another company. Similarly, financial companies are not allowed by law to have a dominant influence over other business groups (Lønroth, Nørreklit, and Sørensen 1997: 7).

9.3.2. *Macroeconomic Policy Priorities*

Danish macroeconomic policy priorities during the postwar period were different from Sweden's. One reason for the difference was Denmark's current account, which displayed a chronic deficit from 1960 onwards. Both the deficit and growing foreign debt, however, were perceived as necessary, both in order to finance modernization of the industrial base and for society as a whole. Over the medium term, it was argued, debt and deficit would help Denmark's small, weak industrial base keep pace with domestic demand and consumption, both private and public.

Nevertheless, Danish industrial policy was not targeted at modernizing the industrial base. It was a weak policy with a laissez-faire attitude toward the regulation of business. In addition, hourly earnings in manufacturing increased at an average yearly rate of 7.3 percent between 1971 and 1975, compared to Germany's 3.5 percent increase. This clearly lowered the price competitiveness of Danish products. The early 1970s saw the government introduce some policies to cool down the inflationary economy, but Danish governments in that decade were generally not as alarmed by the economic situation as they were to become in the 1980s, perhaps because public revenue continued to exceed expenditures until the mid-1970s.

The Danish central bank was not as powerful in the market as its Swedish counterpart. This was due to two factors: the relative weakness of the Danish Social Democratic Party and the chronic current account deficit, which prevented long-term planning that might have ensured low interest rates, assisted investment, and balanced budgets. The tax system was not based on any clear ideas about encouraging the reinvestment of profits. The Danish welfare state was mainly financed out of general revenues. Social security contributions made up a very small share of total revenue, and they even experienced a drastic decline in 1973 when a new sickness insurance reform abolished contributions from the insured. The employers' share remained between 3 and 5 percent for most of the postwar period, through it did increase from 4 percent to 8 percent in 1973 (Johansen 1986: 317).

In the second half of the 1960s, the Danish tax burden increased more rapidly, and to a higher level, than in other Western European countries, even exceeding Swedish levels in the first half of the 1970s. In this period total taxation rose from 26.9 percent to over 44 percent of GDP. The period from 1969 to 1971 alone saw an increase of some 30 percent (Johansen 1986: 231).

Partly as a result of the speed with which the tax burden had grown, the entire postwar tax system came under heavy attack. The tax revolt gave rise to an entirely new parliamentary situation. Representation in parliament had been dominated by the four old parties (Social Democratic, Agrarian, Conservative, and Liberal). But in the general election of 1973, more than 35 percent of the votes were held by five different parties, some of them newcomers, some old splinter parties. Among them was the anti-tax Progress Party, which entered Parliament as the second largest party after the Social Democrats. It had appealed to the electorate by advocating major cutbacks in the state bureaucracy and in social expenditures so as to relieve the tax burden. The success of other parties in the 1973 election, however, suggests that resistance to taxes and the welfare state was not the only issue producing fundamental changes in voter alignments and attitudes during the 1970s.

This interpretation is supported by developments since the 1973 election. The Progress Party gradually lost public support, while—after a brief decline—the tax rate continued to rise. Similarly, surveys have clarified that the vast majority of the numerous social laws passed in the 1960s and 1970s enjoyed broad popular support along with backing from the political parties (Johansen 1986: 368–69).

9.3.3. Labor Market Policy Priorities

Compared to labor markets in most other highly developed welfare states, Denmark's is characterized by liberal (i.e. market-oriented) dismissal rules, considered a prerequisite for economic growth as early as the 'golden age'. These rules allowed firms to compensate for the short-term effects of changes in world markets by making rapid cutbacks in their levels of activity (Nielsen 1991; Lindholm 1994). In general, the state does issue protective regulations governing occupational health and safety, mass redundancies, unemployment, and social security. Nevertheless, wage standards, minimum pay, part-time or temporary employment, and most other conditions of employment have been regulated by collective agreements. outside the domain of state legislation. Denmark also lacked Swedish-style active labor market measures. All in all, the Danish state had less influence over the labor market than its Swedish counterpart.

Denmark's high pay standards in the postwar period were the product of a well-organized, albeit less centralized, labor movement. The same was true for Denmark's high standards on unemployment insurance (especially for low-income groups), which both unions and employers regarded as a necessary compensation for workers forced to accept easy hire-and-fire rules.

The industrial relations system of the 'golden age' was nationally centralized. Every two years wage levels as well as working conditions would be set by high-level agreement between the Employers Federation (DA) and the Federation of Trade Unions (LO). The system of peaceful labor relations, dating back to the 'September Compromise' of 1899, was hardly changed until the 1990s. As a central feature of the system, trade unions were allowed to administer the unemployment insurance funds, whose offices were usually placed either in the same building or near to union offices. As a result, workers applying for unemployment insurance would almost automatically come in contact with a union when they registered for coverage.

But in spite of the high degree of unionization, collective agreements in Denmark always were less far-reaching than they were in Sweden. Only half of all employees are covered by them, and legislation does not automatically extend collective agreements to an entire industry (Lind 1998: 9–10). Moreover, the Danish industrial relations system was never very good at controlling the 'effective wages' paid by firms over and above the contractual minimum. In several different periods, wage increases were well above the OECD average. For as long as the economy was booming, this had no effect on overall employment, which continued to grow.

The growth of public sector employment was directly reflected in rates of female labor force participation, which climbed to over 50 percent of the Danish female population aged 15–66 in the early 1970s (Johansen 1986). Denmark also saw a remarkable increase in part-time employment, to nearly 25 percent by 1980 (Statistics Denmark 1995: 10).

9.3.4. Social Security Priorities

Denmark's unemployment insurance system became as generous as Sweden's in the 1970s. Throughout the postwar period, spending by the insurance funds was already being fully reimbursed by the state. Each fund would then pay the state a fee on behalf of each one of its members. Childcare and elder care arrangements were institutionalized at the municipal level, and both programs expanded rapidly in the 1960s and early 1970s. The same is true for the health care system, organized by local authorities and financed by a combination of fees and state subsidies.

Housing policy, as measured by various forms of state intervention into the housing market like public subsidies and construction, played only a marginal role in the Danish welfare state during the postwar period. In fact, the postwar period witnessed a general withdrawal of the state from the housing market.

The basic old age pension insurance scheme, which had been introduced in 1891, was transformed into a tax-financed basic pension in the 1960s. While the old system had been means- and income-tested, the idea behind the new basic pension was that it should be universal and based on the citizenship principle, and that all income-tested supplements should be replaced by flat-rate benefits. This goal was not fully achieved. Nevertheless, coverage expanded: under the old rules, some 66 percent of those aged 65 and over had received the basic old age pension (Johansen 1986: 319), whereas recipients as a share of the population in that age group grew to 95 percent by 1975 under the new rules.

In addition to the basic pension, Denmark's pension structure rests on three other pillars. The second is the Labor Market Supplementary Pension (ATP)—a mandatory, fully-funded, and contribution-defined scheme covering all wage earners working for an average of 10 hours or more per week. The parties to collective bargaining and the state jointly administer the ATP scheme from a council that also unanimously fixes the annual level of contributions (Kvist 1997: 26). The shares at which employees and employers finance the ATP are one-third and two-thirds, respectively. Coverage varies depending on how many working hours are logged and how long the worker stays connected to the labor market, rather than on earnings. The ATP does not add much to a retired person's income (Johansen 1986). This is symptomatic of the Danish pension system as a whole. Although the full old age pension was introduced in the hopes of lifting average payments to two-thirds of previous earnings, no fixed earnings-replacement ratios (neither de jure nor de facto) have been set in the Danish pension system.

The third pillar in the pension system is constituted by the occupational pension schemes, fully funded and contribution-defined (as a percentage of wages). They differ widely from sector to sector and between branches. This is because these pensions are fixed in decentralized negotiations between the parties to collective bargaining. The fourth pillar in the pension system consists of individualized old age pension arrangements, such as life insurance contracts and savings. Contributions to these schemes vary according to the individual agreements reached between recipients and their banks or insurance companies.

9.3.5. *Institutional Capabilities*

The Danish Social Democratic Party was never as strong as its Swedish counterpart. It never dominated governments to the same degree, and it sometimes headed short-term minority coalition governments with policies shaped by narrow time horizons and changing majorities. The Social Democrats' strength actually declined during the postwar period. After the tax revolt of 1973 the Social Democratic Party remained the largest group in Parliament, but it was dependent on support from the small parties. Its capacity to develop purely social democratic kinds of policy à la Sweden, or simply to pursue long-term goals, was accordingly diminished.

The Danish collective bargaining system is usually described as centralized, but unlike its Swedish counterpart it generated major conflicts and was never able to secure moderate wage growth (Lind 1998: 11). Wage determination proceeds through five stages. First, there are direct negotiations between individual unions and employers' associations. If they are unable to agree, the dispute goes to the central federations, the LO and DA. If no agreement can be reached at this level either, the dispute moves on to a state mediator. The mediator then has three weeks to reach a settlement between the parties before a strike or a lockout can begin. All settlements must be ratified by a vote of the members. If the members do not ratify an agreement, a strike and/or lockout can begin. The government may also intervene, however, if mediation proves unsuccessful. The lack of harmony and the dysfunctional quality of the Danish industrial relations system compared to Sweden's are indicated by the fact that almost every bargaining round in the postwar period ended up in mediation, and that government did intervene whenever mediation failed (Wallerstein and Golden 1997: 720).

Thus, although wage increases at the local level are supposedly bound by general agreements at the national level, the capacity of centralized authorities on both sides of the Danish labor market is too limited to monitor and police local agreements over several years. One reason is that the bargaining system is structured more along craft lines and by skill levels or gender than along industry lines. The skill and craft divisions obviate against coherent union strategies. Thus, the largest employee organization, SiD, a union of unskilled and semi-skilled workers, has opposed centralization, whereas the almost equally large union of skilled metalworkers has been a proponent of centralized bargaining authority (Wallerstein and Golden 1997: 718).

Things became more difficult as employment expanded in the public sector, where pay was centrally determined. Thus, when public sector unions succeeded in pushing for higher incomes, the LO–DA structure of negotiations could not prevent large wage jumps and, as a result, the emergence of intense wage competition across sectors and branches, with additional negative effects on the competitiveness of Danish products.

9.4. Sweden and the Crises of the 1970s

At the end of the 1960s, Sweden seemed to represent a stable configuration of macroeconomic policy, industrial relations, and welfare state arrangements that combined to make high growth compatible with full employment and generous, universal benefits. If there ever was a 'Swedish model', it was certainly at its height in the 1950s and 1960s. There were cracks in the model, such as increasing strains in wage bargaining and rank-and-file dissatisfaction with the consensual tone of relations between the social partners, but on the whole the model did not seem unstable. Almost all the elements of this model-like coherence, however, disappeared rather abruptly in the 1970s.

After a turbulent start to the 1970s, as profits and economic growth fluctuated wildly, Sweden went through a deep and long-lasting economic crisis in the latter half of the decade. Corporate profitability declined, the budget deficit exploded, and growth rates declined (becoming negative in 1977), while wage increases were extremely high in 1976 (Figure 9.2) and inflation went well above the OECD average in both 1977 and 1978 (Figure 9.1). The major achievement of the period was low unemployment. In fact, there was even a small increase in employment at the end of the 1970s (Figure 9.3).

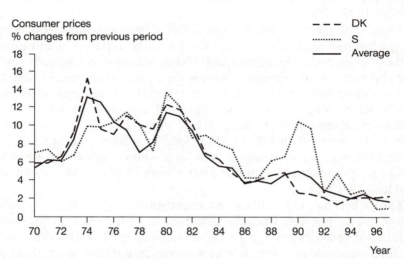

Figure 9.1 Inflation, 1970–1996
Source: OECD, *Economic Outlook* (Paris: OECD, various issues); own calculations.

There are four important themes related to the Swedish economy's unstable development in this period: the weakening of the Swedish model's institutional capacities, the vulnerability of the economic structure following the oil crisis of 1973, the continuing growth of the public sector, and difficulty controlling wage increases.

9.4.1. The Erosion of Institutional Capacities

The first signs of weakening in the tightly integrated Swedish model were already beginning to show in the mid-1960s. Centralized bargaining was

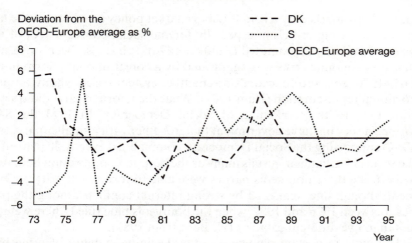

Figure 9.2 Hourly earnings in manufacturing, 1973–1995
Source: OECD, *Historical Statistics* (Paris: OECD, various issues); own calculations.

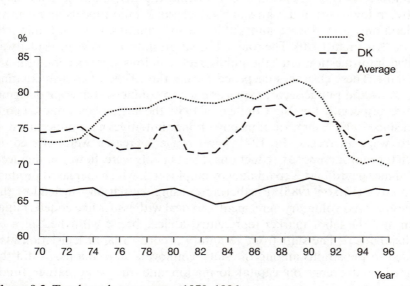

Figure 9.3 Total employment rate, 1970–1996
Source: OECD, *Statistical Compendium: Labour Force Statistics* (Paris: OECD, 1997); own calculations.

increasingly marked by tension. Labor market policy also became the target of increasing criticism, especially for the social consequences of the regional mobility it promoted (Furåker 1976). It has also been suggested that the economic crisis was aggravated by a constitutional reform in the early 1970s that introduced a one-chamber system based wholly on proportional representation (Ruin 1981). What the reform clearly did do was contribute to the weakening of Social Democracy. In 1973 the SAP formed a very unstable government that, together with a smaller party (the VPK) supporting the Social Democrats, commanded exactly 50 percent of the seats in Parliament, just as many as the bourgeois opposition had. And in 1976 the three bourgeois parties were able to form a majority government, though one weakened by strong internal conflicts among the parties: Between 1976 and 1982, when the bourgeois bloc ruled, there were no less than five different cabinets (H. Bergström 1987).

The most important change was the declining stability of wage bargaining. The close understanding that had prevailed between the parties to collective bargaining broke down during the 1960s, at first because of internal friction among different employers and unions within each camp, and then later owing to controversies between unions and employers. The export industries had always been skeptical of centralized wage bargaining and began criticizing the system in a more aggressive tone during the 1960s (Bergom-Larsson 1985). Within the LO, multiple tensions— between low-wage and high-wage associations, union locals and central federations, and private and public sector unions—were beginning to show (Kassman 1990). The role of the export industry as wage leader was called into question, and the public sector unions were becoming more militant. These cleavages deepened during the 1970s, when a fluctuating economy and public sector expansion led to conflicts over wage determination, especially the 'Big Conflict' of 1980, the largest labor market conflict since 1909. A number of incomes policy initiatives were undertaken to curb wage increases. In 1974 lower wage increases were offered in exchange for income tax reductions. The tax cuts were, however, financed by higher payroll taxes (paid only by employers), which increased production costs (Erixon 1985). Furthermore, using legislation—instead of the time-honored voluntary agreement—to deal with issues like codetermination and the labor market represented a clear break with the 'spirit of Saltsjöbaden'. The shift from voluntary accord to labor legislation also added to the strains among the state, employers, and unions, as did the heated controversy on capital formation and the wage earner funds (Stråth 1998).

9.4.2. The Crisis of the Industrial Structure and the Politics of Crisis Management

The 'Swedish model' had produced an industrial structure tailored to the needs of postwar European markets. By the 1970s, however, Sweden's industrial structure had become quite vulnerable to structural changes in the world economy, including market saturation in heavy industry (Schön 1994). Arguably, the economic crisis was also a crisis of the institutions (such as the Rehn–Meidner model) responsible for structural change and industrial rationalization in postwar Sweden. The pattern of growth these institutions produced was not easily reversed, even when altered economic conditions called for change. The oil crisis and the commodities boom of the early 1970s fully exposed these contradictions. Profits for all the major export industries—especially heavy industry (steel and iron), engineering, shipbuilding, paper and pulp—plummeted when the 1972–73 boom was reversed during the next two years. The fluctuating business cycle had other consequences. Wage formation and labor relations were severely disturbed, as extremely high wage increases and taxes in 1975 and 1976 followed the profit boom (and contributed to a deep crisis after 1977).

The crisis was initially viewed as a cyclical variation on the postwar growth pattern and was handled by a policy mix of counter-cyclical macroeconomic measures, state subsidies to ailing industries, labor market training for the unemployed, and public sector expansion (Lundberg 1983). After 1976, when the crisis had deepened, the state took on a more comprehensive role as owner of many important companies in crisis-ridden sectors, such as shipbuilding, paper and pulp, steel, and iron. Subsidies (along with greater labor market training) kept levels of industrial employment virtually intact, while the expanded public services created new jobs, and labor market measures vastly expanded the scope of public relief work (Therborn 1986).

9.4.3. Public Sector Expansion

The crisis of the international economy did not compel Sweden to undertake major changes in social policy or labor market regulation. Despite strongly worded advice from some of Sweden's own experts to reorganize social welfare and labor market policy so that both would now function to contain inflation and facilitate long-term growth, no such policy choices were made (DsJu 1979: 1). If anything, social policy developed along a familiar trajectory during this crisis period, with new reforms like the expansion of parental insurance, a partial pension scheme, lowering the pension age from 67 to 65, introducing dental insurance, and hiring more public sector employees (Furåker 1987). Under bourgeois rule in the late 1970s and early 1980s, there were a number of social policy cutbacks (such as the introduction of one waiting day in the health insurance and the de-indexation of pensions), but on the whole the system was expanded rather than retrenched (Marklund 1990). The same was true of public sector employment, which continued to grow, albeit on a modest scale (Figure 9.6).

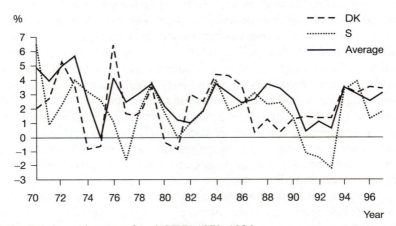

Figure 9.6 Growth rates of real GDP, 1970–1996
Source: OECD, *Economic Outlook* (Paris: OECD, various issues).

9.4.4. The Crisis of Wage Bargaining

Wage bargaining in the latter half of the 1970s did not adjust to higher inflation or the declining international competitiveness of Swedish industry. Indeed, wage negotiations for 1975 and 1976 (which, along with higher payroll taxes, boosted labor costs by 43%) played an important role in the profound crisis of 1977 and 1978. Bargaining after 1976, however, produced more modest wage increases (Rydén 1979). Nevertheless, the leading parts in the drama of crisis adjustment were played by three successive currency devaluations in 1976 and 1977 as well as several subsidies to ailing industries (A. Bergström 1995). The devaluations were, in hindsight, failed attempts at compensating for the declining competitiveness of Swedish industry. At the time, however, they were generally viewed as necessary adaptations to changes in world markets (Lundberg 1983). The brunt of crisis management was borne by the first bourgeois government in four decades, which was reluctant to give up on full employment for political reasons. On the other hand, the government was committed to a 'planned reduction' of the crisis-ridden sectors rather than to its predecessor's program of full-blown nationalization. More than 30 bn Swedish kronor in state subsidies were distributed to ailing industries and sectors, and a large number of companies were temporarily nationalized. The subsidies policy has been portrayed as a reactive policy, but the reorganized crisis industries became fairly successful in terms of employment and profitability by the 1980s (Schön 1994).

9.5. Sweden: Moving from 'Model' to Crisis in the 1980s and 1990s

Many of the policies pursued in Sweden during the 1970s and early 1980s were somewhat fumbling attempts to minimize the impact of world market turbulence and strains on the domestic labor market while simultaneously satisfying demands for social policy expansion. But other policies revealed a more confident approach toward growth and employment in the 1980s. A new model, a new 'third way' avoiding the instability of Keynesianism and the austerity of monetarism, would instead emphasize corporate investments, wage restraint, and curbs on public sector spending as the primary measures for creating balanced growth and full employment. This policy seemed quite successful in the mid-1980s, when Sweden—in contrast to most other European countries—had high growth, low inflation, and low unemployment. For various reasons, ranging from upheaval in the international economy to deregulation of domestic financial markets, the new approach lost its coherence by the end of the 1980s. Recovery now pushed the economy into an 'overheated' stage characterized by labor shortages, high inflation, and low productivity growth. The mechanisms developed to curb these imbalances—various 'non-accommodating' policies, like a fixed currency, as well as a major tax reform—ended up having disastrous consequences for public budgets, employment, and growth rates. The last few years have witnessed a fairly dramatic recovery from the crisis of the early 1990s, on the basis of a floated currency, a stern central bank policy to keep inflation low, and a painful program to balance public budgets by reducing public expenditure and increasing taxes. Unemployment rates are not quite back to the level of the 1980s, but since the mid-1990s they have gone down. The big challenge is to make even lower unemployment possible. But finding a solution to persistent unemployment is still quite controversial, as it touches on many colliding interests, not least of all among the social partners.

9.5.1. The Economic Background

The economic crisis continued into the early 1980s. By postwar standards, unemployment reached record highs (3%–4% open unemployment), corporate profitability went down, investment sunk to record-low levels, and lackluster economic growth even turned negative in 1981. The gross public debt increased to around 60 percent of GDP in the early 1980s, and public deficits to around 7 percent of GDP.

The remainder of the 1980s reversed this downward spiral. Unemployment gradually returned to 'golden age' levels by 1989 (as low as 1.6%), and that same year the employment ratio reached an impressive peak of 80 percent, the highest in Europe at the time. After 1982 corporate profitability was also consolidated, followed by more investment in R & D and new production facilities (Schön 1994). The budget deficit turned into a surplus in 1987. For most of the 1980s, inflation stayed close to the European average. Growth rates were also comparable to those of other European countries.

Yet the Swedish economy also showed signs of instability, especially toward the end of the 1980s. These signs included high inflation (reaching 10% in 1989), productivity growth lower than the OECD average (down to around 1.5%), surging unit labor costs, and a burgeoning flow of international direct investments that reached record levels by the late 1980s (75 bn SEK in 1990) (see Figure 9.2). During this decade employment growth was also concentrated in service production and employment in the sheltered sector.

The big break with the (on balance) successful new economic trajectory came in the early 1990s. Between 1990 and 1992 the employment ratio plummeted from 80 percent to 70 percent, which corresponded to a rise in unemployment from under 2 percent to 8 percent, while real interest rates jumped from 4 percent to 9 percent in the same period as demand fell steeply (e.g. by 5% in 1993). Corporate investments dropped by some 30 percent between 1990 and 1993. At the same time, there was a dramatic increase in public spending, partly to offset a crisis of the financial sector (the state had to channel some 70 bn kronor to financial institutions on the verge of bankruptcy), partly as a reflection of growing pressure on labor market policy to do something about higher unemployment. The budget surplus quickly turned into a record budget deficit (with gross public debt at around 80% of GDP in 1994 and the budget deficit at some 12% of GDP in 1993). Economic growth was negative between 1991 and 1993. Inflation, however, decreased quickly, going from 10 percent to 2 percent between 1990 and 1992. After inflation had been contained, the massive budget deficit was the next political target. Following a series of public spending cuts and tax increases between 1992 and 1996, the deficit turned into a surplus in 1998. Real interest rates have gone down to about 3 percent. Growth rates went up to 3 percent in 1994 and 1995, but decreased to around 2 percent after 1995. Unemployment remains an unsolved issue, although open unemployment at the time of writing (October 1999) is down to some 4.5 percent.

The early 1990s were characterized by lower employment in every segment of the labor market. Within the public sector, job-shedding has been concentrated in the employment-intensive municipalities and counties, where social services, education, and health care are organized (SNA 1995). About 200,000 jobs disappeared from county councils and local municipalities and 30,000 jobs disappeared from the national government sector (Statskontoret 1997). The industrial sector was also badly hit; no fewer than 260,000 manufacturing jobs disappeared between 1990 and 1995 (SNA 1995). Manufacturing and transportation have been particularly vulnerable here, but the same dip in employment can be observed for all sectors of the labor market, with the exception of the category 'ISIC 8' (financing etc.).

9.5.2. Macroeconomic Policy Choices

Swedish macroeconomic policy went through three major phases in the 1980s and 1990s. First, it moved towards a policy using a massive currency devaluation to stimulate competitiveness and corporate profitability in the internationally exposed sector. Devaluation was coupled with wage restraint, a ceiling on public spending, and policies to encourage industrial innovation. This policy mix could be considered a success, generating greater investments, lower inflation, more employment, and a gradual reduction in the budget deficit. The keynote of the second phase, beginning in the mid-1980s, was deregulation of financial markets as a response to changes in domestic and international financial markets. This, together with a tax system left unreformed, caused the domestic economy to overheat with high inflation and conflicts over wage bargaining. The third theme of recent macroeconomic policy, beginning around 1990, took the Swedish economy's various imbalances as its point of departure. The new targets were low inflation and reduced nominal tax rates, to be achieved through a 'non-accommodating policy' based on a hard currency, a reformed tax system, and state intervention in wage bargaining. This shift, even though it was probably necessary to calm down the overheated economy, caused a drastic reduction in market demand, resulting in record-high unemployment and a sharp increase in public deficits. After the krona was floated in 1992, the emphasis shifted to low inflation and a smaller budget deficit. Together with a stabilization of sectoral bargaining after 1995, this new emphasis has improved the Swedish economy's performance considerably, even though unemployment is still much higher than it was in the 1980s.

9.5.2.1. The First Phase—Higher Profits and Wage Moderation (1982–1986)

By the early 1980s there was a widespread belief in Swedish politics that a Keynesian solution to the economic crisis, based on increasing domestic demand, had become unrealistic (Bergström 1987). Sweden's huge budget deficit, its unstable currency, and the discouraging results of the French Keynesian experiment all pointed in this direction. The Social Democrats came to power in 1982 with a program emphasizing that the recovery of the economy should be export-led (SAP 1981). The program, rejecting both the Keynesian cure of a home market stimulus and the Thatcherite remedy of monetarist austerity, referred to itself as a 'third way' between these two alternatives (Government Bill 1982/83: 50).

The keystone of the policy adopted was a 16 percent currency devaluation. Market outcomes had to be accepted as rational and profits as such had to be the labor movement's programmatic goal (Feldt 1985). The basic problem of the Swedish economy, the argument went, was low corporate profitability, which only devaluation could cure. Lower unit labor costs, higher profits, stepped-up production, and greater capacity utilization would lead to higher investment rates even if international economic conditions should prove unfavorable (LU 1984).

An important element of this 'third way' was wage restraint. The devaluation in 1982 was also accepted as a necessary evil by the trade unions. The LO and the TCO did not seek compensation for the effects of devaluation on their members' standard of living; in effect, the unions accepted a decline in real incomes (Elvander 1988: 80; Malm 1994). The trade unions were eager to assist the Social Democratic government in its attempt to construct a new foundation for growth and employment. On the other hand, the government increased corporate taxation so as to diminish shareholders' 'excess profits' (Government Bill 1982/83: 50). Centralized bargaining, however, broke down in 1983 with the industry-level agreement between the Engineering Employers' Association (VF) and the Metalworkers' Union (Metall). In contrast to other employers' associations, the export-oriented multinational companies within the VF had been pushing to decentralize bargaining down to the sectoral level since the early 1970s (and with even greater intensity after the economic turmoil of the early 1980s). The demand for decentralization reflected a view the VF shared with Metall that the engineering industry was the

Swedish economy's growth engine and should therefore be wage leader. This attitude was also in line with the new government's orientation and its policy of redirecting resources from sheltered to exposed sectors (Elvander 1988: 90 ff.). The wage bargaining system established after 1983 therefore became somewhat unstable, though within reasonable limits, until the late 1980s. To control the growth of wages, the government intervened with tax cuts and price controls in 1985, resulting in wage increases at an annual rate of around 5 percent per year between 1984 and 1986 (Elvander 1988: chs. 3, 4).

A third element in the macroeconomic strategy was to limit growth in public spending. As will be discussed in Section 9.5.4, this amounted to freezing the status quo on social welfare expenditure and public sector employment while cutting health care expenditures as a share of GDP.

In addition, the government launched an ambitious industrial policy to strengthen the international competitiveness of Swedish industry. The policy included major investment programs for basic industries, where the supply of raw materials was seen as the main problem. The state established programs for information technology and telecommunications (Glimell 1986). There were also public programs supporting the transfer of resources from one sector to another, for example when the government intervened to support new investment in auto manufacturing facilities as a substitute for the declining shipbuilding (Benner 1997).

9.5.2.2. The Deregulation Strategy and its Effects (1986–1990)

Beginning in the 1970s, a challenge was mounted to Sweden's tightly regulated capital market. Credit regulations and the growing state debt had fostered an expanding 'grey' credit sector outside the reach of regulations established by the central bank. In the 1980s new financial instruments like derivatives emerged on the market, while the public sector (like domestic companies and multinational firms) began looking to the capital market for corporate or municipal bonds to finance investments (Larsson 1998). During the 1980s, the central bank increasingly focused on adjusting monetary policy to changes in the capital market, such as the growing importance of 'grey' financial institutions, the financial internationalization of Swedish enterprises, and the deregulation of foreign capital markets (Svensson 1996).

The bank, together with officials in the Ministry of Finance, was the entrepreneur behind the changes, while the rest of the political system seems to have been passive. Famous is Prime Minister Olof Palme's response when the changes were presented to him by Kjell-Olof Feldt, the Minister of Finance: 'Do what you want to. I don't understand it anyway' (Feldt 1990: 260). What Feldt and the central bank proposed to do in 1986 was to deregulate the credit market and thereby increase the supply of credit (Svensson 1996). Their policy package introduced a market-conforming regulation without lending limits and with market-determined interest rates. Another element in this policy mix was the abolition of currency regulation in 1989 (Werin 1993).

Following deregulation, the growth of the exposed sector came to a halt (Figure 9.7). Instead, deregulation generated an economic expansion in the late 1980s based on the home market and stimulating sectors like construction and retail trade by increasing the supply of capital there (to which higher employment in the sheltered sector testifies, see Figure 9.5). A major mistake of the new policy seems to have been that the old tax system, with its complex array of deductions, was left unreformed. This made loans very attractive to households and companies alike and increased the vulnerability of the financial system (SOU 1995-104). Furthermore, investments in the exposed sector during the late 1980s mainly took the form of foreign direct investments by the capital-intensive and R & D-intensive branches (Jonung 1991). It was therefore outside Sweden where the export sectors grew, on the basis of high profits and in response to the labor shortages created by the home market boom (Swedenborg, Johansson-Grahn, and Kinnwall 1988).

When the economy boomed in the latter part of the 1980s, wages also skyrocketed. Labor agreements in 1989 resulted in wage increases (includ-

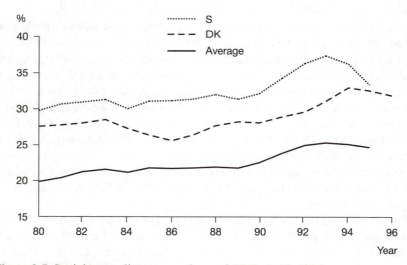

Figure 9.5 Social expenditures as a share of GDP, 1980–1996
Source: OECD, *Social Expenditure Data Base (Work file)* (Paris: OECD, 1998); own calculations.

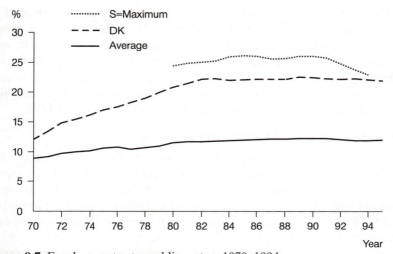

Figure 9.7 Employment rate, public sector, 1970–1994
Source: OECD, *Statistical Compendium: Labour Force Statistics* (Paris: OECD, 1997); own calculations.

ing wage drift) of up to around 10 percent (even higher in the public sector, where police officers and schoolteachers got 25% more). These levels did not correspond to productivity growth or labor unit costs for Sweden's competitors; instead, they reflected labor shortages and wage competition. Inflation rates were up to about 10 percent, the balance of trade deteriorated, growth rates dipped, and productivity increases were alarmingly low.

The late 1980s were marked by wage-inflation spirals, and labor conflicts were mainly based on comparing earnings in different sectors of the economy. This inflationary spiral forced the government to pursue a different strategy based on 'talks' between the parties to collective bargaining and the government about wage formation, complemented by a number of incomes policy initiatives like price and rent controls (Elvander 1988: ch. 3). Furthermore, attempts were made to control the profit explosion by profit funding schemes for training and work development. Companies were obliged to pay a small part of their profits into a working life fund, one for each county. The funds were intended to play the triple role of: (1) calming wage negotiations (a task in which they failed); (2) reducing work injuries; and (3) increasing cooperation, productivity, and work satisfaction on a company level (which succeeded) (Brulin and Nilsson 1994).

To make the situation even more critical, the Social Democratic government abandoned its ambitious industrial policy agenda in the mid-1980s after higher corporate profitability and employment seemed to render the program irrelevant (Benner 1997). Public investments in strategically vital fields such as training, higher education and research, and infrastructure stagnated during the late 1980s (Kaijser 1994). The main emphasis was now shifted to changes in the organization and regulation of public companies, including privatization of some firms, and to deregulation of a number of markets like telecommunications (Fölster 1993).

9.5.2.3. Towards a Hard Currency Policy (1990–)

There was a serious rethinking of macroeconomic policy beginning in the late 1980s. The call for a policy shift came from many influential quarters, ranging from the Productivity Commission (SOU 1991-81) to the labor movement itself (SAP 1989). The recipe suggested was a policy of low inflation and fiscal stringency to foster a more sound pattern of export-oriented growth. The shift rested on a norms-based policy of fixed exchange rates, strengthened by public spending cuts and a tax reform, starting in 1990. This change of course reflected international conditions and constraints in two ways: First, it was an adaptation to the growth policies of most European countries, institutionalized by the Maastricht Treaty's strict convergence criteria on inflation and public deficits. Second, it was a way of bringing inflation and wage increases more in line with Sweden's competitors, without using the devaluation instrument. This kind of policy shift is meant to reduce imbalances in the economy and re-establish a stable foundation for growth and employment, where wage determination is more peaceful, inflation lower, and productivity growth higher.

The change in policy began with the tax reform in 1990. The reform was inspired by international exemplars like the USA, UK, and Denmark. International influence on the tax reform was openly acknowledged by its designers: 'Sweden used to be a model in a world with increasing tax rates but risked becoming an anomaly when the world around Sweden began lowering its tax rates. It was becoming increasingly disadvantageous to deviate from the surrounding world by having considerably higher tax rates when capital, labor, goods and services were becoming internationally mobile' (Fernlund 1990: 21).

The reform was based on a compromise among the Social Democrats, the Liberals, and the Centre Party, with backing from the LO. It introduced a dual income tax system (DIT), where capital incomes were taxed at a peak rate of 30 percent. In addition, the top tax rate on incomes from other sources was reduced to 30 percent, while VAT was broadened to include almost all goods and services. The property tax was set at 1.5 percent instead of the old standard assessment of about 2 percent of ratable value. A similar kind of reform package was introduced for corporate taxation: a nominal tax rate lowered from 50 percent to 30 percent was combined with diminished opportunities for deductions. This system of flat corporate taxation with fewer loopholes was intended to correct the 'lock-in' effects of the previous system, which had led to a concentration of investment in a few sectors.

The second part of the new strategy was the fixed currency. To avoid any speculation that the new devaluation was a 'quick fix' against labor market instability and rampant inflation, the Social Democratic government asserted that price stability would rank ahead of full employment as the overarching target of its 1990 spring budget (Government Bill 1990/91: 100). The key instrument for reducing inflation was to peg the krona to the ECU, and to apply for Swedish membership in the European Union.

The system of wage bargaining became more state-orchestrated after the introduction of the hard currency policy. A wage negotiating group (FHG) was established in 1990. The FHG managed to lay the basis for a two-year central agreement (1991–92) with very low wage increases, abolition of wage indexation, reductions of wage drift, and agreements with retailers and producers to keep prices under control. The outcome of the FHG's negotations represented a significant break with the wage–price spiral of the 1980s, as indicated by the slowdown of wage drift in 1991 and 1992 (Kjellberg 1998: 90), and in spite of centralized bargaining's complete breakdown in 1990, when the SAF closed its central bargaining office.

The bourgeois government that took power in 1991 continued the hard currency policy, but added an ambitious supply-side program to foster new competitive sectors with public support for risk capital formation and high technology development programs. Complemented by changes in labor law (like minor adjustments in job security legislation and a more activating, less generous social policy), the new mixture of supply-side and hard currency policies aimed at developing a flexible socio-economic model capable of adapting quickly to changes in technology and world markets (Bergström 1993). Priorities were suddenly altered when currency speculation returned in 1992. In the fall of 1992 the bourgeois government sided with the Social Democrats to construct two crisis packages (cutting social expenditure and tax increases) to restore the krona. This strategy did not stop speculation, however, and the krona was floated in late 1992. Macroeconomic policy then shifted its focus to smaller public deficits and lower inflation (Wibble 1994). The board of the central bank also decided to set up a new target for monetary policy, namely an inflation level of 2 percent with a tolerance interval of ±1 percent. Price stability thus replaced a fixed exchange rate as the central bank's primary target (SOU 1993-20).

After 1994, when the SAP returned to power, the policy aiming at budgetary balance and low inflation to facilitate new investment and reduce unemployment was continued (Government Bill 1994/95: 25). The main instruments here have been tax hikes, higher individual social security contributions, and cuts in public expenditure. The strategy adopted emphasized that lower budget deficits and interests rates were indispensable to full employment (Persson 1997). The policy was very successful, turning a record budget deficit into a surplus in just four years. Furthermore, institutional mechanisms were introduced to curb imbalances in public budgets, both national and local. A new budget law in 1995 strengthened the government's role and enforced spending limits (SOU 1996-14). Local and regional municipalities have also been forced to balance their budgets by the year 2000. A 1998 reform gave the central bank autonomy, and the ties linking the bank to the Ministry of Finance and Parliament were loosened in accordance with the Maastricht treaty.

After 1994 some taxes were increased to bring down the budget deficit: property tax climbed from 1.5 percent to 1.7 percent, and income taxes went up 5 percent for higher income groups. Surprisingly, tax policy since 1996 has been oriented toward lowering taxes on less mobile sources of revenue, such as food (where the VAT cut by half as a tradeoff for lower replacement rates in several welfare insurance systems) and property taxes, reset at 1.5 percent in 1998. As a result of the intense debate over the effects of personal taxation on the 'business environment' in Sweden, taxes for foreign 'specialists' will also be lowered and the tax increase for higher income groups will be abolished for most middle- and high-income groups.

As mentioned above, industrial relations managed to adapt to the hard currency policy, albeit with some initial help from an interventionist state. Nevertheless, stability in the sectoral bargaining system seemed to remain elusive for a number of years. Bargaining in 1995 was, in fact, the most conflictual since 1980 (Elvander and Holmlund 1997: 31). In that year the LO tried to coordinate wage bargaining through a 'strong norm' for wage increases. Later a 'Europe norm' was outlined by a group of union and employer economists who recommended wage increases of roughly 3.5 percent, equivalent to income growth in other European countries.

Currently, there seem to be two alternative routes wage bargaining could take: a return to centralization or a stabilization of sectoral bargaining. The LO and the current Social Democratic government have been quite actively trying to re-establish central bargaining with the SAF, in the form of talks between the social partners on a 'growth pact'. The SAF, however, has laid down tough conditions for rejoining (some form of) central bargaining: The employers are demanding a political decision to join the EMU, lower taxes, and a reform of labor law (Scharp 1999). In return, SAF was said to be willing to set up a new arbitration board on wage disputes. There is still no 'growth pact', and a return to centralized bargaining seems unlikely. The current Social Democratic government's strategy is to orchestrate a self-regulation of wage bargaining. In its directives to a commission on mediating labor market conflicts, the government has proposed setting up a mediation institute. The proposal is based on the conviction that wage increases must be lower if unemployment is going to be reduced. The institute is intended to play the role of a coordinating agency, analyzing wage increases and the overall development of industrial relations in other European countries, surveying local and sectoral agreements, developing reliable and neutral wage statistics, and reserving the right to intervene in labor market negotiations through compulsory mediation, restrictions on sympathy strikes etc. (SOU 1998-141). The mediating institute would therefore be able to compel controlled wage growth by facilitating self-regulation and cooperation between the parties to collective bargaining. The current government has threatened to establish the institute if wage bargaining does not produce wage restraint (Sahlin 1999).

In the last bargaining round (1997), the sectoral system did in fact produce wage increases in line with those of other countries, thereby confirming the argument made by Hall and Franzese (1998) that an independent central bank and sectoral bargaining can coexist without tensions and state intervention. This was especially true of the industrial sector, where a 'cooperative agreement' covering 800,000 employees was signed in 1996 (Elvander and Holmlund 1997). The LO has nevertheless continued arguing that sectoral bargaining will foster inflationary wage increases and labor market segmentation (Jonsson 1999). Re-centralization of bargaining, however, seems unlikely in light of resistance from the SAF and many LO associations.

9.5.3. Swedish Labor Market Policy from Full Employment to Record-High Unemployment

Labor market policy remained an important instrument for keeping unemployment low during the 1980s, even though unemployment was already on the decline. In 1989, for example, when unemployment was around 1.5 percent, spending on labor market policy as a share of GDP remained almost the same as in 1983, when unemployment was over 4 percent (SOU 1993-43). The makeup of labor market measures also changed somewhat during the 1980s. 'Passive' support (unemployment insurance) peaked, also somewhat surprisingly, in the late 1980s, while 'active' support (through mobility and training programs and support for job creation) became less important. Furthermore, eligibility criteria for unemployment insurance were relaxed in 1987, and the waiting period for insurance was abolished (Korpi 1995: 118). 'Active' labor market policy became less important in the 1980s. Important labor supply measures, such as mobility support and training programs, were cut or even terminated during the late 1980s (SOU 1993-43). The centralized organization of labor market policy was also challenged in this decade. The role of local support in creating jobs, facilitating industrial relocation, and attracting new companies (especially in crisis-ridden regions), was enhanced (Furåker 1989). Municipalities were given limited autonomy to organize and shape labor market assistance (Government Bill 1983/84: 152).

The crisis of the 1990s, like the sudden jump in unemployment, was handled in a rather unexpected fashion by the Social Democratic government. The surge in unemployment after 1990 was not controlled by labor market policy measures; instead, the number of people covered by policy measures declined compared to 1989 (SOU 1993-43: 38). The bourgeois government (1991–94) reversed this pattern and maintained high levels of spending on labor market policy, although the government also made several reforms and cutbacks. It cut replacement rates for unemployment insurance from 90 percent to 80 percent, reintroduced the waiting period, changed the replacement rates for sickness and injury insurance, and introduced tougher qualification criteria in both. Responsibility for the first two weeks of sick pay was also transferred to employers, in an attempt to force them to improve working conditions (Palme and Wennemo 1998).

The SAP used higher unemployment as a key campaign issue in the 1994 election. After being returned to power, the Social Democrats tried a number of ambitious programs to boost employment without cutting taxes, such as general and specific wage subsidies. The rather modest decline of unemployment after 1994, however, indicated that the impact of these stimuli was meager. Also somewhat surprisingly, the Social Democratic government, in opposition to the trade unions, cut the replacement rate for unemployment insurance to 75 percent, though this was compensated by a 12 percent reduction on the VAT for food (Government Bill 1994/95: 100).

A major task for the Social Democratic government after the 1994 election was to halve unemployment. That target was later modified to halving just open unemployment, from 8 percent to 4 percent (Sveriges Regering 1998). Labor market policy's role in relation to this target was to train the unemployed to fill future job vacancies. The quantitative target, which caused tensions between the government and the Labor Market Board (Nyberg and Skedinger 1998), was later replaced with the goal of an 80 percent employment rate. Generally, the government has favored training programs for the unemployed, for example the huge 'competence increase' program (*kunskapslyftet*) for the long-term unemployed with minimal formal qualifications. Some 150,000 unemployed are covered by this program, which is slated to last until 2002. Higher education has also grown dramatically (with some 60,000 additional full-time students), and several new university colleges have been established.

Labor law has been a very complicated issue. The bourgeois government (1991–94) introduced some changes in the 1974 law on job security (LAS) so as to adjust the old 'last in, first out' principle (SOU 1993-32). In addition, the government made changes in unemployment insurance and established a public alternative to the union-organized insurance funds in order to give unorganized employees coverage (Government Bill 1993/94: 80). The Social Democratic opposition and the trade unions interpreted this reform as an attempt to weaken the organizational basis of the trade unions, and the SAP promised to scuttle the reform if returned to power after 1994. The Social Democratic government made good on its promise by restoring job security legislation and shutting down the public unemployment insurance fund, arguably as a concession to LO.

When the SAP returned to power in 1994, it did not want to make any controversial changes in labor law. The design of job security legislation was therefore delegated to a labor market commission composed of representatives from the parties to collective bargaining. They have not been able to agree on reforms, however, since the SAF and LO have presented suggestions that are 180 degrees apart. The SAF wants to substitute legislation for local agreements. All the unions flatly reject this blanket proposal. The government is also struggling with the organization of unemployment insurance. A new commission proposed a public and general system of unemployment insurance (in much the same vein as a 1993 proposal), with a limit of 600 days to strengthen job-seeking incentives (SOU 1996-150). The proposal's hesitant reception reflects the Social Democratic government's fundamental ambiguity on this question. On the one hand, the SAP's orientation toward forcing the unemployed person to adapt (with the assistance of labor market policy, including changes in sick and injury insurance) is a sign of the party's determination to put 'work' before 'benefits'. On the other hand, tough restrictions could lead to a social disaster if the long-term unemployed were excluded from the insurance system. The assumption behind the policy adopted is that benefit recipients continue to identify themselves with the labor market and that generous benefit levels counteract marginalization (Åberg 1997). Nevertheless, the crisis of the early and mid-1990s heightened the importance of social assistance, since there is a growing number of persons who do not qualify for unemployment insurance (Elmér 1998).

9.5.4. Changes in Swedish Social Policy: Adapting to New Conditions

The setup of social policy remained unchanged during the 1980s. Only a few reforms were implemented, mainly when parental insurance was extended and childcare made universally available in 1991, but there were also no drastic cuts or processes of retrenchment. Public sector employment continued to grow, but only slowly. Public sector expenditure as a percentage of GDP did not increase significantly during the 1980s. Social policy reform consisted mainly of administrative changes, including devolution of responsibilities to municipalities and a growing emphasis on lay participation in decision making (Olsson 1990).

In the mid- to late 1980s many observers concluded that it was possible for an advanced redistributive system to coexist with a service-intensive welfare state, full employment, and a vigorous capitalism; the Swedish case exemplified this combination (Therborn 1991). The Swedish welfare state, however, depends on maximum labor market participation to ensure its financial stability (Esping-Andersen 1990). With the dramatic rise in unemployment since the early 1990s, the financial underpinnings of Swedish social policy have been destabilized. Social policy reforms since then, both by bourgeois and (especially) Social Democratic governments, have aimed at controlling and reducing spending on social policy without making systemic changes. This reflects the strong popular and political commitment to the values and tasks of the universal welfare state (Svallfors 1996).

The bourgeois government, for example, was composed of four different parties with four quite distinct welfare ideologies, and where at least one party (the Liberal) strongly favored the traditional Scandinavian model; this made drastic changes in social policy highly unlikely. The Social Democratic Party, which actually contributed to the few changes made by the bourgeois government in its two 1992 crisis packages (such as the work injury insurance reforms and hikes in personal social security contributions), continued the pattern of minor alterations. Faced with a budget deficit, the SAP government followed its bourgeois predecessor's strategy of reforming but not changing the welfare system. Replacement rates were cut even further (down to 75%, though back again to 80% by 1998), while unemployment and sickness insurance were slightly redesigned to boost the role of local initiatives and to make the insurance schemes function as bridges linking sickness, injury, and unemployment to work (Palme and Wennemo 1998).

Nevertheless, the Social Democratic government (1994–) has made some attempts to change social policy's foundations, most notably in the 1995 budget, where replacement rates for social insurance (unemployment, parental, and sickness) were brought down to 75 percent. This was something the government described as a 'structural change' in the welfare system (Government bill 1994/95: 150), since it replaced the income compensation principle with a 'safety net'. After heavy criticism from the trade unions, however, the government later decided to push replacement rates back up to 80 percent.

As indicated by Figure 9.6 and our earlier discussion, reducing public sector employment has played an important role in lowering the budget deficit. There are fewer public sector jobs in both national and county government (in charge of organizing health care) as well as in municipalities (which organize education, childcare, and care for the elderly). This strategy might seem difficult to understand given the importance assigned to public sector employment for promoting female labor market participation since the 1960s. Most of the cuts have been in job categories dominated by women working part-time and with low formal qualifications (Gonäs 1997). The reductions caused strains—but not a revolt—within the labor movement (cf. Feldt 1994). The strategy was based on the Social Democratic government's policy of cutting across the board rather than making radical reductions in specific programs like social insurance. The government thereby avoided a confrontation with the LO, which was highly critical even of the limited cuts that were made in the social insurance system (Gustavsson and Johansson 1995). The Social Democrats calculated that the political price for cutting public sector employment would be lower than the cost of lost constituency support from huge reductions in social insurance. Once the budget deficit was eliminated, the government tried to improve the quality of public services by increasing state support to county councils and municipalities.

The pension system was reformed in 1994 after an agreement between the Social Democrats and the four bourgeois parties. A new pension system will be established in 1999. At the center of the reform is a change from a benefit-defined to a contribution-defined system. The basic pension and ATP will be merged into an income-related pensions system. Pensions will no longer be financed through payroll taxes, but instead through (compulsory) contributions totaling 18.5 percent of wage incomes—16.5 percent will be pay-as-you-go, while 2 percent will be funded. The pension funds will combine a fictitious 'pensions account' kept by the Ministry of Finance with a component chosen freely by contributors from a wide variety of funds, private and public. Pensions will be based on life-long earned incomes, including higher education, parental leave, sick leave or unemployment, and will be linked to GDP growth.

9.6. Denmark: From Crisis Management to Successful Model

9.6.1. *Vulnerability to Economic Internationalization and Other Challenges*

Denmark has an open economy, and the share of state-owned firms is low, so many Danish firms got used to foreign competition at an early stage. Danish exports were traditionally concentrated in mass markets, i.e. for agricultural products, machines and instruments, chemical products, and textile and clothes, where competition becomes fiercer with each passing day. Competition for mass markets in an open economy also meant that the technology content of Danish products and manufacturing processes was comparatively low (Lindholm 1994: 13; Hansen 1994: 33; Hansen and Lunding 1994).

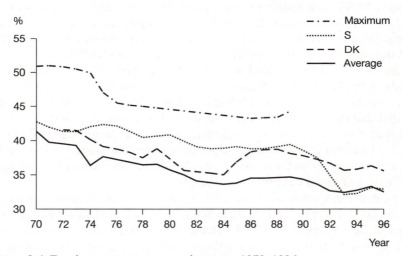

Figure 9.4 Employment rate, exposed sectors, 1970–1996
Source: OECD, *Statistical Compendium: Labour Force Statistics* (Paris: OECD, 1997); own calculations.

Wages in manufacturing were high and generally increased faster than Sweden's during the 1970s (Figure 9.2), so that Danish manufacturing firms became increasingly vulnerable to more intense competition in this period. The failure to control wages has clearly influenced the employment ratio in the exposed sector. Employment in the exposed sector started out at exactly the same level as in Sweden, but higher wages led to a decline in jobs that was earlier and faster than Sweden's (Figures 9.4, 9.7).

Behind the figures also lies a fundamental restructuring of employment in Denmark's exposed sector. The trend has been away from agriculture and fishing, construction, and major areas of manufacturing (especially textiles, foods, stone and glass production) towards business services, financial services, insurance, transport, tourism, etc. In the manufacturing sector, the chemical and pharmaceutical industries increased their employment share. Financial services as a sector maintained its share of employment. The construction sector was the big loser, representing a job loss of more than 1 percentage point from 1989 to 1993. No single countervailing factor—neither German reunification, large wage subsidies to homeowners using professional assistance for house repairs, nor accelerating large public construction projects (i.e. airport, railroad, and road building)—was enough to pull the trend in the other direction.

The shares of low-skill and high-skill unemployment have stayed more or less unchanged. But the figures conceal the fact that the low-skilled share of total employment went from approximately 40 percent to 30 percent between 1970 and 1995 as this group's share of the total labor force fell to the same extent (Finansministeriet 1997). The Danish welfare state is traditionally less dependent on payroll taxes and social contributions than the Swedish. Accordingly, it is less vulnerable to revenue losses when employment goes down. Because its economy's structure of ownership is different, Denmark is also less vulnerable than many other countries, including Sweden, to the effects of more intense international competition for capital investment. Thus, in contrast to the emerging Swedish capital market structure and the traditional capital market structure in the Anglo-Saxon part of the world (De Jong 1997), only 17 percent of the 274 largest Danish companies were characterized by diversified ownership in 1991. 23 percent were individually or family-owned, 18 percent owned by foundations, 7 percent publicly owned, 26 percent owned by a foreign single company or an individual foreign resident, while 10 percent were cooperatively-owned.

Market capitalization is in almost the same situation as it was in the 1970s. It remains low, even now that a small number of Danish companies (253 companies) continues to be listed on the stock exchange. In fact, Danish equity formation even turned negative between 1996 and 1997, and a recent survey indicated that the vast majority of those running Danish companies (70 percent) feels no pressure to maximize short-term profits (Lønroth, Nørreklit, and Sørensen 1997: 17).

It is only recently that Denmark has acquired the ability to practice macroeconomic stability. The situation has always been critical whenever an upswing pushes the Danish economy to expand. Then domestic demand and consumption plus investments cannot be financed out of

Danish exports and savings. Foreign capital must be imported, leading to a growing current account deficit and rising foreign debt.

International capital markets regard the current account as an important indicator of a country's economic health. Therefore Denmark has often been in a situation where a sudden worsening of the current account has put pressure on the Krone as investors began fearing devaluation and requiring higher returns on their investments. Accordingly, the current account has been a major concern of Danish policymakers in the 1980s and 1990s.

Denmark, like Sweden, is a high-tax country. Nevertheless, it is expected to be less vulnerable to intensified tax competition, because it is dominated by small and medium-sized firms which have a harder time than big companies relocating profits. At the same time the Danish welfare state is not as dependent as many other countries, including Sweden, on revenue from the most mobile sources, i.e. the large companies and the large capital owners.

Denmark is vulnerable to tax competition in other ways. One of the clearest examples of this can be found in the Danish preparations for the Single Market. As a response to the removal of the two-day limit on importing consumer goods between EC countries, Danish consumer taxes had to be lowered several times between 1989 and 1992. The problem was that the value-added tax and special excises were (and still are) considerably higher in Denmark than in its main neighbor to the south, Germany (OECD 1977*b*).

9.6.2. *Danish Policy Responses from the 1970s through the 1990s*

Danish adjustment in the postwar period consisted of seven policy shifts. First, Danish policymakers decided to shift to a hard currency policy pegging the Krone first to the Deutschmark and then to the ECU. This required fiscal restraint and wage moderation, which governments and unions gradually exercised from the late 1970s to the late 1980s. An industrial policy, for which there really is no tradition in Denmark, was also adopted. The policies of fiscal restraint, wage moderation, and industrial policy were then complemented by important tax and pension reforms. Finally, Denmark adopted a whole range of active labor market and social policies, which contributed to higher investment.

This series of responses was triggered by—and can only really be understood against the background of—rather dramatic policy failures from the 1970s, which left the Social Democratic government so frustrated that it had to resign without even calling for a new election. No one has offered a convincing explanation as to why the Social Democrats, who were in government for most of the 1970s, responded so poorly to the challenges of that time, but they certainly did not rise to the occasion. Policies intended to restore competitiveness in international product markets were generally lacking. Danish policymakers did not initially use the trick of currency devaluation in any active way, and when they finally did, it only produced a short-term leveling off of the climb toward higher unemployment.

Despite occasional intervention by different Social Democratic governments into collective bargaining rounds, the growing numbers of public sector employees continued to push for higher wages through the 1970s. This led to intensified wage competition among public and private sector unions, and the wage spiral that resulted had a clear negative impact on Danish companies' competitiveness. Since Denmark also refrained from introducing new Swedish-style supply-side measures (like state subsidies, cheap credits, and R & D support for industry) on any larger scale, many small Danish companies had no alternative but to downsize their activities.

Since Denmark also lacked an active labor market policy that might have provided vocational education and training for adult workers on a larger scale, unemployment was allowed to rise freely. The only measure to make a real dent in unemployment was a 1978–79 reform on early retirement, cutting the labor supply.

One could argue that a time of economic crisis is not the right time to introduce new types of benefits. Nevertheless, this is what happened during the 1970s. Despite tighter fiscal constraints, a number of reforms were implemented, notably the 1976 Social Assistance Reform, which boosted compensation for those seeking temporary assistance. At the same time, existing programs were expanded, like the 1971 and 1972/73 social welfare reforms, which brought sickness benefits up to 90 percent of prior earnings, extended coverage to all economically active persons (including the self-employed), and abolished waiting periods.

Finally, there were no serious attempts to increase public revenue. Quite the contrary, as indicated by the 1975 tax reform: in the aftermath of the Danish tax revolt (and because Danish politicians believed that the recession would be short-lived), income taxes were generally lowered in an attempt to ease the crisis. Since access to unemployment benefits was also extended to new groups, the fiscal crisis was aggravated (Johansen 1986: 371).

In the end, it was obvious that something had to be done. Accordingly, discussions began within special semi-autonomous expert planning groups under the auspices of the Danish Technology Council on ways to target and coordinate industrial policies and so improve Danish companies' competitiveness. Also, governmental coordination among the national state, municipalities, and counties (a concertation for which Denmark had no authentic tradition) was initiated. Coordination led to more restrictive agreements with the aim of curbing growth in local public spending. In 1980 local expenditures were allowed to grow only 3 percent, then to 2 percent in 1982, and 1 percent in 1983. Municipalities did what they could to balance their budgets along these lines, but in many cases their only recourse was to short-term measures, i.e. a moratorium on all public building and construction projects.

9.6.2.1. Macroeconomic Policy: Early Orientation towards Germany

In the early 1980s Denmark officially refrained from using devaluation actively to enhance price competitiveness; constraint was sought by tying the Krone to the ECU, in reality to the German mark, the anchor of the EMS. In the 1970s Denmark had been a member of 'the Snake', the forerunner of the EMS.

In spite of participation in the Snake, Denmark's hard currency policy, including inflation and debt fighting, did not begin until the 1980s, following a decade of crisis and dwindling Social Democratic popularity. At first the new hard currency approach appeared successful. The economy grew, and the current account balance improved significantly from 1982 to 1983. At the same time, inflation dropped significantly. So did the nominal interest rate. Unemployment declined sharply.

The fixed value for the Danish Krone was not put to its first real test, however, until after 1983, when the economy started to expand again. As in earlier periods of expansion, the current account deteriorated. This immediately triggered fears of devaluation among financial investors, and the central bank saw no alternative to steady hikes in interest rates as a confidence-building measure for the currency. Pressure on the Krone, however, was unrelenting as the current account continued getting worse. In 1986–87, the current account deficit reached a new low amidst renewed fears of devaluation. On the basis of these fears, the Conservative-led government decided to curb private lending and, by implication, consumption. This ended the upswing.

Denmark now entered a period of slower growth, lasting until 1993. A drop in domestic demand, slow GDP growth, increasing unemployment, and very high wage increases for both private and public sector employees in 1987—all had a clear negative impact on the budget. It went from surplus (2.4% of GDP in 1987) into deficit (2.8% in 1993).

The Conservative-led minority government was nevertheless able to stay in office. The Social Democratic Party could not attract essential support from the smaller parties in Parliament. During the 1980s, crisis awareness among the electorate also grew considerably.

9.6.2.2. Wage Moderation by Consensus and Moderate Decentralization

Once Danish economic policy was oriented toward Germany and relying on a fixed exchange rate, the obvious candidates for best measures to improve the country's competitiveness became wage moderation, productivity growth, and improvements in product quality.

The Conservative-led government's attempt to enforce wage moderation started in 1982 when it abolished automatic annual indexation of private sector wages. In addition, public sector wages were more or less frozen in 1983. Both employers and trade unions accepted these steps as necessary measures in a time of crisis. Against all expectations, however, these steps did not bring about wage moderation.

The reason for the failure of wage restraint was that major wage jumps simply could not be prevented in the absence of indexation and in the wake of an economic upturn driving down unemployment. Accordingly, the Conservative-led government saw no alternative but to intervene in collective bargaining. In 1985 it imposed a statutory wage settlement allowing only very small wage increases. Nevertheless, as in the 1960s and 1970s, government intervention only produced minimal results. It was apparently impossible to impose restrictive wage deals on local unions, employers, and municipalities in a period of high growth.

Between 1984 and 1988, wages in the private sector grew between 4 and 9 percent annually. The blame for this mainly laid at the doorstep of the decentralized industrial relations system, which was unable to prevent wage competition among different sectors and branches or to forestall wage drift resulting from the continuing presence of local bottlenecks in the Danish labor market.

Collective wage agreements in the last half of the 1980s were particularly suggestive in this regard. In 1987, to make up for the previous five years of reduced public sector wage growth, government employees received a large wage increase from a weakened Conservative-led minority government. While public sector unions saw the 1987 accords as a clear victory over the Conservative-led government, private sector unions started to fear that wage drift like this might cost the Danish economy international market share and jobs. On the basis of this insight, they became convinced that there was a need for a more official agreement among the parties to collective bargaining to keep wage claims at a minimum. This led immediately to the '1987 declaration of intent,' in which Danish unions pledged to keep wage increases below the level of Denmark's main trading partners (Due et al. 1995).

This comprehensive agreement, combining a burgeoning crisis awareness with the paradoxical trend in Danish industrial relations known as 'centralized decentralization', helped secure much slower wage growth between 1988 and 1993. In organizational and procedural terms, centralized decentralization has meant a transformation of national bargaining 'from a large number of trade unions and employer organizations to a few, broadly based bodies capable of concluding framework agreements. This centralization is accompanied by a decentralization of competence to make decisions on wages and working conditions for the single workplace at local level, thus allowing maximum flexibility when filling in the details in these framework agreements' (Due et al. 1995: 145). The organizations responsible for setting wages on the employers' side were reduced by two-thirds, from 150 to 50. Trade unions underwent a similarly fundamental change, resulting in the creation of a new cartel for industrial workers. The Danish industrial relations system simultaneously began operating with fewer local bargaining rounds and fewer framework agreements.

In the first half of the 1990s, these changes in both structures and perceptions helped reduce the growth in unit labor costs to a level lower than that of Denmark's main trading partner, Germany. Measured on a national currency basis, the average annual percentage change in Danish unit labor costs for manufacturing was 9.4 between 1973 and 1979, 5.5 between 1979 and 1989, and 1.9 between 1989 and 1995 (Figure 9.2). The corresponding figures for Germany were 4.8, 3.4, and 2.7 (OECD 1997a).

A rather significant shift of income from labor to capital also occurred between 1983 and 1993, indicated by the (mis)match between a rising employment ratio (from 71.5% to 75.9%) and a simultaneous decrease in labor's share of national income (from 68.6% to 67.7%).

Recent wage agreements from 1997 and 1998 indicate that the opposing parties to collective bargaining still feel committed to a labor market that is organized, institutionalized, and controlled. Nevertheless, as more and more employees negotiate salaries, pensions, special bonuses, etc. with their employers on an individual basis, a gradual challenge to centralized decentralization in both the private and the public sector is emerging from outside the system. This individualization is associated with the emergence of a knowledge-based service economy. It also builds on intense competition for skilled labor and expertise. So far these changes have not shown up in the figures on wage inequality. The hierarchy of wage differentials in Denmark continues to be extremely flat.

9.6.2.3. The New Industrial Policy: Developing a Supply Side

In the eyes of policymakers, Denmark's chronic current account deficit was not only the result of wage growth (from an already high plateau) eating away at Danish products' price competitiveness. The low technological content of Danish products and manufacturing processes was also seen as part of the problem.

In order for Danish firms to gain market share, they had to be competitive on the most rapidly expanding markets. These are typically markets with high content in new technologies. Denmark's problem has been an inability to gain or hold market share outside traditional key markets, the very markets that have been 'low growth areas' in international comparison since the 1970s (Lindholm 1994: 34).

Several policymakers also drew attention to the Danish problem of smallness. The structure of industry in Denmark, with its large share of SMEs (small and medium-sized enterprises), was viewed as a weakness rather than a strength, since the country's many small firms were unable to attract capital or cultivate international ties to other firms capable of supplying them with adequate R & D.

Official recognition for the problems of smallness and technological progress in products and production processes led to the introduction of an ambitious, export-oriented technology policy in 1983. The policy included measures to strengthen inter-firm cooperation among SMEs. The aim was to encourage R & D, provide risk capital from patient investors, internationalize technical standards, and make the legal and administrative framework more pro-active in anticipating social and political change (Nielsen 1991: 303–7).

The political decision to deregulate and liberalize telecommunications and infrastructure in 1990 can also be seen in light of this more active industrial and technology policy that began in 1983. Last but not least, the establishment of a large central development fund for SMEs, along with export credits and loans to firms exporting to central and eastern European markets after 1991, symbolized the reorientation of Danish industrial policy in the 1980s and early 1990s.

Measured in export statistics, the new industrial policy was relatively successful. Denmark increased its share of world exports by 0.2 percentage points, from 0.8 percent in 1980 to approximately 1 percent in 1994, while the trade balance improved even more steeply, from −1.3 percent of GDP in 1986 to 6.0 percent in 1993. Along with wage moderation, the new industrial policy contributed heavily to boosting exports of furniture, chemical products, machines and other technical instruments to Germany and the other EU countries. At the same time, other exports (like agricultural products, not promoted by the new program) diminished.

In other sectors undergoing liberalization, like telecommunications and infrastructure, the number of employees was reduced by almost 5 percent between 1988 and 1996, while economic output increased. There have not been job losses in all sectors. In manufacturing, Denmark was able to maintain more or less the same employment ratio from 1982 to 1993 (Figure 9.7), in contrast both to earlier periods and many other OECD countries.

In the 1990s Danish industrial policy was redefined. It shifted away from a focus on individual industries in exposed sectors and product innovation towards a growing emphasis on the 'framework conditions' (i.e. administrative burdens, workforce qualifications, infrastructure, taxation) for the entire Danish business base. Attention simultaneously shifted toward the private service sector as the main engine of growth, employment, and welfare.

As part of the new outlook on services, a 60 percent wage subsidy (maximum DKK 85.00 per hour) has been given to home service companies offering a set of more or less precisely defined services to private households and firms. The purpose of the arrangement was to build up and expand an official home service sector (thereby getting rid of the black market for these services) and create official employment for the low skilled. Since its establishment in 1993, the arrangement has produced approximately 3,000 new jobs. 170,000 households now make use of 'home-services' (Erhvervsministeriet 1997). The number is likely to grow. A recent study has shown that up to 81 percent of the Danish population knows about the home service arrangement and up to 89 percent of the consumers are satisfied with the service they get (SFI 1997).

9.6.2.4. Fiscal Policy: Pro-cyclical Consolidation

Fiscal consolidation was one of the Conservative-led government's first priorities when it came to power in 1982. Its freeze on public sector employment growth was successfully implemented after negotiations between the Finance Ministry and the two associations representing Danish municipalities (the KL) and counties (the ARF). As a result of this accord, the once steady annual growth in public sector jobs leveled off in 1983. That year the peak public sector share of total employment was approximately 22 percent.

Restrictive budget planning for public organizations was also initiated in 1983, under the auspices of the Finance Ministry's Budget Reform Committee (BRU). Acting on the BRU's recommendation, ad hoc budgetary planning was replaced by a 'total frame system' in which the government specified expenditures by public organizations.

Organizations that continued to run deficits over the maximum ceiling were obliged to propose special measures for preventing future deficits. Nevertheless, public spending continued growing even after 1983. In 1982 a new tax was imposed on pension investment returns, followed by a general tax increase in 1983.

It is hard to identify the effects of the cuts in social spending. Expenditures on social transfers declined during the first high-growth/high-employment phase between 1983 and 1986. But by 1993, in the aftermath of an economic downturn, social transfers had risen again, this time to over 20 percent of GDP. Total social expenditures followed the same see-saw pattern: first a considerable decline, then an even larger increase. On average, the Danish social expenditure ratio rose from 28.2 percent in 1982 to 31 percent in 1993.

In some areas the effort to cut spending proved more effective than in others. Danish public health expenditure has been brought down considerably since the 1970s. This happened by closing down numerous hospitals and psychiatric clinics. From 1986 to 1996, 20 out of 102 hospitals and 4 out of 17 psychiatric clinics were closed. The number of places at elderly homes was reduced from 49,487 to 36,444 (Statistics Denmark 1997: 38). All these cuts put pressure on the remaining institutions.

The health care sector stands out because of its strong reliance on private co-payments or insurance contributions. In the health insurance field—largely regulated in Denmark by collective agreements among doctors' associations, municipalities, and counties operating on a 'fee for service' basis—the share of private health insurance contributions grew from 0.6 percent in 1980 to 1.9 in 1994. In the same period patients' direct payments for health care services and products as a share of total health expenditures increased from an average of 10.4 percent to 11.4 percent.

The emphasis on user charges is part of a broader trend shifting the burden of financing from public to private. The clearest example is probably parental contributions to institutions for children, like daycare and after-school programs. A mix of income taxes and private fees has always financed these programs. Since the mid-1980s, however, parental contributions to these programs have increased, on average and in real terms, by some 20 percent (own calculations on the basis of Statistics Denmark 1997: 38).

A number of employment-related social programs, like insurance for occupational injury, unemployment, and sickness, have also been the subject of experimentation in private financing over the last decade. The value of Denmark's still rather small occupational injury programs, privately insured and so far only used to top up publicly funded sickness and invalidity benefits, now amounts to 0.16 percent of GDP according to recent OECD calculations (Adema and Einerhand 1998: 51).

The Social Democrats did not just take over the consolidation priorities of previous Conservative governments. They also had a better sense of timing. In the face of a record-high unemployment in 1993, the new Social Democratic government returned to a traditional expansionary demand-side policy, including an increase in public investment and aid for private building, buttressed by a temporarily under-financed tax reform. The impact was clear for all to see. As early as 1994, the economy began growing at an impressive rate of 4.4 percent. With a slight time lag, private individual and corporate investments followed suit, with positive effects on production and employment.

9.6.2.5. Towards a Broader and More Differentiated Tax System

Between 1986 and the 1990s, the Danish tax system underwent major reforms that reduced tax arbitrage, facilitated flexible adjustment to changes in the international economy, and bolstered other major policy innovations of the 1980s and 1990s (Table 9.1). The overall goal behind the reforms, of course, was to secure stable long-term revenue.

A first important step in this direction was taken by introducing a system of 'Dual Income Taxation' (DIT) in 1987. The underlying idea of the DIT system was to separate taxation of capital gains from taxation of personal income from other sources (i.e. from labor income, private and public pensions, and other social transfers). The committee proposing the reform wanted income from capital to be taxed at a flat rate equal to the corporate income tax rate of 40 percent, and considerably lower than the top marginal tax rate on income from the other sources (Sørensen 1998: 2–4).

A proportional lowering of the capital income tax rate was intended to reduce taxpayers' incentives to invest their savings abroad. Large-scale capital flight would reduce revenue considerably, as it is difficult for tax authorities to monitor and tax capital income from foreign sources effectively in an increasingly internationalized economy. For Denmark, however, there was not much revenue to lose from lowering the capital income tax rate. The Danish tax system was already characterized by favorable options for deducting interest and low taxes both on pension savings and income from owner-occupied housing.

Another reason for introducing a DIT system was that Denmark's high marginal tax rate on capital incomes (together with its generous social security benefits) was seen as a factor contributing to the savings and current account deficit (Sørensen 1998: 18).

At the same time, the reform committee saw separating capital income taxation from labor income taxation as a way of facilitating flexible adjustment to changes in the international economy. The idea was to help Denmark gradually adjust its capital income tax rate downward, should future swings in capital mobility (both up and down) require such incremental adjustments (Sørensen 1998: 15).

Finally, proponents of the DIT system believed it would eliminate certain forms of tax arbitrage and tax avoidance. For instance, the incentive

Table 9.1 *Tax reforms for Sweden and Denmark in the 1980s and 1990s*

Country	Year	Marginal tax rate on personal income (%)	Marginal tax rate on capital income (%)	Tax rate on corporate income (%)	Value-added tax (VAT) rate (%)	Other taxation elements
Sweden	Until 1991	36–72	36–72	52	1980 = 23.5	Broadening of tax base; less tax differentiation by way of fewer tax brackets, deductibility restrictions; lowering of ecological taxes; introduction of contributions paid by the insured in 1993
	1991–1994	31–51	30	30	1992 = 25	
	1994–1995	30–55	30	28		
	After 1995	30–60	30	28		
Denmark	Until 1987	48–73	48–73	40	1980 = 22	Broadening of tax base; stronger tax differentiation through the introduction of more tax brackets,[c] deductibility restrictions; savings-oriented; increase of ecological taxes; introduction of labor market contributions 1993, i.e. for active measures.
	1987–1994	50–68	50–65	50	1992 = 25	
	After 1994	38–58	38–58[a]	34[b]		

[a]The top marginal tax rate on positive net capital income below DKK 20.000 (DKK. 40.000 for married couples is only 44%, and negative net capital income may only be deducted against a top marginal rate of 44% (see Sørensen 1998: 3)).

[b]Introduction of taxation on account. For companies that do not pay an amount on account the corporate income tax rate is 38%.

[c]The introduction of more brackets in the Danish tax structure should be seen against the background of the fact that Denmark had fewer brackets than most other OECD countries prior to the 1980s. Sweden has followed the pattern of most other OECD countries by reducing the number of brackets on the basis of which different incomes are taxed.

Sources: OECD, *The Tax/Benefit Position of Production Workers* (Paris: OECD, 1995); Danish Ministry of Finance, *Danmark som foregangsland: Internationaliseringen og den økonomiske politik* (1997); Sørensen (1998).

to transfer wealth from one family member to another is smaller when all taxpayers face the same capital income tax rate. By the same token, when the capital income tax rate is identical to the corporate rate, tax arbitrage for corporations taking advantage of options for deducting interest and postponing the capital gains tax becomes unprofitable.

Despite these perceived advantages, a pure version of the DIT system was not implemented in Denmark. At the time, the Conservative-led minority government was not able to sell the idea of the DIT system to the Social-Democratic dominated opposition in Parliament. The opposition was especially reluctant to give up on the idea of progressive capital income taxation. Against this background, the final reform package produced by Parliament was a diluted version of the DIT system, maintaining and even raising the marginal tax rate on tangible business investment. This happened at a time when policymakers expected Denmark to go into recession, which prompted an increase in the corporate income tax rate to 50 percent. Tax rates on the two sources of revenue (corporate taxation vs. taxes on capital gains) now moved closer towards each other. Nevertheless, as the corporate income tax rate was being cut in successive steps (to 40% in 1989, 38% in 1991, and 34% in 1992), the divergence between tax rates on the two sources of revenue was maintained, despite similar reductions in marginal tax rates on capital income.

To compensate for the loss of public revenue, the Conservative government introduced a new two-and-a-half percent tax on gross wages, the so-called 'AMBI' (a new labor market contribution). The new tax, however, unleashed a storm of protest from small companies and businesses dependent on imports, because its implementation treated large and export-oriented businesses more favorably (E. Hansen 1994: 75; Statistics Denmark 1995: 41). Firms were compensated for the AMBI tax by having their contributions to the ATP pension supplements lowered proportionally to the number of workers employed in each firm. Denmark's import-dependent and domestic-oriented companies were taxed at full rate, whereas the large export-oriented companies got de facto tax relief from AMBI's implementation (Jensen 1998: 20–21).

MNEs (multinational enterprises) were already taxed at a different rate (40%) than SMEs (small and medium-sized enterprises, at 50%). In addition, Danish law let foreign workers with special skills deemed vital to a given production and development line be taxed at lower level than their native counterparts.

The Social Democratic-led government that took over in 1993 had ideas of its own about the direction that changes in the tax system should take. A top priority of the new government was to ease the almost chronic problems of high unemployment by way of an active labor market policy. But the Social Democrats faced a dilemma in that this aim could not be realized by raising personal or corporate income tax rates.

The solution that was found emphasized a new social security contribution, which was to be phased in gradually as a proportional tax on gross income from work. Effective immediately, the employee's contribution was set at a flat rate of 5 percent, increasing to 8 percent in 1997. The employer's contribution, on the other hand, did not go into effect until 1997, and then at a rate of 0.3 percent of gross wages, increasing to 0.6 percent in 1998. The new social security contribution was earmarked for financing active labor market expenditures as well as unemployment insurance and sickness benefits; this was the government's way of telling taxpayers that the revenue would be used to create employment, and not just go into the general public budget.

The growing emphasis on direct social security contributions was a departure from the traditional Danish mode of financing welfare. The 1994 tax reform was also a small retreat from other principles, most importantly from the principles of the dual income tax system. To receive support for the 1993 reform package, the Social Democratic-led government had to rely on parties to its left in the Danish Parliament, who did not want to give up the idea of a progressive tax system.

Hence, the reform bill that was enacted included a separate two-bracket progressive tax schedule for shareholder income, defined as the sum of dividends and taxable gains on shares (Sørensen 1998: 24). The reform also allowed companies with foreign branches to get a tax break amounting to just 50 percent of the normal Danish corporate income tax levied on the foreign branch's net taxable income. This tax break was to be gradually phased out between 1994 and 1999.

In addition, the government introduced a new energy or environmental tax on plastic bags, gasoline, coal, electricity, water, renovation, etc., which was to be phased in gradually between 1994 and 1998. With the new CO and sulfur tax, real taxes on energy grew steeply to nearly 10 percent of total revenue by 1998. These ecological taxes, however, are unevenly distributed. Companies competing in energy-intensive international markets are reimbursed for their energy tax expenses through subsidies. This is not the case for the small, more nationally oriented companies, firms in the service sector, and households (Kristoffersen, Munksgaard, and Jensen 1997).

To sum up: the Danish tax system has gone through some major changes since the early 1980s, the most prominent of which are differentiation among taxable sources, lower tax rates on corporate and capital incomes, and broadening of the tax base.

9.6.2.6. Social Security Policy: The First Step Away from Generosity

Danish social policy in the 1980s and 1990s was two-sided. On the one hand, it was characterized by continuing—albeit only partly successful—attempts to reduce compensation levels for the unemployed and the sick. On the other hand, benefits for families with children, student benefits, and old age pensions grew considerably.

Denmark's high levels of social assistance in case of unemployment and sickness were increasingly called into question during the 1980s and 1990s. The problem of unemployment, especially for low-skilled groups, was no longer taken to be just a matter of lacking employability or job openings; increasingly it was related to lack of incentives on the part of the unemployed.

The disincentive problem, many policymakers have argued, is caused by the difference between Danish unemployment social assistance, clearly higher than the OECD-18 average, and the negotiated minimum wage (after taxes). The Danish reservation wage, defined as the share of an average worker's wage made up of social assistance and other transfers, is very high by international standards. For many low-skill groups, unemployment compensation exceeds 90 percent of what they could expect to get from a real job. This is due both to relatively high taxation of low incomes in Denmark and to the system of social assistance, which significantly reduces or even eliminates benefits as soon as the recipient has an earned income.

Studies have shown that there is no economic incentive to find work for 3.5 percent of males and 8.5 percent of females. For 30 percent of the males and almost 50 percent of the females, economic gains from work can barely be detected (Andersen 1997: 143; Mogensen 1995). This could be solved by introducing an American-like EITC (earned income tax credit) for low-skilled, low-wage earners.

The Conservative-led governments of the 1980s and early 1990s did not really do much about the disincentive problem for the broader population of low-skilled or unskilled workers. The unemployed between 18 and 24 years of age faced reduced cash assistance, while a freeze on the cash benefit ceiling for the unemployment and sickness insurance schemes mainly affected high-wage groups. Along the same lines, the government introduced a waiting period (for sickness pay) as well as general restrictions on entitlement criteria, making adjustments in social assistance correlate with future expectations about living conditions.

On returning to power, the Social Democrats introduced a tighter policy on unemployment benefits. Lower unemployment from the mid-1980s onward made their task easier, on behalf of the low skilled as well. The law on active social policy, for example, forces unemployed youth under the age of 30 with no direct link to the labor market into activation, meaning that this group has to accept an offer from the municipality, continue education, get training, or take a real job.

13 weeks of passive social benefits are now the maximum allowed before young people are required to enter into such an activation scheme. If they refuse an offer of activation, they lose the right to social assistance. Municipalities do not have the authority to define entitlements to social assistance, but they can tighten controls as they implement the programs.

Municipalities will now no longer offer social assistance to persons with access to other resources, i.e. through marriage or private pension arrangements. Finally, persons who used to receive higher wages cannot get more in social assistance than they would have obtained from joining an unemployment insurance fund. As a result, the purchasing power commanded by unemployment and sickness benefits declined by 17 percent between 1982 and 1987 (Plovsing 1994: 68). In addition, more public expenditures on sickness benefits (as a share of GDP) have been cut in Denmark than in Sweden. Denmark is still above the OECD-18 average, though clearly below the German level.

The de facto level of compensation, however, has not been altered significantly. Unemployment benefits are still very generous in Denmark, with respect to both level of compensation and duration of benefits, although the latter did decline from seven to five years in 1995.

Programs for families with children, students, and old age pensioners have simultaneously been expanded. Maternity leave was extended several times, and in 1993 paid childcare leave, introduced for public sector employees in 1984, was extended to the private sector. Child benefits expanded considerably after the 1987 tax reform. The child benefit is now a flat-rate allowance covering all families regardless of income. As a result, the purchasing power of child benefits was higher in 1988 than in 1976, a positive trend that continued for another decade after 1988. The same has been true of the family cash benefit, which doubled its share of the total social budget between the 1980s and the 1990s.

Student benefits were improved by a reform of the state grants system in 1988. All students above the age of 18 have the right to cheap state-funded loans and very high flat-rate student allowances, which in the 1990s grew to approximately DKK 3,458 for those living away from home and DKK 1,745 for those still living with their parents.

The basic old age pension scheme has also withstood the pressures of retrenchment. It was not subject to the 1983 freeze in benefit ceilings, and the 1987 pension reform actually secured a general increase in cash benefits by the late 1980s. As reflected in OECD aggregate inequality indicators, Denmark was one of the few countries where inequality, as measured by disposable income (after tax and transfers), did not rise between 1986 and 1993 (see OECD 1997*b*: 51). A later OECD estimate suggested that changes in Danish income distribution mainly had a negative impact on higher-income groups (OECD 1998).

In 1989 public sector unions were able to reach agreement with the government on the first general employment-related pension scheme for lower-income public employees. By 1991 this scheme had become a model for similar new arrangements in the private sector, in line with the government's plan to increase savings. As a result, the saving ratio climbed from a low of 12.4 percent of GDP in the 1980s (compared to the OECD average of 22.3%) to a high of 17.8 percent in 1995 (only 1.9 percentage points below the OECD average).

The 1993 tax reform entailed a real improvement in benefit levels, which allowed pensioners' disposable income to grow faster than the disposable income of those active in the labor market (Finansministeriet 1996). Also, in 1996, the Danish ATP was extended to cover most social transfer recipients. As a result of higher benefits, expenditures on public pensions (as a share of GDP) also increased, from way below the OECD-18 average in the 1970s to near that average by the late 1980s (with the biggest growth coming after 1994).

Estimates show that the Danish public pension system and ATP only provide a somewhat 'improved' level of security for the elderly over time. The picture looks slightly different, however, when expanded labor market pensions are included. These pension schemes have recently grown dramatically in importance. If individual personal pensions are included, annual average private pension income rose by 6.2 percent per year in real terms between 1983 and 1993, as compared to 1.6 percent for public pensions (Kvist 1997: 30). At the same time, the number of employees covered by these schemes has almost doubled (Petersen 1995: 11).

9.6.2.7. Danish Labor Market Policy: From Welfare to Work

Under the Conservative-led governments of the 1980s and early 1990s, policies aimed directly at optimizing employment were more or less absent. Job subsidies and other active measures gradually expanded by the Social Democratic governments that had initiated them earlier were brought down to levels just slightly above the OECD-18 average (and well below what was spent on active employment in Sweden). Against this background, total unemployment was allowed to rise dramatically, reaching 11 percent by 1993.

In Denmark persistent high unemployment was not perceived as problematic, possibly because of generous benefits and the way the Danish welfare state was (and, to some extent, still is) financed. With the state financing unemployment benefits at replacement rates varying between 80–90 percent of previous earnings for up to seven years (five years after 1995), the situation for Denmark's unemployed has been more acceptable than for their Swedish counterparts. Employers also clearly support a system in which benefits are financed more out of general revenues than payroll contributions.

While the bourgeois governments of the 1980s and early 1990s hesitated to use active labor market measures as a way of cutting unemployment, the new Social Democratic government has not been so reluctant. For the first time, Denmark got a genuine active labor market policy.

That policy's first major component was a reduction of the period for receiving 'passive' unemployment benefits to four years, followed by a three-year period of 'activation' in the form of training, re-education, or on-the-job experience (seven years) in 1994. It was followed by an additional cutback to two years of passive benefits, accompanied by a three-year activation period, scheduled for gradual phasing in during 1998. Second, rights to passive benefits were restricted for those who had just taken part in subsidized job training activities.

Obligatory and intensified full-time activation through job offers, training, and education within the first two years of unemployment is now also part of the deal. Mandatory activation through education and 50 percent benefit cuts to young people after six months of unemployment have aimed at bringing down youth joblessness. At the same time, policy formulation and implementation were channeled to regional labor market councils, organized along corporatist lines. There are now special programs for activating vulnerable groups, so as to prevent long-term unemployment and reduce labor market bottlenecks. Subsidized jobs for handicapped people have been introduced. Similarly, paid leave schemes for education, job rotation, child supervision, and sabbatical leave have emerged. The influx of 50 to 59 year olds into transitional allowance (pre-early retirement) schemes has been stopped.

The employment effects of the reforms are open to question, especially because the decline in unemployment during the first few years of the new policy's implementation was not matched by an increase in the total employment ratio (from 73.9% to 74.2%). Labor force participation rates also dropped significantly between 1993 and 1994 (from 82.7% to 79.3%) and rose only slightly thereafter. Moreover, the decline in registered unemployment was accompanied by an increase in the number of hidden unemployed, i.e. pensioners and persons on leave.

Since 1995, however, both categories have registered a drop, indicating improvement in labor market performance over time. This trend is partly confirmed by proportional annual figures: the drop in unemployment by approximately 35,000 persons in the first half of 1997 was compensated by a real increase in employment of 26,000, a rise of 2,000 in persons on social benefit programs, an increase in persons on early retirement by another 2,000, and around 6,000 additional persons 'activated' into the labor market.

Fewer employees than expected took advantage of paid leave, and only around 8 percent of the long-term unemployed have entered 'normal' employment (Finansministeriet 1997). If active labor market programs did not exist, the official unemployment figure would more than double (Madsen 1998). Nevertheless, workers taking leave have been replaced by a substitute in 70 percent of all cases, of which 50 percent continued working for the same employer after the original worker returned from leave. About 50 percent of the substitutes were unemployed, but only a few of them long-term.

Many employers have worried that the tighter labor supply resulting from paid leave schemes would fuel wage inflation. This fear was not confirmed, however, since the employees taking leave often come from the public sector, which is less responsive to such changes in the labor market. Yet there has been more pressure on wages and inflation since 1994 than in the period between 1987 and 1994. This is the result of a larger general demand for labor.

The Danish active labor market policy implemented since 1994 also contains a high-skill job creation component. Until recently, a monthly sum of 11,000 Danish kroner was paid for a period of at least a year to any employer who would hire a highly skilled but unemployed worker. 90 percent of the highly skilled beneficiaries of these programs between 1994 and 1996 were still employed (many in the same firm) after the subsidies ran out. Clearly, the participating firms were generally convinced that the high-skilled persons they had hired through the government program helped strengthen the firm in strategically important areas (Akademikernes Centralorganisation 1997).

All in all, the share of labor market program beneficiaries made up of persons using active measures measures grew from 14.7 percent in 1994 to 17.1 percent in 1996, whereas the number of persons taking part in education went up by about 50 percent. The new 1997 law on active social policy built on these participation rates: municipalities in particular are now obligated to activate any person with a problem other than unemployment, e.g. by offering a 50 percent state financed wage subsidy.

9.6.3. Institutional Capacity and Effective Policy Adjustment in Denmark

Denmark's recovery in the 1990s was not only the product of identifiable responses to economic internationalization and other challenges; it was also the outcome of major normative and functional changes in the Danish structure of political governance since the early 1980s.

One of the clearest changes occurred in the parliamentary system and (more specifically) in the relationship between government and opposition parties, as Bille (1998) has argued. While the norm for postwar Denmark was a succession of weak, short-lived governments, often calling for new elections whenever they faced a majority opposed to any single policy, the political system is now one of stable, long-term governments. Since the early 1980s, and through more than a decade of bourgeois Conservative-led governments, a new practice emerged whereby governments now clung to their seats in Parliament despite majorities lined up against even important policies (Bille 1998). Another parliamentary tradition broken in the early 1980s was the norm governing the agreements political parties should and could make. While it was viewed as inappropriate for a 'responsible' political party or government to cut deals with the more extreme parties on the left or right during the 1960s and 1970s, these parties struck several compromises with sitting governments in the 1980s and 1990s. At the same time, the practice whereby governments sought a more or less unified majority behind a package of new laws in a given policy area has been replaced by a parliamentary style of soliciting and securing shifting majorities for different elements of the total legislative package.

Both governments and opposition have become more selective about picking coalition partners. At the same time, and possibly related to the policy and party shopping trend (which makes it harder to affix blame for a 'mistaken' policy), political conflicts are increasingly turned into legal questions invoking the authority of the High Court. While these new practices have clear implications for the theory and practice of democracy, it is also evident that they have improved the capacity of minority governments to initiate and implement policies (over the medium term as well). Parliamentary stability has been restored and this, we argue, is one reason why Denmark has been able to move away from the ad hoc policies of the 1960s and 1970s. The clearest examples of the shift towards broader reform packages in the 1980s and 1990s have been a stable fiscal policy since 1980, the changes in industrial policy, tax reform, and (last but not least) the labor market reform of the 1990s.

In addition to the facilitation of reform coming from changes in the political system, the Danish recovery strategy depended on the active support of trade unions and employers. The structural changes in the industrial relations system known as 'centralized decentralization' were certainly important, but they should not be overestimated. The most important change was normative. During the 1980s and early 1990s, the crisis awareness of the partners to collective bargaining was extremely high. The large and growing current account deficit was an object of concern in almost all wage-setting situations during the 1980s and early 1990s; restoring the trade balance was taken to require wage moderation, less stimulus for economic growth, and higher savings. This still holds true today.

The Danish Economic Council, Danish banks and financial institutions, employers' and employees' organizations alike have all (with the assistance of the OECD) helped diffuse the idea that recovery depends on reducing the vulnerability of the economy to a rapidly growing current account deficit.

In the community of opinion leaders that includes experts and media advocates, there has been almost complete agreement that wage moderation and industrial policy are good for the current account and hence for the economy. The corollaries to this coherent recommendation for improving the current account are that it is also good to lower consumption (both public and private), stop forcing growth, give workers extra payments for their labor market pensions, and favor individual pensions with tax breaks. On this basis, the choices to be made by politicians and actors in the industrial relations system have seemed straightforward.

9.7. Comparing Swedish and Danish Adjustment Processes over Time

Sweden and Denmark did not adjust to economic internationalization along convergent paths leading to uniform policies and outcomes. Sweden has had balanced public budgets since it emerged from the deep crisis of the early 1990s, but it still struggles with high (though falling) unemployment. By contrast, the Danish economy experienced a remarkable recovery in the 1990s, as indicated by its comparatively high growth rates, persistently high (and even rising) employment, low unemployment rates, and greater equality of earnings.

The divergence in performances between Sweden and Denmark during the 1990s was due to differences in the two countries' economic structures as well as in the content and timing of their respective policy responses beginning in the early 1980s. We would also emphasize differences in the structures of governance that affected the two countries' institutional capacities for developing appropriate responses to the problems they were facing. In Sweden 'golden age' institutions and functions were maintained, while in Denmark the traditional institutional boundaries were broken down as new functions emerged.

9.7.1. Sweden: From Model to Failure and Back?

The Swedish narrative contains one puzzle calling for special explanation, namely the causes of the steep and sudden increase in unemployment after 1990. It is a puzzle because the institutional setup was oriented towards the goal of full employment throughout the postwar period. The ideology of full employment and the 'work society' was also deeply embedded in the Swedish social outlook.

The path toward high unemployment in the 1990s was, we argue, a process involving tactical policy mistakes, but also structural problems of the Swedish economy.

The institutional foundations maintaining full employment in the post-war period eroded during the 1980s. The capacity of the Rehn–Meidner model's various components to operate efficiently was circumscribed. Central bank regulation, centralized wage determination, macroeconomic policy, and the 'active' labor market policy changed their orientation during this period. The impact of this institutional erosion was disguised by various devaluations and the economic upswing brought about by the deregulation of the credit market. Full employment, however, stopped being a viable goal when the dismantling of several full employment instruments collided with a recession in the international economy. As Glyn (1998: 11) puts it: 'The . . . collapse in employment showed how vulnerable high employment had become.'

Furthermore, the problems confronting the Swedish economy between 1985 and 1990 were solved in the wrong order. The first thing to happen was an investment boom stimulated by the devaluation. To maximize the stimulus, wages would have had to rise more slowly than profits. But this proved increasingly difficult, at least in the wake of the credit boom after 1987. Incomes policy initiatives taken to calm wage demands failed. Wage bargaining was complicated by the more rapid expansion of the sheltered sectors (compared to internationally exposed sectors) as a result of the credit boom. Until the mid-1980s, the growth pattern had seemed stable: unemployment went down, inflation was relatively low, and there was a process of 'reindustrialization' involving huge investments in new production facilities, machinery, and R & D reinforcing Sweden's traditional specialization in industry and orientation toward exports. The pattern in the mid-1980s was already somewhat different: deregulation (following changes in capital and currency markets, both national and international) combined with the old tax system (and its numerous deduction opportunities) and a 1986 dip in oil prices in 1986 to stimulate an atypical home market-based boom. The next step was to calm this speculative boom. The 1990 tax reform and other 'non-accommodating' policies (most importantly, the fixed exchange rate) stopped some of the heady speculation, but these policies simultaneously aggravated the effects of the new decade's international economic downturn. As a result, the economy was stimulated when it was in need of cooling and put on ice when it needed a modest degree of stimulation.

The Swedish economic system could not adapt to these kinds of changes in such a short period, as was borne out by the massive dip in employment between 1991 and 1993. The transition from an investment-led expansion to a home market-based speculative boom ending in a depressed economy elicited only weak and uncoordinated responses. The policies pursued in the mid-1980s—initiated by the central bank rather than the government—focused on one set of problems, namely the institutional structure of the financial sector, with little concern for the impact on the economy as a whole. This selective focus was, in part, the result of a process replacing centralized economic policymaking, the predominant style of the 1950s and 1960s (when, arguably, both the national and international economic environments were more stable) with a more decentralized model generating more uncoordinated policy initiatives.

Current macroeconomic and labor market policies are geared toward slowly reducing unemployment and stabilizing social spending and organization while simultaneously aiming at keeping inflation low and the state budget in balance. The goal is to avoid exposure to international currency speculation by cutting public deficits, and to keep unit labor costs competitive with other countries by reforming wage bargaining. At the same time, the organization of social policy is being reformed to increase the robustness of the system. The new system in the making includes a stronger emphasis on individual contributions. In other respects, the adaptation to intensified international competition for investment and taxable assets has been less pronounced. The tax system has only been marginally adjusted to international tax competition. Similarly, labor market policy and job security legislation were reformed after unemployment rose.

The most important question is what will happen if unemployment does not go down. The Social Democratic government has committed itself to getting open unemployment down to 4 percent and boosting employment to 80 percent, but without deregulating labor markets, changing job security, reorganizing unemployment insurance, or changing labor market policy. At the same time it has committed itself not to devalue the krona, and not to prop up crisis industries. Its most important instrument for achieving all this is the low interest rate policy, a byproduct of fiscal consolidation and the pledge to run budget surpluses of 2 percent. Dismantling the traditional Swedish investment policy however, has cast greater uncertainty on the direction of future investments. Fighting joblessness has therefore become a troubling issue in Swedish politics, although unemployment has recently been given a boost by a general upswing in the international economy and the home market's recovery after interest rates dropped. There are even reports of labor shortages in certain areas and sectors of the economy, especially for high technology services and in larger cities. Nevertheless, some of the declining unemployment can be explained by targeted programs to train youth and the long-term unemployed, programs that make the declining unemployment figures look more impressive than they actually are. To sum up: many new instruments have been developed to control public expenditure, but fewer have been established to create jobs.

9.7.2. Denmark: The Long Road toward a 'Danish Miracle'

Denmark's commitment to a kind of hard currency policy as early as the 1970s made wage restraint a much more critical precondition for maintaining employment in the private sector. Denmark learned the importance of wage moderation the hard way, by facing large drops in private sector employment after the failure of wage policy for most the 1970s. Pegging the Danish Krone to the ECU (in reality, to the Deutschmark) in 1982 then became an easier choice to make, however, since the country had already learned to accept persistent high unemployment.

After a short, hectic period of economic expansion with significant wage drift between 1983 and 1986, wage increases after 1988 tapered off to a level considerably below that of Denmark's main trading partners, Germany and Sweden. In the 1980s Denmark also introduced a new industrial policy, which included large-scale subsidies and credits to cover the start-up and modernization costs of small firms, guidance and R & D funding, support for product promotion support, and state aid for applications of new technology (especially information technology). In combination with successes on the wage front after 1988, the industrial policy contributed to making Danish export performance more sound and to maintaining employment in the manufacturing sector.

Fiscal consolidation and major tax reforms were equally important steps in the Danish recovery strategy. The tax reforms lowered rates on the most mobile factors and broadened the tax base. Nominal tax rates were lowered, especially on the incomes of the large exporting industries and on capital income. The reforms simultaneously put a stronger emphasis on ecological/energy taxes, social security contributions, and user charges.

This lowered the vulnerability of the Danish tax system to international tax competition and tax arbitrage, but it also favored the large, export-oriented companies in the manufacturing sector at the expense of the smaller, more nationally-oriented companies.

The tax reforms boosted savings incentives, which were complemented by expanded public and private labor market pensions. These changes made an important contribution to success on the wage front and took pressure off the current account problem. Then, after a period of low economic growth and rising unemployment (between 1987 and 1993), a new Social Democratic-led majority government pushed economic growth with an under-financed tax reform and well-timed expansionary fiscal policy that allowed temporary tax cuts to be financed over the medium term.

In combination with some favorable coincidences—the beginning of an international economic upturn, a fall in interest rates, an easing of (loan) conversion rules for households, and an increase in housing prices—the Social Democratic policy contributed to a rapid increase in private consumption, which led in turn to growing individual and corporate investment. These factors—together with successful wage moderation, the modernization of Danish business in the 1980s and 1990s, and German reunification—increased the demand for Danish products and labor. Beginning in 1994, the new government implemented a large-scale active labor market policy that emphasized education, training and job rotation, and decentralization of labor market governance and planning. The new policy, intended partly to prevent local bottlenecks in the labor market causing wage drift, came at just the right time and proved very effective.

All in all, the new 'activating' measures signaled a shift from the de facto 'welfare-without-work' policy of the 1970s and 1980s to the 'work-for-welfare' policy of the 1990s. The latter was emphasized even more after 1996, and it was followed up in practice by the 1996 Social Policy Reform. It meant lowering of taxes and removing old work disincentives for low wage earners and expanding childcare by some 130,000 places since 1993. The goal has been to help the government achieve its goal of increasing the labor supply by some 4 percent over the next decade.

This kind of increase in the labor supply (and, it is to be hoped, in employment as well) will be necessary in order to finance increases in social expenditure expected to accompany the large cohort of elderly Danes over the next several decades. Otherwise, Danish policymakers may have to change some of their social policy priorities. Each year since the 1970s, public sector spending has grown and the Danish welfare state expanded. Denmark's spending on family benefits, for instance, now surpasses Sweden's. Almost all old age pensioners have gotten benefits pushing their incomes higher than the earnings of those still active on the labor market. Finally, unemployment benefits are still very generous compared to comparable policies in Sweden, Germany, and the Netherlands.

Denmark's generous unemployment policy is partly due to the country's easy dismissal rules, which allow Danish firms to add staff and downsize more flexibly than their counterparts in most countries. This not only has a negative effect on employment when the demand for labor declines. When the economy is booming and the demand for labor increasing, Danish employers are also more motivated to hire new workers than employers in other countries. Denmark has one of the most mobile labor forces in the industrial world, surpassed only by Britain and the USA. At the same time, Danish workers perceive their job security to be much higher, which is obviously due to the very generous, state-financed unemployment benefit system (OECD 1997c).

This very system also allows Danish workers to accept the kind of persistent high unemployment that existed in the past. The method of financing Danish unemployment benefits through personal income taxes rather than payroll deductions also helps Danish companies accept prolonged periods of high unemployment.

9.7.3. Emerging New Models: Functional and Normative Implications

Since the early 1990s there has been an attempt to reconstruct the Swedish model of the 1950s and early 1960s, with its stable public finances, low inflation, and peaceful labor relations. The problem that remains is employment. One possible way to increase employment would be to accept a wider wage dispersion in order to foster a more service- and job-intensive economy (Iversen 1998). Another would be to go even further toward exploiting the advantages of highly institutionalized labor markets in a volatile global economy (Garrett 1998). In the interest of avoiding segmentation and social disorganization, however, current policy is choosing neither of these routes. The golden age's highly organized labor relations seem unlikely to re-emerge, given strong resistance both from employers and many unions. Even though the relationship between the social partners is more stable today than in the 1970s or 1980s, it is still marked by distrust, especially at the top. Thus, no uncontested vision like the Rehn–Meider model—promising full employment, economic growth, structural change, and industrial rationalization—seems to be on on the horizon. Sweden has moved from being a model to 'muddling through'.

Although the new Danish model seems more viable than its Swedish counterpart, much still depends on whether Denmark's wage and tax increases can be kept at moderate levels. A moderate wage and tax burden, in turn, depends on what happens with social expenditures. Arguably, if taxes cannot be raised, more social services will have to be funded by private co-payments and provided privately. So far the Social Democratic-led government is progressing only slowly in that direction.

Judging from the expansion in welfare programs aimed at the elderly since the mid-1980s, it is probably not realistic to expect more user charges to be introduced here either. More private financing for health care, which would presumably be followed by a broader use of private mandatory or voluntary health insurance, also faces political constraints. This is true either because of the perceived distributive effects or because (if they are mandatory), they will simply take the form of a normal payroll tax.

By contrast, private financing of education and market capitalization for old state-owned 'public service' companies are two innovations that apparently have a lot more going for them. There is surprisingly little discussion about the normative implications of moving from a single to a three-tier higher education system (traditional public, traditional private, and mixed public-private). Private financing of education will continue to be an important instrument in the government's attempt to increase the labor force cohort with educational qualifications from its current share of 55–60 percent to 80 percent by the year 2020 (Finansministeriet 1996). The same applies to market capitalization of state-owned businesses, where the issue of control, so prominent in the 1970s, has more or less disappeared.

Nevertheless, there have been some changes in the composition of sources financing the welfare state since the early 1970s. The Danish welfare state is still largely financed out of general revenues raised by state and local government. But since the early 1980s, and especially since 1990, the share of revenue from insurance contributions has gone up considerably as the state's tax bite has correspondingly declined. Other changes deserving special mention are the expansion in private co-payment arrangements (i.e. user charges), the extension of labor market pensions, and (last but not least) the increase in labor market contributions.

It is in accordance with these kinds of small, but not insignificant, changes that Sweden's and Denmark's reformed social democratic welfare states have emerged. For Torben Iversen (1998) the question is whether countries shaped as strongly by social democracy as Denmark and Sweden can adapt to the global economy, and whether full employment is compatible with equality. From Iversen's perspective, the challenge of economic globalization is to avoid segmentation on the labor market, where social democratic parties and trade unions run the risk of acting in favor of inside groups at the expense of outsiders (young people, immigrants, the elderly). Sweden to some extent illustrates the dangers of this adherence to an egalitarian tradition still unable to cut unemployment for marginal groups. By contrast, the Danish experience of the 1990s seems to have produced high growth and low unemployment, though at the price of weaker unions and increased labor market segmentation. Our conclusion, then, is that the Swedish experience proves that traditional social democratic policies are not dead, although they do not seem capable of producing full employment anymore. Denmark, on the other hand, is an example of a revitalized, if unorthodox, social democracy. It shows that making many strategically correct decisions can reverse the kind of marginalization that follows high unemployment.

Against this background, it seems that the Scandinavian social democratic welfare state faces a fundamental choice: it can stick to its traditional egalitarian policies, though at the price of higher unemployment, or it can choose new and less orthodox ways to achieve full employment.

REFERENCES

ÅBERG, RUNE (1997). 'Åtstramningspolitik i Återvändsgränd', in Jan Johannesson and Eskil Wadensjö (eds.), *28 recept mot arbetslösheten*. Stockholm: SNS, 22–27.

ADEMA, WILLEM, and EINERHAND, MARCEL (1998). *The Growing Role of Private Social Benefits*. Labour Market and Social Policy Occasional Papers No. 38. Paris: OECD.

Akademikernes Centralorganisation (1997). *Akademikernes erfaringer med Isbryderprojektet*. Copenhagen: AC.

ANDERSEN, TORBEN M. (1997). 'Structural Changes and Barriers in the Danish Labour Market', in Horst Siebert (ed.), *Structural Change and Labour Market Flexibility: Experience in Selected OECD Economies*. Kiel: Mohr Siebeck, 123–49.

AXELSSON, CHRISTINA (1992). *Hemmafrun som försvann*. Stockholm: SOFI.

BENGTSSON, BO (1995). *Bostaden—välfärdsstatens handelsvara*. Uppsala: Statsvetenskapliga inst.

BENNER, MATS (1997). *The Politics of Growth*. Lund: Arkiv.

BERG, OLE (1980). 'The Modernisation of Medical Care in Sweden and Norway', in Arnold J. Heidenheimer and Nils Elvander (eds.), *The Shaping of the Swedish Health System*. London: Croom Helm, 17–43.

BERGOM-LARSSON, MATTS (1985). 'Den svenska modellen ur branschperspektiv', in *Fred eller fejd? Personliga minnen och anteckningar*. Stockholm: SAF, 357–419.

BERGSTRÖM, ASTA (1995). *Åtstramning och expansion*. Lund: Lund University Press.

BERGSTRÖM, HANS (1987). *Rivstart?* Stockholm: Bonniers.

BERGSTRÖM, HANS (1993). 'Flerpartisamarbete i regering och opposition', in Björn von Sydow, Gunnar Wallin, and Björn Wittrock (eds.), *Politikens väsen.* Stockholm: Tiden, 169–205.

BILLE, LARS (1998). *Dansk partipolitik 1987–1998.* Copenhagen: DJØF-Forlag.

BRULIN, GÖRAN, and NILSSON, TOMMY (1994). *Arbetsutveckling och förbättrad produktivitet.* Stockholm: Arbetslivsfonden.

DE JONG, HENK W. (1997). 'The Governance Structure and Performance of Large European Corporations'. *Journal of Management and Governance,* 1: 5–27.

DSJU (Report, Ministry of Justice) (1979: 1). *Vägar till ökad välfärd.* Stockholm: LiberFörlag.

DUE, JESPER, STEHEN MADESN, JØRGEN, KJERULF PETERSEN, LARS, and STRØBY JENSEN, CARSTEN (1995). 'Adjusting the Danish Model: Towards Centralised Decentralization', in Colin Crouch and Franz Traxler (eds.), *Organized Industrial Relations in Europe: What Future.* Aldershot: Avebury, 121–50.

EDEBALK, PER GUNNAR (1975). *Arbetslöshetsförsäkringsdebatten.* Lund: Ekonomisk-historiska institutionen.

EDGREN, JAN, FAXÉN, KARL-OLOF, and ODHNER, CLAS-ERIK (1970). *Lönebildning och samhällsekonomi.* Stockholm: Rabén & Sjögren.

EKLUND, KLAS (1993). *En 'skattereform' för socialförsäkringar?* Stockholm: Fritze.

ELMÉR, ÅKE (1971). *Svensk socialpolitik,* 9th edn. Lund: Gleerup.

—— (1998). *Svensk socialpolitik,* 19th edn. Lund: Studentlitteratur.

ELVANDER, NILS (1966). *Intresseorganisationerna i dagens Sverige.* Lund: Gleerup.

—— (1970). *Svensk skattepolitik 1945–1970.* Stockholm: Rabén & Sjögren.

—— (1988). *Den svenska modellen.* Stockholm: Publica.

—— and HOLMLUND, BERTIL (1997). *The Swedish Bargaining System in the Melting Pot.* Stockholm: Arbetslivsinstitutet.

Erhvervsministeriet (1997). *Erhvervsredegørelsen.* Copenhagen: Erhvervsministeriet.

ERIXON, LENNART (1985). *What's Wrong with the Swedish Model?* Stockholm: SOFI.

—— (1997). *The Golden Age of the Swedish Model.* Stockholm: Department of Economics.

ESPING-ANDERSEN, GØSTA (1990). *The Three Worlds of Welfare Capitalism.* Cambridge: Polity Press.

FELDT, KJELL-OLOF (1985). *Samtal med Feldt.* Stockholm: Tiden.

—— (1990). *Alla dessa dagar . . .* Stockholm: Norstedts.

—— (1994). *Rädda välfärdsstaten!* Stockholm: Norstedts.

FERNLUND, KARL-GUSTAV (1990). *Skattereformen.* Stockholm: Allmänna förlaget.

Finansministeriet (1996). *Ældres Indkomster og Formuer.* Copenhagen: Finansministeriet.

—— (1997). *The Danish Economy—Medium Term Economic Survey.* Copenhagen: Finansministeriet.

Finansministeriet, Erhvervsministeriet, Statsministeriet, Økonomiministeriet (1995). *Velstand og Velfærd—en analysesammemnfatning.* Copenhagen: Kommisionen om fremtidens beskæftigelses- og erhvervsmuligheder.

FÖLSTER, STEFAN (1993). *Sveriges systemskifte i fara?* Stockholm: IUI.

FURÅKER, BENGT (1976). *Stat och arbetsmarknad.* Lund: Arkiv.

——(1987). *Stat och offentlig sektor.* Stockholm: Rabén & Sjögren.

——(1989). *När jobben hotas.* Stockholm: Rabén & Sjögren.

GARRETT, GEOFFREY (1998). *Partisan Politics in the Global Economy.* Cambridge: Cambridge University Press.

GLETE, JAN (1994). *Nätverk i näringslivet.* Stockholm: SNS.

GLIMELL, HANS (1986). 'Den svenska vägen till trängre kretsar', in *Industriförnyelse i Norden.* Roskilde: Forlaget samfundsøkonomi og planlægning, 113–46.

GLYN, ANDREW (1998). 'The Assessment: Economic Policy and Social Democracy'. *Oxford Review of Economic Policy,* 14 /1: 1–18.

GONÄS, LENA (1997). 'Lokala utfall av den offentliga sektorns omvandling', in *Om makt och kön.* Stockholm: Fritze, 103–46.

Government Bill 1982/83-50. Stockholm: Swedish Parliament.

——1982/83-152. Stockholm: Swedish Parliament.

——1990/91-100. Stockholm: Swedish Parliament.

——1993/94-80. Stockholm: Swedish Parliament.

——1994/95-25. Stockholm: Swedish Parliament.

GUSTAFSSON, ROLF Å. (1994). *Köp och sälj, var god svälj?* Stockholm: Arbetsmiljöfonden.

GUSTAVSSON, ULF, and JOHANSSON, GÖRAN (1995).'Sund reaktion fly från s'. *Dagens Nyheter,* 1995-10-01, A4.

HALL, PETER A., and FRANZESE, ROBERT J. (1998). 'Mixed Signals: Central Bank Independence, Coordinated Wage Bargaining, and European Monetary Union'. *International Organization,* 52/3: 505–36.

HANSEN, ERIK D. (1994). *Dansk økonomisk Politik—teorier og erfaringer,* 3rd edn. Copenhagen: Handelshøjskolen Forlag.

HANSEN, POUL E., and LUNDING, CARSTEN (1994). *Dansk Erhvervsliv.* Copenhagen: Handelshøjskolen Forlag.

HELLSTRÖM, MATS (1975). 'Sysselsättning för gemensamma behov', in Daniel Tarschys (ed.), *Offentlig sektor i tillväxt.* Stockholm: SNS, 65–78.

HIRDMAN, YVONNE (1998). *Den kluvna tungan: LO och genusordningen.* Stockholm: Atlas.

ISM (Industri—og Samordningsministeriet) (1994). *Erhvervsredegørelse 1994.* Copenhagen: ISM.

IVERSEN, TORBEN (1998). 'The Choices for Scandinavian Social Democracy in Comparative Perspective'. *Oxford Review of Economic Policy,* 14 /1: 59–75.

JENSEN, BJARNE (1998). 'Den gamle ambi—en saga blot'. *Dansk Told & Skat,* 7: 20–24.

JOHANSEN, LARS N. (1986). 'Denmark' in Peter Flora (ed.), *Growth to Limits: The Western European Welfare States Since World War II,* i. Berlin/New York: Walter de Gruyter, 293–381.

JONSSON, BERTIL (1999). 'Företagsskatten behöver sänkas'. *Dagens Nyheter,* 1999-02-20, A4.

JONUNG, LARS (1991). *Devalveringen 1982—rivstart eller snedtändning?* Stockholm: SNS.

JÖRBERG, LENNART (1982). 'Svensk ekonomi under 100 år', in Bo Södersten (ed.), *Svensk ekonomi.* Stockholm: Rabén & Sjögren, 21–51.

KAIJSER, ARNE (1994). *I fädrens spår.* Stockholm: Carlssons.

KASSMAN, CHARLES (1990). *Arne Geijer och hans tid.* Stockholm: Tiden.

KATZENSTEIN, PETER (1985). *Small States in World Markets: Industrial Policy in Europe.* Ithaca, NY: Cornell University Press.

KJELLBERG, ANDERS (1983). *Facklig organisering i tolv länder.* Lund: Arkiv.

——(1998). 'Sweden: Restoring the Model?', in Anthony Ferner and Richard Hyman (eds.) *Changing Industrial Relations in Europe.* Oxford: Blackwell, 74–117.

KORPI, WALTER (1995). *Arbetslöshet och arbetslöshetsförsäkring i Sverige* Stockholm: EFA.

KRISTOFFERSEN, HANS-ERIK, MUNKSGAARD, JESPER, and JENSEN, METTE (1997). *Energy Taxes and Subsidies in Denmark.* Copenhagen: Institute of Local Government Studies.

KVIST, JON (1997). 'Retrenchment or Restructuring? The Emergence of a Multitiered Welfare State in Denmark', in Jochen Clasen (ed.), *Social Insurance in Europe.* Bristol: Policy Press, 14–39.

LARSSON, MATS (1991). *En svensk ekonomisk historia 1850–1985.* Stockholm: SNS.

——(1998). *Staten och kapitalet.* Stockholm: SNS.

LEWIN, LEIF (1967). *Planhushållningsdebatten.* Stockholm: Almqvist & Wiksell.

LIND, JENS (1998). *Trends in the Regulation of Employment Relations in Denmark.* Copenhagen: Samfundslitteratur.

LINDHOLM, MIKAEL (ed.) (1994). *Danmark i verdensøkonomien.* Copenhagen: Samfundslitteratur.

LO (Landsorganisationen i Sverige) (1941). *Fackföreningsrörelsen och näringslivet.* Stockholm: LO.

——(1951). *Fackföreningsrörelsen och den fulla sysselsättningen.* Stockholm: LO.

——(1961). *Samordnad näringspolitik.* Stockholm: LO.

LØNROTH, HELLE, NØRREKLIT, HANNE, and SØRENSEN, POUL ERIK (1997). 'Capital Market Pressure, Corporate Governance and their Influence on Long-Term Investments: The Case of Denmark'. Working Paper 97-3: Department of International Business. Aarhus: Aarhus Business School.

LU (Långtidsutredningen) (1984). *Långtidsutredningen 1984.* Stockholm: Finansdepartementet.

LUNDBERG, ERIK (1983). *Ekonomiska kriser förr och nu.* Stockholm: SNS.

MADSEN, PER KONGSHØJ (1998). 'Recent Underemployment Trends'. Unpublished draft.

MALM, STIG (1994). *13 år.* Stockholm: Brevskolan.

MARKLUND, STAFFAN (1990). *Paradise Lost?* Lund: Arkiv.

MOGENSEN, GUNNAR V. (ed.) (1995). *Work Incentives in the Danish Welfare State.* Aarhus: Aarhus University Press.

NIELSEN, KLAUS (1991). 'Learning to Manage the Supply-Side: Flexibility and

Stability in Denmark', in Bob Jessop (ed.), *The Politics of Flexibility: Restructuring the State in Britain, Germany and Scandinavia*. Aldershot: Edward Elgar, 282–313.

NYBERG, STEN, and SKEDINGER, PER (1998). *Arbetsförmedlingarna—mål och drivkrafter*. Stockholm: ESO.

OECD (Organisation for Economic Co-operation and Development) (1997*a*). *Economic Outlook*. Paris: OECD.

——(1997*b*). *Economic Surveys: Denmark*. Paris: OECD.

——(1997*c*). *Employment Outlook*. Paris: OECD.

——(1997*d*). 'Income Distribution and Poverty in Selected OECD Countries'. *OECD Economic Outlook*, 62. Paris: OECD.

——(1998). *Income Distribution and Poverty in Selected OECD Countries*. Economic Department Working Papers No. 189.

OLOFSSON, GUNNAR (1993). 'Det svenska pensionssystemet 1913–1993'. *Arkiv för studier i arbetarrörelsens historia*, 58/59: 29–84.

——and PETTERSSON, JAN (1994). 'Sweden', in Frieder Naschold and Bert de Vroom (eds.), *Regulating Employment and Welfare*. Berlin: De Gruyter, 183–246.

OLSSON, ANDERS S. (1989). *The Swedish Wage Negotiation System*. Stockholm: Almqvist & Wiksell.

OLSSON, SVEN E. (1990). *Social Policy and Welfare State in Sweden*. Lund: Arkiv.

PALME, JOAKIM, and WENNEMO, IRENE (1998). *Swedish Social Policy in the 1990s*. Stockholm: Socialdepartmentet.

PERSSON, GÖRAN (1997). *Den som är satt i skuld är icke fri*. Stockholm: Atlas.

PETERSEN, JØRN H. (1995). *Three Essays on Trends towards a Transformation of the Danish Welfare State*. Working Paper 1995:1. Odense: Centre for Health and Social Policy.

PLOVSING, JAN (1994). *Socialpolitik*. Copenhagen: Handelshøjskolens Forlag.

ROTHSTEIN, BO (1996). *The Social Democratic State*. Pittsburgh: University of Pittsburgh Press.

RUIN, OLOF (1981). *Att tänka efter och komma överens före*. Stockholm: Statsvetenskapliga inst.

RYDÉN, BENGT (1979). *Mot nya förlorade år?* Stockholm: SNS.

SAHLIN, MONA (1999). 'Små lönekrav bäst för alla'. *Aftonbladet*, 1999-02-01, 3.

SAP (Sveriges socialdemokratiska arbetarparti) (1980). *Bommersviksseminarium om den offentliga sektorn. 2*. Stockholm: SAP.

——(1981). *Framtid för Sverige*. Stockholm: SAP.

——(1989). *90-talsprogrammet*. Stockholm: SAP.

SCHARP, ANDERS (1999). 'Nu är tillväxten regeringens ansvar'. *Dagens Nyheter*, 1999-01-12, A4.

SCHÖN, LENNART (1994). *Omvandling och obalans*. Stockholm: Fritze.

SFI (Socialforskingsinstituttet) (1997). *Brug og vurdering af Hjemmeservice-ordningen*. Copenhagen: Erhvervsfremmestyrelsen.

SNA (Sveriges Nationalatlas) (1995). *15. Industri och service*. Höganäs: Bra Böcker.

466   *Mats Benner and Torben Bundgaard Vad*

SØRENSEN, PETER BIRCH (1998). *Tax Policy in the Nordic Countries.* London: Macmillan.

SOU (Statens offentliga utredningar) (1961-42). *Mål och medel i stabiliseringspolitiken.*

——(1965-1). *Arbetsmarknadspolitik.*

——(1971-5). *Svensk industri under 70-talet.*

——(1979-24). *Sysselsättningspolitik för arbete åt alla.*

——(1991-81). *Drivkrafter för produktivitet och välstånd.*

——(1993-20). *Riksbanken och prisstabiliteten.*

——(1993-32). *Ny anställningsskyddslag.*

——(1993-43). *Politik mot arbetslöshet.*

——(1995-104). *Skattereformen 1990–1991.*

——(1996-14). *Budgetlag.*

——(1996-150). *En allmän och sammanhållen arbetslöshetsförsäkring.*

——(1998-141). *Medling och lönebildning.*

Statistics Denmark (1995). *50-years-review.* Copenhagen: Statistics Denmark.

——(1997). *10-years-review, 1987–1997.* Copenhagen: Statistics Denmark.

Statskontoret (1997). *Staten i omvandling.* Stockholm: Statskontoret.

STRÅTH, BO (1998). *Mellan två fonder.* Stockholm: Atlas.

SVALLFORS, STEFAN (1996). *Välfärdsstatens moraliska ekonomi.* Umeå: Borea.

SVENSSON, TORSTEN (1996). *Novemberrevolutionen.* Stockholm: ESO.

Sveriges Regering (Swedish Government) (1998). *Avstämning av målet om halverad arbetslöshet.* Stockholm: Ministry of Finance.

SWEDENBORG, BIRGITTA, JOHANSSON-GRAHN, GÖRAN, and KINNWALL, MATS (1988). *De svenska företagens utlandsinvesteringar.* Stockholm: IUI.

THERBORN, GÖRAN (1986). *Why Some Peoples are More Unemployed than Others.* London: Verso.

——(1991). 'Sweden', in Alfred Pfaller, Ian Gough, and Göran Therborn (eds.), *Can the Welfare State Compete?* London: Macmillan, 229–70.

WALLERSTEIN, MICHAEL, and GOLDEN, MIRIAM (1997). 'The Fragmentation of the Bargaining Society: Wage Setting in the Nordic Countries, 1950 to 1992'. *Comparative Political Studies*, 30/6: 699–732.

WERIN, LARS (1993). *Från räntereglering till inflationsnorm.* Stockholm: SNS.

WIBBLE, ANNE (1994). *Två cigg och en kopp kaffe.* Stockholm: Ekerlids.

10

A Fine Balance
Women's Labor Market Participation in
International Comparison

MARY DALY

Even though it may not always be obvious, the female/male balance of employment is a careful one, requiring settlement along a number of different dimensions. The diversity of arrangements across nations suggests not only that different paths are followed but that they sometimes result in similar outcomes. Another striking point in contemporary employment patterns is the degree of change that is underway. In fact, just when it seemed that the arrangements arrived at in the 1970s and earlier were to prove enduring, modernizing forces have thrown open the matter of women and men's share of employment. Internationalization has so far had its greatest impact on male employment patterns—an effect realized especially in the reduction of the demand for low-skilled, industrial labor. How economic and other developments affect women's labor market participation is far from clear. Greater flexibility is likely to accelerate the demand for female labor. Relatedly, service sector growth also tends to be associated with an increased demand for female workers. However, higher demand nowhere automatically provokes increased supply. For women's decision to participate in paid work may not always be founded on a rational calculus or framed within a perspective of self-interest. Such a decision is, rather, governed by a complex series of factors that extend beyond individual choice to embrace key sets of societal relationships. In effect, the balance between female and male levels of labor market participation is embedded in a much larger balance—between the state, market, and family in terms of the distribution of resources and responsibilities in general and in relation to the provision of care.

This chapter seeks to explore the sets of relationships that are involved in the demand for and supply of female labor. It does this by identifying

I would like to thank the editors, Fritz W. Scharpf and Vivien A. Schmidt, for their insightful comments on earlier versions of this chapter and Martin Schludi for his always prompt and helpful assistance with data.

variations in female employment participation patterns and investigating the impact of factors associated with these variations. The approach adopted is comparative, the goal to explore how different constellations of factors operate in particular contexts to affect female employment participation. Taking in a large number of countries helps to expand the range of factors that can be considered. Hence, the chapter will cover more countries than is customary for the volume, focusing on nineteen of the most developed Western economies. The main comparative goal is to explore the conditions under which different types of relations between the demand for and supply of female labor are sustained. The end is not to produce a typology per se—clusters will be used to the extent that they help us to establish how the labor force participation patterns of women are associated with the existence of sets of employment/family systems in the nineteen most-developed economies.

The chapter has both a fact-finding and explanatory mission. In the former regard it will identify the key dimensions of women's labor force participation across nations and how these have changed over time. It should be emphasized that the dependent variable is women's labor force participation, rather than say female/male differences in participation, the types of job held, or the conditions of employment. The point of departure is a set of analyses that will explore the nature of and variation in women's participation in the labor force in a comprehensive manner. These analyses will offer some stylized facts about women's labor supply, sometimes with male patterns as the backdrop. Both status and trends are considered, the latter covering the period between 1970 and 1996. In order to uncover the sociological complexity of female ties to the labor market, crude participation rates will be disaggregated to identify both the amount as well as continuity of women's labor force participation.

The subsequent parts of the chapter devote themselves to both building up a more rounded and robust picture of women's labor force participation and explaining the variations found. The search after explanation will be organized into several stages. The first step will be to consider factors that affect the demand for female labor. In this part of the analysis the structure of the labor market is placed under the spotlight. The second set of explanations considered relate to the supply side. Here the analysis examines the extent to which policy arrangements are seen to covary with the labor supply of certain groups of women. Causality is, however, problematic. Not only is it practically impossible to establish a causal relationship between policy provisions and human behavior but there is the added difficulty in this case of reciprocal causation. Hence, one needs to proceed cautiously towards explanation. Such a need for caution partly explains the delimiting of the dependent variable to female participation rates. All too often female participation in employment is taken as an entrée to other aspects of employment or indeed women's situation in general. I want to hold the attention on participation rates throughout in the belief that this is a phenomenon which is deserving of an analysis that seeks to give due recognition to the complexity occasioned by the high degree of variation within and across nations. For that reason the analysis eschews the application of statistical techniques, such as regression for example, which operate with a narrow understanding of causation. The explanatory approach followed here is one that maps out the broad terrain of covariation, paying due attention to deviating cases, and looking at whether particular paths lead to the same or alternative ends. In a third stage, therefore, the chapter will seek to link the explanatory variables with the patterns found. Here the dependent variable is revisited and a case is made for a more complex understanding of it. A final overview section completes the chapter.

10.1. The Empirical Details of Women's Labor Market Participation

10.1.1. Female Labor Force Participation Rates

The degree of variation in female employment levels across the developed Western nations is striking (Figure 10.1). Measured on the basis of the total female labor force as a proportion of the total population aged between 15 and 64 years, the variation overall in 1996 was in the region of some 30 percentage points. In fact, female labor force participation ranges from a 'high' of 76.3 percent in Sweden to a 'low' of 42.9 percent in Italy.

The cross-national patterning can be seen from Figure 10.1 which presents the female labor force rates in descending order. The 'high' and 'low' nations are clear at a glance. The four Scandinavian countries and the USA cluster together to form a block at the top, with female labor force participation rates in excess of 70 percent. The Mediterranean countries, apart from Portugal, group themselves at the opposite pole. In Greece, Italy, and Spain less than half of all women of working age are economically active. Ireland and Luxembourg tend towards the Mediterranean pattern with the majority of women of working age outside the labor force. Apart from these nations, the patterning among the middle grouping is less definite. What one might call the 'liberal' nations, specifically the UK, Canada, and Australia, tend in the direction of the Scandinavian/USA pattern with female activity rates in the mid- to high sixties. The remaining countries are mainly continental European nations—Austria, France,

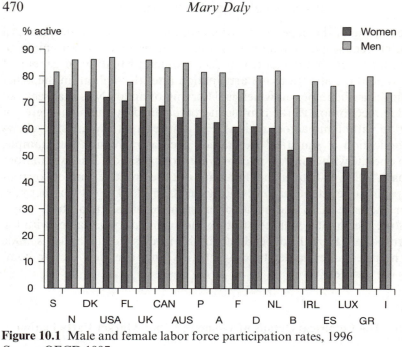

Figure 10.1 Male and female labor force participation rates, 1996
Source: OECD 1997.

Germany,[1] Belgium, and the Netherlands. These nations appear to form a middle way between the Scandinavian route of a highly feminized labor force and the Mediterranean pattern of more home than labor market for women. Around 60 percent of women in these 'middle way' countries are economically active.

Male participation patterns present a stark contrast, in terms of both absolute level and the range of variation (data not shown). Typically, between 80 and 85 percent of men are in the labor force. As is well known, European countries tend to be characterized by low male participation rates—Belgium, Finland, France, Ireland, Italy, Luxembourg, and Spain have rates lower than 80 percent. In general though, the degree of dispersion cross-nationally in male rates is much less than that in female rates. The fact that the variation in male rates is only half that found for women suggests that governments have been more flexible in how they have treated female labor supply. If the Scandinavian countries form the upper

---

[1] It should be noted that throughout this chapter the reference unit for Germany will vary according to the date of the relevant statistics. Where data pertain to the early 1990s and before, the reference unit is the Federal Republic or West Germany; more recent data usually pertain to unified Germany.

end of the continuum of female labor force participation, it is the liberal nations, such as the USA, UK, and Canada, that have the highest male rates. However, Denmark and Norway can match these nations for male participation, although there is no Scandinavian block for men in the same way that there is for women. Finland and to a lesser extent Sweden are actually among the low male participation countries, with activity rates between five and ten percentage points lower than they are in Denmark and Norway. It is important to note, though, that low male rates are a relatively new experience for these countries, especially Sweden where male rates have been on a downward trend in the 1990s.

One of the most revelatory aspects from the point of view of the gender distribution of employment is the relationship between male and female labor force participation rates. Measured in terms of the female/male ratio, the Scandinavian countries are clearly at the top and are unchallenged in this regard. Their high female and relatively low male participation rates place Finland and Sweden in the vanguard, with female/male employment ratios of over 90 percent. They are closely followed by Denmark and Norway, confirming the well-known gender equality orientation of the Scandinavian model. Nations of a liberal provenance—especially Canada and the USA—also have relatively high female/male ratios as does France. The Continental European nations have achieved less gender equality in labor force participation with female/male ratios in the region of 75 percent. Once again, the Mediterranean nations, together with Ireland and Luxembourg, are in a class apart with relatively high male and low female activity rates.

Looking at patterns over time indicates further important differences within and across countries, pinpointing in particular the direction of change, the period when the 'take-off' in women's labor force activity began and the pace of change (Figure 10.2). In contrast to the downward direction in labor market participation generally, the female trend has been determinedly upwards. The 1970s and 1980s were the high points of this trend, all countries except Ireland having seen a steady upward movement in female labor force participation in one if not both decades. Patterns in the 1990s appear to have followed a different course—it is a decade characterized by cross-national diversity. In the northernmost part of Europe, the most recent trend in female labor force participation rates is of decline. Sweden and Denmark have led this trend. Falling female economic activity is not a Scandinavian-wide phenomenon however— Finnish rates are relatively stable and the Norwegian pattern is for continued growth. Indeed so strong and consistent has been the latter rise that Norway has moved over the course of the last two decades from a middling to a leadership position. In some contrast to the Scandinavian pattern, the trend in countries of a liberal provenance in the 1990s has been for stability. However this is a calm after the storm as it were, since the two preceding decades were very active ones indeed for women's labor force participation. Between 1970 and 1990, Australia, Canada, the UK, and the USA witnessed a growth of some 20 percentage points in the female labor force participation rate. The Continental European and Mediterranean nations present evidence of a further trend: women's labor force participation continues to rise in these countries although at a slower pace than in the 1980s. The Netherlands is an exception to all of these trends, having witnessed in the recent past a scale and pace of change that amounts to a veritable transformation in female participation rates. In point of fact, the Netherlands is set apart from all other nations by virtue of the scale and rapidity of the growth it has experienced in women's economic activity. In the twenty-five year period considered here, the participation rate of Dutch women doubled, with the last fifteen years having seen the most growth. These changes transformed the relative position of the Netherlands from a European laggard to an average performer. While no country can rival this pace, there have been periods in other countries when something truly new was taking place. The changes in Sweden in the 1970s, in Australia and Spain in the 1980s, those in Canada and Norway in the 1970s and 1980s, and in Ireland in the 1990s were of such a rapid pace that they must have been associated with considerable upheaval in labor market and family arrangements. One final set of points with regard to the changes in female labor force participation rates over time should be noted. At each of the points in time considered there were:

(1) visible country clusters;
(2) concomitantly, significant gaps between country groupings; and
(3) such gaps, while at their largest in the 1980s, predated this period and remain strong in the current decade.

In other words, the cross-national relationships are not that different over time—female participation seems to occur in bands and country groupings are and have remained fairly firm. Only three countries changed their league position—Canada, the Netherlands, and Norway—over the period considered.

As one might imagine given the scale of these changes, the behavior of women plays a central role in the change that is taking place in the economically active population. Indeed, calculations carried out by EURO-STAT for 1987–92 suggest that the behavior of women rivals the demographic effect (that is, changes in the size of the population of working age) as the main factor accounting for the overall change in the economically active population in the, then twelve, Member States of the EU

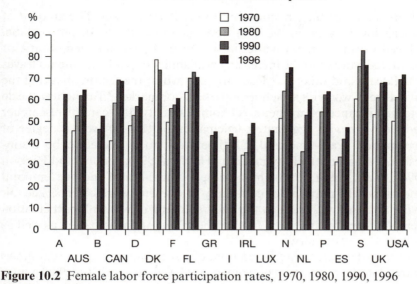

Figure 10.2 Female labor force participation rates, 1970, 1980, 1990, 1996
Source: OECD 1997.

(EUROSTAT 1996: 72). In four countries—Germany, Ireland, Portugal, and the UK—changes in female participation patterns accounted for the bulk of the change in the economically active population and in a further four—Belgium, Luxembourg, the Netherlands, and Spain—they were practically as important as the demographic effect. Only in Denmark, Greece, France, and Italy are changes in female participation patterns relatively unimportant as a factor explaining changes in the economically active population. Moreover, Rubery et al. (1996: 12) demonstrate that when growth in the employment rate occurred in the EU between 1983 and 1992 it was growth in women's rates that accounted for the bulk of it and that without the impact of women's rising participation rates the overall change in the EU employment rates over the period would have been negative rather than weakly positive.

10.1.2. The Amount and Continuity of Women's Labor Force Participation

While participation rates tend to be strongly correlated with, and therefore closely predictive of, full-time employment among men, they have no such singular interpretation for women. One of the most insistent insights from studies of the employment behavior of women is that participation rates per se are relatively poor guides to the extent of women's involvement in and the nature of their relationship to the labor market. The amount of women's involvement in the labor force is, to say the least, problematic. Reduced working time, whether in the form of part-time, temporary, or interrupted work, and the increasing availability of paid and unpaid leaves for childcare and other purposes are just two of the factors masking the real nature of women's attachment to the labor market.[2] To uncover the de facto significance of women's economic activity, the careful researcher needs to work with aggregate participation patterns as well as degree of participation. Part-time and full-time work must therefore be distinguished—a point forcefully made by Hakim (1997), Jonung and Persson (1994), and Zighera (1996) among others. There is also another temporal dimension—the duration or continuity in women's work careers. The following analyses will broaden the understanding of women's participation in employment by analyzing further the extent of participation as well as the degree of continuity.

Towards disaggregating the amount of participation, Figure 10.3 shows the trend in the proportion of women employed on a part-time basis since the 1970s. Taking the general situation first, it is confirmed that part-time work is indeed a very important form and component of female employment. About one-third of employed women across the countries included in the analysis (compared with about 5% of men) work on a part-time basis. The Netherlands is a clear outlier in terms of the significance of part-time work (in its own right and for women's employment). Almost 70 percent of women's employment is part-time there. The Netherlands is followed most closely by Norway, the UK, Australia, and Sweden as the countries where part-time employment is of most significance for women. The Mediterranean countries (together with Finland) make up the opposite pole with about 10 percent of women working on a part-time basis and the Continental European nations together with Canada and the USA occupy the middle ground with about one-quarter of all female employment being part-time. The trends over time indicate diversity. Only in Denmark, Sweden, and Norway is part-time employment as a proportion of women's employment on the decline however. In the Mediterranean and liberal countries it tends towards stability whereas the continental

---

[2] In Sweden e.g. the absences from work are very large. Jonung and Persson demonstrate that, while the difference between male and female labor force participation rates in 1990 was 5 percentage points, the difference between their at work rates was more than double that (11 percentage points) (1994: 42). These authors are of the view that the most accurate measures of women's labor market pattern are either their at work rates (which measure the persons who are actually active in market work during an average week of the year as a percentage of the total population) or the market-hours rate (which measures the total number of hours actually worked in the market per week for a given population group divided by the total size of that population group).

Figure 10.3 Proportion of women's employment that is part-time 1970, 1980, 1990, 1996

Source: OECD 1998*a*.

European nations have seen a steady growth in part-time work as a component of female employment.

Beneath these variations lies a further set of differences in the hours worked, by women especially. For the duration of part-time work itself tends to be, to some extent anyway, country-specific. Not only is there a high level of variation in the hours worked but some nations tend to be long part-time work countries (especially the Scandinavian countries and France) while others (such as Austria, Germany, and the UK) are short or medium part-time work countries (Rubery et al. 1999: 105). Given information shortages, especially in the number of hours worked across nations, it is not possible to standardize case by case. There is some evidence available for the EU Member States however. Zighera (1996) weights female employment rates by hours worked for the, then twelve, Member States of the EU between 1984 and 1991.[3] His data for age cohorts (not shown) demonstrate how misleading absolute participation rates, and country rankings based on them, can be. For when participation

---

[3] He derives his weighting on the basis of employment rate (number of women in employment/total female population aged 20–64) multiplied by the average number of hours worked (total number of hours worked by women/total number of women in employment) (see Zighera 1996: 94–95).

rates are standardized by the hours actually worked by women, Portugal, Denmark, and France are the leading countries in the, then twelve Member State, EU. High part-time work countries, such as the Netherlands and UK, emerge from these figures in a different comparative light, than they do from simple participation rates. In effect the amount of women's labor supply in these countries is lower than the earlier figures suggest. Rates in the Netherlands are especially affected, moving it close to the bottom of the EU (alongside Ireland). Standardizing according to the number of hours worked has, therefore, major comparative implications.[4]

Part-time work is not the only factor complicating women's labor supply. There is also the matter of continuity. Unlike that of men, women's labor force participation tends to be peppered by short and sometimes long interruptions. Again, one is hampered by information shortages from identifying the extent to which women interrupt their labor force participation across nations. However, Zighera's data indicates the stop and start character of female employment. These and other data on age-related patterns for women indicate that there are 'dips' in the years associated with early family formation. Figure 10.4 shows women's participation rates in the EU Member States by age group in 1996. While one must exercise care in reading off behavior over time from these data, they indicate rather a high level of discontinuity from cohort to cohort and also that there is considerable variation across EU Member States in this regard.

The information presented thus far on labor force participation rates is persuasive about a certain commonality of experience amongst the most developed nations in the decades since the early 1970s. The trend in women's rates is upwards and, to the extent that female participation rates have fallen in some of the Scandinavian countries while continuing to grow elsewhere, one could even speak of a convergence. However, while acknowledging elements of a common experience, one must pay due homage to the considerable diversity that characterizes developments in the richest nations over the last two and a half decades. Let us not forget that a gap of over 30 percentage points separates women's economic activity rates in these nineteen highly developed nations. Taking status and trends together, to the extent that there is one overall picture it is of 'organized variation'. In other words, a number of country clusters are identifi-

---

[4] The work of Rubery et al. (1996: 53) has considered some such implications for employment rates. When they recalculated the female employment rate for 1992 in the EU excluding those working less than 10 hours a week, they found that the overall female rate in the EU falls by 1 percentage point and by more than 5 percentage points in Denmark, the Netherlands, and the UK. Unfortunately, the data do not permit us to standardize for hours worked country by country, but they do indicate that other high part-time work countries outside the EU Member States considered by Zighera and Rubery et al. would also be affected by these considerations. These include Australia, Norway, and Sweden.

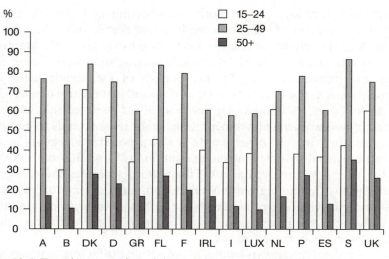

Figure 10.4 Female economic activity rate by age group in EU, 1996
Source: EUROSTAT 1997: table 003.

able. The Scandinavian nations together with the USA are high female activity countries in regard to both the amount and continuity of employment. They are also countries in which women's economic activity rates tend to be relatively stable, although Sweden and Denmark saw some change in a downward direction in the 1990s. These countries are joined by France and Portugal which, when account is taken of both the volume of part-time employment and the degree of continuity in female employment, could also be characterized as 'high female employment' countries. A second grouping of countries consisting of what can be called liberal nations—UK, Australia, and Canada—tends to have somewhat lower female participation rates. Absolute participation rates in these countries are somewhat misleading, since the former two especially are high part-time work countries and in the UK women in relatively large numbers tend to interrupt their employment for child-bearing. In terms of trends over time, these countries saw considerably more growth over the last decades in women's activity rates than the Scandinavian economies but female labor force participation levels may well have peaked here too, for the 1990s have seen more stability than growth. In a third pattern, true especially of Continental European states like Belgium, Germany, Austria, and the Netherlands, the trend in female labor force participation is on a steadily upward course. However with high levels of part-time work (especially in the Netherlands) and an established pattern of women interrupting employment for both child-bearing and child-raising, the actual involvement of women in the labor market is lower than it might seem. A further cluster of countries is formed by the three Mediterranean nations apart from Portugal. In absolute participation terms, these countries have remained solidly at the bottom of the female labor force participation league over the course of time and in a relative context could be described as 'traditional'. However, it should be noted that when they are employed women's attachment to the labor market tends to be continuous and full-time. In other words, a sharp polarization exists in these countries whereby women are either continuously and full-time employed or they are not employed at all. This pattern separates these countries from the two remaining nations of Ireland and Luxembourg where the absolute participation rate resembles the Mediterranean nations but is actually lower when one takes account of the volume of part-time employment that exists in these nations.

This kind of clustering is helpful in indicating the factors that may affect female labor force participation rates. Some of it is also familiar. The Scandinavian nations, for example, are a well-known grouping as are the Mediterranean nations. However obvious this and other patterning, it does not speak automatically to an explanation, since there is a high degree of variation within and across clusters as regards the nature and presence of possible explanatory factors. Given this, the next section moves on to examine how some likely explanatory factors play out within and across nations.

10.2. The Effects of Demand and Supply Factors

The explanatory context is broad, involving along with the structure and organization of the labor market, the arrangement of home and private life as well as the influence of norms and values and their expression in social policies. No single explanation dominates the field but existing research has a tendency to consider explanations in isolation. One way of organizing the field is in terms of factors conventionally regarded as affecting the demand for and/or supply of labor. Such an approach has an appealing simplicity, especially in work like the present which encompasses so many countries. It is an approach with which I begin here. For the purpose of moving towards an explanation and treating different factors in a systematic manner, I will consider in turn the role of a range of demand- and supply-related factors.

A key decision pertains to the approach to be adopted to explanation. Two strategies are possible. The first would be to take the clusters, or a set of exemplar countries of each, and seek to identify the factors that explain their particular configuration(s). The essence of this strategy is to start with the specific case or cases for the purpose of accounting satisfactorily for the experience of that case or set of cases which it represents. The second is a more general strategy. It starts with a set of likely explanatory factors and investigates the extent to which these can account for the experience of all countries in the analysis. The latter strategy is adopted here because it is seen to offer the possibility of a more comprehensive explanation. Comprehensiveness is an important consideration under any circumstances but is especially so given that much of the work in the area of women's labor force participation has tended to focus on particular sets of factors in isolation rather than aiming for a general explanation. Hence in the pages to follow, I will endeavour to ascertain the contribution of each of a set of factors to explaining cross-national variations in the employment participation rate of women. I use the female employment rate rather than the labor force participation rate because it is a truer measure of relevant behavior among women in that it disregards unemployment which tends among women to blur with inactivity (Rubery et al. 1999: 115).

10.2.1. Demand-Oriented Explanations

Economic and structural characteristics and the processes which they engender in the labor market are to the fore as factors theorized to affect the demand for labor. In regard to the pattern of female labor force participation, the temporal and sectoral structure of the labor market as well as the availability and distribution of particular kinds of employment are the most significant factors affecting demand. These are operationalized in the ensuing analyses in terms of the extent of part-time and service sector employment and the size of public sector employment.

10.2.1.1. Part-Time Employment

We have seen earlier (from Figure 10.3) that part-time work is indeed a very important form and component of female employment. It accounts for an average of about one-third of female employment across the countries included in the analysis compared with about 5 percent of that of men. The Netherlands is a clear outlier in terms of the significance of part-time work and it is followed most closely by Norway, the UK, Australia, and Sweden. For the purposes of uncovering the significance of part-time work as a factor affecting the demand for female labor, one question is key: To what extent does the distribution of part-time work covary with the female employment ratio? Figure 10.5 shows the relationship for all

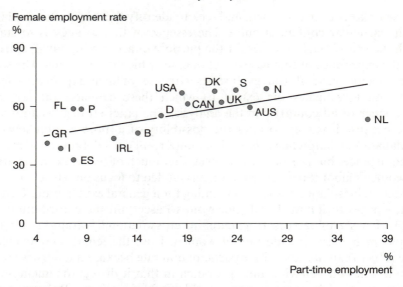

Figure 10.5 Part-time employment (as % of all employment) and the female employment rate, 1996
Source: OECD 1997, 1998*a*.

countries in the analysis except Austria, France, and Luxembourg (for which comparable information on recent female employment rates is not available).

One can see that a good deal of congruence exists between a country's level of part-time employment and its female employment rate. This is a relationship that is especially close in Germany, Australia, the UK, and Canada. To the extent that one can identify the general nature of the relationship it is that the volume of part-time employment tends to co-exist with that of female employment. The Scandinavian nations (except Finland), the UK, and Australia attest to this high part-time/high female employment relation just as the Mediterranean nations, apart from Portugal, support the obverse form of the relationship. However there are some strong exceptional cases also. The Netherlands is the most outstanding exception with the highest share of part-time work of any nation and only moderate female employment rates. Other strong exceptional cases are Portugal and Finland (which also resemble each other very strongly) with high female employment ratios despite a low volume of part-time employment. The USA is another variant of the relation with very high female employment rates but only a moderate level of part-time employment. Given the existence of such strong exceptional cases, one must conclude that there is no automatic or necessary relationship between the volume of part-time employment and the female employment ratio and it is certainly not the case that a large volume of part-time employment is an essential condition of high female employment.

Approaching the question from a somewhat different angle, Rubery et al. (1996) queried the extent to which part-time employment accounted for the growth in female employment in the EU between 1983 and 1992. Their analysis again highlights the Netherlands as a most extreme case in that developments in part-time employment more or less completely explain the changes in women's economic activity rates. The rise in women's labor force participation and that in part-time jobs was virtually synonymous there—86 percent of the new employment created among Dutch women between 1983 and 1992 was part-time. This was much less frequently the case for French (68%) and German and UK women (57%). Unlike France and Germany though, strong growth in part-time female employment stretches back a long way in the UK. Only from 1988 onwards did any genuine increase take place in the volume of female employment in Britain (measured on a full-time equivalent job basis); from 1951 to the late 1980s the continuous rise in female employment rates there consisted entirely of the substitution of part-time for full-time jobs (Hakim 1997: 33).

Overall though, while there is a relationship, the growth in female employment is nowhere solely attributable to an increase in part-time work, except in the Netherlands and to a lesser extent the UK for certain periods. Furthermore, in terms of the more general relation, while high part-time and high female employment tend to go together in many nations, there are too many exceptions for this to be a general relation.

10.2.1.2. Service Sector Employment

Women's employment tends to be closely identified with the service sector also. One could confidently make the prediction that a large service sector is crucial to female employment levels given its tendency to increase the demand for female labor. Following on from this, countries with high rates of service sector employment could be anticipated to have higher female employment levels than those with low service sector employment. Figure 10.6 shows the correspondence between the size of the service sector overall and the female employment rates for all nations (except Austria, France, and Luxembourg for which complete information is missing).

Taking first the overall variation in the size of the service sector, a gap of some 25 percentage points exists in the proportion of employment located in the service sector. Spain has the lowest (at 28.5%) and the USA the highest (53.4%). However, most countries cluster around the average,

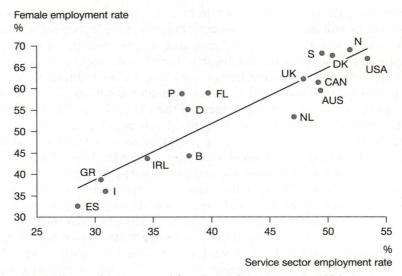

Figure 10.6 The service sector and female employment rates, 1996
Source: OECD 1997.

wherein the service sector accounts for about 40 percent of total employment. The liberal nations tend to have the highest proportion of service-sector employment, together with the Scandinavian nations (except Finland). The Netherlands also has a relatively large service sector. The block at the other end is a familiar one, formed by Spain, Greece, and Italy where the service sector accounts for less than one-third of all employment. In between is a mixed bag of countries, including France, Finland, Portugal, Belgium, and Ireland.

When the size of the service sector and female employment are connected as in Figure 10.6, one can see that there is a close relation. In fact the size of the service sector appears to correspond more closely with the female employment ratio than does the volume of part-time employment. There is a very large group of countries at the top end, comprising the Scandinavian nations (except Finland) and the UK, Canada, Australia, and the USA. At the other end, one sees a correspondence for Greece and Italy—Spain being somewhat adrift of these by virtue of its very small service sector—and indeed Ireland in terms of the co-existence of low service sector employment and low female employment. There are, though, also exceptions. These are becoming familiar at this stage: Portugal and Finland, with their relatively small service sectors and still high female employment rates, are among the most noteworthy of these. Portugal is an interesting case in that the source of its uniqueness lies in the significance of both the primary and manufacturing sectors for women's employment (accounting for over one-third of it). Greece is the country that is closest to Portugal in terms of the significance of the agricultural sector for female employment but its manufacturing sector offers women far fewer opportunities than is the case in Portugal. The importance of both the agricultural and manufacturing sectors for female employment also accounts for Finland's exceptionalism. The Netherlands, with a smaller female employment ratio than might be expected given the size of its service sector, presents another form of exceptionalism. The story in this case is that men tend in the Netherlands to predominate in jobs and sectors (e.g. public administration) which are in most other countries associated with female employment. Overall though, it is interesting to observe that the Continental European nations are quite dispersed here and form no block in terms of the relation between the size of the service sector and female employment.

By way of overview, there is no doubt but that the sectoral location of jobs matters for women's employment. We have identified a fairly consistent relationship cross-nationally between the size of the service sector and female employment participation rates. Such a relationship is especially strong for the Scandinavian and liberal nations—high in both—and the Mediterranean nations together with Ireland—low in both. The variation exemplified by particular cases is quite interesting however. The exceptional cases, especially Portugal and to a lesser extent Finland, suggest that a large service sector is not essential for high female employment and that the agricultural and manufacturing sectors can go considerable distance in raising the female employment ratio. A second form of variation pertains to the source of the jobs within the service sector and in particular whether they originate in the public or private sectors. This tends to separate the Scandinavian from the liberal nations as we shall now see.

10.2.1.3. Public Sector Employment

The dominance of the Scandinavian model in studies of female employment has led to received wisdom in the field to the effect that a large public sector is essential for increasing the demand for female employment. If this were the case, one would expect strong covariation between female employment participation rates and the general prevalence of public employment. In other words, countries with high rates of public sector employment should have higher female employment rates than those with low public sector employment. Government employment will be used here as a proxy for public employment—although of course they are not identical—since information on the former is available on a more detailed and comparable basis than that on the latter.

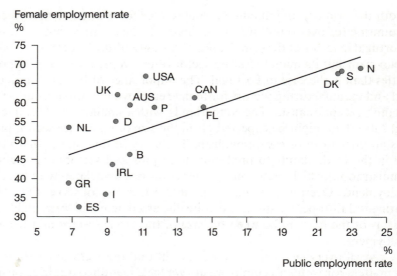

Figure 10.7 The public employment and female employment rates, 1996
Source: OECD 1997.

Figure 10.7 demonstrates how this relationship plays out across countries.

Of the different demand factors considered thus far, the size of the public sector has the least congruent relationship with the female employment ratio. The Scandinavian block, apart from Finland, is not only the most robust but is also the only real cluster. Here the health, education, and social work services as well as public administration are a major source of employment opportunities for women. Apart from the Scandinavian grouping, one has Belgium, Ireland, Greece, Italy, and Spain below the diagonal but in too loose a cluster to confirm any real link between the size of the public sector and women's employment. Another even looser block consists of a motley group of nations: Canada, Finland, and Portugal. In general, though, there are more exceptional than confirmatory country cases. Among the notable exceptions are the USA, UK, and Australia which have relatively high levels of female employment co-existing with a rather small public sector. Women in these countries tend to work in relatively large numbers in the wholesale and retail trades as well as in financial and business services. Hence, it is the private services sector that accounts for high female employment there. Overall the analysis suggests that the Scandinavian route of high public sector employment associated with high female employment is quite exceptional. It is also clear that there is one other route to high female employment as exemplified by countries like the USA, the UK, and Australia where high female employment is more attributable to the private services sector. It is important to point out that this difference may mean qualitative differences for women in terms of their employment, for public sector jobs tend among women to be better paid than private sector jobs (Rubery et al. 1999). Once again, the Continental European nations are quite dispersed.

Overall, the demand factors considered correspond moderately well with female employment ratios. There appears to be a systematic relation between the structure of employment, in particular the prevalence of part-time and service sector employment, and female employment rates. This relationship is particularly robust in the Scandinavian and Mediterranean nations where high or low female employment is associated consistently with variation in both the availability of part-time employment and of service sector employment. In general though, while it confirms this relationship, the analysis speaks against a singular understanding of the factors that shape the demand for female labor. In the liberal nations, it is the private services sector rather than the public sector that exerts the greater influence on female employment rates. In addition, there is no Continental European block in terms of the relationship between either part-time, service sector or public sector employment and the female employment ratio.

10.2.2. Supply-Oriented Explanations

In conventional labor market analysis, supply-side factors tend to be conceived of relatively narrowly, appearing often as human capital stock. Narrow conceptualizations of individual attributes are particularly inappropriate for understanding women's labor market presence for this is a phenomenon embedded in and shaped by, *inter alia*, family considerations and prevalent norms and beliefs. Socio-political traditions and values are the ultimate explanatory root here, the main form in which they find an expression as factors influencing women's ties to employment being social and economic policies. Conventional human capital factors are, therefore, not predictive of women's labor market participation in the same way as they are of that of men. Social and economic policies are especially crucial in the case of women.

While all policies have a potential to influence the labor supply of women, some domains of policy are more in the front line than others. Of primary significance are policies relating to the family, whether they aim to provide financial support or assistance in the form of services. Over time one can see a greater differentiation, even specialization, in family-related policies in developed welfare states, so much so that as an analytic category 'family policy' itself is declining in utility. Against this background, the concept of care has emerged in a literature that has sought to more consciously integrate family and gender into state/market analyses (Daly and Lewis 1998; Knijn and Kremer 1997). This approach spells a broadened frame of analysis, eschewing conventional policy definitions and boundaries to focus upon the political economy of all aspects of policies as they affect the labor and relations involved in caring for the young, the ill, and the elderly and in turn the position of women, the family, and gender relations. The change of analytic approach parallels a qualitative change in welfare state practice. Whereas in the past many activities were privatized to the family, welfare states are increasingly having to concern themselves with and adopt policies on the care of children and the elderly. In fact, this is one of the few growth areas in contemporary European welfare states (Daly 1997).

The increased statutory attention to the family and care has three implications for the type of analysis to be undertaken here. It means, first, that the range of policies to be considered should be broadened beyond what is usually thought of as family policy. Instead of just policies on families with children, the following analyses will also therefore consider how state policies treat caring for the elderly. Second, greater public interest in the care of children and the elderly has occasioned an increasing specialization in state policies in terms of the groups and behaviors which they target. Whereas the dominance of a male breadwinner model in the past made for a relatively uniform role for women as home and family workers, one expression of the modernization of this social model is a greater differentiation in how public policies treat women in particular types of family situation. This kind of a development provides in the present context the analytic opportunity to disaggregate 'women's employment' and investigate the effects of policies on particular groups of women. In this section, therefore, I will allow the dependent variable to vary, hypothesizing as appropriate about the likely effects of policies on the labor supply of particular groups of women. This has the double advantage of specifying further the constituent elements of female employment participation and reflecting the greater specificity in the approach taken to causality. Third, an integrated perspective means overcoming the customary analytic division between cash and services and treating both along with tax provisions as potential influences of female labor supply. Hence in the analyses to follow, policies on caring for children, those on the elderly, and the treatment for taxation purposes of a second earned income will be considered in turn. It should be noted that, as with all the explanatory factors considered, the intention is to focus upon those aspects that impact positively or negatively upon women's participation rate in a comparative context, rather than to provide a comprehensive outline of particular aspects of policy in detail.

10.2.2.1. Policies on Caring for Children

Welfare states have at their disposal a variety of instruments through which they can provide support for child-rearing and childcare-related activities. Kamerman and Kahn (1981), for instance, list nineteen possible policy interventions, ranging through cash allowances, different types of paid and unpaid leaves, social security credits, and services. In terms of the gender dimension of policies (and concomitantly the relations between the market, state, and family), what is of greatest significance is how policy envisions and supports female and male roles. The litmus test of social programs for the present purpose is whether or not they encourage and facilitate employment among mothers. To put this more precisely: public policies on childcare and family support are significant determinants of female labor supply to the extent that they encourage or discourage employment on the part of mothers.

Some types of policies and their constituent features are more telling than others in this regard. The dimensions of policy which I consider as crucial for women's labor market participation are the existence and coverage of childcare services and the existence of and conditions attaching to maternal and parental leaves and benefits. In regard to the latter, the duration and generosity of payment levels are especially important in determining whether women, indeed families, can afford to avail of them or not. If they are unpaid or low paid, they may involve too great a reduction in the family income. Hence one vital criterion with regard to leaves is the proportion which is paid at full pay. Table 10.1 summarizes this and other key features[5] of childcare-related social programs across nations.

It will be apparent that, while most if not all nations have policies on maternity, childcare, and parental leaves, the cross-national variation in the nature of the provisions is striking. There appear to be three general models in operation which could be said to differ from each other in terms

---

[5] It is important to emphasize that these rather general indicators miss some important aspects of variation within and across programs. Among the factors not picked up here are the duration of childcare (in terms of hours per day and up to what age the child is eligible to attend), the costs associated with it, the target group, the funders and providers, the ideological and historical origins of provision as well as the operating conditions (such as staff–child ratios, the content of the care, and so forth). See Kamerman (1991) for a good discussion of some of these factors from a comparative perspective. As regards maternity provisions, what is not considered here is the contribution made by the employer and the legal setting within which the leaves and benefits are granted. Parental leave is also a highly variable entity. What matters most in regard to it apart from the payment level is whether the leave has job guarantees and whether there is a mandatory component for one or both partners.

Table 10.1 *Childcare provision and maternity and parental leave policies in the early to mid-1990s*

	Children (0–3) in publicly funded childcare (%)	Children (3–6) in publicly funded childcare (%)	Paid maternity leave (weeks)	Consecutive weeks of maternity and parental leave	Equivalent weeks of all leave paid at 100%
Austria	3	75	16	112	48
Australia	2[a]	26[b]	12	52	n.a.
Belgium	30	95	15	41	16
Canada	5[a]	35[b]	15	15	n.a.
Denmark	48	82	18	28	21
Finland	21	53	17.5	45	29
France	23	99	16–26	162	14
Germany	2	85	14	162	32
Greece	3	70	16	46	16
Ireland	2	55	14	18	10
Italy	6	91	22	25	25
Luxembourg	2[a]	58[b]	16	n.a.	n.a.
Netherlands	8	71	16	42	16
Norway	31	72	18	94	42
Portugal	12	48	18	118	14
Spain	2	84	16	156	16
Sweden	33	72	12–24	64	43
United Kingdom	2	60	18	40	9
United States	1[a]	14[b]	6	6	n.a.

n.a. = information not available.

[a] Data pertain to children aged 0–2.
[b] Data pertain to children from 3 to school age.

Sources: Bettio and Prechal 1998; Gornick, Meyers, and Ross 1997.

of the degree of choice they offer women (Bettio and Prechal 1998). The first is found in the Scandinavian countries, Sweden and Denmark especially, and it is a strategy of variety. Cash benefits are relatively generous in these countries but so also are leaves and childcare services. The logic of policy seems to be to offer mothers the choice of being employed or not, with the emphasis on facilitating the former—mothers can take leave from the labor market for the purpose of caring for their children or they can remain in the labor market and utilize the relatively widespread public childcare services. The second strategy, found mainly in the Continental European countries, tends to privilege and promote maternal caring. These countries—especially Austria and Germany—offer the most generous provisions with regard to parental leaves and childcare services, while they exist and are widely used, operate mainly on a half-time basis. The orientation of this policy model seems to be to assist the family with, but not substitute for, private or family care. One should note, though, that there are differences among countries here with France quite close to the Scandinavian nations in offering fewer incentives for the mother to remain out of the labor market. In the third pattern, care is also privatized to the family but this occurs because the state provides no alternative. This is a pattern typifying both the Mediterranean countries and the liberal welfare states along with Ireland. Here women have limited choice: little if any paid parental leave exists and the public authorities provide almost no childcare facilities.[6] Hence the family and women are left to their own devices in deciding how to organize for labor market purposes.

If one classifies the different countries in terms of the extent to which their policy package offers women a choice,[7] Table 10.2 shows how they compare, together with the proportion of mothers of children aged under 10 years in each country in employment and of these the proportion in part-time employment.

In general, the orientation of the policy package is quite closely related to mothers' employment behavior. This is to be seen especially in how country groupings distinguish themselves from one another, although there are discrepant relationships or placings for a number of countries within groups and one must be careful here because several factors are involved. Judging from the experience of Scandinavia, it appears that when the policy package offers women a high degree of choice they choose to be in the labor market.[8] Note though that in Sweden especially more

---

[6] What remains unclear is the extent to which childcare services are available on a private (commercial or other) basis. Paid informal and formal care is known to be important in the liberal welfare states and indeed is encouraged in countries where tax reductions are granted for childcare (e.g. the US and more recently Britain). However, no comparable cross-national information exists on the extent of either formal or informal paid or unpaid care. Note though that the publicly-funded services in Table 10.1 are defined as services that are funded at least 75% from public sources.

[7] This is a rather loose classification not least because the different programs cannot be weighted in the same manner. Some of these individual programs have a number of objectives that may not always be congruent with one another. Similarly, the different programs within a welfare state do not always sit well with one another and may even be contradictory. Hence, for example, maternity leave is generally regarded as a provision that enhances the labor market rights of women whereas parental leaves may actually, and are sometimes introduced so as to, discourage women's employment. It is for these kinds of reasons that the three indicators of the proportion of children 0–3 and 3–6 that are catered for in public provision and the equivalent weeks of all leave that are paid at 100% are combined to yield an evaluation of the orientation of policy towards employment on the part of mothers.

[8] Although it should be noted that in Sweden more mothers work part-time than full-time, a point of import in view of the earlier discussion. Belgium and Denmark also tend to have relatively high levels of part-time employment among mothers.

Table 10.2 *Classification of countries on the basis of the degree to which public policies offer a degree of choice to mothers about employment and the proportion of mothers employed in the early 1990s*

	Thrust of policy (degree of choice)	Employment rate of mothers with child aged 0–10 (%)	% of these part-time
Sweden	High	76	53
Denmark	High	74	35
Finland	High	65	15
Norway (1991)*	High	62	n.a.
France	Moderate	60	33
Belgium	Moderate	62	40
Austria	Moderate	64	38
Germany	Moderate	51	n.a.
Netherlands	Moderate	47	87
Australia (1989)*	Low	49	63
Canada (1991)*	Low	61	38
Greece	Low	43	5
Ireland	Low	35	30
Italy	Low	43	12
Luxembourg	Low	42	33
Portugal	Low	71	11
Spain	Low	36	14
United Kingdom	Low	52	65
United States (1991)*	Low	55	32

n.a. = information not available.

Notes: Data are from the European Commission (1997: table 16) and Rubery et al. (1996: fig. 6.1.2) and pertain to 1993 unless marked with an asterisk (*). In the latter case they are from Gornick (1999) and pertain to married mothers between 20 and 59, who have children under 6 and to the year as indicated in brackets after the country's name. For Austria the information is for mothers with children under 15; for Sweden it is for mothers with children under 7 years.

Sources: Bettio and Prechal 1998; European Commission 1997; Gornick, Meyers, and Ross 1997; Gornick 1999.

than half of all employed mothers work only on a part-time basis. Looking further, medium levels of public policy support for maternal employment also appear to have the desired effect. These countries are not always consistent in their approach to maternal employment but they tend to opt for a set of policies that enable (or entice) mothers to be out of the labor market through relatively generous sets of leaves and so on. In France, Germany, and the Netherlands, moderate levels of provision are associated with medium levels of maternal employment. A considerable proportion of these employed mothers work on a part-time basis and in the Netherlands 90 percent are part-time. Low levels of choice are also associated with the expected pattern of maternal employment. However, at least part of the constraint on mothers' employment in Greece, Ireland, Italy, Luxembourg, and Spain is the general low availability of part-time employment.

There are some seemingly exceptional cases also. Perhaps the most striking exceptional group of countries comprises the liberal nations, in particular Canada, the UK, and USA, where mothers' labor force participation is either high or moderate despite a low degree of support from public policies. These might not be as exceptional as they seem though for when they are put together with the other cases the following general explanation of the relation between maternal employment and public policy suggests itself. The employment of mothers depends primarily on the availability of childcare facilities. These can be and sometimes are provided free of charge or subsidized by public facilities (as in Scandinavia). Alternatively, they can be provided by low-cost private facilities. However the existence of the latter is contingent upon low wages and low non-wage labor costs. This is essentially the liberal model. In the Continental European nations, which emerge here as constituting a grouping in their own right, the provision of public facilities is limited but low wage differentials and high non-wage labor costs increase the price of childcare. Hence labor market participation on the part of mothers in these countries is on the low side. It will be obvious that this explanation is relevant also to the demand side for particular constellations of public policies can and do act also to affect the demand for female labor.

So mothers' employment rates cannot be read off as a function of public policies' treatment of families with children. They are shaped by a more complex mix, drawing also upon market factors such as the character of the service sector, wage rates and differentials and non-wage costs. In any case, child-related policies have many objectives and are perhaps better understood as being about balancing a series of aims rather than solely about facilitating maternal employment. The reconciliation of work and family life typically sits alongside other concerns such as the education and welfare of children, the well-being of families, and the balancing of public and private responsibilities more generally. With such a broad range of objectives, the room for ambiguity, contradictions, and perverse effects is large. In the event, family policy in general and policies oriented to the care of children in particular are nowhere unambiguously interpretable as having the support of maternal employment as their primary objective. There is therefore no unidimensional interpretation to these and other policy domains and it is important not to generalize too readily from the Scandinavian model.

A second domain of public policy which may be assumed to affect the supply of female labor is policies on the care of the elderly.

10.2.2.2. Policies on Care of the Elderly

The exigency of having to care for an elderly relative or for adults who are incapacitated or ill is another factor likely to affect labor supply. While men also have caring obligations, as a factor influencing labor supply it is women who are especially affected by family-related responsibilities. The relationship between this type of family responsibility and the labor force participation of women has hardly been investigated. And yet this is a relation that can no longer be ignored because providing for the care of the elderly is proving increasingly problematic and is a domain that is catching the attention of policymakers to an increasing degree. The demographic stretching of the population and the burden placed by greater longevity on the public purse render the care of elderly and ill relatives an extremely important consideration, for individuals, families, states, and societies. Similar to the case of caring for children, women's capacity to participate in the labor market is enhanced to the degree that the state is prepared to provide or subsidize services that assist with or substitute for their private labor. Obviously, caring obligations or demands in relation to the elderly tend to be cohort-specific. Demographic patterns are now such that it is in the middle to late years of the working life that these caring responsibilities are most likely to take effect. One can therefore anticipate that, to the extent that public policies on caring for the elderly have an affect on female labor supply, it should be on the labor force participation rate of women aged between 50 and 64 years.

Three indicators serve to reveal the extent to which public policies support caring for the elderly: expenditure on services for the elderly and disabled as a proportion of GDP; the proportion of the elderly (65 years and over) in residential care; and the proportion of the same age group receiving home help services. Table 10.3 presents this information for the different countries. It shows that, as was the case with children, provision can be divided into three variants. The high and generous providers are the Scandinavian countries and they emerge once again as multiple option countries, providing a range of services and cash benefits. The second grouping of countries, the medium providers, favors the provision of income over services, whereas the third, as the label 'low providers' suggests, basically provides few alternatives to and at the same time little support of private care.

In an attempt to summarize a complex picture, Figure 10.8 shows how those fourteen nations for which full information exists[9] compare on

---

[9] Australia, Canada, Greece, Norway, and the USA are missing from Fig. 10.8.

Table 10.3 *Public and private mandatory expenditures on services for the elderly and disabled persons as percentage of GDP in 1995, the proportion of elderly people in residential care or in receipt of home help services in 1990/1991 and the activity rate of women aged 50 years and over in 1996*

	% of GDP on services	Elderly in residential care (%)	Elderly receiving home assistance (%)	Activity rate of women aged 50 and over (%)
Austria	0.36	4.6	3	27.8
Australia	0.35	6.2	7	26.9
Belgium	0.15	5.2	6	n.a.
Canada	n.a.	7.1	2	35.3
Denmark	3.10	5.2	17	n.a.
Germany	0.58	5.4	1–3	10.5
Greece	n.a.	0.5	n.a.	n.a.
Finland	1.69	7.0	24	19.8
France	0.78	5.0	7	22.8
Ireland	0.48	5.0	3	16.6
Italy	0.20	2.4	1	26.0
Luxembourg	0.46	7.4	n.a.	16.9
Netherlands	0.67	9.1	8	16.6
Norway	3.58	6.8	14	16.6
Portugal	0.23	2.0	1	11.6
Spain	0.26	2.4	2	9.9
Sweden	3.37	5.3	13	27.3
United Kingdom	0.68	5.1	13	12.8
United States	0.05	5.2	4	n.a.

n.a. = information not available.

Sources: OECD 1996, 1998*b*; EUROSTAT 1997: table 003.

expenditure on services for the elderly and disabled and the economic activity rate of women aged 50 and over. There is it must be said relatively little variation on the expenditure variable apart from the Scandinavian countries. This militates against the emergence of a clear causal pattern. Once again one finds that the relationship is at its most consistent for the Scandinavian countries. These are virtually unique in the developed world in terms of the scale of effort they make to provide services for the elderly (and indeed in the degree of congruence between their policies on care for children and that for the elderly). Service provision, both of a residential nature and in the community, is the norm and the model of service provision that prevails is one of public services. These are the only nations to score consistently 'high' when it comes to provision and, as a glance at Figure 10.8 shows, Sweden and Denmark, and to a lesser extent Finland,

tower over all other nations in this regard and also in the extent of labor
force participation of older women. But causality is as ever problematic
and it is readily admitted that other factors, such as pension entitlements,
early retirement, and labor market policies in general, complicate the relationship. The moderately extensive providers of services for the elderly are
by and large a European grouping (France, Germany,[10] the Netherlands,
and the UK). In these countries the level of service provision and the activity rate of older women covary, with the UK as the main exceptions (a high
activity rate in the context of low expenditure). Huddled together at the
low end of service provision are all the Mediterranean nations as well as
Austria, Belgium, Ireland, and Luxembourg. In these countries, expenditure on and the availability of services for the elderly are such that quite a
large 'private' investment, especially in the form of caring in the home on
the part of women, is customary. However, this is the grouping of countries where the relationship between service provision and the extent of
labor force participation among older women is least consistent. Only in
Austria and Ireland is the relationship anyway close. Portugal is once
again the most outstanding outlier.

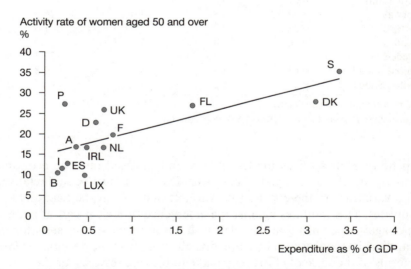

Figure 10.8 Expenditure on services for elderly and disabled people as a percentage of GDP and the activity rate of women aged 50 and over in 1996
Source: OECD 1998*b*; EUROSTAT 1997: table 003.

---

[10] Note that these data will not reflect the effects of the long-term care insurance introduced in Germany in 1996.

Overall, there is only moderate to low support for the expectation that the extent of labor force participation of women in the later phases of the life course is related to the degree of support which welfare states give to the care of the elderly. It would appear that this is a complicated relationship—it is also one that is difficult to identify precisely, mainly because of the inextricability of the effects of this and other factors.

A further factor to be considered for its relationship to women's labor supply is taxation, and in particular the treatment of the income of the second earner.

10.2.2.3. Taxation Policy and the Treatment of Spousal Earnings

When it comes to female labor supply, the most important elements of taxation arrangements reside in the treatment of spousal incomes. What matter especially in this regard are the unit for taxation purposes, the tax allowances for spouses or partners, and how these allowances alter if the second partner has income. In the past taxation systems privileged quite deliberately the one-earner household. This is less common nowadays and to the extent that one can identify a general trend it is in the direction of individualized taxation for spouses or partners. In some ways therefore, the incentives and disincentives around employment on the part of the spouse or partner are now more hidden.

Taxation policies on spouses' incomes speak to the division of labor between husbands and wives, and are relatively insensitive to the presence of children in the family. In other words, it is the labor supply of married women that is targeted by the treatment for taxation purposes of the second income. In order to test for these effects, then, attention should be directed at the labor force participation rates of married women. A likely hypothetical relation could be stated as follows: to the extent that the tax system in general, and the treatment of spousal incomes in particular, is a factor affecting women's labor supply, it will be manifested in the labor force participation rates of married women.

Table 10.4 arrays some relevant features of the tax structure. It also identifies how these and other aspects of taxation arrangements affect the incomes of people by considering the average differential between the tax paid by one-earner couples with two children with that of a single person.[11] On the basis of these data, Table 10.5 presents a classification of the different national taxation systems on their general approach to earned income on the part of the second spouse together with the participation rates of married women. Note though that since this is based on data for

[11] Based on the socio-economic group identified by reference to the average gross earnings from employment of all adult, full-time production workers in the manufacturing sector as carried out by the OECD for 1994.

Table 10.4 *Personal income taxation provisions as of the early 1990s*

	Unit of taxation	Relief for married individuals	Excess of tax paid by single person as compared with a single-earner couple with 2 children as % of gross earnings (1994)*
Australia	Individual	n.a.	1.1
Austria	Individual	Allowance	5.6
Belgium	Splitting	Both spouses receive married person's allowance	12.0
Canada	Individual	n.a.	10.7
Denmark	Individual	Allowance (transferable)	8.4
Finland	Individual	No relief	0.0
France	Family quotient	Income splitting	6.9
Germany	Splitting	Income splitting	10.5
Greece	Individual	Allowance	1.2 (1993)
Ireland	Aggregation	Allowance but individual taxation option also	7.6
Italy	Individual	Allowance	3.7
Luxembourg	Family quotient	Income splitting	n.a.
Netherlands	Individual	Allowance (transferable)	2.7
Norway	Individual	n.a.	4.9
Portugal	Aggregation	Allowance but individual taxation option also	3.5
Spain	Aggregation	Allowance but individual taxation option also	6.8
Sweden	Individual	No relief	0.0
United Kingdom	Individual	Allowance (husband only)	2.4
United States	Individual	n.a.	6.9

*Calculated at the income level of an APW (average production worker).

n.a. = information not available.

Notes: Aggregation: Household taxation is based on the aggregation of the income of married couples.
Splitting: The aggregated income of married couples is divided into two.
Family quotient: Aggregation includes children's income; aggregated income is divided by family quotient which includes an allowance for children.

Sources: European Commission 1997; Lelièvre and Gauthier 1995; OECD 1995; Rubery et al. 1999.

Table 10.5 *Orientation of income tax system and labor force participation rates of married women, 1996*

	Orientation of income tax system toward employment of married women	Participation rate of married women (%)
Australia	Encouraging	n.a.
Finland	Encouraging	62.6
Greece	Encouraging	39.3
Sweden	Encouraging	65.7
Austria	Neutral	51.7
Italy	Neutral	35.7
Netherlands	Neutral	47.0
Norway	Neutral	n.a.
Portugal	Neutral	56.5
United Kingdom	Neutral	57.3
Belgium	Discouraging	45.9
Canada	Discouraging	n.a.
Denmark	Discouraging	63.0
France	Discouraging	53.3
Germany	Discouraging	51.3
Luxembourg	Discouraging	35.7
Ireland	Discouraging	41.0
Spain	Discouraging	35.3
United States	Discouraging	n.a.

n.a. = information not available.

Notes: Countries are classified only on the basis of the gap in tax paid between a one-earner couple and single person (as presented in Table 10.4). They are classified as encouraging if the difference is 2% or less, as neutral if the difference is higher than 2% and less than 6% and as discouraging if the gap is 6% or more.

Sources: European Commission 1997; Lelièvre and Gauthier 1995; OECD 1995; Rubery et al. 1996; EUROSTAT 1997: table 004.

two-earner couples with children—the only known comparative data available—the effects of tax reliefs for children are reflected here for those three countries which in 1994 granted such reliefs (Germany, Ireland, and the USA).

It is first interesting to observe how traditional tax systems remain in their approach to the earnings of the second partner. Only four countries could be said to encourage through their tax system employment on the part of the second partner—Australia, Finland, Greece, and Sweden. In general, national taxation systems tend to be either neutral in regard to earnings on the part of the second partner or to penalize them. With what effect? The relationships between the orientation of the tax system to income of married couples as against that of a single person and married women's labor force participation rates are weaker than those found for public policies on caring for children and the elderly. In only half of all cases (although a majority of those where complete information exists) is there a congruent relationship between the two. The congruence is strongest for countries with tax systems that encourage participation—the Scandinavian countries along with Australia. Among the remaining countries, the level of support in the taxation system and the extent of married women's participation in the labor force are congruent for Austria, Portugal and the UK (moderate in all), and Luxembourg, Ireland and Spain (low in all).

Vermeulen et al. (1995), who considered the effects of the taxation system on married women's labor force participation in seven countries, conclude that there is a lack of perfect correspondence between how taxation systems treat married women's employment and the extent to which such women are active in the labor market. As they rightly point out, the effect of taxation systems overall on married women's employment is difficult to identify, depending on the magnitude of each component's effect and the interaction between effects. The interaction between the taxation and social security systems also needs to be taken into account. The consensus of opinion would appear to be that taxation as a factor affecting women's labor supply cannot be taken alone. However the data on taxation arrangements do contribute towards an explanation of the patterns in some countries. In the light of the above information, taxation incentives may also contribute towards an explanation for the participation rate of Portuguese and British women which appeared to be independent of the level of public support for child and elderly care. Taxation incentives are very likely to play a role in encouraging women in these countries to be in the labor market.

Overall, both congruence and exceptionalism are to be found in the relationship between the labor force participation of different groups of women and public policies on caring for children, the elderly and taxation. Of the different factors considered, childcare policies appear to have the most consistent relation with female labor supply. There may well be two relations at work here: first that the employment patterns of mothers are signally conditioned by childcare policy and provision and second that the employment patterns of mothers have a huge impact on the employment behavior of women in general. The nature of public policies on support for the elderly is also quite important. Looked at in terms of country cases, the policy logic and its effect on the labor supply of women is most easily explained in the Scandinavian countries. One of the most interesting aspects of the Scandinavian countries is the consistency of policy across domains. In other parts of the developed world, public policy is informed by neither so clear nor so consistent a logic. This alerts us to some lack of correspondence between different elements of public policy and between female labor supply and policy provisions in general. It may also, of course, be the case that the factors which I have considered here in isolation have an interactive effect.

In effect, the understanding of women's labor market participation and both the demand and supply factors that influence it have to be revisited.

10.3. Towards an Explanation

Starting with the *explanandum*, it has been emphasized on a number of occasions throughout this chapter that female participation in employment is a complex phenomenon. For one, absolute participation rates are misleading about the extent of women's involvement in the labor force because of the large variation in the hours actually worked. Second, there is the matter of the duration of or continuity in female participation and the need to recognize that women's employment careers are typically of an interrupted character. Only when these two dimensions are related to each other can one achieve a realistic characterization of the phenomenon of female employment participation. To more accurately approach the extent of participation, I utilize full-time equivalent participation rates. This information is available on a comprehensive basis for the Member States of the EU for 1996 (European Commission 1999) but has to be estimated for the four non-EU countries included here.[12] Data shortages prevent us from standardizing for continuity of participation. However, one can approach continuity in a general way by taking the proportion of mothers with children under 10 who are in the labor force (as an, admittedly loose, indicator of the extent to which mothers interrupt their employment career).[13] If one plots the two general variables of extent and continuity of participation, one arrives at what can be called a set of female labor

---

[12] It is estimated on the basis of the general form of the relationship between the total female employment rate and the proportion of female employment that is part-time.

[13] Ideally, continuity should be measured by the number and duration of employment interruptions over the course of the work career. This data is not available however. See Kempeneers and Lelièvre (1991) for this information for the, then twelve, EU Member States in the late 1980s. In the absence of this type of detailed information for all the countries, it was decided to utilize the employment rates of mothers with children under 10 as a proxy. The resultant placings of countries in the four quadrants appear to be robust. I did a modest amount of experimentation with other variables, such as the employment rate of mothers of very young children. The distribution of countries to quadrants did not significantly alter, although in some cases there was variation in where countries were placed within quadrants. The data used in Fig. 10.9 for the EU countries are for 1993 and those for the four other countries are from Gornick (1999). See notes for Table 10.2.

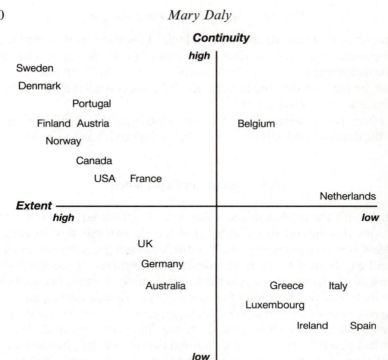

Figure 10.9 Female labor profiles in a cross-national context on the basis of the
continuity and extent of labor force participation

profiles. The following are the profiles together with their cross-national
distribution.

First, there are countries where both participation rates and continuity
tend to be high. This is clearly the most common profile among the developed economies, since it is the quadrant with the largest number (nine) of
countries. There are a number of sub-groupings of countries here though.
Of the clusters I have worked with to date, only the Scandinavian cluster
remains solid. One should note, though, that there are some differences
among the Nordic nations in terms of the actual extent of female labor
force participation and its degree of continuity. Norway is somewhat different from Sweden and Denmark by virtue of its lower extent and more
interrupted pattern of female labor force participation. Portugal is probably the most surprising placing—as a Mediterranean nation it stands
apart from its neighbors with its high level and mostly continuous pattern
of female employment. Also to be found here are the USA and Canada,
both countries where the level of female labor force participation is relatively high but continuity is compromised. Austria and France are also

placed in this cluster although in France both the continuity and extent of female employment tend towards the moderate rather than the high end. In general though, women in all these countries have a firm and fairly continuous attachment to the labor force throughout their life cycle, taking long breaks for child-rearing only in exceptional cases.

The second pattern is of a lower extent (mainly because of a higher volume of part-time work) and a more interrupted pattern of employment. The UK, Germany, and Australia approximate this pattern. Although absolute participation rates are on the high side, the real extent of women's labor force participation in these countries is lowered by the fact that up to 40 percent of all female employment is part-time. Australia and the UK are very close in this regard. Germany fits less well mainly because it has a lower volume of part-time work than the other two nations but its female labor profile in terms of extent and continuity draws it closer to these nations than to any other.

The third pattern is for moderate to high continuity but a lowish level of female participation. The Netherlands and Belgium are the two nations characterized by this pattern. While the two are similar, the Netherlands is set apart by its high volume of part-time work which makes absolute participation rates quite misleading. In fact, Dutch women have a very constrained pattern of labor force participation. In Belgium both the extent and degree of continuity in women's labor force participation are higher than in the Netherlands but in a more general comparison Belgium has a lowish extent of female employment.

The fourth pattern is low on both extent and continuity. This is the most traditional pattern of all—women in Greece, Ireland, Italy, Luxembourg, and Spain have a low extent and continuity of employment. Women in Ireland and Luxembourg tend to drop out of the labor market once they have their first child. In the past this was a more or less permanent exit from paid employment but for younger cohorts of women the birth of children is more likely to spell an interruption in employment rather than a permanent break. Recourse to part-time work in both of these countries is low. The Mediterranean countries, however, tend to have a bipolar female employment pattern. Most women, both mothers and non-mothers, are not active at all in the labor force but, on the other hand, those who are active, even mothers of young children, tend to follow a full-time pattern. There is almost no part-time work in these economies.

If one relates this patterning to what we know about variation in the factors affecting demand and supply, one of the most striking points to emerge is that different combinations of factors are associated with the same outcomes in female labor market participation. Just in the first quadrant alone there is represented almost every variant of policy and labor market structure. The presence of some countries here is more easily explained than that of others. The Scandinavian story, for example, seems most straightforward. Women's labor supply is high and relatively continuous because it is facilitated by policies that at one and the same time create opportunities in the labor market and recognize the special needs of women as workers, providing them and families with a number of options for managing family-related exigencies. Such social policies are complemented by labor market, wage, and taxation arrangements that are consistent in operating to a two-breadwinner logic. The explanation of outcomes in the USA and Canada is not so neat. If anything it seems to be demand factors which make the difference in that these countries have a large service sector and moderate levels of part-time employment. What they do not have, nor does Portugal, is a public policy framework that is highly supportive of female employment. What these three countries share, though, is that they are societies where women have to work: none is a high male breadwinner economy and in the absence of generous social protection a second income is needed. It seems, then, that women in these countries work despite the lack of a supportive infrastructure and that arrangements for the reconciliation of home and work which the Scandinavian welfare states tend to collectivize are actually private solutions in these nations. When one bears in mind that there are two continental European nations—Austria and France— located in this quadrant also, it is striking how quite different policy packages appear to be the functional equivalent of one another. So what the Scandinavian welfare states bring about through massive public expenditure, America, Canada, and Portugal achieve with modest social spending. However, the nuances and tradeoffs involved in policies are important. What seems clear is that the Scandinavian package allows women a high continuity in employment but the high prevalence of part-time work in all except Finland makes for a reduced female presence in the labor market. The tradeoff involved for women in the American and Canadian settings is in the continuity of their labor force participation. They can have a high level of involvement in the labor market but must interrupt this for child-bearing and sometimes child-rearing. Portugal and Finland are very interesting cases because they appear to have no such tradeoffs (at least not on the dimensions that have been considered in this analysis). What seems to draw all of these countries together, though, is the extent to which women have to be employed. On a continuum of choice or constraint in female employment, these are all nations where women are constrained to be in employment, whether for financial reasons as in the USA, Canada, France, and Portugal, or for what one might call 'just society' reasons in Scandinavia.

The composition of the second quadrant—UK, Australia, and Germany—is also challenging to both existing explanations and existing clusters of countries. Both the UK and Australia are countries with a considerable availability of part-time and service sector employment but relatively little public policy supports for female employment. These are not generous welfare states by any means and there is little tradition in these countries of public provision of child-related services. And yet women in these countries manage to maintain relatively high, if rather discontinuous, employment levels. The experience of these countries suggests that the availability of part-time work and a large service sector—in other words high demand—can compensate for the lack of a public support infrastructure. The placing of Germany side by side with these countries reveals another strand to the story of women's relationship to the labor market. The moderate extent and continuity of women's labor supply is very consistent with the configuration of public policies that favors what would today be called a traditional view of marriage. German policies, while they are prepared to support family-based caring, are not willing to supplant it. This makes for practices like half-day childcare facilities and very generous parental leaves. Mothers in this country can work only to the extent that the availability of part-time work and public services allows it.

In some ways Germany has a lot in common with Belgium and the Netherlands, the countries forming the third pattern, especially in terms of the public policy profile. These are also welfare states that are moderately supportive of female employment. Of the two, however, the public infrastructure for the care of children is more wide-ranging and generous in Belgium. Hence Belgian women have a greater chance of being in the labor market than their Dutch counterparts. What gives women the chance of employment in the Netherlands is the high availability of part-time work. As a glance at Figures 10.2 and 10.3 shows, increases in Dutch women's participation in the labor market are very closely related to the growth of part-time work. This is not a country that compares easily with others though. While part-time work allows Dutch women access to employment, one should note that rather high absolute participation rates conceal the second lowest, apart from Spain, extent of female involvement in the market.

The clustering of nations in the fourth grouping—Greece, Ireland, Italy, Luxembourg, and Spain—is the most consistent of all. Notwithstanding some small differences among them, on almost all of the independent variables considered here these countries were similarly placed. The explanation of their particular female labor profile is similar to that for the Scandinavian nations, except in these countries it is the absence of demand and supply factors that makes the difference. They are, for example, nations with a low volume of part-time and service sector employment. The level of caring-related public services is low and the taxation provisions, apart from Italy, are either neutral to or discouraging of employment on the part of the spouse. So neither the demand nor the supply side is right in these countries for large-scale and continuous labor force participation on the part of women.

A number of general insights flow from these patterns. A first is that when it comes to women's labor profile countries do not conform in any simplistic way to existing wisdom about types or systems. True, there are four general types of arrangement but these contain some countries which (1) are generally understood to be very different from each other and (2) are usually grouped with other countries. It would appear, then, that women's labor market participation invokes some new dimensions of national economic and social configurations. Such new dimensions derive, in part anyway, from adding the family to the market-state configuration. The second general insight concerns the role of demand- and supply-related factors. It is easier to identify the impact of supply than demand factors. Supply factors emerge as especially crucial for the continuity of women's employment. Those nations in the two lower segments of Figure 10.9 for example are all nations where neither public services nor taxation arrangements are particularly supportive of women's employment. The effects of demand factors alone as well as those of their interaction with supply factors are more difficult to identify. In some countries—especially the USA, and Canada—demand factors alone appear to make the significant difference. However, in other cases it appears to be the interaction of demand and supply factors that exerts the defining influence on women's labor profile. This seems to be the Scandinavian story and it is an explanation that also fits the French and Austrian cases. But there is no identifiable essential relationship between demand and supply factors and the female labor profile. This leads us to a further but related general insight about functional equivalents. The fact that the same factors are not always present in countries that have similar outcomes suggests that in certain settings one acts as the functional equivalent of another. There is no evidence to assert the causal primacy of any one factor and it is most likely that a satisfactory explanatory frame would embrace not just the factors treated individually here but their interactive effects as well. Fourth, there is the significance of nuances and what in other cases may appear as small-scale variations in labor profile and in policy. A variation of 10 percentage points in female participation rates from one country to another can make the difference between one being a traditional model and the other a non-traditional model. And at the micro-level such a difference spells a huge impact on how women conduct their lives and manage their roles and relations.

10.4. Overview

The standard procedures and concepts for studying labor force and employment participation are less than satisfactory for the purpose of identifying women's relationship to the labor market. Women tend to occupy and move between a range of economic situations at different stages of the life cycle. Hence the conventional rather static perspective of employment advancement as regular and progressive is inappropriate. The analyses undertaken here suggest the need to integrate particular clarifications into the conceptualization and measurement of women's participation in employment. One such clarification is to utilize full-time equivalent rather than absolute participation rates and a second involves integrating into the analysis a measure of continuity/discontinuity in employment participation. In this chapter I have sought not only to utilize these two dimensions to trace female labor profiles across nations but to interrogate the link in a comparative fashion between women's labor force participation and a series of factors typically assumed to be predictive of female labor demand and supply. Although the available information does not allow one to do this on a complete basis, it is possible to identify systematic patterning. Four types of profile, and by implication groupings of countries, emerge.

The first profile is of a high extent and high continuity of female employment. This is the single most common pattern among the nineteen countries studied. A comparatively high and uninterrupted female employment pattern draws together a rather motley group of countries, however, including the Scandinavian nations along with Austria, Canada, France, Portugal, and the USA. The second profile is of a highish extent but low continuity in employment. Women in the nations typified, the UK, Australia, and Germany, are forced to interrupt their employment at least for a period when they have children. Belgium and the Netherlands, as countries with moderate or low female employment rates and high to moderate continuity, comprise the third profile. In these countries part-time work offers women the chance to be in the labor market when they have children, and therefore makes for more continuity in employment than would otherwise be possible. The fourth pattern, which is characterized by a low extent and relatively discontinuous employment, is to be found in the Mediterranean countries of Greece, Italy, and Spain as well as Ireland and Luxembourg. The overall picture in these countries, some internal and cross-national variations notwithstanding, is of women exiting from employment when they have children.

Causally, some factors stand out as being more important than others. On the one hand, the state's support of caring, and to a lesser extent how taxation provisions construct the household as a one- or more breadwinner entity, appear to be fairly strong determinants of the extent to which and how continuously women are economically active. Among these factors the influence of the provisions for families with children and the support for child-rearing, whether in the form of services, leaves, or cash, dominates. On the demand side, the structure of the labor market, especially the extent of part-time and service sector employment, also exerts significant influence on the form of the female labor profile. To the extent that one can identify general patterns of causality three stand out. First, the most widespread situation is where both demand and supply factors are consistent. This is the case in quite a number of countries, including the Scandinavian nations and Greece, Ireland, Italy, Luxembourg, and Spain. In these nations women get a generally clear message: either the public authorities, in terms of their provisions and the extent to which and how they manage the organization of the labor market, facilitate women's involvement in the labor market or they render it difficult. The essential analytical point is that it is not just the content of the policy or set of provisions that matters but also the consistency. By implication one could suggest that the reason why the Continental European nations do not have high female employment is because their policy packages are inconsistent. Second, it appears to be the case that supply factors, in particular the availability of care-related services, affect especially the continuity of women's employment. All of the countries in the two lower quadrants of Figure 10.9, while they have very different kinds of labor markets, share a poor family-related infrastructure. Third, demand factors, conceived of here in terms of the three labor market characteristics mentioned above, appear to be sufficient on their own, at least in the USA and Canada, to draw forth a strong presence of women in the labor market. However given some exceptional cases, especially Portugal, one cannot make statements to the effect that either or both is a sufficient or necessary condition for female labor market participation. If one focuses on the countries where both the extent and continuity of participation are on the high side— Austria, Canada, Denmark, Finland, France, Portugal, Norway, Sweden, USA—it is plausible to suggest a functional equivalent argument. In concrete terms this is to say that in Canada and the USA the private and in particular market sphere acts in some way as the functional equivalent of public services in Scandinavia. While obviously there are differences, not least perhaps in the access to, cost and conditions of the services, the larger point is that there is more than one (the Scandinavian route) to high female employment.

The sets of countries identified conform less than perfectly with existing clusters, either those emanating from conventional or feminist scholarship. This may be because women's labor profile has been peripheral for much of the comparative regime-oriented work. But more than this, it seems that working with the female employment variables we have here serves to uncover new dimensions of national systems. Such dimensions relate to key aspects of gender equality and more widely connote a set of family/employment relations. How else is one to explain the compromised nature of women's labor profile across the developed world. One would at one's peril take women's participation in employment as evidence of gender equality. With the possible exceptions of Finland and to a lesser extent Portugal, absolute participation rates conceal the fact that there are trade-offs involved for women and families in the panoply of employment/family arrangements to be found in the world's most developed nations. In some cases it is the extent of women's labor market participation that is compromised, in others it is its continuity. Trends over time suggest that, when it comes to women's labor market participation, modernization involves adaptation rather than radical change. The meaning of modernization for women may be greater part-time work, an easier shift between part- and full-time work or shorter interruptions of employment for child-related purposes. But almost nowhere does it involve women adopting the typical male pattern. Moreover, trends over time are ambivalent on convergence. True, women's absolute participation rates are climbing or have recently risen but both the clustering of countries and the distances between them and other sets of countries have remained solid. It is as Rubery et al. (1999: 3) point out: the integration of women into the labor market has been associated as much with the maintenance and reinforcement of difference—differences across nations and within them between women and men—as with processes of convergence and equality.

I should draw attention, though, to the particularities of the approach that I adopted here. Not alone have I used an approach that relies on an artificial separation of factors affecting the supply of and demand for female labor but not all possible supply and demand factors have been considered. Because of data unavailability and also in an effort to keep the analysis as manageable as possible, I did not consider, for example, the effects of human capital factors, or of variations in general cultural practices and national value systems. Furthermore, changing patterns of economic activity among women are associated with important demographic and social changes. Reduced fertility rates, an aging population, smaller and different kinds of households, and welfare states that are in the process of modernizing are all being influenced by and influencing the way in which women and men participate in economic life.

In the light of this, one wonders about the extent to which these and other possible influences on the level of female labor force participation

are best captured by more embracing characterizations, through for example the concept of regime. This concept has been implicit in much of this
chapter. So many of the factors considered in this analysis as independent
variables are co-varying that it is practically impossible to say what makes
the difference. It may also be hard to justify treating factors in isolation.
This suggests the benefit of using indicators that encompass a range of
factors. In effect, it does appear as if one is talking about models of
society/public policy rather than individual practices and institutions.
There are also methodological issues. A comprehensive understanding of
women's labor force participation depends as much upon an analysis of
particular cases as it does on the type of large-scale, cross-national analysis undertaken here. The existence of some interesting exceptional cases
suggests the merits of a case study approach. Patterns in Portugal defy
many if not all of the conventional explanatory frameworks and they have
served to challenge at key points the analyses undertaken in this chapter.
It along with the USA and Canada are cases deserving to be studied in
their own right. A case study methodology would also be a welcome complement to the approach adopted here.

It is interesting to ponder the implications of recent developments.
There is clearly a movement of women into the labor force. Moreover, the
extent to which the broad pattern is one of continuity of a long-run trend
lends a certain permanence to the presence of women in the labor market.
A gender analysis makes it clear that women's employment is embedded in
wider social process, involving changes along such dimensions as family,
labor market, public policy. To put it somewhat differently, it is not a phenomenon that can be explained only at micro-level. Moreover, it seems to
be clear that while changing patterns of labor demand may have in the past
been the instigator of increased female employment, the dynamic towards
women's integration into the labor market is over time becoming less
dependent on the level of labor demand (Rubery et al. 1999: 13). In addition, while current developments may have favored a growth in female
employment—by creating jobs that are more flexible and often low-paid—
the next stage of economic development, which will almost certainly render public sector and routine non-manual employment vulnerable, may be
less favorable to the expansion of female employment.

REFERENCES

BETTIO, FRANCESCA, and PRECHAL, SACHA (1998). *Care in Europe*. Brussels:
European Commission, Joint Report of the 'Gender and Employment' and the
'Gender and Law' Groups of Experts.

DALY, MARY (1997). 'Welfare States under Pressure: Cash Benefits in European Welfare States over the Last Ten Years'. *Journal of European Social Policy*, 7/2: 129–46.

——and LEWIS, JANE (1998). 'Introduction: Conceptualising Social Care in the Context of Welfare State Restructuring', in Jane Lewis (ed.), *Gender and the Restructuring of Social Care in Europe*. Aldershot: Ashgate, 1998: 1–24.

European Commission (1997). *Equal Opportunities for Women and Men in the European Union Annual Report 1996*. Brussels: European Commission, Directorate General for Employment, Industrial Relations and Social Affairs.

——(1999). *Employment in Europe 1999*. Brussels: European Commission, Directorate General for Employment, Industrial Relations and Social Affairs.

EUROSTAT (1996). *Social Portrait of Europe*. Luxembourg: EUROSTAT.

——(1997). *Labour Force Results 1996*, Luxembourg: EUROSTAT.

——(1999). *Statistics in Focus, Population Change and Social Condition*. No. 6/99. Luxembourg: EUROSTAT.

GORNICK, JANET (1999). 'Gender Equality in the Labour Market', in Diane Sainsbury (ed.), *Gender and Welfare State Regimes*. Oxford: Oxford University Press, 210–42.

——MEYERS, MARCIA K., and ROSS, KATHERINE E. (1997). 'Supporting the Employment of Mothers: Policy Variation across Fourteen Welfare States'. *Journal of European Social Policy*, 7/1: 45–70.

HAKIM, CATHERINE (1997). 'A Sociological Perspective on Part-Time Work', in Hans-Peter Blossfeld and Catherine Hakim (eds.), *Between Equalization and Marginalization: Women Working Part-time in Europe and the United States of America*. Oxford: Oxford University Press, 22–70.

JONUNG, CHRISTINA, and PERSSON, INGA (1994). 'Combining Market Work and Family', in Tommy Bengtsson (ed.), *Population, Economy and Welfare in Sweden*. Berlin: Springer Verlag, 37–64.

KAMERMAN, SHEILA B. (1991). 'Child Care Policies and Programs: An International Overview'. *Journal of Social Issues*, 47/ 2: 179–96.

——and KAHN, ALFRED J. (1981). *Child Care, Family Benefits and Working Parents*. New York: Columbia University Press.

KEMPENEERS, MARIANNE, and LELIÈVRE, EVA (1991). *Employment and Family within the Twelve*. Brussels: DG5.

KNIJN, TRUDIE, and KREMER, MONIQUE (1997). 'Gender and the Caring Dimension of Welfare States: Towards Inclusive Citizenship'. *Social Politics*, 4/3: 328–61.

LELIÈVRE, EVA, and GAUTHIER, ANNE H. (1995). 'Women's Employment Patterns in Europe: Inequalities, Discontinuities, and Policies', in Anne-Marie Guillemard, Jane Lewis, Stein Ringen, and Robert Salais (eds.), *Comparing Social Welfare Systems in Europe*. Paris: MIRE, 461–86.

OECD (Organisation for Economic Co-operation and Development) (1995). *The Tax/Benefit Position of Production Workers 1991–1994*. Paris: OECD.

——(1996). *Caring for Frail Elderly People: Policies in Evolution*. Paris: OECD.

——(1997). *Statistical Compendium*. Paris: OECD.

——(1998a). *OECD Full-Time/Part-Time Database*. Paris: OECD.

OECD (Organisation for Economic Co-operation and Development) (1998*b*). *Social Expenditure Statistics of OECD Member Countries (work file)*. Paris: OECD.

RUBERY, JILL, SMITH, MARK, FAGAN, COLETTE, and GRIMSHAW, DAMIAN (1996). *Women and the European Employment Rate: The Causes and the Consequences of Variations in Female Activity and Employment Patterns in the European Union*. Brussels: European Commission.

——————————(1999). *Women's Employment in Europe*. London: Routledge.

VERMEULEN, HEDWIG, DEX, SHIRLEY, CALLAN, TIM, DANKMEYER, BEN, GUSTAFSSON, SIV, LAYSTEN, MIKE, SMITH, NINA, SCHMAUS, GUNTHER, and VLASBLOM, JAN DIRK (1995). *Tax Systems and Married Women's Labour Force Participation: A Seven Country Comparison*. Essex: ESRC Research Centre on Micro-Social Change, Paper No. 95-8.

ZIGHERA, JACQUES A. (1996). 'How to Measure and Compare Female Activity in the European Union', in Petra Beckmann (ed.), *Gender Specific Occupational Segregation*. Nürnberg: Institut für Arbeitsmarkt und Berufsforschung der Bundesanstalt für Arbeit, 89–105.

11

Any Way Out of 'Exit from Work'? Reversing the Entrenched Pathways of Early Retirement

BERNHARD EBBINGHAUS

11.1. Introduction

For many industrial societies 'exit' from work has become a major pathway for adapting to economic and social change brought about by international competition, technological change, and social demands. Ever since the rise in mass unemployment following the first oil price shock of 1973, early retirement was thought to be a solution as it would reduce the overall labor supply. Yet industrial societies granted early retirement to older working people not only to alleviate the labor market, but also as a social policy measure. This was particularly fitting in the case of manual workers who had been employed for their entire working lives in often unhealthy mass production factories now threatened with shutdown. While early exit from work became soon a widespread phenomena embracing nearly the entire workforce, there are marked differences in early retirement across OECD countries, variations reflecting different societal choices. Most importantly, the Continental European welfare states have—more or less intention-ally—facilitated early retirement over the last three decades to such a degree that these once industrious societies became 'welfare states without work' (Esping-Andersen 1996a). What was once thought of as a partial cure from the modern ills of large-scale redundancy and mass unemploy-ment is today publicly criticized as the wrong medicine. Instead of creating jobs—that is, increasing the demand for labor—the widely used 'exit' route relies on reducing the supply of labor—a very costly method of using social expenditures and underusing human resources (OECD 1995b, 1998). Those European welfare states that relied most on labor shedding are now suffering from the 'Continental dilemma' (Scharpf 1998): the problem of more and more inactive people becoming dependent on welfare measures financed through social contributions and general taxes that have to be paid by fewer and fewer actively employed people.

The global trend toward early retirement since the 1970s seems to have gone in tandem with growing internationalization and concomitant pressures on employment. Nevertheless, Western welfare states vary in the scope and nature of their initial 'exit' policies, and as a result their recent reform efforts also differ. In order to elucidate the different ways particular countries responded (more or less intentionally) to internationalization, economic restructuration, and social demands, I will compare ten advanced Western economies with dissimilar 'exit' trajectories. The basic assumption of this study is that particular early retirement patterns are outcomes of complex interactions among the particular welfare state regimes, production systems, and state–labor–employer relations. These institutional constraints structure differently the opportunities, incentives, and obstacles under which governments, unions, employers' associations, firms, and workers make their decisions to use (or misuse) the 'exit route' in order to meet their interests. What looks on the surface like a single global tendency toward early withdrawal from the labor market is actually a complex trend concealing very different institutionalized pathways, each with its distinct set of incentives and opportunities for externalizing costs (Casey 1996). Given the multiplicity of actors and the variety of alternative pathways, past efforts to design targeted 'exit' measures often led to unintended consequences. Today many reformers, in light of the new emphasis on 'active aging' and concerns about the financial burdens of an aging society (OECD 1998), wish to reverse the policy course on which they had originally embarked. These reforms' highly contingent nature and the way they have been shaped by a set of multiple, multi-level actors make empirical analysis, general explanations—or, for that matter, policy recommendations—quite intricate and circumstantial. Indeed, the recent reform efforts have shown only mixed results because of cost-shifting, policy substitution, and crowding out by alternatives (Casey 1989, 1996). Moreover, given that these institutionalized pathways are seen by society as 'acquired' social rights, reformers advancing policy reversal face deeply entrenched vested interests.

In this comparative study I seek first of all to describe the trend toward early exit from work before discussing efforts to reverse these policies.[1] I therefore adopt a long-term perspective (looking at the last twenty to thirty years) and compare a selected group of OECD countries from the EU (Germany, the Netherlands, France, Italy, Sweden, Denmark, and UK)

---

[1] This study uses labor force employment rates calculated (subtracting unemployment rates from participation rates) from the OECD, *Labour Force Statistics* (annually). For the policy studies, I have made extensive use of the country chapters from the seminal study by Kohli et al. 1991, and also of more recent studies by Naschold and de Vroom 1994; OECD 1995*a*.

along with just two 'regime' competitors from outside Europe (USA and Japan). The choice of countries—differing somewhat from the countries looked at in the first volume—is motivated by an interest in focusing on different national 'social models' (Ebbinghaus 1999) that combine particular forms of welfare states (Esping-Andersen 1990), production systems (Naschold and de Vroom 1994), labor relations (Crouch 1993), and employment regimes (Kolberg and Esping-Andersen 1991). Most important are the differences in welfare and employment regimes. The Continental European countries have tended to rely more on early retirement as a labor-shedding strategy, while the British, American, and Japanese liberal-residual welfare states provided less public support and Scandinavia's generous welfare states retained their ability to maintain higher employment levels. Not only does the level of public provision play a role; so, too, does the degree to which firms are able to externalize, or are forced to internalize, the costs of early retirement. Also important was the role of the social partners (employers and unions) assuming responsibility for solutions to restructuring and the insider–outsider problem of unemployment.

This chapter is divided into two parts. The first part will describe the phenomenon of early exit and then discuss the 'push' and 'pull' factors that contributed not only to its overall increase, but also to cross-national variations. Indeed, my argument will be that even though 'early exit from work' has been a relatively common trend in advanced capitalist societies as a response to economic and social change, there are marked differences across welfare regimes in providing greater or fewer opportunities for early retirement. There are a multitude of 'pathways' for early retirement, ranging from pre-retirement pensions and disability benefits to employer-initiated policies. In some countries there is a wide range of alternative and even complementary policies available, while in others the choice is rather limited. The second part of the chapter will focus on 'policy reversal', that is, attempts to control the increasingly costly early exit route and shift back to an active (aging) society. Yet such an endeavor remains difficult in the face of entrenched acquired rights, the possible use of 'instrument substitution', and the unintended shifting of costs. Four possible areas of policy reversal will be discussed: extending normal retirement age, closing special early retirement programs, reforming disability insurance, and introducing gradual or part-time retirement.

11.2. 'Exit from Work': Secular Trend or Regime-Specific?

With the expansion of state pensions, the retirement age became a common juncture in the transition from work to retirement—a stage in life. 'As pension systems developed, a norm emerged whereby the life course was divided into three major phases: Youth as the time for education; adult- ɔ hood, for work; and old age, for inactivity' (Guillemard and Rein 1993: ɾ 470). All OECD countries studied here granted state pensions by at leastʁ the age of 65 (except for Denmark, at age 67), which led to a considerable ꟾ decline in—if not the virtual disappearance of—old age employment (at 65 or above), with the significant exception of the self-employed in agriculture and retailing (Jacobs, Kohli, and Rein 1991a, b).[2] In fact, options for early retirement allowed many workers to withdraw from work at an earlier age than 65, and it is this 'early exit from work' (55–64) that I will study here. Moreover, I will concentrate on early retirement by men, not only because it is quantitatively more important but also because a study of female participation rates is complicated by two processes working in opposite directions: an intergenerational increase in women's labor force participation across the postwar period and early exit from work due to early retirement.[3] In addition to analyzing employment trends, I will devote two more sections to discussing those economic 'push' factors and welfare regime-related 'pull factors' that can be linked to early retirement as a global trend with significant cross-national variations.

11.2.1. Cross-National Variations in Early Exit from Work by Men

Early retirement among older men (55–64) became a widespread phenomenon among OECD countries over the last three decades, so there was a corresponding decline in employment rates. Although this is a secular trend, there are also cross-national variations that can be seen most clearly by looking at the two age groups 60 to 64 and 55 to 59 (see Figures 11.1a, 11.1b, 11.2a, 11.2b). Very early exit, before age 60, is relatively common in France and the Netherlands, though also in Germany (and probably in Italy).[4] On

---

[2] In Japan, the USA, UK, and Scandinavia, old age (65+) participation for men has remained relatively high, largely due to widespread self-employment and/or family farming. Japan stands out as a 'work society'—nearly 40% of men 65+ still work, mostly to supplement insufficient pensions. American and Japanese women in post-retirement age (65+) also show a relative high propensity to work (10% and 15%, respectively), mostly (it would appear) as family members helping out in agriculture and commercial shops.

[3] Indeed, most countries show relatively stable employment rates for older women (55–64); it is only in France and Germany that early retirement policies have reduced participation levels significantly during the 1970s. Scandinavian female participation increased so rapidly that it now overcompensates for the (modest) impact of early retirement among women. For details on female labor force participation, see the special study by Daly (this volume).

[4] For Italy, data is only available for the age group 50–59, so that the rate for 55–59 is understated; if estimated separately, the Italian rate for this subgroup would probably be as low as in France (see OECD, *Labour Force Statistics* (annually)).

the other hand, the level of Japanese participation (age 55–59) hardly changed, even increasing slightly. The Scandinavian and Anglo-American work societies' experienced some decline in participation rates for the same age group due to early retirement (less in Scandinavia, more in the UK and USA) but they still remain above the OECD average. The differences become even more obvious when one looks at the second pre-retirement age group (60–64). Japan, Scandinavia, or Anglo-Saxon 'work societies' experienced some long-term decline in participation rates, but remained above the OECD average that fell from just under 80 percent to a bit below 50 percent in three decades (1966–96).[5] By contrast, Continental European societies (with the exception of Italy, a traditionally low employment country) experienced a dramatic decline for older male workers (60–64) during the 1970s, and in France and the Netherlands the decline continued well into the 1980s. The Continental group suffers above all from the 'welfare state without work' syndrome: 'Rather than boost public employment, as in Scandinavia, their main policy response to "deindustrialization" and unemployment had been to induce labor force exit. . . . It has resulted in very unfavorable population dependency ratios due to swelling numbers of retirees coupled to a stagnant and even shrinking workforce' (Esping-Andersen 1996b: 68).

There are also cross-national differences as to the age-specific employment profile, dating back to the time today's older men had initially entered the labor market. Some of these differences are related to the link between longer working lives and family farming, where old age pensions were often insufficient, not mandatory, or initiated late. Familist agrarian countries, especially Japan but also Italy and France, still have large numbers of older agricultural workers. Sweden and Denmark also have a long tradition of farming (see Jacobs and Rein 1994: table 2, p. 25). For the other countries, including the USA, agrarian employment is no longer frequent for the age groups approaching 65. Similarly, working on one's own account was relatively common in commerce and artisan trades when today's pensioners finished their apprenticeship. Again Japan stands out, since older workers there work longer in family firms,[6] though self-employment also plays a role in Italy and France. In general, the share of independent employment among older men is larger (around or above 10%) than in the labor force at large, and these older proprietors are less likely to take the 'early exit' route. Similarly, the self-employed in the

---

[5] The exception is the UK, which follows the (unweighted) OECD average (based on all OECD countries as of the 1980s). Sweden's employment rate declined in the early 1990s due to growing old age employment, but no breakdown by the two age groups (55–59 and 60–64) is available since 1993.

[6] Self-employment is a possible way to gain extra income for those dismissed older Japanese without sufficient pensions and without possibility of re-employment. For a discussion of the importance of Japanese familist traditions, see Esping-Andersen 1997.

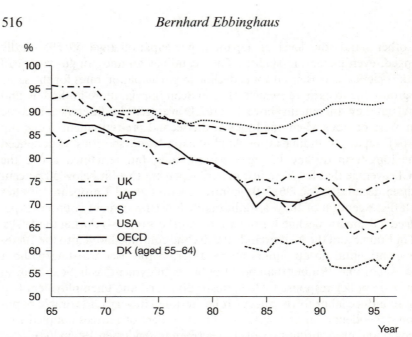

Figure 11.1a Male employment rates, aged 55–59, 1965–1995
Source: OECD, *Labour Force Statistics* (Paris: OECD, various years).

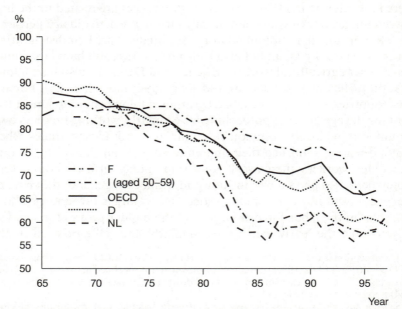

Figure 11.1b Male employment rates, aged 55–59, 1965–1995
Source: OECD, *Labour Force Statistics* (Paris: OECD, various years).

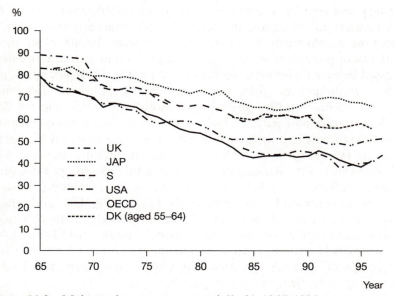

Figure 11.2a Male employment rates, aged 60–64, 1965–1995
Source: OECD, *Labour Force Statistics* (Paris: OECD, various years).

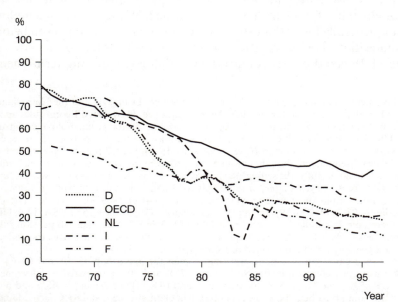

Figure 11.2b Male employment rates, aged 60–64, 1965–1995
Source: OECD, *Labour Force Statistics* (Paris: OECD, various years).

secondary and tertiary sectors are often not or insufficiently covered by public pension programs, and thus cannot profit from early retirement.[7]

Part-time employment is still relatively unusual among older men, despite recent policy initiatives to promote gradual or partial retirement (discussed below). Older male workers tended not to work part-time during their working lives, given traditional male breadwinner roles and work-ethic norms. But there are national exceptions to this rule. Sweden has a long tradition of partial pensions and promoting a gradual transition to full retirement, policies that helped maintain a relatively high activation rate (Wadensjö 1991, 1996): 15 percent of Swedish men (60–64), nearly one-third of the dependent employed in this age group, work only part-time (see Table 11.2). Part-time work among older workers (55–64) is also relatively common in the Netherlands. In the USA, UK, and Japan, at least one in six working men above 60 was employed part-time, though this also reflects difficulties older workers have finding a full-time job.[8] Part-time work is certainly more common among women (in general) and older groups of working age, especially since women during and after child-rearing typically took up only part-time work.[9]

Although seniority dismissal regulations have provided some protection against old age unemployment, older unemployed workers find it difficult to find new employment. In many cases, though, unemployment is not completely involuntary but serves as a 'bridge' or quasi-pension until the age of eligibility for a state pension is reached. While old age unemployment is generally lower than youth unemployment, Germany (even before the unification shock), the UK, and Denmark (the latter not included in Table 11.2), stand out as countries with high levels of long-term unem-

---

[7] Basic pension systems like those in the UK, Sweden, Denmark, and the Netherlands cover all residents, and therefore include the self-employed. However, different rules apply for earnings-related supplementary old age insurance and disability unemployment insurance. US social security and German pension insurance are not compulsory for independent workers (except for German *Handwerker* since 1938). French pre-retirement schemes exclude the self-employed, though they have profited from the lowering of the French state pension age to 60. In Italy, the self-employed are insured by a separate pension scheme, and the pension age is five years later for self-employed Italians than it is for workers there.

[8] Part-time employment among working men (60–64) in 1989/90: Sweden: 31%; the Netherlands: 28% (15% 55–59); Japan: 19%; Denmark: 18%; France: 15%; USA: 14%; UK: 12%; Germany: 7%; Italy: 5% (table 2.6 in OECD 1995*b*: 31). Note that US pension rules lowered pension benefits when working part-time, though these disincentives to combine work and pension have been lowered in recent years (Chen 1996).

[9] Part-time employment among working women for age group 55–59 and 60–64 in 1989/90 was most common in the Netherlands: 77% and 80% (compared to all women: 59%); UK: 54% and 71% (43%); Sweden: 46% and 61% (41%); Denmark: 45% and 60% (38%); less common albeit above the general rate in Germany: 43% and 47% (34%), Japan: 34% and 43% (32%); France: 30% and 34% (24%); USA: 25% and 34% (26%); and very uncommon in Italy: 11% and 10% (10%) (table 2.6 in OECD 1995*b*: 31).

ployment for older workers.[10] German social insurance grants older workers relatively long-term unemployment benefits with high replacement rates, and so do the French, Dutch, and Swedish programs. In these countries, firms that need to restructure or downsize use bilateral agreements to dismiss older workers when they become eligible for long-term unemployment benefits (and until such time as they can start drawing their public pensions). Thus, unemployment insurance can function—whether intentionally or unplanned—as a quasi-early retirement program and 'bridging' pension. Changes in employment rates are therefore better indicators for measuring the extent of 'exit from work' (i.e. non-activity) than participation rates (which include the unemployed).

Table 11.1 *Labor force participation of older men, 1989 (%)*

| Country | Age group | Participation rate | | | 'Exit A' Unemployed | 'Exit B' Retired |
		Self-employed	Full-time employees	Part-time employees		
Sweden	55–59	14.0	67.7	4.7	0.7	12.9
	60–64	12.7	33.9	15.0	1.1	37.3
Germany	55–59	12.6	58.1	0.8	7.1	21.4
	60–64	9.9	21.2	0.9	2.2	65.8
Netherlands	55–59	10.8	43.1	7.7	3.7	34.7
	60–64	8.7	11.0	3.9	0.9	75.5
France	55–59	21.1	39.0	2.4	5.5	32.0
	60–64	11.2	10.8	1.2	0.9	75.9
United Kingdom	55–59	13.7	52.7	1.6	9.4	22.6
	60–64	10.1	37.8	3.3	2.3	46.5
United States	55–59	11.9	57.2	6.9	2.8	21.2
	60–64	10.1	34.2	8.0	1.8	45.8
Japan	55–59	23.5	64.8	0.9	2.4	8.4
	60–64	25.4	40.0	1.8	4.2	28.6

Note: Labor force composition 1989 (Germany: 1987) from EUROSTAT and national surveys; part-time rate for Sweden estimated.

Source: Calculated and compiled from Jacobs and Rein 1994: table. 4, p. 29; no data available for Denmark and Italy.

With these overall trends and the employment profile in mind, we can now summarize patterns of inactivity and link them to some general features of these welfare states. On the one hand, Japan stands out, even among the 'work societies'. Despite the common practice of mandatory

[10] Long-term unemployment among older unemployed men (55+) in 1990 was relatively common in the Netherlands: 86%; France: 68%; Italy: 61%; Germany: 62%; UK: 64%; considerably less common in Denmark: 40%; Japan: 33%; Sweden: 30%; and, given the short duration of benefits, relatively uncommon in the US: 14% (table 2.14 in OECD 1995*b*: 43).

retirement in larger Japanese firms and early eligibility for pensions (around 60), only one in four Japanese men (60–64) has left work thanks to social norms about re-employment. 'Only' one out of three Swedish and Danish men (60–64) has completely withdrawn from the labor market (though many work only part-time). Sweden's limited use of the exit road results from a mixture of reintegration measures, active employment policies, part-time work, and generous partial pensions. The British and American welfare states have less to offer and therefore account for a moderate level of inactivity; that is, one out of two British and American men (60–65) has exited from work, largely due to market pressures (and voluntary policies by firms). Prior to 60, one out of five British or American older men (55–59) has taken the exit route, while in Sweden, Denmark, and Japan the inactivity rate is very small in this somewhat younger age group (55–59), made up largely of the disabled. On the other hand, the Continental European welfare states are known for their heavy reliance on early exit as a labor-shedding strategy. Most dramatic is the extent of early retirement among men (60 to 64): three out of four Dutch, French, and Italian men have retired early, and two out of three German men. The Dutch, French, and Italian 'welfare without work' societies also stand out by virtue of having advanced the early pre-retirement path; thus, one-third of men aged 55 to 59 in those countries have already left the workforce. While this was always the tradition in Italy, France and the Netherlands witnessed a rapid increase in early exit with mass unemployment since the mid-1970s, and one out of five German men (55–59) has used the very early 'exit' route, due to favorable early retirement options. In these countries, labor shedding via early retirement was seen as a major way out of the employment crisis since the mid-1970s.

11.2.2. Push Factors: Economic Restructuring and Labor Shedding

Economic push factors have been held responsible for the need to promote early retirement. Early exit from work would provide a means to help restructure an economy facing deindustrialization, labor-saving technologies, higher skill requirements, a shift toward service sectors, and an oversized public sector. Indeed, special pre-retirement programs were introduced in the mid-1970s (or even earlier) with the intention of easing the industrial restructuring process, especially downsizing of technologically backward and uncompetitive industries. Early retirement in sectors with higher than average old age employment—especially agriculture, mining, and construction—showed an above average trend toward early retirement. Yet there is only limited evidence that early retirement by the 1980s is specific to these downsizing industries, so that a country's mix of industries cannot fully explain the extent of early exit (Jacobs, Kohli, and Rein 1991c: 94).[11] In addition to these specific programs, confined to ailing industries (at least initially), early retirement soon became a more general pathway spreading far beyond the sectors specifically affected by the 'push' of economic restructuring, labor-saving technology, and international competition. Early retirement was also used to accommodate downsizing of the public sector due to financial constraints, EU policies of deregulation and privatization policies since the 1980s (see Héritier and Schmidt, this volume). In fact, in countries like the Netherlands, Germany, France, and Italy, generous early retirement rules for public employees have been used to accommodate downsizing in public employment due to public spending limits, market deregulation, and privatization of the public sector. When in the 1990s, under financial pressures, the Swedish welfare state had to reverse its expansion of public employment and made early retirement more attractive, it did face rising unemployment, especially among older workers. Early exit spread across all sectors, private or public, independent of the need for restructuring or downsizing in the particular sector. Whatever the original intention of its creators, early retirement became a quasi social right claimed by anyone approaching retirement age.

This widespread use of early exit indicates that the economic causes go beyond the need for restructuring in particular sectors, but that the more general 'push factors' are at work (Esping-Andersen and Sonnberger 1991). High unemployment starting in the mid-1970s put special pressure on politicians to attempt to reduce labor supply, in the hope that this might create new employment opportunities for younger job seekers and reduce the costs of underfinanced unemployment programs. In these troubled economies, pre-retirement became not just a legitimate policy for sectoral restructuring but a more general policy of labor shedding (Esping-Andersen 1996b). There is some evidence indicating that unemployment is negatively correlated with early exit trends, while the drop in industrial employment is less significant but positively correlated.[12] But

[11] A shift-share analysis of employment changes by industry during the 1970s for three countries (Germany, the Netherlands, and Sweden) concluded that a 'decrease in employment share of older men within all the industries, rather than changes in the distribution, is the main factor underlying the overall changes in the old-age share of male employment' (Jacobs, Kohli, and Rein 1991c: 83). It is esp. in the public sector that one finds substantial differences among the three countries (in Germany widespread decline, in the Netherlands a moderate decrease, and in Sweden positive growth in public employment among men 60–64).

[12] In a quantitative comparative analysis of early exit in Germany, Sweden, and the USA 'the unemployment variable is significant, and the job loss variable, albeit insignificant, has become stronger' under a model dividing the time-series into pre- and post-1973 periods (Esping-Andersen and Sonnberger 1991: 244).

especially in countries with high unemployment during the 1970s, such as the Netherlands, Germany, and Britain, persistent early retirement 'increasingly took on institutional forms and became increasingly autonomous' (Naschold, de Vroom, and Casey 1994: 451). Thus, the initial rise in unemployment did prove crucial in institutionalizing pre-retirement, but to the degree that early retirement became an acquired social right to all older workers, labor market exit became independent of the ups and downs of the business cycle. Moreover, with growing and persistent mass unemployment in the 1980s, the 'Continental dilemma' (Scharpf 1998) became more intricate: a growing non-active population receiving welfare transfers had to be financed by raising payroll taxes on a shrinking workforce. Hence, early retirement proved to be a very expensive 'way out' of the employment crisis.

Given the different early retirement options but also the specific demographic and labor market profiles, the actual reduction of labor supply through early retirement varies across countries; labor shedding occurred most frequently in Continental Europe.[13] In recent years, exit rates have leveled off and thus led to no or only small additional reductions in labor supply. While early exit by older men helped reduce labor supply, especially in the 1970s and 1980s, the impact of older men retiring was partly offset by the growing participation of women in the workforce, especially in countries like the Netherlands where that growth was substantial. Moreover, early exit by older women played only a minor role, as it was by and large offset by increased overall female labor force participation as women increasingly stayed in the labor market or returned to it after the child-rearing years (see Daly, this volume).

Early retirement was often legitimated by intergenerational solidarity, on the theory that older workers would retire and thus open up job opportunities for younger people. The evidence, however, is rather disappointing, even in the case of special programs requiring employers to hire new (young or unemployed) workers. The French solidarity contracts, which are conditional on a firm's promise to hire a job seeker (Guillemard 1991*a*: 147), show that 'departures on pre-retirement fell far short of reducing by a like number the ranks of unemployed young people. All assessments of pre-retirement have emphasized that the effects on employment were a far cry from the hopes placed in such measures' (Guillemard 1991a: 169).

---

[13] If we compare the different declines in employment ratios of older male workers (55–64) over the last two decades (1975–95), the decline in activity rates has probably reduced overall male labor supply by 3% in the Netherlands and Sweden, around 5% in Germany and UK, and most massively around 7% in France and probably Italy (only data for 50–64: 6.5%) (own shift-share analysis based on Eurostat *Labour Force Survey* 1995 and assuming 1975 employment levels for 1995).

Since the solidarity contracts were only one of several pathways, the replacement of older by younger workers happened only in one out of three cases; most employers reduced their oversized workforce, especially during recessions (Guillemard 1991*a*: 170). Temporary pre-retirement programs in Britain (1977–88) and Germany (1984–88) also required replacement with a job seeker (at least in order to obtain additional subsidies), but these programs were too small to make a major impact on the labor market. Since the most common early exit options are not conditional on replacement by a young person or job seeker, their impact can only be indirect, by way of reducing the overall labor supply. Yet France and Italy, two countries with relatively high levels of early retirement, have disappointingly high levels of youth unemployment.[14]

11.2.3. *Pull Factors: Multiple Pathways to Early Exit*

The analysis of macroeconomic factors contributing to early exit is inconclusive, suggesting merely that early exit is less the direct result of these 'push' factors—of mass unemployment and economic restructuring—than of interaction between these and 'pull factors', in particular, the availability of early retirement options. Opportunities to 'bridge' the transition period between early withdrawal from work and 'normal' retirement age vary among countries and over time. In fact, there are multiple institutional arrangements or 'pathways', to early retirement, often combining different income programs (Kohli and Rein 1991: 6) that can (and sometimes must) be linked sequentially. For instance, a worker who has been dismissed might first receive long-term unemployment insurance, followed by a pre-retirement pension, before finally becoming eligible for a public pension—and each step may have been made conditional on the earlier one. There is no need to assume that all of these institutional arrangements were initially tailored toward advancing early exit from work; many pathways are the unintended consequences of policies designed for quite different purposes (Guillemard 1991*b*). For instance, unemployment benefits were originally extended to older workers as a social policy for the hard to re-employ, though with rising mass unemployment these rights became the first step on an increasingly popular pathway leading to early exit. Thus, it would be misleading to look only at the formal designation, institutional locus, or initial intention of these policies: different pathways may serve the same pre-retirement function.

---

[14] Only one in three young men (15–24) and only one in four young woman was employed in 1990. Yet in France 15% of young men were unemployed, 24% of young women; in Italy, 26% for young men, 38% for young women (OECD, *Labour Force Statistics* (annually)).

Indeed, there is a multitude of possible pathways, yet their availability varies across countries and time (see Figure 11.3).

1. *Lowering 'normal' pension age.* Scandinavians traditionally retired late (at 67), but Sweden lowered its age limit to 65 in 1976, whereas Denmark retained the 67-year limit (Øverbye 1997: 145). On the other hand, the Latin countries and Japan traditionally had a relatively early pension age for industrial workers: most Italian male workers could retire at 60 (or from 50 onwards, if they had 35 years of seniority), since 1983 the French have a right to a full state pension at 60 (after 37.5 years), and Japanese men can draw a public pension at 60. In addition, these three 'familist' countries have granted women the right to draw pensions five years earlier than men (though only prior to 1983 in France), on the grounds that married women (who tended to be younger than their husbands) could retire at the same time as their spouses. Such 'paternalist' policies granting favorable pension rights to women have also been in place in Germany (for small pensions at 60, for normal pensions at 63) and in the UK (at 60), though they also led to comparatively lower pensions due to shorter contribution periods. Yet all these gender gaps have or will be closed, following EU laws on equality. Granting an early 'normal' pension age was largely motivated by social considerations, but de facto it became a labor shedding strategy.

2. *Partial or gradual pensions, providing for a gradual transition from work to retirement.* The first such program, funded by payroll taxes, was introduced by Sweden as early as 1976 (Delsen 1996; Wadensjö 1991) and soon became more widely used than expected after normal retirement age was lowered from 67 to 65. The original program was relatively attractive for beneficiaries; it replaced up to 65 percent of gross earnings lost (depending on how many work hours were reduced, though at least 5 hours per week) without any negative effects on pensions. Other countries, such as France (1985–), Denmark (1987–), and Germany (1989–) later followed the Swedish example, though with more limited success given less favorable terms, more attractive alternatives, and little employer support for part-time jobs. In addition, eligibility rules on 'flexible' pensions also have an important—but often hidden—impact on early exit. Instead of lowering the normal pension age, the Swedish and US American pension systems allow benefits to be drawn prematurely (beginning at 60 and 62, respectively), though with relatively 'fair' actuarial reductions in benefits due to shorter contribution periods, making this option relatively unattractive. Actuarial treatment of benefits plays an important role in the decision to exit either at the first opportunity or later (Casey 1997). In France, for instance, workers have no incentive to continue employment once they have enough contribution years, since benefits will not be raised

with additional years of contribution, and drawing a state pension is incompatible with continuing employment.

3. *Special pre-retirement programs* were set up in the mid-1970s and early 1980s in order to relieve unemployment temporarily by reducing the labor supply. The programs were also meant to help older workers who had only slim chances of being rehired given their age and the labor market situation. Some of these early retirement measures were initially limited to particular industries under pressure from restructuring. Since 1963, the French National Employment Fund (FNE) was a special allocation for dismissed workers (at 60), controlled by public administration and facilitating industrial restructuring, particularly in heavy industry. It was replaced in 1980 by a new, much more widely used special allocation fund that provided for the pre-retirement of redundant workers across all sectors (55/56+). After the 1983 reform of public pensions, the costly pre-retirement programs were replaced by new 'solidarity' contracts that now provided for pre-retirement as early as 55 on condition that the retired worker be replaced by someone younger or unemployed. Special pre-retirement programs like those in France were rather short-lived in other countries. Initially no more than a regional experiment under the British Labour government, the Job Release Scheme (JRS), which also required retiring workers to be replaced, ran for twelve years from 1977 until 1989, when the Conservative government closed it down after numerous stop-and-go changes. The short-lived German Pre-retirement Scheme (1984–1988) was introduced by the conservative-liberal Kohl government at a time when the metalworkers union was fighting for the 35-hour week and the government wanted to side with the moderate unions in favor of reducing lifelong working time instead (Jacobs, Kohli, and Rein 1991*b*: 208–9).[15]

4. *Long-term unemployment* is another major pathway, legitimized not only as a social right for those with long working lives but also as an indirect, 'active' employment measure for young job seekers and the long-term unemployed. In all European countries except the UK, benefits from unemployment insurance (or, in Italy, restructuring funds) were paid to older workers for at least one year (in the Netherlands, up to 5 years for those aged 60 and older). In France, Denmark, and the Netherlands, these unemployment benefits made it possible to 'bridge' the time from dismissal to normal retirement age. The French social partners used their joint unemployment fund to set up guaranteed-income schemes for dismissed workers (above 60) in the private sector (and since 1977 also for voluntary pre-retirement). The Netherlands has developed collective

---

[15] The scheme was relatively favorable and thus costly, paying out about 65% of former earnings (plus social insurance contributions) to 200,000 workers, mostly men (from 58 until normal retirement at 65) during its four years of existence.

schemes for early retirement (VUT), first for one year of 'bridging' unemployment until pension age but later extended to five years. 'The VUT is an example of a scheme that was intended to be temporary but has become semi-permanent (OECD 1995a: 185).[16] As in France, the collective programs are financed on a pay-as-you-go basis, and contributions are part of the wage bill, but in the Dutch case they are negotiated at the branch level. The Danish social partners negotiated a voluntary early retirement benefit (*efterløn*) in 1979, any member of the union-run unemployment fund for at least ten years can draw long-term unemployment benefits from age 60 through 67. By 1986 the program had already reached 100,000 recipients or 60 percent of the insured in this age group (Petersen 1989: 74). In Germany and Sweden, long-term unemployment insurance was the first of several steps toward bridging early retirement, and it was incorporated into employer-worker agreements on voluntary dismissal. Thus German unemployment insurance had provided an alternative pathway to early exit for older jobless workers (aged 60 and over) since 1957. Against the government's intentions, this unemployment provision became 'a vehicle for firms to shed their unwanted workers and to externalize the costs of this [pre-retirement] operation' (Jacobs, Kohli, and Rein 1991b: 202). With mass unemployment growing from the late 1970s onward, negotiated agreements—to dismiss older workers at 59 (the so-called '59er rule'), the age that they can draw on one year of unemployment benefits, followed by five years of pre-retirement benefits for older unemployed workers—became widespread: the firm dismissed the worker but would 'top up' one year of unemployment benefits and the subsequent pre-retirement pension until normal retirement. Similarly, Sweden's long-term unemployed older workers could receive (since 1973) a disability pension (60–65) when unemployed, and could draw (since 1974) on 1 year and 9 months of unemployment benefits. Using the '58.3' rule, companies and unions could agree on shedding older workers (age 58 and 3 months) who could receive first unemployment and then disability pension benefits (Wadensjö 1991: 310). This combination of pathways largely externalizes a firm's restructuring costs, even though firms usually are 'topping up' the lower unemployment benefits to bring them up to previously received net wages. Quite in contrast to the Continental European and Scandinavian welfare states, the liberal-residual Anglo-American and Asian welfare states

---

[16] A few years after its start in 1976, 80% of employees in larger firms were covered by such collective agreements at the branch level (OECD 1995a: 182). Although conditions vary from one branch agreement to another, 80% of gross pay and joint payment of social insurance contributions is common practice. Since 1983 VUT schemes have also existed in the public sector for full (60) and part-time exit (59), and they soon came to cover 45% of VUT beneficiaries. By 1990, 120,000 people, or one in five older persons (60–64), were receiving VUT.

foreclosed the long-term pathway by providing only low, short-term unemployment benefits. In the UK means-tested social assistance, available after one year, was the only 'fall back' for older jobless workers.

5. *Disability insurance.* Another alternative pathway to early retirement has been the use of disability insurance, especially for those workers with age-related health problems after long working lives. In the British and American liberal-residual welfare states, which lack long-term unemployment insurance, disability pensions constitute (with few exceptions) the only public program allowing older workers to receive income support for diminished working capacity in old age.[17] Although the American and British welfare states do not consider the disabled person's chances to find 'commensurate' employment, the number of claims and the acceptance rate for disability awards based on medical indications increased with unemployment. By contrast, the Continental European and Scandinavian welfare states have taken labor market prospects into account; that is, they consider whether an older worker will find it difficult to obtain 'commensurate' employment. These employment considerations were introduced as administrative practices (sometimes advanced by courts) even before the onset of rising mass unemployment in the mid-1970s (Netherlands: 1967 and 1973, Italy: 1970 and 1984; Germany: 1969 and 1976; Sweden: 1973). Disability insurance became very common in the 1980s, most prominently in the Netherlands (Aarts, Burkhauser, and de Jong, 1996*a*) and in Sweden (Wadensjö and Palmer 1996). The incidence of using disability insurance is considerably lower in Germany, given that disability pension awards are less favorable and alternative routes exist (Frick and Sadowski 1996: 118). Italy and France have been applying labor market considerations since the 1970s; older Italian workers with small state pensions have especially profited from these (OECD 1995*a*). Thus, the labor market criterion, initially introduced as a social right, have provided for an important (sometimes unintended) pathway to early exit from work from which workers and firms have profited at the expense of the social insurance schemes. Moreover, disability insurance was in some countries a possible route for early retirement for women, especially when other exit routes were less available.[18]

---

[17] In addition both countries ban discrimination. In 1994 the Americans with Disabilities Act had been passed, guaranteeing civil rights for the disabled and requiring firms (with 15 or more employees) to make 'reasonable accommodation' for disabled workers (Berkowitz and Burkhauser 1996). Similarly, the UK, as early as its 1944 Disabled Persons (Employment) Act, had been relying on a strategy for integrating the disabled into work using quotas, though only rarely were fines actually enforced (Lonsdale and Aylward 1996).

[18] With the exception of British women (60+) who had always been granted early state pensions, every country has witnessed a higher level of disability payments for older female

6. *Employer policies.* Although firms use existing institutional arrangements to externalize their own restructuring costs, they often complement these free public benefits or create alternative routes if public schemes are not attractive enough. It was common practice for German and Swedish employers to rely on unemployment insurance, often backed by collective agreements or the kind of 'social plans' German labor law requires management to negotiate with unions, as a way of dealing with redundancies. Especially where seniority employment rights were relatively strict and unions were strong in sectoral and workplace negotiations, such policies allowed firms to restructure or downsize in a consensual manner. In some countries, the social partners filled the gap left by public policies. The Danish pre-retirement pay scheme, introduced in 1977, stands out as an unusual kind of voluntary and collectively negotiated arrangement.[19] Yet the Dutch social partners also negotiated sectorwide pre-retirement schemes (the VUT) that increasingly compensated for others pathways, such as disability insurance, that were being closed off (de Vroom and Blomsma 1991).

Even where employers were not able to externalize costs, consensual downsizing in workplaces with union-enforced seniority rules was worth some expense to firms (Casey 1992). For instance, larger American companies paid (out of their own pockets) generous 'window plans', providing temporary support to older workers with seniority rights after dismissal. A functional equivalent was the use of the occupational pension funds by British firms.[20] Common social practices also play a role, as in the example of the relatively large severance pay provided by British, Italian, and Japanese firms at the end of long service to a firm. These lump-sum payments are often taxed at favorable rates and are commonly used by retired workers to finance home ownership, a small business, or a private insurance plan. Finally, the practice of finding lighter, possibly less lucrative work for older workers was once a common practice in many firms until

workers than for younger age groups, especially in countries with more generous elibility criteria (esp. Sweden, and less so Denmark, Italy, and Germany) (Aarts, Burkhauser, and de Jong 1996*b*). There are also marked gender differences across countries in how disability benefits are drawn: older men and women in Scandinavia exhibit the same take-up rates, men are more likely to draw benefits in the UK, US, and Germany, while the practice has been more widespread among Dutch women than men since the rules were changed in the 1980s.

[19] Given the late normal retirement age in Denmark (at 67), this voluntary early retirement pay is financed by the union-run unemployment insurance program and allows relatively generous bridging pensions from 60 years onwards. In the 1980s, more than one in two older male or female workers (60–66) insured in a voluntary unemployment scheme received an 'efterløn' (Petersen 1989: 74).

[20] However, this worked only under defined-benefit schemes, when companies subsidized early retirement measures without actuarial reduction (which would be required under defined-contribution schemes).

rationalization measures killed these kinds of jobs in the 1970s. However, these kinds of social norms did remain common in Japan as a way of finding suitable new employment, at least until recently.[21]

In sum, there are multiple pathways to early exit from work; workers and firms in some countries have more options and better opportunities than in others. The Latin 'pensioner' states (France and Italy) have a tradition of granting relatively favorable pre-retirement benefits, while post-agrarian Japan (where re-employment is the social norm) offers early but meager state and private pensions. France adds some special pre-retirement and unemployment options of its own; it is the country with the most widespread early withdrawals from work (while in Italy it is more common to supplement small pensions with illicit employment). The Continental 'welfare without work' societies, the Netherlands and Germany, have relied heavily on tacit pre-retirement policies, though the former favors using disability policy and the latter unemployment and pre-retirement benefits. The Scandinavian 'work societies' (Sweden and Denmark) have also opened up some favorable pathways (largely via the routes of unemployment and partial pensions), yet Scandinavian policies are meant to accommodate an active society where workers make a gradual transition to relatively late retirement. The Anglo-American liberal welfare states provide the fewest opportunities for early retirement, apply stricter criteria to unemployment and disability programs, and grant smaller or shorter benefits. Employers' policies also vary by country: whereas British and American companies provide some voluntary support when it fits their interests, the Continental European and Scandinavian employers often negotiate additional measures in a more consensual style that results in 'topping up' or complementing public benefits. While British and American firms were forced to internalize these restructuration costs and thus use the voluntary pre-retirement route only sparingly, employers in the other countries were able to externalize some of these social costs by shifting them onto a collective or public scheme.

11.3. Policy Reversal

Since the 1980s, the cost pressures of early retirement programs and other pre-retirement pathways have been noted in all OECD welfare states. National governments, employers' associations, and experts now criticize

---

[21] While Japanese firms enforce a mandatory retirement age (at around 60, when the employee pension starts), they see to it that their dismissed workers are re-hired—usually at a lower salary—within their own company, a subsidiary, or an allied firm within the supplier network (Kimura et al. 1994).

the extensive reliance on 'exit from work' as a labor shedding strategy, and instead advocate a policy reversal meant to keep older people working longer and rehire them when unemployed. International organizations ranging from the OECD and IMF to the European Commission have put the financial implications of providing pensions and health care for an increasingly 'aging' population on their agenda (OECD 1995*a*, 1998; European Commission 1997). These organizations have proposed, among other measures, a reversal of pre-retirement pension options. As early as 1982 the European Commission made recommendations on aging, and in 1995 the Commission proposed a 'Council Decision on Community Support for Action in Favor of Older People'. Yet, given vested interests in acquired social rights, changing national pension policies proved relatively difficult, even in countries with conservative governments committed to welfare retrenchment like Reagan's USA and Thatcher's Britain (Pierson 1994). Moreover, reversing one policy could lead to an 'instrument substitution' of one pathway by another (Casey 1989). If one pathway (for instance, pre-retirement through disability pension) is closed, workers, firms, and unions might seek another pathway (for instance, long-term unemployment benefits for older workers) as a second best solution to facilitate early exit. Thus, instead of reducing early retirement and cutting expenses, costs are only shifted from one to another insurance fund, while early exit from work continues. Reversing the course of policy proves difficult to the degree that 'exit' from work is a secular trend, and to the extent that social and economic pressures, that is the push factors, are strong. In the following sections, four different efforts at policy reversal will be reviewed.

11.3.1. Raising Normal Retirement Age

Welfare states that granted women earlier retirement (France, Italy, Germany, UK, and Japan) have now decided to reverse this policy and aim at equalizing retirement by raising the female age limit. Following the European Court of Justice's 'Barber' ruling on equal treatment (Art. 118, Single European Act), every country in the European Economic Area is phasing in equality in pension ages over the next several years. But Japan is also following this global trend as a way of coping with the financial liabilities of a rapidly aging population. Since women have a life expectancy exceeding men's by many years (Bosworth and Burtless 1998), and because women are participating in the labor force at higher rates than they used to, an earlier mandatory retirement age implies higher pension claims. On the other hand, in systems with superannuating in which benefits are linked to the contribution period, an earlier exit from working life might prove disadvantageous to women in light of their—on average—shorter contribution periods (due to family-related interruptions from work). However, a more important method of rolling back the trend toward early exit has been to raise normal retirement age for both men and women.

In order to avoid a social security deficit in the future, the USA was the first country (as early as 1983) to legislate a rise in the normal retirement age, though the change was scheduled to be phased in over several decades.[22] In addition, in 1986 the US Congress made it unlawful to mandate a retirement age in employment contracts; this was after Congress had already extended the age limit to 70 in 1978 (Hutchens 1994: 418). The German pension reform reached by all-party consensus in 1989 foresaw a gradual increase in the female retirement age to 65, along with other measures over a long transition period. But a more highly contested and partisan reform in 1996 anticipated the phasing in of an increase in pre-retirement age from 60 to 65 for the long-term jobless to be accomplished by 2001. In Italy, the 1995 'Dini' pension reform also raised the 'minimum' retirement age step by step from 53 to 54 until 1998, and then (by additional steps) to 57 by 2004, though the public sector was granted a later start on reaching the same new minimum age. Part of the Italian government's compromise with the unions involved waiting until 2004 for public and private sector rules to be harmonized, and not changing pension entitlements for older blue-collar workers and those with long working lives. Similarly, Japan decided in 1989 and 1994 to raise the normal retirement age to 65 for both men and women, yet with a five-year delay for women over the next twenty years. However, the earnings-related portion can still be drawn at 60 in order to supplement lower income from mandatory retirement and subsequent lower paid re-employment, a common practice of many larger firms.[23]

The latest to change were the Scandinavians, but Sweden's dramatic economic and financial problems in the early 1990s soon spurred this country to make major social policy changes within a relatively short span of time (Stephens 1996). Sweden's 1992 crisis pact, supported both by the government and Social Democratic opposition, had foreseen increasing the normal retirement age by one year, but this was later repealed. Yet the

---

[22] The 1983 amendment on raising normal retirement age (from 65 to 66 by 2009 and to 67 by 2025), was expected to remove one-third of the projected actuarial deficit in 2027. Later efforts by Congress to further increase the retirement age were not successful (Chen 1996: 171–72).

[23] The minimum age for receiving a basic pension in Japan will be gradually increased from 60 to 65 by 2013, while the earnings-related benefits can still be drawn from 60 onwards. The basic pension's earnings-test does not include part-time work (less than 33 hrs) or the substantial company bonuses, these 'loopholes' in pension and tax rules allow companies to re-employ their 'retired' workers at lower costs (Takayama 1996: 141–45).

mandatory retirement age will be raised (with the minimum pension age going from 60 to 61) the full normal replacement rate will only be credited at 67, thereby creating an incentive to retire late. Since Denmark had never lowered its normal retirement age of 67, there seemed to be no need for change. But Danes actually retire (on average) at age 61, thanks to programs allowing them to retire early and draw on state pensions in anticipation of retirement. As a consequence, the multi-party 1999 budget settlement, contested by unions and employers, envisaged lowering the normal retirement age to 65 and reducing entitlements accordingly.

Pensions for men in the UK already had an age limit of 65, and pensions there could also be deferred by five years using actuarial treatment, thus benefits will increase with additional contribution years. The pension age for women in the UK will be increased to 65 by 2020. Most surprisingly, France has not attempted to increase the minimum age, probably because 'the French are very much wedded to the idea of official retirement at the age of 60. This entitlement is in many ways a symbol of social progress, something the French have fought for through long years and that was granted them with the advent of a socialist government in 1981' (Reday-Mulvey 1996: 50–51). Yet, de facto, the 1993 Balladur pension reform extended the minimum contribution period from 37.5 to 40 years, so that 'even if retirement at 60 years is now an established right, many are those who will have to work well beyond that age in order to clock-up the requisite 40 contribution years' (Reday-Mulvey 1996: 53).

All countries have decided to raise their normal retirement age gradually, or at least to raise it de facto by changing actuarial calculations in favor of longer contribution periods. Countries that used to have a gender gap have now brought female retirement age up to the norm for men, and no country has chosen to equalize retirement at the more favorable age that used to be the female standard. These measures were less motivated by a desire to retain older workers than by concerns about long-term pension costs in light of currently unfavorable demographic shifts and employment levels. Indeed, every year that a pension is postponed brings additional contributions and delays benefit payments. The widespread use of transitional and gradual measures, which mainly affect new entrants, indicates how difficult it is to change acquired rights; indeed, it is for this very reason that France refrained from altering the age limit explicitly and opted for achieving the same result by indirect means. Moreover, the general strikes over state imposed welfare retrenchment plans, those of the Berlusconi government in Italy in 1994 and the Juppé government in France in 1995 indicate how much veto power unions could still use to block reforms; by contrast, the reforms that the Dini government subsequently negotiated with Italian unions demonstrated the importance of social concertation for bringing about and implementing welfare reform (Ebbinghaus and Hassel 2000). Yet raising the official retirement age does not necessarily lead to an increase in average retirement age or in actual exit rates, since much depends on other pathways and possible adverse effects arising from 'instrument substitution'. Thus, concerted action is needed, both to coordinate different policies and unite all social actors around joint commitments to responsible behavior.

11.3.2. Closing Special Early Retirement Programs

Special early retirement measures were originally created in order to cope with deindustrialization. Yet as mass unemployment started to mount in the late 1970s, these temporary programs experienced a boom. All European countries had these special pre-retirement programs, or at least some special unemployment benefits, by now. Yet fairly soon governments realized that the costs of these relatively generous schemes were beginning to explode as unemployment persisted into the 1980s. The temporary special programs were easier to close down than special provisions in general schemes. Britain's JRS offers an example of the unplanned rise and decline of such a program. The new Conservative government, committed to welfare retrenchment, made several stop-and-go changes to the scheme inherited from the previous Labour government.[24] When the employment situation improved, the government finally phased out the costly program by 1989.

In Germany, it was the conservative-liberal Kohl government which closed its own program after only four years in 1988, despite calls, especially by moderate unions, to prolong it. Not only the government deemed it too costly, employers thought it too expensive and wanted more control over individual retirement decisions (Jacobs, Kohli, and Rein 1991*b*: 209–10). Yet closing down one special program did not put an end to early retirement. In order to curtail the '59er rule', the government introduced a 1982 rule change which sought to force firms which dismiss older workers to cover the additional unemployment benefit costs. However, the rule change 'was not effective because it was immediately challenged in the courts' (Jacobs, Kohli, and Rein 1991*b*: 203), thus it was first suspended

[24] Labor increased the allowance and also lowered the minimum age by two years, though not for women. The Conservatives raised the age limit in 1980, then lowered it gradually in 1982, only to raise it again in 1984 (Laczko and Phillipson 1991: 228). The JRS part-time option was closed down in 1986, and finally JRS was completely closed off to new entrants in 1989, after some 250,000 people had benefited from it (80% men). However, JRS 'was financially unattractive to people who were receiving above average or average wages and who would not be able to supplement JRS with a pension from their employer.' Indeed the majority seemed to have had an additional occupational pension (Laczko and Phillipson 1991: 231).

and when declared constitutional, the court required a costly and cumbersome review of each of the 100,000 pending cases. After ending the special pre-retirement scheme, the government was unable to curtail the use of public programs for early exit. Given the adverse labor market situation, the government even extended unemployment benefits from one to nearly three years, which led to further spread of early retirement, starting now three years ('57er rule') prior to early retirement age 60. Unification made the early retirement route even more indispensable in the East, and difficult to cut back.[25]

France stands out as a country with a number of sequential and parallel early retirement plans, some publicly managed, others negotiated between the social partners (Guillemard 1991*a*). The two pre-retirement schemes, run by the state and by the social partners, were very widespread with over 200,000 beneficiaries for each of the two programs at their peak in 1982–1984 (table 5.4. in Guillemard 1991*a*: 138). 'As a result of increasing competition since 1972 from the guaranteed-income schemes managed by the Unemployment Compensations Fund, the retirement system had been losing its power to regulate definitive exit' (Guillemard 1991*a*: 143). As the state had to increase its subsidies, the social partners 'became aware that the Unemployment Fund's financial difficulties would be blamed on the new early-exit pathways, they decided to curtail pre-retirement arrangements, and decisions were made about sharing costs with the state', (Guillemard 1991*a*: 150) in a 1984 agreement. Moreover, the new Socialist government lowered (for men) the normal retirement age of the public pension scheme to 60, thereby relieving the unemployment fund and FNE, though these programs then financed pre-60 retirement. The government closed after short transitory measures all special state financed pre-retirement schemes except the FNE redundancy allocation, though it raised employer contributions and the minimum age (from 55 to 57) in 1984. Yet the French social partners still maintain their pre-retirement programs, thus only recently (in 1995), a new 'early retirement for new jobs' scheme was collectively negotiated and are part of the social partners' unemployment fund (ARPE).[26]

[25] Even before unification, the GDR government gave pre-retirement benefits to men (at 60) and women (at 55). This was replaced by a special pre-retirement benefit (65% of net earnings) paid by unemployment insurance. About 850,000 East Germans were beneficiaries in 1993, but over the next five years all were transferred to the pension scheme when they reached 60 (Schmähl, George, and Oswald 1996: 74).

[26] ARPE, established by a union-employer agreement (1994), payed pre-retirement pensions to those with 40 years of unemployment insurance contributions, provided that their employer would hire a new employee. Over the first three years of the program there were 122,000 beneficiaries and 111,000 new jobs created, most on permanent contracts (EIRO 1998: fr981143n).

Similarly in Denmark and the Netherlands, governments have only limited capacity to prevent early exit, given the existence of pre-retirement programs run by the social partners. Denmark's voluntary pre-retirement pay (*efterløn*) was initially welcomed, especially by the unions representing unskilled workers, and more recently white-collar and professional employees also profited from such programs. In 1998 the new government introduced some reforms, cutting payments to 91 percent of unemployment benefit (at least for short-term unemployed) (EIRO 1998: dk9812197f). The Dutch VUT scheme, negotiated by the social partners, expanded rapidly and faced rising costs, higher contributions, and problems of moral hazard. Yet a reform of the system proves difficult in light of the need for bipartite consensus and the system's fragmentation into various branch agreements.[27] Following the December 1997 tripartite agreement on state pension reform, VUT has become an issue in collective bargaining rounds, and a number of agreements envisage a transition to a more flexible pre-retirement program with lower benefits and costs (EIRO 1998: nl9809194f).

With the exception of Britain's JRS, only Continental European welfare states advanced special pre-retirement programs. Yet in Scandinavia (especially Denmark), social partners fill the void, and collectively negotiated schemes have also gained in importance on the Continent. As the state retreated and closed down costly special pre-retirement options, collectively negotiated schemes tended to fill the gap. These programs continued to let some firms externalize their restructuration costs, shifting them onto the national (as in France) or the sectoral wage bill (as in the Netherlands). Yet when the costs of these schemes expanded further, an increase in contributions had to be negotiated by the social partners. Once pre-retirement contributions became part and parcel of wage negotiations, wage moderation could be traded off against financing for these new schemes in an exchange benefiting both (restructuring) firms and (older) workers. However, where the state had to underwrite deficits, as in the French unemployment scheme, governments could not remain indifferent to irresponsible behavior, though they had only limited scope to regulate and control the social partners' behavior at different levels or across the whole economy.

11.3.3. *'Curing the Dutch Disease': Reforming Disability Insurance*

Sadly, the (ab)use of disability programs for early exit from work became a notorious symptom of the 'Dutch disease' of the 1980s. Disability

---

[27] The contributions have increased considerably, from 0.6% of the private sector wage bill in 1981 to 2.4% in 1992; in the public sector the increase was even more dramatic, from 0.4% to 6.8% (OECD 1995a: 185).

Table 11.2 *Generosity (1995) and older recipients (1990) of disability benefits*

	Generosity Index	Male recipients recipients (% male LF)	All recipients (1000s)	Recipients (% of age group)					
				Total	Males		Females		
	(1995)	15–64	55–64	55–64	55–59	60–64	55–59	60–64	
Sweden	0.70	7.8	214.8	25.4	16.0	34.3	18.8	32.2	
Denmark	0.39	—	77.0	15.4	11.2	19.5	12.4	18.8	
Germany	0.44	5.5	972.9	14.0	14.1	21.7	8.0	13.1	
Netherlands	0.70	15.2	250.2	30.3	25.8	29.1	40.2	48.5	
France	0.25	—	—	—	—	—	—	—	
Italy	0.36	—	694.0	10.3	8.7	14.9	6.7	11.5	
United Kingdom	0.28	6.8	533.0	9.1	11.8	19.1	4.5	1.9	
United States	0.45	4.3	1,415.0	6.6	7.4	10.7	3.7	5.1	
Japan	0.25	—	—	—	—	—	—	—	

Notes: LF: labor force; Sweden: 1989; Germany, Italy: Population data 1989; Italy: employees only.

Sources: Generosity: OECD 1998: table III.1, 48; male % LF: Aarts et al. 1996b: table 1.1, pp. 4–5) recipients: OECD 1995b: table 4.6, pp. 80–81; own calculations.

transfers were most widespread in the Netherlands (used by 15.2% of working-age population in 1990), followed at a considerable distance by Sweden (7.8%), the United Kingdom (6.8%), Germany (5.5%), and the United States (4.3%) (Aarts, Burkhauser, and de Jong 1996*b*: table 1.1, p. 4). There is an overall correlation between the generosity of disability benefits and disability claims in relation to the workforce and the older age group (see Table 11.2): the generous Dutch and Swedish benefits are paid to 30 percent of the elderly Dutch and 25 percent of older Swedes (55–64), while Britain's (but also France's and Japan's) relatively ungenerous benefits led fewer people there to take up disability insurance.

The Dutch reform process is a telling example of the scope and urgency of the problem to cut back on early exit via disability programs, and it did influence policy debates in other countries (Aarts, Burhauser, and de Jong 1996*a*). Retrenchment was already underway by 1976, when the universalization of benefits to ever larger sections of the population required some cost-saving measures. However, within a decade further contentious retrenchment policies had to be taken against union protest.[28] Yet the cumbersome consensus-driven process and its piecemeal cost-saving measures failed to bring the system under stable control. 'By 1986 employers' organizations and right-wing political parties were arguing that previous reforms had been too small and too late in light of deteriorating economic conditions,' while 'trade unions and left-wing political parties criticized the first series of cost containment proposals for being inequitable' (Aarts and de Jong 1996*b*: 51). The 'social welfare reforms' of 1987 were the first substantial policy reversal, aimed not only at reducing welfare expenditures but also at harmonizing disability with long-term unemployment benefits while abolishing gender inequalities.[29] While the government had expected the reform to cut disability transfers by half, it had to acknowledge two years later that the measures had only brought a small (10%) reduction. Prime Minister Lubbers called the Netherlands a 'sick country', and the new center-left government declared the fight against absenteeism and disability dependence their top priority (Visser and Hemerijck

[28] The labor market consideration, disability awards for older unemployed workers, that was introduced in 1967 and further relaxed in 1973 was applied more strictly after 1978. Even though union protests had blocked a center-left proposal a year earlier, the new center-right coalition was able to reduce replacement rates in 1983. The average net replacement rate was reduced from 87% in 1980 to 72% in 1985 (table 2.6 in Aarts and de Jong 1996*a*: 40), leading to a decrease in disability payments from 22 new awards per 1,000 employed in 1975 to 16 in 1985 (table 2.6. in Aarts and de Jong 1996*a*: 40). Yet in the late 1980s the number of disability benefits, overall costs, and (most worrisome of all) the incidence rate of new awards increased again.

[29] The reforms improved the long-term unemployment situation, especially for married women and older workers, and equalized the benefit-to-wage ratio to 70% for all insured risks—unemployment, sickness, and disability.

1997). Ultimately, only state intervention into the social insurance 'self-administration' (by the social partners) and political compromises were able to alter the rules, at least for younger entrants.[30] In addition to making changes in eligibility and benefits, the government shifted the burden of sick pay costs onto employers, who could now seek private insurance, and reformed the social insurance administration (Aarts and de Jong 1996*b*: 63–65). The measures were initially successful in terminating some benefits, thereby reducing the rate of new awards and improving absenteeism. However, it should also be noted that private employer insurance has filled some of the replacement gap left by the state scheme, since the employers' 'stated interest in reducing labor cost was outweighed by their desire to maintain a generous exit option for their redundant workers' (Aarts and de Jong 1996*b*: 64). The 1990s reform thus proved less capable of foreclosing this exit route altogether, but it did succeed in reducing long-term disability among younger cohorts.

Swedish disability insurance served as a major exit road for older workers: one out of three Swedish men and women (60–64) used this scheme, and it was the second step in the '58.3 rule'. Both 'management and labor often joined forces and used this clause to move older workers off the payroll and onto the disability rolls. Since individual firms and their employees did not bear the direct costs, they were free to push older workers permanently out of the labor force without bearing any of the burden of their actions' (Wadensjö and Palmer 1996: 154). As a consequence, however, 'this rule contributed significantly to increasing national social costs by lowering the *de facto* pension age' (Wadensjö and Palmer 1996: 141). A first intervention by the government in the 1980s banned workplace agreements on using the '58.3 rule' to circumventing employment protection laws. But early retirement still accounted for about half of all disability benefits in the late 1980s (though one-third of disability pensions were part-time). With dramatically rising unemployment and given the financial crisis in the early 1990s, the government finally closed the automatic pre-retirement option of the disability scheme in 1991, as a consequence unemployment among older workers has increased considerably.

Not only was the German disability insurance less generous, and therefore 'only' one in five older men (60–64) and only one in six German women received disability benefits (Frick and Sadowski 1996), the 1984

---

[30] When the tripartite Social Economic Council was unable to come up with a stringent reform proposal, the cabinet abandoned consensus-seeking and presented its own proposal. The reform proposals of 1991 and 1992 made eligibility standards more stringent and planned lower benefits for younger recipients, but after fierce resistance a political compromise left acquired seniority entitlements untouched while still requiring younger beneficiaries under 50 to be re-evaluated thoroughly.

Budget Act already reduced benefits and raised the contribution period to women's detriment, thereby limiting the program's further growth. Nevertheless, the German disability program allowed for disability awards due to old age unemployment (about one-fourth of disability benefits in 1990), and in fact, 'increasingly, labor market problems have been shifted to the disability pension system' (Frick and Sadowski 1996: 121), following the business cycle by and large. Closing this exit route, the Conservative–Liberal government decided in 1996 to phase out the disability pre-retirement program by gradually raising the age from 60 to 63 in 2003 (while the program for the 'severely handicapped' remained in force).

In welfare states with less generous benefits, a reform was less urgent. Still for many Italians, the disability program was the only early retirement option, and it became widespread once the eligibility criteria had been relaxed in 1970/71. After several changes in the 1980s, some 'loopholes' in disability programs were closed in 1995.[31] France stands out in Continental Europe for its low take-up rate, since disability benefits there are relatively meager: just 30 percent of former salary for partial, and 50 percent for full incapacity to work (Palier 1997: 92).[32] Similarly, Japan's disability benefits are relatively low and hardly used as bridging devices for early retirement.

The two existing US programs, the Social Security Disability Insurance (SSDI, originally enacted in 1956) and Supplemental Security Income (SSI, first introduced in 1972), were relatively early subject to retrenchment efforts. In 1977 the Carter administration was using 'moral suasion' to tighten eligibility decisions by state agencies. The Reagan administration used the 1980 reform passed by the Democratic-led Congress to reduce benefits, tighten control, re-evaluate past decisions, and increase work incentives (Sheppard 1991: 278). But under public pressure in 1984,[33] Congress reversed the reform, making it difficult to remove anyone already on the disability rolls. The recession of the early 1990s brought a new wave of applicants.

[31] In 1990, 4 million Italians were receiving 'disability' benefits, though 1.7 million (or 40% of the recipients) were self-employed and only 1 million (or one-quarter of all recipients) were in the age group 55–64 (see OECD 1995b: table 5.2/3, pp. 136–37). The disability insurance provides for medium-term benefits (up to 3 years) after just 5 years of contributions, and for unlimited pensions after 12 years of contributions.

[32] In the 1980s less than 40,000 'disabled' and less than 85,000 'inapt' men and women were held eligible for disability insurance out of around 400,000–500,000 retired (table 5.8 in Guillemard 1991a: 143–44).

[33] The new practice led to half a million removals, most of which led (in turn) to a wave of appeals, a subsequent suit by Social Administration Court judges in 1981, a press campaign about the dire consequences in individual cases, and massive complaints by state governors in 1983 (Berkowitz and Burkhauser 1996).

In 1992 the Conservative Major government stopped the earning-related disability insurance but kept flat-rate benefits and introduced new living and working allowances (subsidies to rent and job-related costs) based on self-assessment rather than means-testing. Both countries, the USA and UK, do not recognize 'commensurate' employment as a labor market criterion in disability insurance, nor does their disability criteria allow for partial work incapacitation out of fear that disability benefits might be abused. Thus, both the American and British disability systems actually produce the strongest disincentives to get out of welfare, as they exclude part-time work while drawing benefits, yet the disability benefits are kept relatively low in order to maintain strong incentives to work.

11.3.4. Gradual and Part-Time Retirement

Gradual and part-time pensions are among the policies recommended by the OECD—not only to reverse the trend toward costly pension expenditures, but also to promote the shift towards an 'active society'. The prime example is the Swedish part-time scheme (1976) which had a take-up rate of 20 percent of the eligible workforce in the early 1980s. Yet the new bourgeois government cut the compensation rate to 50 percent, which led to a near 50 percent drop in the take-up rate (Delsen 1996: 58), while after the return of the Social Democrats in 1987, the replacement rate was raised again. Moreover, with the closure of the alternative '58.3' rule in 1991, the partial pension became widely used again: one-quarter of the eligible older population drew this kind of early partial pension (Delsen 1996: 58). Thus, closing one alternative had led to an instrument substitution, and thus required new action from the government which soon increased the starting age for partial pensions by a year (from 60 to 61, as of 1996), and cut the replacement rate to 55 percent (Wadensjö 1996). A further decline can be expected as a result of new plans aimed at phasing out partial retirement in favor of the less generous part-time 'semi-pension' program.[34]

Denmark introduced a partial pre-retirement scheme only in 1987, a decade after Sweden. It gave workers and the self-employed over 60 an allowance, similar to unemployment benefits, that was proportional to the working hours cut, though the new program had less impact than

---

[34] So far, the part-time early retirement pension has been relatively unpopular. Originally, the scheme allowed only half-time work and semi-pensions, but since July 1993 quarter and three-quarter pensions are also possible. One disadvantage of this special pension is that it leads to actuarial reductions (before 65). Yet in 1993 less than 2,200 men and 500 women were taking part, compared to about 30,000 men and 19,000 women per year in the partial pension scheme before it was reformed (Wadensjö 1996: 33).

expected.[35] Danish unions and employers' associations had long been against gradual pensions, but in 1995 they introduced a new part-time scheme (*delefterløn*) (as part of voluntary unemployment insurance) that is relatively generous, providing about 80 percent of unemployment benefits (Delsen 1996: 60). As in Sweden, the success of partial pensions depends much on the replacement rate, whether a reduction in working time pays off, yet with higher benefits the costs may outdo the gains from allowing a gradual transition from work to retirement.

Similarly, the German pension reform of 1992 which created new rules for gradual retirement by allowing part-time jobs to be combined with partial pensions, failed to be successful due to limited financial incentives and restrictive conditions.[36] New part-time pension schemes, enacted on the initiative of the social partners in 1996, are complemented by collective agreements that cover a part of the pension cuts and guarantee at least 85 percent of net wages (1997: de9708224f). But contrary to the law's intention of a gradual transition, the five years half-pay/half-pension arrangement is used to finance a first period of full-time working and then the remainder as full retirement, thus de facto leading to full early retirement (at 62.5).

Also the French government had only limited success when introducing a partial pension law in 1988, which allows a 60 year-old worker to engage in part-time work while receiving a partial pension (Reday-Mulvey 1996: 54). A new law in 1992 simplified gradual retirement (now 55+), allowed worktime to vary between 40 percent and 50 percent, and abandoned strict replacement requirements in favor of either financial contributions or a recruitment guarantee from the employer. 'A fair number of recent contracts between the social partners contain agreements to keep employees in the firm until the legal retirement age but at the same time to offer

---

[35] The scheme requires a reduction of at least 25% in full-time working hours, not more than 30 hours and not fewer than 15. In 1991 there were only 6,000 beneficiaries per year, less than the 7,500–10,000 expected (Delsen 1996: 56). Indeed, 'because of the high net compensation rate (between 63% and 75%), there is little financial incentive to choose partial rather than full early retirement; and the reduction in working time results in a loss of future supplementary pension entitlements' (Delsen 1996: 60).

[36] Until 65, there is an earnings limit dependent on the share of the pension in overall income (anywhere between around 74% of average earnings for a one-third pension to 37% in the case of two-thirds pension—see table 5.4 in Schmähl, George, and Oswald 1996: 77). In addition, part-time pensioners have to pay income tax and higher social security contributions; thus, net earnings, especially for the half pensions (with 90% replacement rates) and two-third pensions (83%), are relatively close to what they are for full pensions (84%) (table 5.5 in Schmähl, George, and Oswald 1996: 78). 'Regarding net income from pensions and earnings, we can see that a full pension with only marginal employment yields an income at least comparable to that which could be achieved with a partial pension. This might be one of the reasons why little use has been made of this new regulation so far' (Schmähl, George, and Oswald 1996: 78).

them several alternatives for reducing their work hours' (Reday-Mulvey 1996: 55–56). But gradual pensions *à la française* rely largely on state subsidies, negotiated deals with the social partners, and complicated requirements. As a result, it is mostly big firms that take advantage of the program, while most French people still assume a ' "zero sum game" ' of shortening work-life at both ends of the life-cycle' (Reday-Mulvey 1996: 67).

Prospects for gradual retirement in the UK are also limited due to the traditional 'culture of early exit in British industry' and 'little enthusiasm among employers for later or phased retirement' (Taylor and Walker 1996: 108). Yet 'in recent years government policy on older workers has changed from one of encouraging their early retirement to one of trying to increase the supply of older workers and of encouraging employers to utilize this source of labor' (Taylor and Walker 1996: 94). The common defined-benefit occupational pension plans usually require full exit, while the public pension program only allows a retiring employee to begin drawing a pension at 65. The earnings rule was abolished in 1989, which helped older workers combine their pensions with part-time work (60% of workers past normal retirement age work part-time; Taylor and Walker 1996: 95). In the USA, similarly, the combination of partial and gradual retirement was not supported for a long time (neither by public policy nor by employers), and defined benefit employer plans in particular often ruled out part-time early retirement. Moreover, the public pensions' earnings test had been an obstacle to combining work with a pension, though this test was relaxed in 1978 and again in 1990 for those above 65 (OECD 1995*a*: ch. 10).

The Japanese practice of mandatory dismissal (*teinen*) and re-employment (*shukko*) of older workers, together with relatively low pension benefits, functions as a quasi-partial pension program. Japanese workers that meet the earnings test would receive employee pensions beginning at 60 (but not yet the basic benefits) and could thus draw on low-wage supplements (often with shortened working time due to re-employment). Changes scheduled to go into effect in the near future will raise the state pension age and thus leave dismissed workers facing an income gap, which will be even more dramatic as more Japanese firms abandon the *shukko* practice. Thus, in Japan gradual retirement has become a common practice that will increasingly run into problems in the future.

Although gradual retirement used to be the rule before mature public pension systems assumed or even required full withdrawal from work, public policies to support gradual retirement (by encouraging workers to engage in part-time work and/or postpone drawing on their pensions in full) have been late and relatively modest. Political differences and financial constraints have led Sweden to make its gradual retirement less attractive. The relative failure of the Danish, Dutch, French, and German partial pension initiatives results partly from insufficient financial incentives. In addition to relatively low normal benefits, disincentives come from the specific rules applying to public pensions, such as calculating benefits based on the last year's earnings and from the tax treatment of partial pensions. In addition, 'crowding out' by alternative, more generous 'exit' routes can be a major obstacle to gradual retirement. Moreover, the decision to combine part-time work with a partial pension is not a choice reserved exclusively for the beneficiary; it also depends on the employer's willingness to provide part-time employment. Although it might be beneficial to retain older retired workers, especially those with long experience and special skills, many industrial firms are reluctant to do so in the case of shift work and with either unskilled or semi-skilled workers. 'Although overall there has been a relative bottoming-out of the fall of employment rates for older workers,' a comparative study on gradual retirement concludes, 'where not securely articulated into company policies, public policies have not yet necessarily produced the expected results' (Delsen and Reday-Mulvey 1996*b*: 11).

11.4. Conclusion

Early exit from work has been nearly a global phenomena, but the share of employment inactivity of older men in working age have varied considerably across welfare and employment regimes, largely as a function of the availability of pathways for early retirement, (see Table 11.3). As a rule, the Continental European countries that created multiple pathways with often generous pre-retirement benefits also relied most heavily on labor shedding. In contrast, the liberal-residual welfare states (UK, USA, and Japan) and the advanced Scandinavian welfare states maintained a higher level of activity for older people, either by offering insufficient benefits or by trying to promote a gradual transition from work to retirement. Both the 'push' factors set by economic conditions (and the policies of firms) and the 'pull' factors provided by alternative pathways are important for explaining the different patterns of early exit (Esping-Andersen and Sonnberger 1991). It is the 'dialectics of work and welfare' (de Vroom and Naschold 1994) that play out in the interaction of welfare states, production systems, and labor relations. These institutional differences also shape the urgency for change, the scope of the problems, and the very character of policy reversal.

The kinds of welfare and employment regimes in place shaped the decisions concerning the expansion of social and employment rights. The

Table 11.3 *Typology of exit patterns and early retirement regimes*

Regime	Early exit	Welfare regime	Employment regime	Exit pathways	Policy reversal
Latin European (France, Italy)	High	Familist 'pension state': passive transfers	Labor shedding; intergenerational solidarity	Early (seniority) pension; 'bridging' unemployment; state subsidies deficit	Phasing-out; more state intervention; responsible social partner needed
Continental European (Germany, Netherlands)	Medium-high	'Social insurance state': passive transfers	Labor shedding; intergenerational solidarity	Multiple pathways: public and private; externalization of costs	Closing/phasing-out of public schemes; shifting costs on to private actors
Anglo-American (USA, UK)	Medium	Liberal-residual welfare state: low public support	Flexible labor market, but anti-discrimination laws	Narrow pathways: individual cost-sharing; employer sponsored exit	Increase incentives to work longer; shift towards defined-contribution funds
Scandinavian (Sweden, Denmark)	Medium-low	Universal welfare state: gradual but late pensions	Full employment aim and (re)integration policies	Partial pathways: partial or flexible pension	Ending of favorable routes due to financial constraints
Japanese	Low	Familist liberal welfare state: early but insufficient pension	Mandatory retirement, but re-employment norm	Incomplete pathway: re-employment + state pension	Gradual rise in pension age due to demographics

Continental social insurance states and Latin familist 'pension states' relied heavily on passive transfers to shed labor. Largely financed by payroll taxes and administered by the social partners, the early exit pathways in these 'welfare without work' societies, have been relatively susceptible to the externalization of costs by firms and the institutionalization of early retirement as a social right. What started out as temporary redundancy payments or old age unemployment relief became entrenched acquired rights, policy traps in which the search for a solution to rising unemployment via costly labor shedding priced labor even further out of the market. 'Like boats on the river Rhine captured by the temptation of the singing *Loreley* long before they reached their destination, workers in the modern welfare society are lured into early exit pathways long before they reach the age of 65' (Trommel and de Vroom 1994: 52). The Continental European welfare states' 'Loreley effect' had adverse consequences for the financial viability of social insurance systems but also a negative impact on non-wage labor costs (and thus on competitiveness).

The generous Scandinavian welfare states provided similar pathways to early retirement via disability or unemployment insurance, but in contrast to Continental Europe they were able to maintain an active employment policy by integrating older people into the 'work society' and allowing for a more gradual transition from work to retirement (Wadensjö 1996). The traditionally high employment rate among older men in Scandinavia is indeed the result of the late normal retirement age, the opportunities for gradual retirement (combined with part-time work and thus higher employment rates), and the active employment policies (from which also older workers benefit). Yet this success was conditional upon full employment, thus when around 1990, Sweden has experienced a rise in unemployment and was forced to cut back on partial pension and close its disability pension for older unemployed workers, the unemployment rate of older workers has increased considerably.

The Anglo-Saxon liberal-residual welfare states and the Japanese welfare laggard provided narrower pathways to early retirement and subsequently have experienced less early exit from work than Continental European welfare states. Instead of 'pull' through favorable pre-retirement benefits, economic 'push' factors were the driving force behind early exit from work in the flexible labor markets of the USA and UK, but also behind the mandatory retirement practices of large Japanese firms. The liberal-residual welfare states have not had much to offer in the way of state policy, so voluntary employer policies such as window plans (or, in Japan, re-employment) remained the major options. In recent years, companies were less willing to (or capable of) accommodating restructuring by voluntary aid, while downsizing became more and more prominent (also increasingly in Japan). In fact, the Japanese exceptional low rate of early exit from work will be unlikely in the future as companies renounce traditional life-long employment duties, indeed unemployment is rising, particularly among older workers. On the other hand, low unemployment of the currently booming US economy and strong work incentives of the reformed pension system will probably stabilize (if not increase) the current level of employment activity among older workers.

In light of persistent unemployment and financial constraints, all welfare states sought to reverse past early exit routes. This policy reversal was most pressing in the Continental European welfare states, though it was also there that a U-turn proved most difficult in the face of entrenched rights defended by unions, employers' interest in externalizing costs, and the possibility of 'instrument substitution' presented by multiple alternative pathways (some of which were administered by the social partners at various levels). Indeed, closing down special pre-retirement programs or introducing partial pensions did not bring about much change so long as other, more generous alternatives were available. When governments (often against fierce opposition by unions) succeeded in bringing down replacement rates for public benefits programs, private sector actors like the social partners (or simply employers on their own) frequently filled in the gap between the reduced public benefit and former net wages. Given the veto power of unions, as demonstrated by the French strike wave of 1995, governments sought compromises allowing change to be phased in gradually, since more rapid measures would have adversely affected unemployment.

Higher unemployment and financial constraints also induced the Scandinavian welfare states to put on their emergency brakes; thus, Sweden departed from its generous disability and gradual retirement programs, while the Danish government sought to intervene in collectively negotiated pre-retirement schemes. Policy reversal in the liberal-residual welfare states, given how few and limited pathways to early exit were there, was largely driven by long-term concerns about demographic trends and their financial implications. Reforms were phased in to restore long-term solvency and remove any incentives to quit work early. Indeed, disability benefits were always limited to cases of total incapacititation. Similarly, Japan has taken steps to confront its public programs' long-term liabilities. Japan's past reliance on social norms of re-employment, opportunities for secondary employment, and family support seems to be waning, thus undermining the implicit assumptions of old age provision.

Hence, while policymakers in all countries (following the policy recommendations of international agencies) seem to be increasingly persuaded of the need to reverse earlier exit policies, they still find it very difficult to change course by implementing 'best practices' from abroad. Given the entrenched character of acquired social rights and the continued availability of multiple pathways, social compromises are needed to overcome the social partners' blocking power and insure that some reforms can be implemented, at the very least in that policy space shared by Continental Europe and Scandinavia. This will be difficult as long as there exists a social coalition of early exit between firms (which strive for externalizing their restructuration costs and circumvent seniority employment protection) and workers' interests (which perceive an acquired social right to an early retirement given long worklives, substantial contributions, and lacking jobs). Public policy needs to bring the social partner into reform consensus, since a reversal would require the cooperation at several levels (from the national bargaining arena to the workplace) and needs to coordinate changes across different public, bipartite and voluntary policies in order to avoid instrument substitution and mere cost shifting from one scheme to another.

REFERENCES

AARTS, LEO J. M., and DE JONG, PHILIP R. (1996a). 'The Dutch Disabilitiy Program and How It Grew', in Leo J. M. Aarts, Richard V. Burkhauser, and Philip R. de Jong (eds.), *Curing the Dutch Disease: An International Perspective on Disability Policy Reform.* Aldershot: Avebury, 21–46.

——— (1996b). 'Evaluating the 1987 and 1993 Social Welfare Reforms: From Disappointment to Potential Success', in Leo J. M. Aarts, Richard V. Burkhauser, and Philip R. de Jong (eds.), *Curing the Dutch Disease: An International Perspective on Disability Policy Reform.* Aldershot: Avebury, 47–69.

—— BURKHAUSER, RICHARD V., and DE JONG, PHILIP R. (eds.) (1996a). *Curing the Dutch Disease: An International Perspective on Disability Policy Reform.* Aldershot: Avebury.

——— (1996b). 'Introduction and Overview', in Leo J.M. Aarts, Richard V. Burkhauser, and Philip R. de Jong (eds.), *Curing the Dutch Disease. An International Perspective on Disability Policy Reform.* Aldershot: Avebury, 1–19.

BERKOWITZ, EDWARD D., and BURKHAUSER, RICHARD V. (1996). 'A United States Perspective on Disability Programs', in Leo J. M. Aarts, Richard V. Burkhauser, and Philip R. de Jong (eds.), *Curing the Dutch Disease: An International Perspective on Disability Policy Reform.* Aldershot: Avebury, 71–91.

BOSWORTH, BARRY, and BURTLESS, GARY (eds.) (1998). *Ageing Societies: The Global Dimension.* Washington, DC: Brookings Institution.

CASEY, BERNARD (1989). 'Early Retirement: The Problem of "Instrument Subsititution" and "Cost Shifting" and Their Implications for Restructuring the Process of Retirement', in Winfried Schmähl (ed.), *Redefining the Process of Retirement: An International Perspective*. Berlin: Springer-Verlag, 133–50.

—— (1992). 'Paying for Early Retirement'. *JSP*, 21/3: 303–23.

—— (1996). 'Exit Options from the Labour Force', in Günther Schmid, Jacqueline O'Reilly, and Klaus Schömann (eds.), *International Handbook of Labour Market Policy and Evaluation*. Cheltenham: Edward Elgar, 379–401.

—— (1997). *Incentives and Disincentives to Early and Late Retirement*. ILO Conference, Geneva, Sept. 1997.

CHEN, YUNG-PING (1996). 'Gradual Retirement in the United States: Macro Issues and Policies', in Lei Delsen and Geneviève Reday-Mulvey (eds.), *Gradual Retirement in the OECD Countries: Macro and Micro Issues and Policies*. Aldershot: Dartmouth, 164–85.

CROUCH, COLIN (1993). *Industrial Relations and European State Traditions*. Oxford: Clarendon Press.

DE VROOM, BERT, and BLOMSMA, MARTIN (1991). 'The Netherlands: An Extreme Case', in Martin Kohli, Martin Rein, Anne-Marie Guillemard, and Herman van Gunsteren (eds.), *Time for Retirement: Comparative Studies on Early Exit from the Labor Force*. New York: Cambridge University Press, 97–126.

—— and NASCHOLD, FRIEDER (1994). 'The Dialectics of Work and Welfare', in Frieder Naschold and Bert de Vroom (eds.), *Regulating Employment and Welfare: Company and National Policies of Labour Force Participation at the End of Worklife in Industrial Countries*. Berlin: W. de Gruyter, 1–18.

DELSEN, LEI (1996). 'Gradual Retirement: Lessons from the Nordic Countries and the Netherlands'. *EJIR*, 2/1: 55–67.

—— and REDAY-MULVEY, GENEVIÈVE (eds.) (1996a). *Gradual Retirement in the OECD Countries: Macro and Micro Issues and Policies*. Aldershot: Dartmouth.

—— —— (1996b). 'Macro Issues and Policies', in Lei Delsen and Geneviève Reday-Mulvey (eds.), *Gradual Retirement in the OECD Countries: Macro and Micro Issues and Policies*. Aldershot: Dartmouth, 3–12.

EBBINGHAUS, BERNHARD (1999). 'Does a European Social Model Exist and Can it Survive?', in Gerhard Huemer, Michael Mesch, and Franz Traxler (eds.), *The Role of Employer Associations and Labour Unions in the EMU: Institutional Requirements for European Economic Policies*. Aldershot: Ashgate, 1–26.

—— and HASSEL, ANKE (2000). 'Striking Deals: Concertation in the Reform of Contiental European Welfare States'. *JEPP* 7/1: 44–62.

EIRO (*European Industrial Relations Online (EIROnline)*). Dublin: Dublin Foundation <http: //www.eiro.eurofound.ie>.

ESPING-ANDERSEN, GØSTA (1990). *Three Worlds of Welfare Capitalism*. Princeton: Princeton University Press.

—— (ed.) (1996a). *Welfare States in Transition: National Adaptations in Global Economies*. London: Sage.

—— (1996b). 'Welfare States without Work: The Impasse of Labour Shedding and Familialism in Continental European Social Policy', in Gøsta

Esping-Andersen (ed.), *Welfare States in Transition: National Adaptations in Global Economies*. London: Sage, 66–87.

ESPING-ANDERSEN, GØSTA (1997). 'Hybrid or Unique? The Japanese Welfare State between Europe and America'. *JESP* 7/3: 179–89

——and SONNBERGER, HARALD (1991). 'The Demographics of Age in Labor-Market Management', in John Myles and Jill Quadagno (eds.), *States, Labor Markets, and the Future of Old-Age Policy*. Philadelphia: Temple University Press, 227–49.

European Commission (1997). *Supplementary Pensions in the Single Market. A Green Paper*. Brussels: European Commission.

Eurostat (1997), *Labour Force Survey 1995*. Luxembourg: Eurostat.

FRICK, BERND, and SADOWSKI, DIETER (1996). 'A German Perspective on Disability Policy', in Leo J. M. Aarts, Richard V. Burkhauser, and Philip R. de Jong (eds.), *Curing the Dutch Disease: An International Perspective on Disability Policy Reform*. Aldershot: Avebury, 117–31.

GUILLEMARD, ANNE-MARIE (1991a). 'France: Massive exit through unemployment', in Martin Kohli, Martin Rein, Anne-Marie Guillemard, and Herman van Gunsteren (eds.), *Time for Retirement: Comparative Studies on Early Exit from the Labor Force*. New York: Cambridge University Press, 127–80.

——(1991b). 'Pathways and their Prospects: A Comparative Interpretation of the Meaning of Early Exit', in Martin Kohli, Martin Rein, Anne-Marie Guillemard, and Herman van Gunsteren (eds.), *Time for Retirement: Comparative Studies on Early Exit from the Labor Force*. New York: Cambridge University Press, 362–87.

——and REIN, MARTIN (1993). 'Comparative Patterns of Retirement: Recent Trends in Developed Societies'. *ARS* 19: 469–503.

HUTCHENS, ROBERT (1994). 'The United States: Employer Policies for Discouraging Work by Older People', in Frieder Naschold and Bert de Vroom (eds.), *Regulating Employment and Welfare: Company and National Policies of Labour Force Participation at the End of Worklife in Industrial Countries*. Berlin: W. de Gruyter, 395–431.

JACOBS, KLAUS, and REIN, MARTIN (1994). 'Early Retirement: Stability, Reversal, or Redefinition', in Frieder Naschold and Bert de Vroom (eds.), *Regulating Employment and Welfare: Company and National Policies of Labour Force Participation at the End of Worklife in Industrial Countries*. Berlin: W. de Gruyter, 19–49.

——KOHLI, MARTIN, and REIN, MARTIN (1991a). 'The Evolution of Early Exit: A Comparative Analysis of Labor Force Participation Patterns', in Martin Kohli, Martin Rein, Anne-Marie Guillemard, and Herman van Gunsteren (eds.), *Time for Retirement: Comparative Studies on Early Exit from the Labor Force*. New York: Cambridge University Press, 36–66.

——————(1991b). 'Germany: The Diversity of Pathways', in Martin Kohli, Martin Rein, Anne-Marie Guillemard, and Herman van Gunsteren (eds.), *Time for Retirement: Comparative Studies on Early Exit from the Labor Force*. New York: Cambridge University Press, 181–221.

————(1991*c*). 'Testing the Industry-Mix Hypothesis of Early Exit', in Martin Kohli, Martin Rein, Anne-Marie Guillemard, and Herman van Gunsteren (eds.), *Time for Retirement: Comparative Studies on Early Exit from the Labor Force*. New York: Cambridge University Press, 67–96.

KIMURA, TAKESHI, TAKAGI, IKURO, OKA, MASATO, and OMORI, MAKI (1994). 'Japan: Shukko, Teinen and Re-Employment', in Frieder Naschold and Bert de Vroom (eds.), *Regulating Employment and Welfare: Company and National Policies of Labour Force Participation at the End of Worklife in Industrial Countries*. Berlin: W. de Gruyter, 247–307.

KOHLI, MARTIN, REIN, MARTIN, GUILLEMARD, ANNE-MARIE, and van GUNSTEREN, HERMAN (eds.) (1991). *Time for Retirement: Comparative Studies on Early Exit from the Labor Force*. New York: Cambridge University Press.

KOLBERG, JON EIVIND, and ESPING-ANDERSEN, GØSTA (1991). 'Welfare States and Employment Regimes', in Jon Eivind Kolberg (ed.), *The Welfare State as Employer*. Armonk, NY: M. E. Sharpe, 3–35.

LACZKO, FRANK, and PHILLIPSON, CHRIS (1991). 'Great Britain: The Contradictions of Early Exit', in Martin Kohli, Martin Rein, Anne-Marie Guillemard, and Herman van Gunsteren (eds.), *Time for Retirement: Comparative Studies on Early Exit from the Labor Force*. New York: Cambridge University Press, 222–51.

LONSDALE, SUSAN, and AYLWARD, MANSEL (1996). 'A United Kingdom Perspective on Disability Policy', in Leo J. M. Aarts, Richard V. Burkhauser, and Philip R. de Jong (eds.), *Curing the Dutch Disease: An International Perspective on Disability Policy Reform*. Aldershot: Avebury, 93–115.

NASCHOLD, FRIEDER, and DE VROOM, BERT (eds.) (1994). *Regulating Employment and Welfare: Company and National Policies of Labour Force Participation at the End of Worklife in Industrial Countries*. Berlin: W. de Gruyter.

————and CASEY, BERNARD (1994). 'Regulating Employment and Welfare: An International Comparison between Firms and Countries', in Frieder Naschold, and Bert de Vroom (eds.), *Regulating Employment and Welfare: Company and National Policies of Labour Force Participation at the End of Worklife in Industrial Countries*. Berlin: W. de Gruyter, 433–89.

OECD (Organisation for Economic Co-operation and Development) (annually). *Labour Forces Statistics*. Paris: OECD.

——(1995*a*). *The Labour Market and Older Workers*. Paris: OECD.

——(1995*b*). *The Transition from Work to Retirement*. Paris: OECD.

——(1998). *Maintaining Prosperity in an Ageing Society*. Paris: OECD.

ØVERBYE, EINAR (1997). 'Retirement from the Labour Force—a Multiple Choice Exercise? Pre-Retirement in the Nordic Countries in a European Context', in Alessandra Bosco and Martin Hutsebaut (eds.), *Social Protection in Europe: Facing up to Changes and Challenges*. Brussels: ETUI, 139–55.

PALIER, BRUNO (1997). 'A "Liberal" Dynamic in the Transformation of the French Social Welfare System', in Jochen Clasen (ed.), *Social Insurance in Europe*. Bristol: Policy Press, 84–106.

PETERSEN, JØRN HENRIK (1989). 'The Process of Retirement in Denmark: Trends,

Public Discussion and Institutional Framework', in Winfried Schmähl (ed.), *Redefining the Process of Retirement: An International Perspective*. Berlin: Springer-Verlag, 63–81.

PIERSON, PAUL (1994). *Dismantling the Welfare State? Reagan, Thatcher, and the Politics of Retrenchment*. New York: Cambridge University Press.

REDAY-MULVEY, GENEVIÈVE (1996). 'Gradual Retirement in France', in Lei Delsen and Geneviève Reday-Mulvey (eds.), *Gradual Retirement in the OECD Countries: Macro and Micro Issues and Policies*. Aldershot: Dartmouth, 45–68.

SCHARPF, FRITZ W. (1998). 'Employment and the Welfare State: A Continental Dilemma', in GAAC (ed.), *Labour Markets in the USA and Germany*. Bonn: GAAC, 387–404.

SCHMÄHL, WINFRIED, GEORGE, RAINER, and OSWALD, CHRISTIANE (1996). 'Gradual Retirement in Germany', in Lei Delsen and Geneviève Reday-Mulvey (eds.), *Gradual Retirement in the OECD Countries: Macro and Micro Issues and Policies*. Aldershot: Dartmouth, 69–93.

SHEPPARD, HAROLD L. (1991). 'The United States: The Privatization of Exit', in Martin Kohli, Martin Rein, Anne-Marie Guillemard, and Herman van Gunsteren (eds.), *Time for Retirement: Comparative Studies on Early Exit from the Labor Force*. New York: Cambridge University Press, 252–83.

STEPHENS, JOHN D. (1996). 'The Scandinavian Welfare States: Achievements, Crisis and Prospects', in Gøsta Esping-Andersen (ed.), *Welfare States in Transition: National Adaptations in Global Economies*. London: Sage, 32–65.

TAKAYAMA, NORIYUKI (1996). 'Gradual Retirement in Japan: Macro Issues and Policies', in Lei Delsen and Geneviève Reday-Mulvey (eds.), *Gradual Retirement in the OECD Countries: Macro and Micro Issues and Policies*. Aldershot: Dartmouth, 135–63.

TAYLOR, PHILIP, and WALKER, ALAN (1996). 'Gradual Retirement in the United Kingdom', in Lei Delsen and Geneviève Reday-Mulvey (eds.), *Gradual Retirement in the OECD Countries: Macro and Micro Issues and Policies*. Aldershot: Dartmouth, 94–110.

TROMMEL, WILLEM, and DE VROOM, BERT (1994). 'The Netherlands: The Loreley-Effect of Early Exit', in Frieder Naschold and Bert de Vroom (eds.), *Regulating Employment and Welfare: Company and National Policies of Labour Force Participation at the End of Worklife in Industrial Countries*. Berlin: W. de Gruyter, 51–115.

VISSER, JELLE, and HEMERIJCK, ANTON (1997). *'A Dutch Miracle': Job Growth, Welfare Reform, and Corporatism in the Netherlands*. Amsterdam: Amsterdam University Press.

WADENSJÖ, ESKIL (1991). 'Sweden: Partial Exit', in Martin Kohli, Martin Rein, Anne-Marie Guillemard, and Herman van Gunsteren (eds.), *Time for Retirement: Comparative Studies on Early Exit from the Labor Force*. New York: Cambridge University Press, 284–323.

——(1996). 'Gradual Retirement in Sweden', in Lei Delsen and Geneviève Reday-Mulvey (eds.), *Gradual Retirement in the OECD Countries: Macro and Micro Issues and Policies*. Aldershot: Dartmouth, 25–44.

——and PALMER, EDWARD E. (1996). 'Curing the Dutch Disease from a Swedish Perspective', in Leo J. M. Aarts, Richard V. Burkhauser, and Philip R. de Jong (eds.), *Curing the Dutch Disease: An International Perspective on Disablity Policy Reform*. Aldershot: Avebury, 133–55.

12

After Liberalization
Public Interest Services and Employment in the Utilities

ADRIENNE HÉRITIER AND SUSANNE K. SCHMIDT

12.1. Introduction

In European capitalist democracies, the market was contained not only by the formal welfare state, but also by direct state control of the production and distribution of politically salient goods and services. Most important among these were those public interest services that were generally provided by state monopolies. To the extent that direct state control was not explained by military considerations or revenue interests, justifications were generally couched in terms of economic theories of public goods and market failures. Given the dependence of modern economies and private individuals on the 'infrastructure' of transport and communication systems, of energy and water supply, waste disposal, and a wide range of other services and facilities, it was thought nearly self-evident that these could not be provided by private firms operating in competitive markets if these services were going to satisfy politically defined requirements of universal access, security, continuity, and affordability. In fulfilling these infrastructure functions, moreover, the public utilities have become important employers, providing large numbers of 'good' jobs that were secure from market pressures, and that could thus be considered part of the 'informal welfare state' (Schwartz 2000). Since the mid-1970s, however, these sanguine assumptions have been challenged in policy debates focusing not on the original market failures but on failures of the state monopolies that were meant to correct them. These now came under fire for their poor performance in productive efficiency, consumer friendliness, and ser-

We are grateful to Pierre Bauby, Ira Denkhaus, Jean-Michel Glachant, Bruno Jobert, Stephan Leibfried, Herman Schwartz, Mark Thatcher, Bruno Théret, the participants at the Ringberg Conference, and most of all, the editors for helpful comments. Thanks also to Klara Vanek and Maria Byström for research assistance, and to Clare Tame for editorial assistance.

vice innovation. As a consequence, when some countries (foremost among them the United Kingdom) began in the 1980s to follow the American example by privatizing and deregulating their public utilities, countries that had not yet followed suit came under pressure from their export industries, claiming that the high costs and inefficiencies of national infrastructure facilities and services were creating increasingly burdensome competitive disadvantages. Thus, when the European Community, in the course of its Single Market program, came to require the liberalization of service markets, public monopolies in a number of Member States started becoming (and are still being) privatized as utility markets undergo deregulation. So far, this process has mainly transformed the provision of road, air, and rail transport, telecommunications, postal services, and the supply of energy. While some countries took radical measures early on, others have been more hesitant. The experience of the early reformers allows us to tentatively take stock of the situation. In some instances, the privatization of public utilities and the establishment of market competition have reproduced the kinds of problems that had been predicted by theories of market failure. In those countries, the issue has now become the 'reform of the reforms'. While there is no trend toward re-establishing public monopolies, deregulation is generally being followed by re-regulation.

In this paper, we will not be able to assess the extent to which the efficiency goals associated with the liberalization, privatization, and deregulation of public interest services are in fact being achieved. On the basis of current theory and available empirical evidence, we will instead try to answer the following questions: To what extent are the earlier public service goals of universally accessible, secure, continuous, and affordable infrastructure facilities and services still considered important concerns of national public policy? If so, to what extent are they still realized? What are the underlying causes, and what are the lessons for re-regulation?

In contrast to public-service goals, the impact of liberalization, privatization, and deregulation on employment, which is mapped out in the second part of this chapter, has played practically no role in the reform discussions. But since the utilities did make up a significant proportion of the sheltered part of the economy, their exposure to market pressures has made an important contribution to the decline of the 'golden age' welfare state, making it worthwhile to examine these changes in the present chapter as well (Schwartz 2000).

In the following sections, we will first discuss theoretical issues relating to the performance of infrastructure facilities and services that are liberalized, privatized, and exposed to market competition. We then describe examples of 'reformed' structures of service provision and the associated regulatory institutions and practices in order to assess their impact on service provision. The empirical focus here is on the liberalization of net-work-based utilities—rail transport and telecommunications—in Britain, Germany, and France. In the last part of the chapter, we will then assess the impact of liberalization on employment in telecommunications, posts, and railways in a wider range of countries. Finally, some lessons from the reform are drawn.

12.2. The Theoretical and Analytical Background

Even when functions formerly thought to require provision by the state are transferred to the market, those markets' performance is likely to remain an important concern of public policy. For one thing, the privati-zation of a former state monopoly will not by itself create conditions in which the market's expected efficiencies can be realized. And, even under the best of circumstances, market outcomes will not necessarily approxi-mate the substantive and distributive goals to which the state remains committed. Since these goals can no longer be directly pursued through controls exercised by the state-as-owner, the regulation of market activities is likely to gain in importance. In the literature, the question of how regu-lating utilities affects service outcomes in terms of public interest goals is analyzed using theories of market regulation, natural monopolies and public goods, and in the theory of regulatory contracts.

Market-making regulation creates markets and competition by estab-lishing rules specifying the allocation of property rights and terms of 'fair' competition. In sectors dominated by monopolies, restrictions on market access and of fixed prices are abolished, and competition is introduced alongside privatization (Majone 1996). Once created, market processes need to be protected and controlled (Selznick 1985) so as to prevent anti-competitive behavior. Market-making regulation constitutes the essence of public utilities' reform. By increasing the efficiency of utility providers, market-making regulation tries to ensure more customer-friendliness, such as greater accessibility, more innovation, and lower prices. In so doing, market-making regulation links up with the second type of regula-tory activity, market-correcting regulation. Specific outcomes of market processes are considered politically undesirable vis-à-vis specific social goals. The notion that utilities should measure up to public interest goals reflects such a political consensus. Governments decide that user interests not catered to by the market must at least be guaranteed by some kind of affordable minimum service. The underlying political rationality is that politics must defend the interests of utility users who constitute virtually 'the entire voting population of a country' (Levy and Spiller 1996: 3). In light of recent reforms, the crucial question is: 'How can the efficiency-enhancing aspects of the first regulatory activity be reconciled with the conflicting market-correcting goals of the second?'

The interlinking of economic and political logics is influenced by the fact that the services in question are embedded in an infrastructure long regarded as a natural monopoly with the character of a public good. From an economic perspective, a natural monopoly is legitimized by high start-up costs incurred through investment in a technical network whose long-run average costs of production decline only as output increases (Berg and Tschirhart 1988). Being sheltered from competition, however, the provider will be tempted to charge a monopoly price for services unless prevented from doing so by price regulation. The economic justification for a natural monopoly may be challenged as a result of technological developments, in the same way that the automobile and airline industries eventually undermined the old railway monopoly (Nicolaides 1997).

Moreover, there are normative reasons, such as redistribution, employment, or national defense, that have played a role in legitimizing the public monopoly on providing utilities, and that have led to the sort of market correction by regulation discussed above. Thus, public service provision is intended not only to guarantee proper conditions for daily living (*Daseinsvorsorge*, Forsthoff 1968), but also to protect the community and enhance social cohesion. In this way the fixed network (railtrack or cables) vital for the provision of infrastructural services, such as transport or communication, is regarded as a public good with the typical properties of non-excludability and non-subtractability (Samuelson 1954; Hardin 1982) to which the state guarantees equal access. This public service notion reflects the wish to give infrastructure services the quality of a public good (Bazex 1996; Henry 1997; Bauby and Boual 1993).

Thus, railways were long considered a natural monopoly because of high fixed sunk costs in network and rolling stock. (Baumol, Panzar, and Willig 1982). Consequently, they were dominated by single public enterprises owning infrastructure and providing services at the same time. As such, the railways were subject to a kind of state intervention that left limited room for management autonomy, since one goal of public policy was to impose public service obligations on the railway companies (Nicolaides 1997). Similarly, the typical structure in the telecommunications industry was a public or private monopoly. This was also justified by the high sunk costs of network construction, by economies of scope, the scale of service production, the non-storability of output, and by demand that was stochastic and varied by time. In political terms, the monopolistic market structure was legitimized by the need to ensure universal access, that is, to connect remote areas to national networks and provide services at a reasonable and geographically averaged price (Henry 1997; OECD 1997*b*: ii. 48). The public interest aspects of regulation warranted direct subsidization, or cross-subsidization, of some services by other, more profitable activities (Armstrong, Cowan, and Vickers 1994).

Under the impact of economic internationalization, the organization of public service provision has been drastically altered, following the adjustment of other service and industrial sectors to globalization. In some countries that were hesitant to liberalize, this process has been accelerated by European policies favoring liberalization. Moreover, fiscal crises forced states to rid themselves of financial burdens caused by the state-owned railways. In telecommunications, international competition does not allow any country to afford the high costs of an inefficient infrastructure. Thus, in the mid-1980s the notion of 'contested markets' was increasingly applied in order to introduce market elements into 'natural monopoly' sectors under public ownership. While infrastructure was still regarded as a monopoly, service operations were to be handed over to the market. Restrictions to market access were abolished, and nationalized industries under state ownership were transformed into joint stock companies in which the state holds either some or no shares (Levy and Spiller 1996). With sudden exposure to competition, the former monopolists have come under pressure to enhance their productivity.

To spur competition, additional regulatory measures are needed. One response has been to break up the market into regional monopolies, thereby introducing 'yardstick competition' to publicly tender licenses and franchises for the provision of services in these regional markets, and to introduce competition 'for' the market. The presence of separate providers in different regional markets allows the regulator to compare the performance of the different operators. However, additional regulatory measures, such as price regulation or specifying permissible profit rates, are necessary to prevent private regional monopolies from exploiting their market dominance (Nicolaides 1997). The regulator is dependent on the monopolist for information on real costs and to set the 'right' price.[1] In the case of regulating profit rates, although a permissible rate of return can be specified, this does not provide a sufficient incentive for the monopolist to contain costs and improve efficiency.[2]

In all countries public service goals have been maintained in spite of liberalization. As a consequence, the conflicting imperatives of market-

---

[1] If the price ceiling is too low (Nicolaides 1997: 50), the monopolist has no incentive to make long-term investments.

[2] As long as the specified rate of return is generated by a price that is below the profit-maximizing level, costs and prices will be allowed to drift upwards until this point is reached.

making and market-correcting regulation in the liberalized utilities are acutely reflected in the interaction between regulator and regulatee which can be understood as a contract between the principal (regulator) and the agent (regulatee). From both perspectives the contract implies risks and uncertainties. The private service provider is obliged to provide public goods under conditions of competition. As a private provider he must satisfy both consumers and shareholders. From the regulator's side he faces the uncertainty of changing regulations and the risk of being 'expropriated' by political decisions, that is, of being forced for public service reasons to set utility prices below long-term average costs. Frequent changes in regulation disturb long-term investment plans (Nicolaides 1997), so the agent/regulatee prefers a clear and stable regulatory framework, a clearly specified contract, which (by limiting regulators' discretion) prevents utilities from being manipulated (Levy and Spiller 1996).

By contrast, from the viewpoint of the principals (that is, of governments and regulators) regulatory flexibility, and an incomplete contract are desirable, since these enable the principals to keep in touch with newly emerging political needs, and, where necessary, to respond to service providers' unsatisfactory performance. At the same time, the regulator needs to establish incentives that can 'spur investment, efficient pricing, and the introduction of new services and technologies' (Levy and Spiller 1996: 6). In so doing, he finds himself in a situation of informational asymmetry, since he depends upon receiving correct information from the service provider (Majone 1996), who has a monopoly on detailed technical and commercial information. It requires a lot of information to set a price level that can still leave incentives for technological improvements and productivity gains, especially when such data extend across a wide range of quality levels and compacted price structures (Nicolaides 1997). In brief, from the vantage point of the regulator, the principal–agent relationship requires constant fine-tuning (of both instruments and institutions) in order to strike a balance between market efficiency, on the one hand and public-interest goals, on the other (Eberlein 1998).

If economic efficiency considerations prevail, the regulator becomes an instrument of the provider. In cases where rates of return are regulated public interest goals may jeopardize commercial goals, and private providers may have little economic incentive to stay in the game. Most regulatory solutions lie somewhere in-between, and one expects to find specific mixes of goals and instruments reflecting a compromise. Depending on the national regulatory tradition, the specific institutional set-up and instruments used, and on sector-specific factors, these compromises may have an emphasis that is either more commercial or more public-service-oriented.

One of the public interest goals was employment in utility companies. Like the yardstick of service quality, market efficiency has put pressure on employment levels as a way of boosting productivity. However, in contrast to infrastructure concerns, employment has hardly come within the scope of regulatory efforts. Employment cutbacks are negotiated on a company-by-company basis, and the implication of each firm's firing decisions for macroeconomic unemployment and the welfare state's transformation are rarely the object of reflection.

But, in this chapter, questions about service quality will be discussed first. How do the often conflicting goals of market efficiency and public service mesh under the new regulatory regime, and what outcomes does their interaction produce for service performance?

12.3. The New Regulatory Regimes and their Impacts

12.3.1. The Railways

Prior to reform, the rail industries considered here were (as some still are) under public ownership and subject to considerable political intervention. British Rail (BR) consisted of a single, hierarchically structured public entity comprising all functions from the provision and maintenance of infrastructure and rolling stock to freight and passenger operations. Although the management board had substantial autonomy in day-to-day business, it was supervised by the government, and the government intervened to make decisions about finance and investment (Knill 2000). In Germany, where the railways were publicly owned, the Deutsche Bundesbahn (DBB) was an administration with special status under the auspices of the Federal Ministry of Transport, which authorized tariffs, budgets, salaries, and infrastructural investment decisions (Teutsch 2000). The same still holds true for the Société Nationale des Chemins de Fer Français (SNCF), which as an integrated public enterprise is subject to government intervention regarding rates, wages, employment, and levels of service (Douillet and Lehmkuhl 2000).

On a continuum of goals—where public interest goals are at one end and commercial interests at the other—publicly owned railways are positioned close to the former. If, by political fiat, the top priority goes to public service goals, then a high level of service would be expected. However, additional factors like interests of public managers, trade unions, and privileged suppliers claiming a slice of the railway's monopoly profits, can jeopardize this high level of public service. Nevertheless, since public utilities are heavily subsidized, public interest goals may still play an important role, albeit at the cost of running high deficits. However, the very opposite of high-level public service seems indicated by a rough assessment of performance under the old regime, if take-up rates in inter-modal competition with other means of transport are used as the measure of the rail services' success. The market share of rail transport has continually declined from 10.4 percent in 1970 to 6.6 percent in 1993 (Henry 1997). Declining use and accessibility, relatively high prices, and good scores on safety make up the overall picture.

12.3.1.1. Britain: The New Regulatory Regime, Performance, and Reregulation

The most extensive railway reform occurred in Britain in 1993. It transformed British Rail by dividing it into multiple, privately held enterprises linked to each other by contracts (Gibb, Lowndes, and Charlton 1996). Infrastructure and train operation services were separated institutionally. Infrastructure, along with construction, management, and maintenance were transferred to Railtrack, a private monopoly. Train operation was split into twenty-five enterprises, and rolling stock into three leasing companies. Privatization of these services followed. The twenty-five passenger services were franchised to private companies. Railtrack was privatized by stock market flotation.

Two new regulatory authorities were created: in order to offer services, train operators must apply to the Office of Passenger Rail Franchising (OPRAF), now Strategic Rail Authority, for a franchise; to procure access to track, they must obtain a contract with Railtrack and lease rolling stock from the Rolling Stock Companies. Franchises are granted as regional monopolies in competitive bidding 'for' the market for a specified period between seven to fifteen years (interview OPRAF, June 1998). Passenger lines that are not economically profitable but are meant to be maintained for political reasons receive government subsidies that diminish over time. All contracts contain performance rules that offer economic 'benchmark' incentives to help meet contractual conditions. Fines are payable where contract conditions are not honored (interview OPRAF, Sept. 1998). The performance of the regional train operators can be compared (yardstick competition). In addition to the two new regulatory authorities, the Office of the Rail Regulator (ORR) deals with aspects of competition, approves track access agreements and prices, and protects consumer interests (Kay and Thompson 1991). As regards rail safety, HM Railway Inspectorate supervises and issues regulations, and Local Users Councils monitor the service performance of the train operators (interview RI, Oct. 1998).

But just how successful have these attempts been? The results of performance evaluation are paradoxical inasmuch as a clear increase in the use of passenger rail transport services has been offset by a drop in the quality of services offered (interview Rail Users Consultative Committee, RUCC, Oct. 1998). Overall customer satisfaction improved in ten service categories, declined in seven, and stayed roughly the same in two during the period 1997/98 (interview OPRAF, Sept. 1998). Thus, for example, an increase in the number of passengers as a result of improved accessibility (i.e. stopping at more stations) implies longer travel times. Overcrowding has also caused many complaints, and five commuter rail routes into London were officially confirmed as overcrowded in spring 1998 (*The Guardian* 1998*c*). Furthermore, the goal of continuity/reliability, as measured by punctuality and cancellations, has not been reached. The proportion of trains running late increased by 16 percent between April 1997 and April 1998. Fares levied by the twenty-five operators have gone up by more than the 12 percent increase in inflation between 1995 and 1999 (*The Guardian* 1999*a*), with the government controlling fares only within a 50-mile radius around London. The tariff structure is complex and opaque.

Safety has been a salient political issue since accidents on railways increased from 989 to 1,753 in the period 1995/96–1996/97. The network operator, Railtrack, was blamed for poor performance in both track maintenance and signaling.

All in all, the assessment of the operators' performance after liberalization is rather poor. While trains have attracted more passengers, many other things appear to have gone wrong: under-investment, a lack of punctuality, and a drop in safety standards. In order to remedy this situation, two different types of measures have been taken: existing sanctions were used to improve performance, and the institutional arrangements created by the 1993 reform were subjected to a second round of reforms.

Sanctions took the form of fines, stipulated in the contracts, and imposed by the franchise director in order to improve the quality of service. Railtrack's shortage of investment and maintenance work, despite high profits and public subsidies, is regarded as the main reason for declining safety (*The Guardian* 1998*a*). It was therefore asked by the rail regulator, to whom Railtrack is (by contract) publicly accountable for performance, to invest heavily in track expenditure (*The Guardian* 1998*d*). The Rail Inspectorate (RI), responsible for safety, proceeded to undertake nine prosecutions (interview RI, Oct. 1998). The rail regulator also subjected Railtrack to a two-year scrutiny of its access charges to passenger train operators (*Financial Times* 1997), and for the first time the operator was threatened with a large fine for lack of punctuality (*The Guardian* 1999*b*).

In addition to applying measures (like fines) already available, reformers rethought the institutional set-up of reform so as to enhance regulatory powers and political guidance. Thus, attempts have been made to strengthen the regulator's power to sanction operators and Railtrack (interview OPRAF, Sept. 1998). In another effort to boost the authority of regulators, the overlap of functions between the two regulatory agencies, OPRAF and the ORR, was abolished and OPRAF was transformed into the Strategic Rail Authority (SRA) (interview SRA, Sept. 1998; *The Guardian* 1998*b*), and passenger watchdog bodies will have their funding and authority increased.

From the standpoint of the train operators and network and rolling stock companies, this type of 'regulatory turbulence' constitutes precisely the sort of uncertain environment that makes long-term investments in improving services so risky. The regulators' insistence on high-quality service in the public interest is seen as a threat of administrative expropriation, and the prospect that a franchise might only last seven years offers little incentive to invest in new rolling stock.[3] The renegotiation of franchises was taken up earlier than planned. The objective is to strengthen performance requirements, but also to extend the duration of licenses.

Given these contractual conditions, and since the utilities depend on private financing that is in turn dependent on stock market shares, the railways' corporate boards are responsive not only to consumers and the general public, but also to financial markets. In this situation they have frequently tilted toward the latter so that it has been said that 'British utility regulation has fallen victim to the worst excesses of stock-market capitalism' (Wilks 1997: 285). Particularly large shareholder benefits may be achieved if franchises are sold off for as long as subsidies remain high. In the past year, for example, rail companies have repeatedly been taken over by other companies while their senior managers and shareholders made hefty profits. To some extent, however, a change of hands does give the franchise director the opportunity to redefine the terms of service delivery in favor of customers, and transactions have been used to wrestle investments and better services from new owners. Nevertheless, shareholder gains are still disproportionately high in comparison to consumer gains.[4]

---

[3] Operators do, however, receive substantial public subsidies to help them comply with performance goals. The subsidy reduction is intended to provide incentives for cost reductions. Since franchisees can only influence 20% of their costs, while the other 80% are determined by charges for rolling stock and track access, there is limited room for efficiency gains and a tendency to save on costs by cutting services (Knill 2000).

[4] These sales must be viewed against the backdrop of an overly cheap sale of rail assets by the Conservative government (*The Guardian* 1998*c*; Sturm and Wilks 1997).

12.3.1.2. Germany: The New Regulatory Regime, Performance, and
         Further Liberalization

In 1993 the former west German Deutsche Bundesbahn and the east
German Deutsche Reichsbahn were consolidated into a unified joint-
stock company, the Deutsche Bahn AG (DBAG), of which the federal
government is the sole owner. However, government intervention is kept
in check by a legal division of responsibilities among the management
board, the supervisory board, and DBAG shareholders. The rail network
and rail operations were organizationally separated and the network
opened for access by new operators.[5] A new regulatory body, the Federal
Railway Agency, oversees the DBAG and is responsible for licensing railway enterprises and guaranteeing technical safety. The government
assumed all the financial liabilities of the former DBB and still plays a role
in financing regional rail services and infrastructure. Nevertheless, the
pressure on the railways to introduce more rigorous financial accounting
has increased, and a contract-based regime was introduced in regional
passenger transport, which has been put up for tendering. Whereas the
federal government used to pay an annual lump sum to the DBB by way
of compensation for public service obligations, public actors now pay only
for those specific services deemed either necessary or expedient (Teutsch
2000).

In performance terms, the DBAG transported 15.1 percent more passengers in the first four years following reform than it did in the preceding
years (BMV 1998), largely due to regional transport. Despite a downturn
in the long-distance transport market in 1997, long-distance passenger
traffic turnover on ICE and IC/EC trains was positive (Deutsche Bahn
1997), though less so in 1998 (*SZ* 1999*a*). From 1996 to 1997 rail lost out
to air transport, with DBAG losing 2 percent of domestic passenger kilo-
meters, while air transport gained 6 percent (*SZ* 1998), and this trend
became even more evident in 1998. The response to this decline and to the
corresponding loss of earnings was to earmark a number of long-distance
services for abolition. Yet, in 1999 the number of passengers clearly rose
again as compared to the previous year (*SZ* 1999*b*).[6]

Rail fares in Germany are relatively high and reflect an attempt to pursue a policy of economic profitability, though supplemented by a series of
special-rate tariffs. The result is a system that is not particularly transpar-

---

[5] There are indications that the DBAG discriminates against competitors with its oper-
ational branch by granting high discounts to large customers—in effect, to its own opera-
tional units (Teutsch 1998).

[6] There is no legal obligation for rail operators to systematically assess customer satisfaction as there is in Britain.

ent to customers. In order to guarantee rail access in regions with a lower level of demand, Germany has a system of regional tariff balancing (Stoffaes 1997: ii. 727). The state subsidizes regional public transportation.

In view of the rather disappointing results in rail passengers service, there have been calls to accelerate the reform. It is thought that introducing more competition on the rail network and completely separating track from operations will improve both services and pricing. Competition between passenger rail operators on the German network is expected to bring down prices and help make train service affordable as one element of service delivery in the public interest.

12.3.1.3. France: The New Regulatory Regime, Performance, and Further Liberalization

Regulatory reform in France has been characterized by a twofold development. Although the public monopoly of the SNCF in the operation of services has been maintained, the latter has undergone a series of reforms. In 1983 it was transformed into an autonomous public enterprise, and management was given more independence vis-à-vis government. State influence is, however, still pronounced as regards fares, investment decisions, and employment (Douillet and Lehmkuhl 2000). The SNCF comprises all service operations (the *Grandes Lignes,* the suburbs of Paris, regional services, and freight), while a separate railway infrastructure enterprise (Réseau Ferré de France) created in 1997 owns the infrastructure, is responsible for development and planning, and charges SNCF operators for using its network. The SNCF manages the infrastructure on behalf of RFF for public service reasons, that is, to guarantee the safety, accessibility, and continuity of train operations. RFF is responsible for planning and securing the necessary financial means for infrastructure investments (Henry 1997); it also partially absorbed the SNCF debts, while the French government took over another part (Douillet and Lehmkuhl 2000).

The political consensus to maintain a railway committed to the principles of public service has always been strong in France. Unprofitable lines are maintained as a result of political decisions, and the government compensates the SNCF for their continued operation. The SNCF has started to draw up a consumer charter in which it lays claim to a high quality of service, but commitment to the charter remains rather 'soft' and difficult to quantify (Stoffaes 1997: ii. 738).

The performance of the only slightly liberalized SNCF has been mixed. Although the high-speed trains (TGV, *trains à grande vitesse*) have been very successful in attracting passengers, the overall number of rail passengers has been declining since 1989 (Stoffaes 1997: i. 148). The SNCF has shelved any policy of low prices, instead using increased earnings to attract new customers and maximize returns on the profit-producing lines, in particular the TGV. In fact, normal rail transport is becoming increasingly costly for passengers, despite the fact that fares are actually lower than in Britain or Germany as a result of higher government subsidies (Stoffaes 1997: ii. 727). Furthermore, the many offers of reduced fares for business or social travel have created a very complex and opaque tariff structure. A system of regional tariff balancing also guarantees access to rail transport in geographically marginal regions (Stoffaes 1997: ii. 743; Henry 1997).

In comparing the performance of the railway operators in the three countries, it emerges that the quality of services offered is judged unsatisfactory both with and without organizational reform. In Britain with its extensive reform, success in accessibility has been offset by deteriorating service quality, while Germany's half-hearted reform has not produced any significant improvement in service. Although France, with its modest reform, is now providing some high-quality and low-cost services, it still faces problems from overrelying on government subsidies and focusing on the TGV to the neglect of regular passenger services.

12.3.2. Telecommunications

The British Post Office was originally a public corporation under the direct supervision of a ministry that controlled the telephone network and terminal equipment. In 1981 it was converted into two independent public corporations, of which one, British Telecom (BT), was privatized in 1984 (Spiller and Vogelsang 1996). Under the old regime decisions on pricing, investment, and technology were made within a closed network of public monopoly managers, government officials, and the supplier industry (Schneider 1998; Schneider, Dang-Nguyen, and Werle 1994; Spiller and Vogelsang 1996; Thatcher 1997). There was a high degree of political interference and a concomitant lack of managerial incentives (Moore 1986). In Germany and France the basic managerial institutional arrangements under the public monopoly were very similar to those in Britain.

As in the case of the railways, the scope for political intervention to secure general interest goals in service provision was broad leading us to expect a high level of performance. Accessibility, measured by the number of voice telephony lines per 100 inhabitants, rose in France and Germany prior to liberalization. Similarly, access to innovative services increased. Furthermore, the quality of service, as measured by the time necessary to obtain a connection, improved. Charges fell in France and in Germany between 1991 and 1995/97, before liberalization.[7]

The empirical data on market penetration, quality of service, and pricing indicate that the old regime fared relatively well with respect to service provision. It may well be, however, that anticipating liberalization, which had already taken place in other countries such as the UK, was what led to efforts at improved service quality in the other countries. Another reason for this relatively good performance was the availability of new technology. Nevertheless, dissatisfaction remained. Industrial consumers complained that the close interaction among PTTs (Postal, telephone, and telegraph administrations) governments, the domestic equipment industry, labor unions, and households did not allow them to exploit the full potential of technological progress in order to satisfy their demands for communication services that are specialized, international, and cheap. In Britain equipment was considered overpriced, services low in quality, standards idiosyncratic and hence an impediment to innovation, and long-distance tariffs too expensive (Hulsink 1996). These complaints together with the enormous competitive pressure caused by the technology push of the 1980s and the liberalized US market prepared the way for reform in Britain, which was subsequently underlined by European policymaking. The telecommunications industry underwent an extensive transformation. Different types of data transmission services between fixed points gave rise to specialized networks and digital technology. With the new technologies, the cost of extending and maintaining networks declined. Lower costs, in turn changed competitive conditions in the industry and eroded its formerly monolithic structure (OECD 1997*b*: ii. 46).

12.3.2.1. Britain: The New Regulatory Regime, Performance

Barriers to entry have been substantially lowered in Britain. With the industry's privatization in 1984, a duopoly with price-cap regulation was established.[8] This was then abolished in 1991, which rapidly led to new companies entering the telecom market. Despite the large number of licenses granted, the domestic market remains dominated by British Telecom, which accounted for 95 percent of residential call revenues and 79 percent of the business market in 1996. Thus, the newly created market is still biased in favor of the incumbent monopolist, and the market is not very competitive (Bishop, Kay, and Mayer 1995).

---

[7] OECD 1997*a*: i, tables 4.2, 4.8, 7.1, 7.2, and 6.8, respectively.
[8] To increase competition a second operator, Mercury, was granted a license. Both companies were given full access to each others' networks (OECD 1997*b*: ii. 140).

With liberalization a new regulatory structure was established. The Monopolies and Mergers Commission is responsible for problems of competition. Licenses to service providers, specifying obligations and duties, are granted by the Secretary of the State. The regulator is appointed by the government and heads the Office of Telecommunications (OFTEL), a non-ministerial government department responsible for the enforcement of licensing conditions (Helm 1994).

The major regulatory instrument used is the power to set maximum prices at levels calculated to produce 'normal' profits, using the RPI-minus-x-formula.[9] Any profits above these levels can be retained, but every five years price ceilings are adjusted so as to push profits back to the 'normal' level. Consequently, companies must continually strive to increase efficiency so as to maintain their profit stream (Spiller and Vogelsang 1996).

Customers can lodge complaints with OFTEL. British Telecom provides the regulatory authority with monthly statistics about quality of service (OECD 1997*a*: ii. 127), and customers can be compensated in cases of poor service (Armstrong, Cowan, and Vickers 1994).

The basic performance package consists of voice telephony (including fax services), public telephone boxes, and access to emergency services. Performance has improved with respect to the accessibility and standard of services.

Improvement in affordable price performance has been remarkable. Prices for telecom services have fallen sharply in Britain. Relative to the general (retail or consumer) price index, prices have fallen by more than 60 percent since 1985, though they dropped less steeply in the first half of the 1990s (OECD 1997*b*: ii. 50). The price of international calls fell by more than the decline in prices for domestic calls, and business prices dropped further than residential charges (OECD 1997*b*: ii. 140–41). Average annual spending by a business user in 1996 (fixed plus user charges) was lower than in France and the same as in Germany (OECD 1997*a*: ii, table 6.1); residential telephone charges in 1996, by contrast, were clearly lower in Britain than in Germany and France (OECD 1997*a*: ii, table 6.2).

This improvement in performance was not without problems. In the period immediately following privatization, the quality of service was not explicitly regulated and became the subject of widespread criticism. OFTEL intervened in order to improve the quality and transparency of performance by steadily tightening BT's price regulation (Spiller and Vogelsang 1996).

[9] The price formula is RPI-x, where RPI stands for Retail Price Index, and x is the regulator's estimate of the presumed movement of productivity and costs within the industry, normally fixed in advance for a period of four to five years.

Table 12.1 *Great Britain: Accessibility and quality of services after liberalization*

Accessibility	1990	1995
Mainlines (per 100 inhabitants)	44.0	50.2
Cellular phones (absolute numbers)	1,230,000	5,670,000
Internet use (per 100 inhabitants)	4.97	10.09
Public telephones (per 1,000 inhabitants)	5.4	4.9
Quality of service	1987	1991
Residential orders completed in 8 working days (%)	40	83
Failing national calls (%)	4.2	0.5
	1993	1995
Incidence of faulty lines (per 100 lines per year)	15.0	14.0
Repaired faults (within 5–9 working hours, %)	80.2	82.0

Sources: OECD 1997*a*: vol. ii; Armstrong, Cowan, and Vickers 1994.

12.3.2.2. Germany: The New Regulatory Regime, Performance, and Re-regulation

In 1989 the first regulatory reform in Germany—Postreform I—divided the federal post office into three public enterprises (postal services, postbank, and telecoms) and introduced competition into the market for equipment, teletext, satellite communication, and mobile telephony. In 1995 Postreform II transformed the three public enterprises (Telekom, Post, and Postbank) into joint stock companies. Until 1996, when a first batch of shares was floated, all shares were owned by the Bundesanstalt für Post und Telekommunikation. Until 1995, prices were subject to government approval. Starting in early 1998, voice telephony has been completely liberalized, and there has been intensive competition in every service except local voice telephony, where not many new companies are operating yet.

The regulatory authorities underwent change as well. In 1998 the Ministry for Postal Services and Telecoms was dissolved. A new federal regulatory agency—responsible for granting licenses, protecting consumers' interests, and ensuring competition (a function shared with the federal antitrust authority)—was established under the supervision of the Federal Ministry of Economics. Customers can lodge complaints with this new regulatory authority.

The performance package for universal service comprises a minimum of telecom services, voice telephony with ISDN features, free-of-charge information, subscriber directories, and public telephones at affordable prices. Accessibility was improved prior to liberalization.

Table 12.2 *Germany: Service performance*

Accessibility	1990	1995
Mainlines (per 100 inhabitants)	47.5	49.5
Number of cellular phones (in absolute numbers)	430,000	3,750,000
Use of the internet (per 1,000 inhabitants)	4.29	8.84

Service quality	1990	1994
Fault incidence (per 100 lines per year)	16.0	8.7
Faults repaired within 3 working days (%)	81	93

Sources: OECD 1997*a*: vol. i, table 4.4; 72; OECD 1997*a*, vol. ii, table 7.2.

As regards the goal of affordability, prices have fallen steeply relative to the general (retail or consumer) price index in the period 1990–94 prior to liberalization (OECD 1997*b*: ii. 50). It is estimated that deregulation subsequently led to a drop in producer prices of 33 percent (direct effect) and 49 percent (total effect). As compared to the OECD average (= 100%), the basket of total charges for telecommunication services and equipment in January 1997 was 96.5 percent for business and 94.4 for residential users (OECD 1997*b*: ii. 47). In 1999 DT slashed most of its long-distance rates by more than 50 percent (*Herald Tribune* 1999). The regulatory activity of the newly established authority seeking to enhance the competitiveness and customer-friendliness of the liberalized sector led to conflicts with the still powerful DT. Thus, Deutsche Telekom wanted to impose relatively high rates on customers switching to other providers of services for long-distance calls, whereas the regulator granted much lower rates favoring new market entrants and customers.

12.3.2.3. France: The New Regulatory Regime, Performance

In France increased competition in the telecom market has been slow to arrive. France Télécom was, and still is, the dominant provider of telecom services. Until 1998 it held the legal monopoly on fixed-network telephony. The principle of third-party access was not generally applied until 1998, and cable companies are still not allowed to provide telephony services. France Télécom only started to float shares on the stock market in spring 1997, and the government intends to keep a 51 percent stake in the company (OECD 1997*b*: ii. 130).

However a few liberalizing steps were taken earlier in data transmission and mobile telecommunications. An independent regulatory authority, the Autorité de Réglementation des Télécommuncations (ART), was created in 1997 to supervise activities in the market as it was liberalized (OECD 1997*b*: ii. 130). Customers' complaints can be addressed to the regulatory agency, the Ministry for Consumer Affairs, the Business Practices Council, and the courts. The license contract of France Télécom, the incumbent monopolist, stipulates that the company must present an annual performance statement (OECD 1997*a*: ii. 55).

Under this slightly reformed regime, the universal service package is made up of quality telephone service at an affordable price, emergency calls, directory assistance, telephone directories, and public telephones. Accessibility and quality of service improved prior to liberalization.

Table 12.3 *France: Service performance*

Accessibility	1990	1995
Mainlines per 100 inhabitants	47.7	56.3
Cellular phones (absolute numbers)	287,000	1,302,000
	1995	1997
Use of the internet (per 1,000 inhabitants)	1.96	4.22
Service standard	1992	1995
Wait for telephone installation (days)	15	7
	1993	1995
Fault incidence (per 100 lines/year)	7.6	6.3
Faults repaired within 24 hours	86.3	88.3

Source: OECD 1997*a*: vol. ii, tables 4.2, 4.3, 4.8, 7.1, 7.2.

Prices for national and international services have fallen by more than 60 percent, in current prices, since 1985 (OECD 1997*b*: ii. 50).

Table 12.4 *User spending: France, Great Britain, Germany, 1996*

	France	Germany	Britain
Business average annual spending (US$)	997.83	1,258.02	844.43
Residential average annual spending (US$)	799.40	914.37	586.59

Source: OECD 1997*a*,: vol. ii, tables 6.1, 6.2).

Total telecom charges, at 83.7 for businesses and 84.5 for residential use, are in line with the OECD average (= 100%), and in 1996 they were actually below the British level (92.4 business, 93.4 residential) (OECD 1997*b*: ii. 47).

As indicated by the data, the performance of the French telecom industry has in many respects been comparable to Britain's privatized industry where public interest goals are concerned. Customer access is guaranteed, prices are relatively low, and new technological opportunities have been

exploited. Thus, for telecommunications, one can conclude that technological innovation—linked with increased international competition—
was the main thing accelerating improvements in service. However,
increased performance due to technological innovation, which goes hand
in hand with liberalization, still needs regulation in order to maintain general interest goals. In a comparison of the three countries it is interesting
to note that France, with its modest liberalization, performs as well as the
privatized and more liberalized industries of Britain and Germany. The
reason for France's success is its long-term exploitation of, and investment
in, technology.

Reforms in the provision of public services affect more than the quality
of infrastructure services. Liberalization and privatization have significant
implications for employment. Employment levels are being reduced, and
jobs that were traditionally very secure are increasingly being replaced
with much more insecure ones. This development therefore not only matters as a cause of rising unemployment; it is also important in terms of the
kind of comprehensive social protection that was fundamental to the welfare state (Schwartz 2000). This will be analyzed next.

12.4. Restructuring Public Services—The Impact on Employment

Operators of public services are traditionally major employers. Even after
hiving off telecommunications, postal service operators in some countries
remain the largest employers after the state. Among the countries studied
here, experiences with restructuring employment have been quite heterogeneous. A particularly extreme example is New Zealand, which undertook the most radical restructuring of its former government enterprises
during the 1980s and early 1990s. 'During the period of economic liberalization unemployment in New Zealand rose from 3.5 per cent to 11 per
cent, and state enterprises contributed a significant part of this' (Duncan
and Bollard 1992: 171). In the most important state enterprises, aggregate
employment was halved between 1987 and 1992 (Duncan and Bollard
1992: 55). Other countries could not and did not need to copy such rapid
reductions. Employment levels at the outset were very different, on
grounds of productivity and work organization. In addition, reducing
employment levels did not enjoy the same priority in all countries, and
political problems relating to restructuring employment also differed.

In the following, the analysis starts with restructuring employment in
telecommunications. Among all the utilities, it is the sector most affected
by liberalization and privatization, but it also has the most significant
potential for new employment due to rapid growth. In second place there

follows a discussion of postal services. Traditionally managed along with telecommunications in most countries, postal services have been profoundly changed under the impact of telecom reform. For instance, the common practice of cross-subsidizing postal services with telecommunications revenues was stopped. Third, changes in the railways as another traditional large public employer are discussed.

In spite of all the differences among the sectors, there are some things they have in common. For instance, there has been a common incremental approach to introducing liberalization measures in these network industries (cf. Schmidt 1998). For all services, advances in information technology have been important because of how they increased the potential for rationalization and new service offers. Budget constraints are another important factor. They have been particularly prominent as an issue in railways reform but also played a role in postal services. Even in telecommunications, the inability of public operators to rapidly offer all the new networks and services provided an argument for the necessity of opening investment to private actors.

In adapting to far-reaching liberalization measures, established operators in all industries have faced similar challenges. Most of all, rationalization had to be achieved without disruptions in the provision of services, which could have led to significant losses to new competitors or, in the case of railways, to other modes of transport. The generally public nature of employment contracts and the high degree of job security in the public sector made things even more difficult. As a result of job rights and the vulnerability of established operators, significant rationalization has generally been achieved while still safeguarding employees' acquired rights. This development, however, goes hand in hand with highly insecure employment at the new companies that have entered the market for providing telecommunications and postal services. (In rails, the number of new entrants has been small.)

12.4.1. *Restructuring Telecommunications*

'The telecommunications sector is perhaps the most directly affected by regulatory changes and globalization' (ILO 1998: 85).

Among all public services, telecommunications is the one area where liberalization and privatization are connected to a significant growth potential, including hopes for new employment growth. Given the vast scope of restructuring, it is surprising that the impact on employment received so little attention during discussions about reform. One reason for this may be that during the second half of the 1980s, when the foundation for wide-ranging changes was laid, employment remained largely stable and even increased in some countries (Negrelli and Treu 1993: 22), partly because of a parallel modernization of networks. Our graphs (Figures 12.1 and 12.2) illustrate this increase in jobs for Switzerland, Italy, Sweden, and the UK. It is therefore not surprising that the European Commission, which played a special role promoting and harmonizing the liberalization process, spent only a few pages on how liberalization affected employment in its first Green Paper on Telecommunications, published in 1987.

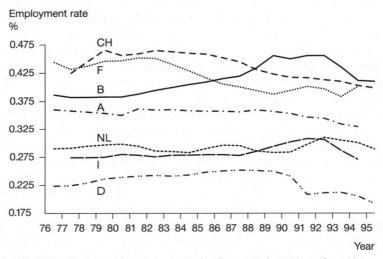

Figure 12.1 Employment in telecommunications services (overview A)
Source: ITU 1998.

But employment in telecoms as a percentage of total national employment in the OECD area then fell from 0.81 percent to 0.67 percent between1982 and 1992 (OECD 1995: 93), which would explain how neglect gave way to concern about employment issues. Thus, in the context of the Commission's 'White Paper on Growth and Competitiveness' published in late 1993, which called for rapid liberalization of telecommunications, Commissioner Bangemann was very careful not to turn employment effects into a major point of contention. In fact, the Commission was rather late in commissioning a study to forecast the employment implications of telecom liberalization. The study did not appear until 1997, at a time when all decisions about liberalization had long been made (European Commission 1997).

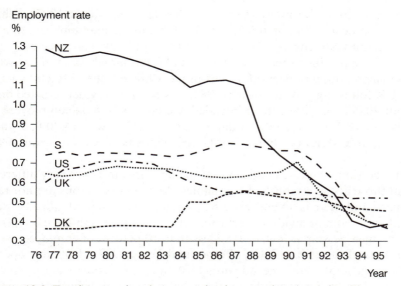

Figure 12.2 Employment in telecommunications services (overview B)
Source: ITU 1998.

In a recent study of the EU-15 Member States, fears of declining employment levels were confirmed. Only under one scenario—rapid liberalization and rapid diffusion of new technologies—were 93,000 new telecom jobs predicted by 2005.[10] This compares to the loss of 216,000 jobs forecast under the worst case scenario of gradual liberalization and slow technological diffusion (European Commission 1997: 13, 268). These developments depend on how many additional jobs are created by the new service providers, which could amount to 162,000 under the best case scenario, as compared to only 55,000 in the worst case. Yet even the job growth at new companies predicted by the positive scenario would be more than canceled out by a forecasted loss of 286,000 jobs at the established operators (European Commission 1997: 18, 14). The report therefore concludes that 'the effects of liberalization on the telecommunications sector itself are negative, jobs created at new operators and service providers and equipment manufacturers and distributors do not offset large redundancies at dominant operators' (European Commission 1997: 60). These forecasts are largely supported by a recent prognosis on

[10] However, this result pertains only when 'direct suppliers to operators' are taken into account (European Commission 1997: 13), a category that is not further explicated in the report. Without this category, all scenarios lead to a negative assessment.

developments in Germany (Elixmann, Keuter, and Meyer 1997). While there is some growth potential (+87,000 jobs) in the medium term due to increased investment, by 2005 an overall loss of 76,000 is expected.

But what has the experience been so far? It has largely been in line with this disappointing projection. For example, while BT shed 110,000 jobs in the UK following privatization in 1984, new service providers created only about 40,000 new jobs: these included Mercury with 8,000 employees in 1994, AT & T UK (6,500), Vodaphone (5,000), Telewest (4,200), Nynex (3,000), and Mercury One-2-One (2,500) (European Commission 1997: 19).

In addition, working conditions at the new operators are very different from those at the established companies. At Mercury unions are not recognized and there is no collective bargaining. Pay is individualized for all employees, and individual performance determines annual pay raises. Union membership is low; in 1994 less than 10 percent of employees were members of the central NCU (Ferner and Terry 1997: 118). New operators, in general, have the advantage of 'human resource management which directly corresponds to their organizational needs' (European Commission 1997: 116). Experience in the USA shows, moreover, that it is difficult for established operators to use higher productivity as a way of outcompeting rivals paying lower wages, so that there is constant pressure to cut jobs. 'Although AT & T operators were 20 percent more productive and had a 50 percent lower error rate in call completion, it was unable to compensate for MCI's 70 percent lower labor costs' (Batt and Keefe 1999).

However, many new jobs are created within other branches due to the increasing differentiation of telecommunications-related jobs. This new employment is covered in other sectoral statistics, and the extent of employment at new operators only accounts for some of the new jobs. The aforementioned study commissioned by the European Commission predicts that up to 1.3 m jobs could be created or maintained throughout Europe by 2005 (European Commission 1997: 24).

12.4.1.1. Mapping Employment Changes

Before discussing these changes in greater detail, we need to comment on the scarcity of existing data, which makes it difficult to establish clearly what developments are going on. Traditionally, employment data refer to the former monopolist. Only slowly are new operators being included in the statistics. Much of the new employment is also not being captured because statisticians tend to group firms according to their main product or service. Liberalized customer premises equipment will thus increase employment in retailing; liberalized services will lead to more jobs in banks and other high-volume telecom users.[11] But the incomplete accounting gets even worse, as many new telecommunications-related activities are not captured at all by the data. This is demonstrated by the OECD's definition: 'In general the data excludes the employees of companies that resell telecommunications capacity, companies that sell value added telecommunications services, companies providing services via alternative information infrastructures (e.g. communication software companies, Internet access providers, cable television companies, satellite communication companies) and companies supplying services to PTOs that they once performed "in-house"' (OECD 1997a: i. 148). The ITU explicitly captures only employment at telecommunications-network operators. To demonstrate the inadequacies of the data, Figure 12.3 shows the development of employment according to the OECD definition in five countries. Figure 12.4, by contrast, builds on ITU data and especially shows how strikingly different developments were in Sweden. These differences and the OECD's already very restrictive definition of data should

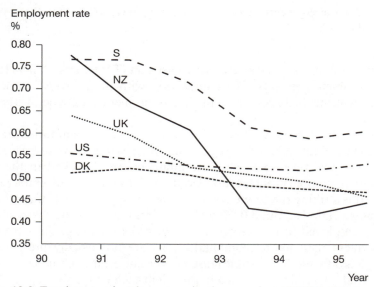

Figure 12.3 Employment in telecommunications services (OECD–Data)
Source: OECD 1995, 1997a.

[11] Another problem is the convergence with cable television. In the UK about 25,000 people are employed, approximately half of them should be added to telecoms (OECD 1995: 97). Data for Germany and Sweden, by contrast, includes Deutsche Telekom's and Telia's cable TV network employment (OECD 1997b: 149).

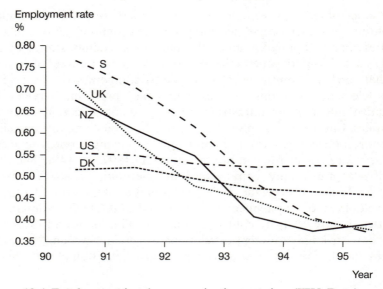

Figure 12.4 Employment in telecommunications services (ITU–Data)
Source: ITU 1998.

be kept in mind, since the analyses are based on ITU figures available from more complete data-sets. The comparison with the (already restrictive) OECD data here cautions that the emerging picture may be overly pessimistic.

In line with all other analyses of this project, employment ratios are presented in the figures. In order to give some further indication of how extensive job losses were, some absolute numbers are also cited in the text. Another preliminary observation needs to be made about employment ratios. It is striking that some countries have a very low ratio: for example, Germany's ratio is around 0.22, while in other countries the share of population employed in telecoms is about twice as high (e.g. the USA). As employment data for telecommunications are not usually presented in ratios, it is difficult to assess the reasons. One important factor is the degree of internal integration that used to prevail in each country's sector. This is particularly noticeable in the case of New Zealand, whose telecom industry started with a very high employment ratio (Figure 12.2) and was well-known for its high degree of internal integration, which even extended to making its own furniture (OECD 1995: 97). Next to differences in the demand for telecommunication services, differences in productivity could be another factor explaining variation in employment ratios. And, indeed, Italy and Germany did have much better productivity figures in 1995 (241 and 178, respectively) than the USA and the UK (144 and 137, respectively), if the traditional indicator of mainlines per employee is used (OECD 1997*a*: i. 151). However, it is doubtful that internal integration, demand, and productivity could account for all the differences.

To interpret the data, one should keep in mind that employment losses appearing in the statistics are only partly a consequence of liberalization. Corporate restructuring, technical change, and different starting conditions also play a role. For instance, of the nine OECD countries where employment fell by more than 10 percent between 1982 and 1992, only five had liberalized markets (OECD 1995: 93). The digitalization of networks has created a significant rationalization potential. Thus, BT cut back its engineering staff from 110,000 to 64,000 between 1985 and 1995 (OECD 1997*a*: i. 150). In the USA, job growth occurred in the competitive sector (e.g. in mobile communications) and job losses in areas where one company had a virtual monopoly (OECD 1997*a*: i. 149). The extent of outsourcing must also be noted. In the UK, BT's outsourcing of building restoration, cleaning, maintenance, and vehicle fleet management was responsible for 19,000 redundancies out of 25,700 in 1985 (European Commission 1997: 95). There are thus three main reasons for employment losses: network renovation was completed, technological developments allowed productivity gains, and liberalization accentuated the repercussions of these other two phenomenon (ILO 1998: 33).

12.4.1.2. Reductions at Established Operators

Among established operators, a two-stage change may be noted. First, one-fourth to one-half of their staff is rationalized. In the second phase the nature of employment is transformed, as operators make permanent adjustments to changing markets and shift alliances among themselves. Hierarchies are becoming flatter, and the status and skills of staff are changing. Given how many jobs had to be cut (see Figure 12.1 and 12.2), these changes have been managed relatively swiftly. Often several measures are combined for the transition: early retirement, voluntary departures, recruitment freezes, retraining, replacing full-time with part-time staff (ILO 1998: 36). The choice of strategy is determined by different factors:

The pace and scope of the reductions being sought by employers, the strength of the trade unions and methods of social consensus, the nature of the operators (. . . public, private or partial control by government), financial situation, degree of population pyramid in the respective operators, amount of funds provided by governments for social measures to accompany staff reductions, aptitude for change, training, occupational and geographical mobility of employees and the interest of the latter in schemes to encourage departures (ILO 1998: 38).

These transition problems are now discussed in greater detail.

Early retirement offers particular advantages, since the average age of the workforce can be lowered, and younger staff is less expensive. It has been very important. Belgacom (Belgium's telecom company) offered early retirement to 25,000 employees. In 1996 France Telecom signed an agreement allowing workers to retire as early as 55, a scheme that could affect 25,000 employees. Because of the overall aging of staff, new posts are planned for 4,800 permanent employees through 2002. In Sweden, by contrast, only a small percentage of staff had a full employment status, so that early retirement was restricted to 2,500 employees, while there were 2,100 layoffs, 2,900 assisted voluntary departures, and 7,500 departures for new jobs between 1990 and 1994 (ILO 1998: 37).

Deutsche Telekom reached an agreement with the dominant union DPG on downsizing in late 1995. Involuntary redundancies were ruled out until 1998. Telekom has offered early retirement to non-managerial staff at 55 and to managers at 60; allowances, in the 80,000–100,000 DM range, are granted for voluntary departures after at least two years of service. The early retirement scheme is constrained by an age structure where 64 percent of workers are forty or under, only 5 percent are over 55, and only 12 percent over 50 (Darbishire 1997: 218 f.).

BT, by contrast, radically cut its workforce from 230,000 to 130,000 between 1985 and 1995 (OECD 1997a: i. 150, 158, 160). However the reduction did not proceed evenly. Between 1982 and 1987 10,000 jobs were shed, resulting in serious problems of service quality. In particular, it became apparent that essential modernization of BT's network (its new competitor Mercury was operating an entirely digital network) could not be achieved without adding manpower. By 1989, staff levels had returned to where they were in 1982. But then nearly 90,000 jobs were shed between 1989 and 1993 (Kelly and Minges 1995: 3). The example of BT shows very clearly how difficult it is to accomplish downsizing when the commitment to strengthen the workforce clashes with demands for cost-cutting and redundancies.

The first stage of redundancies (1984 to 1987) had serious consequences on BTs service quality and as a result, had to be suspended for two years. On the other hand, large numbers of redundancies since then (1990 to 1995) did not cause a decline in service quality or other problems as the firm was more effective at involving staff in the process and used large numbers of subcontractors and temporary workers (non-specified interview quote, European Commission 1997: 110).

BT relied entirely on voluntary redundancy schemes to downsize. Just for the three years between 1993 and 1995, the cost of redundancies amounted to 2.4 bn pounds. On average employees received 35,000 pounds (Ferner and Terry 1997: 109). Even though BT restructured very early, the process is not yet completed. It was expected that BT would see additional job losses of 45,000 to 55,000 by the end of the century (European Commission 1997: 78; ILO 1998: 49). The workforce could be stripped down to 65,000 (Ferner and Terry 1997: 109). However, the experience of the USA advises caution as to whether beneficial schemes have a future. In the course of deregulation, layoffs have become increasingly common, and unionization has declined at the successors to the Bell System (Batt and Keefe 1999).

There have also been attempts to promote more outsourcing. Along with providers of non-core activities, such as caterers and equipment manufacturers, subcontractors were also used to meet peaks in short-term demand for BT's core business, such as network maintenance (Ferner and Terry 1997: 110). Some job losses represent transfers of staff to subcontractors within an overarching attempt to increase flexibility and outsource non-core activities. Between 1980 and 1995, the number of contract workers rose from 10,000 to nearly 22,000 (European Commission 1997: 109). This trend is expected to continue (Ferner and Terry 1997: 112).

In addition to requiring a sheer number of job reductions, liberalization necessitates replacing the old public service logic with a commercial logic, a development that has major consequences for employees as sales and marketing strategies become more important. Whereas the status of employees used to resemble that of public administrations, all of a sudden telecom personnel is supposed to be working for a multinational enterprise. Establishing a number of specialized subsidiaries is often part of this development. Within these subsidiaries, greater management flexibility is being achieved, closer to how the new competitors operate. Employees in the spin-off companies normally have a lower status than they enjoyed in the parent company, and there is a lower level of unionization (ILO 1998: 53).

Another priority is changing the status of employees from public to private law, a requirement of privatization so that management gets greater flexibility. There are different ways to change employees' status: civil service status may be completely replaced by private contracts (as happened in the UK), gradually eliminated with the help of special programs (especially early retirement schemes), or allowed to coexist with private status. France Telecom is keeping its employees under public law until 2002. In Sweden Televerket's transformation into the new company Telia meant that all employees would be subject to common law from mid-1993 onwards. Those who did not renounce their status as public employees (only about 60) remained at Televerket, which will eventually be liquidated. In Denmark and Luxemburg, by contrast, current employees have kept their public law status, while new employees are hired under private law. In Switzerland personnel in the telecommunications branch will be subject to private law from 2001 onwards (ILO 1998: 51 f.). In Germany Deutsche Telekom stopped employing under public law in 1995, and civil servants (54% of the total workforce) were given the opportunity to keep or to change their status.

This change of status does more than cause significant legal problems. Disputes can easily arise when employees whose status differs work together, as in the case of the Dutch KPN, where the conflict between new employees and old civil servants could only be resolved by staff reassignments and departures. To attract high-level external candidates, management had offered generous promotional aid packages. France Telecom's decision not to recruit civil servants after 2002 led to an agreement with the trade unions that civil servants (more than 90% of the workforce) should have the same career opportunities as employees under collective agreements. The number of staff categories was reduced from 116 to 11, and additional annual bonuses were introduced (European Commission 1997: 107). France Télécom also planned to overcome the civil service restrictions by reducing the work week for a portion of staff to 70 percent, while keeping pay and benefits at full-time levels. For every ten employees choosing this mechanism, an additional seven would be hired so that employment goals could be met alongside increased flexibility (European Commission 1997: 111).

Civil servants' pensions have been another difficult issue. In France the state intends to cover pension costs for current employees of France Telecom. In Belgium the private operator had to set up a private pension fund of BEF 140 bn (3.6 bn ECU), the largest in the country (European Commission 1997: 89). In Germany pensions became a major issue in the reform preparing the way for privatization. From 1999 onwards, the federal government has to cover 60 percent of pension obligations, to be financed from the sale of shares (Schmidt 1996: 64).

That all these changes could be managed without major disruptions is largely due to Germany's traditionally high degree of unionization, which makes the search for prior agreement unavoidable. Deutsche Telekom has a 90 percent unionization rate. The union (DPG) demonstrated its opposition to privatization with a 30-day strike in mid-1994, in which it was able to win important concessions. Among these was the DPG's continued role as a negotiating partner with subsidiaries, even though the degree of unionization is lower there (Darbishire 1997: 222).

BT was traditionally a 'closed shop'. Only the Employment Act of 1988 broke with this system that restricted employment to union members in the UK. As a result, almost all of BT's employees were union members just at the time the company was being restructured. Among unions in this sector, the National Communications Union (NCU) was the most important one, representing about half of all employees (Arzt, Bach, and Schueler 1990: 195–97). Collective bargaining continued despite the attempts of the Thatcher government to break the unions. 'Indeed, below the managerial grades, unionism was in relatively good shape, exceptionally so compared with the situation in much of the rest of British industry. This may largely reflect the pragmatism and responsiveness of the NCU, which was prepared to pay the price of its continued influence' (Ferner and Terry 1997: 120). Only certain categories of white-collar, professional, and managerial staff had the rules governing their working conditions switched to individual contracts. Internal pay differentials remained relatively stable between 1984 and 1993, while the overall level of pay in telecommunications fell behind that of the economy as a whole. However directors' pay grew immensely. Measured against a 1984 pay-level index of 100, directors' emoluments had risen to 615 by 1992, with engineering pay at 173 and renumeration for clerical work at 171 (Ferner and Terry 1997: 103).

In sum, telecommunications has gone through significant restructuring, both in terms of lower employment and internal corporate change. While cutting jobs has been a development common throughout the EU, each country's experience has been different. This heterogeneity is due, first of all, to different starting conditions with respect to network modernization, productivity, and internal integration. Second, the degree of unionization, national legal frameworks, and corporate industrial relations largely determine how—and how many—jobs are cut. Because of the generally high level of protection enjoyed by public employees and the special vulnerability of established operators facing competition for the first time, telecom employees have been in a relatively advantageous position despite workforce reductions. Generous schemes made it possible to avoid involuntary redundancies and widespread turmoil in the wake of job cuts. Hiring by new operators could not make up for most of the lost jobs. The newly created jobs tend to be few in number, insecure, and non-union. The more significant employment that telecommunications reform has generated is concentrated in other branches and therefore hard to track.

12.4.2. Restructuring Postal Services

It was common in most countries for a single operator to provide postal and telecommunications services. Dividing the telecommunications branch into separate corporations for later privatization thus had implications for postal services. Although slower than the changes made in telecommunications, comparable reforms were planned and carried out in post offices. Compared to telecommunications, the growth potential is only moderate in this sector, and postal services have not been affected as much by technical change. However, this does not mean that this sector has not been transformed at all. Fully automated sorting centers have been introduced, improved logistics through information and communications technology has allowed new customized services to emerge for tasks like tracing letters and parcels, and the increasing substitution of telecommunications for mail has led to the loss of established markets as well as to new business opportunities.

Within the established postal services, the growth potential is slight. In addition, market segments with above average growth potential are generally the ones that have already been, or are about to be, opened up to competition. Thus, it is expected that the volume of first-class letters will decline by 2 percent between 1995 and 2000, while direct mail, which is increasingly being liberalized, will grow by about 13.5 percent (Price Waterhouse 1997: 66).

Technical and regulatory changes, along with stagnating growth, have all translated into job losses. In 1995 employment at the fifteen public postal operators in the EU was at almost 1.41 million, equal to about 1 percent of the EU's total employment (Price Waterhouse 1997: iv). It had declined by 7 percent, or almost 112,300 employees, between 1990 and 1995—73.6 percent of employers are engaged in mail services, the rest in retail and financial services, a share that is growing. Downsizing at post offices has followed a similar pattern to that of telecommunications, but has progressed more slowly (ILO 1998: 36) (see Figure 12.5).

Because our data in Figure 12.5 stops in 1993, and since then many reductions have taken place some figures shall be quoted. At New Zealand post staff fell from 12,000 to 8,000 between 1987 and 1996, with further losses expected (ILO 1998: 7, 34). In Sweden employment sank from 57,000 in 1990 to 44,000 in 1997 (ILO 1998: 35). And in Denmark the total workforce was reduced by almost 15 percent between 1990 and 1995, with further massive losses expected due to investment in new technology around the year 2000, possibly affecting a quarter of all jobs. These losses are not only due to competition from new operators or alternative means of communications; they also derive from the vast potential for rationalization. An indicator of how much competition established operators are facing from private competitors can be taken from the international parcel volume of the PTTs, one of the most competitive market segments. Between 1990 and 1994 this volume declined by about 18 percent in eleven EU Member States (Price Waterhouse 1997: 63).

The Dutch postal office, a special success story, nicely illustrates the importance of rationalization. Profits more than doubled between 1989

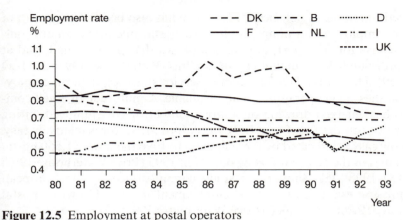

Figure 12.5 Employment at postal operators
Source: Panorama of EC Industry 1997; UPU 1990: 1981–1983 for I: 1981–1987,
for B: 1986, 1987; employees in DK in 1985–1990: 1985: 30,040; 1986: 25,100;
1987: 32,000; 1988: 33,600; 1989: 34,400; 1990: 28,235.

and 1995, going from 301 m guilder to 721 m. These earnings gave the
Dutch PTT twice the profits reaped by its much larger German counterpart, which garnered DM 364 m in 1995 (*Die Zeit* 1996). At the same time,
the Dutch PTT cut employment by 15–20 percent since the beginning of
the 1990s, though without dismissals (ILO 1998: 36). Thereby the Dutch
PTT managed to cut personnel costs as a percentage of turnover from 64
percent in 1989 to 48 percent in 1995. Moreover, additional reductions are
being planned so that the staff level goes down to 40,000 by 2000, compared with 60,000 in 1989 (*Die Zeit* 1996).

Price Waterhouse (1997: x) forecasts that the public postal operators
will cut employment by 108,000 (7.7%) between 1995 (1.41 m) and 2000
(1.3 m). Employment at private operators should increase by 10 percent,
from 400,000 to 440,000, during the same period, so that net job losses
would be around 68,000 or 3.8 percent.

The way this transition is being achieved is similar to what has happened with telecommunications. Just one aspect, employment status, illustrates the parallel: in Sweden, employees lost their civil service status after
the post office became a corporation in 1994. Post Denmark will phase out
civil service employment status by 1998. Similarly, Belgium, the
Netherlands, and the UK no longer have any postal employees under public law. In Austria a new law from 1996 mandated that new contracts have
to come under private law (ILO 1998: 52).

Like telecommunications, the postal sector has been generating new
employment. New jobs have been founded mostly at a growing number of

competitors to the established PTTs. There has also been some growth of indirect employment among suppliers to postal operators, among rail- and airways for transport, among companies that prepare mail, and at mail order and direct mail companies (Price Waterhouse 1997: 26; ILO 1998: 39). Due to the lack of national service statistics, data on employment at these new operators are not available. A multitude of small companies has emerged drawing on a large number of self-employed, hiring one or two full-time staff members. Entry into the sector is relatively easy. Just how easy is indicated by these figures: In 1996 there were 1,550 postal companies in the UK, employing 45,000 in 1995 (Price Waterhouse 1997: 14; ILO 1998: 35). Similarly, a study commissioned by the European Commission estimated that total employment in the EU private postal sector at 350,000 to 400,000 (Price Waterhouse 1997: 22).

In addition to small national private operators, 'global integrators' have been growing. Companies such as UPS, DHL, Federal Express, and TNT 'combine land and air transport services with freight forwarding, customs brokering and other information-intensive activities that enable them to provide efficient pick-up and delivery services. (ILO 1998: 5). The five global integrators operating in the EU (DHL, FedEx, GD Express, TNT and UPS) increased their employment from 35,500 to 52,000 between 1990 and 1995, with about half the growth attributable to acquisitions (Price Waterhouse 1997: 23).

As in telecommunications, employment conditions for postal workers differ widely between new operators and established companies. The strike at UPS, the leading US parcel service, in the summer of 1997 brought this out in the open. The UPS strike was prompted by concerns about employment conditions and differences between full-time staff (with an hourly wage of $20) and part-time workers (paid between $9 and $15). Between 1995 and 1997, 80 percent of new recruitments were part-time (ILO 1998: 80).

Germany, however, illustrates that governments do not have to stand by helplessly and watch traditional operators compete against companies engaging in social dumping. The law there allows licenses to be denied to companies that become competitive through social dumping, for example by employing only part-time workers not required to make social security contributions.

In sum, developments in postal services have been less dynamic than in telecoms, though the experience is similar in other respects. Public operators cut employment, but this is achieved without involuntary redundancies. New operators cannot make up for these losses. Employment there, moreover, is highly insecure, lacking as it does the benefits of public sector contracts.

12.4.3. Restructuring Rails

Like postal services, railways are traditionally important national employers. The continuing decline in the importance of railway transportation, already discussed in the first part of this chapter, is a major cause of the need to restructure. Declining demand goes hand in hand with the public treasury's growing inability to subsidize loss-making activities when public sector deficits are high. Many routes have become unprofitable, but there are political constraints on cutting these. Troublesome industrial relations can inhibit essential job restructuring, a problem best illustrated by the French case. The SNCF's condition has been particularly grave due to its high level of debt, which (at FF 175 bn) was about three times the company's turnover (of FF 57 bn) in 1995. Due to the high staffing level and large number of pensioners, the SNCF's expenses for personnel (FF 43.9 bn in 1995) are almost as high as its turnover (*FAZ* 1996). Retirement age is very low at 60 (and only 50 for train drivers). There are twice as many pensioners as employees, so that the SNCF has to provide FF 27 bn each year in pensions (*FAZ* 1995*b*). Wages are also comparatively high, topped only by the Swiss railway (*Die Zeit* 1995). But as the French public sector strike at the end of 1995 demonstrated, the union's non-compromising stance has made badly needed restructuring extremely difficult.

Given these structural difficulties, railway's slow pace of liberalization is simply exaggerating the problems. So far, there is little scope for new service providers, who would in any case be unlikely to create much new employment. One drawback is the difficulty dominant railway operators have faced capitalizing on the environmental advantages of rail over road traffic. Organizational inflexibilities seem to lie at the heart of the problem. For example, Deutsche Post transferred all its overnight transports from rails to roads in 1995 (*DVZ* 1996*a*).

Figure 12.6 demonstrates how cutting back on employment is an ongoing process. When it was founded in 1938, the French SNCF had half a million employees. In 1995 employment was down to 178,000. An additional loss of 30,000 jobs was feared necessary in order to consolidate the company (*FAZ* 1995*b*). With the change of government in 1997 however, the SNCF was allowed to participate in shaping a new employment program. In 1997 an agreement was reached with the government to offer 1,000 additional permanent posts and employ another 1,000 young people for five years with governmental assistance (*FAZ* 1997*b*). Coming at a time when greater commercial independence was being sought, this renewed political interference was criticized by the SNCF president (*La Vie du Rail* 1997*b*).

Unification and the highly inefficient railway system it inherited from

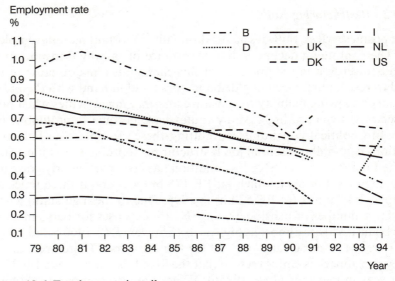

Figure 12.6 Employment in railways
Source: Panorama of EC Industry 1990, 1991/92, 1993, 1994, 1996/97.

east Germany has forced the Deutsche Bahn to make major job cuts. The company became a corporation in 1994, which raised the issue of its employees' civil service status. The solution was to have any Deutsche Bahn employees who refused to change their formal status voluntarily be put on the staff of a new organization that would then hire them out to the DBAG (Lehmkuhl and Herr 1994).

Thanks to a union that acted very cooperatively in spite of this sector's high unionization rate (80%), it was possible to shed 200,000 jobs between 1990 and 1997. In a job pact with the unions reached at the beginning of 1996, the DB agreed not to dismiss any employees until the end of 1998 (*FAZ* 1997a). An extension was negotiated late in 1998. In 1996 DBAG managed to cut its staff by 11 percent (down to 246,859), and in 1997 by 9.5 percent (down to 223,523).[12] As with other public services, there are efforts to rely on early retirement and natural shrinkage of the workforce. It was possible to reduce personnel costs as a percentage of total costs from 60 percent in 1990 to 53.8 percent in 1996 (*La Vie du Rail* 1997a). Nevertheless, in the mid-1990s the DB still had a turnover rate of only 84,000 DM per employee, which was below the French level and rates of 300,000 DM in the USA and 700,000 DM in Japan (*FAZ* 1995a).

Similarly, other European railways are hard-pressed to reduce costs

---

[12] <http://www.bahn.de/Konzern/f-konz.htm>. Geschäftsbericht 1996 and 1997.

and, by implication, employment. The Belgian SNBF will cut personnel from 41,000 to 35,000 between 1996 and 2005, solely by means of early retirement and natural fluctuations. In 1980 the SNCB still employed 67,000. In order to obviate the need for even more reductions, the unions agreed to salary cuts of 2 percent and to a reduction of the working week from 38 to 36 hours, which saved 1,400 jobs (*DVZ* 1996*c*; *La Vie du Rail* 1995). In Italy the staffing level was reduced from 206,000 to 125,000 between 1990 and 1996 without significant social conflict. Italy implemented reforms early: The shift to a statutory organization was enacted in 1986 and the transformation to a shareholder company in 1992 (*DVZ* 1996*b*). In Sweden staff was reduced by around 40 percent between 1988 and 1995. Where dismissals could not be avoided, training opportunities were offered along with help in finding new employment (Lundberg 1997).

In sum, the picture for railways is largely similar to the one for posts and telecommunications. However, so far there have hardly been enough new entrants to make up for at least some of the employment losses (if the example of the UK is excluded, where the divestiture of former monopolist British Rail brought new entrants into the market). In light of what was said earlier about performance, it seems as if employment levels are only likely to stabilize if a determined political effort is undertaken to favor railways over their competitors using roads and airways.

12.5. Conclusion

Since liberalization exposes private providers to conflicting goals—meeting the needs of all types of customers (including economically weak ones) while simultaneously taking shareholders' interests into account—utilities will need intensive re-regulation if they are going to keep attaining their public service objectives.

There are, however, sectoral differences in the conflicting goals that liberalization poses and providers face. The dilemma of re-regulation (and hence its urgency) is particularly acute in sectors like the rail industry, where liberalization's distributive blow (hitting some) is not cushioned by technological innovation's aggregate gains (benefiting all). Moreover, passenger rail transport suffers from harsh competition in the form of air transport and the private car. In the case of British Rail, where reformers undertaking a far-reaching liberalization simultaneously faced a huge need for reinvestment and a low likelihood of obtaining commercial profits, conflicting goals and the resultant urgency of re-regulation on behalf of consumers became particularly acute. Attempts to squeeze profits out of operations directly subjected users to inconveniences like overcrowding, while rapidly selling off stock and changing ownership in order to realize large profits was and remains an attractive perspective.

The conflict between customers' needs and shareholders' gains is less dramatic in sectors where it is mitigated by the impact of rapid technological progress improving mass consumption, as in the case of telecommunications. Here, indeed, market liberalization reinforces and amplifies forces of large-scale innovation greatly benefiting customers and leading to a marked drop in prices that also favors low-income customers. However, it was not the dominant factor. The positive impact of technological innovation on cutting prices and diversifying services and products was evident in France and Germany prior to liberalization. Notwithstanding this technological push favoring more customer-oriented behavior, there is still a need to regulate in favor of customers whose market position is weak, although the urgency is not so great as in passenger rail service.

What, then, can be learned about regulatory design from the empirical evidence about two sectors and three countries? If the regulatory process is viewed as a contractual relation between regulator (or principal) and regulatee (or agent), one may conclude that the relative strength of the regulator vis-à-vis the regulatee depends on the following institutional factors in a given country's overall regulatory order: on the political/institutional side, it is important how much regulatory power has been consolidated. In a fragmented authority structure like the British rail industry, where the functions of rail regulator and franchise director overlap, actors can be played off against one another in a way that weakens regulation.

The position of the regulatee vis-à-vis the regulator is stronger if the former has a dominant market position. In this case much depends on the initial process of privatization and on how far the public monopoly has been dismantled. If privatization merely created a new private monopoly to replace the old public one, the regulator's task is difficult. This difficulty is exacerbated if the regulatee is an international player with greater freedom than any domestic counterpart to withdraw from a national regulatory regime. Once again, Britain's railway sector is a case in point. Privatization was pushed through hastily, with a view toward the approaching general elections, and stock flotation gave industry a favorable deal (Veljanovski 1991). Hence the newly established regulatory authorities must now struggle to correct privatization's initial mistakes; they must try forcing operators into compliance with public service goals as defined in the franchise contracts.

Due to the informational asymmetry between regulator and regulatee over the technicalities and commercial viability of providing goods and services, the regulator depends on the regulatees' willingness to cooperate

(Windhoff-Héritier 1987). The regulator must therefore tread a narrow path between credibly threatening sanctions in case of non-compliance with contracted service standards and building an essential relationship of trust with the regulatee, whose information is crucial for setting incentives.

The regulator's position is defined not only with respect to the regulatee, but also vis-à-vis the government and the public. Some regulators are held more accountable to political decision-makers, while others have a higher degree of professional autonomy (Majone 1996). Autonomy lays regulators open to the accusation of lacking democratic legitimacy. However, their 'seclusion' has been partly counterbalanced by the political salience of the sectors involved, on account of the controversy generated by privatization and deregulation. The private owners of infrastructure and service operators are under close public scrutiny, where transparency is demanded. Better customer representation means that companies are under pressure to comply with public interest goals (Spiller and Vogelsang 1996: 116). This discussion is less pronounced in the German and French rail and telecom industries, where privatization has been less extensive and is still unfolding. However, regulation of liberalized utilities has been subject to ongoing scrutiny, both substantive and institutional, everywhere.

A similar kind of scrutiny and debate has not accompanied the employment effects of liberalization. Unlike quality of service, ongoing job losses have several different sources, not all of them connected to liberalization.

For a variety of technological and political reasons, the large public utility monopolies have come under significant pressure for change. Greater flexibility in markets and differentiation in services dictate a reorganization of former state bureaucracies. Increasing competitive pressures make it necessary to reduce labor costs, and therefore employment, as civil servants are moved into jobs governed by private law contracts. Significant job losses are occurring. Just as with service quality, here, too, a conflict between shareholders and stakeholders may be found. While this conflict is usually solved in ways that benefit current employees, not much is ever done to safeguard overall employment levels.

In none of the sectors—including telecommunications (despite all the promise of growth)—are job losses being compensated by new competitors' hiring. The former public companies find themselves in a difficult situation: if they are too slow to enact necessary reforms, they lose out to competitors. If they change too quickly, unrest among employees can lead to strikes and a decline in standards of service that is also harmful for the company. These major constraints characterize every process of restructuring. Differences between companies in terms of age structure and relationships with unions account for much of the variance in national developments. Notable examples for these different experiences are the Deutsche Bahn, which managed restructuring relatively well thanks to a cooperative union and in spite of the aggravation brought about by German unification. For the SNCF, by contrast, restructuring proved impossible, despite significant pressures for reform.

When the reform of public services takes place within a social dialogue, the major impact of reform on jobs does not attract much public notice. It is surprising how little attention has been paid to this topic, in academic discussions too. Guaranteeing public service functions over the long run has aroused much more concern. The relative lack of concern for job safety does make some sense in light of public employees' status as civil servants enjoying a high degree of social protection. This is a good precondition for finding socially acceptable approaches to restructuring. On the downside, however, a two-tier development is taking place as new employees face even greater insecurity in jobs that are being outsourced or transferred to subsidiaries. Working conditions can be even worse at the new service providers, where even collective bargaining may not be recognized. In addition, our analysis has shown that large job losses seem inevitable. Even companies that managed the reform process very successfully could not avoid shedding jobs, as the example of the Dutch postal office has shown. In all countries, restructuring is an ongoing process.

REFERENCES

ARMSTRONG, MARK, COWAN, SIMON, and VICKERS, JOHN (1994). *Regulatory Reform: Economic Analysis and British Experience.* Cambridge, Mass.: MIT Press.

ARZT, CLEMENS, BACH, KNUD, and SCHUELER, KLAUS W. (1990). *Telekommunikationspolitik in Großbritannien: Auswirkungen von Privatisierung und Liberalisierung.* Cologne: Bund-Verlag.

BATT, ROSEMARY, and KEEFE, JEFFREY (1999). 'Human Resource and Employment Practices in Telecommunications Services, 1980–1998', in Peter Cappelli (ed.), *Employment Practices and Corporate Strategy.* Oxford: Oxford University Press, forthcoming.

BAUBY, PIERRE, and BOUAL, JEAN-CLAUDE (eds.) (1993). *Les Services publics au défi de l'Europe.* Paris: Éditions Ouvrières.

BAUMOL, WILLIAM J., PANZAR, JOHN C., and WILLIG, ROBERT D. (1982). *Contestable Markets and the Theory of Industry Structure.* New York: Harcourt Brace Jovanovich.

BAZEX, MICHEL (1996). 'France', in Loic Grard, Jacques Vandamme, and François van der Mensbrugghe (eds.), *Vers un service public européen.* Paris: ASP Europe, 117–132.

BERG, SANFORD V., and TSCHIRHART, JOHN (1988). *Natural Monopoly Regulation: Principles and Practice*. Cambridge: Cambridge University Press.

BISHOP, MATTHEW, KAY, JOHN, and MAYER, COLIN (eds.) (1995). *The Regulatory Challenge*. Oxford: Oxford University Press.

BMV (Bundesministerium für Verkehr) (1998). *Strukturreform der Bundeseisenbahnen*. Bonn: BMV.

DARBISHIRE, OWEN (1997). 'Germany', in Harry C. Katz (ed.), *Telecommunications: Restructuring Work and Employment Relations Worldwide*. Ithaca, NY/London: ELR-Press, 189–227.

Deutsche Bahn (1997). *Annual Report & Accounts*. Berlin.

DOUILLET, ANNE-CÉCILE, and LEHMKUHL, DIRK (2000). 'Strengthening the Opposition and Pushing Change: The Paradoxical Impact of Europe on the Reform of French Transport', in Adrienne Héritier, Dieter Krewer, Christoph Knill, Dirk Lehmkuhl, and Anne-Cécile Douillet, *Differential Europe: New Opportunities and Restrictions for Policy-Making in the Member States*, 186–253.

DUNCAN, IAN, and BOLLARD, ALAN (1992). *Corporatization and Privatization: Lessons from New Zealand*. Auckland: Oxford University Press.

DVZ (Deutsche Verkehrszeitung) (1996a). 'DB AG steigerte das Konzernergebnis'. (26) 29 Feb.: 1.

——(1996b). C. Bagnai: 'Die FS wachsen vorbildlich: Dank Ökobonus und Bonus Italia-Export den Marktanteil gesteigert'. 2 Mar.: 14 f.

——(1996c). Fred Schreiber: 'Ziel: 2005 soll Belgiens Bahn wieder schwarze Zahlen bringen'. 13 June: 9.

EBERLEIN, BURKARD (1998). 'Regulating Public Utilities in Europe: Mapping the Problem'. Manuscript, Florence: Robert Schuman Centre.

ELIXMANN, DIETER, KEUTER, ALFONS, and MEYER, BERND (1997). *Beschäftigungseffekte von Privatisierung und Liberalisierung im Telekommunikationsmarkt*. Discussion Paper 178. Bad Honnef: Wissenschaftliches Institut für Kommunikationsdienste.

European Commission (1997). *Effects on Employment of the Liberalization of the Telecommunications Sector*. Luxembourg: Office for Official Publications for the European Communities.

FAZ (Frankfurter Allgemeine Zeitung) (1995a). 'Bahnchef Heinz Dürr kündigt den Abbau von 90 000 Arbeitsplätzen an'. 14 Aug.

——(1995b). 'Die streikgeplagte Bahn in Frankreich ist ein Sanierungsfall'. 26 Oct.

——(1996). 'Frankreichs Regierung will die marode Eisenbahn reformieren'. 12 June.

——(1997a). 'Die Bahnreform war ein Erfolg'. (75) 1 Apr.

——(1997b). 'Die SNCF stellt 2000 Mitarbeiter ein'. (160) 14 July.

FERNER, ANTHONY, and TERRY, MICHAEL (1997). 'United Kingdom', in Harry C. Katz (ed.), *Telecommunications: Restructuring Work and Employment Relations Worldwide*. Ithaca, NY/ London: ELR-Press, 89–121.

Financial Times, The (1997). 'UK News Digest: $700 m wiped off Railtrack'. 11 Dec.

FORSTHOFF, ERNST (1968). 'Verfassungsprobleme des Sozialstaats', in E. Forsthoff (ed.), *Rechtsstaatlichkeit und Sozialstaatlichkeit.* Darmstadt: Wissenschaftliche Buchgesellschaft, 145–64.

GIBB, RICHARD, LOWNDES, T., and CHARLTON, CLIVE (1996). 'The Privatisation of British Rail'. *Applied Geography*, 16/1: 35–51.

Guardian, The (1998*a*). 'The Failure of Rail: Tough Regulation is the Answer'. 19 Mar: 9.

——(1998*b*). 'MPs Urge State Holding in Railtrack'. 19 Mar.: 3.

——(1998*c*). 'Rail Operators Given Warning': 27 Mar.: 4.

——(1998*d*). 'Railtrack Ignores Maintenance Warning'. 5 Mar.: 1.

——(1999*a*). 'Rail Fares Speed Ahead of Inflation'. 13 Mar.: 5.

——(1999*b*). 'Railtrack Faces Multimillion Fine for Failure to Reduce Delays'. 10 May: 11.

HARDIN, RUSSEL (1982). *Collective Action.* Baltimore: Johns Hopkins University Press.

HELM, DIETER (1994). 'British Utility Regulation: Theory, Practice and Reform'. *Oxford Review of Economic Policy*, 10/3: 17–39.

HENRY, CLAUDE (1997). *Concurrence et services publics dans l'Union européenne.* Paris: Presses Universitaires de France.

HULSINK, WILLEM (1996). *Do Nations Matter in a Globalising Industry?.* Delft: Eburon.

ILO (International Labour Office) (1998). *Structural and Regulatory Changes and Globalization in Postal and Telecommunications Services: The Human Resources Dimension.* Geneva: International Labour Organization.

International Herald Tribune (1999). 'Phone Wars Flare across Europe'. 27/28 Feb.: 9.

ITU (International Telecommunication Union) (1998). *World Telecommunication Indicators: Chronological Time Series, 1960–1996.* Geneva: ITU.

KAY, JOHN, and THOMPSON, DAVID (1991). 'Regulatory Reform in Transport in the United Kingdom', in David Bannister and Kenneth Button (eds.), *Transport in a Free Market Economy.* London: Macmillan, 19–42.

KELLY, TIM, and MINGES, MICHAEL (1995). *Telecommunications Liberalisation and Employment.* ITU Speeches and Discussion Papers, International Telecommunications Union. <http://www.itu.int/ti/papers/employ/employ. htm>

KNILL, CHRISTOPH (2000). 'Reforming Transport Policy in Britain: Concurrence with Europe but Separate Development', in Adrienne Héritier, Dieter Krewer, Christoph Knill, Dirk Lehmkuhl, Michael Teutsch, and Anne-Cécile Douillet, *Differential Europe: New Opportunities and Restrictions for Policy-Making in the Member States*, 186–253

LEHMKUHL, DIETER, and HERR, CHRISTOF (1994). 'Reform im Spannungsfeld von Dezentralisierung und Entstaatlichung: Die Neuordnung des Eisenbahnwesens in Deutschland'. *Politische Vierteljahresschrift*, 35/4: 631–57.

LEVY, BRIAN, and SPILLER, PABLO T. (eds.) (1996). *Regulations, Institutions, and Commitment: Comparative Studies of Telecommunications.* Cambridge: Cambridge University Press.

LUNDBERG, ANDERS (1997). *Restructuring Experiences in the Swedish State Railways (SJ)*. Manuscript, Stockholm: Statens Järnvägar.

MAJONE, GIANDOMENICO (1996). *Regulating Europe*. London: Routledge.

MOORE, JOHN (1986). 'Why Privatise (1983)?', in John Kay, Colin Mayer, and David Thompson (eds.), *Privatisation and Regulation: The UK Experience*. Oxford: Clarendon Press, 78–93.

NEGRELLI, SERAFINO, and TREU, TIZIANO (1993). 'State, Market, Management and Industrial Relations in European Telecommunications'. *Bulletin of Comparative Labour Relations*, 25: 2–46.

NICOLAIDES, PHEDON (1997). 'The Role of the State in the Single European Market', in *Managing Universal Service Obligations in Public Utilities in the European Union*. Maastricht: European Institute of Public Administration, 39–62.

OECD (Organisation for Economic Co-operation and Development) (1995). *Communications Outlook*. Paris: OECD.

——(1997*a*). *Communications Outlook*, i–ii. Paris: OECD.

——(1997*b*). *Report on Regulatory Reform*, i–ii. Paris: OECD.

OPRAF (1998). 'OPRAF Bulletin: Customer Satisfaction on the Rail Network—Initial Toc Survey Results Published'.

ORR (1997). *New Service Opportunities for Passengers*. London: ORR.

Panorama of EC Industry, Vols. 1990, 1991/92, 1993, 1994, 1996/97, ed. European Union. Luxembourg: Office of Official Publications.

Price Waterhouse (1997). *Employment Trends in the European Postal Sector*. Luxembourg: European Commission.

SAMUELSON, PAUL A. (1954). 'The Pure Theory of Public Expenditure'. *Review of Economics and Statistics*, 36: 387–89.

SCHMIDT, SUSANNE K. (1996). 'Privatizing the Federal Postal and Telecommunications Services', in Arthur Benz and Klaus H. Goetz (eds.), *A New German Public Sector?*. Aldershot: Dartmouth, 45–70.

——(1998). *Liberalisierung in Europa*. Frankfurt: Campus.

SCHNEIDER, FRIEDRICH (1998). *Deregulierung und Privatisierung als Allheilmittel gegen ineffiziente Produktion von öffentlichen Unternehmen?*. Linz: Johannes Kepler Universität Linz.

SCHNEIDER, VOLKER, DANG-NGUYEN, GODEFROY, and WERLE, RAYMUND (1994). 'Corporate Actor Networks in European Policy-making: Harmonising Telecommunications Policy'. *Journal of Common Market Studies*, 32: 473–98.

SCHWARTZ, HERMAN (2000). 'Round Up the Usual Suspects! Globalization, Domestic Politics, and Welfare State Change', in Paul Pierson (ed.), *New Politics of the Welfare State*. Oxford: Oxford University Press.

SELZNICK, PHILIP (1985). 'Focusing Organizational Research on Regulation', in R. Noll (ed.), *Regulatory Policy and the Social Sciences*. Berkeley: University of California Press, 363–67.

SPILLER, PABLO T., and VOGELSANG, INGO (1996). 'The United Kingdom: A Pacesetter in Regulatory Incentives', in Brian Levy and Pablo T. Spiller (eds.), *Regulations, Institutions, and Commitment*. Cambridge: Cambridge University Press, 79–120.

STOFFAES, CHRISTIAN (1997). *Services publics comparés en Europe: Exception française, exigence européenne*, i–ii. Paris: Documentation Française.

STURM, ROLAND, and WILKS, STEPHEN (1997). *Competition Policy and the Regulation of the Electricity Supply Industry in Britain and Germany*. London: Anglo-German Foundation for the Study of Industrial Society.

SZ (Süddeutsche Zeitung) (1998). J. Ludewig: 'Personenverkehr der Bahn leidet unter der Wirtschaftsmisere'. Munich, 6 Mar.: 25.

——(1999*a*). 'Auch die Bahn spricht jetzt vom Wetter als Handicap'. Munich, 9 Mar.: 22.

——(1999*b*). 'Bahn verzeichnet seit Anfang 1999 wieder deutschen Kunden-zustrom'. Munich, 12/13 May: 25.

TEUTSCH, MICHAEL (2000). 'Regulatory Reforms i the German Transport Sector: How to Overcome Multiple Veto Points', in Adrienne Héritier, Dieter Krewer, Christoph Knill, Dirk Lehmkuhl, Michael Teutsch, and Anne-Cécile Douillet, *Differential Europe; New Opportunities and Restrictions for Policy-Making in the Member States*, 255–333.

THATCHER, MARK (1997). 'L'Impact de la Communauté Européenne sur la reglé-mentation nationale: Les Services publics en France et en Grande Bretagne'. *Revue Politiques et Management public*, 15/3: 141–68.

UPU (Union Postale Universelle) (1990). *Statistique des services posteaux 1989*. Bern: Bureau International de l'Union Postale Universelle.

VELJANOVSKI, CENTO (1991). 'The Regulation Game', in Cento Veljanovski (ed.), *Regulators and the Market*. London: Institute of Economic Affairs, 000–00.

Vie du Rail, La (1995). Marc Fressoz: 'Remède de cheval en Belgique'. (2519) 4 f.

——(1997*a*). Christophe Bourdoiseau: 'En 1997, la DB supprime 20 000 postes'. (2607), 9.

——(1997*b*). Francois Dumont: 'Plus d'emplois moins de dette et toujours RFF'. (2606) 4–5.

WILKS, STEPHEN (1997). 'The Amoral Corporation and British Utility Regulation'. *New Political Economy*, 2/2: 279–98.

WINDHOFF-HÉRITIER, ADRIENNE (1987). *Policy-Analyse: Eine Einführung*. Frankfurt: Campus.

Zeit, Die (1995). Fredy Gsteiger: 'Der Zug ist abgefahren'. (52) 22 Dec.

——(1996). Karrem van Gennip: 'Frischer Wind im Kontor'. (37) 6 Sept.

13

Adjusting National Tax Policy to Economic Internationalization
Strategies and Outcomes

STEFFEN GANGHOF

13.1. Introduction

Recent studies in political science have found that despite increased economic internationalization, neither capital (income) tax revenues, nor total tax revenues, nor public expenditures in advanced OECD countries have shown an average downward trend, and that high degrees of global market integration have not systematically translated into lower capital tax revenues, total tax revenues, or public expenditures (Garrett 1998*a*, *b*, *c*; Quinn 1997; Swank 1997). These results are striking. After all, the basic logic of tax competition is convincing, and competitive pressures figure prominently in public debates about tax reform in many countries. Unfortunately, the existing literature is less informative when it comes to explaining systematically why we see so little change on the aggregate level of tax revenues and public expenditures. Common explanations are that adjustment pressures are less strong than many assume, partly because non-tax factors—such as tax-financed public goods in the widest sense—offset the comparative disadvantages of high-tax countries. There is some truth to this view. But it is both imprecise and incomplete.

This chapter tries to give a more complete explanation for the apparent lack of large aggregate effects of competitive pressures by taking a closer

An earlier version of this chapter was presented at the final conference of the MPI Adjustment Project, Ringberg Castle, Munich, 17–20 Feb. 1999, and the conference on 'Globalization, European Economic Integration, and Social Protection' at the European University Institute, Florence, 11–12 Mar. 1999. Thanks to the participants at these conferences as well as Mark Hallerberg, Alex Hicks, Thomas Plümper, Stefan Profit, Claudio Radaelli, Fritz W. Scharpf, Vivien A. Schmidt, and Eric Seils for very helpful comments and suggestions. Special thanks to Philipp Genschel. This chapter grew out of joint work with him, and his help, esp. in the early stages of this project, was indispensable. Thanks also to Duane Swank and Frank Hettich for providing me with parts of their data-sets. All remaining errors are mine.

look at both aggregate budgetary outcomes and the precise nature of adjustment pressures and policies in the eighteen most advanced OECD countries (omitting Iceland and Luxembourg) since the 1970s. I argue that there have been significant and increasing downward pressures on effective tax burdens, especially on corporate and personal income, and (in turn) on tax revenues and public expenditures. However, two (complementary) arguments explain why these pressures have not led to obvious changes in the revenue mix or the level of public expenditures.

First, the downward pressures on capital income tax revenues, total tax revenues, and public expenditures have partly been offset by countervailing—domestic and international—pressures. Pressures to cut effective tax rates on capital income have been balanced by pressures to reduce the tax burden on more 'immobile' tax bases, notably labor. These countervailing pressures have risen both due to international competition in product markets and the severe employment crisis of the last two decades (especially within the EU). Similarly, downward pressures on total tax revenues and public expenditures have partly been offset by parallel downward pressures on public deficits (induced by the debt crisis and the Maastricht criteria) and upward pressures on public expenditures (induced mainly by increasing demands for social expenditures). Given these countervailing forces, the medium-term stability of average capital income tax revenues, total tax revenues, and public expenditures (each as a percentage of GDP) in these eighteen countries has to be seen partly a result of competitive pressures.

Second, given these budgetary constraints for general cuts in effective corporate and personal income tax rates, policymakers have pursued three complementary adjustment policies, which are associated with much smaller (or no) revenue losses. First, given that competitive pressures have not only been due to taxpayers' exit options, but also to new options for international tax avoidance and evasion, countries have taken legal and administrative measures to counteract such behavior. Second, given that the size of competitive pressures varies strongly both within and between the corporate and personal income tax base, many governments differentiated their tax treatment accordingly and focused tax cuts on the tax bases most sensitive to international tax differentials. Finally, given that both international investment flows and options for international tax avoidance partly depend on statutory tax rates, governments have pursued a policy of tax-cut-cum-base-broadening, especially in corporate taxation.

I discuss these three alternative strategies in some detail—their general logic, their effectiveness, and the cross-country differences in pursuing them. Since these strategies have been partly neglected in the existing literature on the political economy of tax competition, this discussion is at times explorative and preliminary. Yet the discussion also suggests that these three policy strategies have led, in part, to new tradeoffs between different goals of national tax policy. Such 'second order effects' of competitive pressures are most obvious with regard to greater differentiation in the tax treatment of different income sources.

The rest of this chapter is divided into five sections. Section 13.2 elaborates the general explanatory framework and gives a stylized description of the relationships between adjustment pressures, strategies, and outcomes. Section 13.3 explores the different adjustment strategies in detail and discusses possible second order effects on national tax policy. Section 13.4 offers an interpretation of the aggregate developments in public budgets, considering the effects of both competitive pressures and domestic economic factors. The chapter concludes with Section 13.5.

13.2. An Extended Explanatory Framework

Policymakers care about the costs of revenue-raising. Both taxation and deficit financing give rise to economic and electoral costs. As to taxation, these costs come in two main forms. First, taxation creates economic inefficiencies (dead-weight losses), which hinder the achievement of economic policy goals like growth or employment. Second, policymakers want to be re-elected, and thus try to minimize the electoral costs associated with high tax burdens.[1] These costs of revenue-raising increase with the size of the tax burden and the public debt.

Policymakers try to design the tax mix, revenue mix, and level of public expenditures so as to balance the marginal costs of taxation against the marginal benefits (both economic and electoral) of public expenditures.[2] Ideally, i.e. in equilibrium, marginal costs and benefits would be equalized. Of course, this is a formidable task for policymakers, especially when the (often uncertain) long-term effects of policies are considered.[3] Yet, for my purposes, it is not important to what extent an equilibrium exists in the real world or to what extent this equilibrium approach can explain the existing cross-country differences in tax systems and expenditure levels. The crucial assumption is rather that policymakers generally do recognize and respond to significant increases in the marginal costs of taxing certain

---

[1] For a fully developed model of taxation, which focuses on the marginal economic and political costs of taxation, see Hettich and Winer 1999. For a careful historical case study from a similar perspective, see Gillespie 1991.

[2] In the following, I neglect benefit-maximizing changes in the structure of public expenditures (see Schulze and Ursprung 1999).

[3] In the following, I largely neglect dynamic aspects of different financing choices, esp. with respect to public deficits.

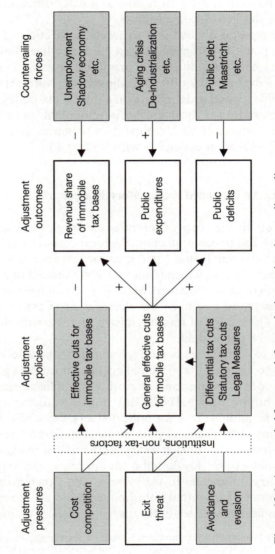

Figure 13.1 An extended framework for analyzing national tax policy adjustment

tax bases—and that they respond in a way that minimizes revenue losses and (by extension) costly expenditure cuts.

Applying these assumptions to the effects of increasing economic integration leads to a basic model of tax policy adjustment that seems to underlie many empirical studies of tax policy adjustment. This model is sketched by the five blank boxes in Figure 13.1. As to adjustment pressures, the emphasis is on the increased exit-threat of mobile resources, most notably capital and a small number of mobile high-income earners. The growing mobility of these resources, it is argued, leads to a sharp increase in the marginal economic costs of taxing them. High taxation would lead to their expatriation (capital flight), so that immobile factors (labor) would end up bearing the burden in the form of lower labor productivity and lower real wages (see e.g. Tanzi 1995).

As a consequence, policymakers will cut effective tax rates on corporate and personal income—and (where the latter is concerned) especially on high-income earners, who are relatively more mobile and/or receive a larger share of income from capital. Such tax cuts lead to revenue losses, which, everything else being equal, can lead to three possible outcomes[4]: (1) the revenue share from immobile tax bases increases (tax mix change), and/or (2) public deficits rise relative to tax revenues (revenue mix change), and/or (3) public expenditures decrease (budget size change). If none of these effects is visible, so the argument goes, it has to be concluded that the adjustment pressures—i.e. the increase in marginal costs—are much weaker than many believe, either because exit is still too costly or because non-tax factors are more important.

I argue that such a conclusion would be premature. This becomes clear when two extensions are added to the simple framework in Figure 13.1. The first extension simply amounts to recognizing that there have been countervailing pressures on the three aggregate policy outcomes just mentioned.[5] With respect to the revenue share of immobile tax bases, these pressures are both domestic and international and mostly concern labor taxes (see shaded boxes in the upper row of Figure 13.1). Policymakers

---

[4] Note that revenue losses are not always inevitable. When countries differ in size, a small country may actually increase its tax revenues—due to an inflow of foreign tax bases—by reducing the effective tax rate on mobile tax bases. In the following, however, I will largely concentrate on a government that has to trade a reduction of tax revenues from mobile tax bases against retained or increased attractiveness for mobile resources. For a short overview of formal models of tax competition, see Schulze and Ursprung 1999.

[5] Similar arguments have been made by Genschel (1999) and Steinmo and Swank (1999) in work in progress. Since I received the draft by Swank and Steinmo only towards the final stage of working on this chapter, the extensive econometric evidence presented in their paper is only partly reflected in the following. Note, however, that in Sections 13.3 and 13.4, I discuss some of the indicators used by Steinmo and Swank.

have had increasing incentives to cut labor taxes (which include social security taxes and, in part, both personal income taxes and consumption taxes) in order to reduce unit labor costs. In addition, there have been increasing downward pressures on taxes on (immobile) property, especially to the extent that they fall on businesses. These downward pressures on immobile tax bases have counteracted a shift in the tax mix towards immobile tax bases.

There have also been well known countervailing pressures on public deficits and expenditures (depicted in the bottom right of Figure 13.1). Potentially exploding public debt burdens and—in Europe—the Maastricht criteria for 'entry' into Euroland have strongly increased the marginal costs of deficit financing. In addition, increasing demands for expenditures—partly due to such factors as demographic change or structural unemployment—have put upward pressures on public expenditures. In turn, both of these forces counteracted changes in the revenue mix and the budget size.

In sum, stability in the three aggregate outcome variables—tax mix, revenue mix, budget size—partly reflects an overall increase in the marginal costs of revenue raising and the marginal benefits of public spending rather than the absence of competitive pressures.

Moreover, in the real world of boundedly rational and myopic policymakers and voters, change may be absent—at least temporarily—even if the long-term marginal economic costs of taxation have become considerably higher than the long-term marginal benefits of expenditures. Change might not happen because the short-term electoral costs of large-scale expenditure cuts may be seen as prohibitive—especially for left-wing parties in office.

My second extension of the analytical framework complements the first and is depicted in the two shaded boxes in the lower left of Figure 13.1. I argue that, given the strong countervailing forces on public budgets just mentioned, governments have pursued three more revenue-preserving adjustment strategies. To understand the logic behind these strategies, one has to paint a somewhat richer picture of competitive pressures. Three observations—to be explained in more detail below—are essential. First, competitive pressures have not only resulted from taxpayers' growing opportunities (given the legal framework of international taxation) to expatriate mobile resources. They also have been due to a rising number of loopholes in the international institutional framework, which create plenty of opportunity for (lawful) international tax avoidance and (fraudulent) evasion (depicted in the lower left box in Figure 13.1). Second, the strength of each type of competitive pressure varies strongly both within and between the corporate and personal income tax base. Some parts of the tax base have become very sensitive to international tax differentials, while others are still fairly unresponsive. Third, especially in the area of corporate taxation, both types of competitive pressures are partly driven by statutory tax rates as such—as opposed to effective tax rates, which also reflect the definition of the tax base.

From these three observations follow three adjustment strategies, more sophisticated than cuts in general effective tax rates on corporate and personal incomes and therefore resulting in lower revenue losses: (1) combining statutory tax cuts with a broadening of the tax base, (2) differentiating between different types of incomes and focusing tax cuts on the most mobile parts of the tax base, and (3) combating international tax avoidance and evasion through legal and administrative measures. To the extent that countries have successfully pursued these policies, they have reduced the need to cut general effective tax rates (see Figure 13.1).

These adjustment strategies have thus allowed governments to defend their revenue base and/or increase their attractiveness for direct investment while simultaneously maintaining a high revenue yield and thus high public expenditures. In turn, they have reduced the tradeoff between possible long-term economic benefits of tax cuts and short-term electoral losses associated with expenditure cuts.

Yet this reconciliation of the two goals of competitiveness and revenue-raising has led, in part, to different tradeoffs in national tax policy. This is most obvious with respect to the policy of increased differentiation of income tax treatment. On the one hand, responding to differences in taxpayers' reactions to taxation by differentiation is no new tendency in the political economy of tax systems (cf. Hettich and Winer 1999: ch. 3). On the other hand, very explicit forms of differentiation—i.e. imposing different statutory tax burdens on different types of incomes—that have resulted, in part, from competitive pressures may contradict traditional notions of tax justice—thus leading to electoral costs—and/or principles of neutral taxation—thus leading to economic (efficiency) costs.

The rest of the chapter uses this extended framework to analyze the empirical evidence on policy outputs and outcomes of the eighteen most advanced OECD countries. The different parts of the argument are also elaborated along the way. For ease of exposition, I start with the second extension in Section 13.3 by taking a comparative look at adjustment pressures and strategies. Section 13.4 then analyzes the development of the main aggregate policy outcomes since 1970.

13.3. Revenue-Preserving Strategies of Tax Policy Adjustment

The argument proceeds in two steps. Sections 13.3.2 to 13.3.5 explore the four main strategies of tax policy adjustment in greater detail: their logic, the determinants of their usage in different countries, and their possible second order effects. First, however, Section 13.3.1 provides the basis for such a discussion by briefly sketching the institutional framework for taxing international income flows. This discussion shows that this framework provides at least some buffer against competitive pressures, that competitive pressures partly arise from taxpayers' options for international tax avoidance and evasion, and that the sensitivity of the capital income tax base to international tax differentials is very heterogeneous.

13.3.1. Adjustment Pressures

In principle, the institutional framework for taxing international flows of corporate and personal income could reduce the competitive pressures arising from economic integration. Income can be taxed according to two different principles, the source principle, and the residence principle. Under the residence principle a country taxes all its residents on their total income, regardless of whether it derives from domestic or foreign sources. Under the source principle, a country taxes the returns from all sources of income within its territory, regardless of whether they belong to residents or non-residents. Broadly speaking, mobility in the income tax base creates problems for national tax policy only if income is effectively taxed under a source-based system. Under a residence-based system, countries can still tax the worldwide income of their residents. In this case, (honest) taxpayers would have to emigrate in order to reduce their tax burden. Investing abroad would not make a difference.

In practice, most countries have adopted a combination of residence- and source-based taxation (see e.g. Zee 1998). Residents are taxed on their worldwide income and non-residents are taxed on their income generated from domestic sources. Therefore, juridical or international double taxation is possible whenever income from domestic sources accrues to non-residents. In order to avoid such a result, the country of residence most commonly provides relief from double taxation by either granting tax credits against domestic tax liabilities of foreign taxes paid or exempting foreign-source income. Consistent application of the tax credit method (full credit) re-establishes the residence principle, because the tax burden on foreign income is lifted or lowered to the domestic level. Consistent application of the exemption method (full exemption) re-establishes the source principle. In practice, most countries impose ceilings on foreign tax credits and limits on tax-exempt foreign-source income, so that the system of international taxation is a mixed one, granting taxing rights to residence as well as source countries. The relative taxing rights of residence and source countries, however, are different depending on the kind of income involved. The rights to tax business (active) income are almost universally granted to the source country. In contrast, the rights to tax portfolio investment (passive) income are generally shared between the source and residence countries—with ceilings imposed on the tax rates on such income in the source country under the model tax convention of the OECD (1996*b*).

While this institutional framework partly works as a buffer against competitive pressure, there clearly are incentives for the expatriation of mobile resources (direct investment). In addition, in a global economy, there are ways to side-step this institutional framework by shifting income into low-tax jurisdictions or evading taxes internationally. To explore these two issues further, I look at corporate and personal taxation separately.

13.3.1.1. Corporate Taxation

Given the institutional framework just sketched, multinational enterprises (MNEs) have a tax incentive to invest abroad whenever their final tax burden is at least partly determined by the tax rate of the source country. There are two basic cases. First, some countries, like Germany, usually exempt repatriated income of foreign branches or subsidiaries so that the tax in the source country is the only tax to be paid. Second, even when a country, like the USA, uses the credit method, this usually does not fully restore the residence principle in an economic sense—for two reasons.[6] For one thing, credit countries invariably do not pay refunds when their taxpayers pay a foreign income tax at a rate that is higher than the domestic rate (OECD 1996*b*: Article 23B). Nor do they allow the excess foreign tax to offset taxes imposed on domestic income (Arnold and McIntyre 1995: 44). As a result of such limitations on the credit, foreign income is typically taxed at the foreign effective tax rate whenever the foreign rate is higher than the domestic rate. Second, income of foreign subsidiaries is assessed differently than domestic income (and foreign income from branches or 'permanent establishments'). Whereas domestic income is taxed continuously as it is produced, income from a foreign subsidiary is taxed only upon distribution, i.e., when the foreign subsidiary pays out a dividend to the parent company. As long as no dividend is paid, the payment of domestic taxes on the foreign-source income is deferred. During

---

[6] Institutional differences between countries with regard to taxing international income flows have been almost completely neglected in quantitative studies of the political economy of tax competition. Yet they may be part of the reason why econometric studies usually find no significant relationship between indicators of capital mobility and indicators of tax policy outcomes (revenues).

this time, the foreign income is only subject to the corporate tax of the source country. Again, the result of such tax deferral is different tax rates for domestic and foreign investments.

In sum, enterprises do often have a tax incentive to invest abroad. But are they really sensitive to tax differentials? It is here that differences within the corporate tax base are important. To put the point in somewhat simplified terms, manufacturing investment does react to tax differentials, but the impact of such differentials on the locational choice is often rather small—non-tax factors are more important (Leibfritz, Thornton, and Bibbee 1997: 31; Ruding Report 1992). By contrast, tax factors are much more important for the location of financial and commercial activities. In general, companies that exercise specific (mostly financial) and centralized activities solely or mainly for the benefit of a MNE react strongly to tax differentials. Examples include coordination centers, distributions centers, financial holding companies, or offshore banking centers (Owens 1993: 27).

This leads me to discuss companies' options for international tax avoidance. As already noted, multinational companies can shift profits from high-tax into low-tax jurisdictions, thus reducing the incentive to relocate production facilities in response to cross-national tax differentials (another reason why such investment reacts only moderately to tax differentials). In other words, the tax base of MNEs might migrate even though mobile resources do not. Two well-known tax avoidance techniques are the manipulation of transfer prices and thin capitalization. Transfer prices are the prices charged in intra-company transactions. They can be manipulated to shift company profits from high-tax to low-tax countries. Since intra-company trade makes up more than 50 percent of international trade in goods and services, transfer pricing is a serious problem for tax administrators (Owens 1993; Tanzi 1998). 'Thin capitalization' means allocation of debt to affiliates in high-tax countries. In general, a parent company can inject equity or issue loans to finance a subsidiary, or the subsidiary can pay for itself out of retained earnings. Since interest expenses are deductible from taxable profits while dividends are not, it is a standard practice to load a subsidiary in a high-tax country with debt. The associated deductible interest expenses will help to keep the subsidiary's taxable profits low, and the interest payments can then be collected (and deferred) by a holding company in a low-tax regime. In general, exploiting the possibility of deferral is another way for MNEs to avoid taxes. They can set up so-called base companies in a low-tax regime that collect the income from foreign subsidiaries. Passive investment income—interest, dividends, rent, royalties, etc.—is stored in the base company in order to prevent its distribution to the parent company, because, once distributed, it would become taxable in the parent's country of residence.[7]

13.3.1.2. Personal Income Taxation

As in corporate taxation, the sensitivity of different types of personal income in the tax base to international tax differentials varies strongly. Most labor income is on the unresponsive end of the continuum. It is very difficult for income from labor to evade taxes, because in most countries it is withheld at the source by the employer. And wage earners usually find it too costly to emigrate for tax reasons. One exception is the highly paid executive or professional.

By contrast, income from financial assets, especially interest income, often finds it easy to evade internationally. If the residence country could ensure effective taxation, it would tax portfolio investment income remitted from abroad—often under the general progressive income tax schedule—and give a tax credit for the foreign withholding tax paid abroad.[8] However, both the absence of international exchange of information and bank secrecy laws usually prevent effective enforcement. Thus, considerable portions of portfolio capital flows bear only the withholding tax in the source country, thus creating an incentive for governments to reduce tax rates both on residents and non-residents.[9]

Finally, the sensitivity of capital income from unincorporated businesses and immobile assets to international tax differentials is somewhere in between the two extremes, but generally still rather small. There may be incentives to invest abroad, especially in countries like Germany that often exempt such foreign income. On the other hand, there are generally few options for international tax avoidance and evasion, and the probability of relocation or emigration due to tax factors is limited.

---

[7] For more extensive and detailed exposition of techniques of international tax planning, see Giovannini 1989 and Arnold and McIntyre 1995.

[8] Withholding tax rates in source countries are established in domestic tax laws, but usually reduced in double taxation treaties. Nowadays, treaty rates on interest and dividends vary between 0 and 15 percent, while non-treaty rates vary between 0 and 40 percent (Zee 1998: 592).

[9] It has been rightly argued that, while international tax evasion is clearly significant, it should also not be exaggerated (BMF 1999: 27–28). For one thing, not all types of investment are well suited to international tax evasion. Evading foreign dividend income is often not worthwhile, because it bears both foreign corporate and withholding taxes, which are not creditable at home in the case of tax evasion. In addition, households are much more likely to make foreign investments through intermediaries, which are subject to stringent accounting rules (OECD 1994: 175). Finally, domestic tax evasion is still an alternative in many countries. All three points are important qualifications. With respect to the last point, however, I argue below that competitive pressures have been partly responsible for greater difficulty and lower success in reducing domestic tax evasion.

Having clarified the precise nature of adjustment pressures in the area of income taxation, the next four sections discuss the main adjustment strategies in more detail.

13.3.2. Adjustment Strategy I: Cutting General Effective Tax Rates

Let us start with corporate taxation and look at the development of general effective corporate tax rates over time. Unfortunately, it is impossible to construct indicators of effective tax rates for the corporate sector as a whole. Effective rates are not only more difficult to measure than statutory rates, but they also vary widely across different sectors, different kinds of investments, or different ways of financing. In fact, part of my argument is

Table 13.1 *Average effective corporate tax rates,[a] 1979–1994*

	Microeconomic indicator			Macroeconomic indicator		
	1979	1994	Change (%)	1970–88	1979–86	1987–94
AUS	29	19	−33	38	35	39
B	n.a.	n.a.	n.a.	37	37	29
CAN	23	20	−13	27	17	16
DK	n.a.	n.a.	n.a.	n.a.	62[b]	45
FL	n.a.	n.a.	n.a.	30	24	33
F	24	14	−41	27	43	25
D	21	20	−5	n.a.	43[c]	28[c]
IRE	19	5	−72	n.a.	n.a.	n.a.
I	13	19	48	141	52	63
JAP	24	25	2	37	45	51
NL	n.a.	n.a.	n.a.	21	21	23
NZ	n.a.	n.a.	n.a.	n.a.	9[d]	13
N	n.a.	n.a.	n.a.	20	47	30
S	n.a.	n.a.	n.a.	56	38	53
SP	19	20	6	n.a.	n.a.	n.a.
UK	24	18	−27	44	54	52
US	22	20	−11	34	26	29
AVERAGE[e]	22	18	−18	40	35	35

n.a. = not available

[a]To nearest percentage point; see text for explanation of the indicators.
[b]Unweighted average for the years 1983–86.
[c]Data on Germany are taken from Genser, Hettich, and Schmidt 1999; averages are for the years 1980–86 and 1987–95.
[d]Unweighted average for the years 1982–86.
[e]Unweighted average; own calculations excluding Denmark and New Zealand for the macroeconomic indicator.

Sources: Chennells and Griffith 1997; Swank 1998; Genser, Hettich, and Schmidt 1999.

about the major differences in effective tax rates within the corporate tax base. Thus, any indicator of effective tax rates should only be seen as a crude proxy of the average corporate tax burden in different countries. Even with these caveats in mind, however, adequate data are hard to find. While quite a few investigations were recently undertaken—partly initiated by government agencies concerned about tax competition—most of them do not cover extended periods of time (see e.g. Baker & McKenzie 1999).

Two of the most useful and widely used indicators are given in Table 13.1. The table displays one microeconomic and one macroeconomic estimate of average effective tax rates for different years and periods and for ten and thirteen countries, respectively.[10] The microeconomic indicator constructs average effective tax rates on the basis of detailed information about a country's tax system. As a result, while these estimates are very precise, they are also highly dependent on the assumptions made about the particular investment project (see Chennells and Griffith 1997; Devereux and Griffith 1998). The macroeconomic indicator of average effective corporate tax rates expresses corporate tax revenues as a percentage of the operating surplus of the corporate sector. Although this indicator has increasingly been used in the political science literature, it is not suitable for an international comparison of the levels of effective corporate tax burdens (see Ganghof 1999a). Any interpretation of this data should be done in conjunction with other indicators and should focus on the time-path of the estimated tax rates.[11]

Despite these caveats, the two indicators taken together clearly show that, on average, there was not a very strong downward trend in effective tax rates between 1979 and 1994. While microeconomic tax rates decreased by 18 percent during this period, macroeconomic estimates show no average downward trend at all. This evidence suggests that competitive pressures on effective corporate tax rates have so far been rather moderate. The average change, however, provides limited information in light of large cross-country differences (see Table 13.1). The microeconomic rates went

[10] Much of the economic literature focuses on marginal effective tax rates (not shown), which measure the effective tax rate applying to an investment project that earns an after-tax rate of return just sufficient to make the initial outlay worthwhile. From a theoretical point of view, while marginal effective tax rates determine the volume of investment at a particular location, the locational decision of (rational) investors is determined by the average effective tax rate.

[11] Even this is quite difficult, however, since a number of countries' macroeconomic estimates are extremely volatile, which makes it hard to see any trends (Ganghof 1999a). Note in addition that while the macroeconomic estimates in Table 13.1 generally come from Swank (1998), the figures for Germany come from Genser, Hettich, and Schmidt (1999). These authors use correct estimates of Germany's corporate operating surplus that are incorrectly reported in OECD National Accounts.

down markedly in Australia, France, the UK, and especially in Ireland, but they went up in Japan, Spain, and quite sharply in Italy.[12] The macroeconomic rates declined strongly in countries such as Norway, Belgium, Denmark, France, and Germany. In France and Germany, they dropped precipitously between 1980 and 1996—by 49 and 57 percent, respectively (see Genser, Hettich, and Schmidt 1999). On the other hand, they increased strongly in countries such as Sweden and Italy.

It is certainly no coincidence that Italy shows large increases on both indicators. Italy's debt problem led to a continuous rise in total tax revenues, which included corporate taxes. In general, both the average stability of general effective corporate tax rates and the cross-countries differences are partly explained by countervailing pressures on public budgets. The correlation between the change of the (microeconomic) effective tax rates and the increase of the total tax burden in the ten countries covered is 0.61. But this brings us to the second main argument of this chapter, which is elaborated in Section 13.4.

As a final caveat, note that corporate tax reform and tax competition did not, of course, disappear from the agenda of OECD countries after 1994. At the time of writing, a number of countries have approved additional cuts in effective tax rates. Even Italy—the most obvious outlier in Table 13.1—started a major overhaul of the corporate tax system in 1997, which reduced the effective corporate tax burden (Bordignon, Giannini, and Panteghini 1999; Giannini 1997). Nevertheless, while effective corporate tax rates surely have a ways to go before reaching a new (temporary) equilibrium, so far one cannot speak of a race to the bottom with respect to general effective corporate tax rates.

Let us finally take a brief look at changes in general personal income tax schedules. As is well known, personal income tax systems have also become flatter, top marginal rates have been reduced, and the tax base has been broadened by measures like limiting exemptions or taxing fringe benefits. With regard to effective tax rates, these reforms, on average, benefited high-income earners more than low-income recipients, which would be consistent with the simple tax competition model. Between 1978 and 1995, average effective tax rates rose considerably at the low end of the earnings scale, but typically increased only modestly or fell for high-income earners (even though patterns varied widely from country to country at the high end) (OECD 1998c: 161).

Yet empirical evidence suggests that it was not mainly competitiveness considerations that drove personal income tax reforms, but rather a

---

[12] Note that the Irish (microeconomic) effective tax rate applies to the manufacturing sector and reflects the preferential tax rate of 10%.

changed philosophy of tax policy and widespread skepticism on the effectiveness of progressive rate schedule (Messere 1997; Owens 1993: 31; Sandford 1993: 20). Unfortunately, quantitative comparative investigations of changes in effective personal income tax rates are rare and often neglect important factors. One of these factors is geographic, cultural, and linguistic 'proximity' between countries. Where the non-tax costs of changing one's domicile decrease, tax differentials become more important. For instance, Canada has for a long time been constrained by US personal income tax policy (Bird and Mintz 1994), and the Canadian policy debates of the last two decades have unambiguously involved arguments to the effect that unmatched rate reductions in the USA might generate an outflow of professional and other higher-income labor from Canada (Albert, Shoven, and Whalley 1992: 10; OECD 1997: 71–106).

13.3.3. Adjustment Strategy II: Cutting Statutory Tax Rates

The first revenue-preserving alternative to effective cuts of general income tax rates has been cuts in the statutory rate plus a simultaneous broadening of the tax base. This policy of tax-cut-cum-base-broadening has been pursued in both personal and corporate income taxation. Yet only with respect to corporate taxation is there clear evidence that competitive pressures have been one of the major driving forces behind this policy. As I have just noted, reforms of personal income tax schedules have mainly been motivated by domestic considerations (Owens 1993: 31; but see Hallerberg and Basinger 1998).

Focusing on corporate taxation, the empirical evidence is clear. As shown in Table 13.2, between 1986 and 1998 almost all eighteen OECD countries significantly cut statutory tax rates, sometimes by almost 50 percent (although this did not lead to cross-country convergence). The average total corporate tax rate (i.e. including profit taxes at sub-national levels) decreased from 48 percent to 37 percent, the median rate from 50 percent to 36 percent. But what does this policy have to do with tax competition? After all, most countries used base broadening to make these reforms more or less revenue-neutral (Garrett 1998c: 90). The answer is that statutory rates as such have important effects on the location of both real investment and the mobile tax bases of MNEs (Ganghof 1999b; Hallerberg and Basinger 1998). Three competitive mechanisms are of special importance.

The first two mechanisms concern competition for real investment. First, companies that have to make locational decisions and are facing very complex tax codes use statutory rates to some extent as proxies for effective rates, because they lack more detailed information—either about

Table 13.2 *Statutory corporate tax rates in 18 OECD countries (%), 1986 and 1998*[a]

	1986	1998	Change (percentage points)
Australia	49	36	−13
Austria[b]	55	34	−21
Belgium[c]	45	40	−5
Canada[d]	52	45	−7
Germany[e]	63	56	−7
Denmark	50	34	−16
Finland	49	28	−21
France[f]	45	42	−3
Ireland	50	38	−12
Italy[g]	46	41	−5
Japan[h]	53	46	−7
Netherlands	42	35	−7
New Zealand	48	33	−15
Norway	51	28	−23
Sweden	52	28	−24
Switzerland[i]	34	34	0
United Kingdom	35	31	−4
United States[j]	51	41	−10
MEAN	48	37	−11
MEDIAN	50	36	−9
COEFFICIENT OF VARIATION	0.14	0.19	

[a]To nearest percentage point; rates given are 'normal rates', including sub-national tax rates and temporary surcharges; in case of progressive rate schedules, top marginal rates are given; when rates on distributed and non-distributed profits differ, the latter are given.
[b]Progressive rate schedule until 1989. Local tax was abolished effective 1994.
[c]Rate for 1998 includes 'crisis surcharge' of 3%.
[d]Rates include local tax averaged over all provinces.
[e]Rates apply to non-distributed profits only. Figures include the (profit-related part) of the local Enterprise Tax (at an approximate rate of 16%). The local tax is deductible from the corporate income tax base. Figure for 1998 also includes a surcharge of 5.5%.
[f]Rate for 1986 applies to non-distributed profits only. Figure for 1998 includes a corporate tax rate of 33.3% and a surcharge of 25%.
[g]Rate for 1986 includes local profit tax (ILOR) partly deductible from the corporate income tax base (IRPEG). The rate for 1998 includes a local tax on value added (IRAP) set at 4.25% which replaced ILOR. After adjusting for the different tax base of IRAP, the Cologne Institute for Business Research estimates the top marginal tax burden on corporations to be 58%.
[h]Rate includes local Corporate Enterprise Tax (deductible from tax base of national Corporation Tax) as well as Corporation Inhabitant Tax.
[i]Progressive schedule until 1997. Rate includes (progressive) sub-national taxes (based on canton and city of Zurich).
[j]Rate includes local tax rate for the state and city of New York.

Sources: Coopers & Lybrand; German Ministry of Finance (BMF); Cologne Institute for Business Research (Institut der deutschen Wirtschaft); own calculations.

effective rates or about the extent to which their future investment profile will enable them to make use of tax relief provisions (e.g. depreciation allowances or investment tax credits) (BMF 1999: 12). Statutory rates thus have an important signaling function for investors. Second, recall that in many countries, like the USA, a domestic parent can claim a foreign tax credit for repatriated profits of a foreign subsidiary and that this tax credit is usually limited to the domestic statutory tax rate. Thus, a US parent pays the US rate on foreign profits as long as the foreign statutory rate is lower than in the USA. If the foreign rate is higher, however, the firm ends up paying the foreign tax. MNEs thus have an incentive to locate subsidiaries in countries with a tax rate lower than or equal to the domestic rate. Governments in turn have an incentive to keep their rate in line with other countries. Considerations like this were especially important with respect to the US. tax reform of 1986. The third mechanism does not concern investment competition, but has to do with international tax avoidance and evasion. Statutory rates directly affect the (re-)location of income by MNEs through techniques like thin capitalization and transfer pricing.

Due to these mechanisms, even countries that wanted to maintain a given effective tax rate had an incentive to restructure their corporate tax system by reducing statutory rates and broadening the tax base (Slemrod 1990). Case studies show that this type of reasoning played a considerable role in the tax reforms of many, albeit not all, OECD countries 'responding' to rate cuts in Great Britain in 1984 and the USA in 1986 (for an overview, see Ganghof 1998). This does not mean, however, that competitive pressures were the only or even most important driving forces behind the tax-cut-cum-base-broadening reforms. In fact, in many countries, domestic considerations were probably more important. Governments turned towards a new philosophy of taxation, aiming primarily at the allocative neutrality of tax systems (for a summary, see Steinmo and Swank 1999).

Quantitative studies also find evidence for both international and domestic determinants of changes in statutory corporate tax rates. Hallerberg and Basinger (1998, 1999), Wagschal (1999a, b), and Ganghof (1999b) used cross-sectional designs to investigate the role of economic and political factors in explaining the magnitude of tax cuts in OECD countries after 1986. Steinmo and Swank (1999) analyze the development of tax rates using a pooled data-set for OECD countries from 1981 to 1995.

Hallerberg and Basinger (1998) as well as Ganghof (1999b) find that higher tax rates in 1986 (the assumed starting year for the tax reform wave) were significantly related to larger tax cuts—indirect evidence for the importance of competitive considerations. As to domestic factors, both studies find that higher real GDP growth was significantly associated with smaller tax cuts, which points towards domestic considerations. In addition, Steinmo and Swank (1999) find that lower rates of domestic investment were significantly related to lower marginal corporate tax rates and that increases in structural unemployment were significantly associated with declines in marginal rates.

There is also evidence that domestic budgetary stress made even statutory (as opposed to effective) tax cuts more difficult. Steinmo and Swank (1999) find that higher public debt was significantly associated with higher corporate tax rates. The prime example for this type of constraint is Italy, which had been the only country to increase—from 46 percent to 53 percent—its general government tax rate after 1986. Only in 1997 did Italy manage to start a major corporate tax reform and reduce the statutory rate by abolishing the local profit tax (see Table 13.2). Similarly, Ganghof (1999b) finds that higher growth of the total tax ratio during the adjustment period was significantly related to smaller cuts in marginal tax rates—a result that is strongly influenced by the high tax cases (Italy and Germany) however.

One mechanism underlying the relationship between statutory tax rates and budgetary constraints may be that, everything else being equal, tax-cut-cum-base-broadening reforms in fact reduce domestic real investment (cf. Sinn 1989, 1997). Both the tax cut and the abolition of investment incentives, depreciation allowances etc. reduce the tax advantage of real investments compared to financial investments. Therefore, even for governments that aim at a more neutral tax system, such a policy may be difficult to pursue if the economic situation is bad or if governments see no budgetary room to compensate (by reducing effective corporate tax burdens or unit labor costs) for the adverse effects on real investments. Such considerations played a role in German tax reform, for instance (Weichenrieder 1996).[13]

Finally, there is disagreement about whether partisan and institutional factors explain international variation in the magnitude of statutory tax cuts. Hallerberg and Basinger (1998; 1999) as well as Wagschal (1999a, b)—focusing on central government rates—find that the number of domestic veto players (e.g. strong second chambers) had a negative effect on the scope of tax reforms. Hallerberg and Basinger also find that left governments pursued deeper statutory rate cuts. By contrast, Ganghof (1999b) argues that total government tax rates (including sub-national

---

[13] In addition, the constraining effect of domestic budgetary tension on statutory corporate tax cuts may result from a strong alignment between corporate and personal income tax rates. See the example of Germany in the next section.

rates) were the strategic variables for governments. On the basis of that assumption he finds that neither the number of domestic veto players nor the partisan composition of the government had a considerable and statistically significant effect on the scope of tax reforms.[14]

In sum, the policy of tax-cut-cum-base-broadening has been an important aspect of recent tax reforms. It has been driven both by competitive pressures and domestic economic considerations. At the same time, domestic budgetary tension seems to have made even statutory tax cuts more difficult.

13.3.4. Adjustment Strategy III: Differential Tax Cuts

In contrast to the policy of tax-cut-cum-base-broadening, the strategy of differentiating tax treatment for different incomes has received almost no mention in the political science literature on tax policy adjustment. Yet the basic logic is perfectly obvious. If the force of competitive pressures varies strongly across different segments of the corporate and personal income tax base, and if countries cannot afford the revenue losses associated with large-scale effective tax cuts for both mobile and immobile factors, they may only be able to achieve effective tax cuts by focusing those cuts on the most mobile tax bases. The most obvious form of differentiation would be between labor incomes and capital incomes within the personal income tax.

But such a schedular tax treatment of different kinds of incomes stands in sharp contrast to the time-honored ideal of comprehensive income taxation, which has been the guiding idea of taxation in most OECD countries (Messere 1993: 224, 237–38). According to this principle, no difference should be made between different forms of income, because they all contribute to a taxpayers' ability to pay. Different types of incomes should be taxed jointly under a common progressive tax rate schedule. Increased differentiation between different forms of incomes may thus go against traditional notions of tax justice. Moreover, it may lead to new domestic options for tax avoidance and arbitrage and reduce the allocative neutrality of the tax system.

In the following, I survey different forms of increased differentiation in corporate and personal income taxation and explore possible conflicts between them and established goals of income taxation. Due to the lack of systematic comparative investigations of these topics, the discussion is often unavoidably anecdotal, additional research is necessary. I deal with corporate and personal income taxation in turn.

---

[14] Note that these results are robust with respect to possible additional veto players in countries with subnational profit taxes (Ganghof 1999*b*: 466 n. 13).

13.3.4.1. Corporate Taxation

In corporate taxation, differentiation has generally taken the form of preferential tax regimes that side-step the general tax system. These regimes offer greatly reduced effective corporate tax rates, which may even be negotiated, to some extent, between the company and the tax authorities at the time of application.[15] These regimes are targeted at the geographically mobile business activities mentioned in Section 13.3.1. While there are no useful quantitative data available on these regimes, their number and scope clearly increased in the last two decades—partly due to competitive bidding (see Baker & McKenzie 1999). For example, many OECD countries have set up special regimes for holding companies, and long-established holding locations like Switzerland recently felt compelled to increase the attractiveness of their regimes (Bonoli and Mach, this volume). Many high-tax countries established preferential regimes or extended existing ones. For instance, France recently extended its headquarter regime (de Drouas 1996), and Denmark introduced one of the world's most attractive holding company regimes, effective 1999 (Baker & McKenzie 1999: 86). This type of competition also forced countries that have traditionally been opposed to any kind of competitive tax policy to match the favorable tax and financial regimes offered by other countries. For example, Australia established a special regime for banking activities in order to avoid having a large portion of its financial activity go offshore to Asian low-tax regimes (McMullen 1994: 21).

In recent years, preferential regimes have received a lot of attention—especially in Europe—as cases of 'harmful tax competition' (for an overview, see CEPS 1999; OECD 1998a). Two aspects, in particular, make them seem 'harmful'. First, the companies attracted by preferential tax regimes often play a crucial role in multinationals' international tax avoidance behavior. They are the low-tax platforms for the (combined) application of techniques such as thin capitalization, transfer price manipulation, or deferral. Preferential regimes thus not only attract mobile resources (direct investment); they also make it easier for multinational corporations to reduce their tax burden in high-tax jurisdictions. Second, many preferential regimes disregard international tax principles, lack transparency, apply only to foreigners, and shelter the domestic economy from the economic effects of the regime (Easson 1998).

---

[15] Note that the attractiveness of a particular regime may not only stem from low corporate income taxes, but also from such features as low capital gains taxes or a country's favorable network of international tax treaties (with low withholding taxes on international income flows as a corollary).

Country-specific evidence suggests that preferential tax regimes may have significant effects on foreign direct investment (for Germany, see Spengel 1998: 16; Weichenrieder 1996). But their effects—both in terms of tax revenues and investment flows—are very difficult to quantify and have not yet received a lot of attention in econometric studies. In addition, little is known about what explains cross-country differences in the reliance on preferential regimes. It is nevertheless clear that preferential tax reductions have been an increasingly important policy, helping defend or increase the attractiveness of a country for mobile (financial) companies (and thus possibly even attracting foreign tax bases) while avoiding the major revenue losses that come from large tax reductions for the bulk of the domestic corporate tax base.

13.3.4.2. Personal Income Taxation

That differentiation in corporate taxation takes the form of preferential regimes is perfectly obvious. It is hard to think of systematic reasons for differential tax treatment of the most mobile kinds of companies, so differentiation takes the form of exceptions. The same thing also happens for personal income taxation, though on a smaller scale. The most obvious example of preferential tax treatment is the special tax reduction (whether low, flat tax rate, or large allowance) for executives of multinational companies temporarily residing in a country hosting an MNE branch, an exemption that exists in many OECD countries. In fact, these so-called expatriate regimes are often integral parts of corporate headquarter regimes, because headquarters imply a large share of foreign expatriates. Anecdotal evidence shows that personal income tax levels for executives may determine locational choices, so that company's competition for top executives translates into tax competition for foreign direct investment. It would be interesting to know to what extent political factors account for the fact that countries like Sweden or Germany have been reluctant to introduce such regimes, but, again, systematic evidence on this is lacking.

Yet in personal taxation this type of preferential tax treatment for certain mobile groups of taxpayers is the exception. Since differences in mobility partly correspond to different types of incomes, a more systematic form of differentiation is possible, pushing tax systems towards a schedular income tax, which, in its purest form, is the exact opposite of a comprehensive (or global) income tax. I shall first briefly sketch different types of differentiation within personal income taxation and then speculate about possible conflicts between these types and the goals of tax justice and allocative neutrality.

There are two basic approaches towards differentiation. The first approach is to remove some forms of capital income from the ambit of the

Table 13.3 *Taxes on interest from bank deposits, 1980 and 1996*

	Tax rates on residents: top personal income tax rate (TP) or final withholding (FW)[a]				Tax rate on non-residents (%)
	1980			1996	1996
A	62	TP	25	FW	0
B	72	TP	15	FW	0
CAN	63[c]	TP	49[c]	TP	25[b]
DK	70	TP	62	TP	0
FL	n.a.	n.a.	28	FW	0
F	25	FW	19	FW	0
D	56	TP	57	TP	0
GR	63[d]	TP	15	FW	15[b]
IRE	60	TP	48	TP	0
I	13[e]	FW	30	FW	30
JAP	20	FW	20	FW	15
LUX	57	TP	51	TP	0
NL	72	TP	60	TP	0
N	n.a.	n.a.	28	FW	0
P	70[d]	TP	20	FW	20
SP	66	TP	56	TP	25[b]
S	50	TP	30	FW	0
CH	43[c]	TP	42[c]	TP	35
UK	75	TP	40	TP	0
US	74[c]	TP	44[c]	TP	0

n.a. = not available
[a]To nearest percentage point.
[b]Various reduced rates and exemptions.
[c]Tax rate varies by state, province, or canton of residence.
[d]Rate for 1985.
[e]Many different rates applicable. The rates given are 'typical'.

Sources: Owens 1993; German Ministry of Finance; Coopers & Lybrand, *International Tax Summaries* (various years).

personal income tax without changing the general approach towards personal income taxation. The most obvious example is income from financial assets, especially interest from bank deposits. Since financial income is most sensitive to international tax differentials, governments have an incentive to cut or abolish withholding taxes on interest for residents and non-residents. Table 13.3 suggests that many governments have at least partly followed this logic. By 1996 only seven of twenty OECD countries levied withholding taxes on the interest income (from bank deposits) of non-residents. More importantly for my point, ten of the twenty countries moved towards low, flat-rate final withholding taxes on the interest income of residents—outside the ambit of the progressive personal income tax.

Growing competitive pressure has been one of the driving forces behind these reforms (see e.g. Müssener 1996).[16]

Another example of the first approach is the differential reduction for unincorporated businesses (which are generally taxed under the progressive personal income tax). In 1994 the German government lowered the top marginal personal tax rate for business income (i.e. income of unincorporated businesses) to 47 percent, whereas the general top personal income rate stayed at 53 percent. The tax reform passed in 1999 will reduce the former rate to 43 percent (by 2000) and the latter to 48.5 percent (by 2002). At the time of writing, Germany's Social Democrat–Green government is planning large-scale cuts for taxes on retained profits of unincorporated businesses. They would be taxed at a flat rate of 25 percent (aligned with the corporate tax rate on retained profits), whereas profit withdrawals and other types of personal income would still be subject to the general progressive rate schedule. Similar rules already exist in Denmark, for example (OECD 1996c: 74). Under the so-called 'company scheme' Danish households' income from unincorporated business activities is subject only to the corporate tax rate, provided household accounts keep the proceeds separate from their other assets. Only when money is extracted from the company scheme it is taxed (again) at a rate equal to the difference between household marginal taxes and the corporate tax rate.

The second approach towards schedular taxation is more consistent. Between 1991 and 1993, the three Nordic countries Sweden, Norway, and Finland changed their general tax system towards a so-called Dual Income Tax (DIT), which treats all kinds of capital income equally for tax purposes, while at the same time entirely separating the taxation of capital and labor income. Capital income is taxed at a proportional tax rate between 25 and 30 percent, while labor income is still taxed progressively and at markedly higher marginal rates (Sørensen 1998). This switch towards the DIT system has explicitly been treated as a response to globalization and tax competition (see e.g. Tikka 1993: 93). However, there were many other motivations, too, such as reducing the distortional effects of progressive income taxation in an inflationary environment, to strengthen private savings incentives, and to limit the scope for domestic tax arbitrage and avoidance (Sørensen 1998).

These forms of schedular taxation are obviously most well suited to reconciling the two goals of revenue-raising (from less vulnerable types of incomes) and competitiveness (with respect to the most sensitive tax bases). However, this 'solution' may conflict with the goals of justice

---

[16] Other aims include mitigating the lack of adjustment to inflation.

and/or neutrality. In the following, I want to take a closer look at both the Dual Income Tax and Germany's reform experience in order to explore possible tradeoffs.

The DIT-approach towards differentiation seems to have avoided conflicts with the neutrality goal of tax policy. In fact, one major goal of the DIT system was to increase the neutrality of capital income taxation by avoiding the kinds of differences in marginal effective tax rates on different types of savings and investment that are inevitable under a real world conventional income tax (see e.g. Cnossen 1995; Sørensen 1998). At the same time, although effective tax rates have strongly declined for some of the most mobile forms of capital incomes, total revenues from capital income taxation either stayed constant or even rose after the DIT reforms (see Table 13.5, as well as Sørensen 1998: 4; Tikka 1993; Zimmer 1993).

The reason for this result is that some forms of capital incomes had always been taxed leniently—or even negatively—under the old income tax.[17] Therefore, the switch to the DIT increased the tax burden on some forms of capital income, e.g. capital gains and income from owner-occupied housing, that are less vulnerable to competitive pressures (cf. Sørensen 1998). This type of tax base broadening accounts for the reconciliation of the two goals of competitiveness and revenue-raising.[18] Thus, in the Nordic countries differentiation in tax treatment did not increase, but changed in a way that made the tax system more robust under international pressure.

Yet the DIT is not without its problems. First, whereas the neutrality goals may have been strengthened, the same cannot be said unambiguously with respect to tax justice. In theory, it is true, the switch to the DIT system has not necessarily increased the injustice of the tax system (Nielsen and Sørensen 1997; Sørensen 1998). From a political economy perspective, however, voters' views on tax justice are more important. In fact, negative views towards the DIT system were part of the reason why Denmark moved back towards a comprehensive income tax in 1993, although the idea of the DIT system actually originated in Denmark and had to some extent been implemented as early as 1987. '[I]t had proved difficult to gain popular acceptance of a tax system which taxes large positive income from wealth at a considerably lower marginal rate than income from labor' (Sørensen 1998: 23).

---

[17] This observation can be made in many OECD countries. In fact, in a number of countries total tax revenues from personal capital income were estimated to be negative (Cnossen 1995: 300–301).

[18] This type of shift of the effective tax burden from 'mobile' to 'immobile' tax bases within the capital income tax base (both personal and corporate) may, in part, explain the stability of total capital income tax revenues in many countries.

The second problem is that the DIT system may not reconcile the three goals of competitiveness, revenue-raising, and neutrality in the future. If competitive pressures in the area of interest taxation increase, further cuts may either lead to revenue losses or have to be restricted to interest income, thus compromising allocative neutrality (cf. Viherkenttä 1996: 136).

A similar tradeoff is already apparent in Germany's experience with differentiation. To make a long story short, the crucial problem is the following: when the German government introduced a lower top marginal tax rate for business income, it mainly did so not out of fear that unincorporated businesses would leave the country, but rather owing to neutrality considerations. Since 1977 the neutrality of taxation with respect to the legal form of business organizations had been guaranteed by aligning the corporate tax rate on profit retention with the top personal income tax rate. This alignment is especially important in Germany, because around 85 percent of all businesses are not incorporated. With the downward pressure on statutory corporate tax rates, the alignment came increasingly under pressure.

In 1990 the corporate-personal tax alignment was loosened for the first time. The corporate tax rate on retained profits fell from 56 percent to 50 percent while the top personal rate fell only to 53 percent. When the next corporate tax cuts—from 50 percent to 45 percent and then to 40 percent—were passed in 1994 and 1999, the government faced a difficult choice. Leaving the top personal rate where it was would have made the differential between the two rates much more severe. On the other hand, simultaneous cuts in the top personal rate by 5 percentage points each time were regarded as impossible to finance, given domestic budgetary tension. The way out of this dilemma was to restrict the cut of the top personal rate to business incomes, thus trading less discrimination between incorporated and unincorporated businesses against differentiation (and therefore more inequality) within the personal income tax system. The top rate for business income fell to 47 percent in 1994 and 45 percent in 1999 (scheduled to be reduced to 43% in 2000), while the normal top marginal personal tax rate stayed at 53 percent until 1999 (scheduled to be reduced to 48.5% by 2002).

Yet this approach was exhausted after the 1999 tax reform. Given high local profit taxes, the total statutory corporate tax rate on retained profits was still above 50 percent—considered too high by 'international standards' (see Table 13.2). Therefore, at the time of writing, the Red–Green (SPD–ecological party) government is planning to cut the federal corporate tax rate on retained profits from 40 percent to around 25 percent. As before, simultaneous cuts in marginal personal tax rates are considered to be too costly. But further differential cuts for unincorporated businesses would not work either. For one thing, the rate differential within the personal income tax would become too large. In addition, the Federal Fiscal Court argued that this specific form of discrimination was unconstitutional. As a result, the government is now trying to push through a reform that only discriminates in favor of unincorporated businesses' retained profits by taxing them at the low corporate tax rate on profit retention. Extracted profits and other types of personal income would still be subject to the general progressive rate schedule. Not surprisingly, the majority of economists rejects this reform proposal, because it would probably make the allocation of capital less efficient by locking in profits.

In sum, there seems to be a three-way tradeoff in Germany's overall system of income taxation among the goals of competitiveness, revenue-raising, and neutrality with respect to the legal form of business organizations or the allocation of capital, a trade-off largely driven by tax competition in corporate taxation. It is ironic that this tradeoff exists even though adjustment in corporate taxation could focus on cuts in statutory (as opposed to effective) tax rates and thus be, to a large extent, revenue-neutral. The reason for this form of 'spillover' is that the kind of base-broadening that would be needed to make simultaneous cuts in personal income taxation revenue-neutral are much more difficult to achieve.

This three-way tradeoff thus also explains much of Germany's exceptional difficulty reducing the statutory corporate tax rate during the 1980s and 1990s (see Section 13.3.3). Since the German government did not want to abandon the goal of a 'level playing field' between incorporated and unincorporated businesses entirely, the fiscal constraints in personal income taxation limited the scope of corporate tax cuts.

To be sure, the specific three-way tradeoff in Germany exists because of how country-specific factors—the large share of unincorporated businesses and the existence of local profit taxes—interact. Moreover, in theory, there are ways to escape the tradeoff. One I have already mentioned: extensive base broadening in personal income taxation. Another way out would be to reform or abolish the local profits tax. However, pursuing these solutions is made difficult by domestic factors—economic, institutional, legal, and political. Thus, it is the combination of competitive pressures and domestic constraints that makes it so difficult for the German government to design a tax reform that would reconcile the major goals of tax policy. It remains to be seen whether the government will eventually find a way to escape the three-way tradeoff. But whatever the choice will be, the constraining effect of intensified tax competition is obvious.

In sum, all the varieties of differentiation that have (at least in part) been induced by competitive pressures seem to have a potential to create severe tensions in a given country's income tax policy. Both the precise form of differentiation and the resulting tradeoffs vary across countries. Since this variation is partly due to political and institutional factors, and given how important the emerging tradeoffs are in economic terms, systematic comparative investigations into the political economy of differentiation seem overdue.

13.3.5. Adjustment Strategy IV: Legal and Administrative Counteraction

The third revenue-preserving policy alternative to making general cuts in effective tax rates has been to pass or strengthen anti-avoidance rules and increase administrative action against international tax evasion. The most important specific anti-avoidance rules deal with the problems of deferral, thin capitalization, and transfer pricing (which were explained in Section 13.3.1). In all three areas, the starting point for understanding the problem and effective countermeasures is the so-called arm's length/separate accounting basis of taxation (hereafter 'AL/SA') utilized by all OECD countries. AL/SA recognizes related corporations as separate entities for tax purposes, with intra-firm transactions booked as though the legal persons were unconnected and dealing with each other at arm's length (OECD 1996a: 10).

As to transfer pricing and thin capitalization, the problem is to make sure that MNEs adhere to the arm's length standard. Transfer pricing rules require related parties to use specific methods for calculating transfer prices for tax purposes. Thin capitalization rules deny deductions for interest paid by a resident corporation to a non-resident shareholder to the extent that the corporation is 'excessively' debt-financed (Arnold and McIntyre 1995). The problem of deferral is not so much poor implementation of the AL/SA standard as the standard itself. In the absence of anti-avoidance legislation, it would be easy for a resident taxpayer in an AL/SA system to avoid domestic taxation on the resident's foreign income by interposing a corporation in a low-tax (preferential) regime to receive such income instead of remitting it to the home country. Therefore, under Controlled Foreign Company (CFC) regimes resident taxpayers controlling a foreign company are required to recalculate the income of the foreign company and pay tax on the latter's retained earnings calculated according to the tax code of the residence state. This is only done in 'abusive' situations, which are defined differently in different countries. Generally speaking, the resident may be taxable only if the non-resident company is subject to an exceptionally low effective tax rate (e.g. in a preferential tax regime) and only on its passive income (OECD 1996a).

In personal income taxation, where the problem is international tax evasion, the main option governments have for dealing with this problem unilaterally is to strengthen enforcement of existing legislation and prosecute tax evaders. Germany, for example, has pursued this option by making large-scale, countrywide investigations of German banks and prosecuting bank employees and managers for aiding and abetting international tax evasion.

There is evidence that such legal and administrative measures can be quite effective in defending a country's revenue base against resourceful taxpayers and preferential tax regimes (see e.g. Ruding Report 1992: 123; Weichenrieder 1996). Therefore, all advanced OECD countries seem to have adopted at least some of these measures. Yet there are two generic limitations. First, rising marginal costs of administration (which show up on the expenditure side of the budget) reduce the benefits of such measures and create a dead weight for the economy (Tanzi 1998). Second, successful countermeasures increase the effective tax burden of MNEs and thus their incentives to relocate. This limitation is exemplified by recent concerns about the tightness of CFC legislation in New Zealand and Germany (Becker 1997; Devereux 1996; see also Owens 1997: 43).

13.4. Countervailing Pressures on Tax Mix, Revenue Mix, and Budget Size

The discussion in Section 13.3 has shown that governments have also pursued other adjustment policies besides cutting effective income tax rates in general. This should have led to smaller revenue losses. Yet these alternative strategies have had their limitations, too, and some countries have implemented general effective tax cuts, especially in corporate taxation. As a consequence, there have been competitive pressures on the tax mix, the revenue mix, and budget size. At the same time, however, there have also been growing countervailing pressures on these three aggregate variables, both domestic and international. In the following, I investigate these countervailing pressures in more detail and review the available data. The next section looks at the tax mix, Section 13.4.2 at the revenue mix and budget size.

13.4.1. Changes in the Tax Mix

13.4.1.1. The Evidence

Figures 13.2 and 13.3 display average revenues (OECD–18) from the major types of taxes as percentages of GDP and total taxation, respec-

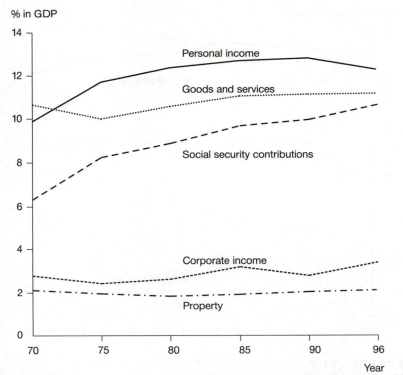

% in GDP

Figure 13.2 Average tax ratios of 18 OECD countries in 1970, 1975, 1980, 1985, 1990, and 1996 (intervening years are not covered)
Note: Unweighted averages.
Source: OECD, *Revenue Statistics 1965–1996* (Paris: OECD, 1997).

tively, between 1970 and 1996. Tax ratios and tax structure paint a similar picture. What we see is a considerable shift in the tax mix towards social security contributions and payroll taxes. Their average share of total taxation rose by around one-third from 19.6 percent in 1970 to 26.3 percent in 1996. While this growth seems consistent with decreasing relative marginal costs for charging taxes on labor, over half the growth (3.9 percentage points) occurred in the five years from 1970 to 1975—at a time when capital was still rather immobile—and mainly constituted a shift away from other 'immobile' tax bases—excises and property taxes. Therefore, this shift had more to do with the growth of the welfare state than with growing tax competition. Between 1975 and 1996, the shift towards social security contributions was more moderate (a rise of 2.8 percentage points). In addition, this shift came increasingly at the expense of the personal

% in total tax receipts

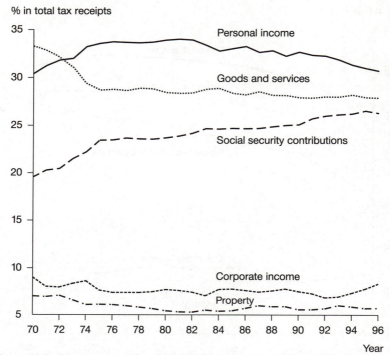

Figure 13.3 Average tax mix of 18 OECD countries, 1970–1996
Notes: Unweighted averages.
Source: OECD, *Revenue Statistics 1965–1996* (Paris: OECD, 1997).

income tax, whose share fell from 34 percent to 30.7 percent between 1981 and 1996. Since the personal income tax is to a large extent a tax on wage income, the shift towards labor may be even more moderate than the shift to social security contributions suggests.

The shares of the other three major types of taxes remained more or less the same (Figures 13.2 and 13.3, Tables 13.4 and 13.5). The share of taxes on goods and services fluctuated at around 28.5 percent, the corporate income tax share at 7.5 percent, and the property tax share around 5.5 percent. Cross-national deviations from this average picture are small enough for the average to be a meaningful summary of the overall development.[19]

[19] However, significant country–country differences with respect to the corporate tax share should be noted (Table 13.5). Between 1985 and 1996, this share remained more or less stable in some countries, decreased markedly in others (e.g. Japan, Norway, and Germany), and increased markedly in still others (Australia, Ireland). While these differences may be explained by a multitude of factors, one particular factor merits attention. A growing corporate income tax share may not always be the result of increasing effective tax

Table 13.4 *Percentage of tax receipts from relatively 'immobile' tax bases in total tax receipts and GDP^a, 1985 and 1996*

| | Social security contributions and payroll taxes as % of | | | | Property taxes as % of | | | | Taxes on goods and services as % of | | | |
| | Total taxation | | GDP | | Total taxation | | GDP | | Total taxation | | GDP | |
	1985	1996	1985	1996	1985	1996	1985	1996	1985	1996	1985	1996
AUS	5	7	1	2	8	9	1	1	33	28	10	9
A	38	41	16	18	2	2	2	3	33	29	14	13
B	32	32	15	15	2	3	1	1	25	27	12	12
CAN	13	16	5	6	9	10	3	4	32	25	11	9
D^b	37	41	14	16	3	3	1	1	23	28	10	11
DK	5	4	2	2	4	3	2	2	34	33	17	17
FL	18	26	7	12	3	2	1	1	34	30	14	15
F	45	45	20	21	4	5	2	2	30	27	13	13
IRE	17	15	6	5	4	5	2	2	44	40	16	13
I	35	34	12	15	3	5	1	2	25	26	9	11
JAP	30	37	8	10	10	11	3	3	14	15	4	4
NL	44	40	20	17	4	4	2	2	26	29	11	12
NZ	1	1	0	0	7	6	3	2	23	35	8	12
N	21	23	9	10	2	2	1	1	38	38	16	16
S	29	32	14	17	2	4	1	2	27	23	13	12
CH	32	37	10	13	8	7	3	2	19	18	56	6
UK	18	17	7	6	12	11	5	4	31	35	12	13
US	25	26	7	7	11	11	3	3	19	17	5	5
OECD-18^c	25	26	10	11	5	6	2	2	28	28	11	11
OECD TOTAL^c	24	26	9	10	5	5	2	2	34	33	11	12

^a To nearest percentage point.
^b United Germany since 1991.
^c Unweighted average.

Source: OECD, *Revenue Statistics 1965–1996* (Paris: OECD, 1997).

Table 13.5 *Percentage of tax receipts from relatively 'mobile' tax bases in total tax receipts and GDP*

| | Personal income taxes as % of | | | | Corporate incomes taxes as % of | | | |
| | GDP | | Total taxation | | GDP | | Total taxation | |
	1985	1996	1985	1996	1985	1996	1985	1996
A	9.7	9.2	22.9	20.9	1.5	1.6[a]	3.5	3.7[a]
AUS	13.6	12.8	45.2	41.2	2.8	4.7	9.4	15.0
B	16.4	14.3	35.0	31.0	2.6	3.1	5.4	6.8
CAN	11.7	13.9	35.2	37.7	2.7	3.3	8.2	8.9
CH	10.7	11.1	34.9	32.0	1.8	1.9	6.0	5.6
D	10.9	9.4	28.7	24.7	2.3	1.4	6.1	3.8
DK	24.6	27.8	50.2	53.2	2.4	2.4	4.9	4.6
F	5.7	6.4	12.8	14.1	2.0	1.7	4.5	3.8
FL	17.0	16.9	41.7	35.0	1.4	3.2	3.5	6.7
I	11.4	10.5	26.7	25.1	3.2	4.0	9.2	9.2
IRL	11.4	10.5	31.3	31.3	1.2	3.2	3.2	9.6
JAP	6.8	5.7	24.7	20.2	5.8	4.7	21.0	16.4
N	9.7	10.7	22.5	26.0	7.4	4.3	17.2	10.5
NL	8.6	7.6	19.4	17.5	3.1	4.1	7.0	9.5
NZ	20.1	15.6	59.8	43.5	2.8	3.5	8.3	9.8
S	19.4	18.4	38.7	35.3	1.7	2.9	3.5	5.6
UK	10.3	9.3	27.4	25.9	4.6	3.8	12.5	10.5
US	9.9	10.7	37.8	37.6	2.0	2.7	7.5	9.6
OECD–18	12.7	12.3	33.1	30.7	3.2	3.4	7.8	8.4

[a]Figure for 1995.

Source: OECD, *Revenue Statistics, 1965–1996* (Paris: OECD, 1997).

Thus, the change in the tax mix (since 1975) seems very moderate. However, this picture is imprecise and may be biased—for two reasons. First, there are no comparable time-series on the relative shares of capital and labor within revenues from the personal income tax, and thus it is unclear to what extent the shift from personal income tax to social security contributions is a shift from capital to labor. Second, the picture does not reflect changes in the shares of capital and labor incomes within national income.

Two types of indicators try to account for such changes by dividing the total tax revenue of a given country into labor, consumption, and capital/

rates, but might be due to an inflow of taxes from foreign sources in response to decreasing tax rates. For example, Ireland's corporate income tax revenues increased strongly between 1985 and 1996: from 1.2 to 3.2 percent of GDP and from 3.2 to 9.6 percent of total taxation (Table 13.5). While this increase is partly due to the Irish economy's rapid growth since 1987, it may also be due to an inflow of foreign tax bases in response to very low (preferential) tax rates.

Table 13.6 *Average/implicit tax rates on capital/other factors of production and labor, 1975–1995*

| | Average effective tax rates | | | | Implicit tax rates | | | |
| | Capital | | Labor | | Other factors | | Labor | |
	1975–85	1985–94	1975–85	1985–94	1976–85	1986–95	1976–85	1986–95
A	20	21	38	41	40[a]	41	39[a]	41
AUS	42	45	18	19	n.a.	n.a.	n.a.	n.a.
B	35	33	37	40	40	36	39	44
CAN	38	44	22	28	n.a.	n.a.	n.a.	n.a.
D	42	42	35	41	31	39	39	45
FL	32	41	31	38	14[a]	21	40[a]	48
F	25	25	37	43	45	45	37	43
D	29	26	35	37	51	41	37	41
I	22	28	28	32	23	32	32	41
I	n.a.	n.a.	n.a.	n.a.	25	22	25	31
JAP	35	44	17	21	n.a.	n.a.	n.a.	n.a.
LUX	n.a.	n.a.	n.a.	n.a.	44	45	33	30
NL	30	31	43	46	35	34	47	51
N	38	37	34	35	n.a.	n.a.	n.a.	n.a.
S	45	58	46	48	32[a]	42	53[a]	55
CH	24	25	26	26	n.a.	n.a.	n.a.	n.a.
UK	60	52	25	21	61	49	28	26
US	42	40	21	23	n.a.	n.a.	n.a.	n.a.
AVERAGE[b]	35	37	31	34	37	37	38	41
STANDARD DEVIATION	10	11	8	9	13	9	8	9

n.a. = not available

[a]1980–1985.

[b]Unweighted average.

Sources: Average effective tax rates: Swank 1998; implicit tax rates: Eurostat 1998.

other factors of production and expressing these revenue components not as shares of GDP or total taxation, but of the underlying aggregate tax base (taken from National Accounts Statistics) (see Table 13.6). Mendoza and colleagues compute 'average effective tax rates' on capital, labor and consumption, while Eurostat gives 'implicit tax rates' on labor, consumption, and other factors of production (i.e. mainly capital) (Eurostat 1998; Mendoza, Milesi-Ferreti, and Asea 1997; Mendoza, Razin, and Tesar 1994).[20]

However, both indicators cannot adequately solve the first problem—lacking a breakdown of capital and labor shares in personal income tax revenues. Mendoza and colleagues simply assume that personal capital and labor incomes are taxed at the same effective rate in all countries and that these effective rates do not vary over time. This assumption may lead to biased estimates in many countries (see Ganghof 1999*a*; Ruggeri, Laroche, and Vincent 1997). Eurostat does estimate the breakdown between capital and labor for each country individually (on the basis of estimates of national administrations) but is not able to adjust this estimate for all countries over time. Thus, both measures are plagued by significant (and possibly systematic) measurement error and are not well suited to capture changes within the structure of the personal income tax over time. Of course, the resulting bias in the breakdown of personal income tax revenues into capital and labor shares also affects the adjustment for changes in the tax base. In sum, the validity of descriptive inferences based on these two indicators seems questionable.

Fortunately, however, it turns out that both measures, while sometimes giving very different estimates for particular countries, paint a broadly similar average picture, which also conveys the same message as simple tax structure data (see Tables 13.4 and 13.5). While the effective tax rate on capital increased only slightly or even remained constant between the mid-1970s and the mid-1990s, the effective tax rate on labor grew more strongly. This relative shift from capital to labor is more pronounced in the Eurostat estimates, which are probably more precise, but only available for EU countries. Thus, taken together the available data suggest that there has been a shift in the tax structure from capital to labor since the mid-1970s—mainly due to increasing social security contributions—but that this shift has so far been fairly moderate.

13.4.1.2. Interpretation

There is a straightforward explanation for the shift towards social security contributions. These contributions are not directly vulnerable to inter-

---

[20] Note that the effective tax rates on capital/other factors of production include not only capital income taxes but also, for example, taxes on immovable property. For a more detailed discussion of these indicators, see Ganghof 1999*a*.

national tax evasion and avoidance since they are withheld at source. Governments may even have to act in order to keep them from rising because they are directly linked to social expenditures, the demand for which has increased strongly due to demographic change and rising unemployment. At the same time, the electoral costs of growing social security contributions may be low compared to other taxes because they are still, at least partly, perceived as insurance contributions.

The fact that the shift has been so moderate is more puzzling. Part of the answer I have already given: institutions and non-fiscal factors have reduced the pressure on national taxation. In addition, countries took advantage of the precise form of these pressures by pursuing revenue-preserving adjustment policies. Now I shall elaborate the second part of my account.

There have been parallel forces, both domestic and international, that have increased the marginal economic costs of taxing 'immobile' tax bases—taxes on labor, (immobile) property, and goods and services— and thus prevented a more pronounced shift in the tax structure. In part, the international forces also have to do with competition—especially, with cost competition. Governments are concerned about the competitiveness of 'national' companies in international product markets and thus have an incentive to limit the tax burden on factors of production. Therefore, both taxes on labor and on business property have also come under pressure.

Let us first look at labor taxes. Three types of taxes are, in effect, taxes on labor. Social security contributions, personal income taxes on wages, and (to a large extent) consumption taxes are all labor taxes. These levies drive a wedge between employers' real labor costs (real product wage) and workers' real take-home pay (real consumption wage). Therefore, to the extent that workers successfully resist reductions in their real consumption wage as a response to labor taxes, real labor costs increase. This rise in labor costs, in turn, reduces the demand for labor, the competitiveness of firms in international product markets, and a country's attractiveness for real investment (Leibfritz, Thornton, and Bibbee 1997: 33–35; Tanzi 1995: 108). Can we also detect a marked tax-induced increase in labor costs for employers empirically? There is no unambiguous consensus in the literature, but it seems clear that the total tax wedge, constituted by all kinds of labor taxes together, has at least a short-run effect on labor costs, which may in fact last quite long (see Leibfritz, Thornton, and Bibbee 1997: 33–46; Nickell and Layard 1999: 3057–61). In any event, many policymakers clearly believe that labor taxes, especially social security contributions, are crucial, and this has led to pressure to reduce or contain them (cf. Genschel 1999).

Similarly, property taxes, even to the extent that they fall on immobile property, have also come under pressure.[21] Whereas options for avoiding or evading taxes on immovable property on an international scale are severely limited, taxpayers may change their residence partly in response to high taxes on immovable property. In addition, taxes on business property increase factor costs. Many governments therefore gave serious consideration to abolishing certain property taxes altogether (Messere 1997: 300). Countries like Austria, Germany, and France abolished or considerably reduced property taxes (especially net wealth taxes) on businesses— and, to some extent, also on individuals.

Finally, taxes on goods and services are relevant not only as part of the tax wedge between consumption and production wage, but also because of how they are subject to competitive pressures stemming from cross-border shopping and bootlegging. This problem, however, is a relatively small one, since consumption taxes are generally levied where the consumption takes place (according to the destination principle) and not where goods and services are produced (origin principle) (Messere 1994). As a consequence, all products compete on the basis of net (pre-tax) producer prices rather than gross (after tax) consumer prices, which ensures that no product is at a competitive disadvantage because it was produced in a high-tax country. The situation is somewhat different within the European Union. In 1993 the EU switched to the origin principle for final consumer purchases (with some exceptions).[22] This creates incentives for legal tax arbitrage in the form of cross-border shopping. But private importation of goods is mainly important for goods subject to high domestic excise taxes. Even sizeable general consumption tax differentials have not led to considerable cross-border shopping (Ratzinger 1997: 469).

Yet this distinction between general consumption taxes (value-added taxes) and taxes on specific goods and services (mostly excises and import duties) opens the door towards seeing that consumption tax revenues have at least partly been influenced by internationalization. In fact, just as the tax competition view of the world would predict in OECD countries, the average revenue share of the generally robust general consumption taxes increased markedly between 1970 and 1996, from 13.5 percent to 17.8 percent. In the same period, the share of specific consumption taxes fell from 20.4 percent to 12.9 percent. This is partly explained by negative fiscal

---

[21] Property taxes are here defined to comprise taxes on immobile property, net wealth taxes, inheritance and gift taxes, and taxes on financial and capital transactions (OECD 1998*b*).

[22] Sales transactions between firms remain subject to the destination principle. In addition, the scope of the origin principle is further diminished. Sales by firms engaged in long-distance selling, purchases of 'new means of transportation' (i.e. cars), and purchases of VAT-exempt firms are exempted from the origin principle.

drag. Since most excises are specific, inflation erodes their real value unless governments adjust the tax rates (which increases the political costs of taxing excises) (Messere 1997: 306). Yet internationalization has played a role as well. Import duties were lowered in the course of trade liberalization, and excises are more vulnerable to cross-border shopping and smuggling than general consumption taxes are.[23]

Now consider the domestic pressures to lower labor taxes, which may have been just as important (if not more so) in preventing more pronounced shifts in the tax mix. These pressures also follow from the effects of the tax wedge between the consumption and production wage. But from a domestic perspective the problem is not one of competitiveness, since all national firms face more or less the same cost increase. The problem is rather that the tax wedge effect is probably more severe in the low-wage service sector (see Scharpf, Volume I). The reason is that market-clearing wages in less productive services may be at or near the effective reservation wage, so that the tax burden cannot be shifted into the consumption wage of employees. Thus, a high tax wedge leads to unemployment—a problem whose significance has increased due to the secular trend towards the service economy. And the tax wedge leads to an ever bigger shadow economy.

Finally, there is also a more political side to the domestic downward pressures on immobile tax bases. Since social security contributions and consumption taxes are in effect rather regressive, raising them may go against the equity demands of many voters, leading to considerable electoral costs. For all of these reasons, there has been increasing pressure to reduce the tax burden on labor (cf. Genschel 1999).

13.4.1.3. What Would Have Happened in the Absence of Competitive Pressures?

In sum, rising downward pressures on mobile tax bases increased significantly but were partly offset by both domestic and international pressures to reduce taxes on 'immobile' tax bases. This implies that capital income tax revenues would probably have increased (in both absolute and relative terms) in the absence of competitive pressures. While this counterfactual

---

[23] Note also that, depending on the size and location of a country, even general consumption taxes might be affected by competitive pressures. Small countries with large borders to 'low-tax' neighbors may shy away from consumption tax increases. As a case in point, recent policy debates in Austria (whose general consumption tax revenues declined from 21.0% to 19.1% of total taxation between 1985 and 1995) focused on options for shifting the revenue burden away from labor. However, policymakers were skeptical about an alternative rise in indirect taxes, since the Austrian standard VAT rate of 20% is higher than in major neighboring countries, notably Germany (which increased its rate in 1997 from 15% to 16%) (see OECD 1998d).

claim can certainly not be quantified, it can be made more concrete by way of example.

As argued above, capital incomes had for a long time provided relatively little revenue for public budgets in most countries—partly due to lenient taxation, exemption, or even subsidization of certain forms of capital incomes, and partly due to domestic tax evasion. Therefore, in the 1980s and 1990s, when many governments tried to make capital income taxation (and personal income taxation in general) more neutral and just, the implied broadening of the tax base and heightened tax enforcement could have led to significantly higher incomes from taxing capital.[24]

One example is the series of Dual Income Tax reforms discussed in Section 13.3. These reforms did not lead to lower tax revenues, though not because the effective tax rate on certain types of capital income increased, but rather because more capital income had to bear the low capital income tax rate. In the absence of competitive pressures, this tax rate might have been set at a higher level.

Other examples are the experiences of Germany and Austria. Austria was one of the countries that removed the taxation of interest from the ambit of the progressive income tax in 1993, thus reducing the marginal tax rate from 62 percent to 22 percent (25 percent since 1996; see Table 13.3). This cut, however, did not lead to large revenue losses, partly because few taxpayers had paid the higher tax rates before—due to both personal tax allowances and domestic tax evasion (Genser 1999: 205; Koman and Wörgötter 1995: 17).[25]

The German government did stick to high marginal tax rates on capital income, but—urged by the German constitutional court—wanted to reduce domestic tax evasion for reasons of tax justice. It therefore introduced a withholding tax on interest payments in 1989—abolished in April of the same year—and again in 1993. These withholding taxes were only pre-payments to the progressive personal income tax, so that their introduction would have increased capital income tax revenues in a closed economy by cutting back on domestic tax evasion. However, when the government announced the introduction of these withholding taxes, taxpayers responded with massive tax flight to countries like Luxembourg (whereas much of the capital was re-channeled into Germany). International tax evasion was thus simply substituted for domestic eva-

---

[24] For a counterfactual argument along similar lines, see Genschel 1999.

[25] In addition, recall that especially small countries may actually increase their revenues from mobile tax bases after cutting tax rates (in a targeted manner), because the inflow of tax bases may over-compensate the reduced revenues from the existing tax bases. In the area of personal capital income taxation, Austria experienced such an inflow of foreign tax bases after cutting the tax rate on interest income (Schuster 1998).

sion.[26] In both cases, the importance of competitive pressures is obvious, but the predicted revenue effects are largely lacking; and in both cases combating domestic tax evasion would probably have led to higher tax revenues if the exit option had not existed.

Leaving the counterfactual world, there is another important implication of my argument. When marginal (economic) costs of taxation increased significantly for both mobile and immobile tax bases—due to competitive and domestic economic forces—this should have led to strong downward pressures on total tax burdens and public expenditures as well as to upward pressures on public deficits—just as the simple tax competition view would predict. The next section takes a closer look at these three variables.

13.4.2. Changes in Budget Size and Revenue Mix

Figure 13.4 plots average total expenditures, total tax revenues and public sector deficits for sixteen OECD countries between 1970 and 1997.[27] Table 13.7 displays periodic averages for these three variables. A casual look at the data conveys three messages. First, until the early 1980s average total tax revenues, public deficits, and public expenditures rose more or less continuously. Second, after the early 1980s there was no clear average medium-term trend anymore towards rising public expenditures. Instead, periods of declining average expenditures (1983–89 and 1993–97) were interrupted by a recessionary period (1989–93) in which average expenditures shot up. Third, the average total tax ratio virtually stagnated after the mid-1980s.

I argue that if countervailing pressures on public expenditures and deficits are taken into account, the medium-term stability of these three budgetary variables does not contradict the existence of considerable competitive pressures. On the contrary, competitive pressures contributed to this stability.

Until the early 1980s, the average OECD–16 government obviously did not consider the marginal costs of revenue-raising a strong constraint on public expenditures. Expenditures rose continuously and taxes had to

---

[26] Note that the introduction of a withholding tax as a prepayment for the progressive income tax has solved the problem of domestic tax evasion only partly. Due to German bank secrecy, many (high-income) taxpayers have still had an incentive not to report their interest income. The German withholding tax has thus partly worked like a final withholding tax as well. Moreover, even since 1993 a large portion of interest incomes has been exempted from tax due to substantial allowances.

[27] New Zealand and Switzerland were omitted due to a partial lack of data. Note also that in Fig. 13.4 public deficits do not equal the difference between expenditures and tax revenues, because non-tax revenues are neglected.

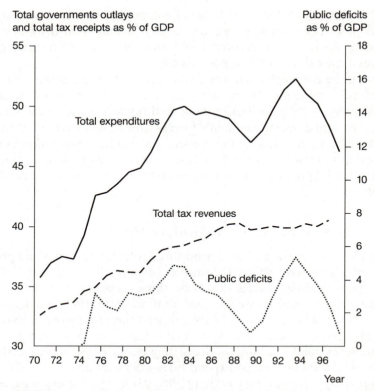

Figure 13.4 Average total government outlays, total tax receipts, and public deficits in 16 OECD countries, 1970–1997

Notes: Unweighted averages.
Source: OECD, *Health Data Base* (Paris: OECD, 1998); OECD, *Revenue Statistics 1965–1996* (Paris: OECD, 1997); OECD, *Economic Outlook* (Paris: OECD, 1998).

follow. Yet taxes rose more slowly, leading to a shift in the revenue mix towards deficit financing. Increasing marginal costs of taxation probably contributed to this shift. In any event, by the early 1980s governments had become aware of the rising economic costs of deficit financing. The high real interest rates of the 1980s combined with the already large stock of public debt to create a potentially explosive debt burden. Internationalized financial markets attached interest rate premiums on countries with high public deficits (Garrett 1998*a*). And in the 1990s the bottleneck of the Maastricht criteria added to the costs of high public deficits for EMU candidates. As a result, there were increasing pressures on governments either to cut spending or increase taxes—or to do both.

Table 13.7 *Percentage of total government outlays, total tax revenues, and public deficits in GDP, 1970–1997*

	Total government outlays % of GDP[a]			Total tax receipts % of GDP[a]			Public Deficits		
	1970–79	1980–88	1989–97	1970–79	1980–88	1989–96	1970–79	1980–88	1989–97
AUS	32	37	38	26	30	30	-0.1	1.7	1.8
A	41	49	50	38	41	42	0.7	3.1	3.4
B	50	61	55	40	46	45	4.7	9.5	5.1
CAN	38	45	48	31	33	36	0.8	4.9	4.6
DK	47	60	60	43	48	50	-1.5	2.8	1.5
FL	36	43	55	37	40	46	-3.8	-2.6	2.1
F	42	51	54	37	43	44	0.3	2.2	3.6
D	45	48	50	36	38	38	1.7	2.3	2.6
IRE	40	51	40	32	37	35	6.6	10.5	1.7
I	37	51	55	27	34	41	8.6	11.1	8.6
J	25	32	33	22	28	29	1.7	1.9	0.6
NL	50	62	56	42	45	45	1.6	5.2	3.4
N	42	46	50	40	43	41	-3.1	-5.6	-2.0
S	50	64	66	45	51	52	-2.6	2.4	3.7
UK	43	46	43	34	37	35	2.4	2.4	4.0
US	32	36	36	27	26	27	1.0	2.7	2.3
AVERAGE	41	49	49	35	39	40	1.2	3.4	2.9
STANDARD DEVIATION	7	9	9	7	7	7	3.2	4.2	2.2
COEFFICIENT OF VARIANTION	0.17	0.19	0.18	0.19	0.18	0.18	2.72	1.23	0.75

[a]To nearest percentage point.

Sources: OECD, *Health Data Base* (Paris: OECD, 1998); OECD, *Revenue Statistics 1965–1996* (Paris: OECD, 1997); OECD, *Economic Outlook* (Paris: OECD, 1998).

Yet increasing taxes was not any easier. High unemployment, sluggish growth, and competition in international product markets increased the marginal costs of taxing labor and consumption; and tax competition, especially in the area of corporate and interest taxation, was a strong constraint on higher tax revenues from capital. The average total tax burden thus virtually stagnated after the mid-1980s. Other factors certainly played a role as well. Low growth reduced tax receipts while simultaneously putting upward pressure on social spending; and increasing the tax burden would have entailed high short-term macroeconomic and electoral costs in the perception of many policymakers.[28] Still, the importance of increasing marginal costs of taxation and capital income tax competition is undeniable—especially within the European Union (cf. OECD 1998*b*: 148–62; 1999).

Finally, rising costs of revenue-raising created downward pressure on public expenditures. At the same time, however, demands for public spending also continued to rise. This has been attributed partly to the economic integration itself, which is thought to generate market dislocations that, in turn, prompt higher demands for social insurance (Garrett 1996, 1998*b*). Other (complementary) explanations stress endogenous developments like the secular shift towards the service economy or population aging (Iversen and Cusack 1998; Pierson 1998). The result was medium-term stability in both average public expenditures and deficits after the early 1980s (Figure 13.4 and Table 13.7).[29]

In sum, fiscal tradeoffs have become much more severe. The economic costs of all forms of revenue-raising have risen—partly owing to economic internationalization—but the demand for government spending has generally risen as well. As a consequence, real-world tax reformers faced difficult electoral tradeoffs. Cuts in effective tax rates on capital (and labor) have increasingly been predicated on expenditure cuts. However, policymakers had to fear short-term electoral losses, even if they believed that spending and tax cuts would boost growth, employment, and thus electoral support over the long run. Thus, governments' ability to play the tax competition game depended to a large extent on their willingness and capacity to cut expenditures.

---

[28] But see the literature on non-Keynesian effects of fiscal contractions, starting with Giavazzi and Pagano (1990).

[29] Two points should be noted. First, the medium-term stability of average public expenditures and deficits certainly does not imply that there was an absolute limit on spending and debt. This is demonstrated by countries like Belgium or Italy, which continued to run high public deficits well into the 1990s (cf. Hallerberg 1999). Second, although the average total tax burden stagnated after the mid-1980s, tax increases did contribute, on a cyclically adjusted basis, to budget consolidation in some countries (OECD 1998*b*: 152).

This perspective throws an interesting light on the large cross-country differences in fiscal policy outcomes shown in Table 13.7. Comparing averages for the periods 1980–88 and 1989–97, the data show that some countries markedly reduced public expenditures and—to a lesser extent—total taxes, while others increased both spending and revenues. These differences translated into different profiles of policy adjustment. Consider the extreme cases of Ireland and Italy that prove to be outliers on many indicators of tax policy change discussed above.

Irish policymakers lowered the public sector share in GDP from 52 percent to 36 percent between 1985 and 1997 (cf. Table 13.7). As a consequence, they were able simultaneously to reach three goals crucial to Ireland's competitive strategy. First, they strongly reduced public deficits and, in turn, the public debt—the overriding objective of Irish fiscal policy after a failed stabilization attempt starting in 1982. Second, the government passed major income tax cuts that facilitated Ireland's consensual wage moderation since 1987 (OECD 1989: 17). Finally, the government was able to reach the first two goals without increasing the effective tax burden on capital, which would have contradicted Ireland's strategy of attracting foreign investment through low tax rates and preferential tax regimes (cf. Aust 1999; Cunningham 1996).[30]

At the other extreme, Italy's governments had—until very recently— been unable to bring down burgeoning public expenditures, and, as a consequence, had to deal with a huge public debt burden. At the same time, belonging to Euroland from the start was one of the overriding objectives of Italy's economic policy. Thus, Italy had virtually no other choice than to keep increasing the total tax burden (OECD 1996*d*: 91–92)—even though competitive pressures on capital income taxation were not absent in Italy (Bordignon, Giannini, and Panteghini 1999; Giannini 1997).

While these examples have to be supplemented by more rigorous data analysis,[31] they suggest that variation in (effective) tax cuts for 'mobile' tax bases may be explained more by differences in governments' capacities (and willingness) to cut expenditures than by differences in competitive pressures. To the extent that this explanation is true, we would expect more

[30] Note that Ireland had relied on tax increases in the first failed stabilization period. This failure sent a strong signal that any second attempt had to rely on expenditure cuts rather than tax hikes.

[31] Fortunately, this is already forthcoming. Steinmo and Swank (1999) find that domestic economic forces (e.g. high structural unemployment, low investment) have put downward pressures on both capital and labor tax burdens (as measured by the average effective tax rates of Mendoza and colleagues), thus constraining a shift from capital to labor. In addition, their evidence suggests (not surprisingly) that higher government spending and public sector debt are significantly related to higher total tax burdens, thus counteracting pressures for tax reductions.

countries to simultaneously pursue budget consolidation and tax cuts in the future. This is already apparent in many countries' recent policy debates. For example, Austria aims at reducing the high burden on labor, but since shifting to taxes on capital and consumption is regarded as difficult—partly due to competitive pressures (see n. 24)—tax reform is inseparable from the heated debate about budget consolidation. Similarly, the new Red–Green government in Germany (following Lafontaine's resignation as Minister of Finance) is pursuing major expenditure cuts in order to create fiscal leeway for cutting both public deficits and the tax burden on businesses.

Many advanced welfare states thus do seem to face 'permanent austerity' (Pierson 1998). While this situation has certainly been driven to a large extent by domestic factors, the contribution of competitive pressures is nevertheless obvious.

13.5. Conclusion

Competitive pressures in corporate and personal income taxation have increased the marginal costs of taxation during the last twenty-five years and contributed to the medium-term stability of average budgetary outcomes among the eighteen most advanced OECD countries since the early 1980s. Three types of factors explain why the increased mobility of the tax base has not led to an average downward trend of capital (income) tax revenues, total tax revenues, or public expenditures.

First, the institutional framework of international taxation and the importance of non-tax factors for international investments have reduced the responsiveness of mobile tax bases to international tax differentials. Second, governments have reduced the revenue losses associated with tax policy adjustment by pursuing a policy of tax-cut-cum-base-broadening, by differentiating their tax treatment and targeting tax cuts to the most mobile segments of the income tax base, and by combating international tax avoidance and evasion through legal and administrative measures. Third, the remaining pressures on the tax mix, the revenue mix, and the budget size have partly been offset by countervailing—domestic and international—pressures.

The aggregate revenue effects of competitive pressures may well continue to grow—in the absence of more international cooperation—as an increasing number of economic actors get more sophisticated at taking advantage of international tax differentials, especially within Euroland. This does not mean, however, that capital tax competition may eventually turn out to be the death blow for the welfare state—simply because taxes on capital have long contributed a minor share to public revenues in most countries. Only if labor mobility were to grow vastly or if the EU were to shift fully toward the origin principle in taxing goods and services would large-scale revenue losses have to be feared.

This limited fiscal importance of capital tax competition, however, should not keep political scientists from studying the politics of tax policy adjustment more closely. I have presented evidence that the revenue-preserving policy strategies pursued by many OECD governments—especially increased differentiation in income tax treatment—partly conflict with established principles of neutral and just taxation. Thus, given strong budgetary constraints on general cuts in effective income tax rates, the impact of competitive pressures has, in part, been a changed and more controversial structure of taxation rather than large-scale revenue losses. The preliminary evidence presented in this chapter suggests that it would be worthwhile to investigate the political economy of these structural changes in more detail.

REFERENCES

ALBERT, WILLIAM T., SHOVEN, JOHN B., and WHALLEY, JOHN (1992). 'Introduction', in John B. Shoven and Whalley John (eds.), *Canada–U.S. Tax Comparisons*. Chicago: University of Chicago Press, 1–23.

ARNOLD, BRIAN J., and MCINTYRE, MICHAEL J. (1995). *International Tax Primer*. Boston: Kluwer Law International.

AUST, ANDREAS (1999). *The 'Celtic Tiger' and its Beneficiaries—'Competitive Corporatism' in Ireland*. Paper presented at the workshop 'Concertation and Public Policy', ECPR Joint Sessions of Workshops, Mannheim, Germany, 26–31 Mar.

Baker & McKenzie (1999). 'Survey of the Effective Tax Burden in the European Union'. Unpublished report, Amsterdam.

BECKER, HELMUT (1997). 'Tax Havens within the EU: Barriers, Harmonization, or Competition?'. *Intertax*, 1997/3: 80–81.

BIRD, RICHARD M., and MINTZ, JACK M. (1994). 'Future Developments in Tax Policy'. *Federal Law Review (Canberra)*, 22/3: 402–13.

BMF (Bundesministerium der Finanzen) (1999). *Reform der Kapitaleinkommensbesteuerung. Gutachten erstattet vom Wissenschaftlichen Beirat beim Bundesministerium der Finanzen*. Bonn: Stollfuß.

BORDIGNON, MASSIMO, GIANNINI, SILVIA, and PANTEGHINI, PAOLO (1999). 'Corporate Taxation in Italy: An Analysis of the 1998 Reform'. *Finanzarchiv*, forthcoming.

CEPS (Centre for European Policy Studies) (1999). 'The Future of Tax Policy in the EU'. Unpublished report, Brussels: CEPS.

CHENNELLS, LUCY, and GRIFFITH, RACHEL (1997). *Taxing Profits in a Changing World*. London: Institute for Fiscal Studies.

CNOSSEN, SIJBREN (1995). 'Towards a New Tax Covenant'. *De Economist*, 143/3: 285–315.

CUNNINGHAM, WILLIAM T. (1996). 'Irish Incentives for Inward Investment'. *Bulletin for International Fiscal Documentation*, 50/9: 394–98.

DEVEREUX, MICHAEL P. (1996). *The New Zealand International Tax Regime*. Report, Keele: Keele University.

—— and GRIFFITH, RACHEL (1998). 'The Taxation of Discrete Investment Choices'. Unpublished manuscript.

DROUAS, DELPHINE DE (1996). 'The French Tax System Challenged by Economic Globalisation'. *Intertax*, 1996/12: 458–59.

EASSON, ALEX (1998). 'Harmful Tax Competition: The EU and OECD Responses Compared'. *EC Tax Journal*, 3/1: 1–8.

Eurostat (1998). *Structures of the Taxation Systems in the European Union. 1970–1996*. Luxembourg: Office for the Official Publications of the European Communities.

GANGHOF, STEFFEN (1998). 'Politische Institutionen im internationalen Steuerwettbewerb. Machen nationale Vetospieler einen Unterschied?'. Diploma Thesis, Free University, Berlin.

—— (1999*a*). *A Note on Comparative Indicators of Tax Burdens*. Paper. Cologne: Max Planck Institute for the Study of Societies.

—— (1999*b*). 'Steuerwettbewerb und Vetospieler: Stimmt die These der blockierten Anpassung?'. *Politische Vierteljahresschrift*, 40/3: 458–72.

GARRETT, GEOFFREY (1996). 'Capital Mobility, Trade, and the Domestic Politics of Economic Policy', in Robert Keohane and Helen Milner (eds.), *Internationalization and Domestic Politics*. Cambridge: Cambridge University Press, 79–107.

—— (1998*a*). 'Global Markets and National Politics: Collision Course or Virtuous Circle?'. *International Organization*, 52/4: 787–824.

—— (1998*b*). *Partisan Politics in the Global Economy*. Cambridge: Cambridge University Press.

—— (1998*c*). 'Shrinking States? Globalization and National Autonomy in the OECD'. *Oxford Development Studies*, 26/1: 71–97.

GENSCHEL, PHILIPP (1999). *Tax Competition and the Welfare State*. Paper. Cologne: Max Planck Institute for the Study of Societies.

GENSER, BERND (1999). 'Konsumorientierung—Realisierungschancen in Österreich', in Christian Smekal, Rupert Sendlhofer, and Hannes Winner (eds.), *Einkommen versus Konsum*. Heidelberg: Physica-Verlag, 197–215.

—— HETTICH, FRANK, and SCHMIDT, CARSTEN (1999). 'Messung der effektiven Steuerbelastung—eine vergleichende Analyse für Deutschland, Österreich und ausgewählte OECD-Staaten'. Unpublished manuscript, University of Konstanz.

GIANNINI, SILVIA (1997). 'The Italian Corporate Tax Reform'. Manuscript (7 Nov.). London: Institute for Fiscal Studies.

GIAVAZZI, FRANCESCO, and PAGANO, MARCO (1990). 'Can Severe Fiscal Contractions Be Expansionary? Tales of Two Small European Countries'. *NBER Macroeconomic Annual*, 5: 75–111.

GILLESPIE, IRWIN W. (1991). *Tax, Borrow and Spend: Financing Federal Spending in Canada, 1867–1990*. Ottawa: Carleton University Press.

GIOVANNINI, ALBERTO (1989). 'National Tax Systems Versus the European Capital Market'. *Economic Policy*, 9: 346–86.

HALLERBERG, MARK (1999). *High Debt Countries in an Integrating World: Why Belgium and Italy Qualified for EMU*. Paper presented at the 1999 American Political Science Association Meetings in Atlanta, Georgia, 2–5 Sept.

——and BASINGER, SCOTT (1998). 'Internationalization and Changes in Tax Policy in OECD Countries: The Importance of Domestic Veto Players'. *Comparative Political Studies*, 31/3: 321–52.

————(1999). 'Globalization and Tax Reform: An Updated Case for the Importance of Veto Players'. *Politische Vierteljahresschrift*, 40/4: 618–27.

HETTICH, WALTER, and WINER, STANLEY L. (1999). *Democratic Choice and Taxation. A Theoretical and Empirical Analysis*. Cambridge: Cambridge University Press.

IVERSEN, TORBEN, and CUSACK, THOMAS R. (1998). *The Causes of Welfare State Expansion: Deindustrialization or Globalization?*. Discussion Paper FS I 98–304, Social Science Research Center, Berlin.

KOMAN, REINHARD, and WÖRGÖTTER, ANDREAS (1995). *Statutory Charges and Economic Functions: The Case of Austria*. Vienna: Institute for Advanced Studies.

LEIBFRITZ, WILLI, THORNTON, JOHN, and BIBBEE, ALEXANDRA (1997). *Taxation and Economic Performance*. OECD Economics Department, Working Papers, No. 176, Paris.

MCMULLEN, SENATOR (1994). 'Australian Tax Policy, the OECD and the Dynamic Asian Economies', in OECD (ed.), *Taxation and Investment Flows: An Exchange of Experiences between the OECD and the Dynamic Asian Economies*. Paris: OECD, 19–23.

MENDOZA, ENRIQUE G., MILESI-FERRETI, GIAN MARIA, and ASEA, PATRICK (1997). 'On the Ineffectiveness of Tax Policy in Altering Long-run Growth: Harberger's Superneutrality Conjecture'. *Journal of Public Economics*, 66: 99–126.

——RAZIN, ASSAF, and TESAR, LINDA L. (1994). 'Effective Tax Rates in Macroeconomics: Cross-Country Estimates of Tax Rates on Factor Incomes and Consumption'. *Journal of Monetary Economics*, 34/3: 297–323.

MESSERE, KEN (1993). *Tax Policy Choices in OECD Countries*. Amsterdam: IBFD Publications BV.

——(1994). 'Consumption Tax Rules'. *Bulletin for International Fiscal Documentation*, 48/12: 665–81.

——(1997). 'OECD Tax Developments in the 1990s'. *Bulletin for International Fiscal Documentation*, 51/7: 298–314.

MÜSSENER, INGO (1996). 'Die Kapitalertragsteuern auf Zinsen und Dividenden im internationalen Vergleich'. *Internationale Wirtschaftsbriefe*/4: 1101–6.

NICKELL, STEPHEN, and LAYARD, RICHARD (1999). 'Labour Market Institutions and Economic Performance', forthcoming in Orley Ashenfelter and David Card (eds.), *Handbook of Labor Economics*. Volume 3C. New York: North Holland, 3029–84.

NIELSEN, SOREN B., and SØRENSEN, PETER B. (1997). 'On the Optimality of the Nordic System of Dual Income Taxation'. *Journal of Public Economics*, 63: 311–29.

OECD (Organisation for Economic Co-operation and Development) (1989). *OECD Economic Surveys: Ireland 1988–1989*. Paris: OECD.

——(1994). *Taxation and Household Saving*. Paris: OECD.

——(1996a). *Controlled Foreign Company Legislation*. Paris: OECD.

——(1996b). *Model Tax Convention on Income and on Capital. September 1996. Condensed Version*. Paris: OECD.

——(1996c). *OECD Economic Surveys: Denmark 1995–1996*. Paris: OECD.

——(1996d). *OECD Economic Surveys: Italy 1995–1996*. Paris: OECD.

——(1997). *Economic Surveys: Canada 1996–1997*. Paris: OECD.

——(1998a). *Harmful Tax Competition: An Emerging Global Issue*. Paris: OECD.

——(1998b). *OECD Economic Outlook 63. June 1998*. Paris: OECD.

——(1998c). *OECD Economic Outlook 64. December 1998*. Paris: OECD.

——(1998d). *OECD Economic Surveys 1997–1998: Austria*. Paris: OECD.

——(1999). *EMU: Facts, Challenges and Policies*. Paris: OECD.

OWENS, JEFFREY (1993). 'Globalisation: The Implications for Tax Policies'. *Fiscal Studies*, 14/3: 21–44.

——(1997). 'Emerging Issues inTaxing Business in a Global Economy', in Richard Venn (ed.), *Taxing International Business*. Paris: OECD, 25–66.

PIERSON, PAUL (1998). 'Irresistible Forces, Immovable Objects: Post-Industrial Welfare States Confront Permanent Austerity'. *Journal of European Public Policy*, 5/4: 539–60.

QUINN, DENNIS (1997). 'The Correlates of Change in International Financial Regulation'. *American Political Science Review*, 91/3: 531–51.

RATZINGER, JÜRGEN (1997). 'Perpektiven für die Umsatzbesteuerung in der Europäischen Union'. *Wirtschaftsdienst*, 77: 464–71.

Ruding Report (1992). *Report of the Committee of Independent Experts on Company Taxation*. Brussels: Commission of the European Communities.

RUGGERI, GIUSEPPE C., LAROCHE, MIREILLE, and VINCENT, CAROLE (1997). *Effective Income Tax Rates In Macroeconomics: An Update for Canada*. Working Paper 97-05, Canada.

SANDFORD, CEDRIC (1993). *Successful Tax Reform: Lessons from an Analysis of Tax Reform in Six Countries*. Fersfield: Fiscal Publications.

SCHULZE, GÜNTHER G., and URSPRUNG, HEINRICH W. (1999). 'Globalization of the Economy and the Nation State'. *World Economy*, 21/3: 295–352.

SCHUSTER, HELMUT (1998). *Die österreichische Abgeltungsteuer—Ein Modell für Deutschland?* Cologne: Bundesverband deutscher Banken.

SINN, HANS-WERNER (1989). 'The Tax Policy of Tax-Cut-Cum-Base-Broadening: Implications for International Capital Movements', in Manfred Neumann and Karl W. Roskamp (eds.), *Public Finance and Enterprises*. Detroit: Wayne State University Press, 153–76.

——(1997). 'Deutschland im Steuerwettbewerb'. *Jahrbücher für Nationalökonomie und Statistik*, 216: 672–92.

SLEMROD, JOEL (1990). 'Tax Principles in an International Economy', in Michael

J. Boskin and Charles E. McLure Jr. (eds.), *World Tax Reform*. San Fransisco: ICS Press, 11–23.

SØRENSEN, PETER B. (1998). 'Recent Innovations in Nordic Tax Policy: From the Global Income Tax to the Dual Income Tax', in Peter Birch Sørensen (ed.), *Tax Policy in the Nordic Countries*. London: Macmillan, 1–27.

SPENGEL, CHRISTOPH (1998). *Unternehmensbesteuerung in Europa—Vergleich und Analyse*. Paper presented at the 'AIESEC Europe Days', 16–18 June, Mannheim.

STEINMO, SVEN, and SWANK, DUANE (1999). *The New Political Economy of Taxation*. Paper prepared for the 1999 Annual Meeting of the American Political Science Association. 1–5 Sept., Atlanta, Ga.

SWANK, DUANE (1997). 'Funding the Welfare State: Globalization and the Taxation of Business in Advanced Market Economies'. *Political Studies*, 46/4: 671–92.

——(1998). '18-Nation Pooled Time Series Data Base on the Political Economy of Advanced Industrial Democracies'. Data Base, Marquette University: Department of Political Science.

TANZI, VITO (1995). *Taxation in an Integrating World*. Washington, DC: Brookings Institution.

——(1998). 'Globalization, Tax Competition and the Future of Tax Systems', in Gerold Krause-Junk (ed.), *Steuersysteme der Zukunft*. Berlin: Duncker & Humblot, 11–27.

TIKKA, KARI S. (1993). 'A 25 per cent Flat Rate on Capital Income: The Finnish Reaction to International Tax Competition', in Nordic Council for Tax Research (ed.), *Tax Reform in the Nordic Countries*. Iustus: Uppsala, 91–108.

VIHERKENTTÄ, TIMO (1996). 'Das Nordische Modell—Ein alternativer Ansatz der Besteuerung von Kapitaleinkommen', in Otto H. Jacobs and Christoph Spengel (eds.), *Aspekte der Unternehmensbesteuerung in Europa*. Baden-Baden: Nomos, 117–38.

WAGSCHAL, UWE (1999a). 'Blockieren Vetospieler Steuerreformen?'. *Politische Vierteljahresschrift:*, 40/4: 628–40.

——(1999b). 'Schranken staatlicher Steuerungspolitik: Warum Steuerreformen scheitern können', in Andreas Busch and Thomas Plümper (eds.), *Nationaler Staat und internationale Wirtschaft*. Baden-Baden: Nomos, 223–47.

WEICHENRIEDER, ALFONS (1996). 'Fighting International Tax Avoidance: The Case of Germany'. *Fiscal Studies*, 17/1: 37–58.

ZEE, HOWELL H. (1998). 'Taxation of Financial Capital in a Globalized Environment: The Role of Withholding Taxes'. *National Tax Journal*, 51/3: 587–99.

ZIMMER, FREDERIK (1993). 'Capital Income and Earned Income Following the Norwegian Income Tax Reform: Is the Dual Income Tax Fair?', in Nordic Council for Tax Research (ed.), *Tax Reform in the Nordic Countries*. Uppsala: Iustus, 141–56.

INDEX

Page numbers in **bold** refer to figures, and those in *italic* to tables.